Lecture Notes in Computer Science   11604

Commenced Publication in 1973
Founding and Former Series Editors:
Gerhard Goos, Juris Hartmanis, and Jan van Leeuwen

More information about this series at http://www.springer.com/series/7407

Edoardo S. Biagioni · Yao Zheng ·
Siyao Cheng (Eds.)

Wireless Algorithms, Systems, and Applications

14th International Conference, WASA 2019
Honolulu, HI, USA, June 24–26, 2019
Proceedings

 Springer

Editors
Edoardo S. Biagioni
University of Hawaii at Manoa
Honolulu, HI, USA

Yao Zheng
University of Hawaii at Manoa
Honolulu, USA

Siyao Cheng
Harbin Institute of Technology
Harbin, China

ISSN 0302-9743   ISSN 1611-3349   (electronic)
Lecture Notes in Computer Science
ISBN 978-3-030-23596-3   ISBN 978-3-030-23597-0   (eBook)
https://doi.org/10.1007/978-3-030-23597-0

LNCS Sublibrary: SL1 – Theoretical Computer Science and General Issues

This Springer imprint is published by the registered company Springer Nature Switzerland AG
The registered company address is: Gewerbestrasse 11, 6330 Cham, Switzerland

Preface

The 14th International Conference on Wireless Algorithms, Systems, and Applications (WASA 2019) was held during June 24–26, 2019, at Honolulu, Hawaii, USA. The conference focused on new ideas and recent advances in computer systems, wireless networks, distributed applications, and advanced algorithms that are pushing forward the new technologies for better information sharing, computer communication, and universal connected devices in various environments, especially in wireless networks. WASA has become a broad forum for computer theoreticians, system and application developers, and other professionals in networking related areas to present their ideas, solutions, and understandings of emerging technologies and challenges in computer systems, wireless networks, and advanced applications.

The technical program of WASA 2019 consists of two keynote talks, 43 regular papers, and 11 short papers, selected by the Program Committee from 143 full submissions in response to the call for papers. All submissions were reviewed by the Program Committee members. These submissions cover many hot research topics, including machine-learning algorithms for wireless systems and applications, Internet of Things (IoTs) and related wireless solutions, wireless networking for cyber-physical systems (CPSs), security and privacy solutions for wireless applications, blockchain solutions for mobile applications, mobile edge computing, wireless sensor networks, distributed and localized algorithm design and analysis, wireless crowdsourcing, mobile cloud computing, vehicular networks, wireless solutions for smart cities, wireless algorithms for smart grids, mobile social networks, mobile system security, storage systems for mobile applications, etc.

First, we like to thank all Program Committee members for their hard work in reviewing all submissions. Furthermore, we like to extend our special thanks to the WASA Steering Committee chairs (Prof. Xiuzhen Susan Chen and Prof. Zhipeng Cai) for their consistent leadership and guidance; we also like to thank the Web chair (Prof. Meng Han), the publication chairs (Prof. Weil Li, Prof. Yibo Xue, Prof. Zhenhai Duan), the publicity chairs (Dr. Cheng Zhang and Prof. Kuai Xu), and the local chairs (Prof. Depeng Li and Prof. Yi Zhu) for their hard work in making WASA 2019 a success. In particular, we would like to thank all the authors for submitting and presenting their exciting ideas and solutions at the conference.

May 2019

Yingfei Dong
Edoardo S. Biagioni
Siyao Cheng
Yao Zheng

Organization

Steering Committee

Xiuzhen Susan Cheng (Co-chair)	George Washington University, USA
Zhipeng Cai (Co-chair)	Georgia State University, USA
Jiannong Cao	Hong Kong Polytechnic University, SAR China
Ness Shroff	The Ohio State University, USA
Wei Zhao	University of Macau, SAR China
PengJun Wan	Illinois Institute of Technology, USA
Ty Znati	University of Pittsburgh, USA
Xinbing Wang	Shanghai Jiao Tong University, China

General Chair

Yingfei Dong	University of Hawaii, USA

Program Co-chairs

Edoardo S. Biagioni	University of Hawaii, USA
Yao Zheng	University of Hawaii, USA
Siyao Cheng	Harbin Institute of Technology

Publication Co-chairs

Wei Li	Georgia State University, USA
Yibo Xue	Tsinghua University, China
Zhenhai Duan	Florida State University

Publicity Co-chairs

Cheng Zhang	George Washington University, USA
Kuai Xu	Arizona State University, USA

Local Co-chairs

Depeng Li	University of Hawaii, USA
Yi Zhu	Hawaii Pacific University, USA

Program Committee

Yu Bai	California State University Fullerton, USA
Pratool Bharti	Communication Concepts Integration
Edoardo S. Biagioni	University of Hawaii, USA
Zhipeng Cai	Georgia State University, USA
Wei Cheng	Virginia Commonwealth University, USA
Changlong Chen	Microsoft
Ionut Cardei	Florida Atlantic University, USA
Sriram Chellappan	University of South Florida, USA
Songqing Chen	George Mason University, USA
Fei Chen	Shenzhen University, China
Qinghe Du	Xi'an Jiaotong University, China
Dezun Dong	National University of Defense Technology
Xiumei Fan	Xi'an University of Technology, China
Xinwen Fu	University of Central Florida, USA
Hui Gao	Beijing University of Posts and Telecommunications, China
Yong Guan	Iowa State University, USA
Xiaofeng Gao	Shanghai Jiao Tong University, China
Baohua Huang	Guangxi University, China
Zaobo He	Miami University, USA
Yan Huo	Beijing Jiaotong University, China
Meng Han	Kennesaw State University, USA
Gaofeng He	Nanjing University of Posts and Telecommunications, China
Yanggon Kim	Towson University, USA
Hwangnam Kim	Korea University, South Korea
Donghyun Kim	Kennesaw State University, USA
Ming Li	University of Nevada, Reno, USA
Zhenhua Li	Tsinghua University, China
Ruinian Li	George Washington University, USA
Feng Li	Indiana University, Purdue University Indianapolis, USA
Yingshu Li	Georgia State University, USA
Sanghwan Lee	Kookmin University, South Korea
Zhihan Lu	University of Barcelona, Spain
Xiang Lu	Chinese Academy of Science, China
Chunchi Liu	Beijing Normal University, China
Bo Mei	Texas Christian University, USA
Liran Ma	Texas Christian University, USA
Jian Mao	National University of Singapore; BeiHang University, China
Linwei Niu	West Virginia State University, USA
Hung Nguyen	Carnegie Mellon University, USA
Anurag Panwar	University of South Florida, USA

Contents

Short Papers

Full Papers

Decomposable Atomic Norm Minimization Channel Estimation for Millimeter Wave MIMO-OFDM Systems

Qianwen An[1], Tao Jing[1], Yingkun Wen[1], Zhuojun Duan[2], and Yan Huo[1(✉)]

[1] School of Electronics and Information Engineering, Beijing Jiaotong University, Beijing 100044, China
{17120039,tjing,16111024,yhuo}@bjtu.edu.cn
[2] Computing Sciences Department, University of Hartford, West Hartford, CT, USA
duan@hartford.edu

Abstract. This paper addresses the problem of downlink channel estimation in millimeter wave (mmWave) massive multiple input multiple output (MIMO)-orthogonal frequency division multiplexing (OFDM) systems, where wideband frequency selective fading channels are considered. By exploiting the sparse scattering nature of mmWave channel, we consider channel estimation as three dimensional (3D) (including angles of departure/arrival and the time delay) line spectrum estimation. To achieve super-resolution channel estimation, we propose a decomposable 3D atomic norm minimization estimation method. This method decomposes the 3D estimation problem into two separate dimensions to reduce the computational complexity, where time delays are estimated only in the OFDM system. Simulation results show that the proposed method can achieve comparable mean square errors as the conventional vectorized ANM at much lower computational complexity.

Keywords: mmWave MIMO-OFDM systems · Channel estimation · Atomic norm minimization · Decomposable ANM

1 Introduction

Millimeter wave (mmWave) communication is considered to be a key technology of the fifth-generation (5G) communication network [1,2]. It brings sufficient bandwidth resources, i.e., ranging from 30 to 300 GHz, to the communication system, and yields Gbps communication data rates. Unfortunately, mmWave communication has some drawbacks. Firstly, due to the extremely high frequency of mmWave, the propagation path loss of mmWave communication is large. Large scale antenna arrays can compensate the significant path loss by providing beamforming gains [1,3]. It is feasible to employ large scale antenna arrays at transmitters and receivers, owing to the size of the antenna is proportional to the wavelength. Secondly, there is serious frequency-selective fading

© Springer Nature Switzerland AG 2019
E. S. Biagioni et al. (Eds.): WASA 2019, LNCS 11604, pp. 3–15, 2019.
https://doi.org/10.1007/978-3-030-23597-0_1

in mmWave wideband communication systems. To combat with the frequency-selective fading, the orthogonal frequency division multiplexing (OFDM) technology divides the wideband channel into multiple parallel flat subchannels [4]. The combination of mmWave massive multiple-input multiple-output (MIMO)-OFDM system is a potential candidate for the 5G wireless communications.

In a mmWave massive MIMO-OFDM system, each antenna requires a radio frequency (RF) chain to match when a digital transceiver is used. Owing to a large number of antennas, the overhead of the RF chains is huge, resulting in high hardware complexity and energy consumption [1]. To reduce the overhead of RF chain, a hybrid analog-digital transceiver architecture is applied [5,6]. This hybrid architecture needs channel state information (CSI) to design beamforming algorithms for implementing directional power gain of the massive MIMO technology. Thus, it is important to estimate channel state for a transceiver when a mmWave massive MIMO-OFDM system employs hybrid analog-digital transceivers. With the development of cognitive radio networks [7,8], Wireless sensor networks [9–12], social networks [13–15] and Internet-of-things systems [16], access devices in the networks have increased significantly, and channel estimation is urgently needed to improve communication quality.

The traditional channel estimation method is not applicable to mmWave massive MIMO channel estimation. Since the channel of mmWave massive MIMO is a sparse multi-path architecture, the channel effective dimension of the mmWave channel is less than the dimension of the traditional channel. Prevalent mmWave channel estimation methods utilize the sparsity of the channel to formulate mmWave channel estimation as a sparse signal recovery [17–19], such as compressed sensing (CS) method, sparse Bayesian learning (SBL), and tensor-based method. There are two disadvantages in the above existing methods. Firstly, on-grid methods have poor channel estimation performance. A CS method discretizes continuous the angles of departure (AoDs) and the angles of arrival (AoAs) in a known grid [17,20]. It cannot estimate arbitrary angular, thus the CS method has a low-resolution of channel estimation, and on-grid CS methods result in grids mismatch and power leakage. Secondly, gridless methods are limited, because these methods require the estimation of channel propagation paths number. For instance, the lower-rank tensor decomposition method in [19,21] can estimate the AoDs and AoAs separately with no grid errors, and the computational complexity of this method is low. If the knowledge of the number of propagation paths is unknown, tensor-based method needs to estimate the order of channel, which increases the computational complexity.

In order to avoid the above disadvantages, the development of the gridless CS method adopts atomic norm minimization (ANM) and semidefinite programming (SDP) to enable recovery of gridless components from compressive measurements [22]. The ANM method is introduced to super-resolution channel estimation without predicting the channel paths number [22–24]. Currently, ANM has been applied to two dimensional (2D) narrowband mmWave channel estimation, then arbitrary AoDs/AoAs can be accurately obtained [22,24]. In fact, mmWave communication is worked on wideband. The sparse scattering path structure of the mmWave massive MIMO-OFDM channel appears in the 3D (AoDs, AoAs, time delays) line spectrum estimation problem. Hence, the 2D ANM cannot be employed to the wideband mmWave massive MIMO-OFDM system that considers frequency selective fading.

In this paper, we propose a decomposable 3D ANM estimation method for a mmWave massive MIMO-OFDM system. The 3D ANM is a three-level Toeplitz structure-based optimization approach. The Vandermonde structure of the transmit/receive and time delay array manifold is captured from the Toeplitz matrix [24,25]. The computational complexity of the ANM method is proportional to the size of the antenna and the number of the subcarrier. For reducing the high computational complexity, the 3D estimation problem is decomposed to the problem of 2D (AoDs, AoAs) and 1D (time delay) angles estimation by exploiting the independence between parameters, where we consider time delays estimation in an OFDM system. The following summarizes the contributions of this paper.

- The proposed decomposable 3D ANM method is suitable for a broadband mmWave system with frequency selective fading.
- Our channel estimation method can gridlessly estimate arbitrary angle and time delay, and the performance of our method is much better than grid-based method.
- The performance of the proposed method is quite close to the traditional vectorized 3D ANM method, and the computational complexity of our method is far less than the 3D ANM method.

The rest of the paper is organized as follows. In Sect. 2, the mmWave massive MIMO-OFDM system model and the downlink channel estimation problem are introduced. In Sect. 3 develops a decomposable 3D ANM method for channel estimation in the frequency domain. The estimation problem is decomposed into two dimensions, including two steps for performing channel estimation. Computation complexity of the proposed method, the vectorized ANM method and the CS method is analyzed in Sect. 4. Simulation results are given in Sect. 5, followed by conclusions in Sect. 6.

2 System Model

We consider a mmWave massive MIMO-OFDM system consisting of a base station (BS) and multiple mobile stations (MSs), assuming that the antenna array is a uniform linear array (ULA). The BS is equipped with N_{BS} antennas and N_{BS}^{RF} RF chains, and the MS is equipped with N_{MS} antennas and N_{MS}^{RF} RF chains. The number of RF chains is usually less than the number of antennas, i.e., $N_{BS}^{RF} < N_{BS}$, $N_{MS}^{RF} < N_{MS}$, and assuming $N_{MS}^{RF} < N_{BS}^{RF}$. As shown in Fig. 1, both the BS and MS adopt hybrid analog-digital precoding architectures that can improve the performance of analog-only precoding solutions and reduce the complexity of full digital precoding solutions [5,6]. The system employs K subcarriers to send N_S data training streams. In addition, only a single MS is considered in the downlink scenario because the channel estimation is conducted by each user individually [4].

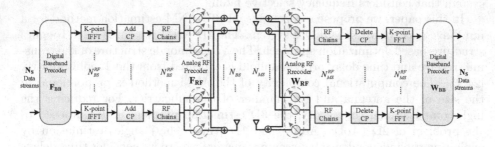

Fig. 1. A block diagram of the OFDM based BS-MS transceiver that employs hybrid analog/digital precoding.

Since mmWave channels have limited scattering in dense-urban non-line of sight (NLOS) environments [26], we adopt a geometric wideband frequency-selective fading channel model with L scatterers between the MS and the considered BS. Then the mmWave massive MIMO-OFDM downlink channel matrix in the delay domain can be modelled as [6,19]

$$\mathbf{H}(\tau) = \sum_{l=1}^{L} \alpha_l \mathbf{a}_{MS}(\theta_l) \mathbf{a}_{BS}^H(\phi_l) \delta(\tau - \tau_l), \tag{1}$$

where α_l is the complex gain of the lth path, $\theta_l \in [0, 2\pi]$ and $\phi_l \in [0, 2\pi]$ denote the AoA and AoD of the lth path, $\mathbf{a}_{MS}(\theta_l)$ and $\mathbf{a}_{BS}(\phi_l)$ are the antenna array response vectors of the MS and BS, and τ_l is the time delay with the lth path. Note that $[\cdot]^H$ represents the conjugate transpose operation of a matrix or vector and $\delta(\cdot)$ denotes the delta function. Since we employ the ULA in our system, the antenna array response vectors $\mathbf{a}_{MS}(\theta_l) \in \mathbb{C}^{N_{MS} \times 1}$ and $\mathbf{a}_{BS}(\phi_l) \in \mathbb{C}^{N_{BS} \times 1}$ can be expressed as

$$\mathbf{a}_{MS}(\theta_l) = \tfrac{1}{\sqrt{N_{MS}}}[1, e^{j(2\pi/\lambda)d\sin(\theta_l)}, \dots, e^{j(2\pi/\lambda)(N_{MS}-1)d\sin(\theta_l)}]^\top,$$

$$\mathbf{a}_{BS}(\phi_l) = \tfrac{1}{\sqrt{N_{BS}}}[1, e^{j(2\pi/\lambda)d\sin(\phi_l)}, \dots, e^{j(2\pi/\lambda)(N_{BS}-1)d\sin(\phi_l)}]^\top,$$

where $[\cdot]^T$ represents the transpose operation of a matrix or vector, λ and d denote the carrier wavelength and the distance between the two adjacent antennas, respectively.

According to the delay domain channel model, the frequency domain channel matrix $\mathbf{H}[k] \in \mathbb{C}^{N_{MS} \times N_{BS}}$ corresponding to the kth subcarrier can be given as

$$\mathbf{H}[k] = \sum_{l=1}^{L} \alpha_l e^{-j2\pi\tau_l f_s k/K} \mathbf{a}_{MS}(\theta_l) \mathbf{a}_{BS}^H(\phi_l), \quad k = 0, 1, \dots, \widetilde{K} - 1, \tag{2}$$

where f_s is the sampling rate, K is the total number of subcarriers, and $\tilde{K}$ represents the number of the subcarriers selected for training[1]. Assuming the symbol sequence of consecutive M frames on the kth subcarrier transmitted by the BS is $\mathbf{s}[k] \in \mathbb{C}^{N_S \times M}$, the received signal $\mathbf{Y}[k] \in \mathbb{C}^{N_S \times M}$ at the MS can be expressed as

$$\begin{aligned}
\mathbf{Y}[\mathbf{k}] &= \mathbf{W}^H[k]\mathbf{H}[k]\mathbf{F}[k]\mathbf{s}[k] + \mathbf{W}[k]\mathbf{N}[k] \\
&= \mathbf{W}^H\mathbf{H}[k]\mathbf{Fs} + \mathbf{WN}[k]
\end{aligned} \tag{3}$$

where $\mathbf{F}[k] = \mathbf{F}_{RF}\mathbf{F}_{BB}[k] \in \mathbb{C}^{N_{BS} \times N_S}$, $\mathbf{W}[k] = \mathbf{W}_{RF}\mathbf{W}_{BB}[k] \in \mathbb{C}^{N_S \times N_{MS}}$ are the precoding matrix of the BS and the combining matrix of the MS, respectively. Both of them consist of a analog RF precoder matrix $\mathbf{F}_{RF}/\mathbf{W}_{RF}$ and a digital baseband precoder matrix $\mathbf{F}_{BB}[k]/\mathbf{W}_{BB}[k]$. Note that the digital precoder is different for every subcarrier. In order to facilitate the development of the channel estimation algorithm, we assume that the precoding/combining matrix and the pilot symbols are the same for different subcarriers. Then the limited scattering characteristic of the mmWave channel is exploited to recast channel estimation as a sparse signal recovery problem.

3   Decomposable 3D Atomic Norm Minimization for Channel Estimation

Our goal is to estimate $\{\mathbf{H}[k]\}_{k=0}^{K-1}$ from the received training signal $\mathbf{Y}$. The channel matrix $\mathbf{H}$ is composed of three independent parameters, i.e., AoAs (θ_l), AoDs (ϕ_l), and time delays (τ_l). Based on the sparse scattering characteristic of mmWave channels, channel estimation can be considered as a 3D line spectrum estimation. To obtain super-resolution parameter estimation, the ANM is used to gridless recover these parameters. Taking advantage of independence between parameters, we decompose 3D ANM channel estimation into a 2D ANM and a 1D ANM estimation problem to reduce the computational complexity.

The ANM is an optimization approach where Vandermonde structures of parameter arrays manifold is captured in the SDP via Toeplitz matrix. The basic idea of the ANM is to represent the signal of interest as a simple linear combination of a few atoms on a known atoms set, and the structural information of the atoms is used to extract the angle information in signals [22].

3.1   2D ANM to Obtain $\hat{\theta}_l$ and $\hat{\phi}_l$

We employ 2D ANM gridless channel estimation to obtain AoDs/AoAs [22, 24]. Since the delay τ_l and AoDs/AoAs θ_l/ϕ_l are independent, we treat τ_l as

---

[1] Since the number of subcarriers used for training is proportional to the computational complexity of channel estimation, the complexity can be mitigated with as few subcarriers as possible.

a constant, setting $\alpha_l e^{-j2\pi \tau_l f_s k/K} = \beta_{l,k}$ for simplified calculation. Therefore, Eq. (2) can be given as:

$$\mathbf{H}[k] = \sum_{l=1}^{L} \beta_{l,k} \mathbf{a}_{MS}(\theta_l) \mathbf{a}_{BS}^{H}(\phi_l), \tag{4}$$

where $\beta_{l,k}$ is the new channel complex gain.

To estimate the angle information AoDs/AoAs and the channel matrix $\mathbf{H}[k]$, we introduce the atomic set, which is the basis of the ANM approach. The channel matrix $\mathbf{H}[k]$ can be written as a linear combination of components in the atomic set. The matrix-form atom set is given by

$$\begin{aligned}
\mathcal{A}_M &= \{\mathbf{A}(\varphi), \forall \varphi \in [0, 2\pi] \times [0, 2\pi]\} \\
&= \{\mathbf{a}_{MS}(\theta)\mathbf{a}_{BS}^{H}(\phi), \forall \theta \in [0, 2\pi], \phi \in [0, 2\pi]\}.
\end{aligned} \tag{5}$$

By selecting the appropriate atoms in the atomic set, we can determine the angular information in $\mathbf{H}[k]$. Therefore, the atomic norm of $\mathbf{H}[k]$ over the atom set $\mathcal{A}_M$ is defined as

$$\|\mathbf{H}[k]\|_{\mathcal{A}_M} = \inf \left\{ \sum_{l=1}^{L} |\beta_{l,k}| \left| \sum_{l=1}^{L} \beta_{l,k} \mathbf{A}(\varphi_l), \mathbf{A}(\varphi_l) \in \mathcal{A}_M \right. \right\}. \tag{6}$$

When the atom is closest to the real θ_l/ϕ_l, the atomic norm $\|\mathbf{H}[k]\|_{\mathcal{A}_M}$ is the smallest. Assuming that θ_l and ϕ_l in $\mathbf{H}[k]$ are independent of each other, $\sin(\theta_l)$ and $\sin(\phi_l)$ satisfy sufficient frequency separation condition [22], which is given as below

$$\begin{aligned}
\triangle_{min,\theta} &= \min_{i \neq j} |\sin(\theta_i) - \sin(\theta_j)| \geq \frac{1}{(N_{MS} - 1)/4}, \\
\triangle_{min,\phi} &= \min_{i \neq j} |\sin(\phi_i) - \sin(\phi_j)| \geq \frac{1}{(N_{BS} - 1)/4}.
\end{aligned} \tag{7}$$

Then the decomposition of $\|\mathbf{H}[k]\|_{\mathcal{A}_M}$ is obtained to be the unique and sparsest, i.e., $\|\mathbf{H}[k]\|_{\mathcal{A}_M} = \sum |\beta_{l,k}|$. The component atoms of $\mathbf{H}[k]$ are determined by solving the atomic norm of (6).

In practice, $\mathbf{H}[k]$ is unknown to the MS. The MS needs to recover $\mathbf{H}[k]$ and θ_l/ϕ_l according to the received training signals $\mathbf{Y}[k]$. Given $\mathbf{Y}[k]$, (6) can be rewritten as a de-noising ANM formulation,

$$\min_{\mathbf{H}[k]} \left\{ \mu \|\mathbf{H}[k]\|_{\mathcal{A}_M} + \|\mathbf{Y}[k] - \mathbf{W}^H \mathbf{H}[k] \mathbf{Fs}\|_F^2 \right\}, \tag{8}$$

where $\|\mathbf{Y}[k] - \mathbf{W}^H \mathbf{H}[k] \mathbf{Fs}\|^2$ is the noise-controlling term, $\|\cdot\|_F$ is the matrix Frobenius norm, and μ is the regularization parameter associated with the noise power. In order to avoid infinite programming, (8) can be calculate via SDP as

$$\min_{\mathbf{H}[k], \mathbf{u}_\theta, \mathbf{u}_\phi} \left\{ \frac{\mu \left(\text{tr}(\mathbf{T}(\mathbf{u}_{\theta,k})) + \text{tr}(\mathbf{T}(\mathbf{u}_{\phi,k})) \right)}{2\sqrt{N_{MS} + N_{BS}}} + \|\mathbf{Y}[k] - \mathbf{W}^H \mathbf{H}[k] \mathbf{Fs}\|_F^2 \right\},$$

$$\text{s.t.} \quad \begin{pmatrix} \mathbf{T}(\mathbf{u}_{\phi,k}) & \mathbf{H}^H[k] \\ \mathbf{H}[k] & \mathbf{T}(\mathbf{u}_{\theta,k}) \end{pmatrix} \succeq 0, \tag{9}$$

where $\mathrm{tr}(\cdot)$ indicates the trace of a matrix, $\mathbf{T}(\mathbf{u}_{\theta,k}) \in \mathbb{C}^{N_{MS} \times N_{MS}}$ and $\mathbf{T}(\mathbf{u}_{\phi,k}) \in \mathbb{C}^{N_{BS} \times N_{BS}}$ are one-level positive semidefinite (PSD) Toeplitz matrices defined by their first rows $\mathbf{u}_{\theta,k} \in \mathbb{C}^{N_{MS}}$ and $\mathbf{u}_{\phi,k} \in \mathbb{C}^{N_{BS}}$, respectively. The PSD matrices $\mathbf{T}(u_{\theta,k})$ and $\mathbf{T}(u_{\phi,k})$ are constructed from the vandermonde matrix—the antenna array response vectors $\mathbf{a}_{MS}(\theta_l)$ and $\mathbf{a}_{BS}(\phi_l)$, respectively, i.e.,

$$\mathbf{T}(u_{\theta,k}) = \sqrt{\tfrac{N_{BS}}{N_{MS}}} \sum_{l=1}^{L} |\beta_{l,k}| \, \mathbf{a}_{MS}(\theta_l)\mathbf{a}_{MS}^{H}(\theta_l), \tag{10}$$

$$\mathbf{T}(u_{\phi,k}) = \sqrt{\tfrac{N_{MS}}{N_{BS}}} \sum_{l=1}^{L} |\beta_{l,k}| \, \mathbf{a}_{BS}(\phi_l)\mathbf{a}_{BS}^{H}(\phi_l). \tag{11}$$

By performing one-level Vandermonde decomposition of the $\mathbf{T}(\mathbf{u}_{\theta,k})$ and $\mathbf{T}(\mathbf{u}_{\phi,k})$, we can acquire the AoAs $\hat{\theta}_l$ and the AoDs $\hat{\phi}_l$. There are many approaches to extract angles, such as the Prony method, the matrix pencil, and the ESPRIT method. In this paper, we use the multiple signal classification (MUSIC) method [27] to get $\hat{\theta}_l/\hat{\phi}_l$ by peak search. Subsequently, the obtained $\hat{\theta}_l$ and $\hat{\phi}_l$ are paired by using a pairing algorithm.

3.2   1D ANM to Obtain Time Delays and Complex Gains

After obtaining $\hat{\theta}_l$, $\hat{\phi}_l$ and $\hat{\mathbf{H}}[k]$ by the above 2D ANM channel estimation, we can get the antenna array response vectors $\mathbf{a}_{MS}(\hat{\theta}_l)$ and $\mathbf{a}_{BS}(\hat{\phi}_l)$. Next, we exploit 1D ANM parameters estimation to obtain the time delay and complex gains [23].

For achieving the estimation of the time delay τ_l and the complex gain α_l, we rewrite the channel as an OFDM channel,

$$h[k] = \sum_{l=1}^{L} \alpha_l e^{-j2\pi\frac{\tau_l}{K}f_s k}, \tag{12}$$

where $h[k]$ is given by the formulation $h[k] = \mathbf{H}[k]\left[\mathbf{a}_{MS}(\hat{\theta}_l)\mathbf{a}_{BS}^{H}(\hat{\phi}_l)\right]^{\dagger}$. Here, $[\cdot]^{\dagger}$ indicates the matrix or vector pseudo-inverse. Set the OFDM channel vector $\mathbf{h} = [h[0], h[1], \cdots, h[\tilde{K}-1]]^{\top} \in \mathbb{C}^{\tilde{K}\times 1}$ corresponding to $\left[\mathbf{H}[0], \mathbf{H}[1], \cdots, \mathbf{H}[\tilde{K}-1]\right]^{\top}$, where subcarrier k is variable. The OFDM channel matrix $\mathbf{h}$ can be expressed as follows.

$$\mathbf{h} = \sum_{l=1}^{L} \alpha_l \mathbf{a}_{\tau}(f_l), \tag{13}$$

where the time delay response vector is defined as

$$\mathbf{a}_{\tau}(f) = \frac{1}{\sqrt{\tilde{K}}}[1, e^{-j2\pi f}, \cdots, e^{-j2\pi(\tilde{K}-1)f}]^{\top} \in \mathbb{C}^{\tilde{K}\times 1}, \tag{14}$$

where the frequency $f_l = \frac{\tau_l}{K} f_s$. Assume that the time delay τ_l satisfies the condition of $0 \le \tau_l \le \frac{f_s}{L_{cp}}$ and L_{cp} is the length of the cyclic prefix. Therefore, the frequency f_l belongs to the interval of $[0, \frac{L_{cp}}{K}]$.

If we want to use the 1D atomic norm to estimate channel states, the frequency f_l needs from the interval $[0, \frac{L_{cp}}{K}]$ mapping to the interval $[0, 1]$. Assuming that the system used a comb pilot allocation type, the positions of the $\widetilde{K}$ pilot subcarriers are randomly selected from L_{cp} ($\widetilde{K} < L_{cp}$) equally spaced position set: $k' \in [0, \frac{K}{L_{cp}}, \cdots, \frac{(L_{cp}-1)K}{L_{cp}}]$. Therefore, the position index k' of the comb pilot subcarrier satisfies the relationship of $k' = \frac{K}{L_{cp}} k$. The OFDM channel at the k'th carrier can be given as

$$h[k'] = h[\tfrac{K}{L_{cp}} k] = \sum_{l=1}^{L} \alpha_l e^{-j2\pi \frac{\tau_l}{L_{cp}} f_s k}, \quad k = 0, 1, \cdots, \widetilde{K}. \tag{15}$$

Now the frequency $f_l = \frac{\tau_l}{L_{cp}} f_s \in [0, 1]$, then we can utilize the atomic norm for the delays estimation. The 1D atomic norm of $\mathbf{h}$ over the atom set $\mathcal{A}_V$ is defined as

$$\|\mathbf{h}\|_{\mathcal{A}_V} = \inf \left\{ \sum_{l=1}^{L} |\alpha_l| \,\Big|\, \sum_{l=1}^{L} \alpha_l \mathbf{a}(f_l), \mathbf{a}(f_l) \in \mathcal{A}_V \right\}. \tag{16}$$

where $\mathcal{A}_V = \{\mathbf{a}(f), \forall f \in [0, 1]\}$.

We assume that the frequency f_l satisfies the frequency separation condition [22], then the atomic norm $\|\mathbf{h}\|_{\mathcal{A}_V}$ can be written as an SDP program:

$$\min_{u,t} \left\{ \frac{1}{2} t + \frac{1}{2\widetilde{K}} \mathrm{tr}(\mathbf{T}(\mathbf{u})) \right\},$$

$$\text{s.t.} \begin{pmatrix} t & \mathbf{h}^H \\ \mathbf{h} & \mathbf{T}(\mathbf{u}) \end{pmatrix} \succeq 0, \tag{17}$$

where $\mathbf{T}(\mathbf{u}) \in \mathbb{C}^{\widetilde{K} \times \widetilde{K}}$ is a PSD Toeplitz matrix constructed form its first row $\mathbf{u}$. $\mathbf{T}(\mathbf{u})$ consists of the one-level vandermonde matrix $\mathbf{A}_V(\mathbf{f})$,

$$\mathbf{T}(\mathbf{u}) = \mathbf{A}_V(\mathbf{f}) \mathbf{D} \mathbf{A}_V^H(\mathbf{f}), \tag{18}$$

where $\mathbf{A}_V(\mathbf{f}) = [\mathbf{a}(f_1), \cdots, (f_L)]$, $\mathbf{D}$ is a semi-positive diagonal matrix. Similarly, we can also extract the frequency $\hat{f}_l$ from $\mathbf{T}(\mathbf{u})$ via the MUSIC method [27].

After obtaining $\hat{\tau}_l$ of the L paths, we can form the delay response vector $\mathbf{a}_\tau(\hat{f})$, then the diagonal matrix of complex path gain $\hat{\mathbf{S}}$ can be calculated by

$$\hat{\mathbf{S}} = \mathbf{A}_\tau(\hat{f})^\dagger \hat{\mathbf{h}}, \tag{19}$$

where $\hat{\mathbf{S}} = \mathrm{diag}([\hat{\alpha}_1, \cdots, \hat{\alpha}_L])$.

Finally, the complete channel matrix $\{\mathbf{H}[k]\}_{k=0}^{K-1}$ can be recovered from the estimation of AoD/AoA, the path gain, and the time delay.

Table 1. Complexity of respective algorithms: $SNR = 20$ dB

ALG	Grid	NMSE	Complexity
D-ANM	–	$1.3e-4$	$O((N+M)^{3.5})$
CS-OMP	$40 \times 40 \times 40$	$7.9e-4$	$O(40^3 + NMK)$
ANM	–	$9.4e-5$	$O((NM\widetilde{K})^{3.5})$

4   Computational Complexity Analysis

We compare the computational complexity of our proposed method versus the vectorized 3D ANM and CS methods. We apply the MUSIC method for both 1D and 2D Vandermonde decomposition. The CS method employs an orthogonal matching pursuit (OMP) algorithm to solve estimation problem and is solved on a $40 \times 40 \times 40$ (AoD-AoA-time delay) grid. If not specifically stated, we denote the decomposable 3D ANM as D-ANM, the vectorized 3D ANM as ANM, the CS as CS-OMP.

From Table 1, we can see that our proposed method has a significant advantage in the computational efficiency of multi-carrier systems for large-scale antenna arrays. The computational complexity of our proposed method is much lower than the ANM and CS methods. In addition, our proposed method achieves a higher estimation accuracy than the CS method.

5   Estimation Accuracy Analysis

In this section, numerical simulation is conducted to evaluate the performance of our proposed decomposable 3D ANM method. We compare the performance of our proposed method with the ANM and CS methods. The ANM algorithms are implemented by using MATLAB CVX toolbox [28]. The mean square error (MSE) of all methods is calculated as a performance criterion. All the results are obtained by averaging over 200 Monte Carlo trials. If not specifically stated, the default simulation settings are listed in Table 2.

We first compare the estimation accuracy of the channel parameters (AoDs, AoAs, and time delays). From Fig. 2, we can see that our proposed method yields accurate estimation of angle parameters. The MSE performance of our proposed D-ANM method is quite close to that of the ANM. The CS method performs much worse due to its discretizing the continuous angle parameters into gird regardless of the SNR range. Then, Fig. 2(b) demonstrates that the proposed method performance is slightly inferior to the ANM, and greatly superior to the CS method. The reason is that time delay is recovered from the estimated channel and the estimation accuracy of delay is limited by the channel accuracy.

Next, we compare the MSE performance of channel estimation achieved by the different channel estimation methods versus SNR. As can be seen from

Table 2. The simulation settings

Parameter	Value
N_{MS}	32
N_{BS}	64
L	4
α_L	Random, Gaussian generated
$\sin(\theta_l)$	Random, uniformly generated
$\sin(\phi_l)$	Random, uniformly generated
τ_l	$(0, 100)$ nanosecond, uniformly generated
f_s	0.32 GHz
f_c	28 GHz
d	$\frac{3.0 \times 10^8}{2 f_c}$
K	128
$\hat{K}$	32
L_{CP}	32
N_S	3
T	6

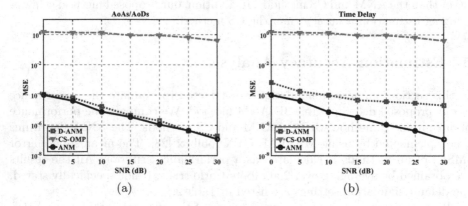

Fig. 2. MSEs associated with different parameters versus SNR.

Fig. 3, the MSEs of all methods decrease as the SNR increases. Our proposed method is comparable to ANM, and their performance is higher than CS. ANM is the development of the gridless CS method, and it recover channel parameters with high accuracy, thus the channel estimation performance of ANM is better than CS.

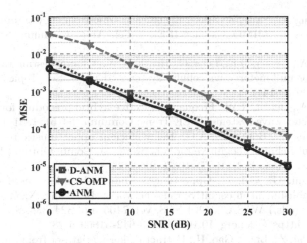

Fig. 3. Comparison of MSE performance versus SNR.

6 Conclusion

We propose a decomposable 3D ANM estimation method for downlink channel of mmWave massive MIMO-OFDM system. By utilizing the sparse multi-dimensional structure of mmWave massive MIMO-OFDM channels, the channel estimation can be formulated as a 3D line spectrum estimation problem. The 3D estimation can be effectively solved based on the decomposable ANM method, and parameters can be extracted from the channel Toeplitz structure. We compare our proposed method with the CS and vectorized 3D ANM methods. The simulation results show that our proposed method has a higher performance than the CS method in terms of both estimation accuracy and computational complexity. The complexity of our proposed method is excellently reduced than traditional vectorized 3D ANM. For future work, it would be interesting to design hybrid analog-digital precoding algorithm based on the known CSI to obtain precoding gains.

Acknowledgments. This work was supported by the National Natural Science Foundation of China (Grant No. 61871023 and 61572070) and the Fundamental Research Funds for the Central Universities (Grant No. 2017YJS035 and 2016JBZ003).

References

1. Heath, R.W., Gonzlez-Prelcic, N., Rangan, S., Roh, W., Sayeed, A.M.: An overview of signal processing techniques for millimeter wave MIMO systems. IEEE J. Sel. Topics Sig. Process. **10**(3), 436–453 (2016)
2. Rangan, S., Rappaport, T.S., Erkip, E.: Millimeter-wave cellular wireless networks: potentials and challenges. Proc. IEEE **102**(3), 366–385 (2014)
3. Larsson, E.G., Edfors, O., Tufvesson, F., Marzetta, T.L.: Massive MIMO for next generation wireless systems. IEEE Commun. Mag. **52**(2), 186–195 (2014)

4. Dai, L., Wang, Z., Yang, Z.: Spectrally efficient time-frequency training OFDM for mobile large-scale MIMO systems. IEEE J. Sel. Areas Commun. **31**(2), 251–263 (2013)
5. Alkhateeb, A., Ayach, O.E., Leus, G., Heath, R.W.: Channel estimation and hybrid precoding for millimeter wave cellular systems. IEEE J. Sel. Topics Sig. Process. **8**(5), 831–846 (2014)
6. Alkhateeb, A., Heath, R.W.: Frequency selective hybrid precoding for limited feedback millimeter wave systems. IEEE Trans. Commun. **64**(5), 1801–1818 (2016)
7. Cai, Z., Duan, Y., Bourgeois, A.G.: Delay efficient opportunistic routing in asynchronous multi-channel cognitive radio networks. J. Comb. Optim. **29**(4), 815–835 (2015). https://doi.org/10.1007/s10878-013-9623-y
8. Duan, Y., Liu, G., Cai, Z.: Opportunistic channel-hopping based effective rendezvous establishment in cognitive radio networks. In: Wang, X., Zheng, R., Jing, T., Xing, K. (eds.) WASA 2012. LNCS, vol. 7405, pp. 324–336. Springer, Heidelberg (2012). https://doi.org/10.1007/978-3-642-31869-6_28
9. Cheng, S., Cai, Z., Li, J., Gao, H.: Extracting kernel dataset from big sensory data in wireless sensor networks. IEEE Trans. Knowl. Data Eng. **29**(4), 813–827 (2017)
10. Li, J., Cheng, S., Li, Y., Cai, Z.: Approximate holistic aggregation in wireless sensor networks. In: 2015 IEEE 35th International Conference on Distributed Computing Systems, pp. 740–741, June 2015
11. He, Z., Cai, Z., Cheng, S., Wang, X.: Approximate aggregation for tracking quantiles and range countings in wireless sensor networks. Theoret. Comput. Sci. **607**, 07 (2015)
12. Cheng, S., Cai, Z., Li, J.: Curve query processing in wireless sensor networks. IEEE Trans. Veh. Technol. **64**(11), 5198–5209 (2015)
13. Mao, J., Tian, W., Li, P., Wei, T., Liang, Z.: Phishing-alarm: robust and efficient phishing detection via page component similarity. IEEE Access **5**, 17 020–17 030 (2017)
14. Mao, J., Tian, W., Jiang, J., He, Z., Zhou, Z., Liu, J.: Understanding structure-based social network de-anonymization techniques via empirical analysis. EURASIP J. Wirel. Commun. Netw. **2018**(1), 279 (2018). https://doi.org/10.1186/s13638-018-1291-2
15. Jia, Y., Chen, Y., Dong, X., Saxena, P., Mao, J., Liang, Z.: Man-in-the-browser-cache: persisting HTTPS attacks via browser cache poisoning. Comput. Secur. **55**, 08 (2015)
16. Mao, J., et al.: Phishing page detection via learning classifiers from page layout feature. EURASIP J. Wirel. Commun. Netw. **2019**(1), 43 (2019). https://doi.org/10.1186/s13638-019-1361-0
17. Berger, C.R., Wang, Z., Huang, J., Zhou, S.: Application of compressive sensing to sparse channel estimation. IEEE Commun. Mag. **48**(11), 164–174 (2010)
18. Wen, C., Jin, S., Wong, K., Chen, J., Ting, P.: Channel estimation for massive MIMO using Gaussian-mixture Bayesian learning. IEEE Trans. Wirel. Commun. **14**(3), 1356–1368 (2015)
19. Zhou, Z., Fang, J., Yang, L., Li, H., Chen, Z., Blum, R.S.: Low-rank tensor decomposition-aided channel estimation for millimeter wave MIMO-OFDM systems. IEEE J. Sel. Areas Commun. **35**(7), 1524–1538 (2017)
20. Gao, Z., Dai, L., Wang, Z., Chen, S.: Spatially common sparsity based adaptive channel estimation and feedback for FDD massive MIMO. IEEE Trans. Sig. Process. **63**(23), 6169–6183 (2015)

21. Nion, D., Sidiropoulos, N.D.: Tensor algebra and multidimensional harmonic retrieval in signal processing for MIMO radar. IEEE Trans. Sig. Process. **58**(11), 5693–5705 (2010)
22. Zhang, Z., Wang, Y., Tian, Z.: Efficient two-dimensional line spectrum estimation based on decoupled atomic norm minimization (2018)
23. Pejoski, S., Kafedziski, V.: Estimation of sparse time dispersive channels in pilot aided OFDM using atomic norm. IEEE Wirel. Commun. Lett. **4**(4), 397–400 (2015)
24. Wang, Y., Xu, P., Tian, Z.: Efficient channel estimation for massive MIMO systems via truncated two-dimensional atomic norm minimization. In: 2017 IEEE International Conference on Communications (ICC), pp. 1–6, May 2017
25. Yang, Z., Xie, L., Stoica, P.: Vandermonde decomposition of multilevel toeplitz matrices with application to multidimensional super-resolution. IEEE Trans. Inf. Theory **62**(6), 3685–3701 (2016)
26. Akdeniz, M.R., et al.: Millimeter wave channel modeling and cellular capacity evaluation. IEEE J. Sel. Areas Commun. **32**(6), 1164–1179 (2014)
27. Zhang, X., Xu, L., Xu, L., Xu, D.: Direction of departure (DOD) and direction of arrival (DOA) estimation in MIMO radar with reduced-dimension music. IEEE Commun. Lett. **14**(12), 1161–1163 (2010)
28. Grant, M., Boyd, S.: CVX: Matlab software for disciplined convex programming, version 2.1, March 2014. http://cvxr.com/cvx

Model Based Adaptive Data Acquisition for Internet of Things

Ran Bi[1(✉)], Jiankang Ren[1(✉)], Hao Wang[2(✉)], Qian Liu[1(✉)],
and Shan Huang[1(✉)]

[1] School of Computer Science and Technology, Dalian University of Technology,
Dalian 116024, China
{biran,rjk,qianliu}@dlut.edu.cn, hs2018@mail.dlut.edu.cn
[2] Department of Computer Science and Technology, Heilongjiang University,
Harbin 150080, China
wanghao@hlju.edu.cn

Abstract. In many IoT applications, sensor nodes are distributed over a region of interests and collect data at a specified time interval. With the development of hardware, the monitoring tasks become diversity. The specified acquisition strategy can not adaptively adjust the sampling interval. Due to the measurement error and the uncertainty of the environment, equi-frequency sampling technique may result in misunderstandings to the physical world. Based on Taylor expansion and time series analysis, this paper presents a sensed data model. The model can be considered as a unified approach, where linear regression or spline interpolation is a special case of our model. A mathematical method for parameter estimation is proposed, which can minimize the measurement error. And we prove the estimation is unbias. An adaptive data acquisition algorithm is proposed. Performance evaluation on the real data set verifies that the proposed algorithms have high performance in terms of accuracy and effectiveness.

Keywords: Data model · Adaptive acquisition · Internet of Things

1 Introduction

The last decade has seen Internet of Things emerging as a new network of computing, where thousands of inexpensive and computational devices can be deployed to monitor the physical components [1,2]. In many IoT applications, sensor nodes are distributed over a region of interests and collect data at a specified time interval [3]. Stationary cycle of data collection is well known and widely recognized in the internet of things. In many applications, sensor node samples data based on equi-frequency sampling (EFS) technique. To reduce the communication cost, most works focus on the approximate data processing, including data collection [4,5], data aggregation processing [6,7], private mechanism [8,9], and curve query processing [10].

© Springer Nature Switzerland AG 2019
E. S. Biagioni et al. (Eds.): WASA 2019, LNCS 11604, pp. 16–28, 2019.
https://doi.org/10.1007/978-3-030-23597-0_2

Data acquisition is a fundamental problem in many IoT applications. As pioneering work [11], Madden et al. provided a statistics prediction model based on multivariate Gaussian distribution. The main challenge of model based data collection approaches are to construct and maintain the availability of the model, so that the accuracy of the estimated data can be guaranteed. However, the model may overlook the complicated spatial-temporal correlations among the sensory data. With the development of hardware, the monitoring tasks become diversity. The specified model can not adaptively adjust the data acquisition strategy. Query driven data collection algorithms are well-designed for a given category of query processing.

There exists few research works focusing on the adaptive sampling in Internet of Things. Since the dataset discretely sampled from the physical world may miss some critical points, and it will result in failures in querying convexity or the interval of critical points. [4] proposed ϵ-Kernel Dataset, which can represent the information of large dataset with small size. In [12], the author proposed an adaptive data acquisition approach, in order to reconstruct the physical world with precision guarantee. According to numerical analysis techniques and Lagrange interpolation, [13] provided a data acquisition algorithm to retrieve the critical points approximately. By Kalman Filter, the authors [14] proposed a strategy to predict the sensory data. The sampling frequency will modify, if the estimation exceeds a given range. However, the proposed adaptive sampling methods depend on some priori knowledge and they overlook the sensing error incurred by the hardware and the environment.

The above facts motivate us to investigate a comprehensive model for data acquisition. We provide a sensed data model based on Taylor expansion and the time series analysis. The proposed model can be considered as a unified approach, where linear regression or spline interpolation is a special case of our model. The spatial-temporal correlation among sensory data of local area is represented as a Gaussian process. By maximizing the log-likelihood function, we can obtain the parameter estimation. To capture the curvity, a model based data acquisition algorithm is provided and the theoretical analysis is given. The contributions of this paper are summarized as follows.

- Sensed data model is given, which integrates the measurement error and spatial-temporal correlation among sensory data of local area. Maximum log-likelihood estimation is applied to achieve the estimations of parameters in the data model.
- We combine likelihood estimation and kernel function. A mathematical method for parameter estimation is proposed, which can minimize the measurement error.
- Based on the model, we propose an adaptive sampling algorithm, which aims at decreasing the data transmission and forward extremum points and inflection points. And we prove the estimation is unbias.
- The extensive simulations on the real data set are conducted. The experimental results show that the proposed algorithm have high performance in terms of accuracy and effectiveness.

The rest of this paper is structured as following. Section 2 introduces Sensed Data Model. Section 3 presents the mathematical foundations of adaptive data acquisition algorithm. Section 4 provides curvity aware data acquisition algorithm and the theoretical performance is analyzed. Experimental results are illustrated in Sect. 5, and Sect. 6 concludes this paper.

2   Sensed Data Model

In this section, we provide a sensed data model based on the time series analysis. By maximizing the joint log-likelihood function, we can obtain the parameter estimation. The proposed model can be considered as a comprehensive approach and a unified model, where linear regression or spline interpolation is a special case of our model.

The data model is similar to that in [15], it integrates global property of sensed data and individual deviation from the mean of sensed data of adjacent area. We will introduce the parameters of the model briefly.

It is assumed that the monitoring area is deployed by m sensor nodes, and the ids of the nodes are $1, 2, ..., m$. During a period of time, the sampled data by the node i are $d_{i1}, d_{i2}, ..., d_{in}$, where d_{ij} represents the sensed data of node i at time t_{ij}. Then sensed data can be described as [16,17]

$$d(t_{ij}) = \alpha(t_{ij}) + v_i(t_{ij}) + \varepsilon_i(t_{ij}) \tag{1}$$

where, $i = 1, 2, ..., m; j = 1, 2, ..., n_i$. $\alpha(t_{ij})$ indicates the mean sensed value of node i at time t_{ij} and $v_i(t_{ij})$ is the individual deviation from $\alpha(t_{ij})$. $\varepsilon_i(t_{ij})$ is the measurement error of node i at time t_{ij}, which is incurred by noise.

In the real application of senor networks, there exists spatial-temporal correlation among sensed data in the local area. $v_i(t)$ can be represented as a Gaussian process with mean μ_i and covariance $Cov_i(t)$. $\varepsilon_i(t)$ can be seen as an uncorrelated Gaussian process with mean 0 and variance function $\sigma^2(t)$. Let $\tilde{d} = \frac{\sum_{i=1}^{m} \sum_{j=1}^{n_i} d_{ij}}{\sum_{i=1}^{m} n_i}$ denote the average of the data in the local area during a given time, and $\tilde{d}_i = \frac{\sum_{j=1}^{n_i} d_{ij}}{n_i}$ denotes the average of the data sampled by node i. Let $C_i = \tilde{d}_i - \tilde{d}$, which is considered as a constant. Then we can have that

$$\begin{aligned} s_i(t_{ij}) &= d_i(t_{ij}) - C_i \\ &= \alpha(t_{ij}) + (v_i(t_{ij}) - C_i) + \varepsilon_i(t_{ij}) \\ &= \alpha(t_{ij}) + \varphi_i(t_{ij}) + \varepsilon_i(t_{ij}), j = 1, ..., n; i = 1, ..., m. \end{aligned} \tag{2}$$

where $j = 1, ..., n; i = 1, ..., m$. $\varphi_i(t)$ and $\varepsilon_i(t)$ are independent, where $\varphi_i(t)$ is a Gaussian process with mean 0. In this paper, the proposed sensed data model is as follows,

$$s_i(t_{ij}) = \alpha(t_{ij}) + \varphi_i(t_{ij}) + \varepsilon_i(t_{ij}). \tag{3}$$

According to Taylor Expansion about t_{ij}, $\alpha(t_{ij})$ and $\varphi_i(t_{ij})$ can be approximated by k-th order polynomials within a neighborhood of t.

$$\alpha(t_{ij}) \approx \alpha(t) + \alpha'(t)(t_{ij} - t) + \cdots + \frac{\alpha^{(k)}(t)}{k!}(t_{ij} - t)^k$$

$$\varphi_i(t_{ij}) \approx \varphi_i(t) + \varphi_i'(t)(t_{ij} - t) + \cdots + \frac{\varphi_i^{(k)}(t)}{k!}(t_{ij} - t)^k, i = 1, ..., m \tag{4}$$

Denote $X_{ij} = (1, t_{ij} - t, ..., (t_{ij} - t)^k)^T, \gamma = (\alpha(t), \alpha'(t), ..., \frac{\alpha^{(k)}(t)}{k!})^T, \psi_i = (\varphi_i(t), \varphi_i'(t), ..., \frac{\varphi_i^{(k)}(t)}{k!})^T$, we have the following,

$$\alpha(t_{ij}) \approx X_{ij}^T \gamma, \varphi_i(t_{ij}) \approx X_{ij}^T \psi_i.$$

then the proposed sensed data model as follows,

$$s_i(t_{ij}) = X_{ij}^T(\gamma + \psi_i) + \varepsilon_i(t_{ij}), j = 1, ..., n_i; i = 1, ..., m. \tag{5}$$

Let $S_i = (s_i(t_{i1}), s_i(t_{i2}), ..., s_i(t_{in_i}))^T, X_i = (X_{i1}, X_{i2}, ..., X_{in_i})^T, \varepsilon_i = (\varepsilon_i(t_{i1}), \varepsilon_i(t_{i2}), ..., \varepsilon_i(t_{in_i}))^T$, we can obtain the following equation.

$$S_i = X_i(\gamma + \psi_i) + \varepsilon_i, i = 1, ..., m \tag{6}$$

where ψ_i follows the distribution of $N(\mathbf{0}, D_i)$ and $D_i = E(\psi_i \psi_i^T)$. Thus we can get to know.

$$\begin{pmatrix} S_1 \\ \vdots \\ S_m \end{pmatrix} = \begin{pmatrix} X_1(\gamma + \psi_1) \\ \vdots \\ X_m(\gamma + \psi_m) \end{pmatrix} + \begin{pmatrix} \varepsilon_1 \\ \vdots \\ \varepsilon_m \end{pmatrix} \tag{7}$$

Let $\mathbf{S} = (S_1^T, ..., S_m^T)^T, \boldsymbol{\varepsilon} = (\varepsilon_1^T, ..., \varepsilon_m^T)^T, \mathbf{Y} = diag(X_1, ..., X_m)$. And similar notations are denoted as $\mathbf{X}$ and $\boldsymbol{\psi}$. We can have the following,

$$\mathbf{S} = \mathbf{X}\gamma + \mathbf{Y}\boldsymbol{\psi} + \boldsymbol{\varepsilon} \tag{8}$$

Since ψ_i follows distribution of $N(\mathbf{0}, D_i)$, then $\boldsymbol{\psi}$ follows normal distribution $N(\mathbf{0}, \mathbf{D})$, in which $\mathbf{D} = diag(D_1, ..., D_m)$. $\boldsymbol{\varepsilon}$ follows normal distribution $N(\mathbf{0}, \mathbf{R})$, where $\mathbf{R} = diag(\sigma_1^2 I_{n_1}, ..., \sigma_m^2 I_{n_m})$ and I_{n_i} is an identity matrix of n_i dimensions.

Based on the above discussion, we get the joint distribution of $\boldsymbol{\psi}$ and $\boldsymbol{\varepsilon}$, the expectation is $\mathbf{0}$ and variance matrix is $\begin{pmatrix} \mathbf{D} & \mathbf{0} \\ \mathbf{0} & \mathbf{R} \end{pmatrix}$.

We denote $\mathbf{D} = \mathbf{D}(\boldsymbol{\tau})$ and $\mathbf{R} = \sigma^2 \Sigma$, where $\Sigma = diag\left(\frac{\sigma_1^2}{\sigma^2} I_{n_1}, ..., \frac{\sigma_m^2}{\sigma^2} I_{n_m}\right) = \Sigma(\boldsymbol{\eta})$. The vectors $\boldsymbol{\tau}$ and $\boldsymbol{\eta}$ are parameters of variance matrix associated with $\mathbf{D}$ and $\mathbf{R}$ respectively. Thus the variance parameter is $\kappa(\boldsymbol{\tau}, \sigma^2, \boldsymbol{\eta})$. $\boldsymbol{\psi}$ and $\boldsymbol{\varepsilon}$ are independent, and thus the variance matrix of $\mathbf{Y}\boldsymbol{\psi} + \boldsymbol{\varepsilon}$ is $\mathbf{Y}\mathbf{D}\mathbf{Y}^T + \mathbf{R}$. Denote $\mathbf{H} = \mathbf{Y}\mathbf{D}\mathbf{Y}^T + \mathbf{R}$, then $\mathbf{S} = \mathbf{X}\gamma + \mathbf{Y}\boldsymbol{\psi} + \boldsymbol{\varepsilon}$ follows multivariate normal distribution $N(\mathbf{X}\gamma, \mathbf{H})$.

The estimations of γ and $\boldsymbol{\psi}$ can be achieved by maximizing the *joint* likelihood of $(\mathbf{S}, \boldsymbol{\psi})$. Actually, the likelihood is not joint, since it is difficult to obtain the vector ψ from the sensed data. Therefore, the joint probability density of $\mathbf{S}$ and ψ can be computed as the product of the conditional density of $\mathbf{S}$.

$$f(\mathbf{S}, \psi; \gamma, \kappa) = f(\mathbf{S}|\psi; \gamma, \eta) * f(\psi; \tau) \tag{9}$$

Since $\mathbf{S}|\phi$ follows normal distribution $N(\mathbf{X}\gamma + \mathbf{Y}\psi, \mathbf{R})$ and ψ follows distribution $N(\mathbf{0}, \mathbf{D})$. The log-likelihood of $\mathbf{S}$ given ψ excepting constant terms as that

$$l(\gamma, \eta; \mathbf{S}|\psi) = -\frac{1}{2}\left(\log|\mathbf{R}| + (\mathbf{S} - \mathbf{X}\gamma - \mathbf{Y}\psi)^T \mathbf{R}^{-1}(\mathbf{S} - \mathbf{X}\gamma - \mathbf{Y}\psi)\right). \tag{10}$$

The log-likelihood of ψ excepting constant terms as follows,

$$l(\tau; \psi) = -\frac{1}{2}\left(\log|\mathbf{D}| + \psi^T \mathbf{D}^{-1}\psi\right). \tag{11}$$

Thus the *joint* log-likelihood, excepting constant terms is given as

$$l(\gamma, \eta; \mathbf{S}|\psi) + l(\tau; \psi) = -\frac{1}{2}\left(\log|\mathbf{R}| + (\mathbf{S} - \mathbf{X}\gamma - \mathbf{Y}\psi)^T \mathbf{R}^{-1}(\mathbf{S} - \mathbf{X}\gamma - \mathbf{Y}\psi)\right)$$
$$-\frac{1}{2}\left(\log|\mathbf{D}| + \psi^T \mathbf{D}^{-1}\psi\right) \tag{12}$$

3   Mathematical Foundation for Parameter Estimation

Property 1. If $\mathbf{c}$, $\mathbf{x}$ and $f(\mathbf{x})$ are $np * 1$ vectors, $\mathbf{P}$ and $\mathbf{Q}$ are $n * n$ matrices. Denote $\dot{\mathbf{P}}_i = \frac{\partial \mathbf{P}}{\partial x_i}$, the following equations are hold.

$$\frac{\partial \mathbf{x}^T \mathbf{P}\mathbf{x}}{\partial \mathbf{x}} = 2\mathbf{P}\mathbf{x} \ (a), \qquad \frac{\partial \mathbf{P}^{-1}}{\partial x_i} = -\mathbf{P}^{-1}\dot{\mathbf{P}}_i\mathbf{P}^{-1} \ (b)$$

$$\frac{\partial f(\mathbf{x})^T \mathbf{P} f(\mathbf{x})}{\partial \mathbf{x}} = 2\frac{\partial f(\mathbf{x})^T}{\partial \mathbf{x}}\mathbf{P}f(\mathbf{x}) \ (c) \qquad \frac{\partial \log|\mathbf{P}|}{\partial x_i} = tr(\mathbf{P}^{-1}\dot{\mathbf{P}}_i) \ (d) \tag{13}$$

$$\frac{\partial (\mathbf{c} - \mathbf{P}\mathbf{x})^T \mathbf{Q}(\mathbf{c} - \mathbf{P}\mathbf{x})}{\partial \mathbf{x}} = -2\mathbf{P}^T \mathbf{Q}(\mathbf{c} - \mathbf{P}\mathbf{x}) \ (e)$$

Lemma 1. *The derivatives of* joint *log-likelihood with respect to* γ *and* ψ *are as follows,*

$$\frac{\partial l(\gamma, \kappa; \mathbf{S}, \psi)}{\partial \gamma} = \mathbf{X}^T \mathbf{R}^{-1}(\mathbf{S} - \mathbf{X}\gamma - \mathbf{Y}\psi)$$
$$\frac{\partial l(\gamma, \kappa; \mathbf{S}, \psi)}{\partial \psi} = \mathbf{Y}^T \mathbf{R}^{-1}(\mathbf{S} - \mathbf{X}\gamma - \mathbf{Y}\psi) - \mathbf{D}^{-1}\psi \tag{14}$$

Proof. Due to the limited space, the details of the proof will omit. Based on formula (12) and (13-e), we have $\frac{\partial(\mathbf{S}-\mathbf{X}\gamma-\mathbf{Y}\psi)^T \mathbf{R}^{-1}(\mathbf{S}-\mathbf{X}\gamma-\mathbf{Y}\psi)}{\partial \gamma} = -2\mathbf{X}^T \mathbf{R}^{-1}(\mathbf{S} - \mathbf{X}\gamma - \mathbf{Y}\psi)$ According to (13-a), we get that $\frac{\partial l(\gamma, \kappa; \mathbf{S}, \psi)}{\partial \psi} = \mathbf{Y}^T \mathbf{R}^{-1}(\mathbf{S} - \mathbf{X}\gamma - \mathbf{Y}\psi) - \mathbf{D}^{-1}\psi$

Lemma 2. *The estimations for γ and ψ can be obtained by maximizing the log-likelihood, and they are equivalent to the solutions of the following equations,*

$$\begin{pmatrix} \mathbf{X}^T\mathbf{R}^{-1}\mathbf{X} & \mathbf{X}^T\mathbf{R}^{-1}\mathbf{Y} \\ \mathbf{Y}^T\mathbf{R}^{-1}\mathbf{X} & \mathbf{Y}^T\mathbf{R}^{-1}\mathbf{Y} + \mathbf{D}^{-1} \end{pmatrix} \begin{pmatrix} \hat{\gamma} \\ \hat{\psi} \end{pmatrix} = \begin{pmatrix} \mathbf{X}^T\mathbf{R}^{-1}\mathbf{S} \\ \mathbf{Y}^T\mathbf{R}^{-1}\mathbf{S} \end{pmatrix} \qquad (15)$$

Proof. For given $\mathbf{R}$ and $\mathbf{D}$, maximizing the log-likelihood are equivalent to solving the following the equations.

$$\begin{cases} \frac{\partial l(\gamma,\kappa;\mathbf{S},\psi)}{\partial \gamma} = 0 \\ \frac{\partial l(\gamma,\kappa;\mathbf{S},\psi)}{\partial \psi} = 0 \end{cases} \qquad (16)$$

$$\Rightarrow \begin{cases} \mathbf{X}^T\mathbf{R}^{-1}(\mathbf{S} - \mathbf{X}\gamma - \mathbf{Y}\psi) = 0 \\ \mathbf{Y}^T\mathbf{R}^{-1}(\mathbf{S} - \mathbf{X}\gamma - \mathbf{Y}\psi) - \mathbf{D}^{-1}\psi = 0 \end{cases} \qquad (17)$$

We know that maximizing the log-likelihood are equivalent to solving Eq. (15).

In the following, we will provide a mathematical methods to compute γ and ψ.

Property 2. If $\mathbf{M}$ is a $m * m$ matrix, $\mathbf{P}$ is a $m * n$ matrix, $\mathbf{Q}$ is a $n * m$ matrix and $\mathbf{D}$ is a $n * n$ matrix, then we have the following,

$$(\mathbf{M} + \mathbf{P}\mathbf{D}\mathbf{Q})^{-1} = \mathbf{M}^{-1} - \mathbf{M}^{-1}\mathbf{P}(\mathbf{D}^{-1} + \mathbf{Q}\mathbf{M}^{-1}\mathbf{P})^{-1}\mathbf{Q}\mathbf{M}^{-1} \qquad (18)$$

Lemma 3. *The matrices in Eq. (15) satisfy the following,*

$$\begin{aligned} \mathbf{R}^{-1}\mathbf{Y}(\mathbf{Y}^T\mathbf{R}^{-1}\mathbf{Y} + \mathbf{D}^{-1})^{-1}\mathbf{Y}^T &= (\mathbf{R} + \mathbf{Y}\mathbf{D}\mathbf{Y}^T)^{-1}\mathbf{Y}\mathbf{D}\mathbf{Y}^T \\ \mathbf{R}^{-1}\mathbf{Y}(\mathbf{Y}^T\mathbf{R}^{-1}\mathbf{Y} + \mathbf{D}^{-1})^{-1} &= (\mathbf{R} + \mathbf{Y}\mathbf{D}\mathbf{Y}^T)^{-1}\mathbf{Y}\mathbf{D} \end{aligned} \qquad (19)$$

Proof. According to Property 2, we can get that

$$\begin{aligned} (\mathbf{R} + \mathbf{Y}\mathbf{D}\mathbf{Y}^T)^{-1} &= \mathbf{R}^{-1} - \mathbf{R}^{-1}\mathbf{Y}(\mathbf{D}^{-1} + \mathbf{Y}^T\mathbf{R}^{-1}\mathbf{Y})^{-1}\mathbf{Y}^T\mathbf{R}^{-1} \\ \Rightarrow \mathbf{R}^{-1}\mathbf{Y}(\mathbf{D}^{-1} + \mathbf{Y}^T\mathbf{R}^{-1}\mathbf{Y})^{-1}\mathbf{Y}^T\mathbf{R}^{-1} &= \mathbf{R}^{-1} - (\mathbf{R} + \mathbf{Y}\mathbf{D}\mathbf{Y}^T)^{-1} \end{aligned} \qquad (20)$$

Both sides of the above equation are left multiplied by $\mathbf{R}$, and rearrange the terms,

$$\mathbf{Y}(\mathbf{D}^{-1} + \mathbf{Y}^T\mathbf{R}^{-1}\mathbf{Y})^{-1}\mathbf{Y}^T\mathbf{R}^{-1} = \mathbf{Y}\mathbf{D}\mathbf{Y}^T(\mathbf{R} + \mathbf{Y}\mathbf{D}\mathbf{Y}^T)^{-1}. \qquad (21)$$

Since $\mathbf{R}$ and $\mathbf{D}$ are symmetric matrices, $\mathbf{R}^T = \mathbf{R}$, and $\mathbf{D}^T = \mathbf{D}$. We know that $(\mathbf{R}^{-1})^T = \mathbf{R}^{-1}$ and $(\mathbf{D}^{-1})^T = \mathbf{D}^{-1}$. We transpose the both sides of Eq. (21),

$$\left(\mathbf{Y}(\mathbf{D}^{-1} + \mathbf{Y}^T\mathbf{R}^{-1}\mathbf{Y})^{-1}\mathbf{Y}^T\mathbf{R}^{-1}\right)^T = \mathbf{R}^{-1}\mathbf{Y}(\mathbf{D}^{-1} + \mathbf{Y}^T\mathbf{R}^{-1}\mathbf{Y})^{-1}\mathbf{Y}^T \qquad (22)$$

$$\left(\mathbf{Y}\mathbf{D}\mathbf{Y}^T(\mathbf{R} + \mathbf{Y}\mathbf{D}\mathbf{Y}^T)^{-1}\right)^T = (\mathbf{R} + \mathbf{Y}\mathbf{D}\mathbf{Y}^T)^{-1}\mathbf{Y}\mathbf{D}\mathbf{Y}^T \qquad (23)$$

Since $\mathbf{Y}^T$ is full rank, we know that

$$\mathbf{R}^{-1}\mathbf{Y}(\mathbf{D}^{-1} + \mathbf{Y}^T\mathbf{R}^{-1}\mathbf{Y})^{-1} = (\mathbf{R} + \mathbf{Y}\mathbf{D}\mathbf{Y}^T)^{-1}\mathbf{Y}\mathbf{D}. \qquad (24)$$

Theorem 1. *The solutions of the following linear equations (15) are as follows,*

$$\begin{cases} \hat{\gamma} = \left(\mathbf{X}^T\mathbf{H}^{-1}\mathbf{X}\right)^{-1}\mathbf{X}^T\mathbf{H}^{-1}\mathbf{S} \\ \hat{\psi} = \mathbf{D}\mathbf{Y}^T\mathbf{H}^{-1}(\mathbf{S} - \mathbf{X}\hat{\gamma}) \end{cases} \tag{25}$$

where $\mathbf{H} = \mathbf{R} + \mathbf{Y}\mathbf{D}\mathbf{Y}^T$.

Proof. For simplicity, let $\mathbf{M}_{ij}$ denote the block matrix, and the Eq. (15) can be rewritten as

$$\begin{cases} \mathbf{M}_{11}\hat{\gamma} + \mathbf{M}_{12}\hat{\psi} = \mathbf{X}^T\mathbf{R}^{-1}\mathbf{S} \\ \mathbf{M}_{21}\hat{\gamma} + \mathbf{M}_{22}\hat{\psi} = \mathbf{Y}^T\mathbf{R}^{-1}\mathbf{S} \end{cases} \tag{26}$$

Based on the second linear equation, we can derive that $\hat{\psi} = \mathbf{M}_{22}^{-1}\left(\mathbf{Y}^T\mathbf{R}^{-1}\mathbf{S} - \mathbf{M}_{21}\hat{\gamma}\right)$. Submit this into the first equation,

$$\hat{\gamma} = \left(\mathbf{M}_{11} - \mathbf{M}_{12}\mathbf{M}_{22}^{-1}\mathbf{M}_{21}\right)^{-1}\left(\mathbf{X}^T\mathbf{R}^{-1}\mathbf{S} - \mathbf{M}_{12}\mathbf{M}_{22}^{-1}\mathbf{Y}^T\mathbf{R}^{-1}\mathbf{S}\right).$$

According to Lemma 3, we have $\mathbf{R}^{-1}\mathbf{Y}\left(\mathbf{Y}^T\mathbf{R}^{-1}\mathbf{Y} + \mathbf{D}^{-1}\right)^{-1}\mathbf{Y}^T = \left(\mathbf{R} + \mathbf{Y}\mathbf{D}\mathbf{Y}^T\right)^{-1}\mathbf{Y}\mathbf{D}\mathbf{Y}^T$. Similarly, we can obtain that $\mathbf{M}_{11} - \mathbf{M}_{12}\mathbf{M}_{22}^{-1}\mathbf{M}_{21} = \mathbf{X}^T\left(\mathbf{R} + \mathbf{Y}\mathbf{D}\mathbf{Y}^T\right)^{-1}\mathbf{X}$, and $\mathbf{X}^T\mathbf{R}^{-1}\mathbf{S} - \mathbf{M}_{12}\mathbf{M}_{22}^{-1}\mathbf{Y}^T\mathbf{R}^{-1}\mathbf{S} = \mathbf{X}^T\left(\mathbf{R}^{-1} - \mathbf{R}^{-1}\mathbf{Y}\left(\mathbf{Y}^T\mathbf{R}^{-1}\mathbf{Y} + \mathbf{D}^{-1}\right)^{-1}\mathbf{Y}^T\mathbf{R}^{-1}\right)\mathbf{S}$. Based on Property 2, we have $\left(\mathbf{R} + \mathbf{Y}\mathbf{D}\mathbf{Y}^T\right)^{-1} = \mathbf{R}^{-1} - \mathbf{R}^{-1}\mathbf{Y}\left(\mathbf{Y}^T\mathbf{R}^{-1}\mathbf{Y} + \mathbf{D}^{-1}\right)^{-1}\mathbf{Y}^T\mathbf{R}^{-1}$.

Denote $\mathbf{H} = \mathbf{R} + \mathbf{Y}\mathbf{D}\mathbf{Y}^T$, we can derive that $\hat{\gamma} = \left(\mathbf{X}^T\mathbf{H}^{-1}\mathbf{X}\right)^{-1}\mathbf{X}^T\mathbf{H}^{-1}\mathbf{S}$.

Since $\hat{\psi} = \mathbf{M}_{22}^{-1}\left(\mathbf{Y}^T\mathbf{R}^{-1}\mathbf{S} - \mathbf{M}_{21}\hat{\gamma}\right) = \left(\mathbf{Y}^T\mathbf{R}^{-1}\mathbf{Y} + \mathbf{D}^{-1}\right)^{-1}\mathbf{Y}^T\mathbf{R}^{-1}(\mathbf{S} - \mathbf{X}\hat{\gamma})$, according to Property 2, $\left(\mathbf{Y}^T\mathbf{R}^{-1}\mathbf{Y} + \mathbf{D}^{-1}\right)^{-1}\mathbf{Y}^T\mathbf{R}^{-1} = \mathbf{D}\mathbf{Y}^T\left(\mathbf{R} + \mathbf{Y}\mathbf{D}\mathbf{Y}^T\right)^{-1}$, and we have $\hat{\psi} = \mathbf{D}\mathbf{Y}^T\mathbf{H}^{-1}(\mathbf{S} - \mathbf{X}\hat{\gamma})$.

Based on Theorem 1, $\hat{\gamma}$ and $\hat{\psi}$ are the estimations by maximizing log-likelihood function $l(\gamma, \kappa; \mathbf{S}, \psi)$. Maximizing log-likelihood function $l(\gamma, \kappa; \mathbf{S}, \psi)$ is equivalent to minimizing the follows,

$$\sum_{i=1}^{m}\left\{\left(S_i - X_i(\gamma + \psi_i)\right)R_i^{-1}\left(S_i - X_i(\gamma + \psi_i)\right) + \psi_i^T D_i^T \psi_i + \log|D_i| + \log|R_i|\right\}.$$

In order to exploit local neighborhood information, we combine likelihood estimation and kernel function. And thus we aim at minimizing the function as that

$$\sum_{i=1}^{m}\left\{\left(S_i - X_i(\gamma + \psi_i)\right)K_{ih}^{1/2}R_i^{-1}K_{ih}^{1/2}\left(S_i - X_i(\gamma + \psi_i)\right) + \psi_i^T D_i^T \psi_i + \log|D_i| + \log|R_i|\right\},$$

where $K_{ih} = diag\left(K_h(t_{i1} - t), ..., K_h(t_{in_i} - t)\right)$ with $K_h(t_{ij} - t) = K\left((t_{ij} - t)h^{-1}\right)h^{-1}$, and h is called bandwidth. With kernel-function, the estimations of γ and ψ are equivalent to the solutions of following equations,

$$\begin{pmatrix} \mathbf{X}^T\mathbf{R}_h\mathbf{X} & \mathbf{X}^T\mathbf{R}_h\mathbf{Y} \\ \mathbf{Y}^T\mathbf{R}_h\mathbf{X} & \mathbf{Y}^T\mathbf{R}_h\mathbf{Y} + \mathbf{D}^{-1} \end{pmatrix}\begin{pmatrix} \hat{\gamma} \\ \hat{\psi} \end{pmatrix} = \begin{pmatrix} \mathbf{X}^T\mathbf{R}_h\mathbf{S} \\ \mathbf{Y}^T\mathbf{R}_h\mathbf{S} \end{pmatrix}$$

in which $\mathbf{R}_h = diag\left(K_h^{1/2}R_1^{-1}K_h^{1/2}, ..., K_h^{1/2}R_m^{-1}K_h^{1/2}\right)$. By two-level kernel weighted function, we can have

$$
\begin{cases}
\hat{\gamma} = \left(\sum_{i=1}^{m} X_i^T \Phi_{ih} X_i\right)^{-1} \left(\sum_{i=1}^{m} X_i^T \Phi_{ih} S_i\right) \\
\hat{\psi}_i = \left(X_i^T \Phi_{ih} X_i + D_i^{-1}\right)^{-1} X_i^T \Phi_{ih} \left(S_i - X_i\hat{\gamma}\right)
\end{cases}
$$

where $V_i = K_{ih}^{1/2} X_i D_i X_i^T K_{ih}^{1/2} + R_i$ and $\Phi_{ih} = K_{ih}^{1/2} V_i^{-1} K_{ih}^{1/2}$. The estimation of $\alpha(t)$ and $\varphi_i(t)$ can be obtained,

$$
\begin{cases}
\hat{\alpha}^{(j)}(t) = j! e_{j+1}^T \left(\sum_{i=1}^{m} X_i^T \Phi_{ih} X_i\right)^{-1} \left(\sum_{i=1}^{m} X_i^T \Phi_{ih} S_i\right) \\
\hat{\varphi}_i^{(j)}(t) = j! e_{j+1}^T \left(X_i^T \Phi_{ih} X_i + D_i^{-1}\right)^{-1} X_i^T \Phi_{ih} \left(S_i - X_i\hat{\gamma}\right)
\end{cases}
\tag{27}
$$

e_{j+1} is a $(k+1)$-dimension vector, where the $(j+1)^{th}$ element is 1 and the others are 0.

4   Curvity Aware Data Acquisition Algorithm

In this section, we provide **C**urvity **A**ware **D**ata **A**cquisition algorithm, named CADA for short. Based on the error between real sensed value and data model, CADD algorithm will adjust the frequency of data acquisition, which aims at decreasing the data transmission and forward extremum points and inflection points.

If the relative error between the model and true sensed value is larger than given δ, then the node will collect sensed data at higher frequency. If the relative error gets smaller, the collection rate will be decreased. Abnormal phenomenon or breakdown of sensor node will cause drastic variation of sensed data, which incurs large error between the real sensed value and the model. Thus more data is helpful to analysis and model revision. Small error implies that sensed data model can effectively reflect the physical world. Less data can meet the requirement. Based on above observation, the sampling interval depends on the relative error.

We consider that the system consists of a base station and m IoT devices, which are divided into l disjoint groups. Each device can communicate with the station through wireless channel. In the initialization, each node will sample the data at maximum frequency f_{max}, in order to construct a more precise data model.

In the maintenance, the sampling frequency is determined based on the relative error between the model and real sensed value. If the relative error is beyond the given threshold, base station update $\hat{\alpha}(t)$ and $\hat{\psi}(t)$. And then it sends the new parameters to the IoT devices in the group. Assuming the sampling interval of node i is h_i.

1. If $\hat{\varphi}'(t) \times \hat{\varphi}'(t + h_i) \leq 0$, it implies that the extremum point will be in the next sampling interval with high probability. And then the length of sampling interval should be decreased.

2. $\hat{\varphi}''(t) \times \hat{\varphi}''(t + h_i) \leq 0$, it means that inflection point is more likely to occur in the next sampling interval. Thus we should decrease the sampling interval.
3. If $\hat{\varphi}'(t) \times \hat{\varphi}''(t + h_i) > 0$, it meas that the first derivative of the sensed data will increases or decreases monotonously, the sampling interval should be increased. However, the relative error is larger than given δ, the node should divert to another group.

Algorithm 1. Curvity Aware Data Acquisition Algorithm

Input: f_{max}, t, δ, Node id for $i = 1, ..., m$
Output: New sampling Interval

1: Initialization, node i will sample the data at maximum frequency f_{max}.
2: **if** $\hat{\varphi}'(t) \times \hat{\varphi}'(t + h_i) \leq 0$ **then**
3: $h_i = \min \left\{ h_i - t, (f_{\max})^{-1} \right\}$;
4: **end if**
5: **if** $\hat{\varphi}''(t) \times \hat{\varphi}''(t + h_i) \leq 0$ **then**
6: $h_i = \min \left\{ h_i - t, (f_{\max})^{-1} \right\}$;
7: **end if**
8: **if** $\left| \frac{s_i(t) - \hat{s}_i(t)}{s_i(t)} \right| > \delta$ **then**
9: **if** $\hat{\varphi}'(t) \times \hat{\varphi}'(t + h_i) > 0$ **then**
10: **if** More than half of member nodes reports relative error larger than δ **then**
11:   **for** Each node in the group **do**
12:    $h_i = \min \left\{ h_i - t, (f_{\max})^{-1} \right\}$;
13:   **end for**
14: **end if**
15: **else**
16: The node should be assigned to another group.
17: **end if**
18: **else**
19: $h_i = h_i + t$;
20: **end if**

4.1 Theoretical Performance Analysis

Theorem 2. *By maximizing the log-likelihood $l(\gamma, \kappa; \mathbf{S}, \psi)$, the estimation of ψ is unbiased.*

Proof. The joint distribution of ψ and $\mathbf{S}$ is that

$$\begin{pmatrix} \psi \\ \mathbf{S} \end{pmatrix} \sim N \left(\begin{pmatrix} \mathbf{0} \\ \mathbf{X}\gamma \end{pmatrix}, \begin{pmatrix} \mathbf{D} & \mathbf{DY}^T \\ \mathbf{YD} & \mathbf{H} \end{pmatrix} \right)$$

The conditional distribution of ψ given $\mathbf{S}$ can be obtained,

$$\psi | \mathbf{S} \sim N \left(\mathbf{DY}^T \mathbf{H}^{-1}(\mathbf{S} - \mathbf{X}\gamma), \mathbf{D} - \mathbf{DY}^T \mathbf{H}^{-1} \mathbf{YD} \right).$$

According to Property 2, $\left(\mathbf{D}^{-1} + \mathbf{Y}^T\mathbf{R}^{-1}\mathbf{Y}\right)^{-1} = \mathbf{D} - \mathbf{D}\mathbf{Y}^T\mathbf{H}^{-1}\mathbf{Y}\mathbf{D}$. Therefore, $\psi|\mathbf{S} \sim N\left(\mathbf{D}\mathbf{Y}^T\mathbf{H}^{-1}(\mathbf{S} - \mathbf{X}\gamma), \left(\mathbf{D}^{-1} + \mathbf{Y}^T\mathbf{R}^{-1}\mathbf{Y}\right)^{-1}\right)$. The estimation of ψ is unbiased.

Theorem 3. *For given $\mathbf{D}$ and $\mathbf{R}$, the error between the real sensed value and the sensed data model is $\mathbf{R}\mathbf{H}^{-1}(\mathbf{S} - \mathbf{X}\hat{\gamma})$.*

Proof. Since C_i can be seen as constant and the estimation for ψ is unbiased. The error is defined as $\hat{\varepsilon} = \mathbf{S} - \mathbf{X}\hat{\gamma} - \mathbf{Y}\hat{\psi}$. We can derive the follows,

$$\hat{\varepsilon} = \mathbf{S} - \mathbf{X}\hat{\gamma} - \mathbf{Y}\mathbf{D}\mathbf{Y}^T\mathbf{H}^{-1}\mathbf{S} + \mathbf{Y}\mathbf{D}\mathbf{Y}^T\mathbf{H}^{-1}\mathbf{X}\hat{\gamma}$$
$$= \left(\mathbf{I} - \mathbf{Y}\mathbf{D}\mathbf{Y}^T\mathbf{H}^{-1}\right)\mathbf{S} - \left(\mathbf{I} - \mathbf{Y}\mathbf{D}\mathbf{Y}^T\mathbf{H}^{-1}\right)\mathbf{X}\hat{\gamma}$$
$$= \mathbf{R}\mathbf{H}^{-1}\left(\mathbf{S} - \mathbf{X}(\mathbf{X}^T\mathbf{H}^{-1}\mathbf{X})^{-1}\mathbf{X}^T\mathbf{H}^{-1}\mathbf{S}\right)$$
$$= \mathbf{R}\mathbf{H}^{-1}\left(\mathbf{S} - \mathbf{X}\hat{\gamma}\right)$$

Theorem 3 implies that the error between the proposed model and real sensed value depends on the variance matrices, which is a multiplier for the difference of local average and the individual sensed data. Larger variance shows drastic variation of physical world, more frequently sampling is necessary.

5 Performance Evaluation

In this section, we conduct a series of experiments to evaluate the performance of the proposed algorithm. The simulated network consists of 100 sensor nodes. It is assumed that the network consists of multiple groups. A group is formed by the set of sensor nodes in a geographical area, where locality of sensory data exists among the sensor nodes. In our setting, the sensed data are based on a real sensor system for temperature and humidity monitoring. The sensed data consists of environmental data regularly sampled by the sensor nodes, which were spread around the lab. The temperature is adopted in our simulations.

The first group of experiments are to investigate the accuracy of the proposed sensed data model. The relative error are calculated based on the real sensory data and the approximation estimated by the sensed data model. Figure 1(a) and (b) present the relative error for inflection points and extremum points respectively, when δ increases from 0.02 to 0.12. We apply second order Taylor expansion to approximate the real sensor data. The estimation of parameters in the model are derived by formula (27). The results show that the proposed model can achieve high accuracy. The sensed data model integrates mean sensed value of adjacent neighbor area and the deviation from the average. Since the proposed CADA algorithm becomes more aggressive for the inflection points and extremum points, and the relative error of other points are higher than that of inflection and extremum points. Experimental results verify the efficiency of the proposed model.

The second group of experiments investigates the recall rate of the proposed algorithm. The recall rate equals to the fraction of the returned points, where

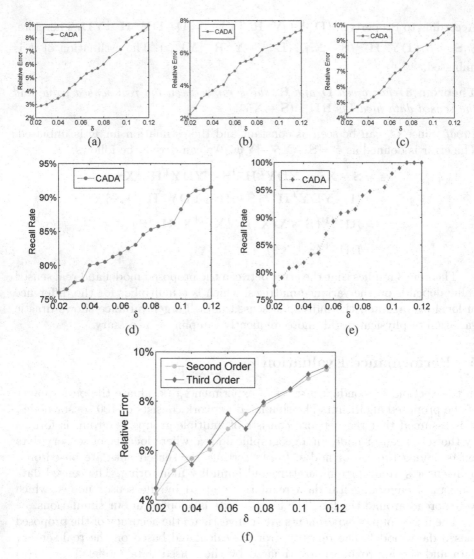

Fig. 1. (a) Inflection points (b) Extremum points (c) Other points (d) Inflection points (e) Extremum points (f) Inflection points

the relative error is less than δ. Figure 1(d) and (e) present the recall rate for inflection points and extremum points respectively, when δ increases from 0.02 to 0.12. We apply second order Taylor expansion and the estimation of parameters in the model are derived by formula (27). The figure demonstrates that the recall rates for inflection and extremum points are improved, when we raise the relative error. When δ is larger than 0.1, the recall rates approach to 100%. It implies that our proposed algorithm can effectively capture the intervals of inflection and extremum points.

The third group experiments investigates the impact of Taylor expansion on the accuracy of the sensed data model. We compare the second order and third order, when δ increases from 0.02 to 0.12. Due to the over-fitting of third order Taylor expansion, the precision of the data model suffers a larger impact than that of second order. The proposed model can achieve a higher accuracy. By increasing the sampling frequency, we can decrease the influence of over-fitting on the accuracy of the data model.

6 Conclusion

There exists few research works focusing on the adaptive sampling in IoT. Since the dataset discretely sampled from the physical world may miss some critical points, and it will lead to a failure in understanding for the physical world. We provide a sensed data model based on Taylor expansion and the time series analysis. The spatial-temporal correlation among sensory data of local area is represented as a Gaussian process. By maximizing the log-likelihood function, we can obtain the parameter estimation. A model based data acquisition algorithm is provided and the theoretical analysis is given. Performance evaluation validates the efficiency of the given algorithms.

Acknowledgments. This work is supported in part by the National Natural Science Foundation of China (61602084, 61602080, 61772112, 61761136019), the Post-Doctoral Science Foundation of China (2016M600202), the Doctoral Scientific Research Foundation of Liaoning Province (201601041), the Fundamental Research Funds for the Central Universities (DUT19JC53).

References

1. Yu, J., Wan, S., Cheng, X., Yu, D.: Coverage contribution area based k-coverage for wireless sensor networks. IEEE Trans. Veh. Technol. **66**(9), 8510–8523 (2017)
2. Yu, J., Huang, B., Cheng, X., Atiquzzaman, M.: Shortest link scheduling algorithms in wireless networks under SINR. IEEE Trans. Veh. Technol. **66**(3), 2643–2657 (2017)
3. Zheng, X., Cai, Z., Li, J., Gao, H.: A study on application-aware scheduling in wireless networks. IEEE Trans. Mob. Comput. **16**(7), 1787–1801 (2017)
4. Cheng, S., Cai, Z., Li, J., Gao, H.: Extracting kernel dataset from big sensory data in wireless sensor networks. IEEE Trans. Knowl. Data Eng. **29**(4), 813–827 (2017)
5. Cheng, S., Cai, Z., Li, J., Fang, X.: Drawing dominant dataset from big sensory data in wireless sensor networks. In: IEEE International Conference on Computer Communications (INFOCOM) (2015)
6. Li, J., Cheng, S., Cai, Z., Yu, J., Wang, C., Li, Y.: Approximate holistic aggregation in wireless sensor networks. ACM Trans. Sens. Netw. **13**(2), 11:1–11:24 (2017)
7. He, Z., Cai, Z., Cheng, S., Wang, X.: Approximate aggregation for tracking quantiles and range countings in wireless sensor networks. Theoret. Comput. Sci. **607**(3), 381–390 (2015)

8. Cai, Z., He, Z.: Trading private range counting over big IoT data. In: The 39th IEEE International Conference on Distributed Computing Systems (ICDCS) (2019)
9. Cai, Z., Zheng, X.: A private and efficient mechanism for data uploading in smart cyber-physical systems. IEEE Trans. Netw. Sci. Eng. (TNSE) Accepted
10. Cheng, S., Cai, Z., Li, J.: Curve query processing in wireless sensor networks. IEEE Trans. Veh. Technol. **64**(11), 5198–5209 (2015)
11. Deshpande, A., Guestrin, C., Madden, S.R., Hellerstein, J.M., Hong, W.: Model-driven data acquisition in sensor networks. In: Thirtieth International Conference on Very Large Data Bases (VLDB), pp. 588–599 (2004)
12. Cheng, S., Li, J., Cai, Z.: $O(\epsilon)$-approximation to physical world by sensor networks. In: IEEE International Conference on Computer Communications (INFOCOM), pp. 3084–3092 (2013)
13. Zhu, T., Wang, X., Cheng, S., Cai, Z., Li, J.: Critical point aware data acquisition algorithm in sensor networks. In: Xu, K., Zhu, H. (eds.) WASA 2015. LNCS, vol. 9204, pp. 798–808. Springer, Cham (2015). https://doi.org/10.1007/978-3-319-21837-3_78
14. Jain, A., Chang, E.Y.: Adaptive sampling for sensor networks. In: 1st International Workshop on Data Management for Sensor Networks: in Conjunction with VLDB 2004, pp. 10–16 (2004)
15. Bi, R., Tan, G., Fang, X.: Critical value aware data acquisition strategy in wireless sensor networks. In: Zou, B., Han, Q., Sun, G., Jing, W., Peng, X., Lu, Z. (eds.) ICPCSEE 2017. CCIS, vol. 728, pp. 148–160. Springer, Singapore (2017). https://doi.org/10.1007/978-981-10-6388-6_13
16. Brockwell, P.J., Davis, R.A., Calder, M.V.: Introduction to Time Series and Forecasting. Springer, New York (2002)
17. Chatfield, C.: The Analysis of Time Series: An Introduction. Chapman and Hall/CRC, London (2016)

Hybrid Low Frequency Electromagnetic Field and Solar Energy Harvesting Architecture for Self-Powered Wireless Sensor System

Di Cao[✉], Jing-run Jia, Min-jie Xie, Yanjing Lei, and Wei Li

School of Computer Science and Technology,
Zhejiang University of Technology, Hangzhou 310023, China
{dicao,2111612044,2111712312,leiyj,leewei}@zjut.edu.cn

Abstract. The development of micro-energy harvesting technology provides a new energy solution for wireless sensor nodes (WSNs). Due to the intermittent power supplied by single environmental energy source, this paper proposes a hybrid energy harvesting architecture that harvest magnetic field (50–60 Hz) and solar energy simultaneously, which aims to provide a sustainable power supply for WSNs. Firstly, the design of free-standing "I-shaped" magnetic field transducer is introduced, which can harvest 0.17–0.46 mW underneath 700 A power transmission line. A further design of a rectifier and matching circuit is conducted and the maximum power point (MPP) of the hybrid energy harvesting circuit is about 60% of the open circuit voltage and the conversion efficiency reaches 61.68%. The experimental results show that the hybrid solar and "I-shaped" transducer can accomplish "cold start" operation of the power management unit (PMU) under magnetic flux density of 4.5 µT and light intensity of 200 lx, which will also provide a promising supply of energy for WSNs.

Keywords: Energy harvesting · Power management ·
Low frequency electromagnetic field harvesting ·
Maximum power point tracking (MPPT) · Wireless sensor network (WSN)

1 Introduction

With the increasing scale of WSN and its the rich and changeable application environments, the sustainable power supply for the WSNs turns to be the main challenge. Due to the drawbacks of using traditional battery power supply, self-powered energy harvesting nodes become an alternative approach to increase the lifetime of the network. By converting solar, mechanical vibration, magnetic field, etc. into electricity, WSNs can sustain in a harsh environment without any maintenances.

Researches on self-powered WSN techniques can be categorized into three directions: (1) Analyze physical properties of environmental energy sources and design of energy transducers [1, 2], which requires the design and implementation of energy transducers to efficiently convert different types of environmental sources into

© Springer Nature Switzerland AG 2019
E. S. Biagioni et al. (Eds.): WASA 2019, LNCS 11604, pp. 29–42, 2019.
https://doi.org/10.1007/978-3-030-23597-0_3

electricity; (2) the study of the power management control schemes [3, 4] aim at improving the energy conversion efficiency and reducing additional circuit loss; (3) Research on the characteristics of information theory, network throughput and network data processing capability based on specific energy harvesting model [5].

The main challenges in the research area (1) and (2) mainly about low output power from the transducer due to its limited weight and contact area for energy conversion [6]. Except for solar cells under sunlight, the power generation level of a single energy harvesting device stays on the order of milli- or micro-Watt level. According to the energy harvesting efficiency in reference [7], the operation of self-powered nodes under sunlight has the highest duty cycle which reaches 45%; The duty cycle for vibration energy transducer is the second, in which the piezoelectric mode has a duty cycle of 6% due to its higher power density; The harvested energy from heat and indoor solar energy cannot supply sufficient power to maintain the operation of a single node.

Therefore, using multiple environmental energy sources is a solution to overcome the shortcomings. In 2017, Akan [8] proposes the idea of multiple energy harvesting IoT network. Comparing with a single environmental source, the multiple sources harvesting system has many advantages based on the analysis of energy model, data model and optimal strategy design. A hybrid energy harvesting model for WSN also been proposed by Kim [9] and Yildiz [10], where the power consumptions during the transmission are quantitatively analyzed relating with the harvesting energy. The models of combining RF energy with other environmental energy is analyzed in [11, 12]. However, integration capability of multiple energy sources and long-term reliability is still a stumbling block [13]. Another critical factor is conversion efficiency degradation during multimode operation. Consequently, maximizing the energy utility and power density from hybrid energy sources will be a priority area of research in the near term.

Thus, this paper proposes a hybrid low-frequency magnetic field and solar energy harvesting system. Based on the hybrid energy harvesting structure, a proper design of the magnetic transducer, rectifier circuit, matching circuit and PMU circuit are given to maximize the energy utility and meanwhile improve energy conversion efficiency. In the end, the experiment is conducted and the results prove that the sustainable power supply of the node from combined energy sources.

2 Hybrid Low Frequency Electromagnetic Field/Solar Harvesting Structure

In order to sustainable energy for WSN, structure of hybrid low frequency electromagnetic field and solar harvesting system is shown in Fig. 1. The structure includes a low frequency (50/60 Hz) electromagnetic field energy transducer, a solar cell, a rectifier circuit, a matching circuit, a PMU, an energy storage unit, an energy-aware switch (EAS), and low power WSNs.

The electromagnetic field energy transducer and the solar panel converts magnetic field and solar energy into electricity. Due to the AC power supply from electromagnetic field energy transducer, additional rectifier and matching circuits are required to perform AC-DC conversion and maximum power conversion.

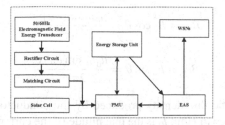

Fig. 1. Block diagram of self-powered wireless sensor node system for hybrid low frequency electromagnetic field and solar energy

The PMU performs the role of a MPPT and DC-DC boost. The energy storage unit is used to store the energy converted by the PMU. The EAS is used to monitor the voltage value of the energy storage unit and control the WSNs to save energy costs.

In the whole hybrid harvesting system structure, more works will be carried out to improve energy conversion efficiency by proper design of energy harvesting transducer and optimization of the power management circuit. Therefore, in the following two chapters, the design of the new low-frequency electromagnetic field transducer and the energy conversion circuit will be introduced in detail.

3   Design of Low Frequency Electromagnetic Field Transducer

The electromagnetic field in power grid is mainly generated by the current on transmission lines and inside of transformer stations. The magnetic field strength near a typical substation is 32 A/m [15], which can act as a reliable energy source for WSNs. The free-standing energy transducer can harvest energy in a certain distance from the power supply equipment. It has great flexibility, and less interferences on the radio communication of WSNs. Meanwhile, the harvested energy is enough to supply the required sustainable energy for WSNs.

3.1   Magnetic Field Model Under Overhead Power Lines

Before the design of electromagnetic transducer, the model of magnetic field generated by the 700 A overhead power lines is studied. Since the power line transmits in a long distance which can be assumed to be an infinitely long wire. And the reflection of magnetic field on a non-ideal ground is relatively small, which can be ignored [17].

According to the quasi-static magnetic field prediction [18], the magnetic flux density of a point relative to the power line and its two components in the horizontal and vertical directions as shown in Fig. 2 can be expressed as:

$$B_0 = \frac{\mu_0 I_0 \sin(\omega t)}{2\pi r} \tag{1}$$

$$B_{0x} = B_0 \cos \theta = \frac{\mu_0 I_0 \sin(\omega t) y}{2\pi r^2} \tag{2}$$

$$B_{0y} = B_0 \sin \theta = \frac{\mu_0 I_0 \sin(\omega t) x}{2\pi r^2} \tag{3}$$

where B_0 is the magnetic flux density produced by the conductor at time T, μ_0 is the permeability of free space in H/m, I_0 is the magnitude of the current passing through the conductor, ω is the angular velocity in rad/s, r is the distance between the conductor and a interest point, x is the horizontal distance between the conductor and a interest point, y is the vertical distance between the conductor and an interest point.

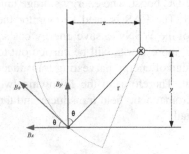

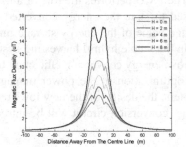

Fig. 2. Magnetic flux density produced by the power line current

Fig. 3. Magnetic field distribution of power transmission line of 700 A dual-loop transmission network

For a balanced three-phase system, the current in each conductor has the same amplitude while the phase is 120° apart from the other two. The flux density at an interest point can be calculated from the sum of the magnetic flux densities generated by the three-phase current:

$$B_x = B_{Ax} + B_{Bx} + B_{Cx} \tag{4}$$

$$B_y = B_{Ay} + B_{By} + B_{Cy} \tag{5}$$

$$B_{total} = \sqrt{B_x^2 + B_y^2} \tag{6}$$

where B_{Ax} represents the magnetic flux density generated by the A-phase conduction current in the X-axis direction, and B_{total} represents the sum of all the magnetic flux densities of a certain point. The simulation in Fig. 3 shows that the magnetic flux density under the dual-loop 700 A power transmission line.

In Fig. 3, the X-axis represents the horizontal distance from the middle of the power line tower, the Y-axis represents the magnetic flux density in μT, and H represents the distance from the ground. It can be seen from that the closer to the power line, the stronger the flux density will be; and the closer to the central axis of the power line, the greater the magnetic field strength. For the convenience of calculation, we use 7 μT (maximum magnetic field strength at 2 m from the ground) and 5.5 μT (maximum magnetic field strength at the ground) as environmental magnetic flux density for further analysis and discussion.

3.2   Design of Electromagnetic Field Transducer

The maximum power that the coil can achieve depends not only on the surrounding magnetic field, but also on the effective coil resistance and the optimized load [16]. Figure 4 shows the equivalent circuit of the free-standing energy transducer with matching load. According to Faraday's law, the induction coil voltage V_{coil} can be expressed as [16]:

$$V_{\text{coil}} = N\omega\mu_{\text{eff}}B_{ex}A \tag{7}$$

where N is the winding turns of the coil, μ_{eff} is the effective magnetic permeability of the transducer core, B_{ex} is the external magnetic flux density (T), A is the effective cross-sectional area of the coil (m^2), and ω is the angular frequency (rad/s).

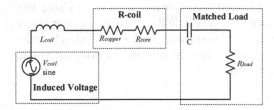

Fig. 4. Far-field energy transducer equivalent circuit with matching load

The effective coil resistance R_{coil} consists of two parts: the enameled wire copper resistance R_{copper} and the equivalent core resistance R_{core}. The copper resistance is the resistance of the longer enameled wire used for the coil wound on the magnetic core.

$$R_{coil} = R_{copper} + R_{core} \tag{8}$$

$$R_{\text{copper}} = \rho_{\text{wire}}l_{wire} \tag{9}$$

where ρ_{wire} is the resistivity (Ω/m) and l_{wire} is the total length (m) of the enameled wire. When the core is affected by a time-varying magnetic field, some of the energy transferred to the load is dissipated as heat in the core, and these losses can be considered as losses due to equivalent core impedance. In order to increase the maximum power from the harvesting coil to the load, the maximum power transfer theory is applied. The coil inductance L_{coil} is eliminated by in series with a compensation capacitor $C = 1/(\omega^2 L_{coil})$ on the harvesting coil. When the load impedance R_{load} match the coil impedance R_{coil}, the electromagnetic field energy transducer harvested power is calculated:

$$P_{\text{EM}} = \left(\frac{V_{coil}}{2}\right)^2 / R_{coil} \qquad (10)$$

The power density of the transducer (harvested power per unit volume) is calculated:

$$S_{\text{power}} = \frac{1}{4}\frac{V_{coil}^2}{R_{coil}} / Vol \qquad (11)$$

where Vol is the total volume (m^3) of the harvesting coil. To maximize the harvested power of the harvesting coil, the coil voltage V_{coil} should be increased and the coil impedance R_{coil} must be minimized. These two variables are closely related to core geometry, core material, and enameled wire properties.

The design of the transducer proposed use a ferromagnetic core due to its high magnetic permeability. The elongated core has a large effective magnetic permeability and can effectively reduce the demagnetization of the core [19]. The transducer adopts Manganese-Zinc (Mn-Zn) ferrite PC40 material (magnetic permeability 2800, conductivity < 0.5 S/m) as the core material of the transducer. The transducer adopts the geometric shape of "I-shaped", as shown in the Fig. 5. Using the larger end faces at both ends can introduce more magnetic flux to strengthen the magnetic field strength in the core. While the thinner intermediate core can effectively reduce the core volume and demagnetization, and meanwhile increase the winding volume and improve the transducer harvested power.

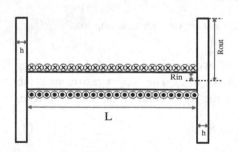

Fig. 5. "I-shaped" low frequency magnetic field energy transducer

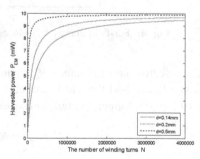

Fig. 6. Relationship between the number of winding turns of different diameters and the harvested power of the transducer ($B_{ex} = 7\,\mu\text{T}$)

To simplify the model operation in the actual calculation process, the transducer can be regarded as a solenoid with a length L (the length of the intermediate core) and a radius r. Since the enameled wire is only wound around the middle core portion of the transducer, the effective permeability μ_{eff} is constant under the condition that the geometry is determined. According to the study by Yuan et al. [16], the effective permeability μ_{eff} varies with the relative magnetic permeability of the core material and the geometry of the core. When the core geometry is determined, the effective magnetic permeability tends to be saturated as the relative magnetic permeability increases.

Since Mn-Zn ferrite is used as the core material, the core loss is negligible when the winding number N is relatively large, so $R_{coil} \approx R_{copper}$. The number of layers of enameled wire K_{layer} can be expressed as:

$$K_{layer} = \frac{N}{L/d_{wire}} \tag{12}$$

The total length l_{wire} of the enameled wire can be expressed as:

$$l_{wire} = 2\pi N \left(\frac{2r + K_{layer}d_{wire}}{2} \right) \tag{13}$$

According to (8), (9), (12) and (13), it can be known that the transducer coil impedance R_{coil} can be derived as:

$$R_{coil} \approx R_{copper} = 2\pi r N \rho_{wire} + \pi N^2 d_{wire}^2 \rho_{wire}/L \tag{14}$$

Using Eqs. (7), (10) and (14), the harvested power P_{EM} of transducer can be expressed as:

$$P_{EM} = N\pi \left(r^2 \omega \mu_{eff} B_{ex} \right)^2 / \left(8r\rho_{wire} + 4\rho_{wire}Nd_{wire}^2/L \right) \tag{15}$$

When the external magnetic field and the geometric structure are fixed, the harvested power of the transducer only depends on the winding volume on the magnetic core. In the case of the external magnetic field $B_{ex} = 7$ μT, the relationship between the number of core winding turns N and the transducer harvested power P_{EM} is as shown in Fig. 6.

According to Fig. 6, as the number of winding turns increases, the harvested power tends to be saturated. The higher N will produce a larger voltage V_{coil}, and at the same time, a larger copper resistance R_{copper} will be produced. The thicker enameled wire has a lower R_{copper} but takes up a lot of space.

Further the open circuit voltage V_{coil}, harvested power P_{EM} and transducer power density S_{power} (enameled wire d = 0.2 mm, $\rho = 0.5441$ Ω/m) at a magnetic field strength of 6 µT, 8 µT, 10 µT, 12 µT are simulated based on different winding number N shown in Figs. 7(a), (b), and (c) respectively.

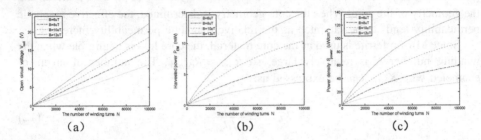

(a)   (b)   (c)

Fig. 7. Under different magnetic fields, relationship (a) between the number of turns of the transducer and the open circuit voltage (b) between the number of turns of the transducer and the harvested power (c) between the number of windings of the transducer and the power density (d = 0.2 mm)

Figure 7(a) shows that when the external magnetic field B_{ex} is constant, the open circuit voltage V_{coil} of the transducer is proportional to the number of winding turns N. Figure 7(b) and (c) show that in the case where the external magnetic field B_{ex} is constant, the harvested power P_{EM} and the transducer power density S_{power} increase with the increase of the number of turns N, and gradually become saturated. When the number of turns N is constant, with the increasing of B_{ex}, P_{EM} and S_{power} also increases.

The low-frequency magnetic field transducer of the "I-shaped" geometry proposed in this paper is compared with the Bow-tie-shaped transducer [16] and the Solenoid-shaped transducer [19] using the same external magnetic field $B_{ex} = 7$ µT. For comparison of the harvesting conditions, the enameled wire ($\rho = 0.5441$ Ω/m) winding with diameter $d = 0.2$ mm is used, and the parameter settings are shown in Table 1.

Table 1. Comparison of four core structure parameters.

Parameter	Solenoid (a) [19]	Solenoid (b) [19]	Bow-tie (c) [16]	I-shaped (d)
R_{out}/cm	5	2	5	5
R_{in}/cm	5	2	1	1.2
L/cm	16	16	16	16
h/cm	0	0	2.4	0.25
Vol/cm^3	1256.6	201.1	206.7	111.7
μ_{eff}	6.48	18.33	130.8	110

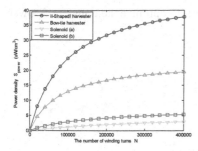

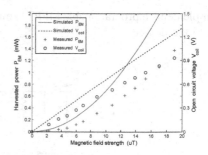

Fig. 8. Comparison of collections of different structure transducers ($B_{ex} = 7\,\mu T$, $d = 0.2$ mm)

Fig. 9. Relationship between magnetic field strength and open circuit voltage and harvested power of the transducer coil

Figure 8 shows that the "I-shaped" transducer has a higher power density than the Bow-tie transducer and the Solenoid-shaped transducer, and the harvesting capability is greatly improved. The number of turns $N = 3700$ and the winding enameled wire diameter $d = 0.2$ mm are used as the standard for both of experiment and simulation. In the phase of the experiment, the Helmholtz coil is used to simulate the uniform magnetic field environment. The comparison results between the experiment and simulation results are shown in Fig. 9. The measured results basically follow the same trend with the simulation results. Due to the magnetic core of the transducer is bonded by several magnetic cores, the integrity of the transducer is affected. And the eddy current loss and demagnetization existing inside the core cause the actual harvested power to be slightly lower than the simulation result.

4 PMU Circuit Design

Since the output of the "I-shaped" transducer is alternating current (AC). The rectifier and matching circuit are required to be implemented. The design circuit is shown in Fig. 10, which mainly consists of: solar cell, magnetic field harvesting coil, rectifier circuit and impedance matching circuit. The rectifier circuit uses full-wave rectification to perform AC-DC conversion. The diode uses BAT54 due to its low forward bias characteristic, small reverse current and high breakdown voltage. The low-frequency magnetic field harvesting coil has a resistance of 158 Ω and an inductance value of 672 H. To maximize power, a L-type matching circuit is selected, in which the capacitance is 14.18 nF and the inductance is 39.26 H. When designing the power management circuit, the power management IC Bq25504 is selected in this paper. The Bq25504 has a self-powered DC-DC converter for "cold start" operation and another for a high efficiency DC-DC converter that provides MPPT for normal operation. The IC is capable of harvesting inputs from microwatts to milliwatts [14]. Its operation is mainly divided into two stages: (1) Under the external input of 330 mV, only the micro watt power is required to start the DC-DC boost converter to realize the "cold start" of the IC. (2) After the cold start is completed, the minimum external input requires only 80 mV to enter the normal working phase, and the Bq25504 also implements a programmable MPPT sampling network to optimize the transfer of power into the device.

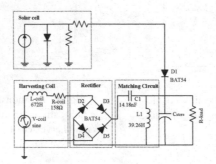

Fig. 10. Hybrid solar and low frequency electromagnetic field transducer circuit

In order to measure the power of the hybrid energy transducer after passing through the full-wave rectification circuit and the impedance matching circuit, the relationship between the output power of the hybrid transducer and the ambient energy is simulated in Fig. 11. The simulation results show that the hybrid solar cell combined with the "I-shaped" transducer gain a higher DC output power. With an external magnetic flux density 4.5 μT, "I-shaped" transducer can support the Bq25504 to work normally under various lighting conditions.

For the hybrid solar and "I-shaped" transducer MPPT design, since the MPP of solar energy is 75%–80% of the open circuit voltage [14], and the MPP of the low frequency electromagnetic field transducer is 50% of the open circuit voltage [16]. Therefore, the MPP after a hybrid structure needs to be redesigned. To obtain the MPP of the hybrid solar and "I-shaped" transducer, the output power is measured by changing the ratio of the open circuit voltage under the pre-designed light intensity and magnetic flux density.

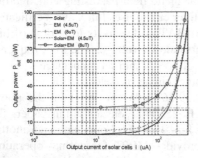

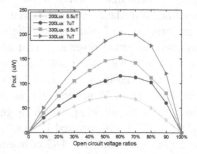

Fig. 11. Relationship between the output power of hybrid solar and low frequency electromagnetic field transducer and the output current I of solar cells

Fig. 12. Relationship between different open circuit voltage ratios and total output power *Pout*

It can be seen from Fig. 12 that under four different environment conditions, the MPP of hybrid structure is about 60% of its open circuit voltage. Further measuring the conversion efficiency of the AC-DC conversion circuit at the MPP. The overall conversion efficiency of the hybrid solar and low frequency electromagnetic field transducer through the AC-DC conversion circuit can be expressed as:

$$\eta = P_{out}/(P_{solar} + P_{EM})$$ (16)

where P_{out} is total output power of the hybrid energy transducer, that is the power at the input end of the PMU, P_{solar} is the collected power of the solar cell, and P_{EM} is the harvested power of the low-frequency electromagnetic field transducer. The experimental results show that the conversion efficiency of the AC-DC converter circuit can reach 61.68% with an illumination intensity of 330 lx and an external magnetic field strength of 5.5 μT.

5 Experiment Results

During the experiment, the hybrid solar energy and "I-shaped" energy harvesting system is shown in Fig. 13. The solar panel is a monocrystalline silicon solar power chip having an outer dimension of 84.5 mm × 55.5 mm. "I-shaped" transducer adopts Mn-Zn ferrite core with relative magnetic permeability $\mu_r = 2800$, geometric size $Rout = 5$ cm, $Rin = 1.2$ cm, $L = 16$ cm, $h = 0.25$ cm, diameter $d = 0.2$ mm enameled wire wound, winding turns $N = 3700$. The experiment measured the illumination intensity parameters by the VICTOR 1010 A digital photometer, and the uniform external magnetic field required for the experiment was generated by the Helmholtz coil, and the magnetic field strength was measured by the LTZ-1000 EMF Tester. The back-end energy management and load circuit adopt Bq25504 power management IC. The system uses dual-storage mode of supercapacitor and lithium battery, and ultra-low power consumption MSP430 chip and NRF24L01 wireless transmission module.

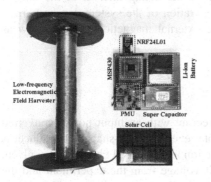

Fig. 13. Hybrid solar and low frequency electromagnetic field energy harvesting system

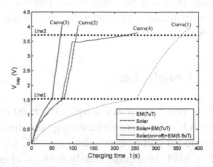

Fig. 14. Relationships between capacitor voltage and charging time under different circumstances

To evaluate the energy harvesting capability and conversion efficiency of hybrid harvesting system, relationships between capacitor voltage and charging time under different circumstances is shown in Fig. 14. The pre-designed circumstances including:

(1) Energy harvesting system with single "I-shaped" transducer ($B_{ex} = 7$ μT);
(2) Energy harvesting system using solar cell under indoor lighting conditions (200 lx);
(3) Energy harvesting system using hybrid solar (200 lx) and "I-shaped" transducer (7 μT);
(4) Energy harvesting system using hybrid solar (200 lx) and "I-shaped" transducer (5.5 μT) to accomplish the "cold start" operation, and then use "I-shaped" transducer work alone.

In Fig. 14, "Line1" indicates a voltage threshold of 1.55 V required to switch from "cold start" to normal operation, and "Line2" indicates a voltage threshold of 3.72 V after charging of the connected storage capacitor. Curve (1) shows that the external magnetic field of 7 μT is the minimum external magnetic field that reaches the Bq25504 "cold start" condition when only the low-frequency electromagnetic field energy transducer participates in the acquisition. It can be seen from the curves (2) and (3) that the charging time of the hybrid solar energy and electromagnetic field energy transducer is significantly reduced. Under the charging conditions (2) and (3), the storage capacitors are charged for 109 s and 71 s, respectively, and the storage capacitor charging time is shortened by about 35%. Curve (4) shows under the external magnetic field of 5.5 μT, the electromagnetic field energy transducer cannot perform the "cold start" operation alone, but with the participation of the solar cell, the hybrid energy harvesting system can bypass the "cold start". The solar intermittent power supply was simulated by covering the solar panels after storage capacitor voltage reaching 3.5 V. The slope of the charging curve is significantly changed near the corresponding time stamp, but since the harvested power satisfies the DC-DC conversion requirement under the 5.5 μT external magnetic field, the final storage capacitor is charged. Experiments have shown that as long as the "cold start" operation is completed when the light is strong, the energy harvesting interval of the normal operation can be completed. And the normal operation of the system can be permanently maintained under the condition that the external magnetic field is as low as 5.5 μT.

6   Conclusion

This paper proposes a hybrid harvesting architecture with an input power converted from low frequency electromagnetic field and solar energy. An "I-shaped" transducer is proposed and a proper design of AC-DC conversion and matched circuit is also given. The MPP is approximately 60% of open-circuit voltage from the experiment and the conversion efficiency reaches 61.68%. The 'I-shaped' transducer is proved to finish "cold-start" operation and normal operation of PMU under an external magnetic field density of 7 μT. By using a hybrid architecture, under the circumstances of a lower magnetic flux density of 4.5 μT and light density of 200 lx, the "cold-start" operation can also be accomplished. In the near future, more work will be carried out in the area of corresponding analysis on the energy management model, and further optimization with the design of low power WSNs. It can also be extended to multi-node WSN which aims to optimize the overall network capability.

References

1. Bito, J., Bahr, R., Hester, J.G., Nauroze, S.A., Georgiadis, A., Tentzeris, M.M.: A novel solar and electromagnetic energy harvesting system with a 3-d printed package for energy efficient Internet-of-Things wireless sensors. IEEE Trans. Microw. Theory Tech. **65**(5), 1831–1842 (2017)
2. Song, C., et al.: A novel six-band dual CP rectenna using improved impedance matching technique for ambient RF energy harvesting. IEEE Trans. Antennas Propag. **64**(7), 3160–3171 (2016)
3. Ruan, T., Chew, Z.J., Zhu, M.: Energy-aware approaches for energy harvesting powered wireless sensor nodes. IEEE Sens. J. **17**(7), 2165–2173 (2017)
4. Chew, Z.J., Ruan, T., Zhu, M.: Strain energy harvesting powered wireless sensor system using adaptive and energy-aware interface for enhanced performance. IEEE Trans. Ind. Inf. **13**(6), 3006–3016 (2017)
5. Smart, G., Atkinson, J., Mitchell, J., Rodrigues, M., Andreopoulos, Y.: Energy harvesting for the Internet-of-Things: measurements and probability models. In: International Conference on Telecommunications, Thessaloniki, pp. 1–6. IEEE (2016)
6. Wu, Y.: Key Technology Research of Energy Harvesting Wireless Sensor Networks. Doctor, Nanjing University of Aeronautics and Astronautics (2013)
7. Li, Y., Yu, H., Su, B., Shang, Y.: Hybrid micropower source for wireless sensor network. IEEE Sens. J. **8**(6), 678–681 (2008)
8. Akan, O.B., Cetinkaya, O., Koca, C., Ozger, M.: Internet of hybrid energy harvesting things. IEEE Internet Things J. **5**(2), 736–746 (2018)
9. Kim, S., et al.: Ambient RF energy-harvesting technologies for self-sustainable standalone wireless sensor platforms. Proc. IEEE **102**(11), 1649–1666 (2014)
10. Yildiz, H.U., Gungor, V.C., Tavli, B.: A hybrid energy harvesting framework for energy efficiency in wireless sensor networks based smart grid applications. In: 2018 17th Annual Mediterranean Ad Hoc Networking Workshop, Capri, pp. 1–6. IEEE (2018)
11. Gu, X.Q., Hemour, S., Wu, K.: Enabling far-field ambient energy harvesting through multi-physical sources. In: 2018 Asia-Pacific Microwave Conference (APMC), Kyoto, pp. 204–206. IEEE (2018)
12. Nguyen, S., Amirtharajah, R.: A hybrid RF and vibration energy transducer for wearable devices. In: IEEE Applied Power Electronics Conference and Exposition, San Antonio, pp. 1060–1064. IEEE (2018)
13. Khan, A.A., Mahmud, A., Ban, D.: Evolution from single to hybrid nanogenerator: a contemporary review on multimode energy harvesting for self-powered electronics. IEEE Trans. Nanotechnol. **18**, 21–36 (2019)
14. Texas Instruments. bq25504-Ultra Low Power Boost Converter with Battery Management for Energy Harvester Applications, Dallas, USA, June 2015
15. EMFs.info: National Grid Substations. http://www.emfs.Info/sources/substations/substations-ng/. Accessed March 2016

16. Yuan, S., Huang, Y., Zhou, J., Xu, Q., Song, C., Thompson, P.: Magnetic field energy harvesting under overhead power lines. IEEE Trans. Power Electron. **30**(11), 6191–6202 (2015)
17. Lunca, E., Istrate, M., Salceanu, A., Tibuliac, S.: Computation of the magnetic field exposure from 110 kV overhead power lines. In: International Conference and Exposition on Electrical and Power Engineering, Iasi-Romania, pp. 628–631. IEEE (2012)
18. Olsen, R.G., Wong, P.S.: Characteristics of low frequency electric and magnetic fields in the vicinity of electric power lines. IEEE Trans. Power Delivery **7**(4), 2046–2055 (1992)
19. Roscoe, N., Judd, M.: Harvesting energy from magnetic fields to power condition monitoring sensors. IEEE Sens. J. **13**(6), 2263–2270 (2013)

Automated and Personalized Privacy Policy Extraction Under GDPR Consideration

Cheng Chang, Huaxin Li, Yichi Zhang, Suguo Du, Hui Cao,
and Haojin Zhu[✉]

Shanghai Jiao Tong University, Shanghai, China
zhu-hj@cs.sjtu.edu.cn

Abstract. Along with the popularity of mobile devices, people share a growing amount of personal data to a variety of mobile applications for personalized services. In most cases, users can learn their data usage from the privacy policy along with the application. However, current privacy policies are always too long and obscure to provide readability and comprehensibility to users. To address this issue, we propose an automated privacy policy extraction system considering users' personal privacy concerns under different contexts. The system is implemented on Android smartphones and evaluated feedbacks from a group of users ($n = 96$) as a field study. Experiments are conducted on both our dataset, which is the first user privacy concern profile dataset to the best of our knowledge, and a public dataset containing 115 privacy policies with 23K data practices. We achieve 0.94 precision for privacy category classification and 0.81 accuracy for policy segment extraction, which attests to the significance of our work as a direction towards meeting the transparency requirement of the General Data Protection Regulation (GDPR).

Keywords: Privacy policy extraction · GDPR ·
Mobile application privacy

1 Introduction

In recent years, we have witnessed a huge growth in emerging mobile techniques such as 5G communication and Internet of Things (IoT). These techniques have empowered the functionalities of mobile devices, and thus service providers (e.g., device OEMs, mobile apps developers) are able to provide more ubiquitous, seamless, and personalized applications to users. However, many of these *mobile applications* (e.g., user-profile-based recommendation, real-time location services, financial apps) widely rely on personal or private information, which brought growing privacy attentions [8,9,16]. The situation can be more serious when personal data are shared with the third party for the advertising purpose [14,22]. To secure users' privacy, one of the critical steps is to let users be aware of potential privacy risks that can be brought by using a mobile app.

© Springer Nature Switzerland AG 2019
E. S. Biagioni et al. (Eds.): WASA 2019, LNCS 11604, pp. 43–54, 2019.
https://doi.org/10.1007/978-3-030-23597-0_4

Until now, privacy policies of mobile apps (e.g., Android apps, web apps) are still the primary channels through which users are able to know their personal data usage. They describe the detailed usage of data collected by apps from a range of aspects, including what and how the data is collected, data security, data retention, user access and control, whether the data is shared with the third party and so on. Ideally, it should be totally decided by users to accept or refuse the policy. In practice, unfortunately, most users just omit to read the privacy policies, as they are always too long and complex [15]. The problem is more pressing after the General Data Protection Regulation (GDPR) went into effect in 2018, as it presents transparency requirement in article 12 that *the controller shall take appropriate measures to provide any information* related to processing the data *in a concise, transparent, intelligible and easily accessible form, using clear and plain language* [19].

Several frameworks were proposed to help fill the gap between the current privacy policy design and the transparency requirement of the GDPR, and most of them focus on the fine-grained policy segment classification to reorganize the policy in a more noticeable security-centric presentation [4,20]. However, users still need to have enough background knowledge about pre-defined terminology and information structure to search and scrutinize their concerned privacy issue. These works are also GDPR-agnostic, causing they lack legal warning to both app providers and users.

In this work, we propose a practical solution that learns users' privacy concerns and automatically extracts corresponding descriptions in privacy policies when users use different kinds of mobile apps. To achieve the goals, the first challenge is to build the user privacy concern profile, since no previous work has provided related datasets. We collect our privacy concern dataset through crowdsourcing and interviewing. Then we aggregate the individual privacy profiles by hierarchical clustering and design a matching mechanism to assign one of the profile clusters to a new user. The second challenge is to automatically analyze privacy policies on a large scale and extract policy segment accurately. To accomplish this task, we deploy a deep Convolutional Neural Network (CNN) followed by a random forest as the core of the policy extraction module. We train the model on OPP-115 dataset [20] containing 115 privacy policies with 23K fine-grained manual annotations, and achieve considerable performance.

Our main contributions are summarized as follows.

- We design and implement a system, which is composed of user privacy profile generation and privacy policy extraction modules. This system automatically provide a user with the descriptions in the app's privacy policy which she most cares about, as well as related GDPR items in order to help her make decisions with enough privacy awareness.
- We build the first dataset depicting the user privacy concern profiles. The dataset is constructed with 252 participants. We further design a matching profile assignment method, which succeeds to fast provide users with according profile identifications in the field study.

- We demonstrate our deep learning based privacy policy extraction model achieving 0.88 F1-score on the OPP-115 datatset [20], which outperforms the state-of-the-art privacy policy analysis system [4].
- We conduct the field study with 96 participants to comprehensively assess our system in practice, where the system achieves 0.81 accuracy on privacy policy presentation.

2 Related Work

Privacy Policy Analysis. Prior work has explored the methods on improving the readability and comprehensibility of privacy policies. Zimmeck *et al.* [23] proposed to classify privacy policies by machine learning. Holtz *et al.* [5] designed simple and obvious icons to represent the contents of privacy policies. However, their taxonomy is somewhat coarse and classification accuracy is relatively low. To this end, Wilson *et al.* [20] created the first public privacy policy corpus and employed three experts to manually label the policies with fine-grained annotations. After that, researchers further implemented online tools to support querying on privacy policies in practice. Oltramari *et al.* [17] designed a semantic framework to visualize the structure of privacy policies. Sathyendra *et al.* [18] proposed an approach towards automatically detecting the provision of choices in privacy policies by NLP techniques. As we know until now, Harkous *et al.* [4] presented the most comprehensive system to enable scalable and multi-dimensional privacy policy analysis. But they all rely on active querying and searching by users and require users to have related background knowledge. Our work is the first to automatically predict mobile users' privacy concerns and then extract the target parts of privacy policy with GDPR consideration.

GDPR Influence. Since the GDPR went into effect in 2018, researchers started to analyze the influence of the GDPR on the current circumstance of privacy policies. Linden *et al.* [11] discovered that, due to the transparency requirement by the GDPR, privacy policies are shown in a more organized structure and have greater number of words. Degeling *et al.* [3] accessed 6357 websites in total and found a 4.9% increase in the number of websites owning a privacy policy. Their work reveals the positive influence of the GDPR. Therefore, we propose to extract related GDPR items to improve the user's privacy awareness.

3 Framework Overview

Figure 1 shows an overview of our system. It comprises two modules: the privacy concern profile generation module and the privacy policy extraction module. The former module is responsible for generating personalized privacy concern profile when a user first signs in the system. We emphasize *user's privacy concerns*, defined as ten categories of security-centric data usage in privacy policies (listed in Table 1). For instance, if a user declares that she worries about whether her personal information is misused by online social apps, *First Party Collection* is

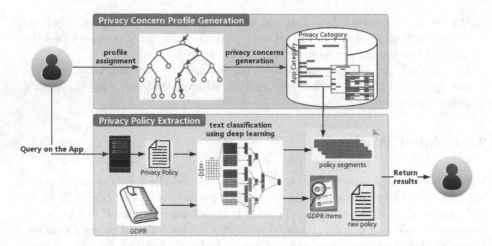

Fig. 1. The high-level overview of the system.

then considered as one of her privacy concerns. The latter module utilizes the strength of deep learning to extract the text segments of the privacy policy and GDPR items, according to the profile generated before. A demo[1] is released to introduce the functionality of our system.

Privacy Concern Profile Generation. This module generates the personalized privacy concern profile for an user in the interactive question-answering form. The user will be asked at most 5 questions about her privacy concerns while using different kinds of apps. The latter question is dynamically elicited by the former answer. According to the answers, a learned profile which is clustered from the profile database is assigned to the user. Then the concern profile is used for the personalized privacy policy extraction.

Privacy Policy Extraction. This module extracts the target segments in the app's privacy policy queried by the user. In this module, a deep learning pipeline, which is comprised of Convolutional Neural Network (CNN) and random forest model, takes as input the segments of the privacy policy scraped from the server and the GDPR. Then the model labels each segment with a set of category-attribute values describing its privacy-related data practice. According to the user profile generated in the previous module, the GDPR-aware query result is the combination of the descriptions in the privacy policy which the user most cares about and the related regulation items in the GDPR. We illustrate the output of our system using an actual example in Appendix A.

4   Privacy Concern Profile Generation

To build the privacy concern profile dataset, we recruited 252 participants on the crowdsourcing platform, Amazon Mechanical Turk (MTurk) [7], to complete

---

[1] https://youtu.be/-0x-HQRnYwQ.

the questionnaire[2] about personal privacy concerns. We cluster the profiles and design a mechanism to assign one of the profiles to a new user.

4.1   Dataset Collection

Questionnaire Design. In order to know a user's personal privacy concerns under different contexts, we ask the participants to list which aspects of privacy they most care about in order while using different kinds of mobile apps. We use app categories from the Google Play and privacy taxonomy from the public dataset OPP-115 [20]. Table 1 describes the adopted privacy categories.

Table 1. The privacy category and description in OPP-115.

Privacy category	Description
First Party Collection	How the app collects user data
Third Party Sharing	How the user data is shared with third parties
User Choice/Control	Choices and control options the app grants to users
User Access and Edit	How users can access or edit their data
Data Retention	How long the app stores the user data
Data Security	How the app protects the user data
Policy Change	How the app informs users about privacy policy changes
Do Not Track	How DNT signals for online tracking is honored
Specific Audiences	Particular policies to some specific groups of users
Other	Introductory information

Participant Recruitment. We also collect users' demographic features and IUIPC score [13] to make the bias of the dataset as low as possible.

We recruited 252 MTurk workers with *Master* qualification and approval rate more than 85%. We paid each participant $2 for the work. On average, the survey lasts about 25 min, which means the participants answered the questions with enough consideration as our expectation. These participants come from different areas (North America 70.2%, Asia 16.7%, South America 10.3%, Europe 2.4%, and Africa 0.4%), have different genders (62.7% male and 37.3% female), own different education degrees (Bachelor's degree 61.1%, graduate degree 13.1%, associate degree or lower 25.8%), and are at different ages (23–30 years old 45.6%, 30–40 years old 31.0%, beyond 40 years old 21.0%, under 22 years old).

IUIPC is a 10-item scale measure of the user's privacy awareness. In each item, the awareness is scaled from 1 to 7. Its effectiveness is demonstrated by some statistic criteria and it is widely used in previous works on privacy research [1,12]. According to [13], people who have stronger privacy awareness should

---

[2] https://www.wjx.top/jq/33235531.aspx.

have higher scores in IUIPC. These recruited participants have an average score of 5.79 and 67.2% of the participants get a score >6 (the maximum score is 7), which shows these participants have strong privacy awareness and thus probably care about the privacy policies.

4.2   Profile Generation

From the dataset, the detailed user privacy profile is constructed in the matrix form, where each row corresponds to a category of apps and the columns represent different privacy category listed in Table 1. If a participant reports that she most cares about privacy j while using apps of category i, the corresponding value at index (i,j) in the matrix is set to 1. Otherwise, the value is set to 0.

Profile Clustering. We apply the technique of hierarchical clustering on the profile matrices. The reason for choosing the hierarchical clustering is that it is non-parametric and able to provide visualized explanations.

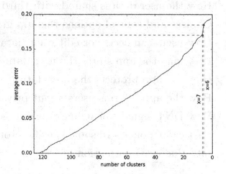

Fig. 2. The average error changes in clustering process.

Figure 2 shows the average error curve while clustering using the bottom-up strategy. The error is calculated by averaging the difference between each profile matrix P and its corresponding cluster C per position, i.e.,

$$cluster\_error = \sum_{\forall(i,j)} |P(i,j) - C(i,j)| \qquad (1)$$

From Fig. 2, we discover that the average error rapidly increases when the remained seven clusters are clustered into six (0.170 to 0.185), which means the information loss is too high to merge the two clusters. Therefore, we choose these seven clusters as typical privacy concern profiles, as it meets both lower information loss and higher profile representativeness.

Profile Assignment. The consequence of the profile clustering is displayed in Fig. 3. Totally, we obtain seven profiles revealing the diversity of privacy concerns. The majority of participants are clustered into Profile 1 and Profile 2, correspondingly occupies 42.9% and 41.3% of the whole. Profile 1 represents participants who most care about data security for most apps. Profile 2 contains the ones who show solicitude for the data collected by the first and the third parties. Profile 6 emphasizes the rights of user control. Profile 7 focuses on data retention and data security for apps related to financial and location information. Profile 3, 4, 5 seem not to mind their privacy, except for some special cases. Profile 5 is like the privacy careless counterpart of Profile 1.

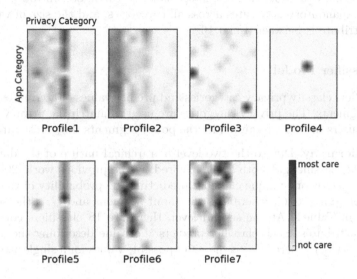

Fig. 3. The clustering results of the privacy profiles.

To assign one of these profiles to a new user, we craft a dynamic interactive question-answering mechanism, where the user is asked at most 5 yes/no questions capturing the discriminative features of profiles, to be eventually assigned to a certain profile. Depending on the user's privacy preferences, the former answer decides the latter question, so different users may answer different set of questions to better personalize their profiles.

5 Privacy Policy Extraction

To extract the concerned information, we deploy a deep learning model as the classifier to label the text segments of the privacy policy. According to the user profile generated as described in Sect. 4, the expected segments are returned to the user, together with related GDPR items to reinforce the privacy awareness.

5.1 Dataset Description

We leverage the public dataset OPP-115 [20] to train our deep learning classifier. The dataset contains 115 privacy policies with 23K fine-grained annotations manually labeled by three experts. The annotation scheme is at two levels. Level 1 annotates each paragraph-sized segment with one or more of ten privacy categories in Table 1. Level 2 is a group of <attribute-value> pairs concretely illustrating the privacy data practice. For instance, if a segment is annotated as *First Party Collection* in level 1, it must contain 3 mandatory attribute annotations: *Collection Action, Information Type* and *Purpose* in level 2. Each attribute has a value coming from its own defined value set. For example, the value set of *Purpose* attribute is: *basic services, advertising, research*, etc. In total, there are 18 distinct mandatory attributes across all categories, and the size of value sets of each attribute is between 4 and 16.

5.2   Classifier Model

The classifiers classify privacy categories and predict values of attributes for policy text segments. The privacy categories are used to match the privacy concern profiles of users so that we can render the policy segments they most care about.

Model Hierarchy. Due to the two-level hierarchical nature of the data label, we train the classifiers at both levels inspired by the previous work [20]. At the first level, there is one unique classifier predicting the probability of the privacy category $p(c_i|s), c_i \in C$, where s is the input segment and C is the set of all categories in Table 1. At the second level, there are 18 classifiers corresponding to 18 attributes. Each classifier predicts the value describing the attribute $p(v_j|s), v_j \in V(a)$, where $V(a)$ is the set of possible values for a single attribute a.

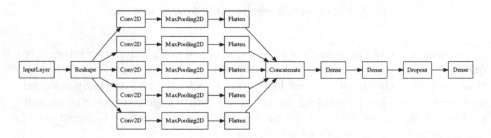

Fig. 4. The CNN structure contains five kinds of filter sizes (from 2 to 6). Each filter size contains a convolutional layer followed by a max-pooling layer. Two fully-connected layers are added after the max-pooling layers. The active function is *sigmoid* for the output layer and *Relu* for convolutional layers and fully-connected layers. A dropout layer is applied to avoid over-fitting.

Classifier Construction. Our classifier contains a CNN followed by a random forest. Figure 4 illustrates the structure of the CNN. Previous work has demonstrated that CNN is appropriate for tasks of text classification [6,10,21]. The output of the CNN, the probability distribution of categories or attribute values, is then fed to a random forest. We constrain the depth of trees no more than 4 to avoid over-fitting.

The model is implemented in Python. A segment is tokenized and embed to a list of word vectors using the *fastText* library [2]. The CNN is constructed by the *Keras*[3] API and the random forest is built using the *sklearn*[4] toolkit.

Model Performance. We randomly select 85 privacy policies in the dataset for training and the remaining 30 policies for testing. The hyper-parameters are obtained by grid-search and 5-fold cross-validation. The CNN converges after 300 epochs.

From Table 2, we can see that on average, our model achieves 0.94 precision, 0.83 recall, and 0.88 F1-score, which are higher than *Polisis*, the state-of-the-art privacy policy analysis system [4]. We also compare our model with approaches of SVM and hidden Markov model (HMM) adopted in OPP-115 as baselines. The results show our model outperforms them with 0.15 to 0.20 degree of metrics.

Table 2. Test results of the category classifier. Hypermeters: word-vector dimension: 300, number of filters for each convolutional layer: 100, intermediate fully-connected layer size: 100, 20, dropout rate: 0.5. batch size: 32.

Privacy category	Precision	Recall	F1-score
First Party Collection	0.94	0.88	0.91
Third Party Sharing	0.92	0.85	0.89
User Choice/Control	0.97	0.71	0.82
User Access and Edit	0.99	0.80	0.89
Data Retention	0.99	0.61	0.76
Data Security	0.94	0.74	0.83
Policy Change	0.88	0.68	0.77
Do Not Track	0.99	0.80	0.89
Specific Audiences	0.99	0.87	0.93
Other	0.92	0.86	0.89
Average	0.94	0.83	0.88
Polisis [4]	0.87	0.83	0.84
SVM	0.66	0.66	0.66
HMM	0.60	0.59	0.60

6   Field Study

We conduct the field study to validate the effectiveness of our system in practice. In this study, we implement our app on Android platform, and deploy the server

---

[3] https://keras.io.
[4] https://scikit-learn.org/.

for privacy policy scraping and text segment extraction. The participants ($n = 96$) are recruited from MTurk. They are asked to assess if our prediction hits the center of their privacy concerns.

Study Procedure. The main goal of this field study is to demonstrate the accuracy of our methods and the feasibility of the system. As described in Sect. 4.2, A participant must pass the dynamic question-answering process to be assigned to one of the seven learned privacy profiles. The questions have two forms: (1) privacy category only, for example, "Do you most care about the *Data Security* contents?" (2) <app category, privacy category> pair, for example, "Do you most care about the *First Party Collection* contents when you use social apps?".

After the assignment, the app connects to the server and transmits the profile index. For each app category, we randomly choose one app from top-50 hots on the Google Play. Its privacy policy is automatically downloaded and divided into segments on the server. At the time, the two-level classification model launches to label all the segments and then extract the concerned ones according to the profile. Subsequently, the raw segments are transmitted to the app, together with related GDPR items. The participants are responsible for judging if the prediction hits their privacy concerns. Finally, the feedback is reported to the server. At the end of the study, the participants are requested to complete the same survey as raised in Sect. 4.1. Each participant is paid $3 after the task.

Study Results. In total, we collect 1910 segment reviews across all the app categories. Figure 5 shows the concrete feedback aggregated by the privacy category. Overall, there are 1548 correctly predicted segments, which means the accuracy is around 0.81. Meanwhile, our system performs extremely well (0.85 accuracy) on the most focused three privacy category (occupying 87% segments).

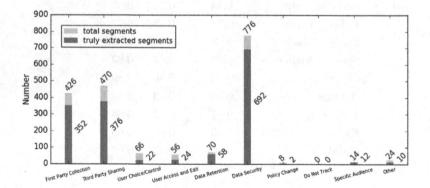

Fig. 5. The concrete feedback results aggregated by the privacy category.

7 Conclusion

In this paper, we create the first system to automatically predict and extract app's privacy policies with personalized privacy concerns. The system is composed of two modules: users' privacy concern profile generation and privacy policy extraction. To generate the profile depicting users' privacy concerns under different contexts, we construct the first dataset and design a matching mechanism to fast assign a learned profile to a user. Then, we deploy a deep learning based NLP model to recognize and elicit the target descriptions in app's privacy policy and related items in the GDPR. The real-world field study demonstrates the effectiveness of our system, where we accurately provide the users with the contents under concerns at 0.81 accuracy.

Acknowledgments. This work was supported in part by National Science Foundation of China under Grant 71671114 and Grant 61672350, and in part by the China Scholarship Council (201806230109).

A   An Example of the System Output

If a user queries the privacy policy of the *WeChat* app, and her privacy concern profile shows solicitude for whether her personal data is secure. Then the system will return a text segment in the *WeChat* privacy policy:

We use a variety of security technologies and procedures for the purpose of preventing loss, misuse, unauthorised access, or disclosure of Information – for example... But no data security measures can guarantee 100% security at all times. We do not warrant or guarantee the security of WeChat or any information you provide to us through WeChat.

And the related regulation items in GDPR is also presented to the user:

...the controller and the processor shall implement appropriate technical and organisational measures to ensure a level of security appropriate to the risk, including inter alia as appropriate:...

References

1. Angst, C.M., Agarwal, R.: Adoption of electronic health records in the presence of privacy concerns: the elaboration likelihood model and individual persuasion. MIS Q. **33**(2), 339–370 (2009)
2. Bojanowski, P., Grave, E., Joulin, A., Mikolov, T.: Enriching word vectors with subword information. Trans. Assoc. Comput. Linguist. **5**, 135–146 (2017)
3. Degeling, M., Utz, C., Lentzsch, C., Hosseini, H., Schaub, F., Holz, T.: We value your privacy... now take some cookies: Measuring the gdpr's impact on web privacy. arXiv preprint arXiv:1808.05096 (2018)
4. Harkous, H., Fawaz, K., Lebret, R., Schaub, F., Shin, K.G., Aberer, K.: Polisis: automated analysis and presentation of privacy policies using deep learning. In: 27th {USENIX} Security Symposium ({USENIX} Security 18), pp. 531–548 (2018)
5. Holtz, L.E., Zwingelberg, H., Hansen, M.: Privacy policy icons. In: Camenisch, J., Fischer-Hübner, S., Rannenberg, K. (eds.) Privacy and Identity Management for Life, pp. 279–285. Springer, Heidelberg (2011). https://doi.org/10.1007/978-3-642-20317-6_15

6. Kim, Y.: Convolutional neural networks for sentence classification. arXiv preprint arXiv:1408.5882 (2014)
7. Kittur, A., Chi, E.H., Suh, B.: Crowdsourcing user studies with mechanical turk. In: Proceedings of the SIGCHI Conference on Human Factors in Computing Systems, pp. 453–456. ACM (2008)
8. Li, H., Zhu, H., Du, S., Liang, X., Shen, X.S.: Privacy leakage of location sharing in mobile social networks: attacks and defense. IEEE Trans. Dependable Secure Comput. **15**(4), 646–660 (2018)
9. Li, H., Zhu, H., Ma, D.: Demographic information inference through meta-data analysis of Wi-Fi traffic. IEEE Trans. Mob. Comput. **17**(5), 1033–1047 (2018)
10. Li, P., Zhao, F., Li, Y., Zhu, Z.: Law text classification using semi-supervised convolutional neural networks. In: 2018 Chinese Control and Decision Conference (CCDC), pp. 309–313. IEEE (2018)
11. Linden, T., Harkous, H., Fawaz, K.: The privacy policy landscape after the GDPR. arXiv preprint arXiv:1809.08396 (2018)
12. Liu, B., et al.: Follow my recommendations: a personalized privacy assistant for mobile app permissions. In: Symposium on Usable Privacy and Security (2016)
13. Malhotra, N.K., Kim, S.S., Agarwal, J.: Internet users' information privacy concerns (IUIPC): the construct, the scale, and a causal model. Inf. Syst. Res. **15**(4), 336–355 (2004)
14. Mayer, J.R., Mitchell, J.C.: Third-party web tracking: policy and technology. In: 2012 IEEE Symposium on Security and Privacy (SP), pp. 413–427. IEEE (2012)
15. McDonald, A.M., Cranor, L.F.: The cost of reading privacy policies. ISJLP **4**, 543 (2008)
16. Meng, Y., Zhang, W., Zhu, H., Shen, X.S.: Securing consumer IoT in the smart home: architecture, challenges, and countermeasures. IEEE Wirel. Commun. **25**(6), 53–59 (2018)
17. Oltramari, A., et al.: PrivOnto: a semantic framework for the analysis of privacy policies. Semantic Web **9**, 1–19 (2017)
18. Sathyendra, K.M., Wilson, S., Schaub, F., Zimmeck, S., Sadeh, N.: Identifying the provision of choices in privacy policy text. In: Proceedings of the 2017 Conference on Empirical Methods in Natural Language Processing, pp. 2774–2779 (2017)
19. The General Data Protection Regulation. https://gdpr-info.eu/
20. Wilson, S., et al.: The creation and analysis of a website privacy policy corpus. In: Proceedings of the 54th Annual Meeting of the Association for Computational Linguistics (Volume 1: Long Papers), vol. 1, pp. 1330–1340 (2016)
21. Zhang, Z., Zou, Y., Gan, C.: Textual sentiment analysis via three different attention convolutional neural networks and cross-modality consistent regression. Neurocomputing **275**, 1407–1415 (2018)
22. Zhou, L., Du, S., Zhu, H., Chen, C., Ota, K., Dong, M.: Location privacy in usage-based automotive insurance: attacks and countermeasures. IEEE Trans. Inf. Forensics Secur. **14**(1), 196–211 (2019)
23. Zimmeck, S., Bellovin, S.M.: Privee: an architecture for automatically analyzing web privacy policies. In: Proceedings of the 23rd USENIX Conference on Security Symposium, pp. 1–16. USENIX Association (2014)

Cooperative BSM Dissemination in DSRC/WAVE Based Vehicular Networks

Lin Chen[1,2], Xiaoshuang Xing[2](✉) (iD), Gaofei Sun[2], Jin Qian[3], and Xin Guan[4]

[1] School of Computer Science and Technology, Soochow University,
Suzhou, Jiangsu, China
20185227092@stu.suda.edu.cn
[2] School of Computer Science and Engineering, Changshu Institute of Technology,
Suzhou, Jiangsu, China
{xing,gfsun}@cslg.edu.cn
[3] School of Computer Science and Technology, Taizhou University, Taizhou, China
qianjin@tzu.edu.cn
[4] School of Data Science and Technology, Heilongjiang University,
Harbin, Heilongjiang, China
guanxin.hlju@gmail.com

Abstract. The dissemination of the basic safety messages (BSMs) is critical to ensure the safety performance of the vehicular networks. The wireless access in vehicular environment (WAVE) protocol restricts the BSM dissemination on the common control channel (CCH) which leads to a low dissemination efficiency. In this paper, we propose to allow the BSM dissemination on both the CCH and the service channels (SCHs). A cooperative BSM dissemination scheme, called as TLMV, is proposed for cooperator selection. The vehicle with short access delay to the SCH, short transmission delay on the SCH, and large number of neighbors working on the SCH is selected as the cooperator to disseminate the BSM on the SCH. Taking into account the fact that a vehicle may have great dissemination efficiency on multiple SCHs, TLMV-M which allows a vehicle to help disseminating the BSM on multiple SCHs is proposed to further improve the dissemination efficiency. Simulation results indicate that our TLMV and TLMV-M significantly reduce the time cost for BSM dissemination and increase the number of vehicles received the BSM compared with the existing workload-balanced shortest processing time first (WSPT) scheme.

Keywords: BSM dissemination · DSRC · WAVE · Vehicular network

1 Introduction

According to the annual reports issued by the National Bureau of Statistics of China, 2.7 million people were injured and more than 70 thousand lives were lost from 2.5 millions of traffic accidents in China from 2007 to 2017. Traffic accidents have become a sever threaten to human lives and improving the safety

© Springer Nature Switzerland AG 2019
E. S. Biagioni et al. (Eds.): WASA 2019, LNCS 11604, pp. 55–66, 2019.
https://doi.org/10.1007/978-3-030-23597-0_5

performance of the traffic system becomes an urgent task to be solved. Dedicated Short-Range Communications/Wireless Access in Vehicular Environment (DSRC/WAVE) based vehicular network has been considered as a promising solution [7]. Two kinds of basic safety messages (BSMs), that are the routine status BSMs (RBSMs) and the event-driven emergency BSMs (EBSMs), are disseminated on the 5.9 GHz frequency band reserved for DSRC. Vehicles make driving decisions, such as decelerate, stop, change lanes, and change driving paths, according to the safety messages to reduce the risk of casualties on the roads. The DSRC frequency band is divided into 1 common control channel (CCH) and 6 service channels (SCHs). WAVE protocol stack, consisting of the IEEE 1609 family, IEEE 802.11p, and the Society of Automotive Engineers (SAE) J2735, regulates the message transmission on these channels. According to WAVE, BSMs and WAVE service advertisements (WSAs) are transmitted on the CCH while other messages are transmitted on the SCHs. Regarding the accessing to the CCH and the SCHs, IEEE 1609.4 [3] proposed the channel coordination model as shown in Fig. 1. It can be seen that time is divided into recurring sync intervals of 100 ms within which there is time slot 0 of 50 ms and a time slot 1 of 50 ms. All vehicles will be tuned to the CCH during time slot 0 to broadcast/receive BSMs and/or WSAs. Once received an interested WSA, a vehicle decides to move to the SCH where the corresponding service will be provided in the following time slot 1. A vehicle will stay on the CCH in the following time slot 1 if there is no interested WSA.

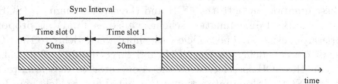

Fig. 1. Channel coordination model

Under the channel coordination model shown in Fig. 1, the EBSMs generated at time slot 1 can not be efficiently disseminated if the BSMs are only transmitted on the CCH. An example is given in Fig. 2. v_1, v_2, v_3, and v_4 are four nearby vehicles driving on the road. At time slot 1, v_1, v_2, and v_4 are tuned to SCH 1, 6, and 3 respectively for interested services. While v_3 stays on the CCH since it has no interested service. At time t_0, v_4 observes a safety related event. It generates an EBSM for this event, hands off to the CCH, and then broadcasts the EBSM. v_3 will successfully get the EBSM since it is on the CCH. However, v_1 and v_2 will not be able to receive the EBSM since they are still working on their SCHs. For the best case, v_1 and v_2 will get the EBSM at the beginning of the next time slot 0 when they move back to the CCH and v_4 are still broadcasting the EBSM. However, there is a worst case that v_1 and v_2 will never get the EBSM if v_4 stops broadcasting the EBSM before the next time

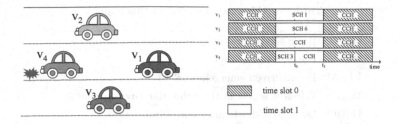

Fig. 2. A toy example of transmitting the BSMs only on the CCH

slot 0. The delayed even missing reception of the EBSM are potential threaten to the safety of the traffic system. As in the example given in Fig. 2, assume the EBSM contains information that a pedestrian is walking to the direction of v_2. If the pedestrian is within the blind area of v_2, he will be in a big danger of being hit by v_2 due to the delayed/missing reception of the EBSM. Therefore, efficient BSM dissemination schemes should be designed to improve the safety performance of the traffic system. In this paper, we design a novel cooperative BSM dissemination scheme to improve the dissemination efficiency. Since the RBSM is generated and transmitted regularly while the EBSMs can be generated at any time when safety related events occur. The dissemination of the EBSMs turns to be a more challenging problem. Therefore, we mainly focus on the dissemination of the EBSMs generated at time slot 1. A safety related event usually affects the safety of a nearby area around the event location, thus we aim to disseminate the EBSM to as many as possible nearby vehicles while keeping the dissemination delay as short as possible [6,13,20]. To achieve this goal, we make the following contributions:

1. We propose a cooperative BSM dissemination scheme, called as TLMV, that allow the EBSM to be transmitted on both CCH and SCHs to improve the dissemination efficiency. Considering the fact that different vehicles may work on different SCHs, we propose to broadcast the EBSM on the CCH immediately after the generation of the EBSM. At the same time, cooperators are selected from the vehicles that received the EBSM on the CCH to disseminate the EBSM on different SCHs.
2. For any vehicle, we define a metric to indicate the dissemination efficiency of the vehicle on an SCH. The metric is designed by considering the access delay to the SCH, the transmission delay on the SCH, and the number of vehicles that can receive the EBSM on the SCH.
3. Taking into consideration the fact that a vehicle may have great dissemination efficiency on multiple SCHs, we propose a scheme, called as TLMV-M, that allows a vehicle to help disseminating the BSM on multiple SCHs. The time cost for finishing the BSM dissemination can be further reduced and more vehicles can receive the EBSM.

For better understanding, we give a list of abbreviations used in this paper in Table 1.

Table 1. Abbreviations used in this paper

BSM	Basic safety message
RBSM	Routine status BSM
EBSM	Event-driven emergency BSM
WAVE	Wireless access in the vehicular environment
DSRC	Dedicated short-range communications
CCH	Control channel
SCH	Service channel
WSA	WAVE service advertisement
WSD	WAVE-enhanced safety message delivery
WSPT	Workload-balanced shortest processing time first

The rest of the paper is organized as following. The related works are discussed in Sect. 2. In Sect. 3, we describe system model and formulate the problem to be solved. The cooperative BSM dissemination schemes TLMV and TLMV-M are designed in Sect. 4. Simulation results are given in Sect. 5 and we conclude the paper in Sect. 6.

2   Related Works

BSM dissemination plays an important role to ensure the safety of the traffic system. The protocol basis of BSM dissemination have been clarified in [8,14]. Recent work on BSM dissemination can be classified into three categories: reliability improvement, congestion control, and efficiency improvement.

[9] and [18] focus on improving the reliability of the BSM dissemination. Reference [9] proposes a scheme which chooses a one-hop neighbor vehicle as a potential forwarder to relay the BSM according to the network properties. More vehicles can receive the BSM and some vehicles can receive several copies of the BSM to improve the reliability of the BSM dissemination. A piggybacked cooperative repetition approach is proposed in [18] where repetitions of the BSM are piggybacked by the newly generated messages to make the dissemination of the BSM more reliable.

When BSMs are frequently broadcasted on the CCH, congestion will cause unsuccessful BSM dissemination and reduce the safety performance of the traffic system [4]. [11,16,17] propose schemes to reduce the frequency that the BSMs are generated and transmitted. While [12] and [15] solve the congestion problem by controlling the transmission power.

All the aforementioned work focuses on the scenarios where the BSMs are disseminated only on the CCH. However, [10] reveals that restricting the transmission of the BSM on the CCH will lead to a low dissemination efficiency. A WAVE-enhanced safety message delivery (WSD) scheme is proposed to explore the SCHs for BSM dissemination and a cooperative WSD is designed to employ cooperators for further dissemination efficiency improvement. A workload-balanced shortest processing time first (WSPT) algorithm is proposed for cooperator selection. The workload of a vehicle is defined as the number of SCHs that its neighbors are working on. The vehicle with small workload will be preferentially selected as a cooperator on the SCH that it has the shortest processing time.

Our idea comes from the work of [10] and we aim at further improving the dissemination efficiency by proposing novel cooperative BSM dissemination scheme. Since the workload defined in [10] only indicates the number of SCHs that a vehicle's neighbors are working on, it contains no information about the number of vehicles working on the SCHs and has little influence on the dissemination efficiency. We focus on selecting cooperators that can disseminate the BSM to as many as nearby vehicles within a time as short as possible. Moreover, we takes into account the fact that a vehicle may have great dissemination efficiency on multiple SCHs and propose a scheme that allows a vehicle to help disseminating the BSM on multiple SCHs.

3   System Model and Problem Formulation

3.1   System Model

We consider a vehicular network consisting of N vehicles, denoted by $V = \{1, 2, \cdots, N\}$. Let C_{ch} denote the CCH and $S_{ch} = \{s_1, s_2, \cdots, s_6\}$ denote the set of SCHs. Each vehicle accesses to the CCH and the SCHs according to the channel coordination model given in Fig. 1. We assume that each vehicle broadcasts a RBSM on the CCH at the beginning of each time slot 0. This assumption is reasonable since the WAVE protocol stack requires the RBSM to be transmitted no less than 10 times per second to guarantee the safety performance. According to [2], the RBSM contains a vehicle's routine status such as the vehicle size, position, speed, and heading acceleration, optional information can be added to the RBSM to satisfy the application requirements. In this paper, we require a vehicle $v \in V$ to add an information c_v to its RBSMs. Here, $c_v \in \{C_{ch} \cup S_{ch}\}$ is the channel that v will work on during the following time slot 1.

Assume that all vehicles have the same transmission range. For a vehicle $v \in V$, other vehicles within v's transmission range are called as v's neighbors. Denote the set of v's neighbors as $N_v = \{v_1, v_2, \cdots, v_{|N_v|}\}$ with $|N_v|$ being the size of N_v. Within each time slot 0, vehicle v will collect a list $L_v = \{c_{v_1}, c_{v_2}, \cdots, c_{v_{|N_v|}}\}$ indicating the set of channels that v's neighbors will be on during next time slot 1. We divide the neighbor set into two subsets N_v^C and N_v^S according to the rule that $\forall v_i \in N_v^C$, $c_{v_i} = C_{ch}$, $N_v^S = N_v \setminus N_v^C$. Then, N_v^C will be the set of neighbors who keep on the CCH and N_v^S will be the set of neighbors who work on the SCHs for next time slot 1. Correspondingly, we divide the list L_v into two sublists with L_v^C for N_v^C and L_v^S for N_v^S. Let $S_v = L_v^S \cap S_{ch}$ denote the set of SCHs that v's neighbors will be on during the next time slot 1. For any $s_i \in S_v$, $i \in \{1, 2, \cdots, 6\}$, let m_i^v denote the number of neighbors that will be on the SCH

s_i for next time slot 1. That is

$$m_i^v = \sum_{v_s \in N_v^S} I_{C_{s_i}(c_{v_s})} \tag{1}$$

Here, $I_{C_{s_i}(c_{v_s})} = 1$ if $c_{v_s} = s_i$ and $I_{C_{s_i}(c_{v_s})} = 0$ otherwise. Therefore, we can formulate a set $M_v = \{m_i^v | s_i \in S_v\}$ for S_v. For better understanding, we summarize the information that a vehicle v will obtain during each time slot 0 in Table 2.

Table 2. Information obtained by vehicle v during time slot 0

Notation	Meaning
N_v	The set of v's neighbors
N_v^C	The set of neighbors who keep on the CCH
N_v^S	The set of neighbors who work on the SCHs for next time slot 1
S_v	The set of SCHs that v's neighbors will be on during the next time slot 1
M_v	The number of neighbors that will be on the SCH s_i for next time slot 1

3.2   Problem Formulation

In the above described vehicular network, we consider the scenario shown in Fig. 3. A vehicle v observes a safety related event and generate an EBSM at time $t = t_0$ during current time slot 1. Let the beginning of the current time slot 1 being the original time that is $t = 0$. According to WAVE, the BSMs should be broadcasted on the CCH. Vehicle v should turn to the CCH and broadcast the EBSM immediately. Considering the fact that there may be some neighbors working on the SCHs during the current time slot 1 and will not be on the CCH until next time slot 0. v should broadcast the EBSM again at the beginning of the next time slot 0 to inform these neighbors. In this case, the number of vehicles being informed of the EBSM within current time slot 1 is

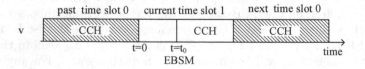

Fig. 3. Generating an EBSM at time slot 1

$$n_{T_1} = |N_v^C| = \sum_{i=1}^{|N_v|} I_{C_{ch}(c_{v_i})} \tag{2}$$

Here $I_{C_{ch}(c_{v_i})} = 1$ if $c_{v_i} = C_{ch}$ and $I_{C_{ch}(c_{v_i})} = 0$ otherwise. The time delay for informing all the neighbors is

$$D = 50 - t_0 + T_a + T_t \tag{3}$$

Here, 50 is the total length of time slot 1, $50 - t_0$ is the rest time of the current time slot 1, T_a indicates the access delay of the CCH, T_t indicates the time needed for transmitting the EBSM.

It can be seen from (2) and (3) that the transmission efficiency of the EBSM is low since limited number of vehicles can be informed during the current time slot 1 and the time delay of informing all the neighboring vehicles are considerable. The low efficiency transmission of the EBSM results in potential threaten to the safety of the traffic system. Therefore, we aim to improve the transmission efficiency of the EBSM by designing a cooperative BSM dissemination scheme. In this scheme, vehicle v who generates the EBSM will turn to the CCH and broadcast the EBSM immediately. At the same time, v will select several neighbors who receive the EBSM to help transmitting the EBSM on the SCHs of S_v. Our objective is to inform as many nearby vehicles as possible while keeping the dissemination delay as short as possible.

4 Cooperative BSM Dissemination Scheme

In this section we solve the cooperative BSM dissemination problem under the scenario given in Fig. 3. We first design a scheme called as Time Least and Most covered Vehicles first (TLMV) which allows a vehicle to help disseminating the EBSM on no more than one SCH in Sect. 4.1. Considering the fact that a vehicle may have great dissemination performance on several SCHs, we propose a TLMV-M scheme by allowing a vehicle to help disseminating the EBSM on multiple SCHs in Sect. 4.2.

4.1 TLMV Scheme Design

As shown in Table 2, each vehicle v get the information of N_v^C, N_v^S, S_v, and M_v during each time slot 0. When v generates an EBSM at time t_0 of the current time slot 1, it turns to the CCH and broadcasts the EBSM. The neighbors within set N_v^C will get the EBSM. Once received the EBSM, vehicle $v_c \in N_v^C$ returns necessary information to participate into the cooperative BSM dissemination[1]. The necessary information includes S_{v_c}, M_{v_c}, and T_{v_c}. Here,

$$T_{v_c} = \{t_i^{v_c} = t_i^{v_c}[a] + t_i^{v_c}[t] \big| s_i \in S_{v_c}\} \tag{4}$$

---

[1] In this paper, we assume that all vehicles are willing to cooperate for BSM dissemination in order to ensure safety. Motivation schemes is outside the scope of this paper.

with $t_i^{v_c}[a]$ being the access delay of v_c to SCH s_i and $t_i^{v_c}[t]$ being the transmission delay of v_c to finish the transmission of the EBSM. $t_i^{v_c}[a]$ can be obtained according to [10] and $t_i^{v_c}[t]$ can be considered as a constant equals to the length of the EBSM divided by the predefined data rate [1].

If $S_{v_c} \cap S_v = S_{v_c}^v \neq \varnothing$, vehicle v_c becomes a candidate cooperator on the SCHs of $S_{v_c}^v$. After receiving the feed back from all the neighbors of N_v^C, vehicle v forms a candidate cooperator list as $L_{s_i}^{CO} = \{(v_c, t_i^{v_c}, m_i^{v_c}) | s_i \in S_{v_c}^v\}$ for any $s_i \in S_v$. Then, vehicle v arrange the cooperator for the SCHs sequentially. The SCH s_i with the minimum channel index i will be arranged first. v_c^* is selected as the cooperator to disseminate the EBSM on s_i according to the rule that

$$\frac{t_i^{v_c^*}}{m_i^{v_c^*}} = \min\left\{\frac{t_i^{v_c}}{m_i^{v_c}}\middle| s_i \in S_{v_c}^v\right\} \tag{5}$$

After the arrangement for each SCH, the selected cooperator will be deleted from the cooperator lists for the unarranged SCHs. Therefore, each vehicle can only help disseminating the EBSM on no more than one SCH.

4.2   TLMV-M Scheme Design

In practical, there exist scenarios where a vehicle have great dissemination performance on several SCHs. For such scenarios, we propose a TLMV-M scheme which allows a vehicle to help disseminating the EBSM on multiple SCHs to further improve the performance of the TLMV scheme.

After forming the candidate cooperator lists for the SCHs in S_v. Vehicle v first selects the cooperator for SCH s_i with the minimum channel index i. v_c^* is selected as the cooperator to disseminate the EBSM on s_i according to the rule given in (5). Then, a time of length $T_{v_c} = t_i^{v_c^*}$ will be cost for v_c to finish the cooperative EBSM dissemination on s_i. As to any unarranged SCHs for which v_c are candidate cooperators, v change the parameter $t_i^{v_c}$ to be $t_i^{v_c} + T_{v_c}$. After that, v arrange the cooperator for the next SCH according to the rule given in (5).

5   Performance Evaluation

In this section we compare the dissemination efficiency of our TLMV and TLMV-M with that of WSPT proposed in [10] through simulation study with MATLAB. Two metrics are defined for performance evaluation

– Dissemination Time: The time cost for disseminating the EBSM on the SCHs of set S_v.
– Dissemination Range: The number of vehicles received the EBSM.

We conduct the simulation study under two scenarios. The simulation results for scenario I-fixed scale vehicular network are given in Subsect. 5.1, and the results for scenario II-scaleable vehicular network are given in Subsect. 5.2.

On the other hand, we assume the traffic flow is subject to Poisson distribution. Then we use the Poisson distribution to randomly generate some numbers obeying the Poisson distribution as the number of vehicles will cooperate with the vehicle A. These vehicles and A form a cooperation vehicles collection. These two cases are specifically analyzed in the following two subsections.

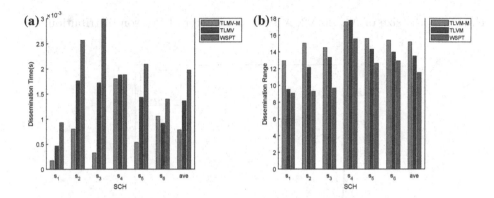

Fig. 4. (a) Total delay of each service channel (b) The number of vehicles covered of each service channel

5.1 Scenario I-Fixed Scale Vehicular Network

In this subsection, we conduct the simulation study in a fixed scale vehicular network. For each vehicle v, the size of N_v^C is fixed to be 20 and the size of N_v^S is randomly generated. The access delay of v_c to SCH s_i is set to be $t_i^{v_c}[a] = 0 \sim 0.025$ s, the length of the EBSM is set to be 200B, and the data rate of a vehicle is set to be $1 \sim 63.5$ Mbits [1,5,10,19]. We conduct 200 times of simulation, the average dissemination time and the average dissemination range on each SCH are given in Fig. 4(a) and (b) respectively. The average dissemination time and dissemination range on all SCHs are also shown with tick "ave" in the figures.

It can be seen that our TLMV and TLMV-M outperform the WSPT in terms of the dissemination time and the dissemination range on all SCHs. The reason is that WSPT considers the workload of the vehicles when selecting cooperators. However, the workload has little influence on the dissemination efficiency. TLMV-M performs better than TLMV since the vehicles with great dissemination efficiency on multiple SCHs are not efficiently utilized in TLMV. For example, vehicle v_c has low dissemination delay on s_1, s_2 and many neighbors are working on s_1, s_2. In TLMV, v_c is assigned to disseminate the EBSM on s_1. Then, s_2 will be assigned to another vehicle whose dissemination delay is bigger than v_c and may have less neighbors working on s_2. However, s_1 and s_2 will both be assigned to v_c in TLMV-M thus leading to a better dissemination efficiency.

5.2   Scenario II-Scaleable Vehicular Network

The density of a network usually follows the Poisson distribution given in (6).
The probability density function for different λ is shown in Fig. 5.

$$P(n) = \frac{\lambda^n}{n!}e^{-\lambda}, n > 0 \tag{6}$$

Here, n is the size of N_v^C or N_v^S, λ is the parameter of Poisson distribution.

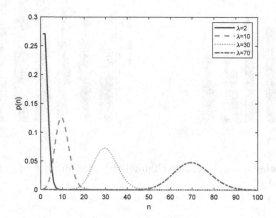

Fig. 5. Probability density function for different λ

In this subsection, we randomly decide the size of N_v^C and N_v^S following the
Poisson distribution to investigate the dissemination performance for different
network scale. For each network scale, i.e. each value of λ, we get the dissemination time and the dissemination range by averaging the results of 4000 times
of simulation. The results are given in Fig. 6(a) and (b).

The results are consistent with that of Fig. 4. TLMV-M performs best and
TLMV outperforms WSPT. The network scale increases with the increasing of
λ. More neighbors will be generated around each vehicle. Therefore, the dissemination range of all schemes increase with λ. When more neighbors are generated around v, there will be more cooperator candidates for v to select. The
probability of selecting better cooperator with lower dissemination delay and
can disseminate the EBSM to a wider range will increase using our TLMV and
TLMV-M. However, the WSPT scheme take the workload as the preference metric. When the network scale increase, the number of vehicles with heavy workload
will increase. These vehicles will not be preferred to be the cooperators in the
WSPT scheme. Vehicle v will choose cooperators from those vehicles with light
workload even if the dissemination delay of these vehicles are longer. Therefore,
we can observe a slightly increase in the dissemination time of WSPT with the
increase of λ.

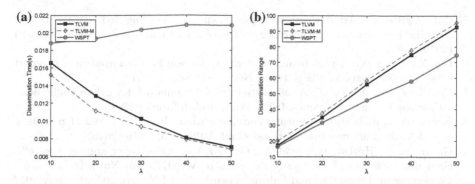

Fig. 6. (a) Total delay of each service channel (b) The number of vehicles covered of each service channel

6 Conclusion

The dissemination of the BSMs plays an important role to ensure the safety performance of the traffic system. In this paper, both the CCH and the SCHs are explored for BSM dissemination. Cooperators are selected for cooperative BSM dissemination by designing the TLMV and the TLMV-M schemes. Simulation results show that our design can significantly reduce the dissemination delay and increase the number of vehicles receiving the BSM.

Acknowledgement. The authors would like to thank the support from the Natural Science Foundation of China (61602062, 61702056, 61802274), the Natural Science Foundation of JiangSu Province (BK20160410), the Natural Science Fund for Colleges and Universities in Jiangsu Province (17KJB520001, 18KJB510044), and the Heilongjiang Provincial Natural Science Foundation of China (F2017027).

References

1. IEEE draft standard for amendment to standard [for] information technology-telecommunications and information exchange between systems-local and metropolitan networks-specific requirements-part ii: Wireless LAN medium access control (MAC) and physical layer (PHY) specifications-amendment 6: Wireless access in vehicular environments. IEEE Std P802.11p/D11.0 April 2010, pp. 1–35, June 2010
2. Dedicated short range communications (DSRC) message set dictionary. SAE J2735, pp. 1–267 (2016)
3. IEEE standard for wireless access in vehicular environments (wave) - multi-channel operation. IEEE Std 1609.4 (Revision of IEEE Std 1609.4-2010), pp. 1–94, March 2016
4. Ahmad, S.A., Hajisami, A., Krishnan, H., Ahmed-Zaid, F., Moradi-Pari, E.: V2V system congestion control validation and performance. IEEE Trans. Veh. Technol. **68**, 2102–2110 (2019)

5. Cai, Z., He, Z.: Trading private range counting over big IoT data. In: The 39th IEEE International Conference on Distributed Computing Systems (ICDCS) (2019)
6. Cai, Z., Zheng, X.: A private and efficient mechanism for data uploading in smart cyber-physical systems. IEEE Trans. Netw. Sci. Eng. 1 (2019)
7. Cai, Z., Zheng, X., Yu, J.: A differential-private framework for urban traffic flows estimation via taxi companies. IEEE Trans. Ind. Inform. 1 (2019)
8. Festag, A.: Standards for vehicular communication—from IEEE 802.11 p to 5g. e & i Elektrotechnik und Informationstechnik **132**(7), 409–416 (2015)
9. Gawas, M.A., Hurkat, P., Goyal, V., Gudino, L.J.: Cross layer approach for efficient dissemination of emergency messages in VANETs. In: Ninth International Conference on Ubiquitous and Future Networks (ICUFN), pp. 206–211, July 2017
10. Ghandour, A.J., Di Felice, M., Artail, H., Bononi, L.: Dissemination of safety messages in IEEE 802.11 p/WAVE vehicular network: analytical study and protocol enhancements. Perv. Mob. Comput. **11**, 3–18 (2014)
11. Gupta, N., Prakash, A., Tripathi, R.: Adaptive beaconing in mobility aware clustering based MAC protocol for safety message dissemination in VANET. Wirel. Commun. Mob. Comput. **2017**, 15 (2017)
12. Joseph, M., Liu, X., Arunita, J.: An adaptive power level control algorithm for DSRC congestion control, pp. 57–62 (2018)
13. Li, J., Cai, Z., Yan, M., Li, Y.: Using crowdsourced data in location-based social networks to explore influence maximization. In: The 35th Annual IEEE International Conference on Computer Communications (INFOCOM), pp. 1–9, April 2016
14. Li, Y.J.: An overview of the DSRC/WAVE technology. In: Zhang, X., Qiao, D. (eds.) QShine 2010. LNICST, vol. 74, pp. 544–558. Springer, Heidelberg (2012). https://doi.org/10.1007/978-3-642-29222-4_38
15. Mughal, B.M., Wagan, A.A., Hasbullah, H.: Efficient congestion control in VANET for safety messaging. In: International Symposium on Information Technology, vol. 2, pp. 654–659 (2010)
16. Ogura, K., Katto, J., Takai, M.: BRAEVE: stable and adaptive BSM rate control over IEEE802.11p vehicular networks, pp. 745–748 (2013)
17. Oliveira, R., Montez, C., Boukerche, A., Wangham, M.S.: Reliable data dissemination protocol for VANET traffic safety applications. Ad Hoc Netw. **63**, 30–44 (2017)
18. Yang, L., Guo, J., Wu, Y.: Piggyback cooperative repetition for reliable broadcasting of safety messages in VANETs. In: 6th IEEE Consumer Communications and Networking Conference, pp. 1–5. IEEE (2009)
19. Yu, J., Huang, B., Cheng, X., Atiquzzaman, M.: Shortest link scheduling algorithms in wireless networks under SINR. IEEE Trans. Veh. Technol. **66**(3), 2643–2657 (2017)
20. Yu, J., Wan, S., Cheng, X., Yu, D.: Coverage contribution area based k-coverage for wireless sensor networks. IEEE Trans. Veh. Technol. **66**(9), 8510–8523 (2017)

TIDS: Trust Intrusion Detection System Based on Double Cluster Heads for WSNs

Na Dang[1], Xiaowu Liu[1(✉)], Jiguo Yu[2], and Xiaowei Zhang[1]

[1] School of Information Science and Engineering, Qufu Normal University,
Rizhao, China
ycmlxw@126.com
[2] Shandong Computer Science Center (National Supercomputer Center),
Jinan, China

Abstract. The efficiency and reliability are crucial indexes when a trust system is applied into Wireless Sensor Networks (WSNs). In this paper, an efficient and reliable Trusted Intrusion Detection System (TIDS) with double cluster heads for WSNs is proposed. Firstly, an intrusion detection scheme based on trust is discussed. The monitoring nodes are responsible for evaluating the credibility of Cluster Member (CM) instead of depending on the feedback between CMs, which is suitable for decreasing the energy consumption of WSNs and reducing the influence of malicious nodes. Secondly, a new trust evaluation method is defined in TIDS and it takes the data forwarding and communication tasks into consideration which may enhance the reliability of Cluster Head (CH). The theoretical and simulation results show that our solution can effectively reduce the system overhead and improve the robustness of WSNs.

Keywords: Wireless Sensor Network · Trust system · Data Aggregation

1 Introduction

The development of micro-chip and short distance communication technique makes WSNs develop in an amazing manner. WSNs are widely deployed in the fields of environmental monitoring, health care and space exploration. Due to the limitation of resource and unattended deploying manner, WSNs are faced with more serious security challenges than the cable networks. Traditional security techniques such as encryption and authentication can protect WSNs from being eavesdropped or tampered. However, these techniques are difficult to be implemented in each node because of the performance limitation of sensors. Therefore, it is necessary to exploit new attack detection and defense techniques for WSNs.

As an active defense technique, intrusion detection can not only identify potential attacks, but also take corresponding protection measures for monitored network [1]. Meanwhile, it provides relevant data records which may be used as the data source to trace the behavior of malicious activity. Because of the limited transmission range of the sensor node, it is almost impossible to directly transmit each sensing data of each node to the Base Station (BS) in a large-scale WSN. Generally speaking, there may be data redundancy between neighbor nodes which cause the unnecessary communication

© Springer Nature Switzerland AG 2019
E. S. Biagioni et al. (Eds.): WASA 2019, LNCS 11604, pp. 67–83, 2019.
https://doi.org/10.1007/978-3-030-23597-0_6

overhead. To solve this problem, the Data Aggregation (DA) is a favorable choice [2]. Although there are a several studies which combined DA with the intrusion detection, the energy efficiency and data precision are important issues in large-scale WSNs. In this paper, we propose a Trusted Intrusion Detection System (TIDS) used in cluster-based WSNs in order to evaluate the reliability of the node and isolate the malicious node from the network.

The remainder of this paper is organized as follows: Sect. 2 describes an overview of related work. Section 3 discusses our network model and some assumptions. The efficient and reliable trust system is analyzed in Sect. 4. Section 5 provides the theoretical and simulation evaluation of TIDS. Section 6 concludes this paper.

2 Related Work

2.1 Clustering Algorithms for WSNs

The sensor node can directly communicate with the BS or interact with each other through relay nodes. The larger the sensor network is, the greater the energy consumes. Therefore, nodes far away from the BS will exhaust their energy at a faster speed than the nearer ones. Faced with this problem, the clustering mechanisms such as LCA [3], LEACH [4], GS^3 [5] and EC [6] were proposed to improve the network scalability and throughput. The nodes in a WSN are divided into different groups and the node with more energy is elected as a CH in a cluster and all CHs of different clusters form a higher-level backbone network. Clustering is an important management strategy which has the ability to facilitate DA technique in a WSN. A double CH model is different from the traditional model, where two cluster heads are selected. Each CH performs DA and its results are sent to BS individually [7]. The BS computes the similarity of two results. If the similarity coefficient does not exceed the pre-defined threshold, the two CHs are added to the blacklist. Meanwhile, the feedback is transmitted from the BS to the trust system which can be used to identify and isolate the compromised sensor nodes in time.

The cluster topology is convenient for creating a trust system locally and carries out DA in a WSN. Furthermore, it simplifies the communication and effectively prolongs the lifetime of network. In addition, a trust system can be applied into the cluster topology easier than other topologies such as tree and ring.

2.2 Trust System for WSNs

The trust system is a favorite scheme which provides a mechanism to monitor the security state of network. For example, it is capable of detecting errors or malicious nodes in a cluster [8]. Many studies have been proposed to discuss the trust systems for WSNs [9–11]. However, these systems suffer from various limitations and consume the overwhelming resources, especially in a large-scale WSN.

Recently, a few trust management systems have been addressed for clustering WSNs. A novel lightweight Group based Trust Management Scheme (GTMS) for clustered WSNs was proposed [12] which divided the trust values into three levels:

sensor node level, CH level and BS level. The innovation of the GTMS was that it evaluated the trust of network from different viewpoints instead of a single trust value. Reliable Data Aggregation and Transmission protocol (RDAT) introduced different functions to compute the reputation and trust values for different activities including sensing, aggregation and routing [13]. The trustworthiness of node is a comprehensive one which depends on the trust of sensing, aggregation and routing protocol.

Improved Reliable Trust-Based and Energy-Efficient Data Aggregation for WSNs (iRTEDA) took the remaining energy and link availability into consideration and prevented the routing path from being overused [14]. Therefore, it ensured that the routing path selected by the trust system was reliable. In addition, watchdog mechanism was employed in many trust systems to monitor the communication behaviors of nodes [7].

2.3 Attack and SDA in WSN

An attacker in a WSN may be an internal node, an external node or both. If the nodes of WSN are equipped with the encryption-based authentication and authorization mechanisms, the external attacks are limited to physical disruption or interference with the communication channel [15]. Internal attacker can initiate various malicious activities such as tampering, eavesdropping and dropping. Among them, packet dropping may have a drastic effect on network performance without being blocked by authentication and authorization [16, 17]. Three typical dropping attacks are described as follows.

- Blackhole Attack. It deserts all received packets and causes the most serious damage to the network. However, it can be easily captured for its activity is rather obvious compared with the normal activity.
- On-Off Attack. When the attack is on, it drops all received packets; when the attack is off, all the received packets are forwarded.
- Selective Forwarding Attack. Different from above mentioned attacks, the selective forwarding attack deserts packet randomly. It may hide the malicious behaviors in normal activities and a sophisticated detection mechanism is indispensable [18].

Recently, several protocols have been proposed for Secure Data Aggregation (SDA) in order to deal with the internal attacks in WSNs. Kefayati discussed a Blind Information Fusion Framework (BIFF) for SDA [19]. The data are transformed from normal space to anonymous space and cannot be deduced after they were fused. A new probabilistic grouping technique, Secure hop-by-hop Data Aggregation Protocol (SDAP), was described which divided the nodes in a tree topology into logical groups (sub trees) of similar size [20]. The commit-and-attest scheme was discussed where the aggregation result could be verified at BS. In addition, trust assessment systems were widely adopted in many protocols including GTMS [12], RDAT [13], Irteda [14] and DCHM [7], which can ensure the security of DA. Therefore, a SDA scheme is proposed in this paper so as to enhance the security of TIDS.

3 Network Model

We develop a trust-based framework for double-CHs-based WSN and design a mechanism to reduce the probability of a malicious node being selected as aggregation node. The nodes in a clustering WSN can be identified as CH and Cluster Member (CM) as shown in Fig. 1.

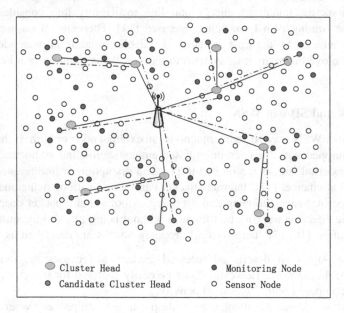

Fig. 1. Network model.

The following assumptions are adopted in our scheme. There are three types of nodes: CM, Monitoring Nodes (MN) and Aggregation Nodes (AN or CH) in a WSN. In addition, we identify a node by a triple $\langle ID, T, S \rangle$ where ID, T and S represent the node identify, the node type and the node subtype, respectively. T defines which type of node is required, such as CM, CH or MN. To prevent trust values from being forged during the transformation from one node to another, a secure communication channel can be established through deploying a key management scheme such as random key distribution mechanism [21].

All nodes are trustworthy in the initial stage and BS is secure with unlimited energy supply. This paper focuses on the selective forwarding which aims to reduce the performance of the network in terms of packet loss rate and prevent the data from being transformed to BS [18]. We propose an intrusion detection mechanism based on Beta model to detect the abnormal behaviors of nodes. The trust value of CM is evaluated by its CHs and MNs when a WSN suffered from an attack. Therefore, each CM does not need to maintain the trust table or communicate with other CMs, which reduces the communication overhead and eliminates the possibility of being attacked by a compromised CM.

4 Trusted Intrusion Detection System with Double CHs for WSNs

The proposed trust intrusion detection system consists of three parts: cluster component, CH component and BS component, as shown in Fig. 2. The main tasks of cluster component are to select CHs, form clusters, monitor the CMs and update the trust system. CH component is in charge of detecting outliers, aggregating data, uploading the aggregation results and trust tables to BS. Two CHs in a cluster execute these operations synchronously with the aim of guaranteeing the reliability of CMs in a cluster and send two aggregation results to BS. According to these aggregation results, BS determines whether the CHs are credible or not.

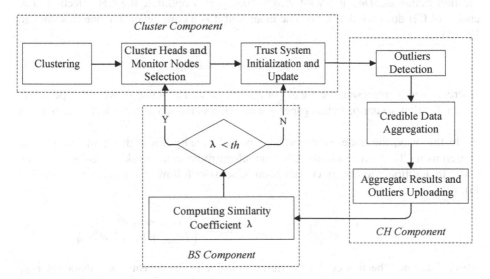

Fig. 2. Overview of the functions of the framework.

4.1 CH Election and Clustering

In the initial phase, sensor nodes are divided into several clusters by improving the clustering algorithm described in DCHM [7]. Different from DCHM, MNs are selected as well when the CHs are selected in our model. MNs need to monitor the behaviors of CMs and maintain a trust table of nodes in a cluster.

The CH and MN selections are two critical parts in the cluster formation. Two indexes are deduced in our model in Eq. (1). The relative residual energy, E_{ri}, can be calculated as

$$E_{ri} = \frac{E_i}{E_{max}} \qquad (1)$$

where E_i and E_{max} are the residual energy and the maximum initial energy of node i, respectively. The greater the relative density of node i is, the higher the correlations between i and its neighbors are.

The relative density, Dn_{ri}, can be obtained by Eq. (2).

$$Dn_{ri} = \frac{Dn_i}{Dn_{max}} \tag{2}$$

where the density of node i is expressed as Dn_i. Dn_{max} refers to the largest density in a network. If the distance between them is not up to the predefined threshold d_0, the two nodes are spatially related.

The density of nodes indicates the number of neighbor nodes within the communication radius d_0. Dn_{ri} is regarded as a principle to optimize the CH selection. The choice of CH does not depend on one index and it is a comprehensive one as shown in Eq. (3).

$$F_i = \alpha_1 \times E_{ri} + \alpha_2 \times Dn_{ri} \tag{3}$$

where α_1 and α_2 represent the weight of E_{ri} and Dn_{ri}. The value of weight depends on the application scenario. In this paper, we take E_{ri} as the main factor in the calculation of F_i ($\alpha_1 > \alpha_2$).

In this way, the node with more energy and density has higher probability to be chosen as a CH. As a result, the CHs can afford more extra workload compared with CMs. In addition, the energy consumption of sensors follows the model as depicted in Eq. (4).

$$E_{TX}(l, d) = E_{TX\_elec}(l) + E_{TX\_amp}(l, d) = \begin{cases} lE_{elec} + l\varepsilon_{fs}d^2, d < d_0 \\ lE_{elec} + l\varepsilon_{mp}d^4, d \geq d_0 \end{cases} \tag{4}$$

where l denotes the number of transmitted bits; d is the transmission distance; E_{elec} indicates the energy required for signal processing; ε_{fs} and ε_{mp} are the energy consumed by the amplifier to transmit data at the shorter distance and the longer distance respectively. Three types of nodes (CH, MN and CM) are deployed in a cluster and these nodes should be initialized before trust system is applied. We choose MNs and CMs according to the following functions.

$$N_{MN} = p \times N_{total}, p \in \left[\frac{1}{4}, \frac{1}{3}\right] \tag{5}$$

$$N_{CM} = N_{total} - p \times N_{total} - 1 = (1 - p)N_{total} - 1 \tag{6}$$

where N_{total} represents the total number of nodes in a cluster, N_{MN} and N_{CM} represent the number of MNs and CMs. Parameter p is the proportion of MNs in a cluster and it is between $\frac{1}{4}$ and $\frac{1}{3}$, which has been proved in [22]. It is indispensable that CHs need to be reselected in the following cases. (i) The energy of CH is lower than the threshold E_{th}. (ii) The CH is detected in an abnormal state. If one or both situations occur, the reselection message is triggered by BS. MCH (Main Cluster Head) keeps in work constantly and CCH (Candidate Cluster Head) sleep and forwards packets periodically. We illustrate the CH selection in Algorithm 1 according to the above-mentioned mechanisms.

Algorithm 1. Cluster Head Selection Algorithm.

Input: Density and energy of node, the energy and trust threshold E_{th}, Θ_T
Output: CHs and MNs

1. **Begin**
2. **If** $E_i \leq E_{th}$ or the Trust value of CH$\leq \Theta_T$ **then**
3. Broadcast a reelection message;
4. Calculate F_i and trust value of CMs according to Equation (3) and (10) in Section 4.3.2;
5.   **If** equality **then**
6.   Select two candidates and MNs according to equation (5);
7.   **Else**
8.   Choose the first and second candidates as MCH and CCH according to F_i;
9.   Select MNs in a descending order;
10.   **End**
11.   Send confirm message to the candidates to ensure that the candidates have enough energy;
12.   **If** energy enough **then**
13.   Select the candidates as the new CH;
14.   **Else**
15.   Repeat line 4 to line 10;
16.   **End IF**
17. **End IF**
18. **End**

4.2   Trust System Initialization

In the initialization stage of trust system, an aggregation tree is needed so that CHs can transmit the aggregation data to BS hop-by-hop. Therefore, it is necessary to build an aggregation tree rooted at BS for organizing sensor nodes in a network. We adopt the algorithm described in [23] to form an aggregation tree and the message is transmitted along the tree from the leaves to root. The initialization of the trust system is consistent with the traditional trust system, such as GTMS, RDAT in [13, 14].

If the original CH is trusted, BS will send the outlier table T_{BS} to all the CHs in the network. Each CH receives the table, T_{BS} as shown in Table 1, and CH shares this table with MNs in the same cluster. Each MN compares its own trust table T_{MN} with T_{BS}. The trust values are updated if T_{BS} and T_{MN} have different items. On the contrary, the update will be ignored. If the original CH is not trusted, the trust value of CH is initialized to zero.

4.3   Trust Intrusion Detection System

As discussed in Sect. 2.3, the internal attack is a serious problem in a WSN and TIDS should decrease the impact of attacks as soon as possible. TIDS detects internal attacks through the following steps.

4.3.1   Monitoring Mechanism

The MN listens to the activities of CH and CM. The monitoring mechanism operates in a way similar to that of watchdog. Each MN monitors the forwarding activity of CHs. A "good" behavior of CH will be recorded if a packet is forwarded; otherwise, a "bad" behavior of CH will be counted. According to the behaviors of CHs, MN store the different numbers of activities in the trust table T_{MN}. MNs also compute trust value of CMs according to the behaviors of CMs. MN only needs to listen to the channel and maintain the trust table, which consumes less energy than data transmission.

Table 1. Trust table in BS (T_{BS}).

Cluster	Node ID	Trust value	Outlier	Bad behavior	Good behavior
Cluster1	MCH_1	0.9167	No	0	10
Cluster1	CCH_1	0.9167	No	0	10
Cluster1	MN_1	0.6923	No	2	8
Cluster1	MN_2	0.9167	No	0	10
Cluster1	MN_3	0.8333	No	1	9
Cluster1	$Node_6$	0.1579	Yes	5	5
Cluster1	$Node_{10}$	0.5000	Yes	3	7
Cluster2	MCH_2	0	Yes	4	6
Cluster2	CCH_2	0	Yes	2	8
Cluster2	......	......	......	......	......
Cluster2	MN_i	0.8333	No	1	9
Cluster2	$Node_1$	0.3043	Yes	4	6
Cluster2	......	......	......	......	......
Cluster2	$Node_m$	0.0725	Yes	6	4
......	......	......	......	......	......

4.3.2   Trust Evaluation

Based on the monitoring mechanism in Sect. 4.3.1, MNs evaluate the trustworthiness of nodes with a trust model. In the Beta trust model, MN_i calculates the reputation $R_{i,j}$ according to the behaviors of CM_j. For example, MN_i counts the number of good and bad behaviors of CM_j as $r_{i,j}$, $s_{i,j}$ and records the credibility of node CM_j using Eq. (7).

$$R_{i,j} = Beta(p|r_{i,j}+1, s_{i,j}+1) \tag{7}$$

Beta model can be represented by a Γ function

$$Beta(p|r_{i,j}+1, s_{i,j}+1) = \frac{\Gamma(r_{i,j}+s_{i,j}+2)}{\Gamma(r_{i,j}+1)\Gamma(s_{i,j}+1)} p^{r_{i,j}}(1-p)^{s_{i,j}} \tag{8}$$

Then the trust value of CM_j in MN_i, $T_{i,j}$, can be expressed as

$$T_{i,j} = E(R_{i,j}) = \frac{r_{i,j}+1}{r_{i,j}+s_{i,j}+2} \tag{9}$$

where $0 \le p \le 1$, $r_{i,j} \ge 0$ and $s_{i,j} \ge 0$. We introduce a parameter θ which is called the attenuation factor and substitute $s_{i,j}$ with $\theta^{s_{i,j}} - 1$ into Eq. (9). $T_{i,j}$ can be transformed to Eq. (10).

$$T'_{i,j} = \frac{r_{i,j}+1}{r_{i,j}+(\theta^{s_{i,j}}-1)+2} = \frac{r_{i,j}+1}{r_{i,j}+\theta^{s_{i,j}}+1} \tag{10}$$

The improved Beta trust model has at least three characteristics compared with the traditional Beta model. (i) The trust value of node decreases dramatically when a bad behavior emerges. (ii) The trust is based on the computation rather than the communication, which consumes less energy. (iii) The data received from the trust nodes will be fused and the other ones will be ignored by CHs, which improve the accuracy of DA.

4.3.3 Intrusion Detection

Each MN generates the trust table for all the nodes in a cluster as shown in Table 2.

Table 2. Trust table in MN (T_{MN}).

Cluster	Node ID	Trust value	Outlier	Bad behavior	Good behavior
Cluster1	MCH_1	0.9167	No	0	10
Cluster1	CCH_1	0.9167	No	0	10
Cluster1	MN_1	0.6923	No	2	8
Cluster1	MN_2	0.9167	No	0	10
Cluster1	MN_3	0.8333	No	1	9
Cluster1	$Node_1$	0.3043	Yes	4	6
Cluster1	$Node_2$	0.9167	No	0	10
Cluster1	$Node_3$	0.9167	No	0	10
Cluster1	$Node_4$	0.5000	Yes	3	7
Cluster1	......	......	......	......	......
Cluster1	$Node_{10}$	0.5000	Yes	3	7

Here, we take cluster 1 as an example to describe the detection mechanism. We divide the intrusion detection into intra-cluster and inter-cluster detections.

(1) Intra-Cluster Detection. The MNs mainly monitor the behavior of CHs and CMs. Assumed that a cluster consists of many sensor nodes, $N = \{n_k|k = 1, 2, ..., n\}$. Take $k = 10$ for example, the number of MNs is 3 (an integer between 10/4 and 10/3 according to Eq. (3)). Three MNs are symbolized as MN_1, MN_2 and MN_3. They are assigned to evaluate the trust values of a CM, CM_j, in the same cluster. They evaluate the trust values, $T'_{1,j}$, $T'_{2,j}$ and $T'_{3,j}$ of CM_j respectively and exchange trust tables with each other. Then, a comprehensive trust value of CM_j and CT_j can be formulized as Eq. (11)

$$CT_j = a_1 T'_{1,j} + a_2 T'_{2,j} + a_3 T'_{3,j} \tag{11}$$

where a_1, a_2, a_3 are the weight of trust values and $a_1 + a_2 + a_3 = 1$. The weight value is based on F_i according to Algorithm 1.

By comparing the comprehensive trust value with a predefined threshold Θ_T, a MN determines whether CM_j is trustworthy or not. A node will be considered as malicious one if CT_j is less than Θ_T. A MN inserts a malicious item into the outlier table. After that, MN shares the table with CHs and other MNs. CH records this outliers table and send it to upstream node in aggregation tree until BS reaches. Then, BS isolates the malicious node from the network according to this outlier table. This process is depicted in Algorithm 2.

Algorithm 2. Intra-Cluster Detection Mechanism.

Input: Original data from CMs, trust value of CMs and the threshold trust Θ_T
Output: Trust data and outliers table T_{MN}
1. **Begin**
2. Compute comprehensive trust value CT_j of CM_j
3. **If**$CT_j < \Theta_T$
4. CM_j is a malicious node, then store it in T_{MN};
5. **Else**
6. CM_j is a normal node and CH accepts its data;
7. **End IF**
8. **End**

(2) Inter-Cluster Detection. Inter-cluster detection is mainly performed at BS and the main work of BS is to calculate the similarity of the aggregated results. The MCH, $MCH_i(i = 1, \ldots, m)$, where m is the number of CH in a WSN, submits the aggregation result R_{MCH_i} and the outliers table T_{MN_i}. The CCH, $H_j(j = 1, \ldots, m)$, keeps sleeping and working according to the sleeping strategy. In a time window t, CCH sleeps $t/2$ and works for $t/2$. In working time, CCH_j sends the aggregation result R_{CCH_j} and the outliers table T_{MN_j} to BS. Then, the similarity coefficient can be verified using Eq. (12).

$$\lambda = \varepsilon_1 * \left(1 - \frac{2 * \left|R_{MCH_i} - R_{CCH_j}\right|}{\left|R_{MCH_i} + R_{CCH_j}\right|}\right) + \varepsilon_2 * \frac{\left|T_{MN_i} \cap T_{MN_j}\right|}{\left|T_{MN_i} \cup T_{MN_j}\right|} \tag{12}$$

where ε_1 and ε_2 are the weights and $\varepsilon_1 + \varepsilon_2 = 1$. $\left|T_{MN_i} \cap T_{MN_j}\right|$ denotes the number of common outliers in T_{MN_i} and T_{MN_j}. $\left|T_{MN_i} \cup T_{MN_j}\right|$ is the number of all outliers in T_{MN_i} and T_{MN_j}. The R_{MCH_i} and R_{CCH_j} will be accepted by BS, if λ is more than a similarity threshold Θ_S. Otherwise, MCH and CCH are both reassigned by BS when $\lambda < \Theta_S$.

Algorithm 3 shows the pseudo code of inter-cluster detection. In this way, BS only accepts the trust aggregation result and the accuracy is ensured.

Algorithm 3. Inter-Cluster Detection Mechanism.

Input: Aggregation results, outliers tables T_{MN} and similarity threshold θ_S
Output: Outliers table T_{BS}

---
1. **Begin**
2.   BS computes the similarity coefficient λ
3.   **If** $\lambda \geq \theta_S$
4. R_{CH}will be accepted by BS;
5.   **Else**
6.   Reelect CHs according to Algorithm 1;
7.   **End IF**
8. **End**

4.4 Trusted Data Aggregation

DA is an effective technology to eliminate data redundancy and improve energy efficiency in a WSN. The basic idea is to fuse the data received from different sources to a single packet and reduce the energy consumption in data transmission. In TIDS, the reliable data are obtained and the malicious nodes are detected. The aggregation is carried out within the trust data. CH calculates the sum of the sensing data and sends the result to BS. Then, the final aggregation result can be expressed as follows:

$$R_{CH_i} = \sum_{i=o}^{k} data_i \tag{13}$$

$$R_{DA} = Avg(R_{CH_1}, R_{CH_2}, \ldots, R_{CH_n}) = \frac{\sum_{i=0}^{m} R_{CH_i}}{m} \tag{14}$$

where k is the number of trust CMs and m is the number of trust ones in n CHs.

5 Simulation

In this section, theoretical analysis and simulation studies will be done to verify our scheme by examining parameters in terms of security, energy consumption and network lifetime. A network with 150 sensor nodes is randomly deployed in a 400 m * 400 m area. The communication radius of the sensor node is 50 m and the transmission rate of the node is 1 Mbps. All the simulation parameters are displayed in Table 3.

As discussed previously, the compromised sensor nodes can attack the network in several traditional ways such as jamming, message dropping and falsifying. In this study, only take dropping attack is considered and packet loss ratio is 50% for a compromised sensor node and 10% for a credible sensor node. Besides, the sensor node measurement model approximately accords with Gaussian distribution.

Table 3. Simulation parameters.

Parameter	Value	Parameter	Value
Packet size	27 bytes	θ	2
E_{max}	0.01 J	α_1	0.6
E_{elec}	50 nJ bit^{-1}	α_2	0.4
ε_{fs}	10 pJ bit^{-1} m^{-2}	ε_1	0.5
ε_{mp}	0.0013 pJ bit^{-1} m^{-2}	ε_2	0.5
E_{th}	0.001 J	a_1	0.5
Θ_T	0.5000	a_2	0.3
Θ_S	0.80	a_3	0.2

5.1   Average Energy Consumption and Network Lifetime

A sensor node is composed of a sensor module, a processing module, a wireless communication module and an energy supply module. The sensing module and the processing module only consume a small amount of energy. The communication module being the most important part needs to be evaluated.

When the node is in a sending state, the relationship between the energy consumption and distance is $E = kd^n$, where n is a signal attenuation index, which is a real number between 2 and 4. In our simulation, the initial energy (E_{max}) of CMs is 0.01 J. According to Eq. (4), the energy consumption of the sender is $E_{TX}(l, d) = E_{TX\_elec}(l) + E_{TX\_amp}(l, d) + l \times E_{elec} + l \times \varepsilon_{fs} \times d^2$ when sending l bit data between nodes. And the energy consumption of the receiver is $E_{RX}(l) = l \times E_{elec}$.

The average energy consumption refers to the ratio of the total dissipation energy of the entire network in one second to the number of all the sensor nodes. The simulation results of average energy consumption and lifetime are shown in Figs. 3 and 4, respectively. It can be found that the average energy consumption of TIDS is smaller than that of DCHM. The energy consumption of TIDS is larger than that of a network without any security mechanism. This is mainly due to the fact that some extra data are calculated, stored, transmitted in TIDS. However, our scheme guarantees the security and accuracy for DA and it is a reasonable tradeoff among different network parameters.

Figure 4 shows the number of surviving nodes in a network. Most of the nodes are active in the initial 6×10^4 s in the condition that $d_0 = 50$ m. But the number of surviving nodes decreases significantly after 6×10^4 s in DCHM. TIDS can keep working in 6.5×10^4 s in TIDS. Although the lifetime of TIDS is shorter than that of the network without any mechanism (7.5×10^4 s), TIDS demonstrates a better performance in lifetime than DCHM. Figures 3 and 4 denote a fact that the energy consumption is an unavoidable overhead when a security mechanism is applied in a WSN and SDA should provide security at a price as low as possible.

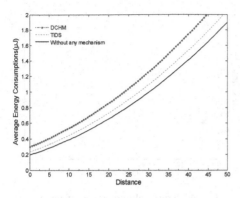

Fig. 3. Average energy consumption.

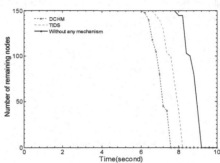

Fig. 4. Number of remaining nodes.

5.2 Security Analysis

The compromised node is a huge threat to a WSN. The performances of TIDS are verified in two cases, compromised CH and the evolution pattern of trust value. Assumed that t_i is the working time of a compromised node, C_i, in a cluster, the probability of C_i being selected as a CH is defined as follows:

$$P_c = \frac{1}{2} \times \frac{t_1}{T_{life}} + \frac{1}{2} \times \frac{t_2}{T_{life}} + \cdots + \frac{1}{2} \times \frac{t_c}{T_{life}} = \frac{\sum_{i=1}^{c} t_i}{2 * T_{life}} \qquad (15)$$

where c is the number of compromised nodes, T_{life} is the lifetime of the whole network. For example, the lifetime of the network is 10000 s when there is no compromised node in cluster 1. In cluster 2, the working time of compromised MCH is 100 s. In cluster 3, the compromised MCH is operated for 500 s and CCH is dominated by a malicious activity for 400 s. Therefore, P_c is equal to 5% according to Eq. (15).

We compared TIDS with DCHM and demonstrated their performances in Fig. 5. The P_c increases linearly with the number of compromised nodes increase if CHs are randomly selected without any security mechanism. Both DCHM and TIDS perform well, especially when the ratio of compromised nodes is less than 10%, and TIDS presents a better performance than DCHM in other cases. Our mechanism is acceptable because P_c is below than 50% even if the compromised nodes are more than 75%.

A normal node should not be reported as a malicious one although it may act as an abnormal one occasionally due to the unreliable channel. In our experiments, TIDS are tested in two situations: (1) a normal node operates in a network scene with communication errors and (2) a normal node operates in a network scene without any communication error. The simulation results are shown in Fig. 6. As time goes on, the trust value of the normal node gradually increases to a higher level. It should be noted that a few errors may result in a severe fluctuation of trust value. This proves that our trust evaluation model in Sect. 4.3.2 can actualize the decline-quick-rise-slow which makes it easier to recognize a malicious node.

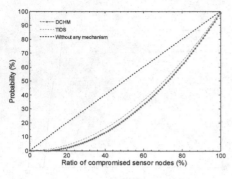
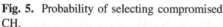

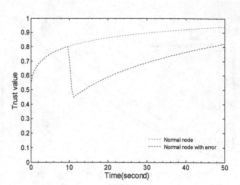

Fig. 5. Probability of selecting compromised CH.

Fig. 6. Trust value changes of node.

5.3 Accuracy of TIDS

The detection rate of malicious nodes is related to the number of malicious nodes. If there are many malicious nodes in a WSN, the detection rate is lower; otherwise, the detection rate is higher. Our experimental network is operated with different proportions of malicious nodes (0%, 10%, 20%, 30%, 40% and 50%) between TIDS and FDSR [22]. For each proportion, our experiment is repeated 20 times with the malicious nodes being deployed to a random location in each experiment. Then, the average detection rate is obtained which is shown in Fig. 7. It is clear that the detection rate keeps declining with the proportion of malicious nodes increasing. Both TIDS and FDSR can detect the malicious nodes at a higher level (more than 90%) when the compromised nodes are less than 10%. However, the detection rate drops to nearly 70% when the proportion of compromised nodes rises to 50%. This illustrates that a more accurate detection mechanism needs to be explored in subsequent studies.

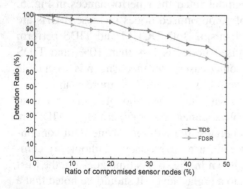

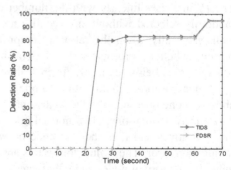

Fig. 7. Detection ratio with compromised nodes.

Fig. 8. Detection ratio changes with time.

The evolution of detection rate is also tested a fixed proportion of malicious nodes (25%) at different times. Figure 8 shows that the detection rate increases with the time goes on. It is obvious that the detection rate of TIDS is better than FDSR, which is mainly because the trust values of nodes may be more accurate with the updating of trust table.

Aggregation accuracy is a key criterion for data aggregation in WSNs. Figure 9 displays a comparison between the FDSR, DCHM and TIDS in accuracy of aggregation. The accuracy of these three protocols grows slowly in the initial stage and the malicious behaviors of the compromised nodes are not detected, which means that the compromised nodes are not excluded from the network. The aggregation accuracy increases sharply after 1200 s because TIDS collects enough malicious behaviors and the trust tables are exchanged among MNs in a cluster. Meanwhile, BS isolates most of the malicious nodes from the network and aggregates the data received from trust nodes only. The aggregation accuracy of TIDS increases to 91.1%, while FDSR is 85.7% and DCHM is 85% after the network runs for 3000 s. Although the improvement of accuracy does not reach a prominent degree, the promotion made by our scheme is significant compared with DCHM and FDSR.

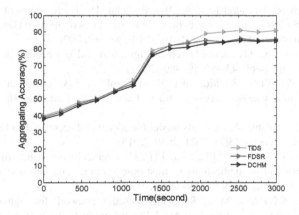

Fig. 9. Comparison of aggregating accuracy.

6 Conclusion

In this paper, we discuss a trust-based intrusion detection mechanism and the secure data aggregation issues in WSNs. We attempt to solve these problems by clustering technique, trust system, and data aggregation. We ensure certain levels of security in case of compromised nodes and prevent the aggregation result from being deviated through trust evaluation, trust exchange and outlier detection. Our scheme promotes the system performance in terms of security and accuracy at a relatively low price of energy consumption. Simulation verifications show that TIDS significantly improves the detection rate, the lifetime and the aggregation accuracy of WSNs. Although TIDS is a favorable trade-off between network security and energy efficiency, we are a long way from a good solution to make the network run in a reasonable manner. For future work, a more accurate aggregation scheme is required and a novel trust model is an important design goal in subsequent studies. In addition, the threshold plays a significant role in trust-based intrusion detection system and an optimal threshold should be determined, which is one of the valuable topics we are pursuing in the future.

Acknowledgements. This work is supported by NSF of China under Grants 61373027 and 61672321; Shandong Graduate Education Quality Improvement Plan (SDYY17138).

References

1. Butun, I., Morgera, S.D., Sankar, R.: A survey of intrusion detection systems in wireless sensor networks. IEEE Commun. Surv. Tutorials **16**(1), 266–282 (2014)
2. Parmar, K., Jinwala, D.C.: Concealed data aggregation in wireless sensor networks. Comput. Netw. **103**(C), 207–227 (2016)
3. Baker, D.: The architectural organization of a mobile radio network via a distributed algorithm. IEEE Trans. Commun. **29**(11), 1694–1701 (2003)
4. Heinzelman, W.R., Chandrakasan, A., Balakrishnan, H.: Energy-efficient communication protocol for wireless microsensor networks. In: Proceedings of the 33rd Hawaii International Conference on System Sciences, pp. 1–10. IEEE, Maui (2000)
5. Zhang, H., Arora, A.: Gs^3: scalable self-configuration and self-healing in wireless sensor networks. Comput. Netw. **43**(4), 459–480 (2003)
6. Wei, D., Jin, Y., Vural, S., Moessner, K., Tafazolli, R.: An energy-efficient clustering solution for wireless sensor networks. IEEE Trans. Wirel. Commun. **10**(11), 3973–3983 (2011)
7. Fu, J.S., Liu, Y.: Double cluster heads model for secure and accurate data fusion in wireless sensor networks. Sensors **15**(1), 2021–2040 (2015)
8. Bao, F., Chen, I.R., Chang, M.J., Cho, J.H.: Hierarchical trust management for wireless sensor networks and its applications to trust-based routing and intrusion detection. IEEE Trans. Netw. Serv. Manag. **9**(2), 169–183 (2012)
9. Ganeriwal, S., Srivastava, M.B.: Reputation-based framework for high integrity sensor networks. In: Proceedings of the 2nd ACM Workshop on Security of Ad Hoc and Sensor Networks, pp. 66–77. ACM, Washington DC (2004)
10. Zhan, G., Shi, W., Deng, J.: Design and implementation of TARF: a trust-aware routing framework for WSNs. IEEE Comput. Soc. **9**(2), 184–197 (2012)
11. Aivaloglou, E., Gritzalis, S.: Hybrid trust and reputation management for sensor networks. Wirel. Netw. **16**(5), 1493–1510 (2010)
12. Shaikh, R.A., Jameel, H., Lee, S., Rajput, S., Song, Y.J.: Trust management problem in distributed wireless sensor networks. In: Proceedings of the 12th IEEE Conference on Embedded and Real-Time Computing Systems and Applications, pp. 411–414. IEEE, Sydney (2006)
13. Ozdemir, S.: Functional reputation based reliable data aggregation and transmission for wireless sensor networks. Comput. Commun. **31**(17), 3941–3953 (2008)
14. Liu, C.X., Liu, Y., Zhang, Z.J.: Improved reliable trust-based and energy-efficient data aggregation for wireless sensor networks. Int. J. Distrib. Sens. Netw. 1–11 (2013)

15. Su, X., Boppana, R.V.: On mitigating in-band wormhole attacks in mobile ad hoc networks. In: Proceedings of IEEE International Conference on Communications, pp. 1136–1141. IEEE, Glasgow (2007)
16. Karlof, C., Wangner, D.: Secure routing in wireless sensor networks: attacks and countermeasures. Ad Hoc Netw. **1**(2), 293–315 (2003)
17. Cho, Y., Qu, G., Wu, Y.: Insider threats against trust mechanism with watchdog and defending approaches in WSN. In: Proceedings of IEEE Symposium on Security and Privacy Workshops, pp. 134–141. IEEE, San Francisco (2012)
18. Cho, Y., Qu, G.: Detection and prevention of selective forwarding-based denial-of-service attacks in WSNs. Int. J. Distrib. Sens. Netw. 1–16 (2013)
19. Kefayati, M., Talebi, M.S., Rabiee, H.R., Khalaj, B.H.: On secure consensus information fusion over sensor networks. In: Proceedings of IEEE/ACS International Conference on Computer Systems and Applications, pp. 108–115. IEEE, Amman (2007)
20. Yang, Y., Wang, X., Zhu, S., Cao, G.: SDAP: a secure hop-by-hop data aggregation protocol for sensor networks. In: Proceedings of the 7th ACM International Symposium on Mobile Ad Hoc Networking and Computing, pp. 356–367. ACM, Florence (2006)
21. Sen, J.: Secure and energy-efficient data aggregation in wireless sensor networks. In: Proceedings of the 2nd IEEE Computational Intelligence and Signal Processing. IEEE, Guwahati (2012)
22. Xiaomei, D.: Secure data aggregation approach based on monitoring in wireless sensor networks. China Commun. **3**(3), 101–148 (2012)
23. Hua, P., Liu, X., Yu, J., Dang, N., Zhang, X.: Energy-efficient adaptive slice-based secure data aggregation scheme in WSN. Procedia Comput. Sci. **129**, 188–193 (2018)

An Efficient Revocable Attribute-Based Signcryption Scheme with Outsourced Designcryption in Cloud Computing

Ningzhi Deng[1], Shaojiang Deng[1(✉)], Chunqiang Hu[2(✉)], and Kaiwen Lei[1]

[1] School of Computer Science, Chongqing University, Chongqing, China
{dnz,sj_deng,chu,leikaiwen}@cqu.edu.cn
[2] School of Big Data and Software Engineering, Chongqing University,
Chongqing, China

Abstract. Sensitive data sharing through cloud storage environments has brought varies and flexible secure demands. Attribute-based signcryption (ABSC) is suitable for cloud storage because it provides combined data confidentiality and authentication, and fine-grained data access control. While, the existed ABSC schemes hardly support efficient attribute revocation. In addition, the heavy computational overhead of ABSC limits the applying resource-constrained device in cloud storage environments. In this paper, to tackle the above problems, we propose an efficiently revocable attribute-based signcryption scheme with decryption outsourcing. The proposed scheme achieves the efficient attribute revocation through delegating the cloud server to update ciphertext without decrypting it. During the decryption phase, it outsource massive decryption operations to the proxy server so that computation cost on user's devices is small and constant. The security analysis proves the correctness, confidentiality, collusion resistance, unforgeability and forward secrecy of our scheme. Furthermore, performance analysis shows that our scheme is efficient in terms of the ciphertext, key size and computation cost while realizing desired functions.

1 Introduction

With widespread popularity of cloud computing, Storaging and sharing sensitive data in cloud computing are used in many domain, such as social networks and personal health record system. In this scenario where the user often stores sensitive data in cloud computing environment, users concern about the privacy of their sensitive data become the main barrier impedes cloud computing from wide deployment and adoption [1,2]. Thus an essential security requirements of data sharing in the cloud computing is to ensure the users' access control of their private data.

In the cloud computing, the access policy should be flexible to support fine-grained access control. The traditional access control system and cryptography methods is difficult to meet these requirements [3,4]. Attribute-based encryption

© Springer Nature Switzerland AG 2019
E. S. Biagioni et al. (Eds.): WASA 2019, LNCS 11604, pp. 84–97, 2019.
https://doi.org/10.1007/978-3-030-23597-0_7

(ABE) [5,6] offers one-to-many encryption by embeding attributes and access policies into the private key or ciphertext. It means that encrypted data can only be decrypted by a private key when the involved attributes match the access policy. To share sensitive data, the data owner can encrypt data using attribute-based access policy before uploading these data to the cloud server. In this way, only users whose attributes satisfy access policy can be allowed to access the sensitive data without knowing the data owner's unique identity information [7,8].

Similarly, Attribute-Based Signature (ABS) [9,10] generates signatures on a message without revealing the identity of the signer. In ABS, a signer who possesses a set of attributes from the authority can sign a message with a predicate that satisfies his attributes. The signature reveals only the fact that a single user with some sets of attributes satisfying the predicate has attested to the message. In order to achieve the confidentiality and authenticity simultaneously, an efficient and flexible method named as Attribute-Based Signcryption (ABSC) is proposed. Signcryption is a cryptographic primitive that can realize signature and encryption simultaneously. Compared with the previously proposed attribute-based encryption scheme, the attribute-based signcryption scheme can not only perform confidential communication but also identity authentication. Meanwhile, our scheme can reduce the communication costs and computational overheads.

Although ABSC is a promising solution for data sharing, the large number of bilinear pairing operations in the ABSC schemes bring high computational cost on the user side. In addition, the frequency of designcryption operation is far greater than signcryption operation. Therefore, how to improve the efficiency of the designcryption algorithms is a key issue. In order to alleviate the computation overhead on the owner and user sides, several outsourced ABE schemes [11–14] transfer the computation to the cloud side, which is extended into our signcryption scheme.

In this paper, we further study the aforementioned problems and propose a revocable attribute-based signcryption scheme with outsourced designcryption. Our main contributions are outlined as follows:

- We construct an efficent revocation ciphertext-policy attribute-based signcryption scheme, which integrates encryption and signature without requiring any certificate for verification and supports efficient attribute revocation.
- We provide an immediate revocation approach with high efficiency. In our scheme, the attribute authority delegates the ciphertext update procedure to cloud server. Benefiting from that the users' computation and communication has been obviously alleviated.
- We theoretically prove the correctness of the proposed scheme and analyze its efficiency and feasibility. In particular, Our scheme is proven to be confidentiality under adaptive chosen plaintext attack. And the security analysis also shows the resistant against collusion attacks, unforgeability and forward secrecy.

The rest of the paper is organized as follows. Section 2 overviews the related work. We present the system and security model in Sect. 3. Our CP-RABSC construction is described in Sect. 4. In Sects. 5 and 6, security analysis and performance analysis are discussed. Finally, we conclude the paper in Sect. 7.

2   Related Work

The attributes revocation is an essential mechanism in ABE applications for real-world applications. Because the users'attributes may change frequently in the system. Boldyreva et al. [15] proposed an attribute revocable ABE schemes, which extended from their main contribution, a revocable IBE. They realize revocation by update attribute secret key periodically. This approaches has two main problems: (i) there is a vulnerability span of time, which is not backward and forward security [16]. (ii) The periodically key update could be a heavy computation burden for the key authority and all non-revoked users. To overcome the problem, Attrapadung et al. [17] proposed a new revocable ABE scheme, in which data is encrypted with a list of revoked user index and a set of attributes or a policy. The revoked users cannot decrypt data and non-revoked users do not need to update their private keys periodically any more, but the data owner needs to manage the revocation list. The shortcoming of this mechanism is that it does not support the attribute-level revocation which means revocation of user's attributes.

In recent years, Yu et al. [18] proposed a method to achieve immediate attribute revocation. The method implemented attribute revocation by employing the proxy re-encryption, which allows an untrusted server (such as the cloud) to convert a ciphertext into a new ciphertext without decrypting it. Li et al. [19] presented an efficient CP-ABE scheme with user revocation, and the lower computation cost through outsourcing both encryption and decryption to cloud servers. Later They also presented a CP-ABE scheme [20] with attribute revocation, which resists collusion attack by existing users and revoked users.

Signcryption is a cryptographic primitive that simultaneously performs the functions of both digital signature and encryption in a single logical step. The attribute-based signcryption (ABSC), first introduced by Gagne' et al. [21], integrates attribute-based encryption and attribute-based signature with restriction that the access structure is fixed in the setup phase. Recently, many ABSC schemes have been proposed [22–29]. Wang et al. [22] introduced an attribute-based signcryption with ciphertext-policy and claim-predicate mechanism, which combines data encryption and signing by a expressive access tree. Emura et al. [23] put forward a supporting dynamic encryptor attribute-based signcryption scheme, which means that users are free of being involved in the key updating procedure. And they proved its secure in the standard model. Hu et al. [24] proposed a fuzzy attribute-based signcryption scheme supporting error tolerance for the attributes in the body area network. Liu et al. [25] proposed a secure sharing scheme for a personal health records system based on ciphertext-policy ABSC. Later, Rao [26] proved that Liu's scheme fails to provide confidentiality and public ciphertext verifiability. And they also presented a provable secure CP-ABSC scheme for cloud-based PHR sharing system that has ability to provide confidentiality, authenticity, signcryptor privacy and public verifiability, simultaneously. Yu *et al.* [27] proposed a hybrid access policy ABSC scheme based on key-policy signature and ciphertext-policy encryption. Nevertheless the above ABSC schemes did not consider revocability. Meng *et al.* [28] proposed a novel decentralized key-policy attribute-based signcryption scheme, which applies the multi authority and the decentralized authority can reduce the communication cost and the collaborative cost. Deng *et al.* [29] proposed a ciphertext-policy attribute-based signcryption with outsourced designcryption scheme in the cloud-based personal health records system, which eliminate the computational overhead of the designcryption process at user side. However, their scheme required large computation and communication cost to support attribute revocation.

3   Preliminaries and System Model

In this section, we summarize some mathematical backgrounds related to bilinear mapping, which can be used to design attribute-based signcryption schemes.

3.1   Preliminaries

Bilinear Maps. Let G_0 and G_T be two multiplicative cyclic groups with the prime order p. A bilinear map $e : G_0 \times G_0 \to G_T$ satisfying the following properties:

(1) Bilinear: for all $P, Q \in G_0$ and $a, b \in Z_p^*$, the equation $e(P^a, Q^b) = e(P, Q)^{ab}$ is true.
(2) Non-degeneracy: The generator g satisfies $e(g, g) \neq I$, where I is the identity element of group G_T.
(3) Computability: There is an effective polynomial time algorithm to compute $e(P, Q)$, for all $P, Q \in G_0$.

Decisional Bilinear Diffie-Hellman Problem (DBDH). Given (g, g^a, g^b, g^c, h) where $h \in G_2$ and $a, b, c \in Z_p^*$ are previously unknown random numbers, the *Decisional Bilinear Diffie-Hellman* problem is to decide whether $h = e(g, g)^{abc}$.

Access Structure. Let $P = \{P_1, P_2, ..., P_n\}$ be a set of parties. A collection $\mathbb{A} \subseteq 2^P$ is monotone if $\forall B, C$, we have that if $B \in \mathbb{A}$ and $B \subseteq C$ then $C \in \mathbb{A}$. An access structure (monotone access structure) is a collection (monotone collection) $\mathbb{A} \subseteq 2^P \backslash \emptyset$. The sets in $\mathbb{A}$ are called the authorized sets, and the sets not in $\mathbb{A}$ are called the unauthorized sets.

Access Tree. Let $\mathcal{T}$ be a tree representing an access structure. Each non-leaf node of the tree represents a threshold gate, described by its children and a threshold value. Let num_x and k_x be the number of children and the threshold value of a node x, respectively. When $k_x = 1$, the threshold gate is an **OR** gate and when $k_x = num_x$, it is an **AND** gate. Each leaf node x of the tree is described by an attribute and a threshold value $k_x = 1$.

Secret Share Scheme. We utilize the secret sharing scheme introduced by Shamir [30] to embed a random number into the access tree in the signcryption procedure. To illustrate that, we define a algorithm **divide**$(\mathcal{T}, t)$ that takes an input an access policy tree $\mathcal{T}$ and a secret t and return a set of secret shares corresponding each leaf node x of $\mathcal{T}$, $\{q_x(0)\}$. The algorithm is described as follows.

- Choose a polynomial $q_x()$ for each non-leaf node x in the tree $\mathcal{T}$. These polynomials are chosen in a top-down manner, starting from the root node.
- For each node x in the tree, set the degree d_x of the polynomial $q_x(\cdot)$ to be one less than the threshold value k_x of that node, i.e., $d_x = k_x - 1$.
- Starting with the root node r, set $q_r(0) = t$, and choose d_r other points of the polynomial $q_r()$ randomly to define it completely. For any other node x, set $q_x(0) = q_{parent}(x)(index(x))$ and choose d_x other points randomly to completely define $q_x(\cdot)$.
- Finally, for each leaf node x in the tree, the secret share is $q_x(0) = q_{parent}(x)(index(x))$.

We also define the Lagrange coefficient

$$\Delta_{i,\mathbf{S}}(x) \stackrel{def}{=} \prod_{\substack{j \in \mathbf{S} \\ j \neq i}} \frac{x - j}{i - j}$$

for $i \in \mathbb{Z}_p$ and a set $\mathbf{S}$ of elements in $\mathbb{Z}_p$.

3.2 Network Architecture

The network architecture of our scheme is shown in Fig. 1. It consists of four entities, which are data owners, cloud server, attribute authority and data users. The attribute authority generates initial private keys for users including data owners and data users, and distributes the private keys to users through secure channels. It is also responsible for updating users private key when attribute revocation occurs. A data owner uploads signcrypted data to the cloud server. The cloud server stores the encrypted data with its signature and provides them to the data users. Data users downloads the encrypted data from cloud server and unsigncrypt them for further application.

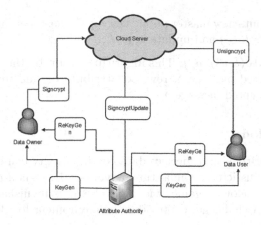

Fig. 1. Network architecture of our scheme.

3.3 Algorithm Definitions

Our scheme consists of the following algorithms:

Setup(1^λ): This algorithm is run by the attribute authority. On input security parameter λ, it returns the master public key mpk and master secret key msk. mpk is shared by users while msk is kept secret by the system.

sExtract(mpk, msk, A_s): This algorithm is run by the attribute authority. On input the master public key mpk, master secret key msk and a user's signing attribute set A_s, it generates signing secret keys SK_{A_s} for a user.

dExtract(mpk, msk, A_d): This algorithm is run by the attribute authority. On input the master public key mpk, master secret key msk and a user's decryption attribute set A_d, it generates decryption secret keys SK_{A_d} for a user.

Signcrypt($m, mpk, SK_{A_s}, \pi_s, \mathbb{A}$): This algorithm is run by a data owner. On input the plaintext m, master public key mpk, predicate π_s of data owner and a ciphertext access policy $\mathbb{A}$ it outputs the ciphertext δ.

OutDesigncrypt($\delta, mpk, tk, \pi_s, \mathbb{A}$): This algorithm is run by the cloud server. On input the ciphertext δ, master public key mpk, the transforamtion key tk, predicate π_s of data owner and the ciphertext access policy $\mathbb{A}$, it outputs either the transformed ciphertext δ'.

UserDesigncrypt($\delta, \delta', mpk, SK_{A_d}, \pi_s, \mathbb{A}$): This algorithm is run by a data user. On input the ciphertext δ, the transformed ciphertext δ', master public key mpk, the decryption secret key SK_{A_d}, predicate π_s of data owner and the ciphertext access policy $\mathbb{A}$, it outputs either the plaintext m or rejection symbol $\perp$.

UpdateKeyGen(mpk, msk, a_k): This algorithm is run by the attribute authority. On input the master public key mpk, master secret key msk and the revoked attribute a_k it outputs new master public key mpk', master secret key msk', user secret key $(\widehat{SK}_{A_s}, \widehat{SK}_{A_d})$ and update key uk_j.

CiphertextUpdate(δ, uk_k, a_k): This algorithm is run by the cloud server. On input the signcrypted message δ, revoked attribute a_k and update key uk_k it outputs new signcrypted message $\tilde{\delta}$.

3.4   Security Model

The notion of security with respect to data confidentiality can be captured by a game. If no probabilistic polynomial time adversary has a non-negligible advantage in winning the following game, it is said to be indistinguishable under chosen plaintext attacks. A challenger $\mathcal{C}$ provides the enviroment for the attack, and $\mathcal{A}$ is an adversary.

Setup: The challenger $\mathcal{C}$ runs the *Setup* algorithm on input a security parameter λ, gives public parameters mpk to the adversary $\mathcal{A}$ and keeps the master key msk secret.

Query Phase 1: The adversary $\mathcal{A}$ makes the following queries.

sExtract: $\mathcal{A}$ queries a signing attribute set A_s, $\mathcal{C}$ answers by running algorithm **sExtract**(mpk, msk, A_s).

dExtract: $\mathcal{A}$ queries a decryption attribute set A_d, $\mathcal{C}$ answers by running algorithm **dExtract**(mpk, msk, A_d).

Signcrypt: $\mathcal{A}$ queries a signing attributes set A_s, a ciphertext policy $\mathbb{A}_d$ and a message m, $\mathcal{B}$ runs algorithm **sExtract**(mpk, msk, A_s) and **Signcrypt**$(m, mpk, SK_{A_s}, \pi_s, \mathbb{A})$ returns the ciphertext δ to $\mathcal{A}$.

Challenge: The adversary $\mathcal{A}$ submits two equal length messages m_0 and m_1 to the challenger $\mathcal{C}$ with signing attribute and access policy. The attribute sets which satisfy the access policy must be not queried in **Query Phase 1**. $\mathcal{C}$ picks $b \in_R \{0, 1\}$ and signcrypt the message m_b by run algorithm **Signcrypt**$(m, mpk, SK_{A_s}, \pi_s, \mathbb{A})$. Then return δ_b^* to $\mathcal{A}$.

Guess: Finally, the adversary $\mathcal{A}$ outputs a guess bit $b' \in \{0, 1\}$ and wins the game if $b = b'$.

The advantage of the adversary $\mathcal{A}$ in the above game is defined as $Adv(\mathcal{A}) = |Pr(b = b') - \frac{1}{2}|$.

4   CP-RABSC Construction

In this section, we present the specific construction for our revocable attribute-based signcryption scheme with outsourced designcryption.

4.1 System Initialization

Setup. G_0 and G_T are both cyclic groups of prime order p, while g is the generator of G_0. Let $e : G_0 \times G_0 \to G_T$ be a bilinear pairing. For each attribute a_i in the global attribute set $\mathcal{U}$, this algorithm chooses a random number $v_i \in Z_p^*$ and calculates $V_i = g^{v_i}$. Besides, it picks another secret number $\alpha \in_R Z_p^*$ and calculate $A = e(g, g)^\alpha$. And it defines two hash functions: $H_1 : \{0,1\}^* \to G_1$ and $H_2 : \{0,1\}^* \to Z_p^*$.

It sets the master secret keys as $msk = \{\{v_i\}_{a_i \in \mathcal{U}}, \alpha\}$, and the master public key as $mpk = \{g, G_0, p, A, \{V_i\}_{a_i \in \mathcal{U}}\}$.

4.2 User Key Generation

dExtract. The algorithm selects random number $r_d, \beta \in Z_p^*$ for each decryption user. And according to the user's attribute set A_d, it randomly chooses $\{r_{d,i} \in Z_p^*\}_{a_i \in A_d}$. Then it computes $D_d = g^{\alpha - r_d}, D_{d,i} = g^{r_d/\beta} H_1(a_i)^{r_{d,i}/\beta}, D'_{d,i} = H_1(a_i)^{r_{d,i}/v_i \beta}$.

It sets transformation key as $tk = \{(D_{d,i}, D'_{d,i})\}_{a_i \in A_d}$, retrieval key as $rk = \beta$ and the decryption secret key as $SK_{A_d} = (D_d, tk, rk)$.

sExtract. The algorithm selects random number $r_s \in Z_p^*$ for each signer. And according to the signer's attribute set A_s, it randomly chooses $\{r_{s,i} \in Z_p^*\}_{a_i \in A_s}$. Then it computes $D_s = g^{\alpha - r_s}, D_{s,i} = g^{r_s} H_1(a_i)^{r_{s,i}}, D'_{s,i} = H_1(a_i)^{r_{s,i}/v_i}$.

It sets the signing secret key as

$$SK_{A_s} = (D_s, \{(D_{s,i}, D'_{s,i})\}_{a_i \in A_s}).$$

4.3 Data Signcryption

Signcrypt. For the predicate π_s of the data owner and ciphertext access policy $\mathbb{A}$, the algorithm defines two corresponding access tree $\mathcal{T}_s$ and $\mathcal{T}_e$. It picks a random number $s \in Z_p^*$ and runs the algorithm **divide**$(\mathcal{T}_e, s)$, **divide**$(\mathcal{T}_s, s)$. These algorithm return the shares of s: $\{q_i(0)\}_{a_i \in A_e}, \{q_j(0)\}_{a_j \in A_s}$. A_e, A_s are sets of attributes in $\mathbb{A}$ and π_s, respectively. It computes $C_0 = m \cdot A^s$, $C'_0 = g^s$, $C_i = g^{q_i(0)}$, $C'_i = V_i^{q_i(0)}$.

Then it picks a random number $t \in Z_p^*$ and computes $V = e(C'_0, g^t)$, $h = H_2(m, V, \mathcal{T}_e, \mathcal{T}_s)$, $R = g^t \cdot D_s^h$, $R_j = D_{s,j}^{q_j(0)}$, $R'_j = (D'_{s,j})^{q_j(0)}$.

The ciphertext is:

$$\delta = (C_0, C'_0, \{(C_i, C'_i)\}_{a_i \in A_e}, h, R, \{(R_j, R'_j)\}_{a_j \in A_s}, \mathcal{T}_e, \mathcal{T}_s)$$

4.4   Data Designcryption

OutDesigncrypt. When the user receives the ciphertext δ, the algorithm transforms the ciphertext under transformation key tk as follows.

For each tuple in tk, it computes

$$F_{d,i} = \frac{e(C_i, D_{d,i})}{e(C_i', D_{d,i}')} = e(g,g)^{r_d q_i(0)/\beta},$$

and assigns this value to according leaf node in $\mathcal{T}_e$.

Then, it can recover the value of a non-leaf node z with leaf node set S_x as

$$F_{d,z} = \prod_{z \in S_x} F_{d,z}^{\Delta_{i,S_x}(0)} = e(g,g)^{r_d q_z(0)/\beta}$$

or return $\perp$. It repeats above steps up to the root node to get $F_{d,root} = e(g,g)^{r_d s/\beta}$.

For each tuple in $\{(R_j, R_j')\}$, it computes

$$F_{s,j} = \frac{e(R_j, g)}{e(V_j, R_j')} = e(g,g)^{r_s q_j(0)},$$

and assigns this value to according leaf node in $\mathcal{T}_s$.

Then, it can recover the value of a non-leaf node z' with leaf node set $S_{x'}$ as

$$F_{s,z'} = \prod_{z' \in S_{x'}} F_{s,z'}^{\Delta_{i,S_{x'}}(0)} = e(g,g)^{r_s q_{z'}(0)}$$

or return $\perp$. It repeats above steps up to the root node to get $F_{s,root} = e(g,g)^{r_s s}$.

Finally, it sends the transformed ciphertext $\delta' = (F_{d,root}, F_{s,root})$ to the data user. **UserDesigncrypt.** When receiving the transformed ciphertext δ', the data user exploits the retrieval key $rk = \beta$ to recover the message and verify the signature as follows. It computes

$$Y = e(D_d, C_0') \cdot F_{d,root}^\beta, m = \frac{C_0}{Y}, V' = \frac{e(C_0', R)}{(Y \cdot F_{s,root}^{-1})^h}.$$

Then, it outputs m if $h = H_2(m, V', \mathcal{T}_d, \mathcal{T}_s)$ holds. Otherwise it outputs $\perp$.

4.5   Attribute Revocation

UpdateKeyGen. When an attribute a_k is revoked from some users, this algorithm chooses a new random number $\bar{v}_k \in Z_p^*$ and computes $\tilde{V}_k = g^{\bar{v}_k}$ to replace v_k and V_k for that attribute. Then, it updates influenced user secret key part $\tilde{D}_{d,k}' = H_1(a_k)^{r_{d,k}/\bar{v}_k}$, $\tilde{D}_{s,k}' = H_1(attr_k)^{r_{s,k}/\bar{v}_k}$ and distributes to those users who still possess that attribute.

Besides, it generates the update key $uk_k = \frac{v_k}{\bar{v}_k}$ and send to cloud proxy re-signcryption service.

SigncryptUpdate. When the data owner receives the update key uk_k, it updates the influenced ciphertext as follows.

It computes $a_i \neq a_k$, $\tilde{C}'_i = C'_i$, $\tilde{R}'_i = R'_i$; $a_i = a_k$, $\tilde{C}'_i = (C'_i)^{uk_k}$, $\tilde{R}'_i = (R'_i)^{uk_k}$

The updated ciphertext is

$$\bar{\delta} = (C_0, C'_0, \{C_i, \tilde{C}'_i\}_{i \in \Omega_e}, h, R, \{R_i, \tilde{R}'_i\}_{i \in \Omega_s}, \mathcal{T}_e, \mathcal{T}_s).$$

5   Security Analysis

Confidentiality. The proposed scheme is IND-(CP-ABSC)-CPA secure under the DBDH assumption in the random oracle model.

Theorem: If an adversary $\mathcal{A}$ can break the IND-(CP-ABSC)-CPA secure of our scheme that makess q times queries with a non-negligible advantage ε, then there is another challenger $\mathcal{C}$ with algorithm $\mathcal{B}$ can solve the DBDH problem with a non-negligible advantage.

Due to the space limited, we will give the proof in the extended version.

Collusion Attack Resistance. In the proposed scheme, the secret sharing is embedded into the ciphertext instead to the private keys of users so the private keys of users are randomized by r_d, r_s such that they cannot be combined in the proposed scheme. In order to unsigncrypt a ciphertext, a user or a colluding attacker should recover $e(g,g)^{\alpha s}$. To recover this, the attacker must pair C_i, C_i' from the ciphertext and D_i, D_i' from some colluding user's private key for an attribute $attr_i$ that the attacker does not hold. However, this results in the value $e(g,g)^{\alpha s}$ is blinded by r_d, r_s which is randomly assigned to each user. This value can be blinded out if and only if the user has the enough key components to satisfy the secret shared in the ciphertext. Therefore the proposed scheme is secure against collusion attacks.

Unforgeability. The adversary who wants to forge the signcryption ciphertext must have the secret key of sensitive data owner and the random factor t. However, it cannot forge the private key $SK_{A_s} = (D_s, \{D_{s,i}, D'_{s,i}\}_{attr_i \in A_s})$ because the secret number r_s and $\{r_s, i\}$ are chosen randomly. Additionally, the attacker cannot falsify a valid signcryption ciphertext from exist ciphertexts. Even if the adversary changes the ciphertext, the receiver can still verify the integrity and legitimacy of the ciphertext by algorithm *Unsigncrypt*.Thus the proposed scheme is unforgeable under chosen message attacks.

Table 1. Communication cost

	Size
Ciphertext	$(2l_e + 2l_s + 2)|G_0| + |G_T| + |Z_p|$
Decryption Key	$(2|A_d| + 1)|G_0| + |Z_p|$
Signing Key	$(2|A_s| + 1)|G_0|$

Table 2. Computation cost

	Cost
Signcryption	$(2l_e + 2l_s + 3)E_0 + 2E_T + P$
Designcryption	$E_0 + E_T$

6   Performance Analysis

In this section, we analyze the communication and computation cost of our proposed scheme. For the computational cost of decryption, we only consider the computation on the user side. We assume that the size of access structure and hash computation cost are not included in the calculation (Tables 1 and 2).

We analyze the ciphertext, decryption key and signging key size of our proposed scheme as follows. The ciphertext is $\delta = (C_0, C_0', \{(C_i, C_i')\}_{a_i \in A_e},$ $h, R, \{(R_j, R_j')\}_{a_j \in A_s})$. The total size is $|C_0| + |C_0'| + |A_e|(|C_i| + |C_i'|) + |h| +$ $|R| + |A_s|(|R_j| + |R_j'|) = (2l_e + 2l_s + 2)|G_0| + |G_T| + |Z_p|$. The decryption key and signing key is $SK_{A_d} = (D_d, tk = \{(D_{d,i}, D_{d,i}')\}_{a_i \in A_d}, rk), D_s = g^{\alpha - r_s},$ $D_{s,i} = g^{r_s} H_1(a_i)^{r_{s,i}}, D_{s,i}' = H_1(a_i)^{r_{s,i}/v_i}$. The size can be calculated as $|D_d| +$ $|A_d|(|D_{d,i}| + |D_{d,i}'|) + |rk| = (2|A_d| + 1)|G_0| + |Z_p|, |D_s| + |A_s|(|D_{s,i}| + |D_{s,i}'|) =$ $(2|A_s| + 1)|G_0|$.

The major concern for the computation cost is the exponentiation and pairing operations in signcryption and designcryption algorithm. In our scheme, the Signcrypt algorithm calculates $C_0, C_0', \{(C_i, C_i')\}_{a_i \in A_e}, h, R, \{(R_j, R_j')\}_{a_j \in A_s},$ $V = e(C_0', g^t)$, which need $(2|A_e| + 2|A_s| + 3)$ times exponentiation operation in G_0, two times exponentiation operation in G_T and one pair operation. And the UserDesigncrypt algorithm calculates $Y = e(D_d, C_0') \cdot F_{d,root}^{\beta}, V' =$ $e(C_0', R)/(Y \cdot F_{s,root}^{-1})^h$, which only need one exponentiation operation in G_0 and one exponentiation operation in G_T.

Due to the space limited, the performance evaluation is omitted here, we will evaluate our scheme performance in terms of storage overhead and time complexity in the extended version.

7 Conclusion

In this paper, we present an efficient revocation attribute-based signcryption scheme for data sharing in the cloud storage system. In our scheme, only users whose attributes satisfy the access policy defined by data owner can have access to the encrypted data. And data users can check the data authenticity and integrity with the signing attributes which hide the specific identity of the data owner. Besides, the proxy re-signcryption serivices reduce the computaion and communication overhead when attributes revocation. The security analysis showed its confidentiality, anonymous collusion attack resistance, unforgeability and forward securecy. The performance analysis indicated that our scheme has low computation overhead of decryption and attribute revocation.

Acknowledgments. This research was partially supported by the National Natural Science Foundation of China under grants 61702062, 61672119, the Chongqing Research Program of Basic Research and Frontier Technology with Grant (No. cstc2018jcyjAX0334), the Fundamental Research Funds for the Central Universities (No. 2019CDQYRJ006), and Overseas Returnees Innovation and Entrepreneurship Support Program of Chongqing (cx2018015).

References

1. Wang, S., Liang, K., Liu, J.K., Chen, J., Yu, J., Xie, W.: Attribute-based data sharing scheme revisited in cloud computing. IEEE Trans. Inf. Forensics Secur. **11**(8), 1661–1673 (2016)
2. Yu, L., Cai, Z.: Dynamic scaling of virtual clusters with bandwidth guarantee in cloud datacenters. In: IEEE INFOCOM 2016-The 35th Annual IEEE International Conference on Computer Communications, pp. 1–9. IEEE (2016)
3. Hur, J., Noh, D.K.: Attribute-based access control with efficient revocation in data outsourcing systems. IEEE Trans. Parallel Distrib. Syst. **22**(7), 1214–1221 (2011)
4. Lei, Y., Shen, H., Cai, Z., Liu, L., Calton, P.: Towards bandwidth guarantee for virtual clusters under demand uncertainty in multi-tenant clouds. IEEE Trans. Parallel Distrib. Syst. **29**(2), 450–465 (2018)
5. Sahai, A., Waters, B.: Fuzzy identity-based encryption. In: Cramer, R. (ed.) EURO-CRYPT 2005. LNCS, vol. 3494, pp. 457–473. Springer, Heidelberg (2005). https://doi.org/10.1007/11426639_27
6. Alrawais, A., Alhothaily, A., Chunqiang, H., Cheng, X.: Fog computing for the internet of things: security and privacy issues. IEEE Internet Comput. **21**(2), 34–42 (2017)
7. Lewko, A., Waters, B.: Decentralizing attribute-based encryption. In: Paterson, K.G. (ed.) EUROCRYPT 2011. LNCS, vol. 6632, pp. 568–588. Springer, Heidelberg (2011). https://doi.org/10.1007/978-3-642-20465-4_31
8. Yu, L., Chen, L., Cai, Z., Shen, H., Liang, Y., Pan, Y.: Stochastic load balancing for virtual resource management in datacenters. IEEE Trans. Cloud Comput. (2016)
9. Chunqiang, H., Li, H., Huo, Y., Xiang, T., Liao, X.: Secure and efficient data communication protocol for wireless body area networks. IEEE Trans. Multi-scale Comput. Syst. **2**(2), 94–107 (2016)

10. Maji, H.K., Prabhakaran, M., Rosulek, M.: Attribute-based signatures. In: Kiayias, A. (ed.) CT-RSA 2011. LNCS, vol. 6558, pp. 376–392. Springer, Heidelberg (2011). https://doi.org/10.1007/978-3-642-19074-2_24
11. Chunqiang, H., Li, W., Cheng, X., Jiguo, Y., Wang, S., Bie, R.: A secure and verifiable access control scheme for big data storage in clouds. IEEE Trans. Big data **4**(3), 341–355 (2018)
12. Green, M., Hohenberger, S., Waters, B.: Outsourcing the decryption of abe ciphertexts. In: Proceedings of the 20th USENIX Conference on Security, SEC 2011, p. 34. USENIX Association, Berkeley (2011)
13. Lei, Y., Shen, H., Sapra, K., Ye, L., Cai, Z.: Core: cooperative end-to-end traffic redundancy elimination for reducing cloud bandwidth cost. IEEE Trans. Parallel Distrib. Syst. **28**(2), 446–461 (2017)
14. Xing, K., Chunqiang, H., Jiguo, Y., Cheng, X., Zhang, F.: Mutual privacy preserving k-means clustering in social participatory sensing. IEEE Trans. Ind. Inform. **13**(4), 2066–2076 (2017)
15. Boldyreva, A., Goyal, V., Kumar, V.: Identity-based encryption with efficient revocation. In: Proceedings of the 15th ACM Conference on Computer and Communications Security, CCS 2008, pp. 417–426. ACM, New York (2008)
16. Rafaeli, S., Hutchison, D.: A survey of key management for secure group communication. ACM Comput. Surv. **35**(3), 309–329 (2003)
17. Attrapadung, N., Imai, H.: Conjunctive broadcast and attribute-based encryption. In: Shacham, H., Waters, B. (eds.) Pairing 2009. LNCS, vol. 5671, pp. 248–265. Springer, Heidelberg (2009). https://doi.org/10.1007/978-3-642-03298-1_16
18. Yu, S., Wang, C., Ren, K., Lou, W.: Attribute based data sharing with attribute revocation. In: Proceedings of the 5th ACM Symposium on Information, Computer and Communications Security, ASIACCS 2010, pp. 261–270. ACM, New York (2010)
19. Li, J., Yao, W., Zhang, Y., Qian, H., Han, J.: Flexible and fine-grained attribute-based data storage in cloud computing. IEEE Trans. Serv. Comput. **10**(5), 785–796 (2017)
20. Li, J., Yao, W., Han, J., Zhang, Y., Shen, J.: User collusion avoidance CP-ABE with efficient attribute revocation for cloud storage. IEEE Syst. J. **12**(2), 1767–1777 (2018)
21. Gagné, M., Narayan, S., Safavi-Naini, R.: Threshold attribute-based signcryption. In: Garay, J.A., De Prisco, R. (eds.) SCN 2010. LNCS, vol. 6280, pp. 154–171. Springer, Heidelberg (2010). https://doi.org/10.1007/978-3-642-15317-4_11
22. Wang, C., Huang, J.: Attribute-based signcryption with ciphertext-policy and claim-predicate mechanism. In: 2011 Seventh International Conference on Computational Intelligence and Security, pp. 905–909, December 2011
23. Emura, K., Miyaji, A., Rahman, M.S.: Dynamic attribute-based signcryption without random oracles. Int. J. Appl. Cryptogr. **2**(3), 199–211 (2012)
24. Hu, C., Zhang, N., Li, H., Cheng, X., Liao, X.: Body area network security: a fuzzy attribute-based signcryption scheme. IEEE J. Sel. Areas Commun. **31**(9), 37–46 (2013)
25. Liu, J., Huang, X., Liu, J.K.: Secure sharing of personal health records in cloud computing: ciphertext-policy attribute-based signcryption. Future Gen. Comput. Syst. **52**, 67–76 (2015). Special Section: Cloud Computing: Security, Privacy and Practice
26. Rao, Y.S.: A secure and efficient ciphertext-policy attribute-based signcryption for personal health records sharing in cloud computing. Future Gen. Comput. Syst. **67**, 133–151 (2017)

27. Gang, Y., Cao, Z.: Attribute-based signcryption with hybrid access policy. Peer-to-Peer Netw. Appl. **10**(1), 253–261 (2017)
28. Meng, X., Meng, X.: A novel attribute-based signcryption scheme in cloud computing environments. In 2016 IEEE International Conference on Information and Automation (ICIA), pp. 1976–1979, August 2016
29. Deng, F., Wang, Y., Peng, L., Xiong, H., Geng, J., Qin, Z.: Ciphertext-policy attribute-based signcryption with verifiable outsourced designcryption for sharing personal health records. IEEE Access **6**, 39473–39486 (2018)
30. Shamir, A., Rivest, R.: How to share a secret. Commun. ACM **22**(11), 612–613 (1979)

Massive MIMO Cognitive Cooperative Relaying

Son Dinh[1], Hang Liu[1(✉)], and Feng Ouyang[2]

[1] The Catholic University of America, Washington, DC, USA
liuh@cua.edu
[2] Johns Hopkins Applied Physics Laboratory, Laurel, MD, USA

Abstract. This paper proposes a novel cognitive cooperative transmission scheme by exploiting massive multiple-input multiple-output (MMIMO) and non-orthogonal multiple access (NOMA) radio technologies, which enables a macrocell network and multiple cognitive small cells to cooperate in dynamic spectrum sharing. The macrocell network is assumed to own the spectrum band and be the primary network (PN), and the small cells act as the secondary networks (SNs). The secondary access points (SAPs) of the small cells can cooperatively relay the traffic for the primary users (PUs) in the macrocell network, while concurrently accessing the PUs' spectrum to transmit their own data opportunistically through MMIMO and NOMA. Such cooperation creates a "win-win" situation: the throughput of PUs will be significantly increased with the help of SAP relays, and the SAPs are able to use the PU's spectrum to serve their secondary users (SUs). The interplay of these advanced radio techniques is analyzed in a systematic manner, and a framework is proposed for the joint optimization of cooperative relay selection, NOMA and MMIMO transmit power allocation, and transmission scheduling. Further, to model network-wide cooperation and competition, a two-sided matching algorithm is designed to find the stable partnership between multiple SAPs and PUs. The evaluation results demonstrate that the proposed scheme achieves significant performance gains for both primary and secondary users, compared to the baselines.

Keywords: Massive MIMO · Non-orthogonal multiple access ·
Dynamic spectrum access · Relay selection · Cooperative spectrum sharing

1 Introduction

Mobile traffic is growing at a very rapid rate. Massive multiple-input, multiple-output (MMIMO) and non-orthogonal multiple access (NOMA) are two essential enabling technologies for next-generation (5G & beyond) mobile networks to achieve necessary performance improvement in spectrum efficiency and network capacity for meeting ever increasing user demands. Traditional MIMO networks typically use a few of antennas to transmit and receive signals. Massive MIMO (MMIMO), on the other hand, is a MIMO system using an antenna array with a large number of elements at the base stations (BSs) or access points (APs) [1, 2]. Advanced signal processing techniques can be employed to leverage the large number of antennas and concurrently generate multiple directional signal beams, each focusing a great amount of signal

© Springer Nature Switzerland AG 2019
E. S. Biagioni et al. (Eds.): WASA 2019, LNCS 11604, pp. 98–110, 2019.
https://doi.org/10.1007/978-3-030-23597-0_8

energy on an intended mobile user (MU). Beamforming enables the BS/AP to transmit/receive multiple signal beams simultaneously to/from multiple MUs on the same frequency channel with a high signal gain. The more antenna elements the BS/AP is equipped with, the more possible signal paths and the higher total throughput. The emerging 3GPP 5G New Radio (NR) standards [3, 4] support MMIMO in both mmWave bands and sub 6 GHz bands with up to 64 logical antenna ports, and the number of antenna elements is expected to increase in the future standard releases. NOMA is another technique to improve spectrum efficiency and network throughput [5, 6]. With NOMA, a user receiving the superposition transmission with its own signal sent in lower power can decode the stronger signal components for other users and then cancel them out to get its own signal, thus yields a significant spectral efficiency gain over conventional orthogonal multiple access. These new radio techniques can potentially significantly enhance the network performance and distinguish 5G systems from 4G systems.

In addition, 5G NR will support services with different spectrum licensing terms [7], including exclusive-use licensed spectrum, shared spectrum, and unlicensed spectrum. In particular, dynamic access to shared spectrum through cognitive radio (CR) capability can make more efficient use of spectrum, alleviate the spectrum scarcity problem, and provides new services. For example, non-operator organizations can use shared spectrum to deploy private networks in public venues, workplaces, or industrial facilities, which will unlock opportunities for innovative deployment models and take advantage of 5G technology to extend mobile networking ecosystem.

It is vital to have efficient and reliable mechanisms to optimize dynamic spectrum access (DSA) to the shared spectrum. There can be different models for DSA [8]. In interweave or underlay DSA models that most existing research focused on, unlicensed secondary users (SUs) of spectrum can access the licensed spectrum bands of primary users (PUs) to transmit data only when the PUs are not using the spectrum or when the interference from the SUs are tolerable by the PUs, i.e. below certain threshold, through techniques such as spectrum sensing and interference management. Alternatively, the PUs and SUs can cooperate in DSA, termed cooperative DSA [9, 10], also known as cooperative cognitive radio network (CCRN) model, to achieve flexible spectrum sharing. The cooperative spectrum sharing can perform more efficiently than uncooperative shared access and benefit both parties. Novel network architecture and protocols are needed to facilitate the cooperation. Specifically, it is worth to investigate whether joint optimization of various elements in the network system is possible and design efficient algorithms to leverage advanced physical-layer technologies such as MMIMO and NOMA in cooperative cognitive radio networks for significant performance gains and new network functionalities.

In this paper, we propose a novel cooperative transmission scheme of PUs and SUs by exploring new radio technologies such as MMIMO and NOMA in dynamic spectrum access and sharing. We study a deployment scenario consisting of a cellular macrocell network and multiple cognitive small cells, in which the incumbent macrocell network owns the spectrum band and is the primary network (PN), and the small cells act as the secondary networks (SNs). The macrocell network serves a group of primary users, and small cell networks serve their own secondary users. The secondary access points (SAPs) of the small cells equip with cognitive radio capability with MMIMO beamforming and NOMA technologies. A SAP can dynamically access the spectrum owned by the macrocell network to help the incumbent BS to relay the primary traffic to the PUs while simultaneously transmit its own data with MMIMO and NOMA. Such cooperation creates a "win-win" situation: the throughput of PUs will be significantly increased with the assistance of SAP relays, and the SAPs can serve their SUs opportunistically. In this way, the dynamic spectrum access by the small cells will not congest the licensed spectrum, but improve the performance of the incumbent primary network. The interplay of these advanced radio techniques is analyzed in a systematic manner, and a framework for the joint optimization of relay selection, NOMA and MMIMO transmit power allocation, and transmission scheduling is proposed and investigated. Further, to model network-wide cooperation and competition, a two-sided matching algorithm is designed to find stable partnership between the SAPs and PUs in the network. The evaluation results demonstrate that the proposed scheme greatly improves the utilities of both primary and secondary users.

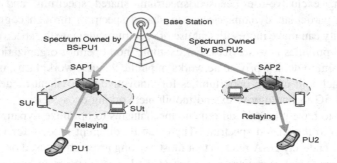

Fig. 1. A scenario for cognitive cooperative relaying with MMIMO and NOMA.

2   System Model

As shown in Fig. 1, there exist a group of small cells in the coverage area of an incumbent macrocell base station (BS) that is the owner of a spectrum band. The incumbent BS serves a number of PUs. We assume that a PU is allocated a licensed sub-channel for data delivery in a time slot via orthogonal frequency-division multiplexing (OFDM). Thus, we define a link between the macrocell BS and PU as the primary link (PL). For simplicity, we assume the incumbent BS and PUs are equipped with a single antenna and no NOMA capability.

Each small cell SAP is assumed to have MMIMO and NOMA interference cancellation capability, which can dynamically access to the sub-channels in the licensed spectrum of the incumbent PUs to serve its SUs opportunistically. Under the proposed cooperative DSA framework, a SAP can dynamically relay the traffic for the PU, while borrowing PU's sub-channel to transmit/receive the secondary data to/from its SUs using its MIMO and NOMA capabilities. We design the algorithms for a PU to select a SAP as relay and the SAP to control the power for transmitting SU data in the small cell and relaying PU data to optimize overall system performance. The SUs in a small cell are served opportunistically. For system fairness and simplicity, we allow one PU at most has one small cell SAP as its relay in a time slot. A SAP can only help one PU and access the PU channel that it is in cooperation with. In addition, we consider the downlink data communication from the macrocell BS to the PUs, whereas both uplink and downlink transmissions are considered for the SN. For the uplink from PU to the macrocell BS, symmetric analysis can be applied.

If a PU_i does not have a relay during a transmission time slot t, the BS will directly send data to PU_i on the subchannel allocated to PU_i. If a SAP_j acts as a relay for a PU_i in a time slot t, we call SAP_j and PU_i forms a partnership. Let $\mathcal{S}_j$ denote a set of SUs in small cell j associated to SAP_j. Thus, the time slot t is divided into two subslots as shown in Fig. 2. In subslot 1, the BS will transmit PU_i's data on the subchannel allocated to PU_i, and the partner SAP_j will receive the PU_i's data. Meanwhile, SAP_j will schedule K SUs in its small cell, $SU_k, k \in \mathcal{S}_j$ to transmit secondary uplink traffic and utilize its MMIMO beamforming and NOMA signal cancellation capabilities to receive the secondary uplink traffic, while receiving the primary data. In subslot 2, the SAP_j forwards the primary data to PU_i and also sends K downlink secondary traffic beams to its SUs in the small cell, $SU_k, k \in \mathcal{S}_j$, with MMIMO and NOMA. We will consider the case where an SAP is equipped with M antennas ($M > K$) and a SU has a single antenna.

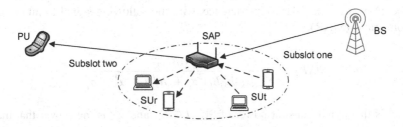

Fig. 2. MMIMO NOMA transmissions.

Assume the slot duration is T, subslot 1 duration $\delta T (0 \leq \delta \leq 1)$, and subslot 2 size $(1 - \delta)T$. In subslot 1, an SAP_j accesses the subchannel allocated to its partner PU_i and receives the signal sent from the incumbent BS to PU_i, along with the uplink signals from K SUs. Let y_m be the baseband signal output at the m-th element of the SAP_i antenna array. The $M \times 1$ signal vector at the array output, $\mathbf{y_j} = [y_{1j}, y_{2j}, \ldots, y_{mj}, \ldots y_{Mj}]^T$ can be represented by [11]

$$\mathbf{y_j} = \mathbf{h_{bj}} x_{bi} + \mathbf{H_j} \mathbf{x_j} + \mathbf{n_j} \tag{1}$$

where x_{bi} is the primary message sent from the incumbent BS to PU_i and the elements of $K \times 1$ vector $\mathbf{x_j} = [x_{1j}, x_{2j}, \ldots, x_{kj}, \ldots x_{Kj}]^T$, represent the messages transmitted from each of K SUs in the small cell $\mathcal{S}_j$. $\mathbf{n_j}$ is noise, and $\mathbf{H_j}$ is the $M \times K$ channel matrix between the SAP_i and its SUs. The column of the channel matrix, $\mathbf{H_j} = [\mathbf{h_{1j}}, \ldots, \mathbf{h_{kj}}, \ldots \mathbf{h_{Kj}}]$, represent the channels or spatial signatures associated with each SU. The channel vector with a linear antenna array can be modelled as [12]

$$\mathbf{h_{kj}} = \frac{\beta_{kj}}{1 + b_{kj}^e} [1, e^{-j\pi\varphi_{kj}}, \ldots, e^{-j\pi(M-1)\varphi_{kj}}] \tag{2}$$

where b_{kj} is the distance between the SAP$_j$ and SU k, $k \in S_j$, e is the pathloss exponent, φ_{kj} is the normalized direction, and β_{kj} is the fading attenuation coefficient. $\mathbf{h_{bj}}$ is the channel vector between the incumbent BS and partner SAP$_i$ that can be modeled in the same way. We are considering a flat Rayleigh block-fading channel model [10] to simplify our problem description, with which the channel is invariant and flat within each slot, but generally varying over the slots. For a large M value in MMIMO, a simple conjugate beamforming structure, i.e. a maximum-ratio-combining (MRC) beamformer with $\mathbf{w_{kj}} = \mathbf{h_{kj}^H}$ at SAP can yield good performance [13]. The symbol from the k-th user can thus be decoded by applying $\mathbf{w_{kj}} = \mathbf{h_{kj}^H}$ to the array output:

$$\hat{x}_{kj} = \mathbf{w_{kj}}\mathbf{y_j} = \mathbf{h_{kj}^H}\mathbf{h_{bj}}x_{bi} + \mathbf{h_{kj}^H}\mathbf{H_j}\mathbf{x_j} + \mathbf{h_{kj}^H}\mathbf{n_j} \tag{3}$$

SAP decodes the message from each of the SUs by treating the signal from the incumbent BS and other SUs as interference, with the following signal-to-interference-plus-noise ratio (SINR):

$$SINR_{kj} = \frac{|\boldsymbol{h}_{kj}^H\boldsymbol{h}_{kj}|^2\alpha_{kj}^2}{\Sigma_{l\in\mathcal{S}_j\backslash k}|\boldsymbol{h}_{kj}^H\boldsymbol{h}_{lj}|^2\alpha_{lj}^2 + |\boldsymbol{h}_{kj}^H\boldsymbol{h}_{bj}|^2\alpha_{bi}^2 + \sigma_j^2} \tag{4}$$

where α_{lj}^2 is the signal transmit power of SU$_l$, $l \in \mathcal{S}_j$, and α_{bi}^2 is the power that the BS transmits the primary data to PU$_i$, and σ_j^2 is the noise power. Then the achievable data rate from SU k to SAP j can then be expressed as $R_{kj} = B\log_2(1 + SINR_{kj})$. The data throughput from SU k to SAP j during subslot 1 can then be expressed as

$$C_{kj} = \delta TR_{kj} = \delta TB \log_2(1 + SINR_{kj}) \tag{5}$$

After SAP$_j$ decodes the messages from its SUs, it subtracts these messages from the superposed signal it received by carrying out successive interference cancellation (SIC) [5, 6], and decode the information from the incumbent BS for PU$_i$ using a MRC beamformer with $\mathbf{w_{bj}} = \mathbf{h_{bj}^H}$. The SINR for decoding the PU$_i$ information is given by

$$SINR_{bj} = \frac{|\mathbf{h}_{bj}^H\mathbf{h}_{bj}|^2\alpha_{bi}^2}{\sigma_j^2} \tag{6}$$

Note that if there is no NOMA SIC, the SINR for the PU$_i$ message received by relay SAP$_j$ is less due to the interference of the SUs, which is

$$SINR_{bj} = \frac{|h_{bj}^H h_{bj}|^2 \alpha_{bi}^2}{\Sigma_{l \in S_j} |h_{bj}^H h_{lj}|^2 \alpha_{lj}^2 + \sigma_j^2} \tag{7}$$

By applying SIC, the interference to the PU information is removed before decoding so that its SINR is improved. The achievable data rate for the link from the incumbent BS to SAP$_j$ can be expressed as: $R_{bj} = B \log_2(1 + SINR_{bj})$. The corresponding data throughput for the link from the incumbent BS to SAP$_j$ in subslot 1 is

$$C_{bj} = \delta T R_{bj} = \delta T B \log_2(1 + SINR_{bj}) \tag{8}$$

It is possible to apply SIC in decoding the messages from the SUs. However, this will significantly increase the signal processing complexity and the SUs are served opportunistically, thus we only use SIC for PU message decoding to improve PU's performance. The SU message decoding depends on MMIMO beamforming. In addition, we assume each SU uses a fixed power to transmit its uplink traffic as the uplink power control introduces a large overhead and complexity.

In subslot 2, the SAP$_j$ relays the primary data x_{ji} to the PU$_i$ and simultaneously transmits K secondary downlink messages, $\mathbf{x_{jd}} = [x_{j1}, x_{j2}, \ldots, x_{jk}, \ldots x_{jK}]^T$, one message to a SU, on the PU$_i$'s subchannel with MMIMO beamforming and NOMA. Similar analysis can be performed. Let $\hat{x}_{ji}$ be the signal received by the PU$_i$ and vector $\hat{\mathbf{x}}_{jd} = [\hat{x}_{j1}, \hat{x}_{j2}, \ldots \hat{x}_{jk}, \ldots \hat{x}_{jK}]^T$ contain the signals received at each of the SUs, respectively, which can be described by

$$\hat{x}_{ji} = \mathbf{h}_{ji}^H \mathbf{w}_{ji} x_{ji} + \mathbf{h}_{ji}^H \mathbf{W}_j \mathbf{x}_{jd} + n_i \tag{9}$$

$$\hat{\mathbf{x}}_{jd} = \mathbf{H}_j^H \mathbf{w}_{ji} x_{ji} + \mathbf{H}_j^H \mathbf{W}_j \mathbf{x}_{jd} + \mathbf{n_d} \tag{10}$$

where $\mathbf{w_{ji}}$ is the M $\times$ 1 MMIMO precoding vector applied to x_{ji} before transmitting it by the M antenna elements of the SAP$_j$ to PU$_i$, and $\mathbf{W}_j$ is the $M \times K$ MMIMO precoding matrix applied to the secondary signal vector sent to its SUs by the SAP$_j$ for the transmit beamforming. The downlink channel matrix $\mathbf{H}_j^H$ from the SAP$_j$ to the SUs is considered as the conjugate transpose of the uplink channel matrix due to channel reciprocity. $\mathbf{h_{ji}}$ is the channel vector between the SAP$_j$ and PU$_i$, and n_i is noise. We consider that the maximum ratio transmission (MRT) precoding [11] is used to transmit the primary and secondary messages to individual users, that is, $\mathbf{w_{ji}} = \mathbf{h_{ji}}$ and $\mathbf{W}_j = \mathbf{H}_j$.

An incumbent PU$_i$ receives a superposition of the messages for itself as well as the SUs. It treats the SUs' information as noise and decodes its own message with the following SINR:

$$SINR_{ji} = \frac{\mathbf{h}_{ji}^H \mathbf{h}_{ji} \alpha_{ji}^2}{\Sigma_{l \in S_j} \mathbf{h}_{ji}^H \mathbf{h}_{lj} \alpha_{jl}^2 + \sigma_i^2} \tag{11}$$

The achievable data rate of an incumbent PU_i during subslot 2 is then $R_{ji} = B \log_2(1 + SINR_{ji})$, and the corresponding PU_i throughput in subslot 2 is

$$C_{ji} = (1 - \delta)TR_{ji} = (1 - \delta)TB \log_2(1 + SINR_{ji}) \qquad (12)$$

Assume that SUs have NOMA capability. After a SU receives the superposed signal, it may try two approaches to obtain its message, depending on its MMIMO channel state and SAP_j's power allocation strategy:

(1) a SU_k, $k \in \mathcal{S}_j$, can try to decode the PU_i's message and then use SIC to subtract this message from its observation, and finally decode its own information. For the PU_i message decoding at SU_k, the SINR is given as:

$$SINR_{jk\_ji} = \frac{\mathbf{h}_{kj}^H \mathbf{h}_{ji} \alpha_{ji}^2}{\sum_{l \in \mathcal{S}_j} \mathbf{h}_{kj}^H \mathbf{h}_{lj} \alpha_{jl}^2 + \sigma_k^2} \qquad (13)$$

The data rate for PU_i is R_{ji} and let $\varepsilon_{ji} = (2^{R_{ji}/B} - 1)$. If $SINR_{jk\_ji} \geq \varepsilon_{ji}$, SIC can be carried out successfully at SU k and the SINR for decoding its own message is given by

$$SINR_{jk} = \frac{\mathbf{h}_{kj}^H \mathbf{h}_{kj} \alpha_{jk}^2}{\sum_{l \in \mathcal{S}_j \setminus k} \mathbf{h}_{kj}^H \mathbf{h}_{lj} \alpha_{jl}^2 + \sigma_k^2} \qquad (14)$$

(2) If SU_k cannot successfully decode the PU_i signal, i.e. $SINR_{jk\_ji} < \varepsilon_{ji}$, it will decode its own message directly by treating PU_i's information as noise. The SINR of SU_k signal is then

$$SINR_{jk} = \frac{\mathbf{h}_{kj}^H \mathbf{h}_{kj} \alpha_{jk}^2}{\mathbf{h}_{kj}^H \mathbf{h}_{ji} \alpha_{ji}^2 + \sum_{l \in \mathcal{S} \setminus k} \mathbf{h}_{kj}^H \mathbf{h}_{lj} \alpha_{jl}^2 + \sigma_k^2} \qquad (15)$$

The achievable data rate for SU_k is thus $R_{jk} = B \log_2(1 + SINR_{jk})$, and the corresponding data throughput for SU_k in subslot 2 is

$$C_{jk} = (1 - \delta)TR_{jk} = (1 - \delta)TB \log_2(1 + SINR_{jk}) \qquad (16)$$

Moreover, If the incumbent BS transmits data to PU_i directly on its subchannel without cooperative relaying, the achievable rate is a function of the BS transmit power α_{bi}^2 and the complex channel gain h_{bi} between BS and PU_i, which can be expressed as [11], $R_{bi,dir} = B log_2(1 + \frac{\alpha_{bi}^2}{\sigma_i^2}|h_{bi}|^2)$ where σ_i^2 is the noise power. The PU_i throughput without the cooperative relaying in time slot T is

$$C_{bi,dir} = TR_{bi,dir} = TB log_2(1 + \frac{\alpha_{bi}^2}{\sigma_i^2}|h_{bi}|^2) \qquad (17)$$

3   System Optimization

From the above analysis, we can see that a set of strategies affect the achievable throughput of PU and SAP transmissions, including (i) a PU should decide whether to use its frequency channel for direct transmission from BS to PU, or for SAP relaying. (ii) In the latter case, the best MMIMO-NOMA SAP relay for a PU should be selected. (iii) After a SAP relay is selected, how are the resources shared in the PU and SU data transmissions? That is, the MMIMO-NOMA relay transmission and power allocation strategies should be decided, including the size of subslots 1 and 2 as well as the SAP power allocation for transmitting PU data and SU data. We model the system of multiple PUs and multiple SAPs as a two-side matching problem, and study the relay selection, relay transmission, and power allocation strategies for overall system optimization.

3.1   System Utility Maximization

Let $\mathcal{P}$ denote the set of PU links and $\mathcal{S}$ the set of MMIMO-NOMA small cells each led by a SAP. We define the utility that each party can earn as its throughput, which is a function of relay selection, subslot partition, transmit power allocation, and MMIMO-NOMA transmission states. If PU link $i, i \in \mathcal{P}$ uses SU $j, j \in \mathcal{S}$ as a relay, the utility of PU$_i$ is defined as the throughput with this partnership, $U_{i,j}^p = C_{bj} = C_{ji}$. Here, we assume that the SAP$_j$ relay should forward all the data received from the incumbent BS to the cooperating PU$_i$, that is, satisfying the flow conservation constraint $C_{bj} = C_{ji}$, because the primary data has higher priority. The utility of SAP relay j is the sum of the throughput that it receives and transmits its own data on the subchannel leased from PU link i, $U_{i,j}^s = \sum_{k \in \mathcal{S}_j} (w_u C_{kj} + w_d C_{jk})$ where w_u and w_d, $0 \leq w_u, w_d \leq 1$, are the weight factors that are put on the SU uplink and SU downlink transmissions, respectively.

In the case of direct transmission from the BS to PU$_i$ without cooperative relaying, the utility of PU$_i$ is $U_i^{dir} = C_{bi,dir}$. The utility of SAP$_j$ without cooperation is $U_j^{dir} = C_{kj} = C_{jk} = 0$ because the SAP does not have spectrum to transmit without cooperation. A PU$_i$ selects a SAP$_j$ as the cooperative relay only when its utility through the relay is greater than that of the direct transmission, i.e. $U_{i,j}^p = C_{bj} = C_{ji} > U_i^{dir} = C_{bi,dir}$. For a SU, the requirement is that its utility with cooperation should be greater than zero, i.e. $U_{i,j}^s = \sum_{k \in \mathcal{S}_j} (w_u C_{kj} + w_d C_{jk}) > U_j^{dir} = 0$. In addition, the transmit power allocation of the SAP should be subject to the SAP total power constraint: $\alpha_{ji}^2 + \sum_{k \in \mathcal{S}_j} \alpha_{jk}^2 \leq P_{max}$, where P_{max} is the maximal total transmission power of SAP.

Let us first assume that PU$_i$ has selected SAP$_j$ as its cooperative relay. The relay selection optimization problem will be discussed in the next section. Then, the objective is to maximize the total utility $U_{i,j}^p + U_{i,j}^s$ by jointly determining the optimal subslot length δ and the power allocation of the SAP MMIMO-NOMA PU data relay and secondary data transmission to SU_k, $k \in S_j$, subject to the above flow conservation and power constraints. The optimization problem can be formulated as

$$\max_{\delta, P_{ji}, P_{jk|k \in S_j}} \left\{ U_{i,j}^p + U_{i,j}^s \right\} = \max_{\delta, P_{ji}, P_{jk|k \in S_j}} \left\{ C_{ji} + \sum_{k \in S_j} \left(w_u C_{kj} + w_d C_{jk} \right) \right\} \quad (18)$$

$$\text{s.t. } C_{bj} = C_{ji} > C_{bi,dir}, \sum_{k \in S_j} \left(w_u C_{kj} + w_d C_{jk} \right) > 0,$$

$$\alpha_{ji}^2 + \sum_{k \in S_j} \alpha_{jk}^2 \leq P_{max}, \quad 0 < \delta < 1$$

The above constrained optimization problem can be solved with gradient ascent algorithms [14].

3.2 Two-Sided Matching

Next, we will focus on the cooperation and relay selection problem among multiple PU links and MMIMO-NOMA-empowered SAPs, and aim to optimize the utilities of all the entities with fairness. There exist competitions among the PUs, as well as among the SUs during relay selection and partner matching. The optimal strategy of an entity depends on the behaviors of other entities.

In practice, the SAP$_j$ can estimate the channel vectors $\mathbf{h}_{bj}$ and $\mathbf{H}_j = [\mathbf{h}_{1j}, \ldots,$ $\mathbf{h}_{kj}, \ldots \mathbf{h}_{Kj}]$ in its small cell and determine the power allocation and beamforming for its MMIMO-NOMA transmission. The PU$_j$ estimates the channel coefficients h_{bi} and $\mathbf{h}_{ij}$. We assume that a common control channel is available for exchanging messages among the entities involved in cooperation. Then, BS, PUs and SAPs periodically exchange control messages within their transmission range, i.e. local neighborhood. All the achievable link rates can be then derived. We consider the scenario without global information. The partnerships are formed through local information exchange among the BS, PUs and SAPs. Under this setting, we find our problem is best modeled using two-sided matching theory [9, 15, 16]. Based on this theory, we define the following concepts.

Definition 1: An entity is *individual rational*, if it will only cooperate with others when such a partnership improves its utility, i.e., $U_{i,j}^p > U_{i,dir}^p$, $\forall i \in \mathcal{P}$ and $U_{i,j}^s > 0$, $\forall j \in S$.

Definition 2: A *blocking pair* is a pair (PU$_i$, SAP$_j$) who both already have their respective partners $n(i)$ and $n(j)$, but prefer each other rather than their partners, i.e., $U_{i,n(i)}^p < U_{i,j}^p$ and $U_{n(j),j}^s < U_{i,j}^s$.

We can easily see that, if there exists a blocking pair, the entities involved have an incentive to break up from their existing partnership and form a new pair. Therefore, the current matching is unstable and not desirable. The definition of matching stability is given as follows.

Definition 3: A matching is stable if and only if every participating PU and SAP is individual rational and if there is no blocking pair in the network.

Based on the given definitions, our objective is to find a stable matching in the primary and secondary markets. It has been proven that a stable matching always exists for a two-sided market [15], and PUs and SAPs can find their partners using the following matching algorithm.

```
For each PU p ∈ 𝒫:
    Initialize the preference list by ranking the PU's utility in
    partnership with each of available SAP relays, p.list();
    p.partner ← free; end ← false;
    while end != false
        if p.partner = free and p.plist != ∅ then
            s ← pop(p.plist());
            Send a "propose" message to s;
        if p receives an "accept" message from s then
            p.partner ← s;
        if p receives a "reject" message then
            delete the message sender from p.plist();
            If the message sender is the current partner of p then
                p.partner ← free;
    Algorithm end when no message to issue and no response re-
    ceived from SAPs.
```

```
For each SAP s ∈ 𝒮:
    Initialize the preference list by ranking the SU's utility in
    partnership with each of available primary links, s.list();
    s.partner ← free; end ← false;
    while end != false
        if s receives a "propose" message from p then
            if p ∉ s.list()then
                s sends a "reject" message to p;
            else
                s.partner ← p;
                s sends an "accept" message to p;
                for each PU p' with a rank lower than p in s.list()
                    s sends a "reject" message to p';
                    remove p' from s.list();
    Algorithm end when no message received from PUs and no re-
    sponse to send.
```

The above algorithm is an extension of [16], which is a distributed version of the Gale–Shapley algorithm [15]. It can be proven that the algorithm finishes in $O(N_P + N_S)$ iterations and results in a stable matching that is optimal for the PUs [15], where N_P is the number of PUs and N_S is the number of SAP relays. Note that since the PUs represent the owners of the channel and can proactively lease the channel for higher utilities, the result of our mechanism is therefore desirable.

4 Evaluation Results

In this section, we evaluate the performance of the proposed MMIMO-NOMA-based cognitive cooperative relaying framework. We consider that N_P PUs are randomly located in a semicircle with a radius of 100 m centered at the incumbent BS. Moreover,

N_S MMIMO-NOMA SAP relays are randomly distributed within the same semicircle. Each SAP serves a small cell with 8 active SUs, 4 transmitters and 4 receivers, besides relaying data for the PU. The SUs are randomly placed in a circle centered at the SAP with a radius of 25 m. A SU receives or sends the secondary data from or to the SAP. In addition, we assume that the subchannel bandwidth for a PU link is 1 MHz. The thermal noise level is set to be −100 dBm. The transmission power of the incumbent BS, P_{bs}, is set to be a value such that the average channel SNR of the PUs is 0 dB. The maximum transmission power of a SAP and a SU is set to be $1.0 \times P_{bs}$ and $0.5 \times P_{bs}$, respectively. We further assume that the incumbent BS and PUs are equipped with a single antenna. The SAPs are equipped with MMIMO and NOMA transceivers, and the SU has a single antenna, but has NOMA capability. As discussed before, the channel is modeled as a flat block-fading channel [10] and line-of-sight propagation between the sender and receiver with a path loss exponent of 3 and a small-scale Rayleigh fading component $\sigma = 1$.

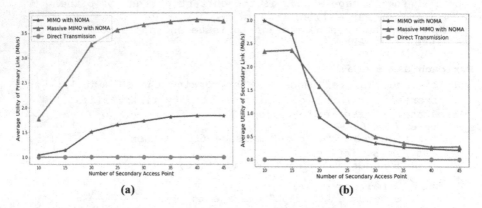

Fig. 3. (a) Average utility of primary users, (b) Average utility of secondary access points versus the number of secondary access points for difference schemes.

Figures 3(a) and (b) illustrates the average utilities of PUs and SAP relays, respectively, versus the number of SAPs. The number of PU links, N_P is set to be 20. The "Direct Transmission" in the figures means that there is no cooperative SAP relaying, and the incumbent BS directly transmits its data to a PU. For the "MIMO with NOMA" scheme, the SAP relay has only two antenna elements. With massive MIMO and NOMA, the SAP equips with a 32-element MMIMO antenna array. Figure 3(a) shows the average PU utility for the relaying schemes improves as the number of SAPs increases because more SAPs result in more opportunities for the PU links to find suitable cooperative relays. Figure 3(b) shows that the SU utility for the relaying schemes decreases as the number of SAPs increases because more SAPs compete to access the limited spectrum resource. We can see from the figures that by exploiting cooperative SAP relaying with massive MIMO and NOMA, the proposed scheme significantly outperforms the direct transmission and MIMO-NOMA relaying schemes in terms of PU's utility. The MIMO-NOMA relaying scheme sometimes achieves a little better SAP utility than the MMIMO-NOMA relaying scheme, especially in the case of fewer SAP relays, because the SAP relays may not be at a good location and need to greedily allocate more power to transmit the PU data, but leave less power for SU data transmission.

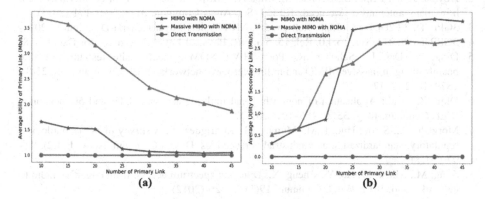

Fig. 4. (a) Average utility of primary users, (b) Average utility of secondary access points versus the number primary users for difference schemes.

Figures 4(a) and (b) shows the utilities of PUs and SAPs versus the number of PU links, respectively, when the number of SAPs, N_s is 20. In Fig. 4(a), the average PU utility decreases for the relaying schemes as the number of PUs increases because more PU links compete for good SAP relays, and some of PUs may not be able to find suitable relays. In Fig. 4(b), the SAP utility improves with more PUs because a SAP is more likely to be selected as a relay for a PU link and access the PU's spectrum for its own data transmission. The MMIMO-NOMA based cooperative relaying scheme achieves much higher PU utility than the baselines. Due to the greedy allocation of the SAP transmit power to maximize the PU utility, the SU utility of the MMIMO-NOMA relaying scheme is less than that of the MIMO-NOMA relaying scheme in some cases. The results validate that our MMIMO-NOMA cooperative relaying framework can achieve win-win gains for both PUs and SUs.

5 Conclusions

In this paper, we present a novel framework that enables multiple PUs and multiple MMIMO-NOMA empowered SAPs to cooperate in traffic relaying and dynamic spectrum sharing. By leveraging the MMIMO and NOMA capabilities, SAPs help relay traffic for PUs while concurrently accessing the PUs' spectrum to transmit their own data. The optimization algorithms for the SAP relay selection and data transmission are proposed and analyzed. Evaluation results show that both PUs and SAPs can benefit from this proposed framework.

References

1. Lu, L., Li, G.Y., Swindlehurst, A.L., Ashikhmin, A., Zhang, R.: An overview of massive MIMO: benefits and challenges. IEEE J. Sel. Top. Sign. Process. **8**(5), 742–758 (2014)
2. Hoydis, J., ten Brink, S., Debbah, M.: Massive MIMO in the UL/DL of cellular networks: how many antennas do we need? IEEE J. Sel. Areas Commun. **31**(2), 160–171 (2013)
3. 3GPP TS 38.201, ver. 15.0.0, Rel. 15, 5G; NR Physical Layer General Description (2018)
4. 3GPP TS 38.214, ver. 15.4.0, Rel. 15, 5G; NR; Physical Layer Procedures for Data (2018)
5. Ding, Z., Dai, L., Schober, R., Poor, H.V.: NOMA meets finite resolution analog beamforming in massive MIMO and millimeter-wave networks. IEEE Commun. Lett. **21**(8), 1879–1882 (2017)
6. Ding, Z., et al.: Application of non-orthogonal multiple access in LTE and 5G networks. IEEE Commun. Mag. **55**(2), 185–191 (2017)
7. Morgado, A., Saidul Huq, K.M., Mumtaz, S., Rodriguez, J.: A survey of 5G technologies: regulatory, standardization and industrial perspectives. Digital Commun. Netw. J. **4**(2), 87–97 (2018)
8. Song, M., Xin, C., Zhao, Y., Cheng, X.: Dynamic spectrum access: from cognitive radio to network radio. IEEE Wirel. Commun. **19**(1), 23–29 (2012)
9. Hua, S., Liu, H., Zhuo, X., Wu, M., Panwar, S.: Exploiting multiple antennas in cooperative cognitive radio networks. IEEE Trans. Veh. Technol. **63**(7), 3318–3330 (2013)
10. Zhang, J., Zhang, Q.: Stackelberg game for utility-based cooperative cognitive radio networks. In: Proceedings of the ACM MOBIHOC (2010)
11. Biglieri, E., et al.: MIMO Wireless Communications. Cambridge University Press, Cambridge (2007)
12. Gao, X., Dai, L., Sun, Y., Han, S., Chih-Lin, I.: Machine learning inspired energy-efficient hybrid precoding for mmWave massive MIMO systems. In: Proceedings of IEEE International Conference on Communications (ICC), Paris, pp. 1–6 (2017)
13. Ngo, H., Larsson, E., Marzetta, T.: Energy and spectral efficiency of very large multiuser MIMO systems. IEEE Trans. Commun. **61**, 1436–1449 (2013)
14. Papadimitriou, C., Steiglitz, K.: Combinatorial Optimization, Algorithms and Complexity. Dover Publication Inc., New York (2014)
15. Roth, A.E., Sotomayor, M.A.O.: Two-Sided Matching: A Study in Game-Theoretic Modeling and Analysis. Cambridge University Press, Cambridge (1992)
16. Brito, I., Meseguer, P.: Distributed stable matching problems. In: van Beek, P. (ed.) CP 2005. LNCS, vol. 3709, pp. 152–166. Springer, Heidelberg (2005). https://doi.org/10.1007/11564751_14

Minimum Control Cost of Weighted Linear Dynamic Networks

Zhaoquan Gu[1](✉), Yuexuan Wang[2,3], Yijie Wu[3], Yongcai Wang[4],
and Yueming Wang[2]

[1] Cyberspace Institute of Advanced Technology, Guangzhou University,
Guangzhou, China
zqgu@gzhu.edu.cn
[2] College of Computer Science and Technology, Zhejiang University,
Hangzhou, China
[3] Department of Computer Science, The University of Hong Kong,
Hong Kong, China
[4] Department of Computer Sciences, Renmin University of China,
Beijing, China

Abstract. Controlling a weighted linear dynamic network is important
to various real world applications such as influencing political elections
through a social network. Extant works mainly focus on minimizing the
number of controllers that control the nodes in a network, but ignore the
cost of controlling an individual node. Apparently, controlling a journal-
ist or a mayor in a city has largely different costs, and we show that
the aggregated control cost in extant works is often prohibitive. In this
paper, we formulate the minimum control cost (MCC) problem in a
weighted linear dynamic network, which is to find the set of controlled
nodes with minimum sum of control costs. We show that the MCC problem is NP-hard by reducing the set cover problem to it. We also derive the
lower/upper bounds and propose two approximation algorithms. Extensive evaluation results also show that the proposed algorithms have good
performance compared to the derived lower bound of the problem.

1 Introduction

Weighted dynamic networks have been employed as a model in various areas,
including transportation networks [16], social networks [1] and network flow control [21]. In a weighted linear dynamic network, each node has a state value that
changes with time by a linear transformation model, each edge has a weight
that models the connection between the nodes, and each node has a weight that
identifies the hardness of controlling it (we call it control cost). In real world
applications, it is an important and challenge problem to control a weighted linear dynamic network [2,11,12,17,19,20,22,23] which targets at driving all nodes
towards designated states by controlling only a small subset of the nodes.

This work is supported by the National Natural Science Foundation of China under
Grant No. U1636215 and National Key R&D Program of China 2018YEB1004003.

E. S. Biagioni et al. (Eds.): WASA 2019, LNCS 11604, pp. 111–123, 2019.
https://doi.org/10.1007/978-3-030-23597-0_9

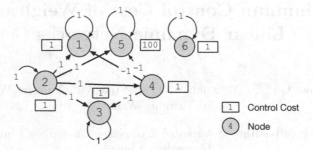

Fig. 1. An example with 6 nodes: exact control may find {1, 2, 3, 5, 6} as the controlled nodes with a total cost 104, while a better set {1, 2, 3, 4, 6} has a minimum cost 5.

For instance, in a mayoral election, it is possible for some parties to control the voters through social networks such as Twitter. Directly controlling different voters in a city may incur different costs. Even in a small town, it is economically prohibitive to control all voters. Therefore, it is more preferable to control only a small portion of voters with minimum cost and let these voters influence other voters in the network.

However, extant works ignore minimizing this cost and they typically focus on minimizing the number of controllers [11,22]. A controller is a node added to a network which can impose the same control signal onto all its controlled nodes. For instance, the exact controllability theory (in short, exact control) [22] which offers a method to find the minimum number of controllers and to discover a set of nodes to be controlled. However, this approach does not consider the cost of controlling an individual node, and our example in Fig. 1 shows that their control cost can be extremely high.

In this paper, we formulate the problem of controlling a weighted linear dynamic network with minimum control cost (MCC). Controlling different nodes may take different costs and the problem targets at finding a set of nodes controlled by external controllers that minimizes the total cost. If the control cost of each node is uniform, it would be straightforward to find the minimum number of controlled nodes, which also minimizes the total control cost. If the control cost of each node varies, the problem becomes much more difficult. In the paper, we prove that the MCC problem is NP-hard, no matter the control costs are uniform or not. We then propose two approximation algorithms to tackle it. The main contributions of the paper are:

(1) We formulate the MCC problem of weighted linear dynamic networks for the first time, and prove its NP-hardness;
(2) We propose two approximation algorithms: the HR's algorithm computes the control cost in a short time, but incurs quite large approximation ratio without guarantee, while the Headhunter's algorithm achieves $\ln N$-approximation ratio with time complexity $O(N^3)$ (N is the number of nodes in the network);

(3) We conduct extensive evaluations on real data and the results also corrobo-
rate the theoretical analyses.

The remainder of the paper is organized as follows. In the next section, we
introduce the system model and formulate the MCC problem. Section 3 highlights existing works related to the MCC problem. In Sect. 4, we prove the NP-
hardness of the problem and derive the lower/upper bounds. In Sect. 5, we propose two efficient approximation algorithms. We present the evaluation results
in Sect. 6 and conclude the paper in Sect. 7.

2 Preliminaries

2.1 System Model

Considering a weighted network $G(A)$ with the node set $V = \{v_1, v_2, \cdots, v_N\}$,
denote $\overrightarrow{x(t)} \in \mathbb{C}^N$ as the state values of the N nodes at time t. The matrix
$A = (a_{ij})_{N \times N} \in \mathbb{C}^{N \times N}$ is called the *coupling matrix* of the network $G(A)$. For
directed networks, if there exists a directed link from v_j to v_i, the edge-weight a_{ij}
is nonzero. For undirected networks, $a_{ij} = a_{ji}$ for all i, j, thus A is symmetric.

Definition 1. *A **controller** is an external node that can inject signals to change
the state values of the nodes in the network.*

Definition 2. *A **controlled** node in a network is a node directly controlled by
one or more controllers.*

Suppose we use M controllers $\{c_1, c_2, \ldots, c_M\}$ to control $G(A)$. Denote
$B = (b_{ij})_{N \times M} \in \mathbb{C}^{N \times N}$ as the *controlling matrix*, in which b_{ij} is the constant scaling factor that amplify or diminish the same signal from controller c_j
to the controlled node v_i. We say node v_i is a controlled node if $\exists j, b_{ij} \neq 0$
(that is, the i-th row of B has nonzero entries), and network $G(A, B)$ is called
a controlled network. Time is discretely measured in slots of equal length, and
network $G(A, B)$ fits the linear time-invariant (LTI) dynamics:

$$\overrightarrow{x(t+1)} = A \cdot \overrightarrow{x(t)} + B \cdot \overrightarrow{u(t)}, u(t) \in \mathbb{C}^M.$$

A linear dynamic network $G(A, B)$ is said to be **controllable** if it can be
driven from any start state to any final state in finite time steps by imposing
time-variant signals via the controllers. Suppose each node v_i in the network
$G(A, B)$ has a cost w_i. Denote $\overrightarrow{w} = [w_1, \ldots, w_N]$ as the cost vector of all nodes,
and denote w_{min}, w_{max} as the minimum and maximum cost to control the nodes.
For a controllable network $G(A, B)$, denote the set of controlled nodes as C,
which consists of the indices of non-zero rows in B.

Definition 3. *The control cost of network $G(A, B)$ is the total cost of the controlled nodes, i.e. $\sum_{j \in C} w_j$*

Remark 1. We do not consider the cost of the controllers, because they are virtual nodes without defined costs. Even assigned with homogeneous cost, ECT [22] already proves the minimum number of controllers needed for full control is the largest geometric multiplicities of the coupling matrix. So their minimum cost is fixed given the network.

2.2   Problem Formulation

We formulate the Minimum Control Cost (MCC) problem as follows:

Problem 1. For a weighted dynamic network $G(A)$ with cost vector $\vec{w}$, find a controlling matrix B such that $G(A, B)$ is controllable and the control cost of $G(A, B)$ is minimized.

The decision version of the problem is: given a budget K, decide whether there exists a controlled network $G(A, B)$ with control cost no larger than K.

2.3   Mathematical Basics

We introduce related mathematical concepts briefly which can be found in well-organized textbooks on linear algebra (e.g., [10]).

Let I_n denote the $n \times n$ identity matrix; we omit the subscript if not causing confusion. Let e_k denote the k-th column vector of I_n, and all the n unit vectors e_k ($1 \leq k \leq n$) together form the natural basis for the n-dimensional linear space. Let θ denote the zero vector.

For a matrix A, denote A^H as the conjugate transpose. If $AA^H = I$, then A is *unitary*, and the column vectors of A form an orthogonal basis. If there exists matrix A^{-1} such that $AA^{-1} = I$, A is *invertible*, and A^{-1} is the *inverse matrix*. Denote $r(A)$ as the rank of A, which is the maximal number of linear independent row vectors (or column vectors) in the matrix A. The proof of the following lemma can be found in [10].

Lemma 1. *Suppose P is an $N \times N$ invertible matrix, Q is an $M \times M$ invertible matrix and A is an $N \times M$ matrix, $r(PAQ) = r(A)$.*

For the block matrix $[A, B]$, we may denote its rank as $r(A, B)$ for convenience.

Throughout this paper, we assume the $N \times N$ matrix A has s distinct eigenvalues $\lambda_1, \ldots, \lambda_s$ with the algebraic multiplicity α_i and the geometric multiplicity μ_i for λ_i. The *geometric multiplicity* $\mu_i = N - r(A - \lambda_i I)$ is the dimension of the eigenspace $\mathrm{Ker}(A - \lambda_i I) = \{x \in \mathbb{C}^N | (A - \lambda_i I)x = \theta\}$. That is, μ_i is the maximal number of independent eigenvectors corresponding to λ_i. The *algebraic multiplicity* is defined in the characteristic polynomial: $f_A(\lambda) = \det(\lambda I - A) = \prod_{i=1}^{s}(\lambda - \lambda_i)^{\alpha_i}$, where α_i is the dimension of the root subspace $U_{\lambda_i} = \{x \in \mathbb{C}^N | \exists m > 0, (A - \lambda_i I)^m = \theta\}$. Then, it is shown in [10] that $\sum_{i=1}^{s} \alpha_i = N$. The Jordan normal form (JNF) of matrix A is $J = \mathrm{diag}(J_{\lambda_1}, \ldots, J_{\lambda_s})$ such that there exists an invertible matrix P suits $A = PJP^{-1}$.

In linear algebra, the size of J_{λ_i} equals α_i, and the number of Jordan blocks in J_{λ_i} equals μ_i. If J_{λ_i} is diagonal, i.e. all Jordan blocks are 1×1, $\alpha_i = \mu_i$ can be deduced. The column vectors in matrix P are the *generalized* eigenvectors of A, which form a complete basis of the N-dimensional linear space. In fact, we can transform a matrix to its JNF by changing from natural basis to the basis formed by generalized eigenvectors.

3 Related Works

In control theory, $G(A, B)$ is controllable if and only if it satisfies the **PBH rank condition** [7]: $r(\lambda_i I_N - A, B) = N$ for every eigenvalue λ_i of A. We introduce two types of controllability.

3.1 Structural Controllability Theory (SCT)

In some applications, edge-weights cannot be easily measured. Structural controllability [11] reveals the controlling property related to the topological structure of the network. SCT split each node into an in-node and an out-node, and each directed edge is mapped to an edge between the in-node of its starting node and the out-node of its ending node, resulting in a bipartite graph. Through maximum cardinality matching on the bipartite graph, a set of unmatched in-nodes are identified in time $O(m\sqrt{n})$ [8]. The corresponding nodes in the original graph each should be directed controlled by one controller. There are also isolated components without unmatched nodes (usually forming circles), to which there is no directed path from those other unmatched nodes, so at least one node in each isolated component should be directly controlled by the controllers. That is the main reason that the SCT do not always optimize the control cost, since the selection of these additional controlled nodes is uncertain.

3.2 Exact Controllability Theory (ECT)

Exact controllability is introduced in [22], which computes the minimum number N_D of controllers to fully control an arbitrary network as $N_D = \max_{1 \leq i \leq s} \mu_i$, i.e., the largest geometric multiplicity. Using the equation $r(\lambda I - A, B) = r(\lambda I - J, P^{-1}B)$, ECT also propose a method to design the controlling matrix B, which finds $P^{-1}B$ and then generates $B = P(P^{-1}B)$.

4 Problem Hardness of the MCC Problem

We rewrite the PBH rank condition as follows.

Lemma 2. *Suppose $A = PA'P^{-1}$ where P is invertible; the PBH rank is*

$$r(A - \lambda I, B) = r(A' - \lambda I, P^{-1}B). \tag{1}$$

This lemma can be deduced from Lemma 1 directly since $[A' - \lambda I, P^{-1}B] = P^{-1}[A - \lambda I, B]\text{diag}(P, I)$. From Lemma 2, we can change to a more convenient basis to facilitate the process of finding such e_k (the k-th column vector of I). One of such bases is formed by generalized eigenvectors. By using an invertible matrix P such that $A = PJP^{-1}$, we only need to satisfy $r(J - \lambda_i I, P^{-1}B) = N$ for each λ_i to control the network.

4.1 NP-Hardness

We show the MCC problem is NP-hard by reducing the Minimum (weighted) Set-cover problem (whose decision version is NP-complete [9]). A weighted Set-cover instance is characterized by:

(1) a set of points $V = \{v_1, v_2, \ldots, v_n\}$,
(2) a multi-set[1] of sets $\mathcal{S} = \{S_1, \ldots, S_m\}$, $S_i \subset V$ and it has the weight $w(S_i)$; for $1 \leq i \leq m$ and $\bigcup_{i=1}^{m} S_i = V$, and
(3) the incidence matrix $Q = (q_{ij})_{n \times m}$ such that $q_{ij} = 1$ iff S_j covers point v_i.

The minimum set cover problem is to find the optimal cover $\mathcal{S}_{OPT} \subset \mathcal{S}$ satisfying **validity** ($\bigcup_{S \in \mathcal{S}_{OPT}} S = V$) and **optimality** ($\sum_{S \in \mathcal{S}_{OPT}} w(S_i) = OPT$ is the minimum among all valid covers). In the unweighted version, $w(S_i) = 1$ for $1 \leq i \leq m$. In the decision version, the problem is to decide whether there exists a valid cover of size k for any given constant k.

We first transform a set-cover instance $(V, \mathcal{S}, w, Q)$ to $(V', \mathcal{S}', w', Q')$ such that $|V'| = |\mathcal{S}'| = m + n$. Suppose all weights are in the range $[w_{min}, w_{max}]$. We add n dummy sets $S'_{m+i}(1 \leq i \leq n)$ and m dummy points $v_{n+i}(1 \leq i \leq m)$. Specifically, we construct the instance as follows:

(1) $V_{dummy} = \{v_{n+i} | 1 \leq i \leq m\}$, and $V' = V \cup V_{dummy}$.
(2) $S'_i = S_i \cup V_{dummy}$, $w'(S_i) = w(S'_i)$, for $1 \leq i \leq m$; $S'_{m+i} = \{v_i\} \cup V_{dummy}$, $w'(S'_{m+i}) = W$ for $1 \leq i \leq n$; and $\mathcal{S}' = \{S'_j | 1 \leq j \leq m + n\}$.
(3) Q' is an $(m + n) \times (m + n)$ matrix, whose first n rows are $[Q, I_n]$ and the last m rows are all 1's (corresponding to the V_{dummy}).

The transformation preserves the validity and the matrix Q' is invertible. We omit the proof due to page limits. Then, we can modify the non-zero entries in Q' to get an invertible matrix $Q_1 = (q_{ij})_{N \times N}$, where $N = m + n$ is the size of the matrix Q_1. Let $P = Q_1^{-1}$ and J be any diagonal matrix with N distinct eigenvalues, such as $J = \text{diag}(1, 2, \ldots, N)$. Then we can transform the set cover instance into an MCC instance with the coupling matrix $A = PJP^{-1}$ and the cost to control node v_j is $w_j = w'(S'_j)$ ($1 \leq j \leq N$).

Suppose a set of node indices $C = \{c_1, \ldots, c_M\} \subset [N]$ is chosen as controlled nodes, the controlling matrix is $B = [e_{c_1}, \ldots, e_{c_M}]$, and the cover $\mathcal{S}_C = \{S_{c_1}, \ldots, S_{c_M}\}$. Then, we can deduce that $G(A, B)$ is controllable iff the cover $\mathcal{S}_C$ is valid. Therefore the above polynomial reduction from the weighted minimum Set-cover problem to the MCC problem reveals the NP-hardness.

---

[1] Different elements in $\mathcal{S}$ may coincide.

Theorem 1. *The minimum control cost (MCC) problem is NP-hard.*

4.2   Lower and Upper Bounds

When one controller only controls one node, the columns of B are restricted to unit vectors e_k, and the MCC problem is equivalent to the minimum number of controller problem where all nodes have uniform weights (such as $w_i = 1$ for node $v_i \in V$). For a controllable network $G(A, B)$, the PBH rank condition should be satisfied. Note that $r(A - \lambda_i I) = n - \mu_i$, and thus we need to pick an optimal set C such that $e_k (k \in C)$ can compensate for the μ_i defective (missing) dimensions of the column space of $A - \lambda_i I$ for each λ_i.

Let $N_C = |C|$ denote the number of controlled nodes and $OPT = \sum_{j \in C} w(j)$ denote the minimum control cost. The cost of each node is in the range $[w_{min}, w_{\max}]$.

Theorem 2. $\max_i \mu_i \leq N_C \leq \sum_i \mu_i$ *and* $w_{min} \max_i \mu_i \leq OPT \leq w_{max} \sum_i \mu_i$.

Proof. (sketch) Note that for each λ_i there are μ_i defective dimensions $A - \lambda_i I$ to be covered by μ_i linearly independent column vectors of P^{-1}, so $N_C \geq \max_i \mu_i$. Since each chosen column covers at least one extra defective dimension (otherwise it can be removed from the optimal set), and so $N_C \leq \sum_i \mu_i$. Since $w_{min} N_C \leq OPT = \sum_{j \in C} w_j \leq w_{max} N_C$, we have $w_{min} \max_i \mu_i \leq OPT \leq w_{max} \sum_i \mu_i$.

5   Approximation Algorithms

We propose two approximation algorithms called the HR's Algorithm and the Headhunter's Algorithm. We introduce the intuitive ideas behind the names of the algorithms. Suppose a multinational company is recruiting a think tank to help the company adapt to various challenges. The column vectors in A represent the abilities of current employees. $A - \lambda_i I$ represents their abilities under challenges (there is one challenge for each eigenvalue). For each challenge, there are missing dimensions of abilities among the current employees. The column vectors in the matrix B represent the abilities of new employees in the think tank, restricted to unit vectors e_k; and there are various bases to measure the abilities. To meet the challenges, a minimum number of new employees talented at those missing dimensions is desirable, in order to satisfy the PBH rank condition $r(A - \lambda_i I, B) = N, \forall \lambda_i$.

The HR department of the company can recruit new employees without the help of the headhunter, who simply recruits enough people to overcome each challenge separately. However, the headhunter is able to measure the abilities of the candidates from multiple dimensions, and can recommend appropriate candidates who overcome multiple challenges.

5.1   The HR's Algorithm

We present the HR's algorithm in Algorithm 1. After computing all eigenvalues of A (Line 4), the algorithm generates corresponding controlled nodes for each eigenvalue as Lines 6–9. This process is similar as recruiting enough people to overcome each challenge (i.e. eigenvalue) without the help of headhunter.

Algorithm 1. The HR's Algorithm

1: **Input:** the coupling matrix A and the weight vector w;
2: **Output:** the set C of node indices, the control cost;
3: $C := \emptyset$;
4: Compute all the eigenvalues of A: $\{\lambda_1, \lambda_2, \cdots, \lambda_s\}$;
5: **while** $i \leq s$ **do**
6:     Compute matrix $D = \lambda_i I_N - A$;
7:     Use Gauss-Jordan elimination with partial pivoting to transform D into column canonical form and get a set of indexes of maximal linear independent rows with indices in $V = \{c_1, c_2, \cdots, c_r\}$;
8:     Compute the complement set V^* of V;
9:     $C := C \cup V^*$;
10: **end while**
11: cost := $\sum_{j \in C} w_j$.

Theorem 3. *Suppose B is formed by column vectors $e_k(k \in C)$ where C is given by the HR's Algorithm, then $G(A, B)$ is controllable.*

Proof. In each iteration, the unit vectors e_j for $j \in V^* \subset C$ are linearly independent of the columns of $\lambda_i I - A$, so the PBH rank condition is satisfied for λ_i. Therefore, the network is controllable.

We adopt Gauss-Jordan elimination(Line 7), of which the time complexity is $O(N^3)$, and so the time complexity of the HR's Algorithm is $O(N^4)$. The algorithm is straightforward but the approximation ratio can not be guaranteed.

5.2   The Headhunter's Algorithm

The headhunter is able to measure the abilities of the candidates in more convenient bases other than the natural basis as in the HR's algorithm. At the beginning, the headhunter performs a preparatory step, after which μ_i row vectors (representing the abilities of candidates with respect to those defective dimensions) are identified for each λ_i. We calculate the Jordan normal form $J = P^{-1}AP = \text{diag}(J_1, \ldots, J_s)$ where $J - \lambda_i I$ contains exactly μ_i empty rows (each being the last row of a Jordan block). The corresponding rows (with the same row indices) in P^{-1} are selected and stacked vertically to form the $N_1 \times N$ matrix Q. The headhunter selects columns in Q to "cover" the defective dimensions. The weight for the j-th column is the cost w_j of node v_j. The headhunter can use exponential-time search over all possible combinations of columns, and iterate on all possible value $K = \sum_{j \in C} w_j$ in the range $[w_{min} \max_i \mu_i, w_{max} N_1]$. Each inner verification only takes time $O(KN_1 \max_i \mu_i)$. Even with dynamic programming to reuse the column canonical forms, such exact algorithm is still not practical for real-world networks with hundreds of nodes.

Algorithm 2. The Headhunter's Algorithm

1: **Input:** the $N \times N$ coupling matrix A and the weight vector w;
2: **Output:** the set C of selected node indices, the control cost;
3: Initialize $C := \emptyset$;
4: Prepare the $N_1 \times N$ matrix Q, formed by rows $q_k^i (1 \le i \le s, 1 \le k \le \mu_i)$;
5: Let the round number $t = 0$.
6: **while** there are non-zero entries in any row vector q_k^i **do**
7:    $t := t + 1$.
8:    Calculate $ecc_j(t) := |\{i | \exists 1 \le k \le \mu_i, q_{k,j}^i \ne 0\}|$ for each column j.
9:    $j(t) := \operatorname{argmax}_{1 \le j \le n} \frac{ecc_j(t)}{w(j)}$;
10:    $C := C \cup \{j(t)\}$;
11:    **for** each covered eigenvalue λ_i by the column $j(t)$ **do**
12:      Perform the following Gaussian elimination to erase non-zero entries in the first covered row q_k^i such that $k = \min\{h | 1 \le h \le \mu_i, q_{h,j(t)}^i \ne 0\}$:
13:      **for** each j s.t. $q_{k,j}^i \ne 0$ **do**
14:         $q_{h,j}^i := q_{h,j}^i - \frac{q_{k,j}^i}{q_{k,j(t)}^i} q_{h,j(t)}^i$ for $1 \le h \le \mu_i$.
15:      **end for**
16:    **end for**
17: **end while**
18: $cost := \sum_{j \in C} w_j$.

To be efficient, the headhunter greedily selects the columns and we describe the algorithm in Algorithm 2. Define the effective covering count $ecc_j(t)$ as the number of dimensions newly covered if the j-th column of Q is selected at round t. In one round, an eigenvalue is covered at most once. If the newly selected columns are linearly dependent on previously selected columns within μ_i dimensions for λ_i, then λ_i is not covered at this round.

The headhunter prefers the greedy method that selects the controlled node with the lowest average cost $\frac{w_j}{ecc_j(t)}$ (for $ecc_j(t) > 0$) in each round. Assume the row vectors corresponding to λ_i in Q are $q_1^i, q_2^i, \ldots, q_{\mu_i}^i$ where $q_k^i = [q_{k,1}^i, q_{k,2}^i, \ldots, q_{k,N}^i]$. We show the correctness and time complexity as follows.

Theorem 4. *The time complexity of the Headhunter's Algorithm is $O(N^3)$.*

Proof. We show the sketch of the proof. Each λ_i can be covered μ_i times, and we perform at most $O(N\mu_i^2)$ operations for each λ_i. Therefore the time complexity is $O(N \sum_i \mu_i^2) = O(NN_1 \max_i \mu_i) = O(N^3)$.

Theorem 5. *The Headhunter's Algorithm has an approximation ratio of* $\log N$.

It follows a similar proof as that of the greedy algorithm for Minimum Set-cover problem. We omit the details. In fact, the approximation ratio is asymptotically optimal, by the inapproximability results of Set-cover Problem [4].

6   Evaluation

We evaluated the algorithms in terms of control cost with various weight settings, and obtained the computation time. We used a single machine equipped with an Intel i7 3.5Ghz CPU, 16G memory and 1T SSD. As shown in Table 1, we use 10 real datasets of various network types such as social networks and citation networks. We also generated datasets using the ErdosRènyi [5] (ER) model.

Table 1. Evaluation datasets

Dataset name	Nodes (N)	Edges	Weight
Prison inmate [13] (PI)	67	182	Unweighted
Organization Consulting [3] (OC)	46	879	Unweighted
Organization Freeman [6] (FM)	34	695	Unweighted
Florida Baydry [18] (FD)	128	2137	Weighted
Florida Baywet [18] (FW)	128	2106	Weighted
Mangrove [18] (MG)	97	1492	Weighted
Electronic circuits [14] (EC) - s208a	122	189	Unweighted
Electronic circuits [14] (EC) - s420a	252	399	Unweighted
Electronic circuits [14] (EC) - s838a	515	819	Unweighted
Co-authorships [15] (NS)	1461	2742	Weighted

6.1   Control Cost

For each algorithm, we compute control cost in three weight settings. In the first setting, we assume the weight of a node is $d+1$ (d is the out degree of the node); in the second setting, each node's weight is generated randomly ranging from 1 to 5; in the third setting, the weight of a node is equal to 1 (uniform).

Figure 2 shows the total control cost and the corresponding lower and upper bound in 10 real datasets when the node weights are $d+1$, random, and uniform. In Fig. 2(a) and (b), control costs by HR are much lower than the upper bound. On the other hand, Headhunter shows an optimized cost which is near the lower bound. In selecting nodes to control, HR finds a possible solution without considering the cost, while Headhunter puts the cost of controlling a node into consideration. When the node weights are uniform, the control cost is equal to the number of nodes that need to be controlled in the network; Fig. 2(c) shows that both HR and Headhunter achieve good results near the lower bound.

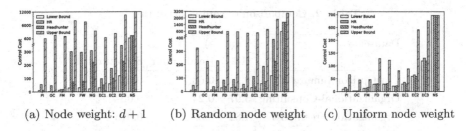

(a) Node weight: $d+1$ (b) Random node weight   (c) Uniform node weight

Fig. 2. Control cost of real networks with different node weights. The y axis is cut to show the upper bound. See Table 1 for the description of the datasets.

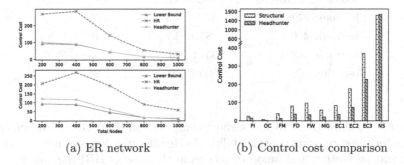

(a) ER network   (b) Control cost comparison

Fig. 3. (a) Control cost of ER network with random (upper) and $d+1$ (lower) node weights; (b) Control cost comparison of structural algorithm and Headhunter.

Figure 3(a) shows the control costs on the generated network by the ER model with random or $d+1$ as node weights. In the ER model, an edge between two nodes exists with the same probability p. We set $p = 0.005$ and generate a network with number of nodes ranging from 200 to 1000. Notice that the network is not restricted to be fully connected. As shown in the figure, Headhunter has found controlled nodes which is near optimal cost in each case. As the number of nodes increases, the generated network becomes much more connected; the number of nodes that need to be controlled as well as the corresponding costs decrease. Although structural controllability is a less constrained model, we compare the cost with structural controllability algorithm in [11]. As shown in Fig. 3(b), the control cost of structural controllability is much higher than Headhunter. This is because the structural controllability algorithm does not consider the cost of controlling each node, so a node with high control cost may be chosen even if there are other nodes with lower costs.

6.2 Computation Time

We also evaluated the total computation time for finding the valid set of controlled nodes and the corresponding control cost. The computation time is important as the network may be large and it can take infeasible amount of time to compute. Table 2 shows the comparison of the three algorithms including HR, Headhunter and Structural Controllability (structural).

Table 2. Comparison of computation time

Dataset	Time (s)		
	HR	Headhunter	Structural
Trust-prison inmate	9.2	0.63	0.03
Organizational-Consulting	5.97	0.24	0.02
Organization-Freeman-1	4.82	0.32	0.016
Foodweb-Florida Baydry	42.5	0.46	0.13
Foodweb-Florida Baywet	31.8	0.45	0.14
Foodwebmangrove66	15.2	0.32	0.12
Electronic-s208a	87.1	1.3	0.05
Electronic-420a	287.1	8.7	0.19
Electronic-s838a	5573	75	0.59
Co-authorships	505.1	49	2.28

The results show that HR has a short computation time while Headhunter is much faster to get to exact controllability. As Headhunter does not need excessive matrix transformation and union of sets as in the case of HR, the computation time is greatly reduced. Structural has a short computation time, but it cannot provide exact control when edge weights are given (Sect. 3). In contrast, HR and Headhunter guarantee exact controllability.

Evaluation results show that our algorithms can attain the set of controlled nodes with total control cost close to the theoretical lower bound, while the computation cost is reasonable.

7   Conclusion

In this paper, we formulate the minimum control cost (MCC) problem of weighted linear dynamic networks. We proved its NP-hardness by reducing the set-cover problem to its decision version and derived the lower/upper bounds. We present two approximation algorithms, of which the Headhunter's algorithm achieves $\log N$-approximation ratio with $O(N^3)$ time complexity. Our evaluation has shown that the proposed algorithms could find controlled nodes with control costs that are close to the lower bound.

References

1. Berger-Wolf, T.Y., Saia, J.: A framework for analysis of dynamic social networks. In: Proceedings of the 12th ACM SIGKDD International Conference on Knowledge Discovery and Data Mining. ACM (2006)
2. Chen, Y.Z., Wang, L.Z., Wang, W.X., Lai, Y.C.: Energy scaling and reduction in controlling complex networks. Roy. Soc. Open Sci. **3**, 160064 (2016)

3. Cross, R.L., Parker, A.: The Hidden Power of Social Networks: Understanding How Work Really Gets Done in Organizations. Harvard Business Review Press, Brighton (2004)
4. Dinur, I., Steurer, D.: Analytical approach to parallel repetition. In: the Forty-Sixth Annual ACM Symposium on Theory of Computing, pp. 624–633. ACM (2014)
5. Erdos, P., Rényi, A.: On the evolution of random graphs. Publ. Math. Inst. Hung. Acad. Sci. **5**, 17–61 (1960)
6. Freeman, S.C., Freeman, L.C.: The networkers network: a study of the impact of a new communications medium on sociometric structure. School of Social Sciences University of California (1979)
7. Hautus, M.L.J.: Controllability and observability conditions of linear autonomous systems, Nederl. Akad. Wetensch. Proc. Ser. A **72**, 443–448 (1969)
8. Hopcroft, J.E., Karp, R.M.: An $n^{5/2}$ algorithm for maximum matchings in bipartite graphs. SIAM J. Comput. **2**(4), 225–231 (1973). https://doi.org/10.1137/0202019. http://epubs.siam.org/doi/10.1137/0202019
9. Karp, R.M.: Reducibility among combinatorial problems. In: Miller, R.E., Thatcher, J.W., Bohlinger, J.D. (eds.) Complexity of Computer Computations. Springer, Boston (1972). https://doi.org/10.1007/978-1-4684-2001-2_9
10. Lancaster, P., Tismenesky, M.: The Theory of Matrices: With Applications. Elsevier, Amsterdam (1985)
11. Liu, Y.Y., Slotine, J.J., Barabási, A.L.: Controllability of complex networks. Nature **473**, 167 (2011)
12. Lombardi, A., Hörnquist, M.: Controllability analysis of networks. Phys. Rev. E **75**(5), 056110 (2007)
13. Milo, R., et al.: Superfamilies of evolved and designed networks. Science **303**, 1538–1542 (2004)
14. Milo, R., Shen-Orr, S., Itzkovitz, S., Kashtan, N., Chklovskii, D., Alon, U.: Network motifs: simple building blocks of complex networks. Science **298**, 824–827 (2002)
15. Newman, M.E.: Finding community structure in networks using the eigenvectors of matrices. Phys. Rev. E **74**, 036104 (2006)
16. Ni, C.C., Su, Z., Gao, J., Gu, X.D.: Capacitated kinetic clustering in mobile networks by optimal transportation theory. In: IEEE INFOCOM 2016 (2016)
17. Czeizler, E., Gratie, C., Chiu, W.K., Kanhaiya, K., Petre, I.: Target controllability of linear networks. In: Bartocci, E., Lio, P., Paoletti, N. (eds.) CMSB 2016. LNCS, vol. 9859, pp. 67–81. Springer, Cham (2016). https://doi.org/10.1007/978-3-319-45177-0_5
18. Ulanowicz, R.E., DeAngelis, D.L.: Network analysis of trophic dynamics in south Florida ecosystems. US Geol. Surv. Prog. South Florida Ecosyst. **114**, 45 (2005)
19. Wang, L.Z., Chen, Y.Z., Wang, W.X., Lai, Y.C.: Physical controllability of complex networks. Sci. Rep. **7**, 40198 (2017)
20. Wang, W.X., Ni, X., Lai, Y.C., Grebogi, C.: Optimizing controllability of complex networks by minimum structural perturbations. Phys. Rev. E **85**, 026115 (2012)
21. Wen, J.T., Arcak, M.: A unifying passivity framework for network flow control. In: INFOCOM 2003. IEEE (2003)
22. Yuan, Z., Zhao, C., Di, Z., Wang, W.X., Lai, Y.C.: Exact controllability of complex networks. Nat. Commun. **4**, 2447 (2013)
23. Yuan, Z., Zhao, C., Wang, W.X., Di, Z., Lai, Y.C.: Exact controllability of multiplex networks. New J. Phys. **16**, 103036 (2014)

Privacy Protection for Context-Aware Services: A Two-Layer Three-Party Game Model

Yan Huang$^{(\boxtimes)}$, Zhipeng Cai, and Anu G. Bourgeois

Georgia State University, Atlanta, GA 3030, USA
yhuang30@student.gsu.edu, {zcai,abourgeois}@gsu.edu

Abstract. In the era of context-aware services, users are enjoying remarkable services based on data collected from a multitude of users. However, in order to benefit from these services, users are enduring the risk of leaking private information. Game theory is a powerful method that is utilized to balance such tradeoff problems. The drawback is that most schemes consider the tradeoff problem from the aspect of the users, while the platform is the party that dominates the interaction in reality. There is also an oversight to formulate the interaction occurring between multiple users, as well as the mutual influence between any two parties involved, including the user, platform and adversary. In this paper, we propose a platform-centric two-layer three-party game model to protect the users' privacy and provide quality of service. One layer focuses on the interactions among the multiple asymmetric users and the second layer considers the influence between any two of the three parties (user, platform, and adversary). We prove that the Nash Equilibrium exists in the proposed game and find the optimal strategy for the platform to provide quality service, while protecting private data, along with interactions with the adversary. Using real datasets, we present simulations to validate our theoretical analysis.

1 Introduction

Due to the rapid development and popularity of context aware services, people's lives have become more comfortable and convenient than ever before. Applications include health care, smart grid, industrial services [48], social network platforms, and transportation, to name a few [5,7]. Smart transportation [6,15,32] provides drivers the optimal path based upon current traffic conditions, e-health [46] platforms are able to continuously monitor a patient's health status and facilitate communication with the healthcare specialist, and the smart grid [31] improves power management by monitoring usage patterns and balancing loads. Typically, it is only with the users' information that these context aware applications can provide and maintain any service and the quality of the service is often directly dependent upon the quantity and quality of collected data. As a result, users must consider the cost of leaking private information in order to benefit

© Springer Nature Switzerland AG 2019
E. S. Biagioni et al. (Eds.): WASA 2019, LNCS 11604, pp. 124–136, 2019.
https://doi.org/10.1007/978-3-030-23597-0_10

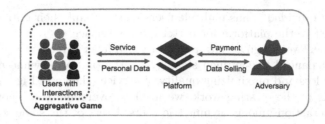

Fig. 1. Two-layer three-party game model

from such services. There is, of course, always a threat of private information being captured during data transmission. However, in recent years, private data leakage, as well as intentional data sale/reuse is more likely from the service provider platform [3,4,16,18,25,26,49]. In recent news we learned of Facebook improperly sharing data that impacted 87 million users [2] and Equifax [1] compromised private information of 143 million users. In spite of this, users still employ these applications, as the services are deemed essential to many people, thus positions the provider platforms in a dominant capacity [14].

This has led to considerable research on techniques to protect a user's private data from being leaked and/or sold. Most of the privacy protection algorithms, e.g. k-anonymity [40,41], l-diversity [30,33], t-closeness [22], and differential privacy [36,50], protect the data by adding noise, but this in turn will decrease the quality of the services provided. Therefore, several game theory based models have been proposed to balance the trade-off between service quality or reward and privacy protection.

Most of the game theory based research has a drawback, in that they only focus on the interaction between two parties, i.e. the user with an untrusted platform, or the user with an adversary (an entity trying to purchase or steal data) [13,27,28,44]. A more realistic model should consider the interactions of the three parties: the user, platform, and adversary. These two-party models ignore or fail to formulate the interaction between each pair of parties (3 such pairings). More recently, diverse three-party game models have been proposed to provide a more realistic interaction analysis [21,23,24,39,42,43]. Yet there is still a shortcoming, as they can only provide binary strategies, meaning the decision for users to submit or not submit their data. Instead, it would be beneficial to have a fine-grained strategy to provide a protection level ranging between 0–1, which is what we propose in this paper.

Another deficiency with the current n-player game models (those with n users) [13,28,29,44,45,47] is that they only consider the interaction between the users and other parties (either the platform or adversary). They fail to represent the interaction between asymmetric users, where users have individual privacy protection expectations. To demonstrate the impact, let us consider a transportation application. A user is able to get accurate traffic status without submitting any personal information to the platform, provided other users do submit their information. If multiple users stop submitting their information, the service quality will decrease, and if no users submit their information, minimal service can be provided. Thus multiple users must submit their data to provide enough context to the platform for better quality service.

In this paper, we design a platform centric two-layer three-party game model to provide a balanced fine-grained strategy for the platform, while minimizing users' privacy loss and maximizing quality of service (shown in Fig. 1). To avoid the drawbacks of the existing work, we need to overcome the following challenges: (i) Interaction among asymmetric users. Users of the same service have interactions and each user has a different privacy protection expectation. Thus, the interactions among the users increase the difficulty in addressing the users' strategy selection. (ii) Complicated game structure. Users' strategies are not only influenced by other users, but also by the platform's strategy, as well as the adversary's strategy. We formulate this by using two-layer game model – a game model among asymmetric users and a game model among users, platform and adversary. (iii) Theoretical analysis and solution. The complicated game structure and asymmetric users increases the difficulty to perform a theoretical analysis of Nash equilibrium and determining proper strategies for users and platforms.

The following methods are implemented to address the above challenges in this paper. Firstly, we utilize a quasi-aggregative game model to formulate the interactions between asymmetric users and utilize a contract model to formulate the interactions between the platform and adversary. Secondly, based on the proposed two-layer three-party game model, we analyze the Nash equilibrium to find the proper fine-grained strategies for all users and the platform. Finally, we perform simulations based on real datasets to validate the theoretical analysis.

To the best of our knowledge, we are the first to provide a privacy protection framework from the perspective of the platform, since the platform is in the dominate position, as described above. The main contributions of this paper are summarized as follows:

- A platform-centric two-layer three-party game model to capture the interactions among asymmetric users, and the interactions between users, the platform, and adversary. This will provide proper guidance for both the users and platforms.
- The theoretical Nash equilibrium analysis to find the proper fine-grained guidance for all the asymmetric users and the platform.
- Simulations with real datasets to validate the theoretical analysis and evaluate the performance of the proposed two-layer three-party game.

The rest of the paper is organized to introduce the system model in Sect. 3. We analyze the optimal strategies for asymmetric users and platforms in Sect. 4. Section 5 presents the simulations to validate the theoretical analysis and we conclude the paper and discuss future work in Sect. 6.

2   Preliminary

In this section, we present previous results that are fundamental to the work proposed in this paper. Let $\Gamma = (\tilde{\pi}_i, S_i)_{i \in \mathscr{I}}$ denotes a non-cooperative, pure strategy game with a finite set of players $\mathscr{I} = \{1, ..., I\}$, and finite dimensional strategy sets $S_i \subset R^N, s_i \in S_i$. The joint strategy set $S = \prod_{i \in \mathscr{I}} S_i$, is assumed to be a compact metric space, and payoff functions $\tilde{\pi}_i : S \to R, i \in \mathscr{I}$, are assumed to be upper semi-continuous. Then the Quasi-Aggregative Game can be defined as follows.

Definition 1 *(Quasi-Aggregative Game)* [17]. *The game* $\Gamma = (\tilde{\pi}_i, S_i)_{i \in \mathscr{I}}$ *is a quasi-aggregative game with aggregator* $g : S \to \mathbb{R}$, *if there exist continuous functions* $F_i : \mathbb{R} \times S_i \to \mathbb{R}$ *(the shift functions), and* $\sigma_i : S_{-i} \to X_{-i} \subset \mathbb{R}, i \in \mathscr{I}$ *(the interaction functions) such that each of the payoff functions* $i \in \mathscr{I}$ *can be written:* $\tilde{\pi}_i = \pi_i (\sigma_i (s_{-i}, s_i), s_i)$, *where* $\pi_i : X_{-i} \times S_i \to \mathbb{R}$, *and:* $g(s) = F_i (\sigma_i(s_{-i}), s_i)), \forall s \in S, i \in \mathscr{I}$. *Agent* i's *best-replies, depend on* $x_{-i} = \sigma_i(s_{-i})$, *is given by* $R_i(x_{-i}) = arg \max \pi_i(x_{-i}, s_i) : s_i \in S_i$.

Theorem 1. *The quasi-aggregative game has a pure strategy Nash equilibrium (PSNE) the following two assumptions holds* [17].

Assumption 1. *Each correspondence* $R_i : X_{-i} \to 2^{S_i}$ *is strictly decreasing.*

Assumption 2. *The shift-function* F_i, $i \in \mathscr{I}$, *all exhibit strictly increasing differences in* x_{-i} *and* s_i.

3   System Model

In this section, we formulate the interactions between asymmetric users, as well as the interactions among the three parties and introduce the proposed game model.

3.1   Users Model

Assume a set of users $N = \{1, 2, ..., n\}$ use a client of a platform to get context-based service. Each user $i \in N$ will submit a dataset $D_i = \{d_{i1}, d_{i2}, ..., d_{im}\}$ with m attributes to the platform. The client has a local privacy protection algorithm installed which satisfies strict privacy protection standards, such as Local Differential Privacy [36]. Thus, the platform can only get anonymized data or noise-added data from users.

Even if the client has a privacy protection algorithm installed, the anonymized data or noise-added data can still leak some information to the platform, the privacy leakage level depends on the privacy protection setting of the client. Without loss of generality, we define the privacy protection level of attribute j as $\delta_j \in [0, 1]$.

When $\delta_j = 1$, the platform cannot retrieve any information about users' attribute j. When $\delta_j = 0$, the platform can retrieve all the information about users' attribute j. To get statistical result from users, the platform has to set the same $\boldsymbol{\delta} = \{\delta_1, \delta_2, ..., \delta_m\}$ for all the users [9,11,20,38]. According to privacy protection laws, such as General Data Protection Regulation within the European Union and the European Economic Area, the platform should use strongest privacy protection strength in the client by default. Thus, the default setting of privacy protection level vector is $\delta = \{1, 1, ..., 1\}$.

However, by using the strongest privacy protection strength, the platform cannot collect usable information from users, resulting in worst service quality. Thus, to collect information from users, the platform has to offer a δ with lower privacy protection level.

Users have the right to accept or reject the platform's offer δ. We define user i's strategy for attribute j as $a_{ij} \in [0, 1]$, which defines the probability of user i accept the privacy leakage level δ_j. Therefore, the strategy vector of user i is $a_i = \{a_{i1}, a_{i2}, ..., a_{im}\}$ and the strategy vector of all users is $a = \{a_i, a_j, ..., a_n\}$.

The service quality depends on the users' strategy, and one user's strategy has a marginal impact on service quality. The service quality of user i received from the platform depends not only on its strategy a_i, but also on the strategy of other users a_{-i}. Formally, for a specific privacy protection level, the expected received service quality of user i is determined by the strategy of user i and other users' strategy, which can be defined as $Q_i(a_{-i}, a_i)$.

Meanwhile, the platform may resell users' data to a adversary resulting in privacy loss to the users. Assume each user has a constant privacy cost estimation vector $c_i = \{c_{i1}, c_{i2}, ..., c_{im}\}$, where c_{ij} defines the privacy cost of attribute j's privacy leakage. We can define the total cost estimation of user i as follows:

$$C_i^u(a_i) = \sum_{j=1}^{m} c_{ij} a_{ij} \left(s_j + (1 - \delta_j) \right), \tag{1}$$

where $s_j \leq \delta_j$ is privacy leakage level when the platform resells the users' dataset.

Thus, we can derive the expected utility function of user i as follows.

$$U_i^u(a_i, a_{-i}) = Q_i(a_{-i}, a_i) - C_i^u(a_i). \tag{2}$$

3.2   Platform Model

The quality of service depends upon the number of users that accept the privacy protection level of attributes. For this reason, the platform entices uses to accept the offer with higher privacy leakage level by providing more accurate service quality. We define $\sigma_j(a)$ as the expected number of users that accept the information leakage level δ_j for attribute j, and calculate $\sigma_j(a)$ as

$$\sigma_j(a) = \sum_{i=1}^{n} a_{ij}. \tag{3}$$

The value of δ_j reveals the privacy leakage of users' attribute j and also reveals the information that can be retrieved by the platform. According to the research of privacy protection algorithms [10, 11, 37], the service quality based on attribute j can be defined as a logarithmic function of privacy leakage level δ_j, and is affected by the number of users that accept the privacy leakage level δ_j as a law of diminishing marginal utility. Therefore, we can derive that the service quality depends on a single attribute j as $log((1-\delta_j)+1)\sigma_j^b(\boldsymbol{a})$, where $0 < b < 1$ is the parameter revealing the impact of $\sigma_j^b(\boldsymbol{a})$. The value of b is decided by the local privacy protection algorithm.

Meanwhile, attribute i and attribute j may have a correlation. Thus, the information of attribute i not only contributes to the service which is based on attribute i but also contributes to the service which is based on attribute j, if there is a correlation between attribute i and j. We define the correlation between attribute i and attribute j as e_{ij}. Therefore, the information of attribute i also contributes to the expected service quality which is based on attribute j with the correlation coefficient e_{ij}. Accordingly, we can define the total expected service quality Q as

$$Q(\boldsymbol{\delta}, \boldsymbol{a}) = \sum_{j=1}^{m} \left(1 + \sum_{k=1, k\neq j}^{m} e_{jk} \right) log((1-\delta_j)+1)\sigma_j^b(\boldsymbol{a}). \tag{4}$$

The collected dataset from users can generate income for the platform. The expected income form data is also affected by the privacy leakage level $\boldsymbol{\delta}$ and the number of users who accept the platform's offer. According to data aggregation research [19] and the standard form of Cobb-Douglas production function [34], the expected data value to the platform can be defined as

$$V^p(\boldsymbol{\delta}, \boldsymbol{a}) = \alpha \sum_{j=1}^{m} (1-\delta)_j^{\zeta} \sigma_j^b(\boldsymbol{a}), \tag{5}$$

where α is the total value productivity of the platform, and $\zeta \in (0,1)$ is the platform's value output elasticities of each attribute.

To get extra profit, the platform could sell the collected data to an adversary. The platform may choose a different privacy leakage level vector $\boldsymbol{s} = \{s_1, s_2, ..., s_m\}$ for the resale dataset. And for each unit of privacy leakage level of attribute j, the platform asks for a price p_j for each user's data. The price vector of the dataset is defined as $\boldsymbol{p} = \{p_1, p_2, ...p_m\}$, which is determined in a contract with the adversary. Thus, the total expected price is defined as

$$P(\boldsymbol{s}, \boldsymbol{p}, \boldsymbol{a}) = \sum_{j=1}^{m} p_j s_j \sigma_j^b(\boldsymbol{a}). \tag{6}$$

However, the data resale incurs a cost due to reputation loss to the platform. If we define r_j is the unit cost for reselling one user's attribute j with privacy leakage level s_j, we can derive the expected cost due to reputation loss as

$$\sum_{j=1}^{m} r_j s_j \sigma_j^b(\boldsymbol{a}). \tag{7}$$

Meanwhile, the platform has a constant running cost c_p. Thus, the total expected cost of the platform is $C^p(\boldsymbol{s}, \boldsymbol{a}) = \sum_{j=1}^{m} r_j s_j \sigma_j^b(\boldsymbol{a}) + c_p$.

To sum up, the expected utility of the platform is $U^p(\boldsymbol{\delta}, \boldsymbol{s}, \boldsymbol{p}, \boldsymbol{a}) = V^p(\boldsymbol{\delta}, \boldsymbol{a}) + P(\boldsymbol{s}, \boldsymbol{p}, \boldsymbol{a}) - C^p(\boldsymbol{s}, \boldsymbol{a})$. The platform will maximize its utility by achieving a Nash Equilibrium with the users and adversary.

3.3   Adversary Model

To get users information, the third party can purchase data from the platform. By using purchased data, the adversary can generate value according to its type γ, where θ is its value productivity, and γ is its value output elasticities of each attribute. According to data aggregation research [19] and the standard form of Cobb-Douglas production function [34], the expected data value to the adversary can be defined as

$$V_t\left(\boldsymbol{s}, \boldsymbol{a}\right) = \theta \sum_{j=1}^{m} s_j^{\gamma} \sigma_j^b(\boldsymbol{a}). \tag{8}$$

Thus, the expected utility function of the third party is

$$U^t\left((\boldsymbol{p}(\gamma), \boldsymbol{s}), \boldsymbol{a}\right) = V_t\left(\boldsymbol{s}, \boldsymbol{a}\right) - P\left((\boldsymbol{p}(\gamma), \boldsymbol{s}), \boldsymbol{a}\right). \tag{9}$$

4   Game Model

In this section, we formulate the problem with a two-layer three-party game and analyze its Nash Equilibrium.

4.1   Aggregative Game Model

In this paper, we assume users do not exchange information with the other users. Each user's action influences the other users' utility. With a specific privacy leakage level $\boldsymbol{\delta}$, we can use quasi-aggregative game model to formulate the interactions among users.

To maximize utility, a user chooses a proper privacy leakage level for each attribute. According to [17], we define the interactions among users as m quasi-aggregative games, e.g., $\Gamma_j = (\tilde{\pi}_{ij}, A_i), \forall j = 1, 2, ...m$, where A_i is user i's strategy space. The payoff function of each player in this game can be defined as $\tilde{\pi}_{ij} = U_{ij}^u(\sigma_{ij}(\boldsymbol{a}_{-i}), a_{ij})$; the aggregator can be defined as $g_j(\boldsymbol{a}) = F_{ij}(\sigma_{ij}(\boldsymbol{a}_{-i}), a_{ij}) = \sigma_{ij}(\boldsymbol{a}_{-i}) + a_{ij}$; the interaction functions vector can be defined as $\sigma_{ij}(\boldsymbol{a}_{-i}) = \sum_{k \in N, k \neq i} a_{kj}$. User i in the game Γ_j aims to maximize its utility by properly choosing a strategy vector $\boldsymbol{a}_i$ such that $\boldsymbol{a}_i = \arg\max_{a_{ij}} U_i^u(\sigma_i(\boldsymbol{a}_{-i}), a_{ij})$.

According to the property of quasi-aggregative game theory [17], we can derive the following theorem.

Theorem 2. *The game $\Gamma_u = (\tilde{\pi}_i, A_i)_{i \in N}$ has a pure strategy Nash equilibrium (PSNE) for any privacy leakage level $\boldsymbol{\delta}$.*

Proof. When the integrated value σ_{-i} increases, user i can get increased payoff. Thus, user i can increase its payoff by decreasing the value of strategy s_i. As a result, the best-reply correspondence of user i is strictly decreasing. It is obviously that the shift function F_i (Sect. 4.1) exhibits strictly increasing differences in x_{-i} and s_i. According to [17], the theorem is proved.

4.2   Contract Model

The platform makes a contract with the adversary. Assume the adversary announces its type is γ, $\gamma \in (0,1)$. The platform provides a menu of contracts $\{(\boldsymbol{p}(\gamma), \boldsymbol{s})\}$ to the adversary. According to contract theory [35], to incentivize the adversary to accept the contract designated for him rather than choosing other contracts or refusing any contract, the menu of contracts should satisfy both the individual rationality condition and the incentive compatibility condition defined below.

Condition 1 *(Individual Rationality (IR)). A menu of contracts $\{(\boldsymbol{p}(\gamma), \boldsymbol{s})\}$ satisfies the individual rationality constraints if it yields to the adversary a non-negative payoff, i.e., $\forall \gamma \in (0,1)$, $U^t(\boldsymbol{p}(\gamma), \boldsymbol{s}) \geq 0$, where $U^t(\boldsymbol{p}(\gamma), \boldsymbol{s})$ is the utility of adversary with type γ.*

Condition 2 *(Incentive Compatibility (IC)). A menu of contracts $\{(\boldsymbol{p}(\gamma), \boldsymbol{\delta})\}$ satisfies the individual compatibility constraints if the best response for the adversary with type γ is to choose the contract $(\boldsymbol{p}(\gamma), \boldsymbol{s})$ rather than other contracts, i.e., $\forall \gamma, \hat{\gamma} \in (0,1)$, $U^t(\boldsymbol{p}(\gamma), \boldsymbol{\delta}) \geq U^t(\boldsymbol{p}(\hat{\gamma}), \boldsymbol{s})$.*

Therefore, the objective of the platform is to maximize its utility by properly creating a menu of contracts. We formalize the optimization problem of the platform as follows.

$$\max_{\{(\boldsymbol{p}(\gamma), \boldsymbol{s})\}} \quad U^p(\boldsymbol{\delta}, \boldsymbol{s}, \boldsymbol{p}(\gamma), \boldsymbol{a}),$$

subject to Condition 1 and 2.
$$\tag{10}$$

According to the aggregative model and contract model, we can see that the platform needs to properly choose the privacy leakage level $\boldsymbol{\delta}$ for all users and create the contract menu for the adversary to maximize its utility. Therefore, the Nash Equilibrium can be derived by solving the combined optimization problem:

$$\max_{(\boldsymbol{\delta}, \{(\boldsymbol{p}(\gamma), \boldsymbol{s})\})} \quad U^p(\boldsymbol{\delta}, \boldsymbol{s}, \boldsymbol{p}(\gamma), \boldsymbol{a}^*),$$

subject to Condition 1 and 2.
$$\tag{11}$$

where $\boldsymbol{a}^*$ is the PSNE of the aggregative game.

5   Simulation

In this section, we study the interactions in the proposed two-layer three-party game. In the simulation, we utilize a parallel machining learning algorithm termed Particle Swarm Optimization (PSO) [8] to find the optimal strategies for the user and the platform.

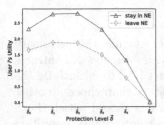 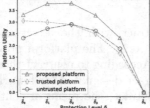 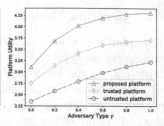

Fig. 2. User utility vs. protection level. (Color figure online)

Fig. 3. Platform utility vs. protection level. (Color figure online)

Fig. 4. Optimal strategy of user under various. (Color figure online)

5.1   Simulation Setting

We use real datasets as the inputs of the user and platform. More specifically, based on the Data Protection Survey published by SANA [12], we extract four protection levels for income, age, and race. As shown in Table 1, δ_1, δ_2, δ_3, and δ_4, are the protection levels used by Retail platforms, Healthcare platforms, Government platforms, and Financial platforms, respectively.

Table 1. Extracted strategies

Application	{Income, Age, Race}
Retail	$\delta_1 = \{0.2, 0.3, 0.4\}$
Healthcare	$\delta_2 = \{0.3, 0.4, 0.5\}$
Government	$\delta_3 = \{0.4, 0.5, 0.7\}$
Financial	$\delta_4 = \{0.6, 0.7, 0.8\}$

We set the correlation coefficient between income and age as 0.1, the correlation coefficient between income and race as 0.01, and the correlation coefficient between age and race as 0. We also tried the other correlation coefficient values and find out that the correlation coefficient is not a key factor. The privacy costs of users have normal distribution with parameters: $\mu_{income} = 10, \mu_{age} = 6, \mu_{race} = 2$ and $\sigma^2 = 1$. The total value productivity of the platform is $\alpha = 6$ and the output elasticity is $\zeta = 0.6$. The total value productivity of the adversary is $\theta = 8$ and the output elasticity is $b = 0.6$. The reputation cost for the attributes are $r_{income} = 3$, $r_{age} = 2$, $r_{race} = 1$. We choose the best strategy from running the algorithm 100 times, where each run consists of 10,000 iterations.

5.2   Users Interaction

Figure 2 shows the utility of user i when it performs different actions under different privacy protection levels. The x axis is the protection level, where $\delta_0 =$

$\{0, 0, 0\}$ is the lowest protection level and $\delta_5 = \{1, 1, 1\}$ is the highest protection level. δ_1 to δ_4 are the increasing protection levels, as in Table 1. The solid red line in Fig. 2 shows the utility of user i when it stays in the Nash Equilibrium, and the dashed green line is when it leaves the Nash Equilibrium. As we can see, the user's utility increases at first and then decreases as the protection level increases. The reason for utility increasing, is that the rate of the user's privacy loss decreasing is larger than that of service quality decreasing. However, the user's utility decreases after the maximum point, because the rate of service quality decreasing is larger than that of privacy loss decreasing. User i has utility 0 with the strongest protection level δ_5 because the user cannot get any service quality and has no privacy loss. Figure 2 also shows us that the utility of user i when it stays in NE is higher than that when it leaves NE. This proves the existence of NE in the aggregative model and that users cannot get higher utility if they use non-NE strategies.

5.3   Platform Comparison

We compare the proposed platform with a trusted platform and an untrusted platform. We assume the trusted platform keeps users' data safe and will not trade the data, while the untrusted platform sells all its collected data.

As shown in Fig. 3, the utility of the proposed platform (solid red line) increases at first and then decreases as the protection level increases. The utility increases because the rate of payoff increasing is larger than that of reputation loss increasing and the utility decreases because the rate of payoff increasing is less than that of reputation loss increasing. This proves the NE existence of the two-layer three-party game because the platform cannot increase its utility by simply decreasing the privacy protection level.

Figures 3 and 4 compare the utility of three types of platforms with different protection levels and different adversary types, respectively. As shown in Fig. 3, the trusted platform has higher utility than the untrusted platform with protection level δ_0 to δ_1 because the trusted platform has no reputation loss and the selling profit of untrusted platform cannot make up its reputation loss. The untrusted platform has higher utility than the trusted platform with protection level δ_2 to δ_5 because the payment from selling data can dominate the reputation loss, thus has more profit than the trusted platform. This explains why the platforms usually sell users data in real life.

However, the platform does not need to sell all the users' data to maximize its utility. From Figs. 3 and 4, we can see that the proposed platform in this paper has the highest utility because it balances the tradeoff between payoff (from data collection and selling data) and reputation loss. It will choose a proper protection level and selling strategy to maximize its utility. Therefore, we can conclude that the proposed framework can provide balanced strategies for the platform. By using the proposed model, the platform will properly choose the data selling strategy, thus decreasing users' privacy loss.

6   Conclusion

The use of context-aware services are integrated into the majority of people's daily lives. By utilizing these services, one must provide certain private information in order to receive better outcomes. Users risk leaking private data, as service platforms are sometimes willing to sell this information to a third party, or adversary to gain more profit, thus resulting in conflicting goals.

This paper studies the interactions among the three parties by proposing a platform-centric two-layer three party game. In the proposed game model, we theoretically formulate the behaviors of each party and the interactions among the three parties by using an aggregate game model and contract model. We run simulations with real datasets to validate the effectiveness of the proposed game model. We show that the proposed model can provide the proper strategy for the platform to balance the payoff and reputation loss, thus increasing privacy protection of the users. This work will enable platforms, such as Facebook, to provide quality service and protection to its users, but also provide a means to profit from a balanced strategy. To further investigate more realistic privacy protection issues, this work will be extended to a model that considers the influence of temporal data. Therefore, the users and platform need to consider the privacy protection for not only the current status, but also previous and future conditions.

Acknowledgments. This work is partly supported by the National Science Foundation (NSF) under grant NOs. 1252292, 1741277, 1704287, and 1829674.

References

1. The Equifax data breach. https://www.ftc.gov/equifax-data-breach
2. Facebook security breach exposes accounts of 50 million users. https://www.nytimes.com/2018/09/28/technology/facebook-hack-data-breach.html. Accessed 28 Sept 2018
3. Cai, Z., He, Z.: Trading private range counting over big IoT data. In: The 39th IEEE International Conference on Distributed Computing Systems, July 2019
4. Cai, Z., He, Z., Guan, X., Li, Y.: Collective data-sanitization for preventing sensitive information inference attacks in social networks. IEEE Trans. Depend. Secure Comput. **15**(4), 577–590 (2018)
5. Cai, Z., Zheng, X.: A private and efficient mechanism for data uploading in smart cyber-physical systems. IEEE TNSE 1 (2018)
6. Cai, Z., Zheng, X., Yu, J.: A differential-private framework for urban traffic flows estimation via taxi companies. IEEE Trans. Ind. Inform. (2019)
7. Capurso, N., Mei, B., Song, T., Cheng, X., Yu, J.: A survey on key fields of context awareness for mobile devices. JNCA **118**, 44–60 (2018)
8. Clerc, M., Kennedy, J.: The particle swarm - explosion, stability, and convergence in a multidimensional complex space. IEEE TEC **6**(1), 58–73 (2002)
9. Cormode, G., Jha, S., Kulkarni, T., Li, N., Srivastava, D., Wang, T.: Privacy at scale: local differential privacy in practice. In: SIGMOD, pp. 1655–1658 (2018)
10. Dewri, R.: Local differential perturbations: location privacy under approximate knowledge attackers. IEEE TMC **12**(12), 2360–2372 (2013)

11. Erlingsson, U., Pihur, V., Korolova, A.: Rappor: Randomized aggregatable privacy-preserving ordinal response. In: CCS. ACM (2014)
12. Filkins, B.: Sensitive data at risk: the SANS 2017 data protection survey, September 2017
13. Freudiger, J., Manshaei, M.H., Hubaux, J.P., Parkes, D.C.: Non-cooperative location privacy. TDSC **10**(2), 84–98 (2013)
14. He, Z., Cai, Z., Yu, J.: Latent-data privacy preserving with customized data utility for social network data. IEEE Trans. Veh. Technol. **67**(1), 665–673 (2018)
15. Hu, Q., Wang, S., Hu, C., Huang, J., Li, W., Cheng, X.: Messages in a concealed bottle: achieving query content privacy with accurate location-based services. IEEE Trans. Veh. Technol. **67**(8), 7698–7711 (2018)
16. Huang, Y., Cai, Z., Bourgeois, A.G.: Search locations safely and accurately: a location privacy protection algorithm with accurate service. J. Netw. Comput. Appl. **103**, 146–156 (2018)
17. Jensen, M.K.: Aggregative games and best-reply potentials. Econ. Theory **43**(1), 45–66 (2010)
18. Jia, Y., Chen, Y., Dong, X., Saxena, P., Mao, J., Liang, Z.: Man-in-the-browser-cache: persisting https attacks via browser cache poisoning. Comput. Secur. **55**, 62–80 (2015)
19. Jugel, U., Jerzak, Z., Hackenbroich, G., Markl, V.: M4: a visualization-oriented time series data aggregation. VLDB **7**(10), 797–808 (2014)
20. Kairouz, P., Oh, S., Viswanath, P.: Extremal mechanisms for local differential privacy. In: Advances in Neural Information Processing Systems, vol. 27, pp. 2879–2887. Curran Associates, Inc., Red Hook (2014)
21. Karimi Adl, R., Askari, M., Barker, K., Safavi-Naini, R.: Privacy consensus in anonymization systems via game theory. In: Cuppens-Boulahia, N., Cuppens, F., Garcia-Alfaro, J. (eds.) DBSec 2012. LNCS, vol. 7371, pp. 74–89. Springer, Heidelberg (2012). https://doi.org/10.1007/978-3-642-31540-4_6
22. Li, N., Li, T., Venkatasubramanian, S.: t-closeness: Privacy beyond k-anonymity and l-diversity. In: ICDE, pp. 106–115, April 2007
23. Li, W., Song, T., Li, Y., Ma, L., Yu, J., Cheng, X.: A hierarchical game framework for data privacy preservation in context-aware IoT applications. In: 2017 IEEE Symposium on Privacy-Aware Computing (PAC), pp. 176–177, August 2017
24. Li, W., Hu, C., Song, T., Yu, J., Xing, X., Cai, Z.: Preserving data privacy in context-aware applications through hierarchical game. In: SPAC, Washington DC, USA, September 2018
25. Liang, Y., Cai, Z., Han, Q., Li, Y.: Location privacy leakage through sensory data. Secur. Commun. Netw. **2017** (2017)
26. Liang, Y., Cai, Z., Yu, J., Han, Q., Li, Y.: Deep learning based inference of private information using embedded sensors in smart devices. IEEE Netw. **32**(4), 8–14 (2018)
27. Liu, C., Wang, S., Ma, L., Cheng, X., Bie, R., Yu, J.: Mechanism design games for thwarting malicious behavior in crowdsourcing applications. In: IEEE INFOCOM 2017 - IEEE Conference on Computer Communications, pp. 1–9, May 2017
28. Liu, X., Liu, K., Guo, L., Li, X., Fang, Y.: A game-theoretic approach for achieving k-anonymity in location based services. In: IEEE INFOCOM, April 2013
29. Ma, R., Xiong, J., Lin, M., Yao, Z., Lin, H., Ye, A.: Privacy protection-oriented mobile crowdsensing analysis based on game theory. In: IEEE TBDI, pp. 990–995, August 2017
30. Machanavajjhala, A., Venkitasubramaniam, M., Kifer, D., Gehrke, J.: l-diversity: Privacy beyond k-anonymity. In: ICDE, p. 24, April 2006

31. Maharjan, S., Zhu, Q., Zhang, Y., Gjessing, S., Basar, T.: Dependable demand response management in the smart grid: a stackelberg game approach. IEEE TSG **4**(1), 120–132 (2013)
32. Mahrsi, M.K.E., Côme, E., Oukhellou, L., Verleysen, M.: Clustering smart card data for urban mobility analysis. IEEE TITSyst. **18**(3), 712–728 (2017)
33. Mao, J., Tian, W., Jiang, J., He, Z., Zhou, Z., Liu, J.: Understanding structure-based social network de-anonymization techniques via empirical analysis. EURASIP JWCN **2018**(1), 279 (2018)
34. Meeusen, W., van Den Broeck, J.: Efficiency estimation from Cobb-Douglas production functions with composed error. Int. Econ. Rev. **18**(2), 435–444 (1977)
35. Miltiadis, M.: The theory of incentives: the principal-agent model. Econ. J. **113**(488), F394–F395 (2001)
36. Pastore, A., Gastpar, M.: Locally differentially-private distribution estimation. In: IEEE ISIT, pp. 2694–2698, July 2016
37. Qin, Z., Yang, Y., Yu, T., Khalil, I., Xiao, X., Ren, K.: Heavy hitter estimation over set-valued data with local differential privacy. In: CCS. ACM (2016)
38. Thakurta, A.G., et al.: Emoji frequency detection and deep link frequency (2017)
39. Vakilinia, I., Tosh, D.K., Sengupta, S.: 3-way game model for privacy-preserving cybersecurity information exchange framework. In: MILCOM, October 2017
40. Wang, J., Cai, Z., Li, Y., Yang, D., Li, J., Gao, H.: Protecting query privacy with differentially private k-anonymity in location-based services. Pers. Ubiquitous Comput. **22**, 453–469 (2018)
41. Wang, S., Hu, Q., Sun, Y., Huang, J.: Privacy preservation in location-based services. IEEE Commun. Mag. **56**(3), 134–140 (2018)
42. Wang, S., Huang, J., Li, L., Ma, L., Cheng, X.: Quantum game analysis of privacy-leakage for application ecosystems. In: MobiHoc, July 2017
43. Wang, S., Li, L., Sun, W., Guo, J., Bie, R., Lin, K.: Context sensing system analysis for privacy preservation based on game theory. Sensors **17**(2), 339 (2017)
44. Wu, X., Dou, W., Ni, Q.: Game theory based privacy preserving analysis in correlated data publication. In: ACSW, February 2017
45. Xu, L., Jiang, C., Qian, Y., Li, J., Zhao, Y., Ren, Y.: Privacy-accuracy trade-off in differentially-private distributed classification: a game theoretical approach. IEEE TBD 1 (2017)
46. Yi, C., Cai, J.: A priority-aware truthful mechanism for supporting multi-class delay-sensitive medical packet transmissions in e-Health networks. IEEE TMC **16**(9), 2422–2435 (2017)
47. Ying, B., Nayak, A.: Location privacy-protection based on p-destination in mobile social networks: a game theory analysis. In: IEEE CDSC, pp. 243–250, August 2017
48. Zheng, X., Cai, Z., Li, J., Gao, H.: Location-privacy-aware review publication mechanism for local business service systems. In: IEEE INFOCOM, pp. 1–9, May 2017
49. Zheng, X., Cai, Z., Li, Y.: Data linkage in smart internet of things systems: a consideration from a privacy perspective. IEEE Commun. Mag. **56**(9), 55–61 (2018)
50. Zheng, X., Cai, Z., Yu, J., Wang, C., Li, Y.: Follow but no track: privacy preserved profile publishing in cyber-physical social systems. IEEE Internet Things J. **4**(6), 1868–1878 (2017)

Who Leaks My Privacy: Towards Automatic and Association Detection with GDPR Compliance

Qiwei Jia, Lu Zhou, Huaxin Li, Ruoxu Yang, Suguo Du, and Haojin Zhu[✉]

Shanghai Jiao Tong University, Shanghai, China
{jiaqiwei,zl19920928,lihuaxin003,yangruoxu,sgdu,zhu-hj}@sjtu.edu.cn

Abstract. The APPs running on smart devices have greatly enriched people's lives. However, they are collecting personally identifiable information (PII) secretly. The unrestricted collection, processing and unsafe transmission of PII will result in the disclosure of privacy, which cause losses to users. With the advent of laws and regulations about data privacy such as GDPR, the major APP vendors have become more and more cautious about collecting PII. However, the researches on detecting privacy leakage under GDPR framework still receive less attention. In this paper, we analyze the clauses of GDPR about privacy processing and propose a method for PII leakage detection based on Association Mining. This method assists us to find many hidden privacy leakages in traffic data. Moreover, we design and implement an automated system to detect whether the traffic data sent by the APPs reveals users' PII. We have tested 509 APPs of different categories in the Google Play Store. The result shows that 76.23% of the APPs would collect and transmit PII insecurely and 34.06% of them would send PII to third parties.

Keywords: GDPR · Privacy leakage · Association mining

1 Introduction

The widespread use of smart devices has led to the development of various APPs. While providing users with services, these APPs also collect users' personally identifiable information (PII) [1,4]. Researches show that the proportion of APPs leaking personal data has increased exponentially in recent years, and significant numbers of APPs leak personal data to third-parties [5,15].

In order to regulate the data collection, transmission and processing behavior of operators, many countries have enacted different laws and regulations, such as EU General Data Protection Regulation (GDPR), American California Consumer Privacy Act (CCPA) of 2018, and People's Republic of China Network Security Law. Among these laws and regulations, GDPR is considered as the most important change in data privacy regulation in 20 years [13,22].

The GDPR reshapes the way in which data is collected, transmitted and processed. Compared with previous laws, it expands the material and territorial

© Springer Nature Switzerland AG 2019
E. S. Biagioni et al. (Eds.): WASA 2019, LNCS 11604, pp. 137–148, 2019.
https://doi.org/10.1007/978-3-030-23597-0_11

scope of protection, and is known as the most advanced and strict law on data protection and privacy. With the implementation of the GDPR, it is necessary to recheck the privacy leakage problem in APPs.

Existing detection methods for APP privacy leakage include the following two aspects: analyzing APPs and detecting traffic data. Analyzing APPs by static or dynamic methods often results in high false positives, and it is difficult to form an automated system [1, 4–8, 14, 21]. Detecting traffic data are mainly based on string search and regular matching. Although precise PII strings can be detected, there are still many potential privacy leakages if the APP developers deliberately modify the keywords in the traffic data to evade detection [2, 3, 9–12, 20].

In order to mine hidden information which cannot be shown by simple string search and regular matching, we propose a novel detection method, association mining based on the iterative key-value pair matching, to detect the APP privacy leakage under the GDPR environment. The main idea of this method is that personal data such as personal identifier, device identifier and location information on a single terminal will not be changed in an experimental environment. Therefore, the associations between keys and values can be used to mine more indirect associations among different keys and discover the hidden information.

The contributions of this paper are summarized as below:

- We analyze the GDPR clauses regarding the data collection, transmission, and processing, and find out the differences from other privacy laws.
- We propose a novel detection method, association mining based on the iterative key-value pair matching, to explore the potential privacy leakage issues hidden in traffic.
- We implement a privacy leakage detection system based on association mining and detect the top 509 Android APPs in Google Play Store. The result shows that 76.23% of the APPs are collecting and transmitting privacy data insecurely, and 34.06% will send PII to third parties at least once;

The rest of the paper is organized as follows. Section 2 lists related works about privacy leakage detection. Section 3 gives the interpretation of GDPR and puts forward the subjects of study. Section 4 introduces the methodology. Section 5 gives the design and implementation of the privacy leakage detection system. Section 6 evaluates the APPs in Google Play by our system. Section 7 concludes the paper.

2   Related Work

2.1   The Analysis of APP Programs

As is mentioned above, the static analysis is a method of analyzing the program file without executing it. The most popular static analysis techniques include dataflow analysis, symbol execution and so on. Using static analysis methods, we can reach each accessible branch of the program and track the data flow.

However, in actual works, many branches in a program are actually unreachable, which may cause false positives, and the dataflow-tracking may cause path explosion, which will increase the number of calculations exponentially [1, 4–6].

Dynamic analysis means to analyze an APP when it is running on a real or virtual device. During the process of analyzing, the analyst may use hook functions and debug tools to observe APP behaviors and data transmissions. Sometimes, the analysts should modify or customize the systems, and a large number of operations rely on manual works. Therefore, it is difficult to develop an automated detection system, and the efficiency is relatively low [7, 8].

2.2 The Analysis of Traffic Data

The existing researches include TaintDroid developed by Enck et al. [8], which provides real-time privacy analysis using Android's virtualized execution environment. Ren et al. implemented a cross-platform privacy leakage detection system Recon, and it shows privacy leakage during APPs running in a visual way [3]. Reyes et al. tested 5,855 children's apps on Google Play and found that 73% of them transmit sensitive data over the Internet [2]. The above works have promoted the development of privacy leakage detection on a single terminal. However, after analyzing plenty of traffic packages, we found that many of them contain hidden privacy leakages, especially customized or ambiguous keywords that can not be detected by previous methods.

2.3 The Analysis Based on the GDPR

Some articles combined with the GDPR to detect privacy leakages mainly have two ideas: one is to define the scope of the privacy according to the GDPR, then apply machine learning, string search and other methods to detect privacy leakages during the execution of the APPs. For example, Tesfay et al. subdivided Privacy Sensitive Information (PSI) into 13 types, then use machine learning to classify the unstructured texts from Twitter, and analyze whether they contain PSI or not [17]; the other idea is to check the APPs' compliance with a certain clause of the GDPR. Ferrara et al. designed a method of taint analysis to merge all sources of sensitive data, then reconstruct the data flow, and finally generate a report of the GDPR analysis [18]. Kammüller took advantage of the Attack Trees to verify GDPR compliance and illustrated on the example of a healthcare IoT [19]. The two ideas do not actually interpret the GDPR, or just make a static detection which has the problem of path explosion.

3 GDPR and Privacy Leakage Detection

The General Data Protection Regulation (GDPR) [22], passed by the European Union in April 2016 and came into effect on May 2018, is a regulation with the aim of strengthening personal data and privacy protection for residents of the EU. With the implementation of GDPR, many APP vendors have adjusted their privacy policies and become more cautious in collecting and processing privacy.

3.1 Scope and Definition

Chapter 1 Article 3 of GDPR stipulates the territorial scope, it applies to the personal data controllers and processors in the EU, wherever they work. APPs storing or processing personal data of the EU citizens, regardless of whether they have businesses in the EU, must meet with the GDPR [22].

Chapter 1 Article 4 of GDPR defines several keywords. 'Personal data' includes the name, identification number, address, an online or social identifier of a natural person. By processing 'personal data', the individual's performance, economic status, health, personal preferences, interests, reliability, behavior, location or whereabouts, etc., collectively called 'profiling', can be evaluated. In mobile, 'personal data' usually includes the following parts:

- Personal identifier (PI): name, gender, date of birth, email address, etc.
- Device identifier (DI): network, hardware information, phone number, etc.
- Location information: longitude, latitude, base station information, etc.

3.2 Data Collection and Secure Transmission

Chapter 2 Article 6 of GDPR states that the legality of processing, including collection, storage, modification, transmission, etc., must first satisfy the condition that 'the data subject has given consent'. When installed or running, the APP may apply for many unnecessary permissions and collect irrelevant users' personal data, which violates the GDPR.

In terms of data transmission, Chapter 4 Article 32 stipulates that measures such as anonymization and encryption should be adopted to ensure security when processing personal data. If the APP transmits personal data using plain text or a simple encryption algorithm, users' information would be easily stolen.

3.3 Third-Party Privacy Disclosure

It is clarified in Article 13 of Chapter 3 that 'when collecting personal data, the APP should provide with the identity details of the data controller, and the purposes as well as the legal basis for the processing, and the recipients of the personal data'. APPs may send data to third parties for reasons such as remote calls, information collection, etc., and this further increases the risk of privacy disclosure. From the terms of the GDPR, the behavior that APPs transmit personal data to third parties without users' explicit knowledge, violates the regulations of the GDPR.

4 Methodology

4.1 Data Extraction

In mobile, most of the APPs transmit data through the HTTP/HTTPS protocol. The substance of privacy leakage detection is analyzing specific HTTP/HTTPS packages in the network. Figure 1 shows a typical HTTPS request package. Three sections in request packages, i.e., (a) the request line, (b) the Referer header field and Cookie header field, and (c) the request data, may contain a large amount of valid personal information, as they are used as the carriers of request parameters or APP data.

(a) POST https://lf.xxxxxx.com/pgc/ma/
    ?cityid=361&tengxun_new&aid=1&max_behot_time= HTTP/1.1
    Host: lf.xxxxxx.com
    Connection: keep-alive
    Accept: application/json, text/javascript
    User-Agent: Mozilla/5.0 (Linux; Android 4.4.2; MI 6 Build/NMF26X)

(b) Referer: https://lf.xxxxxx.com/user/profile/native_index/
    ?user_id=2935892161&is_following=0

(c) data=%7B%22bssid=28%3AC2%3ADD%3A4D%3AFC%3AA9%2C%22location%22%3Atrue%2C
    %22phone%22%3Atrue%2C%22storage%22%3Atrue%7D%2C%22night_mode%22%3A%2C%2
    2apn_notify%22%3A1%2C%22switch_domain%22%3A0%2C%22video_nowifi_notice_m
    ode%22%3A0%2C%22refresh_mode%22%3A0%2C%22comment_mode%22%3A0

Fig. 1. Example of HTTPS packages.

The contents of the Referer header field and the request header both consist of a domain name and several parameters. The format of parameters is key-value pairs like 'key1=value1&key2=value2&key3=value3&...', where the equal sign (=) is an assignment character, and the ampersand (&) is a connector. The key is a name defined by developers, while the value is its corresponding content. In most cases, the actual meaning of the key value can be inferred by the name.

The cookie field and request data contain the cache information and form information sent by the APP. Although having no fixed assignment characters and connectors, they usually appear as key-value pairs. Valid key-value pairs can also be extracted as long as the assignment characters and connectors are effectively recognized.

4.2   Association Mining

In general, a key can express its actual meaning, so analysts can examine whether the key carries personal data or not [10]. However, after analyzing a large amount of traffic data, we find that it is impossible to filter all the packages containing personal data through common keys. In some cases, the developer deliberately modifies the key in order to evade the detection. Thus, simple common keys matching cannot accurately infer whether a package carries personal data. For example, the key-value pair 'bssid=28%3AC2%3ADD%3A4D%3AFC%3AA9' in Fig. 1 is actually the MAC address rather than a Basic Server Set id. In this case, such APPs can leak a large amount of privacy without being noticed.

To address this problem, we propose the key-value association mining. Its main idea is that: (a) pre-set a collection of keys as a key set; (b) collect and analyze traffic data for a large number of APPs on a single terminal, extract all key-value pairs; (c) for each key in key set, extract the associated values in all key-value pairs to expand the value set; (d) for each value in the value set, extract the associated keys in all key-value pairs, expand the key set and remove duplication; (e) repeat (c) (d) until the key set and the value set no longer grow, and the matching is completed.

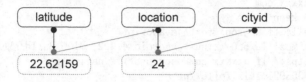

Fig. 2. The process of association.

The main assumption of this method is that personal data such as the personal identifier, device identifier and location information on a single terminal in a session will not be changed. So the associations between keys and values are used to discover more indirect associations among different keys, and thus enlarge the coverage of privacy leakage detection. As shown in Fig. 2, the key 'latitude' finally matches a key-value pair of 'cityid=24' which can not be easily found through common methods.

5   System Design and Implementation

We design and implement our system prototype on Android OS, which is running on more than 85% smart devices. We setup our detection system on Android Emulators to automatically examine APPs' privacy leakage. The detection system includes three modules: APP Crawler, Automation Platform, and PII Detector in Fig. 3.

5.1   APP Crawler

The APP Crawler is responsible for collecting APPs from APP stores (e.g., Google Play), and storing them by categories. Robustness and parallelism are considered when crawling, so techniques such as error handling and multi-threading are used in the implementation.

In our experiments, the Crawler starts with reading the APP category names and links on the main page of Google Play. Then for each category, it goes to sub-pages and downloads the top 20 APPs of each category. The automation was implemented by the Beautiful Soup library[1] in Python. In the end, we have downloaded 509 APPs of 27 categories from Google Play and saved them with their package names.

---

[1] https://www.crummy.com/software/BeautifulSoup/.

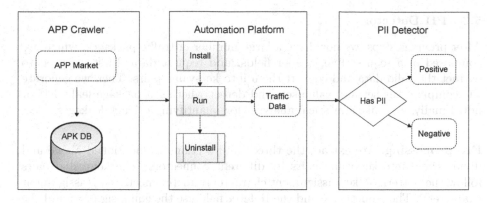

Fig. 3. Privacy leakage detection system.

5.2 Automation Platform

The Automation Platform is responsible for installing, running and uninstalling the APPs. It would manipulate user interface for 15 min, capturing and saving the traffic data. The platform must ensure that only one APP is running at a time in order to eliminate interference from the other APPs. APPs connect to the Internet through a Man-in-the-Middle (MIM) proxy, while the traffic capture tool working on the proxy collects traffic data for further analysis.

APPs Runtime Emulation. We use Yeshen Emulator[2] in our prototype. Yeshen Emulator is a popular Android emulator that can customize a virtual Device id, SIM number, IMEI, IMSI and other private parameters of Android OS. It can also set virtual GPS data. ADB (Android Debug Bridge) debugging tools are integrated into Yeshen Emulator and we use the ADB Monkey tool to send some pseudo-random user events (such as clicking, returning, back to the desktop, etc.) to emulate UI operations.

Traffic Data Capture. We capture traffic data by Fiddler2[3], which integrates the functions of MIM proxy, traffic interception, and HTTPS decryption. We only need to store the traffic data for the APPs being tested, so we want to discard the traffic data not generated from the emulator (e.g., traffic data from other hosts in LAN or physical machines) and traffic data generated by Android system APPs and pre-installed APPs in the emulator. So we set Fiddler2 to filter traffic packages in the network and only save packages by Yeshen Emulator. Then we run 'iptables firewall' through the ADB shell, set firewall rules to prevent the other APPs from connecting the Internet.

---

[2] https://www.yeshen.com.
[3] https://www.telerik.com/fiddler.

5.3   PII Detector

After previous steps, we now have a large number of traffic packages, which are composed of a request line, header fields, and request data. First we need to extract the valid data and convert them into key-value pairs. Then we generate the complete key set and value set, and detect whether a package leaks PII or not. Finally, we make statistical analyses for quantifying privacy leakages.

Pre-processing. We extract the three valid sections as mentioned above and divide them into key-value pairs by different connectors. The key-value pairs follow the pattern of 'key(assignment character)value(connector)key(assignment character)'. The request line and the Referer field use the equal sign (=) and the ampersand (&) as the assignment character and connector respectively, while the cookie field and request data have no fixed formats and characters. Some common characters we have seen are :=/ (assignment characters) and ,;&+— (connector). Therefore, we use a simple statistical method to solve the challenge, that is, counting the numbers of assignment characters or connectors respectively in the sections, and selecting the most ones.

Besides, there are many binary data and other invisible characters, as well as a lot of newline characters, brackets, quotation marks in a real traffic package. In addition, the generated key-value pairs contain many invalid data, such as random strings, domain names, etc. These data are filtered and removed in pre-processing as well.

Privacy Pairs Generation. We conduct association mining as described in Sect. 4.2 to generate more complete key set and value set and expand them until they cannot grow anymore. In order to avoid the explosion of associated keys/values that are added into the sets, we only expend frequent keys/values whose number of appearance is larger than a threshold (=3 in our experiment) in each round. This can avoid a large number of random keys/values that are not related to user privacy.

We set the initial key set with some common device identifier and location information keywords including 'phoneNumber', 'imei', 'imsi', 'androidid', 'mac', 'longitude', 'latitude'. At the end of the expansion, many other keys related to PII or sensitive data in the key set, such as 'system_info', 'deviceid', 'devicename', 'providceId', 'city_i', 'areaId', 'mypos', 'adCode', are found with our methods in the experiment. Some keys/values that are not related to privacy may be included. In this case, we filter and remove values which are obviously not related to user privacy.

In the end, we analyze the privacy leakage of APPs by the key set and value set. When the key and the value of a key-value pair are both in the set, the pair is evaluated as a privacy pair. A package which includes one or more privacy pair is classified as a privacy-sensitive one.

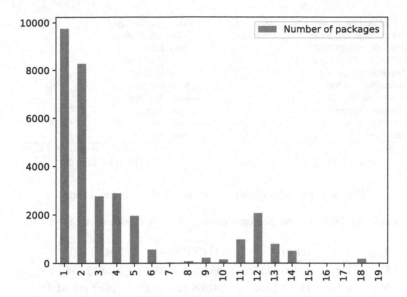

Fig. 4. The distribution of privacy-sensitive key-value pairs in packages.

6   Evaluation

In our experiments, we have crawled 509 APPs of 27 categories from Google Play, captured 169,326 packages, and extracted 629,217 valid key-value pairs. The overall analysis result shows that the privacy-sensitive key-value pairs have appeared in about 34.0% of all captured packages and on average each one carries 3.716 pieces of privacy, as shown in Fig. 4.

Unconsented Data Collection. For the analysis of APPs, we find that 388 out of the 509 APPs transmit personal data over the Internet, accounting for 76.23%. These personal data are captured and transmitted in our automated detection system without 'the data subject's consent', so the APPs do not conform to Chapter 2 Article 6 of GDPR. This proportion is higher than 61.9% or 63.3% by the other existing methods [6,16], which shows the effectiveness of our method. Among them, APP categories such as Jobs, Cars, Medical and News transmit more personal data, while Novel, Personalization, Audio and Entertainment APPs seem more secure, as shown in Fig. 5.

Unencrypted Personal Data Transmission. Device identifiers (e.g., android id, IMSI, etc.) are observed to be the most personal data collected by APPs. The APP vendors leverage them to identify devices and target ads to users. When transmitting personal data, more than 39% APPs use the unencrypted HTTP protocol, though decreased 9% in the past 2 years, which are considered insecure and violate Chapter 4 Article 32 of GDPR. The different personal data and their transmitting methods are shown in Table 1.

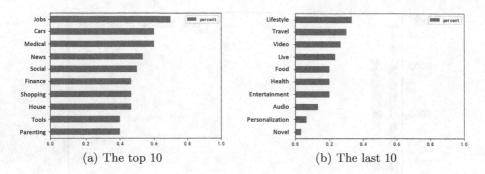

(a) The top 10   (b) The last 10

Fig. 5. Categories ranking in transmitting personal data.

Table 1. The different personal data and their transmitting methods.

Type	HTTP	HTTPS	Total
Device ID	50408 (23.56%)	65424 (30.38%)	115832 (54.14%)
Network Info	11534 (5.39%)	30268 (14.15%)	41802 (19.54%)
Location	21622 (10.11%)	34394 (16.08%)	56016 (26.18%)
Others	92 (0.04%)	192 (0.09%)	284 (0.13%)
Total	83656 (39.10%)	130278 (60.90%)	213934 (100%)

Third-party Data Disclosure. Sending personal data to a third-party without consent is likely to violate Article 13 of Chapter 3 of GDPR. We extract the SLD (second-level domain) from the Host header filed of a package, then judge whether the host is a third-party or not according to the attribution of SLD. We find that 173 of the 509 APPs have sent personal data to third-parties, accounting for 34.06%. The Keywords that are most concerned by third-parties are listed in Table 2.

Table 2. The Keywords that are most concerned by third-parties.

Keyword	Frequency	Keyword	Frequency
imei	19204	device_type	7891
device_id	11955	imsi	6266
os	10644	lat	6095
os_version	9176	lng	6063
uuid	8921	mac	5610

Power of Association Mining. After analyzing the key set and value set generated in our association mining, we find that many different keys have the same values, which are their actual meanings, as shown in Table 3. Analysts would miss a lot of privacy leakages if they only search for sensitive key names in network traffic.

Table 3. Actual meanings and related keys appeared in packages.

Actual meaning	Related keys
imsi	net_oper, sim_serial, iccid, AD9, deviceid
android_id	aid, deviceId, distinct_id, did, openudid, uuid
imei	uuid, deviceToken, deviceId, devkey, meid
mac	mac_address, device_id, bssid, m
longitude	lng, lng_pos, currentLng, x1
latitude	lat, lat_pos, mypos, y1, geoia, latlng, X1, Coordinate

7 Conclusion

While changing people's lives, the APPs running on smart devices are collecting our privacy. With the implementation of laws and regulations such as GDPR, this problem has not been greatly improved. Some APP developers are even deliberately concealing the transmission of users' PII in traffic data, and it is difficult to detect this case by previous methods. In this paper, we propose a privacy leakage detection method based on Association Mining, design and implement a detection system, then apply it to the APPs in Google Play Store, and the result is as we expected.

We should know that the key-value matching can extend the boundary of privacy leakage detection and reduce false negatives, but it also increases false positives to a certain extent. By filtering key set and value set we can slow down the occurrence of false positives, but it cannot be completely avoided.

In future research, Combining the static or dynamic detection method with the analysis of data flow to infer the actual meanings of keys, the effect may be further improved.

Acknowledgments. This work was supported in part by National Science Foundation of China under Grant 71671114 and Grant 61672350, and in part by the China Scholarship Council (201806230109).

References

1. Rui, H., Jin, Z., Wang, B.: Investigation of taint analysis for smartphone-implicit taint detection and privacy leakage detection. EURASIP J. Wirel. Commun. Netw. **2016**, 227 (2016)
2. Reyes, I., et al.: Won't somebody think of the children? Examining COPPA compliance at scale. PoPETs **2018**(3), 63–83 (2018)

3. Ren, J., Rao, A., Lindorfer, M., Legout, A., Choffnes, D.R.: ReCon: revealing and controlling PII leaks in mobile network traffic. In: MobiSys, pp. 361–374 (2016)
4. Zimmeck, S., et al.: Automated analysis of privacy requirements for mobile apps. In: NDSS 2017 (2017)
5. Nan, Y., Yang, Z., Wang, X., Zhang, Y., Zhu, D., Yang, M.: Finding clues for your secrets: semantics-driven, learning-based privacy discovery in mobile apps. In: NDSS 2018 (2018)
6. Li, L., et al.: IccTA: detecting inter-component privacy leaks in android apps. In: ICSE, no. 1, pp. 280–291 (2015)
7. Razaghpanah, A., et al.: Haystack. In Situ Mobile Traffic Analysis in User Space. CoRRabs/1510.01419 (2015)
8. Enck, W., et al.: TaintDroid: an information-flow tracking system for realtime privacy monitoring on smartphones. ACM Trans. Comput. Syst. **32**(2), 5:1–5:29 (2014)
9. Continella, A., et al.: Obfuscation-resilient privacy leak detection for mobile apps through differential analysis. In: NDSS 2017 (2017)
10. Liu, Y., Song, H.H., Bermudez, I., Mislove, A., Baldi, M., Tongaonkar, A.: Identifying personal information in internet traffic. In: COSN, pp. 59–70 (2015)
11. Xia, N., et al.: Mosaic: quantifying privacy leakage in mobile networks. In: SIGCOMM, pp. 279–290 (2013)
12. Xiang, C., Chen, Q., Xue, M., Zhu, H.: APPCLASSIFIER: automated app inference on encrypted traffic via meta data analysis. In: GLOBECOM, pp. 1–7 (2018)
13. Greengard, S.: Weighing the impact of GDPR. Commun. ACM **61**(11), 16–18 (2018)
14. Li, H., Zhu, H., Du, S., Liang, X., Shen, X.: Privacy leakage of location sharing in mobile social networks: attacks and defense. IEEE Trans. Dependable Sec. Comput. **15**(4), 646–660 (2018)
15. Li, H., Xu, Z., Zhu, H., Ma, D., Li, S., Xing, K.: Demographics inference through Wi-Fi network traffic analysis. In: INFOCOM, pp. 1–9 (2016)
16. Zhang, D., Guo, Y., Guo, D., Wang, R., Yu, G.: Contextual approach for identifying malicious inter-component privacy leaks in android apps. In: ISCC, pp. 228–235 (2017)
17. Tesfay, W.B., Hatamian, M., Serna, J., Rannenberg, K.: PrivacyBot: detecting privacy sensitive information in unstructured texts. In: ICICS 2018, p. 156 (2018)
18. Ferrara, P., Olivieri, L., Spoto, F.: Tailoring'taint analysis to GDPR. In: Medina, M., Mitrakas, A., Rannenberg, K., Schweighofer, E., Tsouroulas, N. (eds.) APF 2018. LNCS, vol. 11079, pp. 63–76. Springer, Cham (2018). https://doi.org/10.1007/978-3-030-02547-2_4
19. Kammüller, F.: Attack Trees in Isabelle. In: ICICS, pp. 611–628 (2018)
20. Li, H., Zhu, H., Ma, D.: Demographic information inference through meta-data analysis of Wi-Fi traffic. IEEE Trans. Mob. Comput. **17**(5), 1033–1047 (2018)
21. Zhou, L., Du, S., Zhu, H., Chen, C., Ota, K., Dong, M.: Location privacy in usage-based automotive insurance: attacks and countermeasures. IEEE Trans. Inf. Forensics Secur. **14**, 196–211 (2018)
22. General Data Protection Regulation (GDPR). https://gdpr-info.eu

Trustroam: A Novel Blockchain-Based Cross-Domain Authentication Scheme for Wi-Fi Access

Chunlei Li[1,2], Qian Wu[1,2], Hewu Li[1,2(✉)], and Jun Liu[1]

[1] Institute of Network Sciences and Cyberspace,
Tsinghua University, Beijing, China
lichunle16@mails.tsinghua.edu.cn, {wuqian,lihewu}@cernet.edu.cn,
juneliu@tsinghua.edu.cn
[2] Beijing National Research Center
for Information Science and Technology (BNRist), Beijing, China

Abstract. Cross-domain roaming in Wi-Fi networks is ubiquitous and the frequency of global roaming of users has increased dramatically in recent years. To ensure network security, it is important to authenticate users belonging to different domains. Existing solutions like eduroam leverage a centralized and hierarchical architecture to authenticate users, which leads to serious performance and security issues in practice. In this paper, we propose Trustroam, a novel cross-domain authentication scheme in Wi-Fi networks based on blockchain. Different from traditional hierarchical solutions, Trustroam authenticates users and servers in a distributed and anonymous manner, avoiding several serious problems such as single point of failure and privacy leakage. Through the distributed consensus mechanism and mutual authentication, our scheme is highly fault tolerant to handle compromised server attacks. We implemented the Trustroam prototype in a real testbed. Experimental and evaluation results show that our scheme is superior to existing hierarchical solutions in terms of scalability, security and privacy preserving. Besides, Trustroam is an effective solution that can be conveniently and incrementally deployed in practical environments.

Keywords: Cross-domain authentication · Eduroam · Consensus · Blockchain · Security

1 Introduction

There are massive requirements of Wi-Fi access every day in the world. In order to enhance the network security and management, users should be authenticated before connecting to the network. In Wi-Fi networks, it is a ubiquitous phenomenon that users roam between different access points (APs), institutions, regions and countries. According to [1], there are more than 500,000 international cross-domain access requests between academic institutions every day. A secure

E. S. Biagioni et al. (Eds.): WASA 2019, LNCS 11604, pp. 149–161, 2019.
https://doi.org/10.1007/978-3-030-23597-0_12

and scalable cross-domain authentication scheme is needed to coordinate the current roaming scenarios in the Wi-Fi network.

Eduroam [2] is a solution to this problem. It allows users to obtain Internet connectivity at visiting institutions with the personal credentials distributed by their home institutions. The visiting and home institutions establish trust between them through a hierarchical RADIUS [4] system. However, the normal operation of the entire system depends on the trust of a few nodes in such an architecture, which will lead to several problems. First of all, it introduces a single point of failure and the hierarchical trust fabric has caused great performance and operations bottlenecks on the aggregation proxies in practice [3]. Secondly, the central nodes of the hierarchy are vulnerable to varieties of attacks, which will seriously affect the security of system services. Finally, once the node of the hierarchical fabric is compromised or hacked, the privacy of users will be ruthlessly leaked.

Blockchain [6] technology has the features of decentralization, distributed consensus, and anonymity. In the blockchain network, a distributed ledger called blockchain is jointly maintained by all nodes, and revisions to the blockchain depend on the consensus of most nodes. The blockchain technology has been applied to many sectors in recent years. Some studies [7,8] have tried to use blockchain for authentication in wireless networks. However, merely using the blockchain as a database, these authentication methods are so rough and rudimentary that they have low fault tolerances and inadequate anonymity, which leads to security and privacy leakage problems.

In this paper, we propose a novel cross-domain authentication scheme in Wi-Fi networks based on blockchain. Different from traditional hierarchical solutions, we utilize blockchain to authenticate the users and the authentication server (AS) in a distributed way. Based on the distributed consensus mechanism, the normal operation of the authentication system is determined by the stability and trust of most nodes rather than a few central servers. Therefore, it has a strong fault tolerance.

The main contributions of this paper are:

- We propose Trustroam, a novel blockchain-based distributed authentication scheme for cross-domain roaming. It prevents the single point of failure and privacy leakage problems facing the hierarchical authentication architecture like eduroam.
- We design a mutual authentication protocol to verify both the users and the AS, which improves the reliability of the AS node and thus enhances the access security.
- We implement a prototype of Trustroam in a real testbed. The experimental results and comprehensive analysis show that our scheme is superior to existing hierarchical cross-domain roaming authentication solutions in terms of scalability, security and privacy preserving.

The rest of this paper is organized as follows. The related researches are shown in Sect. 2. The detailed design of Trustroam is described in Sect. 3. In

Sect. 4, we introduce our testbed implementation and evaluation of our scheme. In Sect. 5, we make a discussion and finally we draw a conclusion in Sect. 6.

2   Related Work

Eduroam [1] is a world-wide roaming access service for the international research and education community. Authentication in eduroam is achieved based on a hierarchical fabric which typically consists of three levels (organizational, national, and global) of RADIUS [4] servers. Before a user accesses the network service of the visiting institution, an authentication will be performed between the user and his or her home institution, during which the RADIUS hierarchy is responsible for routing and forwarding the authentication packets. However, this hierarchical architecture has led to great performance and operation problems on the aggregation proxies. Especially when a single point of failure happens, a large scale of service will be down or affected. What's worse, user's identity information may be leaked to other institutions due to the certificate forgery.

Researchers [3] presented a new trust fabric based on RADIUS/TLS [9] to enhance the security and reduce the routing complexity of eduroam. Authors in [5] made an investigation of identity theft vulnerabilities and MITM (Man in the Middle) attacks in eduroam and provided some countermeasures to resist these attacks. To overcome the shortcomings of unstable and slow user authentication, [10] proposed a disruption-tolerant authentication architecture to improve the performance and stability of eduroam. However, these enhanced solutions for eduroam cannot address the problems of single point of failures and internal compromised server attacks.

Blockchain has attracted widespread attention in recent years. [7] proposed an authentication method using bitcoin 2.0 to enhance the security in Wi-Fi access. Based on consortium blockchain, [8] proposed a cross-domain authentication scheme to authenticate users roaming among multiple areas in Vehicle-to-Grid networks of smart grid. However, these methods simply use blockchain as a database to store users' credentials, which is vulnerable to compromised server attacks and privacy leakage.

3   Proposal Design

In Wi-Fi networks, there are two typical roaming scenarios, intra-domain and inter-domain (cross-domain). In this paper, we are mainly focusing on the cross-domain roaming scenario, in which a user belonging to institution A roams to institution B and requests to access the Wi-Fi network service. To ensure network security, the institution B should verify the identity and validity of the access users. The notations are listed in Table 1.

Table 1. Notations and parameters of process and algorithm

Notation	Description
U	User
C_u, C_s	Challenge string generated by user and AS
SK_u, SK_s	Secret key of user and AS
$ADDR_u$, $ADDR_s$	Node address of user and AS
L_{TA}	List of trusted AS address
L_{RU}	List of registered user address
$H(\cdot)$, $Sig(\cdot)$	Hash and signature function
R	Result of authentication
TX_n	Transaction for triggering authentication

3.1 Trustroam Process

Different from the existing hierarchical solutions like eduroam, we leverage the distributed consensus mechanism of blockchain to verify the user and AS. The node address issued by the blockchain is used as the user's credential to be authenticated. Generally, the node address is derived from the public key of the user. With the appropriate encryption algorithm like ECDSA [14], we can recover the node address from the user's digital signature. In our proposal, both the user's device and the AS are the blockchain node, which means they have their own node address and secret key and they can generate and send transactions. So, the authentication for the user and AS can be performed by verifying appropriate digital signatures.

Users should first register in their home institutions with their identity information and node addresses. The node address used to identify a user across multiple domains will be stored in the blockchain at the registration step. Then, the home authentication server responses to the user with a list of trusted AS address (L_{TA}) which would be used to verify the visiting AS when the user roams to other institutions.

After the successful registration, users can access to the Wi-Fi networks of the participating institution (namely the institution that has deployed Trustroam) through authenticating their registered node address. Fig. 1 shows the process of authentication protocol of Trustroam.

(1) U requests to access the network service. Then the AS sends C_s to U.
(2) U generates C_u and signs C_s and C_u with SK_u. Then U sends $Sig(H(C_s,C_u))$, C_u and $ADDR_u$ to AS.
(3) AS generates TX_u and sends it to the blockchain network to authenticate U distributedly. After reaching a consensus, the blockchain network will notify AS of the result R. If success, AS accepts U, signs C_s, C_u and R with SK_s, and sends $Sig(H(C_s,C_u,R))$, R and $ADDR_s$ to U; otherwise, AS notifies U of the error type and detailed messages.

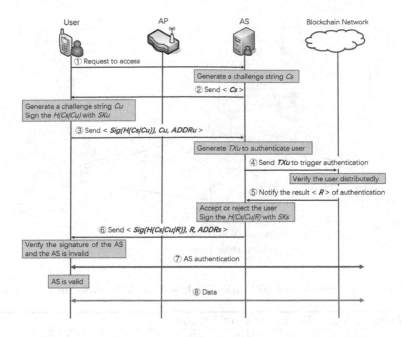

Fig. 1. Authentication protocol of Trustroam.

(4) U verifies the signature of AS and checks whether the $ADDR_s$ is in the local L_{TA}. If yes U notifies AS of the result; otherwise U requests to check whether AS is a new trusted AS or an invalid one. If it is a new trusted AS, then U updates the local L_{TA}; otherwise U can reject to access to the network.

The L_{TA} is designed for fast authentication of AS. It is maintained by the blockchain network and the user device and it can be updated according to the verification result of AS.

3.2 Distributed Consensus and Authentication

In order to reach a consensus among massive peer nodes, researchers have proposed many consensus mechanisms, such as Proof of Work (PoW) [11], Proof of Stake (PoS) [12], Delegate Proof of Stake (DPoS) [13] and so on. Based on these mechanisms, we propose to authenticate users through multiple AS nodes belonging to different participating institutions which join together to form a blockchain network. The authentication code is written in the blockchain in advance. A transaction that encapsulates the input parameters of the authentication function should be sent to trigger the execution of the authentication procedure which is also called smart contract [15].

As shown in Fig. 2, when a user sends his or her digital signature to AS for authentication mentioned above, the AS node will generate a transaction TX_u and broadcasts it to all the peer nodes. Each node receiving the transaction

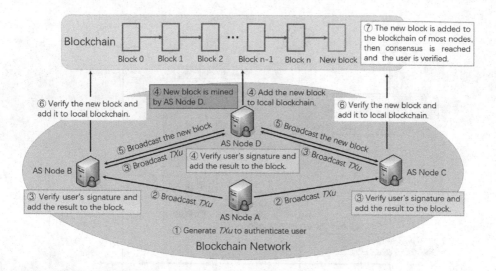

Fig. 2. Process of distributed authentication based on PoW consensus mechanism.

Algorithm 1. Algorithm for user verification

Input: $Sig(H(TX_u))$, $H(TX_u)$, $ADDR_s$, $Sig(H(C_s,C_u))$, $H(C_s,C_u)$, $ADDR_u$;
Output: (True or False, Reason);

1: // The function retrieveaddr() recovers the node address of the signer from the signature and message.
2: require($ADDR_s$ in L_{TA} and $ADDR_u$ in L_{RU});
3: $RADDR_s$ = retrieveaddr($Sig(H(TX_u))$, $H(TX_u)$, $HashType$);
4: **if** $RADDR_s$!= $ADDR_s$ **then**
5:    return (False, AS signature invalid);
6: **end if**
7: $RADDR_u$ = retrieveaddr($Sig(H(C_s,C_u))$, $H(C_s,C_u)$, $HashType$);
8: **if** $RADDR_u$!= $ADDR_u$ **then**
9:    return (False, User invalid);
10: **end if**
11: generate result R and stage it in a block;
12: **return** (True, Success);

---

will be triggered to authenticate the user. The detailed process is presented in Algorithm 1. At the same time, the full nodes (namely the AS node acting as a miner) try to solve a hash puzzle to compete for the right to write the blockchain under the PoW consensus mechanism. Once a node solves the problem, it adds the authentication results to a new block and broadcasts the block to all the peers. Other nodes will check the received block and its contained results. If the block or included results is invalid, then it would be dropped; otherwise the new block will be added to their local blockchain. After that, most of the nodes will reach a consensus on the validity of the access user. The security of PoW is based on the assumption that a majority of computation power is controlled by honest nodes. Our scenario meets this precondition because the 51% attack [6] can be easily detected and the participating institutions will adjust their computational power dynamically for their own benefit.

In Algorithm 1, the node first parses the received transaction and retrieves the input parameters including the signatures of the user and AS. Then it checks whether the AS is trusted and whether the user is registered. This check point prevents the access of illegal users or AS.

3.3 AS Verification

To enhance the access security, users are supposed to initiate an authentication for the AS which is not included in the local L_{TA} before accessing to the network. The AS verification is completed by the distributed nodes. Randomly selected N (its value is predefined by the participating institutions) trusted AS nodes will verify the untrusted AS and sign the authentication result. The untrusted AS should redirect the results to the user. If all the signatures are valid and signed by the trusted AS and the results are not tampered, the AS will be added to user's local L_{TA}; otherwise it would be an illegal AS and the user is able to determine not to connect to the visiting network. The AS verification process is shown in Algorithm 2.

Algorithm 2. Algorithm for AS verification

Input: $Sig(H(TX_s))$, $H(TX_s)$, $ADDR_s$, N;
Output: (True or False, Reason, Signature);
1: // N is the number of AS signers; $ADDR_s$.sn is the number of AS signers that have already authenticated $ADDR_s$; L_{sig} is the list of signed AS.
2: **if** N $\leq$ $ADDR_s$.sn **then**
3:     return (True, Success, Null);
4: **end if**
5: **if** $ADDR_s$ not in L_{TA} **then**
6:     return (False, AS invalid, Null);
7: **end if**
8: $RADDR_s$ = retrieveaddr($Sig(H(TX_s))$, $H(TX_s)$, $HashType$);
9: **if** $RADDR_s$!= $ADDR_s$ **then**
10:     return (False, AS signature invalid, Null);
11: **end if**
12: **if** $ADDR_s$.sn == N - 1 **then**
13:     $ADDR_s$.sn = 0;
14:     return (True, Success, Sig(H(Success,$ADDR_s$)));
15: **end if**
16: $ADDR_s$.sn += 1;
17: randomly select a trusted AS TA_n in (L_{TA} - L_{sig});
18: send TX_n to TA_n to trigger the next verification;
19: **return** (True, Success, Sig(H(Success,$ADDR_s$)));

The Algorithm 2 is executed in the full node and triggered by the AS verification transaction TX_s generated by the user. On receiving the TX_s, the AS signs the hash of TX_s with its private key and sends a transaction to authenticate itself. If the number of signers that have verified this untrusted AS ($ADDR_s$.sn) is less than N, the current node will generate and send a new transaction to trigger the next verification. In this case, the authentication is secure and credible since the result is determined by multiple nodes.

4   Implementation and Evaluation

4.1   Implementation

We implemented the Trustroam prototype in a real testbed, which consists of multiple authentication domains and a blockchain network. Figure 3 shows the topology of the testbed.

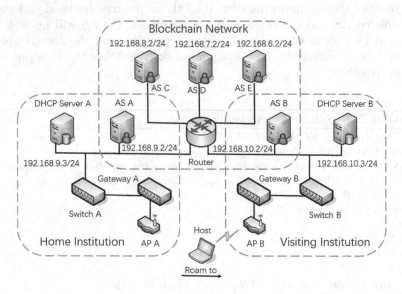

Fig. 3. Topology of Trustroam testbed.

We use Ethereum [14] as the blockchain technology, based on which we developed a smart contract [15] and wrote about 200 lines of Solidity code to implement distributed authentication function. Five ASes are connected together to form a blockchain network through a Peer-to-Peer protocol and a private Ethereum blockchain is maintained by these ASes. Open vSwitch [16] is deployed as the gateway to detect the access request and control the network connection of the user.

Modules mentioned above are deployed in the Dell PowerEdge R730 Server (Intel Xeon 2.20 GHz 20 CPU, 32 GB Memory, 2 TB Hard-disk and 81 Gbps network-cards), with Ubuntu 16.04 LTS operating system installed. Several laptops of Thinkpad T450 are used as the roaming hosts for testing.

As shown in Fig. 3, when roaming to a visiting institution, the host will first associate with AP B and get an IP address. Then the Gateway B will temporarily block the data traffic of the host and notify the AS B to authenticate the host. After the successful mutual authentication, the Gateway B will be notified of the authentication result and forward user's data packets normally. The following experiments are carried out based on such roaming scenario.

4.2   Evaluation

Security and Anonymity. Our solution resolves the management and security issues of eduroam by flattening the network. Compared to eduroam, Trustroam leverages the distributed consensus mechanism to authenticate the access user, which has no single point of failure problem built on a peer-to-peer network. In this case, a small amount of compromised servers have little impact on the authentication result since it is determined by the consensus of most AS nodes. Therefore, anyone who forges the authentication result to spoof the user and the trusted AS will be blocked. The AS verification algorithm and mutual authentication protocol allow our proposal to better defend against MITM attacks because the untrusted AS will be elaborately verified by the user and the blockchain network.

In addition, we use the blockchain node address to uniquely identify a user, and no extra credentials will be provided to the AS during authentication phase. Users are anonymous to the visiting institution. So we can infer that our scheme enhances the access security, anonymity and privacy preserving of cross-domain roaming compared to eduroam.

Scalability. We compare the scalability between the eduroam and Trustroam by evaluating the authentication load of the AS node. Suppose there are N participating institutions, $S_{national}$ ASes of national level and S_{global} ASes of global level in eduroam and f full nodes in Trustroam, then the authentication load of global AS L_{global}, national AS $L_{national}$, and Trustroam AS node $L_{trustroam}$ is presented as follows.

$$L_{global} = \frac{\alpha \cdot n_a}{S_{global}} \tag{1}$$

$$L_{national} = \frac{n_a}{S_{national}} \tag{2}$$

$$L_{trustroam} = \frac{(1+f) \cdot n_a}{N} \tag{3}$$

where n_a denotes the number of cross-domain authentication packets in unit time of the entire network. α represents the ratio of the number of authentication packets of global level to the number of all the cross-domain authentications.

Figure 4 shows the variety of AS load with n_a and α under the condition of $N = 1000$, $S_{global} = 2$, $S_{national} = 25$, $f = 100$. We can see that the AS load of Trustroam is relatively greater than that of eduroam. It is because that the

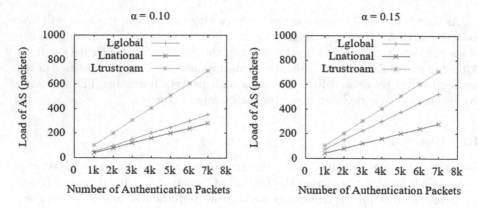

Fig. 4. Load of AS in Trustroam and eduroam.

user is authenticated by multiple nodes simultaneously to enhance the security in our consensus-based proposal, which leads to additional overhead. However, due to the hierarchical trust fabric, a large scale of traffic will cause a serious performance bottleneck on the aggregation proxies in eduroam. According to the result, the load of the central sever (e.g. AS of global level) grows with the increase of α, while Trustroam is barely affected by the global authentication traffic. When $\alpha > 0.20$, its load will exceed that of the node in Trustroam. So, we can infer that our scheme is more scalable than eduroam in the practical environment, especially with a large scale of international authentications.

Authentication Latency. Since it is difficult to measure the authentication latency of eduroam and Trustroam in a large scale, we compare their perfor-

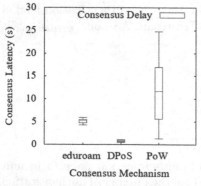
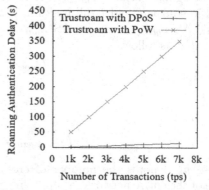

(a) Authentication latency of different mechanisms

(b) Roaming delay varies with authentication traffic size in Trustroam

Fig. 5. Trustroam shows comparable performance in terms of authentication latency and has high throughput in practice.

mance in our local testbed. In addition to PoW, we also measure other consensus mechanisms.

The result of our measurement is shown in Fig. 5(a). We can observe that the consensus mechanism has an important effect on the authentication latency of Trustroam. According to the measurement result, the authentication latency of eduroam, Trustroam with PoW and Trustroam with DPoS is 5.65 s, 11.68 s and 0.72 s respectively. Under the premise of ensuring the security and trust of the system, the participating organizations can implement Trustroam with DPoS to reduce the latency in practice.

As shown in Fig. 5(b), we also measure the roaming authentication delay of Trustroam under the condition of a large amount of authentications. We can see that the authentication delay grows linearly with the number of transactions increasing and the throughput is about 15tps and 500tps of the PoW and DPoS respectively. So it can provide services for a large number of users.

Overhead. To evaluate the signaling overhead, we measure the data size and number of packets transmitted in 5 s between the user and the AS with the number of users increasing. The results is shown in Fig. 6. We can observe that Trustroam has much lower signaling overhead than eduroam because Trustroam has no complex key negotiation and certificates exchange that is done in eduroam. In addition, with the increase of concurrent authentications, eduroam shows a high packet loss rate due to the bottleneck of the central server, while Trustroam is less affected by large-scale of traffic because of its distributed architecture.

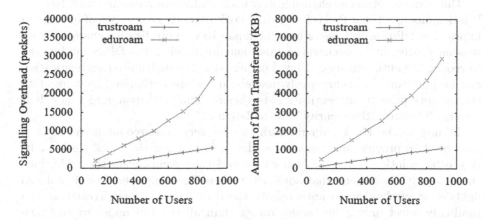

Fig. 6. Signaling overhead of Trustroam and eduroam.

We analyze the computation and storage overhead of our proposal for authenticating n users. The computation overhead $P_{computation}$ and storage overhead $P_{storage}$ are represented as follows.

$$P_{computation} = m \cdot \left(\sum_{i=1}^{n} C_i + \sum_{j=1}^{k} Q_j \right) \tag{4}$$

$$P_{storage} = s \cdot R_n + n \cdot R_u + m \cdot \sum_{l=1}^{k} B_l \tag{5}$$

where m is the number of full nodes of the blockchain network. C_i is the cost of smart contract execution including the digital signature verification for the user and AS. The complexity of C_i is O(1). Q_j is the overhead to solve the hash puzzle. Its complexity is O($\log 2^d$), in which d is the value of the difficulty to solve the problem. So the computation complexity of $P_{computation}$ is O($m \cdot k \cdot \log 2^d$), where k is the number of generated blocks. s is the number of AS nodes. R_n and R_u denote the item size of the L_{TA} and L_{RU} respectively. B_l is the size of a new generated block. The storage cost of $P_{storage}$ is O($m \cdot k$), in which the storage overhead of the L_{TA} and L_{RU} is too small and ignored.

5   Discussion

The security of Trustroam depends on the security of the blockchain technology, which is open to everyone in the network. An adversary can simply launch a node to interact with the blockchain. Therefore, it is important to guarantee the trust of AS nodes. Our scheme can be deployed incrementally. A new AS or institution should be carefully checked before it participates in the blockchain network. For example, its credentials must be verified by multiple participants before joining the network.

   Different consensus mechanisms may lead to different authentication latency. It is demonstrated that PoS is faster than PoW to reach a consensus of blockchain in practice. DPoS is even faster but will impair its decentralization characteristics to some degree. In the scenario of cross-domain roaming, the DPoS can be used to reduce the authentication delay. Furthermore, the distributed authentication can be performed asynchronously, namely, users are authorized to connect to the network prior to authentication, further reducing the roaming latency. It is a tradeoff between the security and the latency.

   Mining in the blockchain network can be very resource-intensive, so it is important to provide an incentive for the node to mine the block sustainably. A feasible solution is to charge the user and then compensate the node. Furthermore, we recommend that administrators utilize a more environmental and lightweight mechanism to authenticate the user. For instance, Trustroam can randomly select only a few nodes rather than all the full nodes to authenticate the user, which will greatly reduce the authentication overhead. Due to the random selection for AS nodes, its security is barely impaired in this way.

6   Conclusion and Future Work

In this paper, a novel cross-domain authentication scheme in Wi-Fi networks based on blockchain is proposed and the design of our proposal is described in detail. Through the distributed consensus mechanism and mutual authentication, Trustroam avoids the problems of single point of failure and privacy leakage, which enhances the security of cross-domain roaming and has a strong fault tolerance to deal with compromised server attacks. We implemented the Trustroam prototype in a real testbed and carried out experiments and evaluations on the proposal. The results show that our scheme is feasible, effective and convenient to deploy. Compared to existing hierarchical solutions, our scheme has the advantages at scalability, security and privacy preserving. In future work, we will focus on the optimization of its performance on latency and resource consumption and design a lightweight consensus mechanism to make the proposal more efficient.

Acknowledgement. This work is supported by the National Key Research and Development Plan of China (2017YFB0801702).

References

1. Eduroam. https://www.eduroam.org/wp-content/uploads/2016/05/The-Global-Village.pdf. Accessed 19 Jan 2019
2. Eduroam. https://www.eduroam.org. Accessed 17 Jan 2019
3. Wierenga, K., Winter, S., Wolniewicz, T.: The Eduroam architecture for network roaming. RFC 7593, September 2015
4. Rigney, C., Rubens, A., Simpson, W., Willens, S.: Remote authentication dial in user service (RADIUS). RFC 2865, June 2000
5. Brenza, S., Pawlowski, A., Pöpper, C.: A practical investigation of identity theft vulnerabilities in Eduroam. In: Proceedings of ACM WiSec 2015, New York City, USA, June 2015
6. Swan, M.: Blockchain: Blueprint for a New Economy. O'Reilly Media Inc., Newton (2015)
7. Sanda, T., Inaba, H.: Proposal of new authentication method in Wi-Fi access using bitcoin 2.0. In: Proceedings of IEEE GCCE 2016, Kyoto, Japan, December 2016
8. Liu, D., Li, D., Liu, X., Ma L., Yu, H., Zhang, H.: Research on a cross-domain authentication scheme based on consortium blockchain in V2G networks of smart grid. In: Proceedings of IEEE EI2 2018, Beijing, China, October 2018
9. Winter, S., McCauley, M., Venaas, S., Wierenga, K.: Transport layer security (TLS) encryption for RADIUS. RFC 6614, May 2012
10. Liu, H., Goto, H.: Certificate-based, disruption-tolerant authentication system with automatic CA certificate distribution for Eduroam. In: 2014 IEEE 38th International Computer Software and Applications Conference Workshops (COMPSACW), Vasteras, Sweden, September 2014
11. Dwork, C., Naor, M.: Pricing via processing or combatting junk mail. In: Brickell, E.F. (ed.) CRYPTO 1992. LNCS, vol. 740, pp. 139–147. Springer, Heidelberg (1993). https://doi.org/10.1007/3-540-48071-4_10
12. Buterin, V.: What proof of stake is and why it matters, August 2013
13. EOSIO White Paper v2. https://github.com/EOSIO/Documentation/blob/master. Accessed 27 Jan 2019
14. Ethereum. https://www.ethereum.org. Accessed 29 Jan 2019
15. Ethereum White Paper. https://github.com/ethereum/wiki/wiki/White-Paper. Accessed 19 Jan 2019
16. Open vSwitch. https://www.openvswitch.org. Accessed 5 Jan 2019

Joint Optimization of Routing and Storage Node Deployment in Heterogeneous Wireless Sensor Networks Towards Reliable Data Storage

Feng Li[1], Huan Yang[2], Yifei Zou[3], Dongxiao Yu[1(✉)], and Jiguo Yu[4]

[1] School of Computer Science and Technology,
Shandong University, Qingdao, China
{fli,dxyu}@sdu.edu.cn
[2] College of Computer Science and Technology,
Qingdao University, Qingdao, China
cathy_huanyang@hotmail.com
[3] Department of Computer Science,
The University of Hong Kong, Hong Kong, China
yfzou@cs.hku.hk
[4] School of Computer Science and Technology,
Qilu University of Technology, Jinan, China
jiguoyu@sina.com

Abstract. The penetration of *Wireless Sensor Networks* (WSNs) in various applications poses a high demand on reliable data storage, especially considering sensor networks are usually deployed in harsh environment. In this paper, we introduce *Heterogeneous Wireless Sensor Networks* where robust storage nodes are deployed in sensor networks and data redundancy is utilized through coding techniques, in order to improve the reliability of data storage. Taking into account the cost of both data delivery and storage, we propose an algorithm to jointly optimize data routing and storage node deployment. This problem is a binary non-linear combinatorial optimization, and it is highly non-trivial to design efficient algorithms due to its NP-hardness. By levering the Markov approximation framework, we elaborately design a *Continuous Time Markov Chain* (CTMC) based scheduling algorithm to drive the storage node deployment and the corresponding routing strategy. Extensive simulations are performed to verify the efficacy of our algorithm.

Keywords: Reliable data storage · Routing ·
Storage node deployment · Heterogeneous sensor networks

This work is partially supported by Shandong Provincial Natural Science Foundation, China (Grant No. ZR2017QF005) and NSFC (Grant No. 61702304, 61832012, 61602195, 61672321 and 61771289).

E. S. Biagioni et al. (Eds.): WASA 2019, LNCS 11604, pp. 162–174, 2019.
https://doi.org/10.1007/978-3-030-23597-0_13

1   Introduction

Recent years have witnessed the advancement of *Wireless Sensor Networks* (WSNs) in various applications [1]. Nevertheless, due to the penetrations of WSNs with big sensory data [5,6,12,15], how to store the sensed data becomes a very challenging problem. Since sensor nodes usually have limited resources and thus cannot provide qualified data storage service, specialized storage nodes are deployed to form the so-called *Heterogeneous Wireless Sensor Networks* (HWSNs) such that the data sensed by the regular sensor nodes are delivered to the storage nodes through multi-hop transmissions.

Unfortunately, sensor networks may be deployed in hash areas, and the resulting vulnerability (especially for the storage nodes) is a considerable threat for data storage, and thus is supposed to be concerned. One choice is to introduce data redundancy. For example, by applying erasure codes, the reliability of the data storage can be significantly improved [2,9]. Nevertheless, the induced data redundancy also increases data traffic in the sensor network, while the sensor nodes usually have quite limited energy (e.g. in [14]). Moreover, the increasing network scale also induces inevitable overhead in data storage.

To this end, we aim at seeking a tradeoff between the storage reliability and the energy efficiency of data delivery and storage in this paper, by jointly optimizing routing and storage node deployments. Specifically, by leveraging the notation of *Markov approximation* [4], we design a *Continuous Time Markov Chain* (CTMC) based algorithm, to adaptively tuning the deployment of the storage nodes as well as the corresponding data routing scheme. The cost in data delivery and storage is (nearly) minimized with data storage reliability ensured. We also verify the efficacy of our algorithm through extensive simulations.

The rest of this paper is organized as follows. We introduce our system model and formulate our optimization problem in Sect. 2. Our algorithm as well as related analysis are presented in Sect. 3. We evaluate our algorithm through extensive simulations in Sect. 4. We then survey related literatures in Sect. 5 and finally conclude our paper in Sect. 6, respectively.

2   System Model and Problem Formulation

2.1   System Model

We model a WSN as a digraph $\mathcal{G} = (\mathcal{N}, \mathcal{E})$. $\mathcal{N} = \{n_i\}_{i=1,\cdots,|\mathcal{N}|}$ denotes a set of $|\mathcal{N}|$ sensor nodes. For each pair of sensor nodes, e.g., n_i and $n_{i'}$, if $n_{i'}$ is within the maximal communication range of n_i, there exists a directed transmission edge $(n_i, n_{i'}) \in \mathcal{E}$. Assume $\mathcal{S} = \{s_j\}_{j=1,\dots,|\mathcal{S}|}$ is a set of $|\mathcal{S}|$ storage nodes. We denote by τ_j the *data storage cost* we have to pay to place one unit of data at s_j. Specifically, the storage cost not only involves the energy consumption to receive the data packets from sensor nodes, but also more significantly stems from maintaining the received data. We suppose that the storage nodes are equipped with mobile mechanisms (e.g., as shown in [16,18]), if re-deployment is demanded for adapting to the dynamics of network states. We also assume the storage nodes are equipped with long-range communication modules to exchange messages with each other for cooperations and to handle remote queries.

We denote by $\mathcal{U} = \{u_k\}_{k=1,\ldots,|\mathcal{U}|}$ ($|\mathcal{U}| \geq |\mathcal{S}|$) a finite set of sites where we are allowed to deploy our storage nodes. We then extend the WSN graph $\mathcal{G}$ by $\mathcal{N} \leftarrow \mathcal{N} \bigcup \mathcal{U}$ and $\mathcal{E} \leftarrow \mathcal{E} \bigcup \{(n_i, u_k)\}$. In particular, if u_k is within the maximal communication range of n_i, then there exists a directed edge $(n_i, u_k) \in \mathcal{E}$. In such an extended graph, we define a cost assignment $\gamma : \mathcal{E} \rightarrow \mathbb{R}^+$ to represent the *data delivery cost*, i.e., the energy consumed on carrying a unit of data along a transmission edge $e \in \mathcal{E}$.

2.2   Reliable Data Storage

The reliability of data storage can be achieved by replication or coding. In the former solution, individual data have multiple copies, each of which is placed at distinct storage node, while in the latter one, the original data can be encoded by, e.g., *Maximum Distance Separable* (MDS) codes first, and each of the encoded data is then placed in distinct storage node. The above two solutions share the same idea in the sense that the reliability is guaranteed by introducing data redundancy, such that the original data can be recovered even some of the storage nodes (and thus part of the data) are corrupted.

Take coding technique as an example. Let λ_i be the amount of data sensed by node n_i in each sensing-storage period[1]. The original data can be encoded through, e.g. MDS codes parameterized by (μ_i, λ_i). In particular, the λ_i original data can be encoded into $(\mu_i - \lambda_i)$ parity data. Both the original data and the parity ones are then delivered from source node n_i to μ_i distinct storage nodes. We hereby call both of them encoded data for brevity, as the original data can be treated as the one encoded by identity matrix. The storage reliability lies in the fact that the original data can be recovered by accessing any λ_i of the μ_i encoded data. In another word, the corruptions of any less than $(\mu_i - \lambda_i)$ storage nodes (or encoded data) will not prohibit the recovery of the data sensed by n_i. Therefore, we tolerate at most $\min_i \{\mu_i - \lambda_i\}$ storage node failures.

In data replication solution, if each sensor node replicates its data for μ_i times, it is sufficient to access one of the copies. Since the copies are placed at different storage nodes, at most $\min_i \{\mu_i - 1\}$ storage node corruption can be tolerated. By this way, we save the computation overhead in encoding process but have to spend more energy on data delivery, since node n_i should deliver μ_i full copies of its sensed data to distinct storage node. In fact, as shown later, our optimization framework is readily compatible to both replication and coding-based solutions by scaling the cost of data delivery and storage; nevertheless, we currently focus on redundant coding scheme in the following.

---

[1] We assume that the data storage is performed periodically in individual nodes. In each period, the data cumulated in the sensing phase are encoded and delivered to the storage nodes.

2.3 Problem Formulation

In this paper, we aim at minimizing the costs induced by both data delivery and storage, while ensuring the storage reliability, by jointly optimizing routing and storage node deployment. Let $x_{i,k} \in \{0,1\}$ denote if node $n_i \in \mathcal{N}$ transmits one of its encoded data to the storage node deployed at u_k (if any) along multi-hop transmissions. Specifically, for the purpose of cost minimization, data are delivered along the "shortest" paths under cost assignment γ^2. Assume $c_{i,k}$ denotes the minimum cost to deliver a unit of data from n_i to u_k. We also suppose $y_{j,k} \in \{0,1\}$ indicates if storage node s_j is placed at u_k. Given a coding scheme $\{(\mu_i, \lambda_i)\}_{i=1,\cdots,|\mathcal{N}|}$, we formulate our optimization problem of *Joint roUting and Storage node deploymenT* (JUST) as follows

$$\min \sum_{i=1}^{|\mathcal{N}|} \sum_{k=1}^{|\mathcal{U}|} c_{i,k} x_{i,k} + \beta \sum_{i=1}^{|\mathcal{N}|} \sum_{k=1}^{|\mathcal{U}|} \sum_{j=1}^{|\mathcal{S}|} \tau_j x_{i,k} y_{j,k} \tag{1}$$

$$\text{s.t.} \sum_{k=1}^{|\mathcal{U}|} x_{i,k} = \mu_i, \ \forall n_i \in \mathcal{N} \tag{2}$$

$$\sum_{j=1}^{|\mathcal{S}|} y_{j,k} - x_{i,k} \geq 0, \ \forall n_i \in \mathcal{N}, u_k \in \mathcal{U} \tag{3}$$

$$\sum_{j=1}^{|\mathcal{S}|} y_{j,k} \leq 1, \ \forall u_k \in \mathcal{U} \tag{4}$$

$$\sum_{k=1}^{|\mathcal{U}|} y_{j,k} \leq 1, \ \forall s_j \in \mathcal{S} \tag{5}$$

$$x_{i,k}, y_{j,k} \in \{0,1\}, \ \forall n_i \in \mathcal{N}, s_j \in \mathcal{S}, u_k \in \mathcal{U} \tag{6}$$

The above optimization problem is composed by a quadratic objective function as well as a set of linear constraints, and thus is a *Quadratic Integral Programming* (QIP) problem. In the objective function (1), the first item indicates the data delivery cost, while the second one represents the storage cost. We introduce parameter β to make a tradeoff between them. The objective function is minimized with the following constraints respected: (2) the storage reliability is ensured (i.e., each sensor node n_i places its μ_i encoded data in distinct storage nodes); (3) for each pair of n_i and u_k, there exists a storage node deployed at u_k if n_i delivers one of its encoded data to u_k; (4) at most one storage node is deployed at each u_k; (5) each storage node is deployed in at most one site.

The NP-hardness of the optimization problem can be proved even in a homogeneous setting, where the storage nodes have identical storage cost (i.e., $\tau_j = \tau$ for $\forall s_j \in \mathcal{S}$), such that our problem is reduced to minimizing $\sum_{i,k} c_{i,k} x_{i,k}$ with the constraints (2)–(6). Specifically, we aims at *choosing a subset of $\mathcal{U}$ to deploy*

---

[2] The shortest paths can be calculated through applying many state-of-the-art algorithms, as we will show in Sect. 3.1 later.

the given storage nodes $\mathcal{S}$ such that the induced data delivery cost is minimized with the storage reliability also guaranteed by a given coding scheme. Therefore, by adopting homogeneous storage nodes, our JUST problem actually can be transformed into a *Fault Tolerate k-Median Facility Placement* (FTkMFP) problem and thus is NP-hard.

3 Jointly Optimizing Routing and Storage Node Deployment Towards Reliable Data Storage

In this section, we leverage the Markov approximation framework [4] to resolve our combinatorial problem. We first discuss a simplified case where storage nodes are fixed in Sect. 3.1, to inspire the application of Markov approximation to our problem in Sect. 3.2. We then present the details of our algorithm and give corresponding discussion in Sect. 3.3.

3.1 What If Storage Nodes Are Fixed?

When the storage nodes are fixed (i.e., $\{y_{j,k}\}_{j,k}$ are knowns), our aim becomes seeking for the optimal routing scheme to deliver each of the encoded data from its source sensor node to destination storage nodes, such that the induced overhead (including both data delivery cost and storage cost) is minimized. Hence, in our JUST problem, we minimize $\sum_{i,k}(c_{i,k} + \beta \sum_j \tau_j y_{j,k})x_{i,k}$, subjected to $x_{i,k} \leq \sum_{j=1}^{|\mathcal{S}|} y_{j,k}$ for $\forall n_i \in \mathcal{N}$ and $u_k \in \mathcal{U}$. Since the storage node locations are given, the cost associated with each $x_{i,k}$, i.e., $c_{i,k} + \beta \sum_j \tau_j y_{j,k}$, is also known. Hence, the optimal solution in this case is to let each source sensor node $n_i \in \mathcal{N}$ delivers its encoded data to the μ_i "nearest" storage nodes with less overheads. Apparently, the above μ_i-*Nearest storage Nodes* (μ_i-NN) policy is based on polynomial-time graph shortest path algorithm, e.g., Dijkstra's algorithm or Floyd-Warshall algorithm, or other state-of-the-art distributed shortest path algorithms [11,13]. Although introducing a new freedom of storage node deployment has the potential of decreasing the cost of distributed data storage, the problem becomes very hard such that only nearly optimal solution can be achieved, as we have demonstrated in Sect. 2.3.

3.2 Markov Approximation

Assume $\mathcal{F} \subset \{0,1\}^{|\mathcal{S}| \times |\mathcal{U}|}$ is a set of feasible deployment strategies, and c_f denotes the total cost induced by a given $f \in \mathcal{F}$. Specifically, $f = \{y_{j,k}\}_{j,k}$, which respects constraints (4) and (5). Recall that, given $\forall f \in \mathcal{F}$, the data routing strategy (as well as the induced cost c_f) can be calculated according to μ_i-NN policy, as shown above. In fact, our optimization framework accommodates various routing subroutines which may be aimed at distinct objectives (e.g., in terms of energy). Our JUST problem (1)–(6) is equivalent to

$$\min_{f \in \mathcal{F}} \{c_f\} \tag{7}$$

The above objective function can be approximated by a log-sum-exp function parameterized by θ:

$$\phi_\theta(\{c_f\}_{f \in \mathcal{F}}) = -\frac{1}{\theta} \log \left(\sum_{f \in \mathcal{F}} \exp(-\theta c_f) \right) \tag{8}$$

where θ is a positive constant. According to [3], we have

Theorem 1. $\min_{f \in \mathcal{F}} \{c_f\}$ *can be approximated by* $\phi_\theta(\{c_f\}_{f \in \mathcal{F}})$, *owing to the following tight bound*

$$0 \leq \phi_\theta(\{c_f\}_{f \in \mathcal{F}}) - \min_{f \in \mathcal{F}} \{c_f\} \leq \frac{1}{\theta} \log |\mathcal{F}| \tag{9}$$

The approximation difference gets close to zero, as ϕ approaches infinity, i.e.,

$$\min_{f \in \mathcal{F}} \{c_f\} = - \lim_{\theta \to \infty} \frac{1}{\theta} \log \left(\sum_{f \in \mathcal{F}} \exp(-\theta c_f) \right)$$

By associating each $f \in \mathcal{F}$ with weight $p_f \in [0, 1]$, our problem formulation (7) has the same optimal value as

$$\min \sum_{f \in \mathcal{F}} c_f p_f \tag{10}$$

$$\text{s.t.} \sum_{f \in \mathcal{F}} p_f = 1 \tag{11}$$

$$p_f \geq 0, \forall f \in \mathcal{F} \tag{12}$$

where $\{p_f\}_{f \in \mathcal{F}}$ are variables. The weight p_f can be regarded as the time fraction of adopting the deployment strategy f in a long run. The equivalence is obtained by letting $p_f = 1$ for the optimal deployment strategy and 0 for the others.

Considering our problem (7) has an approximation $\phi_\theta(\{c_f\}_{f \in \mathcal{F}})$, its unique properties can be exploited to drive our algorithm design. In more details, the log-sum-exp function $\phi_\theta(\{c_f\}_{f \in \mathcal{F}})$ has a convex and closed conjugate function

$$\phi_\theta^*(\{p_f\}_{f \in \mathcal{F}}) = -\frac{1}{\theta} \sum_{f \in \mathcal{F}} p_f \log p_f$$

where $p_f \geq 0$ for $\forall f \in \mathcal{F}$ and $\sum_{f \in \mathcal{F}} p_f = 1$. In another word, $\phi_\theta(\{c_f\}_{f \in \mathcal{F}})$ is the same as the optimal value of the following optimization problem (so-called "JUST-Approx")

$$\min \sum_{f \in \mathcal{F}} c_f p_f + \frac{1}{\theta} \sum_{f \in \mathcal{F}} p_f \log p_f \tag{13}$$

$$\text{s.t.} \sum_{f \in \mathcal{F}} p_f = 1 \tag{14}$$

$$p_f \geq 0, \quad \forall f \in \mathcal{F} \tag{15}$$

Based on the *Karush-Kuhn-Tucker* (KKT) conditions, we have the optimal solution to our JUST-Approx problem

$$p_f^* = \frac{\exp(-\theta c_f)}{\sum_{f' \in \mathcal{F}} \exp(-\theta c_{f'})}, \quad \forall f \in \mathcal{F} \tag{16}$$

According to Theorem 1, this result gives a nearly optimal solution to the JUST problem with an optimality gap bounded by $\theta^{-1} \log |\mathcal{F}|$. In particular, the cost is (nearly) minimized by time-sharing across different deployment strategies in a long run according to $\{p_f^*\}_{f \in \mathcal{F}}$. Unfortunately, since the size of $\mathcal{F}$ is exponentially large, it is highly non-trivial to explicitly calculate p_f^* according to (16).

3.3 Algorithm

To solve the above JULY-Approx problem (and thus to address the JULY problem with approximation optimality), we design a homogeneous *Continuous-Time Markov Chain* (CTMC) $\{F(t)\}_{t \geq 0}$, where t denotes time and $F(t) \in \mathcal{F}$ is a random variable indicating the storage node deployment at time t, so as to drive the adaptive deployment of the storage nodes. In the CTMC, state transitions (i.e., storage node re-deployments) may occur at any point in time, and can be specified by *transition rates*. In particular, we assume that two states are linked by re-deploying only one storage node. The assumption does not compromise the reachability between the states and thus the irreducibility of the Markov chain.

Due to the state finiteness and irreducibility of CTMC $\{F(t)\}_{t \geq 0}$, it has a *unique* stationary distribution. In the Markov approximation framework, we design a *time-reversible* CTMC $\{F(t)\}_{t \geq 0}$, such that its stationary distribution respects the following *detailed balance equation*

$$p_f^* q_{f,f^+} = p_{f^+}^* q_{f^+,f} \tag{17}$$

where q_{f,f^+} and $q_{f^+,f}$ denote the transition rates from f to f^+ and the one from f^+ to f, respectively. In this paper, we defined the transition rates q_{f,f^+} as

$$q_{f,f^+} = \delta \frac{\exp(-\theta c_{f^+})}{\exp(-\theta c_f) + \exp(-\theta c_{f^+})} \tag{18}$$

where δ is a constant. Recalling the definition of q_f^* (for $\forall f \in \mathcal{F}$) in Eq. (16). The above definition apparently satisfies the balance equation (17).

We implement CTMC $\{F(t)\}_{t \geq 0}$ based on the following propositions [10]:

Proposition 1. *The sojourn time in each state f is an exponential random variable with rate defined by*

$$v_f = \sum_{f' \in \mathcal{F}(f)} q_{f,f'} = \delta \sum_{f' \in \mathcal{F}(f)} \frac{\exp(-\theta c_{f'})}{\exp(-\theta c_f) + \exp(-\theta c_{f'})} \tag{19}$$

where $\mathcal{F}(f)$ denotes the set of states adjacent to f.

Proposition 2. *The transition probability from f to $f^+ \in \mathcal{F}(f)$ is defined as*

$$p_{f,f^+} = q_{f,f^+}/v_f \tag{20}$$

if we consider the discrete-time counterpart of the CTMC.

Remark 1. *According to the above two propositions, the optimality of the CTMC-driven method can be explained from two folds: we spend more time on sojourning in the storage node deployment with lower cost, while it is more likely to move to the lower-cost storage node deployment.*

By the above two propositions, a straightforward way is to adaptively deploy the storage nodes in a centralized manner as follows: (i) supposing the current storage node deployment is f, we set up a count down timer initialized by an exponential random value $\Delta t \sim \text{Exponential}(v_f)$; (ii) when the timer expires, we transit to a new storage node deployment $f^+ \in \mathcal{F}(f)$ according to the transition probabilities defined in (18). Nevertheless, this approach entails some central infrastructures, and thus cannot be adapted to distributed sensor networks.

Algorithm 1. Algorithm for jointly optimizing storage node deployment and routing (in each epoch)

---

1 Initialization: randomly initialize the storage node deployment f;
2 **foreach** *epoch* **do**
3   Calculate an routing strategy according to f;
4   **foreach** $s_j \in \mathcal{S}$ **do**
5   Generate an exponential random variable $\Delta t_j \sim \text{Exponential}(v_j)$;
6   Set up a count down timer initialized by Δt_j;
7   **if** *No notification message is received* **then**
8   When the timer expires, move to a new site according to (21), and broadcast a notification message;
9   **else**
10   Stop the timer;
11   **end**
12   **end**
13 **end**

We hereby propose an algorithm in Algorithm 1, to implement CTMC in a distributed manner. We assume that the storage nodes $\mathcal{S}$ are initially deployed at $\mathcal{U}$ in a randomized fashion (see Line 1). The lifetime of the sensor network can be divided into a set of epochs, and a new epoch begins when some storage node changes its location. In each epoch, we first calculate a routing strategy according to the current storage node deployment f by the μ_i-NN policy (see Line 3). In every epoch, each storage node s_j generate an exponential random variable $\Delta t_j \sim$ Exponential(v_j) where $v_j = \sum_{f' \in \mathcal{F}_j(f)} q_{f,f'}$ and $\mathcal{F}_j(f)$ is the subset of feasible storage node deployments with only s_j placed at different sites from the one in f (see Line 5). Each storage node s_j then sets up a count-down timer initialized by Δt_j (see Line 6). According to Lines 7–11, when the timer expires, s_j broadcast a notification message, while the ones received the message before the expirations of their timers stop counting down. Assuming $j^* = \arg\min_j \{\Delta t_j\}_{j=1,\cdots,|\mathcal{S}|}$, storage node s_{j^*} is the one whose timer expires first, the time span of the current epoch is Δt_{j^*}. As shown in Line 9, we re-deploy s_{j^*} according to the probabilities

$$p_{f,f^+} = q_{f,f^+}/v_{j^*}, \quad \forall f^+ \in \mathcal{F}_{j^*}(f) \tag{21}$$

The algorithm complexity mainly stems from computing c_{f^+}, i.e., calculating routing strategy and the corresponding cost. Since the sensor nodes are fixed and the sites for storage node deployment are knowns, the shortest paths from the sensor nodes to the sites (as well as the resulting data delivery cost) can be calculated by state-of-the-art polynomial-time algorithms (e.g., Dijkstra method with a time complexity of $O(|\mathcal{N}|^2)$). The results can be pre-loaded in the storage nodes, especially considering the storage nodes usually have sufficient memory space. Moreover, when a storage node moves to a new site, it notifies the other storage nodes of its new position by broadcasting $O(\log|\mathcal{U}|)$-length notification messages to the associated sensor nodes, such that all storage nodes can calculate c_{f^+} locally. In fact, the storage nodes can forward the notifications to the sensor nodes by piggybacking the received new storage node deployment in the acknowledgments. Furthermore, for each sensor node, when getting the notification messages from the storage nodes, it could quickly calculate the cost to place a data unit in the re-deployed storage node and then update the routing scheme according to the μ_i-NN policy.

In the above implementation, each storage node only needs to maintain a local timer. One question is that, does it still realize CTMC $\{\mathcal{F}(t)\}_{t\geq 0}$ by respecting Propositions 1 and 2? We then have the following theorem, where it is implies that using a set of local timers instead of a centralized one does not compromise the optimality of $\{\mathcal{F}(t)\}_{t\geq 0}$ in solving our JULY-Approx problem.

Theorem 2. *In Algorithm 1, the sojourn time for each state f is exponentially distributed with rate v_f (19), and the transition probability from f to f^+ ($f^+ \in \mathcal{F}(f)$) is $p_{f,f^+} = q_{f,f^+}/v_f$ (20).*

Proof. For each storage node deployment f, the sojourn time $\Delta t(f)$ can be defined as $\Delta t(f) = \min\{\Delta t_j\}_{j=1,\cdots,|\mathcal{S}|}$, according to Algorithm 1. Since $\Delta t_j \sim$ Exponential(v_j), we have $\Delta t(f) \sim$ Exponential$(\sum_j v_j)$. In another word, $\Delta t(f)$ is a random variable following an exponential distribution with rate defined by

$\sum_j v_j = \sum_j \sum_{f' \in \mathcal{F}_j(f)} q_{f,f'}$. Also, as $\bigcup_j \mathcal{F}_j(f) = \mathcal{F}/\{f\}$ and $\bigcap_j \mathcal{F}_j(f) = \emptyset$, we obtain $\sum_j v_j = \sum_{f' \neq f} q_{f,f'} = v_f$. Hence, $\Delta t(f) \sim \text{Exponential}(v_f)$.

Suppose $j^* = \arg\min_j \Delta t_j$. Recalling $\Delta t(f) \sim \text{Exponential}(\sum_j v_j)$, the probability of $\Delta t(f) = \Delta t_{j^*}$ can be defined by $\Pr(\Delta t(f) = \Delta t_{j^*}) = v_{j^*}/\sum_j v_j$. Therefore, for $\forall f^+ \in \mathcal{F}(f)$, we define p_{f,f^+} as

$$p_{f,f^+} = \Pr(\Delta t(f) = \Delta t_{j^*}) \times p_{j^*}(f') = \frac{v_{j^*}}{\sum_j v_j} \cdot \frac{q_{f,f^+}}{v_{j^*}} = \frac{q_{f,f^+}}{v_f}$$

where s_{j^*} is the storage node redeployed provided that transition $f \to f^+$ happens, and $p_{j^*}(f^+)$ is the probability that $f \to f^+$ happens.

4   Simulations

In this section, we evaluate the efficacy of our algorithm by extensive simulations. We assume 200 sensor nodes are uniformly deployed in a $100\,\text{m} \times 100\,\text{m}$ targeted area. Each senor node sets its storage reliability requirement uniformly in a range of $[1, 4]$. For simplicity, we assume the sensor nodes have identical transmission power and receiving power, such that the data delivery cost associated with each edge can be normalized to 1. We suppose the system involves 10 storage nodes whose storage costs are uniformly chosen from $[1, 4]$. We assume $\beta = 1$ such that we equally consider the cost of data delivery and the one of storage.

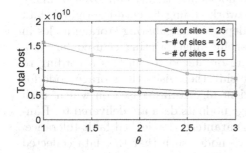

Fig. 1. Total cost.   **Fig. 2.** Optimality gap.

We first illustrate the total cost of our algorithm (including both data delivery cost and data storage cost) under different numbers of sites where we deploy the storage nodes. The results are given in Fig. 1. It can be shown that, increasing the number of the sites results in decreased total cost, since we have much larger space of feasible solutions. Another observation is that, taking smaller value for θ implies lower total cost, which is consistent with the fact that we approach the optimum by increasing the value of θ (see Theorem 1).

We also compare the results of our algorithm with the optimal ones. Due to the computational intractability of large system settings, we assume the storage nodes have identical storage cost to "shrink" the domain of feasible solutions. We shown the optimality gaps (defined in Eq. (9)) in Fig. 2. It can be demonstrated that, increasing θ results in smaller optimality gap, which confirms Theorem 1 again. Another interesting observation is that, although setting more sites to deploy the storage nodes leads to lower total cost, the corresponding optimality gap is larger than the cases with less sites. This can be explained by re-visiting Eq. (9) Theorem 1: more sites implies larger $\mathcal{F}$, and the optimality gap is inversely proportional to $|\mathcal{F}|$.

5   Related Work

There have been a vast body of proposals investigating data collection issues by one or multiple sink nodes, e.g, [8, 22]. Although we borrow the idea of employing mobile sinks, these algorithms cannot be applied to the storage problem as they do not take into account storage reliability as well as the cost in data storage, which are the main concerns in the context of data storage.

Some of the exiting proposals aim at distributing the sensed data among sensor nodes. For example, [19] chooses a subset of non-root sensor node to store the data delivered from the downstream ones in a tree-structure sensor network. [20,23] integrate compress sensing and probabilistic broadcasting to decrease data traffic and energy consumption. In [17,25], a quorum-based data storage strategy is proposed, using data replication to ensure storage reliability.

To handle increasing demand on data storage posed by large-scale deployments of sensor networks, specific storage nodes are usually employed in many recent proposals. [24] utilizes random network coding to encode original data and distributes the encoded data to pre-deployed neighboring storage nodes in a randomized manner. Besides, homomorphic fingerprinting is used for data maintenance. In [18], the sensor nodes are organized to clusters according to pre-deployed storage nodes, and a mobile sink then visits the storage node for data collection. [21] proposes energy-efficient algorithms, based on which, each sensor node can determine to which storage node its data are delivered to. Random linear network coding is applied to guaranteed the desired fault-tolerance. In [7], storage nodes are treated as "relay" nodes such that the data collected at sensors are first delivered to storage nodes for compress, and the compressed data are then forwarded to a sink node. The energy consumption is minimized by optimally deploy the storage nodes, but no storage reliability is considered.

6   Conclusion

To address the problem of minimizing data delivery and storage cost with storage reliability guaranteed, we have proposed a CTMC-based algorithm in this paper, by leveraging the framework of Markov approximation, such that the deployment of the storage nodes are adaptively scheduled, while the routing scheme is updated accordingly. The performance of our algorithm has been verified by theoretical analysis and numerical simulations.

References

1. Akyildiz, I., Su, W., Sankarasubramaniam, Y., Cayirci, E.: Wireless sensor networks: a survey. Comput. Netw. **38**(4), 393–422 (2002)
2. Albano, M., Chessa, S.: Distributed erasure coding in data centric storage for wireless sensor networks. In: Proceedings of IEEE ISCC, pp. 22–27 (2009)
3. Boyd, S., Vandenberghe, L.: Convex Optimization. Cambridge University Press, Cambridge (2004)
4. Chen, M., Liew, S., Shao, Z., Kai, C.: Markov approximation for combinatorial network optimization. IEEE Trans. Inf. Theory **59**(10), 6301–6327 (2013)
5. Cheng, S., Cai, Z., Li, J.: Curve query processing in wireless sensor networks. IEEE Trans. Veh. Technol. **64**(11), 5198–5209 (2015)
6. Cheng, S., Cai, Z., Li, J., Gao, H.: Extracting kernel dataset from big sensory data in wireless sensor networks. IEEE Trans. Knowl. Data Eng. **29**(4), 813–827 (2017)
7. D'Angelo, G., Diodati, D., Navarra, A., Pinotti, C.: The minimum k-storage problem: complexity, approximation, and experimental analysis. IEEE Trans. Mob. Comput. **5**(7), 1797–1811 (2016)
8. Deng, R., He, S., Chen, J.: An online algorithm for data collection by multiple sinks in wireless-sensor networks. IEEE Trans. Control Netw. Syst. **5**(1), 93–104 (2018)
9. Dimakis, A., Prabhakaran, V., Ramchandran, K.: Decentralized erasure codes for distributed networked storage. IEEE Trans. Inf. Theory **52**(6), 2809–2816 (2006)
10. Gallager, R.: Stochastic Processes: Theory for Applications, 1st edn. Cambridge University Press, Cambridge (2014)
11. Ghaffari, M., Li, J.: Improved distributed algorithms for exact shortest paths. In: Proceedings of the 50th ACM STOC, pp. 431–444 (2018)
12. He, Z., Cai, Z., Cheng, S., Wang, X.: Approximate aggregation for tracking quantiles and range countings in wireless sensor networks. Theor. Comput. Sci. **607**(3), 381–390 (2015)
13. Holzer, S., Wattenhofer, R.: Optimal distributed all pairs shortest paths and applications. In: Proceedings of ACM PODC, pp. 355–364 (2012)
14. Li, F., Yang, Y., Chi, Z., Zhao, L., Yang, Y., Luo, J.: Trinity: enabling self-sustaining WSNs indoors with energy-free sensing and networking. ACM Trans. Embed. Comput. Syst. **17**(2), 57:1–57:27 (2018)
15. Li, J., Cheng, S., Cai, Z., Yu, J., Wang, C., Li, Y.: Approximate holistic aggregation in wireless sensor networks. ACM Trans. Sens. Netw. **13**(2), 11:1–11:24 (2017)
16. Liu, Q., Zhang, K., Liu, X., Linge, N.: Grid routing: an energy-efficient routing protocol for WSNs with single mobile sink. Int. J. Sens. Netw. **25**(2), 93–103 (2017)
17. Luo, J., Li, F., He, Y.: 3DQS: distributed data access in 3D wireless sensor networks. In: Proceedings of IEEE ICC, pp. 1–5 (2011)
18. Maia, G., Guidoni, D., Viana, A., Aquino, A., Mini, R., Loureiro, A.: A distributed data storage protocol for heterogeneous wireless sensor networks with mobile sinks. Ad Hoc Netw. **11**(5), 1588–1602 (2013)
19. Sheng, B., Li, Q., Mao, W.: Data storage placement in sensor networks. In: Proceedings of ACM MobiHoc, pp. 344–355 (2006)
20. Talari, A., Rahnavard, N.: CStorage: decentralized compressive data storage in wireless sensor networks. Ad Hoc Netw. **37**, 475–485 (2016)
21. Tian, J., Yan, T., Wang, G.: A network coding based energy efficient data backup in survivability-heterogeneous sensor networks. IEEE Trans. Mob. Comput. **4**(10), 1992–2006 (2015)

22. Wang, J., Cao, J., Sherratt, R., Park, J.: An improved ant colony optimization-based approach with mobile sink for wireless sensor networks. J. Supercomput. **74**(12), 6633–6645 (2018)
23. Yang, X., Tao, X., Dutkiewicz, E., Huang, X., Guo, Y., Cui, Q.: Energy-efficient distributed data storage for wireless sensor networks based on compressed sensing and network coding. IEEE Trans. Wirel. Commun. **12**(10), 5087–5099 (2013)
24. Zeng, R., Jiang, Y., Lin, C., Fan, Y., Shen, X.: A distributed fault/intrusion-tolerant sensor data storage scheme based on network coding and homomorphic fingerprinting. IEEE Trans. Parallel Distrib. Syst. **23**(10), 1819–1830 (2012)
25. Zhang, C., Luo, J., Xiang, L., Li, F., Lin, J., He, Y.: Harmonic quorum systems: data management in 2D/3D wireless sensor networks with holes. In: Proceedings of IEEE SECON, pp. 1–9 (2012)

Fusing RFID and Computer Vision for Occlusion-Aware Object Identifying and Tracking

Min Li[1,2,3($\boxtimes$)], Yao Chen[2,3], Yanfang Zhang[2,3], Jian Yang[2,4], and Hong Du[1]

[1] Beijing Jiaotong University, Beijing, China
{limin,duhong}@iie.ac.cn
[2] Institute of Information Engineering, Chinese Academy of Sciences, Beijing, China
{limin,chenyao,zhangyanfang}@iie.ac.cn,
jyang@bit.edu.cn
[3] School of Cyber Security, University of Chinese Academy of Sciences, Beijing, China
[4] School of Optics and Photonics, Beijing Institute of Technology, Beijing, China

Abstract. Real-time identifying and tracking monitored objects is an important application in a public safety scenario. Both Radio Frequency Identification (RFID) and computer vision are potential solutions to monitor objects while faced with respective limitations. In this paper, we combine RFID and computer vision to propose a hybrid indoor tracking system, which can efficiently identify and track the monitored object in the scene with people gathering and occlusion. In order to get a high precision and robustness trajectory, we leverage Dempster-Shafer (DS) evidence theory to effectively fuse RFID and computer vision based on the prior probability error distribution. Furthermore, to overcome the drift problem under long-occlusion, we exploit the feedback from the high-confidence tracking results and the RFID signals to correct the false visual tracking. We implement a real-setting tracking prototype system to testify the performance of our proposed scheme with the off-the-shelf IP network camera, as well as the RFID devices. Experimental results show that our solution can achieve 98% identification accuracy and centimeter-level tracking precision, even in long-term occlusion scenarios, which can manipulate various practical object-monitoring scenarios in the public security applications.

Keywords: RFID · Visual tracking · DS evidence theory · Occlusion-aware

1 Introduction

Nowadays, with the increasing number of thefts in museums, important venues, etc., anti-theft systems are gradually integrating with industries such as Closed Circuit Television [1] and intelligent electronic device [2, 3]. However, these anti-theft products can only deal with those cases in which the object is stolen, but fail to identify

© Springer Nature Switzerland AG 2019
E. S. Biagioni et al. (Eds.): WASA 2019, LNCS 11604, pp. 175–187, 2019.
https://doi.org/10.1007/978-3-030-23597-0_14

and track the thief bringing with the object when multiple people are gathering, which is more and more mentioned as the advanced public security services [4].

Intuitively, both RFID and computer vision are potential solutions for above public security services. RFID has been widely used in many fields because of its light volume, non-line-of-sight propagation, automatic identification, and low cost [5]. A RFID reader can efficiently identify the tag people are wearing within the working range. However, it is very difficult to accurately track moving people based on passive RFID system alone, in which the positioning accuracy is usually at the meter level, such that fine-grained identification and tracking of tagged objects cannot be achieved within this range. On the other hand, computer vision has achieved remarkable accuracy in tracking individual objects and is currently broadly applied in many areas, such as robotics, surveillance, human motion analyses and so on. Nevertheless, the fatal problem faced by computer vision based tracking systems lies in that, such a system can be easily dysfunctional when occlusion occur over the monitored object or the thief [6]. Besides, computer vision cannot distinguish similar items, such as documents, valuable assets, thus it is unfeasible to track these objects solely with computer vision. Furthermore, suppose that there are multiple people gathering, the monitored object is being stolen with a sever occlusion on it. In such a scenario, neither RFID nor computer vision can solely help the safeguard identify who is stealing the object and what track the thief is running out.

To solve such a practical problem, in this paper, we propose a fusing scheme to combine the advantages of RFID and computer vision for online identifying and tracking. More specifically, if the RFID tag is pre-attached to the object in visual surveillance scenarios, we can identify the thief by determining which track is the closest one to the trajectory of the tag. When an item is lost in a multiple-people gathering scenario, the camera detects and tracks all of the individuals in the surveillance area, while the RFID reader detects the tag on the item and tracks the tag. The position and speed of the thief and the tagged stolen item at the same time are often the closest. Therefore, for the detected RFID tag, we try to match it to one of the people that is most likely to be the thief by using a distance and velocity probability matrix in the sliding window. Due to the low accuracy of the RFID trajectory and the fragility of the visual trajectory to occlusion, neither RFID nor visual can solely help a fine-grained and robust tracking. Unfortunately, previous studies only employ the visual trajectory or simple weighting method to obtain the final trajectory [15, 16], which results in a dramatic trajectory error. For this task, we introduce DS evidence theory to fuse the RFID position and the visual position based on a priori probability error distribution to obtain an accurate and robust trajectory. Additionally, visual tracking is prone to fail when the thief is occluded, especially under long-term occlusion. Thereby, the position matrix and peak information of correlation filter are used to determine and correct the false tracking under occlusion.

Contributions: In summary, this paper makes the following contributions:

- First, we propose an innovative combination of RFID signals and visual signals for online identification and high-precision tracking, which can be applied to find person stealing the tagged object.

- Second, DS evidence theory based on prior error distribution is used to fuse the position information of visual and RFID, which can obtain the fusion trajectory with high robustness and precision.
- Third, a template update strategy and the RFID signal are used to adjust the search box of correlation filter for visual tracking under long-term occlusion.
- Fourth, we implement the system with off-the-shelf camera and RFID products. It's validated that the tracking accuracy is set to the centimeter level and the matching accuracy is 98%. More importantly, the object can be tracked correctly even in long-term occlusion.

The rest of the paper is organized as follows. Section 2 introduces related research. The main design of our scheme is over viewed in Sect. 3. We describe the technical details of our approach to people tracking and identification in Sect. 4. Section 5 presents experimental results of the system. Finally, Sect. 6 concludes the paper.

2   Related Work

Recent studies have shown that people tracking and identification can be accomplished using RFID. The mainstream method in RFID-based people tracking solutions is to leverage Received Signal Strength (RSS) as fingerprints or distance ranging metrics [7]. Mehmood et al. [8] used Artificial Neural Networks (ANN) to learn the intrinsic link between RSS fingerprints and position coordinates. Figuera et al. [9] added the spectral information of the training data to the Support Vector Machine (SVM). Dwiyasa et al. [10] applied Extreme Learning Machine (ELM) to position fingerprint localization algorithm. However, the tracking accuracy of these methods in a complex experimental environment is still low, and it is not possible to accurately locate the tagged object.

On the other hand, recent years have witnessed the rapid advance of computer vision, making it possible for reliable object tracking. Since 2013, Correlation filter-based tracking strategies have been widely studied due to their high efficiency and strong robustness, and its representative method is the Kernelized Correlation Filter (KCF) [11]. Correlation filter predicts the region in the image related to the position of the last frame of the object and then extracts the object region. After a series of transformations, such as Fast Fourier transform, the region with the maximum response in the result is considered as the object's position. Unfortunately, Vision-based tracking is susceptible to illumination, distortion, occlusion, and fast motion, which ultimately leads to a failed tracking [6].

There are some researches focus on the combination of RFID and computer vision for identifying and tracking in different applications. A robot with RFID antennas and camera was used for people tracking in a crowded environment, and this approach was refined by using a fixed camera and RFID antennas [12]. Reference [13] introduce an approximate aggregation for tracking quantiles and range countings in wireless sensor networks. Xuan et al. introduce the fusion of electronic and visual signals, but it focuses on the matching algorithm, and the final positioning accuracy is low [14]. Reference [15] performed better in the theory, but the experimental environment was very small and the phase measurement was complicated.

3   Scheme Overview

To address our scheme clearly, we first introduce our scheme overview, as shown in Fig. 1. The whole scheme needs two kinds of input information, RFID information and computer vision information. For RFID part, we need the tag's ID, tracking trajectory, and velocities in all trajectory points. For visual part, we need the detected persons, tracking trajectories and also velocities in all trajectory points. Then, the data processing procedure is composed of three phases, association, fusion and occlusion-aware processing.

The association phase aims to match the RFID tag to the visual thief, we calculate the distance and velocity probability matrix in the time window, and select the person corresponding to the tag with the largest probability. The fusion phase is to get an accurate and robust trajectory. We employ DS evidence theory to fuse the coordinate information of the two sensors based on the prior error distribution, and obtain a fusion trajectory superior to the single sensor trajectory. The occlusion-aware processing intends to correct false tracking in case of occlusion when tracking the thief, we use the feedback information from the tracking results and the probability matrix of the two sensors, so that the tracker can still track correctly after long-term occlusion.

Based on the scheme architecture, we then introduce the technic details of the scheme in the next section.

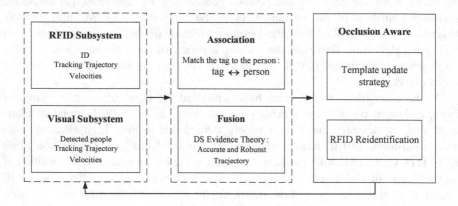

Fig. 1. System architecture

4   Detailed Scheme

4.1   Signal Acquisition

Signal acquisition primarily uses RFID and vision sensors to detect and track objects and obtain their own trajectories. For the RFID subsystem, we need to obtain the tag's ID and the tracking trajectory. We choose ANN [8] to locate RFID tags and get the tracking trajectory for two reasons. First, compared to online learning methods such as Landmarks, ANN only requires reference labels offline for easy deployment. Second,

ANN has a greater impact on nonlinear fitting and positioning accuracy compared to machine learning methods such as SVM [9]. For ANN, in the offline phase, the reference tags are placed 60 cm apart from one another to obtain the training data, which including the RFID signals and the coordinates of the reference tags. In the online phase, the input of the ANN network is the RSS of the four antennas, and the output is the coordinate of the tagged object. Thus, we can get the trajectory of the tagged object.

For the visual subsystem, we need to obtain the detected people and their tracking trajectory. Firstly, to get the detected people, we choose YOLO [16] for pedestrian detection, which has high precision and can run in real time. Secondly, since we need to specifically track the thief, we choose the single object tracking algorithm based on Efficient Convolution Operator (ECO) [17] is used to get the tracking trajectory. ECO is improved on the basis of correlation filter, which is a state-of-the art algorithm. When using the hand-craft features, the speed of ECO can reach 66 fps, which enables real-time tracking. ECO specifies that the template is updated every six frames. But when the model is updated while it is occluded, the template will drift to the occlusion object and lead to false tracking, we will improve the template update strategy in Sect. 4.3.

4.2 Association and Fusion

The two described subsystems provide a set of tags T and a set of visions V, incorporating the identifier and location estimates for every tag and vision, respectively. From these two sets, we want to establish an assignment between individual tags and visions such that a subset T_i is assigned to a particular vision V_j. The described problem can be formulated in a data association context which considers the spatial distance $d_{ij} = \sqrt{x_{ij}^2 + y_{ij}^2}$ between tag T_i and visual V_j. Depending on the localization uncertainty of the RFID and visual system, a zero-mean Gaussian kernel with specific covariance (σ_x, σ_y) is obtained. Then, the spatial distance can be transformed into a probability measure, we have:

$$p_{i,j} = \frac{1}{2\pi\sigma_x\sigma_y} \exp\left(\frac{-x_{i,j}^2}{2\sigma_x^2} + \frac{-y_{i,j}^2}{2\sigma_y^2} \right) \tag{1}$$

On the other hand, the tag and the pedestrian speed are defined as the derivative of the trajectory with respect to time, we have:

$$V_i = \frac{dX_{T_i}(t)}{dt} \tag{2}$$

We can extend them to a function of time, and build an assignment matrix that holds the individual probability measures for each RFID $\leftrightarrow$ visual pair. Tag T_i can then be assigned to the most likely class V_j by finding the maximum value within the sliding window time.

Existing systems and algorithms only focus on visual trajectories, or use simple weighting methods. However, visual tracking is easy to fail due to problems such as occlusion. Therefore, we use DS evidence theory to combine the trajectories of RFID and visual object based on the priori error distribution to obtain robust and accurate results. DS evidence theory fuses basic probability assignment functions in the iden- tification framework through combination rules and finally makes decisions, which is introduced as follows [18].

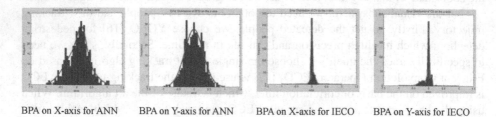

BPA on X-axis for ANN   BPA on Y-axis for ANN   BPA on X-axis for IECO   BPA on Y-axis for IECO

Fig. 2. The basic probability distribution function (BPA) for ANN and IECO without occlusion.

Identification Framework: We define the identification framework $\Theta = \{H_1, H_2, ..., H_M\}$ as a set of discrete locations within the object space region, which is the mean error distance from the real position.

Basic Probability Assignment Functions (BPA): The probability values of RFID positioning error and visual positioning error in the identification framework are cal- culated separately. Thus, we get the BPA m_1, m_2 of ANN and IECO under different areas based on the Gaussian distribution. Figure 2 shows the BPA without occlusion, while the BPA under occlusion in discussed in Sect. 4.3.

Combination Rules: The combination rule based on evidence credibility can be defined as follows:

$$\begin{cases} m(H) = p(H) + K \cdot \varepsilon \cdot q(H), \\ m(\emptyset) = 0, \\ m(\Theta) = p(\Theta) + K \cdot \varepsilon \cdot q(\Theta) + K \cdot (1 - \varepsilon) \end{cases} \tag{3}$$

for $H \neq \emptyset, \Theta$, where $p(H)$ represents the combination mass without normalization, and $q(H)$ represents the average support of proposition H. ε is the evidence credibility. We have:

$$p(H) = \sum\nolimits_{\cap_{i=1}^N H_i = H} m_1(H_1) m_2(H_2) \cdots m_n(H_N) \tag{4}$$

$$q(H) = \frac{1}{N} \sum\nolimits_{i=1}^N m_i(H) \tag{5}$$

By taking consideration the local conflict degrees, the evidence credibility ε can be calculated. Thus, the introduction of the local conflict concept is the innovation of this modified combination method. We therefore have

$$\varepsilon = e^{-K} \tag{6}$$

$$\bar{K} = \frac{1}{N(N-1)/2} \sum_{i<j<N} K_{ij} \tag{7}$$

$$K_{ij} = \sum_{H_i \cap H_j = \emptyset} m_i(H_i) m_j(H_j) \tag{8}$$

where K_{ij} is the local conflict of evidence m_i, m_j. While $\bar{K}$ is the average conflict degree of all local conflict K_{ij}, (i, j = 1, 2, ..., N), which represents the global conflict of system.

4.3 Occlusion-Aware

Most existing trackers are prone to long-term or short-term occlusion because of obstacles, pedestrians, etc. However, these phenomena will lead to drifting problems and missed the thief. In the proposed method, we use template update strategies and RFID signals to solve occlusion problems in visual tracking.

In correlation filter, the ideal response map should have only one sharp peak and the waveform is smooth in other areas when the detected object is highly matched to the correct object. Otherwise, when the object is occluded or has undergone violent deformation, the entire response map will fluctuate intensely. Therefore, the peak value and the fluctuation of the response map can reveal the confidence degree of the tracking results to a certain extent. Hence, we explore a high confidence feedback mechanism with two criteria. The first criterion is the maximum response score. The F_{max} of the response map $F(s, y; w)$ can be defined as follows:

$$F_{max} = \max F(s, y; w) \tag{9}$$

The second criterion is a novel one to measure the Fluctuation of the Waveform named F_w measure. We have

$$F_w = \frac{|F_{max} - F_{min}|}{mean\left(\sum_{w,h}(F_{w,h} - F_{min})^2\right)} \tag{10}$$

where F_{max}, F_{min} and $F_{w,h}$ denote the maximum, minimum and the w-th row h-th column elements of $F(s, y; w)$. When the two criteria F_{max} and F_w of the current frame are lower than their respective historical average values with certain ratios $\beta 1$ and $\beta 2$, the correlation filter will not be updated, which can reduce the impact of short term occlusion.

Furthermore, in addition to the above two indicators, when both the distance probability matrix and the velocity probability matrix in the sliding time window are larger than the experimentally set threshold $\beta 3$ and $\beta 4$, we can conclude that the object tracking fails due to long-term occlusion. In the sliding time window, we mainly focus on the BPA of RFID, while the visual BPA is negligible due to occlusion. To correct the occlusion, the search box of the correlation filter is adjusted to the position of the RFID, thus the tracking is performed again.

5   Experimental Results

In this section, we conduct performance evaluation of the hybrid scheme in our lab environment.

5.1   Evaluation Methodology

We conduct indoor experiments in a laboratory (10 m × 7 m) by using an off-the-shelf camera and four RFID antennas with different population sizes, RFID antennas are placed at the center of each side. In the scene, there are multiple individuals, with one of them (the thief) having an attached RFID tag (the tagged object). The surveillance camera is calibrated with known intrinsic parameters, including focal length, lens distortion, and relative rotation and translation with respect to the scene, so that image coordinates can be transferred to world coordinates. Ground truth was annotated by clicking on individuals' head in each image and using calibration information to reconstruct their coordinates. The hybrid system runs on a computer with CPU, and its running speed is 66 fps, which enables real-time tracking. We adopt the error distance, defined as the Euclidean distance between the result and the ground truth, as our base metric.

5.2   Performance of Matching

For the thief identification, we test our ability to identify the thief with multiple people moving in the experimental area. The matching accuracy rate R denotes the success rate of matching the tagged object to the thief, which can be defined as follows:

$$R = \frac{of\ successful\ matches}{of\ experiments\ in\ total} \times 100\% \tag{11}$$

The experiments in Table 1 show that system has perfect performance, which demonstrates the effectiveness of our association algorithm. Besides, with the number of people increasing, the performance gets worse because people movement cause signal reflection and extra visual noise.

Table 1. Matching accuracy with different numbers of people

# of tracks	1	2	3	4
Matching accuracy	100%	99%	99%	98%
Localization accuracy	10 cm	21 cm	29 cm	39 cm

When matching the thief, the length of the sliding window, i.e., the number of location points, usually affects the success rate of matching. We set the number of locations from 10 to 80 at an interval of 10, and for each case, we test on 2, 3 and 4 trackers respectively. Figure 3 describes how the matching accuracy changes along with the sampling number. When the number of location points increases, the accuracy also tends to increase, i.e., from 59% when the location number is 5 to 98% when the location number reaches 80. In practical experiments, we set the number of points to 60, which not only obtains relatively higher matching accuracy but also reduces the complexity of the experiment.

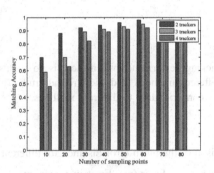

Fig. 3. Matching accuracy ratio vs position number

5.3 Performance of Fusing Algorithm

We then evaluate the thief tracking accuracy of our scheme and compare the performance with other well-known systems. As shown in Fig. 4(a), the path of RFID is dispersed to a large extent, while the video and the fusion paths are closer to the real path. Besides, the Cumulative Distribution Functions (CDF) of the error distance for different methods are shown in Fig. 4(b). For RFID-only method, most of the errors are within 100 cm. While 90% of the errors are less than 30 cm with the fusion method and video tracking.

The mean error distance of our fusion approach is compared with methods using only RFID or camera for people tracking (Table 2). The ANN model has better performance than SVM [8] while the ultimate positioning accuracy is at the decimeter level. In terms of visual methods, the improved ECO (IECO) has higher position accuracy than the original ECO [24]. The fusing approach has better results than the RFID-only and visual-only approach, and its positioning error is 0.097 m, which demonstrates that our fusion method is effective.

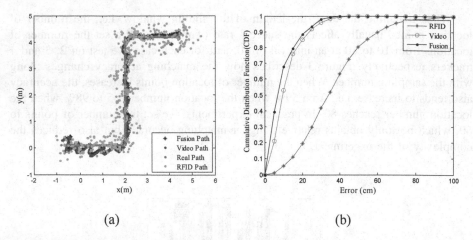

(a)   (b)

Fig. 4. Comparison of tracking performance when there is no occlusion. (a) Shows the paths corresponding to three different methods and the ground truth. (b) Shows the cumulative distribution function (CDF) corresponding to different methods.

Table 2. Comparison of the mean error distance for different tracking systems

System	Sensor type	Error (m)	Error in x-axis (m)	Error in y-axis (m)
SVM	Passive RFID	0.530	0.310	0.263
ANN	Passive RFID	0.400	0.279	0.234
ECO	Camera	0.124	0.086	0.089
IECO	Camera	0.118	0.063	0.081
Fusion	RFID and camera	0.097	0.039	0.070

5.4   Performance of Occlusion-Aware

The experiments on long-term occluded scenes are also validated. As shown in the first row of Fig. 6, the IECO algorithm drifts after the object is occluded for a long time and then tracks another object. For the fusion algorithm, the object is completely occluded in frame 516 and lost for a certain time. However, after performing the correction using RFID signal, the object is correctly tracked in the 886th frame.

The path of the occlusion experiments is shown in Fig. 5(a), the trajectory of the visual-only (IECO) tracking method is completely erroneous after being occluded, while the RFID and fusion methods do not deviate from the true trajectory. As shown in Fig. 5(b) and Table 3, the mean error distance of the RFID-only method is 0.52 m, and 90% of the errors is within 0.9 m. Although the video path is concentrated, the error is increased due to the tracking error caused by the occlusion. However, the fusion error is 0.2 m, which has better results. Furthermore, 90% of the errors are within 50 cm, which suggest enhanced performance compared to the single sensor. Therefore, our fusion method can still track the thief correctly under long-term occlusion, and has higher tracking accuracy than the single sensor.

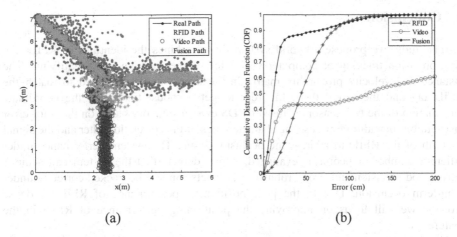

(a)   (b)

Fig. 5. Comparison of tracking performance under occlusion. (a) Shows the paths corresponding to different methods and (b) shows the cumulative distribution function (CDF) corresponding to different methods.

Table 3. Performance comparison of different tracking systems

System	Sensor type	Error (m)	Error in x-axis (m)	Error in y-axis (m)
SVM	Passive RFID	0.656	0.410	0.346
ANN	Passive RFID	0.52	0.32	0.34
ECO	Camera	2.224	1.886	1.689
IECO	Camera	1.95	1.69	0.94
Fusion	RFID and camera	0.21	0.12	0.15

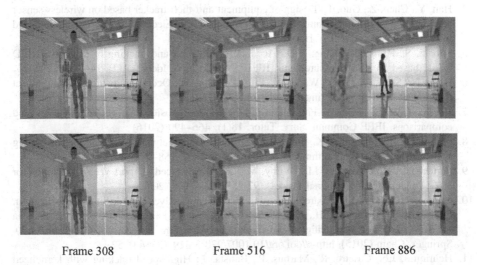

Frame 308   Frame 516   Frame 886

Fig. 6. Comparison of tracking performance under occlusion. The top row is the visual tracking method (IECO), and the second row is the fusion tracking method.

6 Conclusion

In this study, we propose a hybrid system that combines the identities of RFID and high-precision tracking of computer vision for online tracking and identifying. The distance and velocity probability matrix in the time window are used to match the RFID tag and the visual thief. In order to get a robust trajectory, the coordinate information of the two sensors is fused by DS evidence theory based on the prior error distribution. In addition, we use the characteristics of the correlation filter and the signal strength of the RFID to address the occlusion issue. The system performance under different number of people is evaluated, which depicts that the system can achieve fairly good precision and strong robustness, objects can still be tracked correctly under long-term occlusion. Due to the poor positioning performance of RFID in dense crowds, we will focus on improving the positioning performance of RFID in the feature.

Acknowledgement. This work was supported by Collaborative Fund of China Electronics Technology Group Corporation (Project No. 6141B08080401).

References

1. Alshammari, A., Rawat, D.B.: Intelligent multi-camera video surveillance system for smart city applications. In: 2019 IEEE 9th Annual Computing and Communication Workshop and Conference (CCWC), Las Vegas, pp. 0317–0323, IEEE (2019)
2. Liang, Y., Cai, Z., Yu, J., Han, Q., Li, Y.: Deep learning based inference of private information using embedded sensors in smart devices. IEEE Netw. **32**(4), 8–14 (2018)
3. Zheng, X., Cai, Z., Yu, J., Wang, C., Li, Y.: Follow but no track: privacy preserved profile publishing in cyber-physical social systems. IEEE Internet Things J. **4**(6), 1868–1878 (2017)
4. Han, Y., Chen, Z., Guo, T.: Design of equipment anti-theft tracker based on wireless sensor network. In: 2017 First International Conference on Electronics Instrumentation and Information Systems (EIIS), Harbin, pp. 1–5. IEEE (2017)
5. Subedi, S., Pauls, E., Zhang, Y.D.: Accurate localization and tracking of a passive RFID reader based on RSSI measurements. IEEE J. Radio Freq. Identif. **1**(2), 144–154 (2017)
6. Dong, X., Shen, J., Yu, D., Wang, W., Liu, J., Huang, H.: Occlusion-aware real-time object tracking. IEEE Trans. Multimed. **19**(4), 763–771 (2017)
7. He, S., Chan, S.H.G.: Wi-Fi fingerprint-based indoor positioning: recent advances and comparisons. IEEE Commun. Surv. Tutor. **18**(1), 466–490 (2016)
8. Mehmood, H., Tripathi, N.K.: Optimizing artificial neural network-based indoor positioning system using genetic algorithm. Int. J. Digit. Earth **6**(2), 158–184 (2013)
9. Figuera, C., Rojo-Álvarez, J.L., Wilby, M., et al.: Advanced support vector machines for 802.11 indoor location. Signal Process. **92**(9), 2126–2136 (2012)
10. Dwiyasa, F., Lim, M.H.: Extreme learning machine for active RFID location classification. In: Handa, H., Ishibuchi, H., Ong, Y.S., Tan, K.C. (eds.) Proceedings of the 18th Asia Pacific Symposium on Intelligent and Evolutionary Systems. PALO, vol. 2, pp. 657–670. Springer, Cham (2015). https://doi.org/10.1007/978-3-319-13356-0_52
11. Henriques, J.F., Caseiro, R., Martins, P., Batista, J.: High-speed tracking with kernelized correlation filters. IEEE Trans. Pattern Anal. Mach. Intell. **37**(3), 583–596 (2015)

12. Yuan, J., Chen, H., Sun, F., Huang, Y.: Multisensor information fusion for people tracking with a mobile robot: a particle filtering approach. IEEE Trans. Instrum. Meas. **64**(9), 2427–2442 (2015)
13. He, Z., Cai, Z., Cheng, S., Wang, X.: Approximate aggregation for tracking quantiles and range countings in wireless sensor networks. Theor. Comput. Sci. **607**(3), 381–390 (2015)
14. Teng, J., Zhang, B., Zhu, J., Li, X., Xuan, D., Zheng, Y.F.: EV-Loc: integrating electronic and visual signals for accurate localization. IEEE ACM Trans. Network. **22**(4), 1285–1296 (2014)
15. Duan, C., Rao, X., Yang, L., Liu, Y.: Fusing RFID and computer vision for fine-grained object tracking. In: IEEE INFOCOM 2017 - IEEE Conference on Computer Communications, Atlanta, pp. 1–9. IEEE (2017)
16. Redmon, J., Divvala, S., Girshick, R., Farhadi, A.: You only look once: unified, real-time object detection. In: Proceedings of the IEEE Conference on Computer Vision and Pattern Recognition (CVPR), Las Vegas, NV, pp. 779–788 (2016)
17. Danelljan, M., Bhat, G., Shahbaz Khan, F., Felsberg, M.: ECO: efficient convolution operators for tracking. In: Proceedings of the IEEE Conference on Computer Vision and Pattern Recognition (CVPR), pp. 6638–6646 (2017)
18. Wang, J., Liu, F.: Temporal evidence combination method for multi-sensor object recognition based on DS theory and IFS. J. Syst. Eng. Electron. **28**(6), 1114–1125 (2017)

Spatiotemporal Feature Extraction for Pedestrian Re-identification

Ye Li[1], Guangqiang Yin[1(✉)], Shaoqi Hou[1], Jianhai Cui[2], and Zicheng Huang[2]

[1] University of Electronic Science and Technology of China, Chengdu, China
liye@std.uestc.edu.cn, yingq@uestc.edu.cn,
shaoqi.hou@foxmail.com
[2] People's Public Security University of China, Beijing, China
cuijianhai@139.com, huangzcg@sina.com

Abstract. Video-based person re-identification (ReID) is a problem of person retrieval that aims to match the same person in two different videos, which has gradually entered the arena of public security. The system generally involve three important parts: feature extraction, feature aggregation and loss function. Pedestrian feature extraction and aggregation are critical steps in this field. Most of the previous studies concentrate on designing various feature extractors. However, these extractors cannot effectively extract spatiotemporal information. In this paper, several spatiotemporal convolution blocks were proposed to optimize the feature extraction model of person Re-identification. Firstly, 2D convolution and 3D convolution are simultaneously used on video volume to extract spatiotemporal feature. Secondly, non-local block is embedded into ResNet3D-50 to capture long-range dependencies. As a result, the proposed model could learn the inner link of pedestrian action in a video. Experimental results on MARS dataset show that our model has achieved significant progress compared to state-of-the-art methods.

Keywords: ReID · Spatiotemporal feature · Mixed convolution · Non-local block

1 Introduction

Person ReID aims to use computer vision technology to match person under two different cameras that has non-overlapping, which has aroused attention among researchers in recent years for the wide range of application, such as intelligent security, intelligent video surveillance and criminal investigation. In order to monitor the whole social region, it is necessary to use cameras to cover social region completely. Unfortunately, it is a real challenge to transmit the real-time video data, for each cameras has a separate line. With remarkable progress of technology of wireless network transmission, wireless network transmission algorithm could realize data interaction between front-end acquisition equipment and background analysis equipment. Moreover, multiclass classification [1] and feature selection [2, 3] are vital for information processing.

© Springer Nature Switzerland AG 2019
E. S. Biagioni et al. (Eds.): WASA 2019, LNCS 11604, pp. 188–200, 2019.
https://doi.org/10.1007/978-3-030-23597-0_15

In general, according to different sampling rules, person ReID methods can be classified two categories: image-based which use video as training sample and video-based which use image as training sample. A majority of the previous work use image-based approach [4–9], while only a few use video-based approach [10–14]. Compared to static image feature extraction, the temporal component of videos provides additional information for identification, as the same person is easier to be re-identified based on the motion information. However, Video-based person ReID system needs to capture pedestrian video that contain complete walking movements, and send the video data back to back-up server by wireless network transmission algorithm. In order to solve the problem that the amount of video data is too large to transmit, we optimize the algorithm of wireless network transmission to raise efficiency of data transmission or simplify the model to reduce the requirement of data volume.

Person ReID system generally involve three important parts: feature extraction, feature aggregation and loss function. Feature extraction and feature aggregation attract more attention in recent work [11]. These work proposed several methods of feature aggregation, including average or maximum temporal pooling method, RNN based method, and temporal attention method. But those methods failed to capture long-range dependencies and track spatial alignment simultaneously. [13] proposed using the jointly attentive spatial-temporal scheme, but failed to optimize the networks under severe occlusion. In conclusion, those approaches cannot effectively extract spatial-temporal information.

In this work, we adopt a novel scheduling policy to transmit video data [15] and devise an end-to-end deep convolutional network that is used to extract spatial-temporal features. Inspired by the recent success of mixed convolutional model on video action recognition [16], we directly use a hybrid model of 2D and 3D convolution to extract spatial-temporal features. It can integrate feature extraction and feature aggregation into one step. Then the non-local block is embedded into model to capture long-range dependencies. We summarize the contributions of this work in three-folds.

- Propose to use 3D convolution model to extract and aggregate spatial-temporal features.
- Propose a new model that contain 2D and 3D convolution to extract and aggregate features.
- Combine non-local block with Residual model to extract and aggregate spatiotemporal features, which is capable of mining the dependencies among frames.

In the following, we discuss some related works in Sect. 2, and introduces the details of the proposed model in Sect. 3. Section 4 introduces the experiment configuration states and experimental results. At last, some conclusions are stated for this research in Sect. 5.

2 Related Work

In this section, we will discuss some of the research progress in person ReID field, especially video-based deep neural network. Then we will summarize the mixed convolution in action recognition. At last, we will discuss the non-local block which has achieved excellent performance in feature extraction of video.

2.1 Person ReID

Image-Based Person ReID. Corresponds to an approach that extract pedestrian features from a single image, which pays more attention to some external information such as mask, pose, and skeleton. Gheissari et al. [17] proposed a method of representing the shape and structure of human body with multiple triangles. Douglas Gray et al. [18] proposed the most effective feature selection method from different perspectives through feature learning. Bazzani et al. [19] proposed using the cumulative HSV color histogram of the multi-frame image of pedestrians to represent the global characteristics of pedestrians. Zhao et al. [20] proposed a partial alignment representation method for body part misalignment problems. These method mainly solve problems of person misalignment, and is difficult to cope with complex environment changes such as illumination and occlusion.

Video-Based Person ReID. Corresponds to an approach that extract pedestrian features from video sequences, which pays more attention to motion information. Wang et al. [21] firstly proposed a new video ranking model to select discriminative spatial-temporal feature representations. McLanghlin et al. [12] utilized RNN to integrate the temporal information among frames. Chung et al. [22] presented a two-stream convolutional neural network to learn spatial and temporal information separately. Zhou et al. [10] proposed temporal attention model for feature learning. Liu et al. [23] designed a Quality Aware Network, which obtained sequence features with higher discriminative power and solved a series of practical problems in illumination blur.

2.2 Mixed CNN

Mixed CNN is a neural network model that contains 2D CNN and 3D CNN. 2D CNN is used to extract spatial features, while 3D CNN is used to extract spatiotemporal features [24]. Tran et al. [24] proposed using 3D CNN in action recognition, and found that 3D ConvNets are more effective in spatiotemporal feature learning than 2D ConvNets. Considering the problem of a large amount of calculation, Qiu et al. [25] proposed a P3D ResNet, which replaced one $3 \times 3 \times 3$ convolution kernel with one $1 \times 3 \times 3$ convolution kernel on spatial domain plus one $3 \times 1 \times 1$ convolution kernel on temporal domain. Considering the solid performers of 2D CNN in action recognition, Tran et al. [16] proposed a method that use MCx and rMCx to extract spatial-temporal features.

2.3   Non-local Block

Non-local technique [26] is a filtering algorithm which computes a weighted average of all areas that are similar to the current area. Inspired by this technique, Wang et al. [27] proposed a non-local block to capture long-range dependencies in video-based feature extraction. Particularly non-local block is an independent block that could be embedded into any neural network. Moreover, in [27], the author showed the performance of non-local block for the task of video segmentation, and action recognition.

3   The Proposed Approach

We introduce detailed settings of the proposed model in this section. We divided the person ReID system into two parts: feature extractor and loss function. Feature extractor consists of feature extraction and feature aggregation, which is mainly used to extract spatiotemporal features from continuous video clip, and loss function is used to optimize feature extractor.

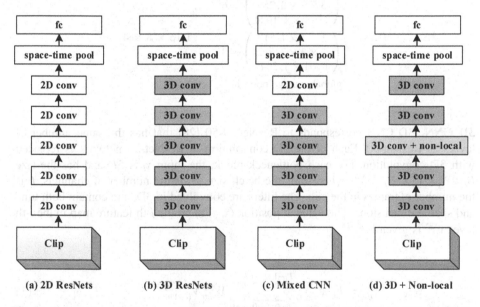

Fig. 1. Proposed model for person ReID. (a) 2D ResNets; (b) 3D ResNets; (c) Mixed CNN, which contains 3D convolution and 2D convolution; (d) 3D + non-local.

3.1   Spatiotemporal Feature Extraction and Aggregation

In this part we use ResNet-50 (see in Fig. 1(a)) as basic network that utilizes x to denote the input clip of size $b \times 3 \times W \times H$, where b is the batch size, 3 is the channel of image, W and H are the width and height of the frame. Only bottleneck blocks are considered, and the details of network are shown in Table 1. In this work, we reconstruct the convolution unit with several different spatiotemporal convolutional variants, such as 3D convolution, mixed convolution and non-local block. Then, we will explain each neural network in more detail.

Table 1. Our ResNet3D-50 model for video-based. The size of the input image is 256×128. Residual blocks are shown in brackets.

	Layer	Output size
conv$_1$	$7 \times 7 \times 7$, 64, stride 1, 2, 2	$T \times 128 \times 64$
pool$_1$	$3 \times 3 \times 3$ avg, stride 1, 2, 2	$T/2 \times 64 \times 32$
res$_2$	$\begin{pmatrix} 1 \times 1 \times 1, 64 \\ 3 \times 3 \times 3, 64 \\ 1 \times 1 \times 1, 256 \end{pmatrix} \times 3$	$T/2 \times 64 \times 32$
res$_3$	$\begin{pmatrix} 1 \times 1 \times 1, 128 \\ 3 \times 3 \times 3, 128 \\ 1 \times 1 \times 1, 512 \end{pmatrix} \times 4$	$T/4 \times 32 \times 16$
res$_4$	$\begin{pmatrix} 1 \times 1 \times 1, 256 \\ 3 \times 3 \times 3, 256 \\ 1 \times 1 \times 1, 1024 \end{pmatrix} \times 6$	$T/8 \times 16 \times 8$
res$_5$	$\begin{pmatrix} 1 \times 1 \times 1, 512 \\ 3 \times 3 \times 3, 512 \\ 1 \times 1 \times 1, 2048 \end{pmatrix} \times 3$	$T/16 \times 8 \times 4$
	global average pool, fc	$1 \times 1 \times 1$

3D CNN. 3D CNN corresponds to ResNet3D-50 [28] that has the same number of layers as ResNet-50. Each of the 2D convolution in ResNet-50 network is replaced with 3D convolution. For each bottleneck block, the input x_i is $5D$ and has the size $B_i \times N_i \times L \times H_i \times W_i$, where B_i is the batch size, N_i is the number of channels, L is the number of frames in the clip. The filters are convolved in 3D, and contain both time and spatial dimensions. The value at position (x, y, z) on the j-th feature map in the i-th layer v_{ij}^{xyz} is given by:

$$v_{ij}^{xyz} = b_{ij} + \sum_m \sum_{p=0}^{P_i-1} \sum_{q=0}^{Q_i-1} \sum_{r=0}^{R_i-1} W_{ijm}^{pqr} V_{(i-1)m}^{(x+p)(y+q)(z+r)} \tag{1}$$

Where P_i and Q_i denote the height and width of the kernel, respectively. R_i denotes the size of the 3D kernel along with the temporal dimension, W_{ijm}^{pqr} denotes the (p, q, r) th value of the kernel connected of the m-th feature map in the previous layer v_{i-1}, and b_{ij} denotes the bias. The 3D CNN architecture is illustrated in Fig. 1(b).

Mixed CNN. Mixed CNN corresponds to a mix of 2D convolution and 3D convolution. [16] has demonstrated that 3D convolutions are particularly useful in the early layer, while 3D convolutions are not necessary in the later layers. Thus a new architecture may use 3D convolutions in the bottom layer and switch to using 2D convolutions in the top layers. In this work ResNet3D-50 is considered having 5 groups of convolutions (Fig. 1(b)), our new architecture consists in replacing all 3D convolutions in group 5 with 2D convolutions. The Mixed CNN architecture is illustrated in Fig. 1(c).

3D CNN NL. 3D CNN NL corresponds to ResNet3D-50 which contains non-local blocks. Inspired by the non-local mean operation [26, 27] define a generic non-local operation as:

$$y_i = \frac{1}{C(x)} \sum_{\forall j} f(x_i, x_j) g(x_j) \tag{2}$$

Where y is the output signal and x is the input signal (image, video, features) of the same size as y. i represents the index of an output position whose response is to be computed, and j represents the index that enumerates all possible positions. The function f computes a correlation coefficient between i and all of the j. The function g computes a response of the input signal at the position j. $\forall j$ represents all positions of j. At last the factor $C(x)$ is used to normalize the response.

There are several versions of f and g, and experiments show that the non-local operation is not sensitive to these choices. For simplicity, we only consider g as: $g(x_j) = w_g x_j$, where w_g is a weight matrix to be learned, and we consider f as:

$$f(x_i, x_j) = e^{x_i^T x_j} \tag{3}$$

Where $x_i^T x_j$ is dot-product similarity. And the normalization factor is considered as:

$$C(x) = \sum_{\forall j} f(x_i, x_j) \tag{4}$$

The non-local operation is warped into a block that can be embedded into plenty of existing architectures. The non-local block is defined as:

$$z_i = W_z y_i + x_i \tag{5}$$

Where x_i is the input and "$+x_i$" represents a residual connection [29]. y_i is given in Eq. (2). The non-local block is illustrated in Fig. 2.

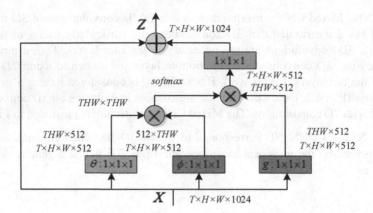

Fig. 2. A spacetime non-local block.

The feature maps are shown in Fig. 2 as the shape of their tensors, e.g., T × H W × 1024 for 1024 channels (proper reshaping is performed when noted), where "⊗" denotes sum, and "⊗" denotes multiplication. The blue boxes denote $1 \times 1 \times 1$ convolutions. "X × X × X × X" denotes the size of input or output after the operation.

For non-local operation is an efficient, simple and generic component for capturing long-range dependencies, it is embedded in the group 2 of ResNet3D-50 network. This type of the CNN architecture is illustrated in Fig. 1(d).

3.2   Loss Function

Our loss function consists of a softmax cross-entropy loss function with label smoothing regularization [30] and a triplet loss function.

The triplet loss function used in this paper was originally proposed in [31], named as Batch Hard triplet loss function. To form a batch of samples, we randomly sample P identities and randomly sample K tracks for each identity (each track contains T frames); totally there are $P \times K$ clips in a batch. For each sample a in the batch, the hardest positive and the hardest negative samples within the batch are selected when forming the triplets for computing the loss $L_{triplet}$.

$$L_{triplet} = \overbrace{\sum_{i=1}^{P} \sum_{a=1}^{K}}^{all\ anchors} [m + \overbrace{\max D\left(f_a^i, f_p^i\right)}^{hardest\ positive} - \underbrace{\min_{\substack{j=1...P \\ n=1...K \\ j \neq i}} D\left(f_a^i, f_n^j\right)}_{hardest\ negative}]_+ \tag{6}$$

The original Softmax cross-entropy loss function is given by:

$$L_{softmax} = -\frac{1}{P \times K} \sum_{i=1}^{P} \sum_{a=1}^{K} p_{i,a} \log q_{i,a} \tag{7}$$

Where $p_{i,a}$ is the ground truth identity and $q_{i,a}$ is the prediction value of sample $\{i, a\}$. The label-smoothing regularization is proposed to regularize the model and make it more adaptable with:

$$L'_{softmax} = -\frac{1}{P \times K} \sum_{i=1}^{P} \sum_{a=1}^{K} p_{i,a} \log((1-\varepsilon)q_{i,a} + \frac{\varepsilon}{N}) \tag{8}$$

Where N is the number of classes. This can be considered as a mixture of the original ground-truth distribution $q_{i,a}$ and the uniform distribution $u(x) = 1/N$.

$$L = L'_{softmax} + L_{triplet} \tag{9}$$

4 Experiments

In this section, our proposed approach is evaluated on MARS [32]. Our approach is compared with the state-of-the-art approach, and experimental results demonstrate that our proposed method can enhance the performance of feature extraction and feature aggregation.

4.1 Datasets

There are three public video datasets for person ReID, including MARS, iLIDS-VID [21], and PRID-2011 [33]. All proposed models are evaluated on the MARS dataset, which is the largest. MARS is an extension of the Market-1501 dataset. MARS contains 1261different persons, 625 are used for training and 636 for testing. Each person is captured by at least 2 cameras. Given a query tracklet, MARS aims to retrieve tracklets that contain the same ID.

4.2 Experimental Setup

In this part, we detail the experimental configurations for training and testing.

Training. The sequence length can be set to any value, but considering the limitation of GPU memory and the long dependence of tracklet information, 4 or 8 for each identity is set for the training process. For instance, 8 frames are adopted as an input tracks in training term, and randomly be chosen 8 from a tracklet, then another 8 frames are randomly chosen from remaining frames of the tracklet. Finally one tracklet was divided into multiple input tracks, which constitutes our training sample set. The spatial size of input images is 256 × 128, and is randomly cropped from a tracklet whose size is randomly enlarged by 1\8 with a probability of 0.5. Batch size is set to 64. Adaptive Moment Estimation (Adam) [34] is adopted with a weight decay of 0.0005 when training. The model is trained for 60 epochs, beginning with a learning rate of 0.0003 and reducing it by exponential decay with decay rate 0.1 at 20 epochs and 40 epochs. The model was pre-trained on Kinetics and UCF101 dataset.

Testing. All proposed models are tested on MARS dataset, which contains 1980 query tracklets and 9330 gallery tracklets. Cumulated Matching Characteristics (CMC) and mean average precision(mAP) are used to evaluate the performance. Considering the convenience of experiment comparison, only the CMC at rank-1, rank-5, rank-10 and mAP are reported. Batch size is set as 1. During testing, the video is divided into some clips, and clip level representation is extracted. The video level representation is the average of all clip level representations.

4.3   Component Analysis of the Proposed Model

In this part, the performance of 3D convolution, Mixed convolution and 3D convolution with non-local block separately are reported separately.

Different Convolution Units: 2D vs 3D. 2D CNN, 3D CNN and Mixed CNN on MARS dataset are shown in Table 2. 2D CNN is baseline that is image-based ResNet-50 network. 3D CNN is video-based train model that is pre-trained on Kinetics and UCF101 dataset. Mixed CNN is our proposed model which has 2D convolution and 3D convolution. The 3D CNN improves the mAP of 2D CNN counterparts (+1.5 point accuracy), results shows that 3D convolution is more effective than 2D convolution in spatiotemporal feature extraction. It is noted that Mixed CNN has 64.3% accuracy, slightly higher than the 3D CNN's 64.0%, which demonstrates that temporal modeling is more necessary in early layer while it is not necessary in the later layer.

Table 2. Component analysis of the proposed approach: 2D CNN is the Resnet-34, 3D CNN is the ResNet3D-34, Mixed CNN is the ResNet-34, which contains 2D convolution and 3D convolution.

Methods	CMC-1	CMC-5	CMC-10	mAP
2D CNN	74.2	88.1	91.7	**62.5**
3D CNN	75.8	89.2	92.6	**64.0**
Mixed CNN	75.3	89.7	92.2	**64.3**

Different Length Settings: T = 4, 8, 16. The sequence length of the input image is a key factor in determining the effectiveness of the model. ResNet3D-50 network is used to study the correlation between sequence length and accuracy. The results in Table 3 show that T = 8 performs better than T = 4 and T = 16. When T is small, the model is prone to overfitting because the input contains less information. However, when T is large, the model is difficult to train because the input contains more information. T = 8 is more suitable for video-based problem. In the rest of this paper, T is set as 8 by default.

Table 3. Comparison of different sequence length T = 4, 8, 16

Length	CMC-1	CMC-5	CMC-10	mAP
T = 4	71.0	84.7	88.3	**56.6**
T = 8	74.6	89.1	91.7	**63.1**
T = 16	72.3	86.7	89.8	**59.9**

Different Embedding Position: Non-local Block. Considering the non-local block can be embedded into any position, Resnet3D-34 model was used to study the correlation between inserting position and accuracy. Table 4 shows that the performance of a non-local block on res_2 is slightly higher than on res_2, which demonstrates big spatial size is sufficient to provide spatial information.

Table 4. Comparison of different embedding position of non-local block

Position	CMC-1	CMC-5	CMC-10	mAP
res_2	74.1	87.9	91.4	**61.8**
res_3	73.9	88.3	91.5	**61.4**
res_2 & res_3	74.1	86.6	90.9	**60.3**

4.4   Comparison with State-of-the-Art Methods

The best parameter setting is selected in our proposed model, and their performance is compared in MARS dataset, with the result shown in Table 5.

Table 5. Comparison with state-of-the-art methods

Methods	CMC-1	CMC-5	CMC-10	mAP
Zheng et al. [32]	65.0	81.1	–	45.6
Li et al. [35]	71.8	86.6	–	56.1
Liu et al. [23]	73.7	84.9	–	51.7
Zhou et al. [10]	70.6	90.0	–	50.7
Hermans et al. [31]	79.8	91.4	–	67.7
Liu et al. [36]	68.3	–	–	52.9
Li et al. [14]	82.3	–	–	65.8
Ours (3D CNN)	80.7	91.0	93.4	**69.9**
Ours (3D + non-local)	79.6	90.7	92.8	**67.3**

It is clearly showed that the accuracy of video-based is higher than that of image-based model, which shows that 3D convolution is more effective than 2D convolution. Zhou et at. [10] used a very complex feature extraction model that combined Spatial RNN, temporal attention and temporal RNN. However the mAP is only 50.7%. In contrast, we adopt a simple model that is based on ResNet3D-50, and the mAP achieve

69.9%. The mAP of [14] is only 65.8%, our proposed model (3D + non-local) can achieve 67.3%, and we believe the improvement mainly comes from the use of non-local block that could capture the linkages intrinsic among tracklets.

5   Conclusion

Video-based person ReID is a significant research, which has made a great progress. In this paper, several end-to-end models are proposed that are used for feature extraction and aggregation. The experiment is designed to demonstrate the effectiveness of each model. Experimental results show that 3D convolution could more effectively fuse spatiotemporal features and non-local block could capture long-range dependencies. While our study was focused on feature extractor, we will try to find more suitable convolution unit and improve the performance of loss function in the future.

References

1. Cai, Z., Goebel, R., Salavatipour, M.R., et al.: Selecting dissimilar genes for multi-class classification, an application in cancer subtyping. BMC Bioinform. **8**(1), 206 (2007)
2. Guo, J., et al.: An XGBoost-based physical fitness evaluation model using advanced feature selection and Bayesian hyper-parameter optimization for wearable running monitoring. Comput. Netw. **151**, 166–180 (2019)
3. Song, T., Cheng, X., Li, H., Yu, J., Wang, S., Bie, R.: Detecting driver phone calls in a moving vehicle based on voice features. In: INFOCOM 2016, pp. 1–9 (2016)
4. Cheng, D., Gong, Y., Zhou, S., et al.: Person re-identification by multi-channel parts-based CNN with improved triplet loss function. In: Computer Vision and Pattern Recognition. IEEE (2016)
5. Liu, H., Feng, J., Qi, M., et al.: End-to-end comparative attention networks for person re-identification. IEEE Trans. Image Process. 1 (2017)
6. Wang, F., Zuo, W., Lin, L., et al.: Joint learning of single-image and cross-image representations for person re-identification. In: 2016 IEEE Conference on Computer Vision and Pattern Recognition (CVPR). IEEE Computer Society (2016)
7. Wu, L., Shen, C., Hengel, A.V.D.: PersonNet: person re-identification with deep convolutional neural networks (2016)
8. Xiao, T., Li, H., Ouyang, W., et al.: Learning deep feature representations with domain guided dropout for person re-identification (2016)
9. Xiao, T., Li, S., Wang, B., et al.: End-to-end deep learning for person search (2016)
10. Zhou, Z., Huang, Y., Wang, W., et al.: See the forest for the trees: joint spatial and temporal recurrent neural networks for video-based person re-identification. In: IEEE Conference on Computer Vision and Pattern Recognition, pp. 6776–6785. IEEE (2017)
11. Gao, J., Nevatia, R.: Revisiting temporal modeling for video-based person reid. CoRR, abs/1805.02104 (2018)
12. McLaughlin, N., del Rincon, J.M., Miller, P.: Recurrent convolutional network for video-based person reidentification. In: The IEEE Conference on Computer Vision and Pattern Recognition (CVPR), June 2016

13. Xu, S., Cheng, Y., Gu, K., Yang, Y., Chang, S., Zhou, P.: Jointly attentive spatial-temporal pooling networks for video-based person re-identification. In: The IEEE International Conference on Computer Vision (ICCV), October 2017

14. Li, S., Bak, S., Carr, P., Wang, X.: Diversity regularized spatiotemporal attention for video-based person reidentification. In: The IEEE Conference on Computer Vision and Pattern Recognition (CVPR), June 2018

15. Zheng, X., Cai, Z.: Real-time big data delivery in wireless networks: a case study on video delivery. IEEE Trans. Ind. Inf. 1 (2017)

16. Tran, D., Wang, H., Torresani, L., et al.: A closer look at spatiotemporal convolutions for action recognition (2017)

17. Gheissari, N., Bab-Hadiashar, A., Suter, D.: Parametric model-based motion segmentation using surface selection criterion. Comput. Vis. Image Underst. **102**(2), 214–226 (2006)

18. Gray, D., Tao, H.: Viewpoint invariant pedestrian recognition with an ensemble of localized features. In: Forsyth, D., Torr, P., Zisserman, A. (eds.) ECCV 2008. LNCS, vol. 5302, pp. 262–275. Springer, Heidelberg (2008). https://doi.org/10.1007/978-3-540-88682-2_21

19. Bazzani, L., Cristani, M., Murino, V.: Decentralized particle filter for joint individual-group tracking (2012)

20. Zhao, L., Li, X., Wang, J., et al.: Deeply-learned part-aligned representations for person re-identification (2017)

21. Wang, T., Gong, S., Zhu, X., Wang, S.: Person re-identification by video ranking. In: Fleet, D., Pajdla, T., Schiele, B., Tuytelaars, T. (eds.) ECCV 2014. LNCS, vol. 8692, pp. 688–703. Springer, Cham (2014). https://doi.org/10.1007/978-3-319-10593-2_45

22. Chung, D., Tahboub, K., Delp, E.J.: A two stream siamese convolutional neural network for person re-identification. In: Proceedings of the IEEE Conference on Computer Vision and Pattern Recognition, pp. 1983–1991 (2017)

23. Liu, Y., Yan, J., Ouyang, W.: Quality aware network for set to set recognition. In: The IEEE Conference on Computer Vision and Pattern Recognition (CVPR), July 2017

24. Tran, D., Bourdev, L., Fergus, L., Torresani, L., Paluri, M.: Learning spatiotemporal features with 3D convolutional networks. In: ICCV (2015)

25. Qiu, Z., Yao, T., Mei, T.: Learning spatio-temporal representation with pseudo-3D residual networks (2017)

26. Buades, A., Coll, B., Morel, J.M.: A non-local algorithm for image denoising. In: 2005 IEEE Computer Society Conference on Computer Vision and Pattern Recognition (CVPR 2005), vol. 2, pp. 60–65, June 2005

27. Wang, X., Girshick, R., Gupta, A., He, K.: Non-local neural networks. In: The IEEE Conference on Computer Vision and Pattern Recognition (CVPR), June 2018

28. Hara, K., Kataoka, H., Satoh, Y.: Can spatiotemporal 3D CNNs retrace the history of 2D CNNs and imagenet? CoRR, abs/1711.09577 (2017)

29. He, K., Zhang, X., Ren, S., Sun, J.: Deep residual learning for image recognition. In: Computer Vision and Pattern Recognition (CVPR) (2016)

30. Szegedy, C., Vanhoucke, V., Ioffe, S., Shlens, J., Wojna, Z.: Rethinking the inception architecture for computer vision. In: The IEEE Conference on Computer Vision and Pattern Recognition (CVPR), June 2016

31. Hermans, A., Beyer, L., Leibe, B.: In defense of the triplet loss for person re-identification. CoRR, abs/1703.07737 (2017)

32. Zheng, L., et al.: MARS: a video benchmark for large-scale person re-identification. In: Leibe, B., Matas, J., Sebe, N., Welling, M. (eds.) ECCV 2016. LNCS, vol. 9910, pp. 868–884. Springer, Cham (2016). https://doi.org/10.1007/978-3-319-46466-4_52

33. Hirzer, M., Beleznai, C., Roth, Peter M., Bischof, H.: Person re-identification by descriptive and discriminative classification. In: Heyden, A., Kahl, F. (eds.) SCIA 2011. LNCS, vol. 6688, pp. 91–102. Springer, Heidelberg (2011). https://doi.org/10.1007/978-3-642-21227-7_9
34. Kingma, D.P., Ba, J.: Adam: a method for stochastic optimization. CoRR, abs/1412.6980 (2014)
35. Li, D., Chen, X., Zhang, Z., et al.: Learning deep context-aware features over body and latent parts for person re-identification (2017)
36. Liu, H., Jie, Z., Jayashree, K., et al.: Video-based Person Re-identification with Accumulative Motion Context. IEEE Trans. Circ. Syst. Video Technol. 1 (2017)

Detecting Android Side Channel Probing Attacks Based on System States

Qixiao Lin[1], Jian Mao[1(✉)], Futian Shi[1], Shishi Zhu[1], and Zhenkai Liang[2]

[1] Beihang University, Beijing 100083, China
maojian@buaa.edu.cn
[2] National University of Singapore, Singapore 117417, Singapore

Abstract. Side channels are actively exploited by attackers to infer users' privacy from publicly-available information on Android devices, where attackers probe the states of system components (e.g., CPU and memory), APIs, and device sensors (e.g., gyroscope and microphone). These information can be accessed by applications without any additional permission. As a result, traditional permission-based solutions cannot efficiently prevent/detect these probing attacks. In this paper, we systematically analyze the Android side-channel probing attacks, and observe that the high frequency sensitive data collecting operations from a malicious app caused continuous changes of its process states. Based on this observation, we propose SideGuard, a process-state-based approach to detect side-channel probing attacks. It monitors the process states of the applications and creates the corresponding behavior models described by feature vectors. Based on the application behavior models, we train and obtain classifiers to detect malicious app behaviors by using learning-based classification techniques. We prototyped and evaluated our approach. The experiment results demonstrate the effectiveness of our approach.

Keywords: Side-channel attack · Supervised learning ·
Android system state · Application behavior model

1 Introduction

Android has the leading market share among mobile operating systems, with 85.9% of global market share in the first quarter of 2018 [1]. Mobile applications (apps) in the Android platform provide convenient services in different aspects, e.g., social life, health care, e-commerce, business, etc. Most of these apps carry and process users' private information that should be protected from unauthorized access of other applications. To enforce this security requirement, the Android platform deploys a sandbox-based security model where each app runs in its application-sandbox and cannot access other apps' data. In addition, Android uses a permission system to regulate apps' access to resources and services. Though the above security mechanisms make it difficult for attackers to

© Springer Nature Switzerland AG 2019
E. S. Biagioni et al. (Eds.): WASA 2019, LNCS 11604, pp. 201–212, 2019.
https://doi.org/10.1007/978-3-030-23597-0_16

directly access other apps' information, research has shown that side-channel attacks can still infer users' sensitive information from the publicly-available information from the shared resources [5,9,20], e.g., the states of system components (e.g., CPU and memory), APIs, and device sensors (e.g., gyroscope, microphone, etc.).

More seriously, the aforementioned side-channel information can be obtained without additional permissions. For example, the states of system components are obtained from Android's public interfaces, including `procfs` and `sysfs`. One of typical side channel attacks using system states infers browsing history and UI transition based on data resident size and shared virtual memory size extracted from `procfs` [5,9]. APIs are designed for applications' access to system resources, but they are abused for side channel information acquisition and transmission [4,22]. Different kinds of sensors collect diverse personal information to enhance functions that improve user convenience. However, large amounts of sensors provide more potential targets for side channel probing attacks. Researches have shown that sensor data can be used to infer users' input on the screen [15] and location [7,10].

To defend against side channel attacks, traditional detection schemes usually adopt data flow analysis, control flow analysis, or both. TaintDroid [6] is a typical detection scheme based on data flow. By analyzing the flow of sensitive information in the application, data flow analysis detects the application behaviors of transmitting sensitive information outside in different ways, such as through network socket. The control flow analysis captures the application's behaviors by analyzing API calls and their trigger conditions to detect side channel attack. However, these traditional detection schemes are not designed specifically for detecting side-channel information leakage that can be bypassed by well-designed side-channel attacks. For example, Babil et al. [2] presented various side-channel attacks that can bypass TaintDroid's taint tracking detection. Determining the fundamental features of the side-channel behavior to defend against probing attacks with high effectiveness is still a critical challenge in mobile data security, especially, privacy preserving.

Our Observation. To infer user's sensitive data effectively, malicious apps typically need to access/probe the resources leading to side-channel attacks repeatedly at a high frequency. These probing operations result in a continuous change of malicious apps' process states. Similar to probing attack detection using process states (e.g., UI state inference attack [5]), side-channel attack behaviors can also be "leaked" (or identified) via process states. An approach designed under the similar inspiration, APPGuardian [21], simply considered CPU schedule status from `schedstat` in `/proc` as behavior features to detect malicious data-collection behaviors, which may not have enough sensitivity and result in false positive.

In this paper, we propose SideGuard, an approach to detect side-channel probing attacks based on system states in Android. SideGuard works as an independent app installed on Android devices. It monitors system states and collects app behaviors for applications running in the system based on the system state changes. SideGuard adopts learning-based classification techniques, such as SVM and Random Forest, to train a behavior classifier to identify the malicious apps that is carrying out probing attacks. SideGuard is a lightweight detection method without any modifications in Android system or applications.

Contributions. In summary, we make the following contributions in this paper.

- We systematically analyze typical Android side-channel probing attacks, and observe that the high frequency sensitive data collecting operations from a malicious app will inevitably cause continuous changes of its process states.
- We propose a system-state-based approach, SideGuard, to detect the Android side channel probing attacks. Our approach monitors and takes the changes of the system states as the critical features to identify the dynamic behaviors of an application. We train a behavior classifier and detect the probing attacks according to the application's system-state behavior model.
- we prototype and evaluate our approach. The experiment results illustrate the effectiveness of SideGuard, which can detect six different types of probing attacks, and the best F1 score achieves 0.99.

Paper Organization. The rest of this paper is organized as follows. Section 2 presents the overview of our approach; Sect. 3 proposes our approach and illustrates the critical components in detail; Sect. 4 presents the implementation and evaluation results of our approach; Sect. 5 discusses related work; and Sect. 6 concludes the paper.

2   Overview

2.1   The Influence of Probing Behaviors on System States

A side-channel probing attack typically consists of two steps: public information collection and privacy inference. Malicious applications that perform side-channel probing attacks collect public information through different side channels, and send them to attackers that carry out analysis and inference remotely. The side-channel attacks have high stealthiness because attackers only collect public-available information without additional permissions, which can hardly be detected by conventional malware detection approaches. How to distinguish side-channel probing attacks and the normal access to the system resources is the main challenge to effectively defend against the side-channel attacks.

To address this problem, we first analyze typical side-channel attacks by executing side-channel probing operations and monitoring the corresponding dynamic behaviors and system states. Specifically, we developed an application that performs side-channel probing behaviors and collects mobile usage data tcp_snd from procfs. We monitored the process state of this application in every second. Figure 1 illustrates the change of voluntary context switches, one of process state data that indicates the switching number of the CPU from one process to another. The attack behavior started from the fourth second and

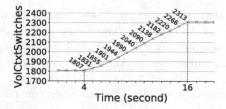

Fig. 1. Number of voluntary context switches during an attack behavior

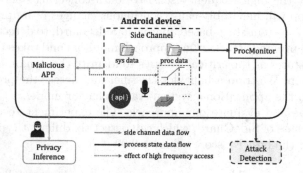

Fig. 2. Side channel probing attack and our approach

ended at the sixteenth second. Figure 1 shows that the number of voluntary context switches increased during the attack and all variation between time periods were nearly same. The reason of this constant increase is that although the application were running in the background, it collected data at the high sampling frequency and needed to occupy CPU continuously. This is just one example of the "visibility" of such probing attacks. There are other kinds of system states that also changed when probing behaviors happen.

Based on the experiments, we found that to accurately infer users' sensitive information, malicious apps need to collect a large amount of side-channel information with high frequencies. Highly frequent side-channel data collection causes aggressive utilization of CPU, shared memory and other shared resources and presents continuous changes of process states. Therefore, the change pattern of process state data can be used to reveal application behaviors, and further, to detect these attacks.

2.2   Approach Overview

The aforementioned analysis discloses that the high frequency operations collecting system states from a malicious app will inevitably cause continuous changes of its own system states. Based on this finding, we propose SideGuard, a system-state-based approach to defend against side-channel probing attacks. As shown in Fig. 2, SideGuard consists of two main components, the ProcMonitor module and the Attack Detection module. The ProcMonitor module collects process-

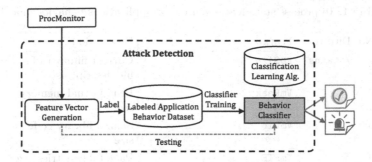

Fig. 3. Attack detection module of SideGuard

related states, e.g., data from `procfs`, and extracts apps' dynamic behavior features for side-channel probing detection. The Attack Detection module takes the apps' dynamic behavior feature vectors as inputs and detect the unexpected behaviors based on learning algorithms.

3 Design

In this section, we present the design of SideGuard. We first identify the process states that are related to probing attacks. Shown in Fig. 3, SideGuard collects the states using its ProcMonitor. Upon receiving the states, SideGuard converts them into feature vectors for training and detection. Training datasets from benign/malicious samples are used to train a behavior classifier, which is then used to detect probing attacks based on suspicious app states.

3.1 System States Selection

Process states of applications can be divided into three categories by their changing modes, namely, *constant* states, *increased-decreased* states and *accumulative* states. *Constant* states are irrelevant to applications behavior and remain unchanged after processes are created. Most of them are attribute value of applications, such as process ID (`pid`), user ID (`uid`), etc. *Increased-decreased* states refer to those states varying with applications behaviors, such as memory usage or CPU share of the process. As for *accumulative* states, e.g., CPU scheduling times and interruption times, they continually accumulate while apps are running. Our approach focuses on *increased-decreased* states and *accumulative* states.

We build an Android application behavior model based on 16 process state features as representation of applications behaviors, which are illustrated in Table 1. These features include various of processor, memory, scheduler and file system states, namely, the number of file descriptor slots allocated (Feature 1), states related to virtual memory (Feature 2–8), the number of context switches (Feature 9–10), the number of threads in process containing this thread (Feature

Table 1. 16 process state features used for applications behavior model

No	Directory	Feature	Description
1	/status	FDSize	Current number of file descriptors
2		VmPeak	Peak virtual memory size
3		VmLib	Shared library code size
4		VmPTE	Page table entries size
5		VmSize	Virtual memory size
6		VmHWM	Peak resident set size
7		VmRSS	Resident set size
8		VmData	Size of data segments
9		VoluntaryCtxtSwitches	Number of voluntary context switch
10		NonVoluntaryCtxtSwitches	Number of involuntary context switch
11		Threads	Number of threads in process
12	/stat	Utime	CPU time spent in user code
13		STime	CPU time spent in kernel code
14	/statm	Size	Total program size
15		Resident	Resident set size
16		Share	Resident shared pages

11), CPU usage time (Feature 12–13) and the data related to memory (Feature 14–16). Details of the features are also shown in Table 1. They are extracted from /proc/⟨pid⟩/status, /proc/⟨pid⟩/s-tat and /proc/⟨pid⟩/statm.

3.2 Data Collection and Feature Vector Generation

In our approach, ProcMonitor is an independent Android app runing on the Android device to extract required process state data from Android system for the follow-up attack detection. ProcMonitor reads user-specified pid, loads its process state files, including status, stat, and statm. ProcMonitor stores all process state data for feature vector generation.

Because an application behavior changes different process state data in different association patterns, we generate feature vectors according to the analysis of association patterns between side channel behaviors and application states. Basically, there are two types of association patterns.

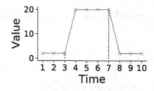

Fig. 4. Values of the process state feature with the first association pattern during an attack.

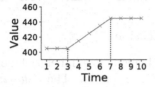 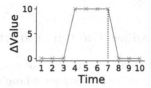

Fig. 5. Values of the process state feature with the second association pattern during an attack.

- In the *first association pattern*, values of process state features increase significantly at the moment when malicious apps launch side-channel probing attack. The value stays high until the attack operations stop, after which they decrease to the original level. Process state features with this association pattern can only be *increased-decreased* states. For instance, malicious apps produce new threads to collect sensitive data, which increases number of threads (`status.Threads`, *increased-decreased* states); when data collection is finished, the number of threads decreases accordingly, as shown in Fig. 4.
- In the *second association pattern*, values of process state features show a rising trend for the duration of side-channel attacks and the increase is almost constant. Process state features with this association pattern can be *increased-decreased* or *accumulative* data. For example, malicious apps need CPU scheduling continually, which means applying for CPU usage and handing over CPU. Thus, CPU scheduling times (`status.NonvoluntaryCtxtSwit ches`, *accumulative* data) increase continuously, as shown in Fig. 5(a), and the increment is constant, as shown in Fig. 5(b). Another example is that process memory size (`statm.Size`, *increased-decreased* state) increases during the moment that malicious apps store collected state information in memory, then either temporarily store it in local storage or send it to a remote server.

Among the 16 process state features, Feature 1, 2, 3, 4, 11 are associated with application behaviors in the first pattern, which require no preprocessing. And other features are associated in the second pattern, for them, we utilize increments of their value instead of themselves to present the implicit correlation in multiple moments.

Given the process state feature set $\{F1_i, F2_i, ..., F16_i\}$, which is collected from the Android device at the i-th time, we calculate the increment of the features with the second association pattern as follows (take Feature No. 5 as an example):

$$\Delta F5_i = F5_i - F5_{i-1} \tag{1}$$

Then we generate feature vector $\vec{v_i}$ as follows:

$$\vec{v_i} = (F1_i, F2_i, F3_i, F4_i, \Delta F5_i, \Delta F6_i, \Delta F7_i, \Delta F8_i, \Delta F9_i, \Delta F10_i, F11_i, \\ \Delta F12_i, \Delta F13_i, \Delta F14_i, \Delta F15_i, \Delta F16_i) \tag{2}$$

3.3 Classifier Training and Attack Detection

We collect process state data of malicious and benign apps, label each generated feature vector and construct a labeled app behavior dataset. The *Behavior Classifier* is trained based on the dataset. For our approach, the real-time collected process data of suspicious apps will be converted into a feature vector to be tested by the Feature Vector Generation module. Then the feature vector will be entered into the Behavior Classifier, which will predict the behavior is benign or malicious.

4 Implementation and Experimentation

In this section, we introduce the implementation and discuss results from experiments.

4.1 Side-Channel Behavior Simulation

We developed three malicious apps that can perform six types of side-channel attacks based on existing research. We named these three applications as *ProcReader*, *APICaller* and *SensorSniffer*. ProcReader reads mobile data usage and shared-memory size in `procfs` with the time period of 50 ms to re-perform Twitter Identities Inference [22] and UI Inference [5]. APICaller invokes MediaRecorder and isMusicActive, which are APIs exploited by Audio Recording [2] and Driving Route Inference [22]. SensorSniffer collects accelerometer and gyroscope data to re-perform TouchLogger [3] and Voice Eavesdropping [12].

We perform the aforementioned typical side-channel attacks and extracted these applications' process states as attack behavior samples when they run in the background.

4.2 Process State Extraction

To build our behavior model, ProcMonitor extracts required process state data from `procfs`. ProcMonitor lists the process ID and the name of applications on the main interface so that users can choose the process they intend to monitor and input the process ID according to the list. For example, if an attack that

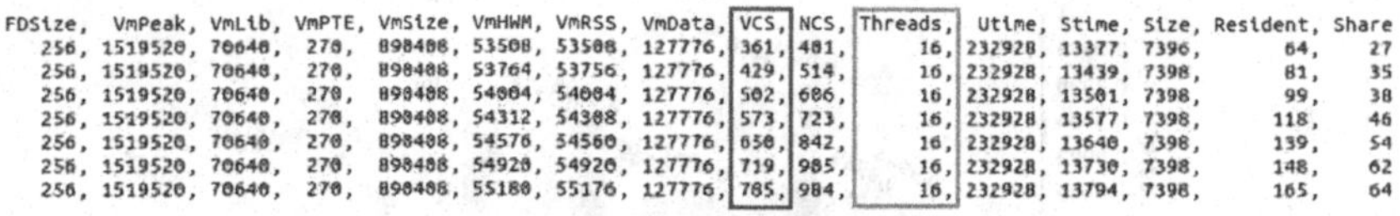

FDSize	VmPeak	VmLib	VmPTE	VmSize	VmHWM	VmRSS	VmData	VCS	NCS	Threads	Utime	Stime	Size	Resident	Share
256,	1519520,	70640,	270,	890488,	53508,	53508,	127776,	361,	481,	16,	232928,	13377,	7396,	64,	27
256,	1519520,	70640,	270,	890488,	53764,	53756,	127776,	429,	514,	16,	232928,	13439,	7398,	81,	35
256,	1519520,	70640,	270,	890488,	54004,	54004,	127776,	502,	686,	16,	232928,	13501,	7398,	99,	38
256,	1519520,	70640,	270,	890488,	54312,	54308,	127776,	573,	723,	16,	232928,	13577,	7398,	118,	46
256,	1519520,	70640,	270,	890488,	54576,	54560,	127776,	650,	842,	16,	232928,	13640,	7398,	139,	54
256,	1519520,	70640,	270,	890488,	54928,	54920,	127776,	719,	985,	16,	232928,	13730,	7398,	148,	62
256,	1519520,	70640,	270,	890488,	55180,	55176,	127776,	785,	984,	16,	232928,	13794,	7398,	165,	64

Fig. 6. Process state data of ProcReader received in the server (Color figure online)

read `tcp_snd` data is performed by ProcReader, to monitor its process state, we need to run ProcMonitor, find ProcReader's process ID on the main interface and enter it in the input box. Then the process state of ProcReader will be sent to the server. The data received are shown in Fig. 6. The `Threads` data in the red box are associated in the first pattern, and the `VoluntaryCtxtSwitches` data in the blue box are associated in the second pattern. Therefore, we need to convert raw data to the behavior feature vectors as we described in Sect. 3.2.

4.3 Experimentation and Results

We run these malicious applications in the background to simulate data collection progress in side channel and collected their process states as attack behavior samples. In addition, we collected normal behavior samples for training by running three benign applications in the background, including Google Chrome, WPS Office and QDreader, ranking highly at Google Play Store.

For each malicious app run in the background, we collected 1,000 set of data as specific attack behavior samples at the interval of one second. To ensure no bias on the sample data, there are 1,000 normal behavior samples that we collected for training phase, which consists of 400 sample data collected when Google Chrome runs, 300 sample data collected when WPS Office runs and 300 sample data collected when QDreader runs.

We deployed seven learning algorithms, including SVM, MLP, RandomForest, DecisionTree, ExtraTrees, AdaBoost and GradientBoosting, and trained the corresponding classifiers respectively. For each algorithm, we trained the One-vs-One Classifier and the One-vs-Rest Classifier. We used ten-fold cross validation for testing and chose $Precision = \frac{TP}{TP+FP}$, $Recall = \frac{TP}{TP+FN}$ and $F1 = \frac{2*Precision*Recall}{Precision+Recall}$ to measure the performance of a classifier.

The $F1$ results of different classifiers are summarized in Fig. 7. The experiments show that all classifiers, expect SVM, have good performances and their F1 scores are beyond 0.99.

5 Related Work

Linux layer side channel uses `procfs` (proc file system) and `sysfs` (sys file system) that are inherited from Linux system. A typical side channel probing attack is to infer users' browsing history exploiting related data about memory

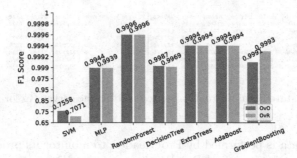

Fig. 7. Evaluation results of one-vs-one and one-vs-rest classifiers trained by different learning algorithms

usage of applications in procfs, including data resident size [9] and data resident size [5], as we presented in Sect. 1. Power consumption of devices reflects the state of applications and the behavior of users and Yan et al. [19] presented a side channel probing attack to infer four kinds of privacy information utilizing the change of power consumption, including front-end running applications, current browsing UI, the length of password user inputs and user's location. Michalevsky et al. [13] performed another location inference attack by analysis of the distance between user's location and the base station based on the power consumption of mobile device. Spreitzer et al. [17] proposed ProcHarvester, an systemic automated technique to assess the leaking of information from procfs, which is a common source of side channel information. ProcHarvester located the first procfs side channel in Android O.

Android layer side channel mainly refers to API provided by Android system. Apps can read mobile usage data through a public API class called android.net.TrafficStats. Based on the data obtained through it, Zhou et al. [22] designed a packet sequence comparison method to identify specific Twitter ID. And even the packets are encrypted, Taylor et al. [18] can identify applications' state by data transmission direction, data packet length and so on. In addition to that, API could be utilized to send sensitive information secretly. For example, Chandra et al. [4] designed two malicious applications that sent information through received intervals of battery change broadcast, and Marforio et al. [11] exploited volume change broadcast to launch similar attack.

Hardware layer side channel includes built-in equipment in Android devices, e.g., different kinds of sensor, camera, microphone and so on. They collect users personal information for function enhancement, but provide potential targets for side-channel probing attacks because applications can access these collected data without additional permissions required. For instance, Cai et al. [3] infered users' passwords according to the relation between input number and acceleration sensor. Combined with acceleration sensor and gyroscope sensor, Ping et al. [16] performed an attack that inferred input text. In addition to input inference, data from different sensors can be exploited to infer location. For example, user's vehicle can be inferred by acceleration sensor [7]; user's driving route can be inferred by barometric sensor [8], acceleration sensor and gyroscope sensor [14].

6 Conclusion

In this paper, we analyze the correlation between the side-channel-attack behaviors and application process states. Based on our observations, we propose SideGuard, a learning-based approach to defend against side-channel probing attacks. SideGuard works as an independent app on the mobile device that monitors the process states and infers the runtime behaviors of other apps. It extracts 16 process state features and creates corresponding application behavior models. We train the detection classifiers using different machine learning algorithms based on our application behavior model to detect side channel attack. The experiment results show that the F1 score of SideGuard are beyond 0.99.

Acknowledgement. We thank the anonymous reviewers for their valuable comments. This work was supported in part by the National Key R&D Program of China (No. 2017YFB080 2400), in part by the National Natural Science Foundation of China (No. 61402029, No. 61871023, No. U11733115), and in part by Singapore Ministry of Education (under NUS Grant No. R-252-000-666-114).

References

1. Share of Android OS of global smartphone shipments from 1st quarter 2011 to 2nd quarter 2018. https://www.statista.com/statistics/236027/global-smartphone-os-market-share-of-android/. Accessed 3 Mar 2019
2. Babil, G.S., Mehani, O., Boreli, R., Kaafar, M.A.: On the effectiveness of dynamic taint analysis for protecting against private information leaks on Android-based devices. In: 2013 International Conference on Security and Cryptography (SECRYPT), pp. 1–8. IEEE (2013)
3. Cai, L., Chen, H.: Touchlogger: inferring keystrokes on touch screen from smartphone motion. HotSec **11**, 9 (2011)
4. Chandra, S., Lin, Z., Kundu, A., Khan, L.: Towards a systematic study of the covert channel attacks in smartphones. In: Tian, J., Jing, J., Srivatsa, M. (eds.) SecureComm 2014. LNICST, vol. 152, pp. 427–435. Springer, Cham (2015). https://doi.org/10.1007/978-3-319-23829-6_29
5. Chen, Q.A., Qian, Z., Mao, Z.M.: Peeking into your app without actually seeing it: UI state inference and novel android attacks. In: 23rd USENIX Security Symposium (USENIX Security 14), pp. 1037–1052 (2014)
6. Enck, W., et al.: TaintDroid: an information-flow tracking system for realtime privacy monitoring on smartphones. ACM Trans. Comput. Syst. (TOCS) **32**(2), 5 (2014). https://doi.org/10.1145/2619091
7. Hemminki, S., Nurmi, P., Tarkoma, S.: Accelerometer-based transportation mode detection on smartphones. In: Proceedings of the 11th ACM Conference on Embedded Networked Sensor Systems, p. 13. ACM (2013). https://doi.org/10.1145/2517351.2517367

8. Ho, B.J., Martin, P., Swaminathan, P., Srivastava, M.: From pressure to path: Barometer-based vehicle tracking. In: Proceedings of the 2nd ACM International Conference on Embedded Systems for Energy-Efficient Built Environments, pp. 65–74. ACM (2015). https://doi.org/10.1145/2821650.2821665
9. Jana, S., Shmatikov, V.: Memento: learning secrets from process footprints. In: 2012 IEEE Symposium on Security and Privacy, pp. 143–157. IEEE (2012). https://doi.org/10.1109/SP.2012.19
10. Liang, Y., Cai, Z., Han, Q., Li, Y.: Deep learning based inference of private information using embedded sensors in smart devices. IEEE Netw. Mag. **32**(4), 8–14 (2018)
11. Marforio, C., Ritzdorf, H., Francillon, A., Capkun, S.: Analysis of the communication between colluding applications on modern smartphones. In: Proceedings of the 28th Annual Computer Security Applications Conference, pp. 51–60. ACM (2012). https://doi.org/10.1145/2420950.2420958
12. Michalevsky, Y., Boneh, D., Nakibly, G.: Gyrophone: recognizing speech from gyroscope signals. In: 23rd USENIX Security Symposium (USENIX Security 14), pp. 1053–1067 (2014)
13. Michalevsky, Y., Schulman, A., Veerapandian, G.A., Boneh, D., Nakibly, G.: PowerSpy: location tracking using mobile device power analysis. In: 24th USENIX Security Symposium (USENIX Security 15), pp. 785–800 (2015)
14. Narain, S., Vo-Huu, T.D., Block, K., Noubir, G.: Inferring user routes and locations using zero-permission mobile sensors. In: 2016 IEEE Symposium on Security and Privacy (SP), pp. 397–413. IEEE (2016). https://doi.org/10.1109/SP.2016.31
15. Owusu, E., Han, J., Das, S., Perrig, A., Zhang, J.: Accessory: password inference using accelerometers on smartphones. In: Proceedings of the Twelfth Workshop on Mobile Computing Systems & Applications, p. 9. ACM (2012). https://doi.org/10.1145/2162081.2162095
16. Ping, D., Sun, X., Mao, B.: TextLogger: inferring longer inputs on touch screen using motion sensors. In: Proceedings of the 8th ACM Conference on Security & Privacy in Wireless and Mobile Networks, p. 24. ACM (2015). https://doi.org/10.1145/2766498.2766511
17. Spreitzer, R., Kirchengast, F., Gruss, D., Mangard, S.: Procharvester: fully automated analysis of procfs side-channel leaks on android. In: Proceedings of the 2018 on Asia Conference on Computer and Communications Security, pp. 749–763. ACM (2018). https://doi.org/10.1145/3196494.3196510
18. Taylor, V.F., Spolaor, R., Conti, M., Martinovic, I.: Robust smartphone app identification via encrypted network traffic analysis. IEEE Trans. Inf. Forensics Secur. **13**(1), 63–78 (2018). https://doi.org/10.1109/TIFS.2017.2737970
19. Yan, L., Guo, Y., Chen, X., Mei, H.: A study on power side channels on mobile devices. In: Proceedings of the 7th Asia-Pacific Symposium on Internetware, pp. 30–38. ACM (2015). https://doi.org/10.1145/2875913.2875934
20. Zhang, L., Cai, Z., Wang, X.: Fakemask: a novel privacy preserving approach for smartphones. IEEE Trans. Netw. Serv. Manag. **13**(2), 335–348 (2016)
21. Zhang, N., Yuan, K., Naveed, M., Zhou, X., Wang, X.: Leave me alone: app-level protection against runtime information gathering on android. In: 2015 IEEE Symposium on Security and Privacy, pp. 915–930. IEEE (2015). https://doi.org/10.1109/SP.2015.61
22. Zhou, X., et al.: Identity, location, disease and more: inferring your secrets from android public resources. In: Proceedings of the 2013 ACM SIGSAC Conference on Computer & Communications Security, pp. 1017–1028. ACM (2013). https://doi.org/10.1145/2508859.2516661

Online DAG Scheduling with On-Demand Function Configuration in Edge Computing

Liuyan Liu, Haoqiang Huang, Haisheng Tan$^{(\boxtimes)}$, Wanli Cao, Panlong Yang, and Xiang-Yang Li

School of Computer Science and Technology,
University of Science and Technology of China, Hefei, China
{hstan,plyang,xiangyangli}@ustc.edu.cn,
{liuliuy,PB1998,cwl233}@mail.ustc.edu.cn

Abstract. Modern applications in mobile computing become increasingly complex and computation intensive. Task offloading from mobile devices to the cloud is more and more frequent. Edge Computing, deploying relatively small-scale edge servers close to users, is a promising cloud computing paradigm to reduce the network communication delay. Due to the limited capability, each edge server can be configured with only a small amount of functions to run corresponding tasks. Moreover, a mobile application might consist of multiple dependent tasks, which can be modeled and scheduled as Directed Acyclic Graphs (DAGs). When an application request arrives online, typically with a deadline specified, we need to configure the edge servers and assign the dependent tasks for processing. In this work, we jointly tackle on-demand function configuration on edge servers and DAG scheduling to meet as many request deadlines as possible. Based on list scheduling methodologies, we propose a novel online algorithm, named OnDoc, which is efficient and easy to deploy in practice. Extensive simulations on the data trace from Alibaba (including more than 3 million application requests) demonstrate that OnDoc outperforms state-of-the-art baselines consistently on various experiment settings.

Keywords: Edge Computing · DAG scheduling ·
Function configuration · Online algorithm

1 Introduction

With the development of cloud computing [1,2], resource-limited mobile devices can significantly expand their capability by offloading computational-intensive tasks to the remote cloud. However, due to the long distance between mobile devices and the remote cloud, serious communication delay is inevitable. It is

---

The first two authors have equal contribution.

© Springer Nature Switzerland AG 2019
E. S. Biagioni et al. (Eds.): WASA 2019, LNCS 11604, pp. 213–224, 2019.
https://doi.org/10.1007/978-3-030-23597-0_17

even worse when a large amount of data needs to be transferred. Such long latency can not meet the demand of delay-sensitive applications with strict deadlines, e.g., Automatic Drive and VR applications. To mitigate this problem, *edge computing* is proposed as a new cloud computing paradigm [3,4]. By deploying relative small-scale edge servers at the edge of the Internet (e.g., wireless access points), edge computing can provide nearby rich computing resources to the mobile users so that the propagation delay can be decreased significantly.

The resource and computation ability of edge servers are relatively constrained compared with a remote cloud. We should carefully configure the functions (i.e. computation modules of applications) that an edge server supports. At the same time, modern applications might consist of multiple dependent functions whose dependency can be modeled as DAGs (Seen in Fig. 1). Furthermore, in edge computing, mobile users come online and generate requests on some applications, which are typically latency-sensitive and require an immediate response. Assigning requests deadline is common practice in real-time systems to guarantee the quality of service. Therefore, it is of great importance to study how to configure edge servers and schedule the tasks to each server so that as many request deadlines can be satisfied as possible.

Task offloading [5–10] has been a major research topic because of its difficulty and importance. A notable work by Topcuoglu et al. [6] aimed to make suitable decisions to improve performance by reducing makespan. Inspired by list scheduling schemes, they proposed an insertion-based heuristic algorithm called HEFT [6]. Minimizing the overall cost is also a practical objective in task offloading. Neto et al. [7] tried to reduce the energy consumed by mobile devices and designed a flexible and innovative computation offloading framework. Sundar et al. [8] considered the execution and communication cost jointly to minimize the total cost subject to the application deadline. By appropriately allocating the application deadline among individual tasks, the tasks were scheduled in a greedy manner. All aforementioned works assumed that the edge servers can serve any requests assigned, which is impractical. Due to the limited resource (e.g. memory and CPU), an edge server cannot configure all the functions simultaneously.

The scheduling of dependent tasks represented as a DAG, called *DAG scheduling* for short, has also been extensively studied [6,11–14]. Based on their techniques, the existing DAG scheduling schemes can be classified into three categories [15,16]: *list scheduling* [6,17], *cluster-based scheduling* [11,18] and *task duplication-based scheduling* [15,19]. However, all these work focused on scheduling tasks of one DAG in offline manner. In the real scenario in edge computing, users' requests come in arbitrary order and time and we cannot know any information about these requests until their arrivals. To tackle the scheduling problem in this manner, we need an online algorithm.

A common practical method for function configuration is on-demand configuration (e.g., Azure Functions [20]): when a task is assigned to some edge server without the corresponding function for it, the edge server will first copy the function image from the remote cloud and deploy it locally to serve the task. In this work, we consider on-demand function configuration and DAG scheduling jointly in edge computing. Our objective is to satisfy as many request deadlines as possible. The problem, even its special case, has been proved to be NP-Hard [8]. Based on *list scheduling* methodology, we then propose an efficient and effective online DAG scheduling with on-demand function configuration algorithm, named OnDoc.

Our main contributions can be highlighted as follows:

- We formulate the online function configuration and DAG scheduling problem in edge computing where multiple application requests, with specific deadlines, are generated online in arbitrary time and order. The objective is maximizing the number of requests that satisfy the deadlines.
- We design a scheduling algorithm to meet as many request deadlines as possible. To the best of our knowledge, this is the first work that studies function configuration and DAG scheduling jointly in an online manner in edge computing. Our algorithm OnDoc maintains multiple task scheduling lists to reduce idle time of edge servers dramatically. Besides, OnDoc is easy to implement and does not introduce large scheduling overhead.
- We conduct extensive emulations under Alibaba data trace [21]. The evaluation results show that our online algorithm, OnDoc, can adapt well to different network environments and perform consistently better than the heuristic baselines on various experiment settings, e.g., the number of requests satisfying their deadline by OnDoc can be at least **1.9×** that of the baselines.

The rest of this paper is organized as follows. In Sect. 2, we present the model and problem formulation. In Sect. 3, we present OnDoc in detail. Section 4 illustrates our simulation results, and Sect. 5 concludes the whole work.

2 System Model and Problem Definition

Network: The network consists of heterogeneous edge servers and a remote cloud, denoted as $S = \{s_1, s_2, ..., s_m\}$. Each edge server s_i has a limited capacity C_i, which means that the multi-dimension resources (e.g. CPU, I/O, and storage) available in s_i can maximally configure a number of C_i functions (i.e., deploying functions and serving the corresponding tasks) simultaneously. Note that there is a special server s_m to represent the remote cloud, where we assume it has enough resources to configure all functions. The data rate between server s_i and s_j is denoted as $d_{i,j}$. We set $d_{i,j} = d_{j,i}$ and $d_{i,j} = +\infty$ if $i = j$.

Application and Request: There are multiple applications in our edge computing system and each request invokes one of them with initial data. Each application is modeled by a directed acyclic graph (DAG) $G(\mathcal{V}, \mathcal{E}, \mathcal{W})$, to depict the dependence among all the functions. Here, $\mathcal{V}$ is the set of nodes denoting the tasks, $\mathcal{E}$ is the set of directed links defining the dependence among tasks, and the set $\mathcal{W}$ depicts the amount of required data transferred from the predecessor task to the successor on each link. For instance, a link (v_i, v_j) with weight $w_{i,j}$ specifies that there is $w_{i,j}$ amounts of data transferred from task v_i to v_j. Hence,

v_j cannot start before the data transfer is finished. The computation and communication of one task cannot overlap. Then if two tasks are placed at different servers s_x and s_y, the communication delay, e.g., $w_{i,j}/d_{x,y}$, should be considered.

Each request is submitted to the edge system from one edge server termed *the initial server*, which will call for an application denoted by a DAG. Given the DAG of a request, a task without any predecessor tasks is called *the entry task* and a task without any successor tasks is called *the exit task*. For ease of presentation, we let the *exit (entry) tasks* all connect to a *pseudo exit (entry) task* which does not take any processing time or resources, so that there will be exactly one pseudo exit (entry) task in each DAG. The weight of links adjacent to the pseudo exit task is the amount of the output data produced by the exit tasks. For the pseudo entry task, the weight of the additional links is the amount of initial data received by each entry task. The pseudo entry and exit task must be processed in the initial server of the request, which means that initial data must be transferred from and the result must be sent back to the initial server.

Function Configuration: Without loss of generality, we assume that each type of task exactly maps to one function. We define a function $map : V \to F$. V is the set of all tasks and F is the set of all functions. For any $v \in V$ and $f \in F$, $map(v) = f$ means that task v is to be processed by function f. To process task v_j on server s_i, s_i must have configured the corresponding function $f_j = map(v_j)$ locally. Specifically, when task v_j is assigned to edge server s_i without function f_j, s_i has to suffer configuration time, denoted as $\mathcal{C}_{i,f_j}$, to download the function from the remote cloud and deploy it. Each deployed function on a edge server can process one task at one moment, which means that the queuing delay is considered. Recall that we assume the remote cloud has configured all functions, where all tasks assigned can be processed at their arrival. An edge server can configure a new function directly as long as it has enough capacity. Otherwise, we need to release some configured functions for the new one.

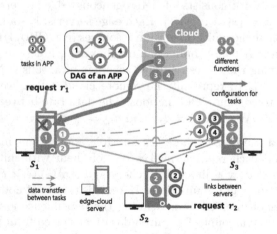

Fig. 1. A simple case of system model

Problem Formulation: Here, we consider a series of requests arriving *online* in arbitrary time and order, denoted as $\mathcal{R} = \{r_1, r_2, \ldots\ldots\}$. Each request r_k calls for one application in the edge system with a deadline L_k. Except for the parameters of the network and the DAGs of all applications, we cannot know any information of a request before its arrival, e.g., the application it calls for, the amount of initial data, the initial edge server, and its deadline. Let v_i^k denote the i-th task of request r_k. The processing time for v_i^k at server s_j is $p_{i,j}^k$, which can be known at the request's arrival. The assumption is practical since that we can estimate the processing time well based on the previous record. Note that since the initial data of each request might be different, the processing time of the same task from different requests of the same application might be different. When r_k arrives at server s_j in time $t_k^\uparrow$, we decide where to process each task (called *task assignment*). Here, if task v_i^k is assigned to a server s_j, we should first configure the corresponding function $map(v_i^k)$ if s_j does not hold it. If a task is assigned to the remote cloud, we can process it as soon as it arrives at the cloud. As the granularity of tasks is relatively small, we do not consider task preemption to avoid extra processing overhead. That is to say, once one task is started, it will be continuously processed until its completion. The completion of the exit task indicates the completion of the request, which should be before the deadline. Under the aforementioned model, our goal is to satisfy as many request deadlines as possible.

A simple example of our model is illustrated in Fig. 1. Specifically, there is an edge-cloud system containing 3 edge servers and a remote cloud. The capacity of edge servers is all set to 2, while the cloud holds all functions. Two requests, r_1 and r_2, call for the same application with their own initial data arriving at server s_1 and s_2, respectively. We take r_1 as an example, whose task 1 and 2 are assigned to edge server s_1, and task 3 and 4 to s_2. s_1 then need download function 2 from the remote cloud and choose to drop the existing function 4. Besides, task 2 can be processed only if function 2 has been deployed on s_1 and its predecessor node (i.e., task 1) has been finished.

3 Algorithms

We describe the details of OnDoc (Algorithm 1) in this section. OnDoc is a variant list scheduling scheme, which remains simplicity and efficiency of many prevalent list scheduling schemes of DAG scheduling. The main idea of list scheduling is to define priorities of tasks and assign tasks to the server in priority order. Besides, we have to modify the function configuration of each edge server simultaneously due to the limited capacity. Hence, OnDoc is composed of three parts: priority-calculating strategy, task-assigning strategy, and function-configuring strategy. We next present these strategies specifically.

Priority Calculation: When addressing DAG scheduling with list scheduling strategies, a useful method that can prioritize the tasks efficiently and simply is significant. Shin et al. [16] classifies task priorities applied by most list scheduling heuristics into three types: *S-level, B-level, T-level. S-level*, called static level, is the longest path from the task to the exit task with computation cost taken into consideration only. *B-level* is also calculated from bottom (exit task) to top (entry task). The difference between *S-level* and *B-level* is that communication cost is taken into consideration by *B-level* as well. *T-level*, namely, is the sum of computation cost and communication cost of the longest path from the entry task to the concerned task. After computing task priorities, we can prioritize these tasks corresponding to the decreasing (increasing) order of *S-level, B-level* (*T-level*). However, all these task priorities are static and can only prioritize tasks from one request. The challenge remaining is that we have to schedule tasks from multiple requests concurrently in most cases and we cannot employ these task priorities to determine the priority of tasks from different requests.

To tackle the aforementioned challenge, we maintain multiple task scheduling lists $Q = \{l_1, l_2, ...\}$ rather than follow the idea of list scheduling methodology to merge tasks form all request to construct one prioritized list. Q is the set of prioritized lists of requests. Let Q be empty initially. When $t = t_k^{\uparrow}$, request r_k arrives at initial server s_j with deadline L_k, we employee the *B-level* as task priorities to get a scheduling list l_k of r_k and insert l_k into Q instantly (Line 1–4 in Algorithm 1). Every time when we are scheduling, we only take the head of all the scheduling lists in Q into consideration. To choose an appropriate task to assign, we first determine the target server based on the *Task-assigning strategy* for all candidate tasks. Then leaded by the idea to reduce the idle time of edge servers, we choose the task that can start execution at earliest time in its target server among all the candidate tasks to assign (Line 6–7). Each scheduling process ends with the chosen task is already starting execution in its target server, then the chosen task is deleted from its scheduling list and the next scheduling begins. If the scheduling list of request r_k is empty or request exceeds the corresponding deadline, we delete it from Q (Line 9–10).

Task-Assigning Strategy: We greedily assign each task to the server which can finish it as early as possible besides the pseudo exit (entry) task whose target sever is initial server under our model. Let $EFT_{i,j}^k$ denote the <u>e</u>arliest <u>f</u>inish <u>t</u>ime of task v_i^k on server s_j and $EST_{i,j}^k$ be the <u>e</u>arliest <u>s</u>tart <u>t</u>ime corresponding. As illustrated above, $EFT_{i,j}^k$ and $EST_{i,j}^k$ are two most important attributes. We follow the steps below to calculate them.

When determining $EFT_{i,j}^k$, it is obvious that we should obey two constraints: precedence constraint and capacity constraint. Precedence constraint means that tasks cannot start execution before the data of its precursors transferring to server s_j. Capacity constraint means that tasks have to wait until server s_j has spare capacity. To articulate the two constraints, we formulate them as following.

For ease of formula, we record status of edge servers all the time. For instance, we maintain a set $A_j = \{(v_1', r_1'), (v_2', r_2'), ..., (v_n', r_n')\}$ (without pseudo entry task) for server s_j, when task v_i^k is assigned to server s_j, we insert a tuple (i, k) to A_j. Without loss of generality, we assume that

$$EFT_{v_1',j}^{r_1'} \geqslant EFT_{v_2',j}^{r_2'} \geqslant ... \geqslant EFT_{v_n',j}^{r_n'}$$

and denote $A_j(m) = \{(v_1', r_1'), (v_2', r_2'), ..., (v_m', r_m')\}$. For convenience, if $m \geq |A_j|$, we fill the set up with $(m - |A_j|)$ virtual tuples (v_{entry}, r_k).

Then we define an indicator binary variable as following:

$$x_{i,j} = \begin{cases} 0 & \text{if } i = j \\ 1 & \text{if otherwise} \end{cases} \tag{1}$$

For (pseudo) entry task v_{entry}, we have

$$EST^k_{v_{entry}, j} = EFT^k_{v_{entry}, j} = t^\uparrow_k, \forall j \in S \tag{2}$$

The *precedence constraint* is denoted as

$$EST^k_{i,j} \geq \max_{i' \in pre(i,k)} EFT^k_{i', tar(v_{i'}^k)} + \frac{w^k_{i',i}}{d_{tar(v_{i'}^k), j}} \tag{3}$$

Here, $tar(v_{i'}^k)$ denotes the target server of $v_{i'}^k$ and $pre(i, k)$ represents the set of predecessor tasks of v_i^k. Also, the communication delay is included in the Eq. (3) and $w^k_{i',i}$ denotes the amount of data transfer from $v_{i'}^k$ to v_i^k.

The *capacity constraint* is

$$EST^k_{i,j} \geq \min_{i', r' \in A_j(C_j)} EFT^{r'}_{i', j} + C_{j, map(v_i^k)} * x_{map(v_i^k) map(v_{i'}^{r'})} \tag{4}$$

As a result, $EST^k_{i,j}$ can be computed as below:

$$EST^k_{i,j} = \max\{ \max_{i' \in pre(i,k)} EFT^k_{i', tar(v_{i'}^k)} + \frac{w^k_{i',i}}{d_{tar(v_{i'}^k), j}},$$
$$\min_{i', r' \in A_j(C_j)} EFT^{r'}_{i', j} + C_{j, map(v_i^k)} * x_{map(v_i^k), map(v_{i'}^{r'})}\} \tag{5}$$

Obviously, we have:

$$EFT^k_{i,j} = EST^k_{i,j} + p^k_{i,j} \tag{6}$$

Then we tentatively enumerate tasks' EFT in each server to determine their target server. For any task v_i^k (i is not entry or exit), we have $tar(v_i^k) = \min_{s_j \in S} EFT^k_{i,j}$.

Function-Configuring Strategy: In Eq. (5), when $x_{map(v_i^k), map(v_{i'}^{r'})}$ equals to 1, it means that we have to configure the corresponding function to allow the task to begin executing. First, we have to check whether there is enough capacity for configuration. If so, we just take up the spare space simply, if not, we need to decide which function will be replaced. In OnDoc, to allow the configuration to start as soon as possible, we always choose the function which can be replaced at the earliest time to drop. If there are many candidate functions that can be replaced at the same time, we choose one uniformly random (Line 8).

Algorithm 1. OnDoc

---

1 set $Q \leftarrow \emptyset$;
   /* Thread for maintaining Q */
2 if *new request r arrives* then
3      $l \leftarrow$ scheduling list of r;
4      $Q \leftarrow Q \cup \{l\}$;
   /* Thread for assigning tasks and configuring functions   */
5 while $Q \neq \emptyset$ do
       /* H consists of head of each scheduling list in Q */
6   Construct set H ;
7   We assign task v^* to server $tar(v^*)$
8   Configure $tar(v^*)$ with corresponding function before v^* executed;
9   if $\exists l \in Q$ *and* $l = \emptyset$ then
10   delete l from Q;

---

4 Performance Evaluation

In this section, we conduct extensive emulations to evaluate OnDoc based on an 8-day data trace from Alibaba [21] and compare our algorithm with two heuristic baselines. The emulation results show that the number of requests satisfying their deadline by OnDoc can be at least **1.9×** that of the baselines. Besides, we investigate the impact on OnDoc of various parameter settings and demonstrate that the performance of OnDoc is stably better the baselines.

4.1 Experiment Settings

Workloads: We use an 8-day data trace from Alibaba [21] as our workload. The data trace contains more than 3 million jobs (called requests of applications in this work) with the DAG information and the start time. We randomly choose multiple requests consecutively each day to get 8 different sets and take the start time of each request as its release time. Besides, to be more consistent with the real scenario of edge computing, where requests need to be processed in real time, we scale all the processing time to milliseconds. We conduct experiments on 8 request sets independently and analyze the average performance.

Default Setting: We simulate an edge computing system with 5 heterogeneous edge servers and one remote cloud. The available capacity of edge servers is limited to 3, while the remote cloud has all functions preloaded. The configuration time for each function is set to 500 ms. And the data transmission time from server to the cloud, which is by default set as 20 times of that between two edge server, is set $[100, 2000]$ ms. And we conduct experiments to study the impact of these parameters. If not specified explicitly, the processing time in the remote cloud is set $0.75\times$ (in average value) of that in edge servers [5] as the remote cloud typically has more resources than edge servers.

4.2   The Heuristic Baselines

Due to the lack of work jointly studying online DAG scheduling and function configuration, we adopt two classical schemes as our baselines, which are

- **Local Heuristic (Local):** when an application request arrived at **initial server**, the local heuristic will process it in it. Precisely, we limit the target server of each task to its initial edge server in Algorithm 1. This baseline makes sense to verify that task assignment of one request should be considered even with induced communication cost.
- **First-Come-First-Serve (FCFS):** *FCFS* is a popular scheduling policy which is commonly used by the methods based on queuing theory [5]. We implement it by converting multiple task scheduling lists to a single list with respect to the releasing order and always assigning the task in the head of the list to its target server.

Moreover, the two baselines employ the same task priorities and function configuration strategy as OnDoc.

4.3   Experiment Results

In this part, we first illustrate the overall performance. The result shows that OnDoc outperforms other baselines dramatically. The number of deadlines which are satisfied is at least **1.9×** of that of the baselines under default setting. Furthermore, we conduct multi-group experiments to study the influences of different settings of various parameters (i.e., the offload overhead to the cloud and the capacity of the edge servers).

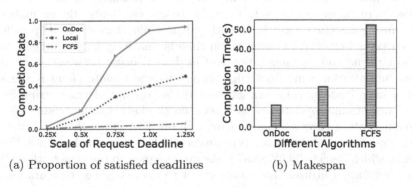

(a) Proportion of satisfied deadlines   (b) Makespan

Fig. 2. Overall performance of different algorithms

Overall Performance. Figure 2 demonstrates the performance of all algorithms on the workloads from Alibaba. We scale the deadline of each request from 0.25x to 1.25x of the original value in the default setting with other parameters remaining as the default value. Figure 2(a) depicts that the performance of all algorithms get better with the deadlines increasing. Meanwhile, OnDoc out-performs the baselines dramatically. Under the default setting, the number of requests that satisfy their deadline in OnDoc is 1.9×, 51.6× that of *Local* and *FCFS* respectively. Furthermore, the makespan, the gap between the release time of the first request and the completing time of the lasted completed request, of our scheduling is minimum, which is a surprising byproduct shown by Fig. 2(b).

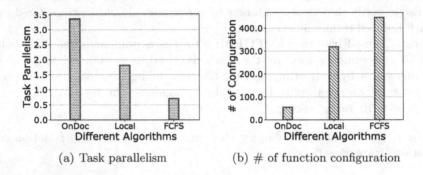

(a) Task parallelism   (b) # of function configuration

Fig. 3. Task parallelism and # of function configuration of different algorithms

To understand why OnDoc outperforms the baselines, we conduct some fur-ther analysis. (1) From the perspective of the parallelism between tasks from different or even the same request, Fig. 3(a) demonstrates that OnDoc can exploit the parallelism well. Task parallelism is defined as the average number of run-ning tasks at every moment. Figure 3(a) depicts that task parallelism of OnDoc is the highest. It means that OnDoc utilizes the resources of edge servers to process more tasks concurrently than the baselines. Hence, OnDoc makes use of computing resources more sufficiently. Meanwhile, it exploits the parallelism between tasks better. (2) Configuration time is relatively larger compared with processing time and communication cost of data transfer between edge servers. The communication time from edge servers to the remote cloud is the same order of magnitude as configuration time if the amount of transferring data is large. Thus, an appropriate trade-off between the long distance communication and configuration plays a significant role. Figure 3(b) shows that the number of function configuration by OnDoc is dramatically less than the baselines. Further analysis, which depicts 39.5% of all tasks are assigned to the remote cloud, illus-trates that OnDoc utilizes the remote cloud to decrease the configuration cost without inducing notable communication cost. Almost all the tasks assigned to remote cloud request for a relatively small amount of data, which means that OnDoc assigns tasks with a large amount of input data to edge servers to avoid notable communication delay. Meanwhile, OnDoc employs cloud to mitigate edge servers' pressure to avoid repeating configuration.

Sensitivity Analysis. We also conduct abundant experiments to investigate the impact of different settings. Figure 4(a) demonstrates the performance of all

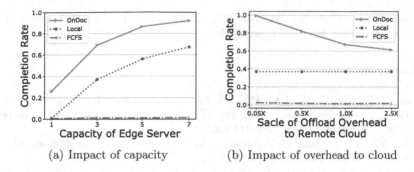

(a) Impact of capacity   (b) Impact of overhead to cloud

Fig. 4. The proportion of requests satisfying deadlines with different settings of the capacity of edge servers and the overhead to the cloud

algorithms under different capacity setting. OnDoc and *Local* are affected significantly because more capacity means more computing resources. The number of function replacing decreases due to the increase in capacity. On the one hand, some repeating configurations are avoided. On the other hand, more capacity can support more task execution simultaneously, which can exploit the parallelism between tasks better. To study the impact of communication time to the remote cloud, we scale it from 0.05× to 2.5× of the default value. Figure 4(b) illustrates when communication time is 0.05×, OnDoc can finish all requests before their deadline. Since the communication time to cloud equals to that between edge server, the cloud can provide powerful computing resources (i.e., infinite capacity, no function configuration time, faster task processing) without inducing more communication cost than edge servers. It is easily understood that *Local* is not affect by the overhead for it only uses edge servers. *FCFS* performs badly and is not sensitive to the above parameters since its task assignment policy is the main bottleneck constraining performance. The requests needing large processing time will block the execution of all requests that released after it.

5   Conclusion

In this work, we study task scheduling with function on-demand configuration in edge computing where requests for some application with specific deadlines and initial data arrive online in arbitrary time and order. We construct a general model for this problem with the goal to meet as many request deadlines as possible. An efficient heuristic algorithm, named OnDoc, is proposed, which is the first online algorithm to solve this problem to the best of our knowledge. Specifically, OnDoc is based on list scheduling schemes and can be implemented easily in practice. Besides, extensive experiments validate that OnDoc has a stable and superior performance compared with the baselines.

Acknowledgments. This work is supported partly by the National Key R&D Program of China 2018YFB0803400, China National Funds for Distinguished Young Scientists No. 61625205, NSFC Grants 61772489, 61751211, Key Research Program of

Frontier Sciences (CAS) No. QYZDY-SSW-JSC002, NSF ECCS-1247944, NSF CNS 1526638, and the Fundamental Research Funds for the Central U.

References

1. Chun, B.G., Ihm, S., Maniatis, P., Naik, M., Patti, A.: Clonecloud: elastic execution between mobile device and cloud. In: ACM Proceedings of the Sixth Conference on Computer Systems, pp. 301–314 (2011)
2. Zhao, Y., Liu, X., Qiao, C.: Job scheduling for acceleration systems in cloud computing. In: IEEE ICC, pp. 1–6 (2018)
3. Satyanarayanan, M., Bahl, P., Caceres, R., Davies, N.: The case for VM-based cloudlets in mobile computing. IEEE Pervasive Comput. **4**, 14–23 (2009)
4. Garcia Lopez, P., Montresor, A., Epema, D., Datta, A., Higashino, T., Iamnitchi, A., et al.: Edge-centric computing: vision and challenges. ACM SIGCOMM CCR **45**(5), 37–42 (2015)
5. Tan, H., Han, Z., Li, X.Y., Lau, F.C.: Online job dispatching and scheduling in edge-clouds. In: IEEE INFOCOM, pp. 1–9 (2017)
6. Topcuoglu, H., Hariri, S., Wu, M.: Performance-effective and low-complexity task scheduling for heterogeneous computing. IEEE TPDS **13**(3), 260–274 (2002)
7. Neto, J.L.D., Yu, S.Y., Macedo, D.F., Nogueira, M.S., Langar, R., Secci, S.: ULOOF: a user level online offloading framework for mobile edge computing. IEEE TMC **17**(11), 2660–2674 (2018)
8. Sundar, S., Liang, B.: Offloading dependent tasks with communication delay and deadline constraint. In: IEEE INFOCOM, pp. 37–45 (2018)
9. Zhang, W., Wen, Y., Wu, D.O.: Energy-efficient scheduling policy for collaborative execution in mobile cloud computing. In: IEEE INFOCOM, pp. 190–194 (2013)
10. Guo, H., Liu, J., Zhang, J.: Efficient computation offloading for multi-access edge computing in 5G HetNets. In: IEEE ICC, pp. 1–6 (2018)
11. Palis, M.A., Liou, J.C., Wei, D.S.L.: Task clustering and scheduling for distributed memory parallel architectures. IEEE TPDS **7**(1), 46–55 (1996)
12. Darbha, S., Agrawal, D.P.: Optimal scheduling algorithm for distributed-memory machines. IEEE TPDS **9**(1), 87–95 (1998)
13. Sakellariou, R., Zhao, H.: A hybrid heuristic for DAG scheduling on heterogeneous systems. In: IEEE IPDPS, pp. 111 (2004)
14. Deng, M., Tian, H., Fan, B.: Fine-granularity based application offloading policy in cloud-enhanced small cell networks. In: IEEE ICC, pp. 638–643 (2016)
15. He, K., Meng, X., Pan, Z., Yuan, L., Zhou, P.: A novel task-duplication based clustering algorithm for heterogeneous computing environments. IEEE TPDS **30**(1), 2–14 (2019)
16. Shin, K., Cha, M., Jang, M., Jung, J., Yoon, W., Choi, S.: Task scheduling algorithm using minimized duplications in homogeneous systems. Elsevier JPDC **68**(8), 1146–1156 (2008)
17. Liu, G.Q., Poh, K.L., Xie, M.: Iterative list scheduling for heterogeneous computing. Elsevier JPDC **65**(5), 654–665 (2005)
18. Ali, J., Khan, R.Z.: Optimal task partitioning model in distributed heterogeneous parallel computing environment. AIRCC Int. J. Adv. Inf. Technol. **2**(6), 13 (2012)
19. He, K., Zhao, Y.: A new task duplication based multitask scheduling method. In: IEEE Grid and Cooperative Computing(GCC), pp. 221–227 (2006)
20. Azure Functions. https://azure.microsoft.com/en-us/services/functions
21. Alibaba trace (2018). https://github.com/alibaba/clusterdata

Magnetic Beamforming Algorithm for Hybrid Relay and MIMO Wireless Power Transfer

Bin Ma[1,2], Yubin Zhao[1(✉)], Xiaofan Li[3], Yuefeng Ji[4], and Cheng-Zhong Xu[5]

[1] Shenzhen Institutes of Advanced Technology,
Chinese Academy of Sciences, Beijing, China
{bin.ma,zhaoyb}@siat.ac.cn
[2] University of Chinese Academy of Sciences, Beijing, China
[3] State Radio Monitoring Center Testing Center, Beijing, China
lixiaofan@srtc.org.cn
[4] Beijing University of Posts and Telecommunications, Beijing, China
jyf@bupt.edu.cn
[5] State Key Lab of IoTSC and Department of Computer and Information Science,
University of Macau, Macau, China
czxu@um.edu.mo

Abstract. Using magnetic beamforming, the power transmission efficiency can be highly increased for realizing the practical near-field magnetic resonant coupling (MRC) wireless power transfer (WPT). The usage of relay coils is also of great benefit for power transmission in the WPT system containing multiple transmitters (TXs) each with a coil. In this paper, we study the influence of relay coils and the magnetic beamforming for a MRC-WPT system with multiple TXs, relay coils and a single receiver (Rx), called multi-relay WPT (MWPT) system. The optimization problem is formulated to design the currents flowing through TXs in different places so as to maximize the power delivered to the RX load, subject to a given constraint of summational power consumed by all resistances in the MWPT system. In general, the problem is a non-convex quadratically constrained quadratic programming (QCQP) problem, which can be solved with relaxation of the Lagrange multiplier. Numerical results show that by comparing with equal-current and magnetic beamforming mode, relay coils significantly enhances the power transmission efficiency over the longer distances, and magnetic beamforming with passive relay coils significantly improve the transmission power, efficiency and distance.

Keywords: Multi-relay wireless power transfer ·
Magnetic resonant coupling · Beamforming

Y. Zhao—This work was partially supported by National Nature Science Foundation of China (No. 61801306), Shenzhen Fundamental Research (No. JCYJ20180302145755311), CAS/SAFEA International Partnership Program for Creative Research Teams, Open Fund of IPOC (No. IPOC2018B002).

E. S. Biagioni et al. (Eds.): WASA 2019, LNCS 11604, pp. 225–234, 2019.
https://doi.org/10.1007/978-3-030-23597-0_18

1 Introduction

Wireless power transfer has been deemed as a promising technology, bringing convenience for powering up electronic portable smart device (mobile phone, laptop, wearable product, etc.) and electric vehicle [1–3]. Three prime visions of WPT technology are inductive coupling, magnetic resonance and microwave radiation. Inductive coupling certainly has restrictive condition in the transmission distance, and microwave radiation is of weak performance with its low energy transfer efficiency. Magnetic resonance has the advantages of having relatively long power transfer distance and high power transmission efficiency [4]. The professional standards development organization, AirFuel, based on magnetic resonant technology with the frequency (6.78 MHz) is vigorously promoting the design of more practical wireless charging standards and provide a safe, reliable and interoperable charging solution [5–7].

Designing a high quality electronic components (adjustable capacitance and resistance, coil, etc.) or circuit is the traditional way to enhance the energy transmission efficiency [8,9]. Currently, the study of algorithm for multiple transmitters proposed to charge one receiver (MISO) has been investigated in [10,11], which studied the MRC-WPT system with only two Txs and a single Rx. While the obtained results cannot be directly extended to the cases that have more than two TXs. The relay coils can also enhance the power transmission efficiency of WPT system. The feasibility of relay coils for MRC-WPT system to prolong the power transmission distance has been proved by Dionigi and Mongiardo [12]. In the paper, they came up with a common attribute that can be used to design a wireless power transfer network with relay elements by considering a simple but rigorous equivalent network [13]. The current can be optimally controlled through model analysis and experiment to achieve maximum power transfer efficiency of the MRC-WPT system [14]. For the same relay resonator, the resonator current should be equalized to achieve the highest system power level. Uniform current distribution and uniform spacing distribution with equal reflection impedance were analyzed. The latter was proved to achieve approximately equal current and relatively high efficiency [15].

In this paper, we construct a MISO MRC-WPT system with multiple Txs, relay coils and a single Rx. All the coils in the system are horizontally placed to a same plane. While the positions of Txs and relay coils are fixed and uniform spatial distribution. The Txs are keeping in contact with the Rx via bluetooth communication in the controller module. We propose the magnetic beamforming algorithm based on solving a QCQP problem, which adjusts each Tx current to maximize the Rx load consumed power with the given sum-power of whole WPT system. To solve the problem, we derive the lagrangian function and its Karush-Kuhn-Tucker (KKT) conditions. And by doing a relaxation of the Lagrange multiplier, we obtain the optimally allocated Tx currents to achieve the objective function [16]. We compare the performances of same-set MWPT system with each Tx equal-current allocated and common WPT system with each Tx equal-current allocated and beamforming. Then we make comparison between the MWPT system with equal Tx current and with the magnetic beamforming, respectively. Numerical results are observed to verify the advance of relay coils and the magnetic beamforming algorithm.

2   System Model

As shown in Fig. 1, we consider an MWPT system with $N_T \geq 1$ TXs each equipped with a single coil, indexed by $Tx(n)$, where $n \in N_T$, $N_L \geq 1$ relay resonators each equipped with a coil, indexed by $Rel(m)$, where $m \in N_L$, and a single Rx with a coil. There is a controller module, which can build a communication link between Txs and Rx to allocate the current to each Tx for magnetic beamforming. The relay coils are passive coils, which contain no battery, no load or communication module. Each TX is connected to a stable energy source supplying sinusoidal voltage over time given by $\tilde{v}_{Tx(n)}(t) = Re\{v_{Tx(n)}e^{jwt}\}$, with the complex $v_{Tx(n)}$ denoting an adjustable voltage and $w > 0$ denoting its operating angular frequency. Let $\tilde{i}_{Tx(n)}(t) = Re\{i_{Tx(n)}e^{jwt}\}$ $(\tilde{i}_{Rel(m)}(t) = Re\{i_{Rel(m)}e^{jwt}\})$ denote the steady-state current flowing through Tx_n $(Rel(m))$, with the complex current $i_{Tx(n)}$ $(i_{Rel(m)})$. Likewise, define $\tilde{i}_0(t) = Re\{i_0 e^{jwt}\}$ as the steady-state current in the RX, with the complex current i_0.

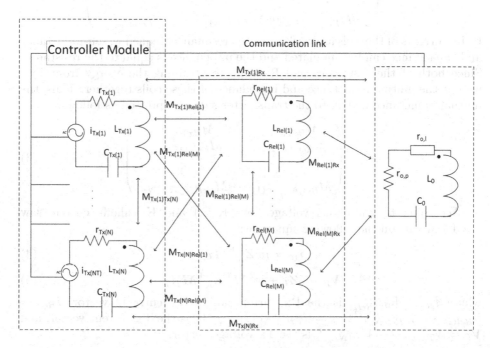

Fig. 1. System model of an MRC-MWPT system

Let $r_{Tx(n)}$ $(r_{Rel(m)})$, $L_{Tx(n)}$ $(L_{Rel(m)})$ and $C_{Tx(n)}$ $(C_{Rel(m)})$ denote the parasitic resistance, self-inductance and capacitance for $Tx(n)$ $(Rel(m))$. Let L_0

and C_0 denote self-inductance and capacitance for Rx. The resistance of the Rx, denoted by $r_0 > 0$, contains the parasitic resistance $r_{0,p} > 0$ and the load resistance $r_{0,l} > 0$, i.e., $r_0 = r_{0,p} + r_{0,l}$. The load resistance $r_{0,l}$ is considered to be purely resistive. We use $M_{Tx(n)Rel(m)}$, $M_{Tx(n)Rx}$, $M_{Rel(m)Rx}$, $M_{Tx(n_1,n_2)}$, and $M_{Rel(m_1,m_2)}$ to denote the mutual inductance between the n-th TX coil and the m-th relay coils, between the n_1-th TX coil and n_2-th TX coils, between the m_1-th and the m_2-th relay coils, between the n-th TX coil and the Rx coil, and between the m-th relay coil and the Rx coil, respectively. These mutual inductance can be obtained by Conways mutual inductance formula [17]. Then, we define the impedance and mutual inductance of Txs, relay coils and in the matrix form as follows:

$$\boldsymbol{Z_T} = \begin{pmatrix} Z_{Tx(1)} & jwM_{Tx(1,2)} & \cdots & jwM_{Tx(1,N_T)} \\ jwM_{Tx(1,2)} & Z_{Tx(2)} & \cdots & jwM_{Tx(2,N_T)} \\ \vdots & \vdots & \ddots & \vdots \\ jwM_{Tx(N_T,1)} & jwM_{Tx(N_T,2)} & \cdots & Z_{Tx(N_T)} \end{pmatrix} \quad (1)$$

$$\boldsymbol{Z_R} = \begin{pmatrix} Z_{Rx} & jwM_{RxRel(1)} & \cdots & jwM_{RxRel(N_L)} \\ jwM_{Rel(1)Rx} & Z_{Rel(1)} & \cdots & jwM_{Rel(1,N_L)} \\ \vdots & \vdots & \ddots & \vdots \\ jwM_{Rel(N_L)Rx} & jwM_{Rel(N_L,1)} & \cdots & Z_{Rel(N_L)} \end{pmatrix} \quad (2)$$

If the currents of the coils are working at the resonance frequency, self-inductance and capacitance can be eliminated and the impedance is equal to the resistance. Since both of the relay coils and Rx coil are attaining the energy from Txs, we put the mutual inductance and impedance of these coils together. Thus, the mutual inductance matrix to the transmitter side is expressed as follows:

$$\boldsymbol{M} = \begin{pmatrix} M_{RxTx(1)} & \cdots & M_{RxTx(N_T)} \\ M_{Rel(1)Tx(1)} & \cdots & M_{Rel(1)Tx(N_T)} \\ \vdots & \ddots & \vdots \\ M_{Rel(N_L)Tx(1)} & \cdots & M_{Rel(N_L)Tx(N_T)} \end{pmatrix} \quad (3)$$

According to Kirchhoffs voltage law (KVL) and Kirchhoffs current law (KCL), we attain the following equations:

$$\boldsymbol{i_R} = jw\boldsymbol{Z_R^{-1}}\boldsymbol{M}\boldsymbol{i_T} \quad (4)$$

$$\boldsymbol{V_T} = (\boldsymbol{Z_T} + w^2\boldsymbol{M^T}\boldsymbol{Z_R^{-1}}\boldsymbol{M})\boldsymbol{i_T} \quad (5)$$

where $\boldsymbol{i_R} = [i_0, i_{Rel}^T]$, is the Rx current and relay currents vector, $\boldsymbol{i_{Rel}} = [i_{Rel(1)}, \cdots, i_{Rel(N_L)}]^T$; $\boldsymbol{i_T} = [i_{Tx(1)}, \cdots i_{Tx(N_T)}]^T$ is the Tx current vector; and $\boldsymbol{V_T} = [V_{Tx(1)}, \cdots, V_{Tx(N_L)}]^T$ is the Tx voltage vector.

3   Problem Formulation

The total power consumption is the sum of Txs, relay coils and the Rx, which is $P = P_{Rx} + P_{Rel} + P_{Tx}$. Consider $P_{Rx} = i_0^H r_0 i_0$, $P_{Rel} = \boldsymbol{i_{Rel}^H} \boldsymbol{R_{Rel}} \boldsymbol{i_{Rel}}$, and $P_{Tx} =$

$i_T^H R_{Tx} i_T$, where R_{Tx} and R_{Rel} is $diag[r_{Tx(1)}, \cdots, r_{Tx(N_T)}]$ and $diag[r_{Rel(1)}, \cdots, r_{Rel(N_L)}]$. Then we give a constant value, called P_{max}, to be the constraint of the problem for maximizing the power delivered to RX load, which is $P_{Rx,l} = i_0^H r_{0,l} i_0$. Then we can obtain:

$$P = i_T^H [w^2 M^T (Z_R^{-1})^H R Z_R^{-1} M + R_{Tx}] i_T \qquad (6)$$

$$P_{Rx,l} = w^2 r_{0,l} i_T^H M^T z_R^H z_R M i_T \qquad (7)$$

where $R = diag[r_0, r_{Rel(1)}, \cdots, r_{Rel(N_L)}]$, and z_R is the first row vector of Z_R^{-1}. So, we can formulated the problem, indexed by (P), as follows:

$$(P) : \max_{i_T} \quad w^2 r_{0,l} i_T^H M^T z_R^H z_R M i_T$$
$$\text{s.t.} \quad i_T^H [w^2 M^T (Z_R^{-1})^H R Z_R^{-1} M + R_{Tx}] i_T \le P_{max} \qquad (8)$$

4   Optimal Solution

P is a complex-valued non-convex QCQP problem [16]. The optimal current solution i_T can be obtained by leveraging the KKT conditions of the optimization problem. Let $\lambda \ge 0$ denote the Lagrange multiplier corresponding to the constraint in (8). Because the imaginary-part of $i_{Tx(n)}$ contribute in the same way to P_{Tx}, P_{Rel} and P_{Rx}, we can set the imaginary-part of $i_{Tx(n)}$ equal to 0, which means that $i_T^H = i_T^T$. The lagrangian equation of (P) is given by:

$$L(i_T, \lambda) = w^2 r_{0,l} i_T^T M^T z_R^H z_R M i_T + \lambda \{ P_{max} - i_T^T [w^2 M^T (Z_R^{-1})^H R Z_R^{-1} M + R_{Tx}] i_T \} \qquad (9)$$

Then, the KKT conditions contain the feasibility conditions for the primal and dual solutions, the condition that is due to the fact that the gradient of the lagrangian equation in regard to i_T must vanish, and the condition that stands for the complimentary slackness, which are given by:

$$i_T^T [w^2 M^T (Z_R^{-1})^H R Z_R^{-1} M + R_{Tx}] i_T \le P_{max} \qquad (10)$$

$$\lambda \ge 0 \qquad (11)$$

$$i_T^T \{ w^2 M^T [r_{0,l} z_R^H z_R - \lambda (Z_R^{-1})^H R Z_R^{-1}] M - \lambda R_{Tx} \} I_T = 0 \qquad (12)$$

$$\lambda \{ P_{max} - i_T^T [w^2 M^T (Z_R^{-1})^H R Z_R^{-1} M + R_{Tx}] i_T \} = 0 \qquad (13)$$

where I_T is $[1, \cdots, 1]^T$. To figure out the set of equations in (10)–(13), we consider two possible cases as follows.

• Case 1: $\lambda = 0$. It can be confirmed that any i_T satisfying $w^2 r_{0,l} M^T z_R^H z_R M = 0$ can satisfy the KKT conditions (10)–(13) in this case. However, this result of i_T will make the objective function equal to zero, which is not the optimal solution for (P). Thence, this case cannot lead to the optimal solution to (P).

• Case 2: $\lambda > 0$. The equation can be deduced as follows:

$$w^2 M^T [r_{0,l} z_R^H z_R - \lambda (Z_R^{-1})^H R Z_R^{-1}] M - \lambda R_{Tx} = 0 \qquad (14)$$

According to (14), we denote the following singular-value-decomposition (SVD):

$$w^2 r_{0,l} \boldsymbol{M}^T \boldsymbol{z}_R^H \boldsymbol{z}_R \boldsymbol{M} [\boldsymbol{R}_{Tx} + w^2 \boldsymbol{M}^T (\boldsymbol{Z}_R^{-1})^H \boldsymbol{R} \boldsymbol{Z}_R^{-1} \boldsymbol{M}]^{-1} = \boldsymbol{U} \boldsymbol{\Gamma} \boldsymbol{U}^H \qquad (15)$$

where $\boldsymbol{U} = [\boldsymbol{u}_1 \cdots \boldsymbol{u}_{N_T}]$ is orthogonal, and $\boldsymbol{\Gamma} = diag[\gamma_1, \cdots, \gamma_{N_T}]$. Choosing the minimum value, γ^*, from γ_n ($1 \leq n \leq N_T$), it can be a relaxation that make λ equal to γ^*, which applies that lagrange dual function (11) is minimized. Updating the value of λ in (14), we denote the following SVD:

$$w^2 \boldsymbol{M}^T [r_{0,l} \boldsymbol{z}_R^H \boldsymbol{z}_R - \lambda (\boldsymbol{Z}_R^{-1})^H \boldsymbol{R} \boldsymbol{Z}_R^{-1}] \boldsymbol{M} - \lambda \boldsymbol{R}_{Tx} = \boldsymbol{V} \boldsymbol{K} \boldsymbol{V}^H, \qquad (16)$$

where $\boldsymbol{V} = [\boldsymbol{v}_1 \cdots \boldsymbol{v}_{N_T}]$ is orthogonal, and $\boldsymbol{K} = diag[\kappa_1, \cdots, \kappa_{N_T}]$. Choosing the maximum value, κ^*, from κ_n ($1 \leq n \leq N_T$) and the eigenvector, $\boldsymbol{v}^*$, corresponding to κ^*, the optimal current is given by:

$$\boldsymbol{i}_T^* = \beta \boldsymbol{v}^*, \qquad (17)$$

where β is a constant satisfying that (10) holds with equality.

5   Numerical Results

As shown in Fig. 2, we assume that the WPT system consists of $N_T = 5$ Tx coils, $N_L = 3$ relay coils and a single Rx coil, each of which has 80 turns and a radius of $0.1\,\mathrm{m}$. The wires of all coils are made by cooper and with radius of $1\,\mathrm{mm}$. All the coils are horizontal relative to the xy-plane. The coils of Tx, relay, and Rx are same with resistance equal to $0.2688\,\Omega$ ($r_{0,p} = 0.2688\,\Omega$). And load resistance $r_{0,l} = 100\Omega$ is set on the Rx. We choose all the capacitors adapted to the resonance angular frequency $\omega = 6.78 \times 10^6\,\mathrm{rad/s}$. Let h_{TR} denote the vertical dimension between Txs and Rx. We consider that relay coils are always placed in the middle flat of Txs and Rx on z-axis. And we assume that the Rx can move in a disk of the xy-plane at $z = 1\,\mathrm{m}$ with radius of $1\,\mathrm{m}$.

The experimental group is a MWPT system set as Fig. 2 with equal Tx current mode (ETCM). For control groups, we construct a basic WPT system that has only 5 Txs and Rx placed in the same way as Fig. 2. The benchmarks are the WPT system with ETCM, denoted as $B1$, and with magnetic beamforming, denoted as $B2$. And $B1$, $B2$ and experimental group are subject to the sum-power constraint, $P_{max} = 100\,\mathrm{W}$, of TXs and Rx (and relay coils). Let η denote the efficiency of WPT, which is defined as the proportion of the Rx load consumed power $P_{Rx,l}$ to the total system power P_{max}, ie., $\eta = \dfrac{P_{Rx,l}}{P_{max}}$.

In Fig. 3, three curves are plotted and corresponding to the maximum of energy transmission efficiency η in $B1$, $B2$ and experimental group versus the vertical dimension h_{TR} between Txs and Rx. We compare the three curves and obtain that the relay coils do the same performance of energy transmission efficiency ($\eta = 60.44\%/73.59\%$) as $B1/B2$ at $h_{TR} = 0.8829\,\mathrm{m}/0.9906\,\mathrm{m}$, and do make great progress in energy transmission efficiency over the longer vertical

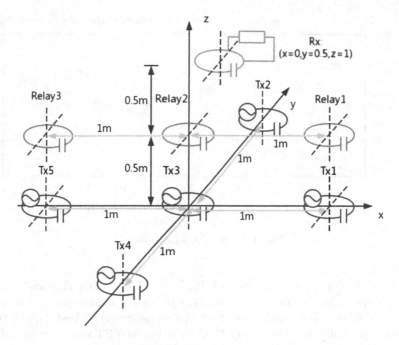

Fig. 2. System setup

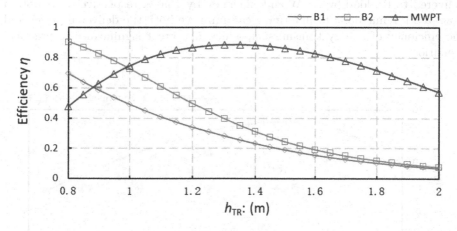

Fig. 3. Efficiency v.s. transmission distance.

transfer distances. It can be explained that MWPT system comes into being overcoupling, which expresses as that the maximum of power delivered to the RX load in MWPT system is less than the same value in $B1$ ($B2$) when h_{TR} is less than $0.8829\,\mathrm{m}$ ($0.9906\,\mathrm{m}$).

Figure 4 plots the power delivered to Rx load, $P_{Rx,l}$, versus the consumed power of whole system, P_{max}, in the case that position of Rx is $x = 0\,\mathrm{m}$,

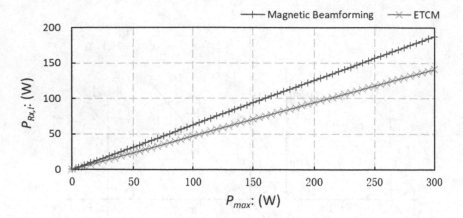

Fig. 4. Power v.s. sum-power.

$y = 0.5$ m, $z = 1$ m. For the case of $P_{max} = 50$ W, using the beamforming algorithm can delivers more power up 31.3 W to Rx load resistance with the efficiency of 62.6%; nevertheless the ETCM can delivered at best 23.5 W to Rx load resistance with the efficiency of 47%. By using MWPT magnetic beamforming, the performance of WPT system is better because of the increase of power delivered to Rx load by 7.8 W and efficiency by 15.6%, respectively. We obtain that MWPT magnetic beamforming can improve both the delivered power and the efficiency of energy transmission, which has great significance in practical scenarios.

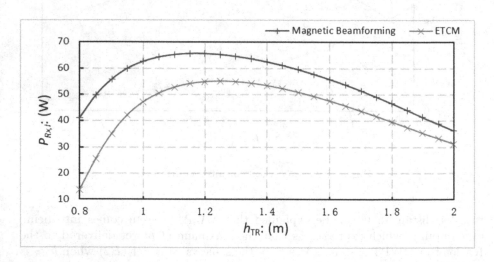

Fig. 5. Power v.s. the vertical dimension with $P_{max} = 100$ W.

In Fig. 5, there are two marked curves that are plotted by the power of Rx load, $P_{Rx,l}$, versus the vertical dimension, h_{TR}, in the case that Rx has fixed coordinate on x, y axis, yet its z-axis coordinate changes with the varying h_{TR} with the $P_{max} = 100$ W. The power of Rx load can get highest value 65.64W at $h_{TR} = 1.15$ m with magnetic beamforming, meanwhile the maximum of $P_{Rx,l}$ with ETCM is 55.12 W at $h_T R = 1.248$ m. The maximum difference of $P_{Rx,l}$ between magnetic beamforming and ETCM is 24.4558 W when h_{TR} is getting to 0.8 m. It can be readily observed that magnetic beamforming has preferable performance comparing to ETCM. With h_{TR} increasing, the decline of system transmission efficiency causes that the difference value of $P_{Rx,l}$ between magnetic beamforming and ETCM gets less. Besides, we obtain that magnetic beamforming can keep higher power level in the larger area to prolong the transmission distance.

6   Conclusion

In this paper, we study an beamforming algorithm for MWPT System by magnetic resonant coupling. Firstly, the problem is formulated as a QCQP problem that maximizes the power delivered to Rx load by jointly adjusting the currents of different Txs with the constraint of the total system consumed power. For solving the problem, we derive the lagrangian equation of the problem and do a relaxation of the Lagrange multiplier to obtain the feasible solution. Then we construct two distributed WPT systems: a multi-relay WPT system with ETCM and benchmarks that use ETCM and magnetic beamforming without relay coils. Firstly, by comparing the MWPT system and benchmarks, it can be observed that relay coils can greatly enhance the efficiency of WPT system. Then we verify that the beamforming algorithm presented in this paper makes great improvements in both transmission power, efficiency and distance by comparing the performances of the magnetic beamforming algorithm and ETCM in MWPT system. For future work, we will study the optimal relay coils placement to maximize the energy transmission efficiency and avoid the overcoupling in the WPT system.

References

1. Shin, S., et al.: Wireless power transfer system for high power application and a method of segmentation. In: 2013 IEEE Wireless Power Transfer (WPT), pp. 76–78, May 2013
2. Gupta, A., Ghosh, S., Chatterjee, S., Iyer, A.: System for metered wireless power transfer for low voltage application. In: 2017 Progress in Electromagnetics Research Symposium - Fall (PIERS - FALL), pp. 886–891, November 2017
3. Shin, J., et al.: Contactless power transfer systems for on-line electric vehicle (OLEV). In: 2012 IEEE International Electric Vehicle Conference, pp. 1–4, March 2012

4. Hu, H., Georgakopoulos, S.V.: Wireless power transfer in human tissue via conformal strongly coupled magnetic resonance. In: 2015 IEEE Wireless Power Transfer Conference (WPTC), pp. 1–4, May 2015

5. Kong, S., Bae, B., Kim, J.J., Kim, S., Jung, D.H., Kim, J.: Electromagnetic radiated emissions from a repeating-coil wireless power transfer system using a resonant magnetic field coupling. In: 2014 IEEE Wireless Power Transfer Conference, pp. 138–141, May 2014

6. de Rooij, M., Zhang, Y.: eGAN FET based 6.78 MHZ differential-mode ZVS class D airfuel class 4 wireless power amplifier. In: PCIM Europe 2016; International Exhibition and Conference for Power Electronics, Intelligent Motion, Renewable Energy and Energy Management, pp. 1–8, May 2016

7. Shi, T., Wiener, P.: High power constant current class EF2 GaN power amplifier for AirFuel magnetic resonance wire-less power transfer systems. In: PCIM Europe 2018; International Exhibition and Conference for Power Electronics, Intelligent Motion, Renewable Energy and Energy Management, pp. 1–4, June 2018

8. Masuda, S., Hirose, T., Akihara, Y., Kuroki, N., Numa, M., Hashimoto, M.: Impedance matching in magnetic-coupling-resonance wireless power transfer for small implantable devices. In: 2017 IEEE Wireless Power Transfer Conference (WPTC), pp. 1–3, May 2017

9. Beh, T.C., Kato, M., Imura, T., Oh, S., Hori, Y.: Automated impedance matching system for robust wireless power transfer via magnetic resonance coupling. IEEE Trans. Ind. Electron. **60**, 3689–3698 (2013)

10. Yoon, I., Ling, H.: Investigation of near-field wireless power transfer under multiple transmitters. IEEE Antennas Wirel. Propag. Lett. **10**, 662–665 (2011)

11. Ahn, D., Hong, S.: Effect of coupling between multiple transmitters or multiple receivers on wireless power transfer. IEEE Trans. Ind. Electron. **60**, 2602–2613 (2013)

12. Dionigi, M., Mongiardo, M.: Magnetically coupled resonant wireless power transmission systems with relay elements. In: 2012 IEEE MTT-S International Microwave Workshop Series on Innovative Wireless Power Transmission: Technologies, Systems, and Applications, pp. 223–226, May 2012

13. Menon, K.A.U., Gungi, A., Hariharan, B.: Efficient wireless power transfer using underground relay coils. In: Fifth International Conference on Computing, Communications and Networking Technologies (ICCCNT), pp. 1–5, July 2014

14. Shin, J., Shin, S., Kim, Y., Lee, S., Song, B., Jung, G.: Optimal current control of a wireless power transfer system for high power efficiency. In: 2012 Electrical Systems for Aircraft, Railway and Ship Propulsion, pp. 1–4, October 2012

15. Zhang, Y., Zhao, Z., He, F., Chen, K., Lu, T., Yuan, L.: Increasing power level of resonant wireless power transfer with relay resonators by considering resonator current amplitudes. In: 2015 IEEE Energy Conversion Congress and Exposition (ECCE), pp. 3077–3081, September 2015

16. Boyd, S., Vandenberghe, L., Faybusovich, L.: Convex optimization. IEEE Trans. Autom. Control **51**(11), 1859–1859 (2006)

17. Conway, J.T.: Inductance calculations for noncoaxial coils using bessel functions. IEEE Trans. Magn. **43**, 1023–1034 (2007)

Self-attention Based Collaborative Neural Network for Recommendation

Shengchao Ma and Jinghua Zhu[⊠]

School of Computer Science and Technology, Heilongjiang University,
Harbin 150080, China
zhujinghua@hlju.edu.cn

Abstract. With the rapid development of e-commerce, various types of
recommendation systems have emerged in an endless stream. Collaborative filtering based recommendation methods are either based on user
similarity or item similarity. Neural network as another choice of recommendation method is also based on item similarity. In this paper, we
propose a new model named Self Attention based Collaborative Neural
Network (SATCoNN) to combine both user similarity and item similarity. SATCoNN is an extension of Recurrent Neural Network (RNN).
SATCoNN model uses self-attention mechanism to compute the weight
of products in multi aspects from user purchase history which form a
user purchase history vector. Borrowing the idea of image style transfer,
we model the users' shopping style by gram matrix. We exploit the max-
pooling technique to extract users style as a style vector in gram matrix.
The experimental results show that our model has better performance
by comparison with other recommendation algorithms.

Keywords: Deep neural network · Collaborative filtering ·
Self-attention · Recommendation · User style

1 Introduction

With the development of Internet technology and e-commerce, e-shopping websites are full of a large amount of product information. Recommendation system
can help users avoid information overload and improve user's shopping efficiency.
Many companies use recommendation based system to improve the sales of products,
such as the famous company Amazon, Alibaba, YouTube, and all, especially
in recent years, with the e-commerce has developed spurt, the recommendation
system plays an increasingly important role in it, and even Netflix has set up
the Netflix Prize to promote the development of the recommendation system.

With the rapid development of e-commerce, various types of recommendation
systems have emerged in an endless stream [22–24]. The traditional recommendation system uses collaborative filtering to recommend products. Collaborative
filtering based methods are either based on user similarity or item similarity

---

Supported by the National Science Foundation of China (61602159, 61100048).

E. S. Biagioni et al. (Eds.): WASA 2019, LNCS 11604, pp. 235–246, 2019.
https://doi.org/10.1007/978-3-030-23597-0_19

separately [12,13]. Recently, neural network has been used in recommendation system, however, it is also based on item similarity which recommend product according to similarity between the target item and the user purchase history. Until now, no model has been proposed to combine these two kinds of similarity for recommendation system.

Traditional collaborative filtering algorithms are generally divided into two categories. One is based on the user similarity, these algorithms recommend the products to the users according to user similarity, one is based on the similarity of the items, they make recommendation by item similarity. Matrix factorization is one of the most used models by collaborative filtering algorithm. Matrix factorization uses a latent vector to represent a user and a product respectively, and then through the dot product of the user vector and the item vector to obtain the user's score on the item, and is optimized by minimizing the root mean squared error (RMSE), and the item is recommended to the user through the obtained score. Since the interaction between user and item is too sparse, coupled with the limitations of the matrix decomposition technology itself, the above model cannot generate good recommended results. With the great success of deep learning, more and more people will apply deep learning in the recommendation system, deep learning has powerful data representation ability, feature abstraction ability and model expression ability, it can better extract features from heterogeneous data and then alleviate the problems of data sparseness and cold start.

But regardless of the traditional recommendation system or the new neural-based recommendation system, only utilize the unilateral similarity, either the similarity between the products, or the similarity between the users. Without getting rid of the dilemma of using a single method, we propose a new model that combines these two methods, when calculating the recommended probability of a new product, not only considers the similarity between items, but also considers the similarity between target user and the users have brought the target item. The traditional recommendation system based recurrent neural network, using vanilla attention, only considering the importance of each product from a certain aspect, which will limit the expression ability of the model. We introduced a self-attention mechanism to consider the importance of the products from different aspects, we use the GRU model and the self-attention mechanism to model the user history purchase sequence. The traditional method is to use the vector obtained by the GRU and attention mechanism as an abstract representation of the user history. We use the gram matrix in the image style transfer to model the users shopping style separately, and use the max-pooling to extract the users style. Because in the real world, the amount of implicit feedback is much larger than explicit feedback, so the entire framework builds the relationship between users and products based on implicit feedback. It uses a binary classfication approach, using three embedding layers: user layer, item layer and target layer.

2 Related Works

2.1 Traditional Recommendation Techniques

Most of the traditional recommendation algorithms are based on matrix factorization techniques and probabilistic models. The most classic model is the item-based collaborative filtering recommendation algorithm [9] proposed by Sarwar, Karypis, Konstan, and Riedl in 2001. They explored item-based collaborative fltering techniques, and first analyzed the user-item matrix to identify relationships between different items, and then used these relationships to indirectly compute recommendations for users. In 2007, Salakhutdinov and Mnih [10] presented the Probabilistic Matrix Factorization (PMF) technique, which can performed well on the large, sparse and very imbalanced dataset. In 2009, Rendle, Freudenthaler, Gantner and Schmidt-Thieme [3] presented a generic optimization criterion BPR-Opt for personalized ranking that is the maximum posterior estimator derived from a Bayesian analysis of the problem. They also provide a generic learning algorithm for optimizing models with respect to BPR-Opt. In 2011, Wang and Blei [11] proposed an algorithm to recommend scientific articles to users of an online community, their approach combined the merits of traditional collaborative filtering and probabilistic topic modeling.

2.2 Recommendation Based on Neural Network

With the great success of deep learning in natural language processing, speech recognition and computer vision, more and more people apply deep learning in the recommendation system [17–20]. In 2015, Wang, Wang, and Yeung [5] proposed a hierarchical Bayesian model called collaborative deep learning (CDL), which jointly performs deep representation learning for the content information and collaborative filtering for the ratings (feedback) matrix. In 2016, Tan, Xu and Liu [7] further studied RNN-based models for session-based recommendations, and proposed the application of two techniques to improve model performance, namely, data augmentation, and a method to account for shifts in the input data distribution. In 2017, He, Liao and Zhang [4] explored neural network architectures for collaborative filtering. They devised a general framework Neural network-based Collaborative Filtering (NCF), and proposed three instantiations—GMF, MLP and NeuMF—that model user-item interactions in different ways. In 2018, Wang, Zhang, Xie, and Guo [2] proposed DKN, a deep knowledge-aware network that takes advantage of knowledge graph representation in news recommendation to addresses three major challenges in news recommendation.

3 Preliminary

3.1 Implicit Feedback

Among user product interactions, there are many behaviors that can be used to infer user preferences, such as click, browse, favorite, etc. These behaviors do not explicitly show the preferences of the user. The amount of implicit feedback is much larger than explicit feedback. The explicit feedback is that the user clearly expresses that he likes a item. For example, a user gives a item 5 points and give another item 0 points. This paper mainly models the implicit feedback behavior between users and items. Assume there are m users and n items, we define implicit user item interaction matrix $R \in R^{m \times n}$ [4] as

$$R_{ij} = \begin{cases} 1, \ if \ user \ i \ interacted \ the \ item \ j; \\ 0, \qquad\qquad otherwise. \end{cases} \tag{1}$$

When the element value of the user-item interaction R_{ij} is 1, it means that there is interaction between user i and item j, Note that $R_{ij} = 1$ does not mean that the user i likes item j. Similarly, $R_{ij} = 1$ in the matrix does not mean user i don't like item j. The observed phenomenon reflects at least the user's interest in the item. The unobserved entry is just a missing value and lacks negative feedback, but can be considered as a mixture of negative information and potential interactions, the user might not like item, or user is just not aware of this item.

3.2   Recurrent Neural Network

The Recurrent Neural Network (RNN) implements one of the most popular models for solving the time series problem today. There are two main models in the recurrent neural network, one is Long Short-Term Memory (LSTM), the other is Gated Recurrent Unit (GRU), both models can alleviate the problem of the vanishing gradient of the recurrent neural network, but the GRU model need fewer parameters than the LSTM model and in various studies, e.g., in [16] and the references therein, it has been noted that GRU is comparable to, or even outperforms, the LSTM in most cases [15]. So we use the GRU model to encode the user's historical sequence.

3.3   Attention Mechanism and Self-attention Mechanism

The attention mechanism was first used in image processing and machine translation models [1], because it has achieved excellent results in both models, more and more people apply it to other deep learning models. However, the core idea is consistent. The candidate elements are given different weights by the relationship between the target and the candidate set. Finally, the weighted average vector of the candidate elements is obtained as the vector we want to use. The usual attention mechanism is Bahdanaus additive style. First we calculate the score between the target and the candidate set:

$$score(h_t, h_c) = v_a^T tanh(W_1 h_t + W_2 h_c) \tag{2}$$

where the weight of the candidate set element is given by the following formula:

$$\alpha_{tc} = \frac{exp(score(h_t, h_c))}{\sum_{c=1}^{C} exp(score(h_t, h_c))} \tag{3}$$

the weighted average of the candidate set elements is:

$$c_t = \sum_{C=1}^{C} \alpha_{tc} h_c \tag{4}$$

Finally, we can get our attention vector by the following formula:

$$a_t = f(c_t, h_t) = tanh(W_c[c_t; h_t]) \tag{5}$$

We represent the item vector in the user history as $H = (h_1, h_2, \ldots h_n)$. The attention mechanism takes the H as input, and outputs a vector of weights **a**:

$$\mathbf{a} = softmax(\mathbf{w}_{s2} tanh(W_{s1} H^T)) \tag{6}$$

The standard attention mechanism that assigning a single importance value to a item makes the model focus on only one specific aspect of items. Thus, to capture the user preference from different aspects, we need to perform multiple hops of attention [25]. so the vector $\mathbf{w}_{s2}$ become a matrix. We get the weight:

$$A = softmax(W_{s2} tanh(W_{s1} H^T)) \tag{7}$$

The attention matrix is as the following:

$$M = AH \tag{8}$$

4 Self-attention Based Collaborative Neural Network for Recommendation

4.1 Time-Aware User History Sequence Features

The extraction framework for timing features is as shown in Fig. 1: First, We get the user's history item vectors $Hist_u$ from the item embedding. $Hist_u$ is a $d_1 \times N$ matrix. d_1 indicates the dimension of the item vector. N indicates the number of the items in user's history. Connecting the item vectors obtained from the item embedding layer with their corresponding tags, we get $Hist_{u\_tag}$. $Hist_{u\_tag}$ is a $(d_1 + d_2) \times N$ matrix. d_2 indicates the dimension of the tag vector. We use the user vector to initialize the hidden state, We enter the $Hist_{u\_tag}$ into the GRU model to get the output vectors H_{out}. We use H_{out} as the input for self-attention:

$$A_h = softmax(W_1 tanh(W_2 H_{out}^T)) \tag{9}$$

$$M_h = A_h H_{out} \tag{10}$$

Finally, we get an abstract representation of the user's history:

$$\mathbf{u}_h = a_t(M_h w_1 + b_1) \tag{11}$$

a_t indicates the active function,w_1 indicates a vector.

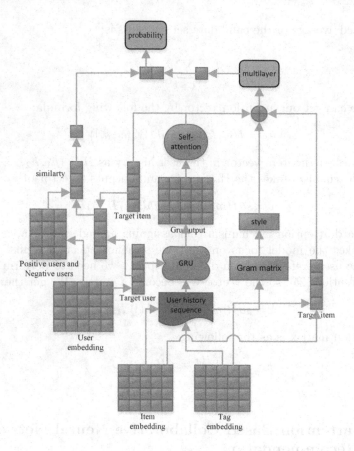

Fig. 1. SATCoNN model

4.2 Shopping Style Model

In this section, we use the gram matrix in the image style transfer to model the users shopping style. The gram matrix can extract the correlation between features. We make the dot product of the matrix $Hist_{u\_tag}$ and its own transpose to get the gram matrix S. S is a $(d_1 + d_2) \times (d_1 + d_2)$ matrix. For each element S_{ij} in the S matrix is obtained by:

$$S_{ij} = H_{i1} * H_{1j} + H_{ik} * H_{kj} + \cdots + H_{iN} * H_{Nj} = \sum_{k=1}^{k=N} H_{ik} * H_{kj} \qquad (12)$$

For the simplicity of the formula, we simplify $Hist_{u\_tag}$ to H. S_{ij} represents the sum of the correlation strengths of the i-th feature and the j-th feature on each item, we only take the largest element in each row, so we use the max-pooling to extract the users style:

$$u_s = max - pooling(S) \qquad (13)$$

u_s is the user's style vector.

4.3   User Similarity Model

In this section, we mainly model the relationship between users and users. We call these users who interactive the target item i_t as positive users U_p and call these users who dose't interactive the target item as negative users U_n. The target item vector i_t contains its corresponding tag vector. According to the assumption of collaborative filtering, similar users are more likely to purchase similar items, therefore, we sample multiple positive users, and obtain the similarities between the target user and the positive users through the cosine similarity. We want to consider the similarity between the target user and the positive users under the condition of the target item, which is a bit like the conditional Gan model, so we concatenate the target user u_t and the target item, and through a linear transformation. We use sim_p represent the similarity vector between positive users and target user. We also sample multiple negative users. If the target users are more similar to these users, the target users are less likely to interact with the target item. Of course, these similarities are calculated under the condition of the target item. We use sim_n represent the similarity vector between negative users and target user. Here, we do not use the vanilla-attention mechanism, mainly because we want to highlight similar strength, and using the vanilla-attention mechanism will loss similar strength information. We use the cosine similarity to calculate the similarity vector between the target user and the candidate users, then we use $0.5 + 0.5cos(\Theta)$ to normalize the cosine similarity. We concatenate sim_p and $1 - sim_n$ to get a vector sim, Then we pass the vector sim through the multi-layer perceptrons and relu function get a scala sup. sup indicates the support strength of these candidate users to the target users.

$$sim = cat(SIM(U_p, Wcat(i_t, u_t)), 1 - SIM(U_n, Wcat(i_t, u_t)))) \quad (14)$$

cat is the concatenate function, W is the linear transformation. SIM is the similarity function.

4.4   Combined Model and Loss Function

We connect the user history vector u_h, the user style vector u_s, the target user vector u_t, and the target item vector i_t to get the vector v. Then we pass the vector v through the multi-layer perceptrons, and get a scala r. We consider the final problem as a binary classification problem. We take the support we get in the third quarter and the scala r through linear combination and sigmoid activation function to obtain the predicted probability p_{ui}. The probability p_{ui} represents how likely user u is relevant to item i. We optimize the results by minimizing the negative logarithm of the likelihood:

$$J(\theta) = - \sum_{(u,i) \in R} y_{ui} log p_{ui} + (1 - y_{ui}) log(1 - p_{ui}) \quad (15)$$

y_{ui} is 1 indicating that user u has a relationship with item i, and 0 otherwise. We use the stochastic gradient descent method (SGD) to optimize the loss function.

For negative samples, we treat items that have not interacted with the user as negative samples and take a sample to obtain negative samples. In order to prevent overfitting, we will add L2 regularization term to the loss. We also made some restrictions on the similarity. We hope that the similarity between the positive users and the target item is greater, while the similarity between the negative users and the target item is smaller. The total loss is as follows:

$$loss = J(\theta) + \lambda_u \|u_t\|_2^2 + \lambda_i \|i_t\|_2^2 + \lambda_n mean(U_n i_t) - \lambda_p mean(U_p i_t) \quad (16)$$

λ_u, λ_i, λ_n, and λ_p are hyperparameters that control the weight of each loss term. *mean* is the mean function.

5   Experiments Evaluation

We conducted a lot of experiments to evaluate the performance of our model, our model shows good performance by comparison with other models. In this section, we mainly introduce our experiment part, including the detailed introduction of the experiment data set, the evaluation criteria of the experiment, the setting of the specific parameters of the experiment and the comparative experiments of this paper.

5.1   Datasets and Evaluation Metrics

We used two public datasets for training. The two datasets are Amazon (Electro)[1] [21] and MovieLens (1M)[2]. The dataset of Amazon (Electro) is mainly related to electronic products. There are various information such as price, description, category, and user's review information, there are 192,403 users, 63,001 items, 801 product categories and 1,689,187 interaction in the Amazon (Electro) dataset. The MovieLens (1M) dataset is mainly related to movies, with a total of 6,040 users, 3706 items, 18 product categories and 1,000,209 interactions.

Table 1. Dataset statistics

Dataset name	Domain			
	Users	Items	Categories	Interactions
Amazon (Electro)	192,403	63,001	801	1,689,187
MovieLens (1M)	6,040	3,706	18	1,000,209

In this experiment, we followed the common strategy that randomly samples 100 items that are not interacted by the user, ranking the test item among the 100 items. we mainly use the AUC [6] to evaluate our model.

---

[1]   http://jmcauley.ucsd.edu/data/amazon/.
[2]   https://grouplens.org/datasets/movielens/.

5.2   Parameter Settings

In the experiment, we set the user vector, item vector, and label vector dimensions to 128, 64, 64, respectively, We used the Matrix factorization technology to pre-train user embedding, item embedding and tag embedding. we will add the drop-out layer [8] during training to prevent overfitting, and drop-out rate is 0.5. We choose the relu activation function to activate. We use the stochastic gradient descent method (SGD) to optimize the loss function. The learning rate is set to 2e−4. For each positive sample, we extract [1–5] negative samples for training. But, for BPR model, it only extract 1 negative sample for each positive sample in the training. The regularization hyperparameters λ_u, λ_i are set to 3e−5 and λ_n, λ_p are set to 4e−5. and we clip the gradient of the backpropagation during training.

5.3   Baselines

The comparison algorithm of this paper is as follows:

- **BPR** [3]: This mainly adopts matrix factorization and probability model, and optimizes the pairwise loss to obtain the user's item ranking.
- **GRU RNN** [6]: We used the comparison model in [6], we changed the LSTM unit in the model to the GRU unit, the stacked depth is set to be 1.
- **GRU+Attention** [6]: We introduced the attention mechanism based on the above GRU RNN model.

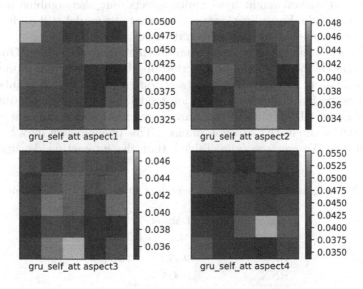

Fig. 2. The attention weight from different aspect

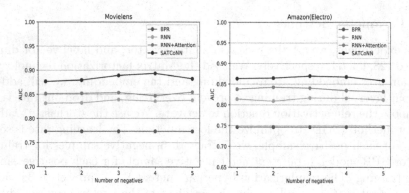

Fig. 3. The AUC in different number of negative samples per positive instance

Figure 2 shows the weight of self-attention on 25 different items of 4 aspects on the MovieLens. For the convenience of display, we reshape the weights of 25 items into a 5 × 5 matrix. We can see that the same item has different weights in different aspects.

From Fig. 3, we can see that our models are significantly better than other models under different sampling strategies on the MovieLens, the rnn+attention is not significantly improved relative to the RNN model, which might because the RNN+Attention model only compute the attention weight from single aspect. Our model is much better than the best performing model RNN+Attention model in all the comparison models, which might because our model not only compute the attention weight from multi aspects, but also combine user similarity and user style. From Fig. 3, we can see that our model still performs well relative to other models on the Amazon dataset.

The Table 2 is the mean of AUC from different sample strategy. Our model is 3.26% points higher than the best performing RNN+Attention model in the MovieLens dataset. In the Amazon dataset, our model is 2.73% points higher than the best-performing RNN+Attention model. From the Table 1, under the same model, the AUC value in the MovieLens dataset is significantly higher than the AUC value in the Amazon dataset. This phenomenon may be related to the dataset. We can see from Table 1 that the interaction density in the

Table 2. The mean AUC of different sampling strategy on various algorithms

Algorithm name	Dataset	
	MovieLens	*Electro*
BPR	*0.7732*	*0.7463*
RNN	*0.8352*	*0.8134*
RNN+Attention	*0.8516*	*0.8373*
SATCoNN	*0.8842*	*0.8646*

MovieLens dataset is greater, while in the Amazon dataset, the interaction of user item interaction is very sparse, but we can see our model still show excellent performance on sparse dataset.

6 Conclusion

In this paper, we combine the model based on user similarity with the model based on item similarity to solve the shortcomings of insufficient expression ability using a single model, and for the first time, we apply the Gram matrix in image style transfer to the recommendation system to model the users preference style, and use the max-pooling to extract the abstract representation of users preferences style, and we introduced the self-attention+gru model to compute the weight of products from multi aspects. For future work, we still have some room for improvement, such as the price of the item, the user's review information, and the user's different behaviors such as clicks, browsing, etc., which have not been fully utilized. These jobs hope to be solved in the future.

References

1. Bahdanau, D., Cho, K., Bengio, Y.: Neural machine translation by jointly learning to align and translate. In: International Conference on Learning Representations (2015)
2. Wang, H., Zhang, F., Xie, X., et al.: DKN: deep knowledge-aware network for news recommendation. In: The Web Conference, pp. 1835–1844 (2018)
3. Rendle, S., Freudenthaler, C., Gantner, Z., et al.: BPR: Bayesian personalized ranking from implicit feedback. In: Proceedings of the Twenty-Fifth Conference on Uncertainty in Artificial Intelligence, pp. 452–461. AUAI Press (2009)
4. He, X., Liao, L., Zhang, H., et al.: Neural collaborative filtering, pp. 173–182 (2017). https://doi.org/10.1145/3038912.3052569
5. Wang, H., Wang, N., Yeung, D.-Y.: Collaborative deep learning for recommender systems. In: KDD, pp. 1235–1244 (2015)
6. Zhou, C., Bai, J., Song, J., et al.: ATRank: an attention-based user behavior modeling framework for recommendation. In: Proceedings of 32th AAAI Conference on Artificial Intelligence (2018)
7. Tan, Y.K., Xu, X., Liu, Y.: Improved recurrent neural networks for session-based recommendations. In: Conference on Recommender Systems, pp. 17–22 (2016)
8. Srivastava, N., Hinton, G.E., et al.: Dropout: a simple way to prevent neural networks from overfitting. JMLR 15(1), 1929–1958 (2014)
9. Sarwar, B., Karypis, G., Konstan, J., et al.: Item-based collaborative filtering recommendation algorithms. In: WWW, pp. 285–295 (2001)
10. Mnih, A., Salakhutdinov, R.: Probabilistic matrix factorization. In: Neural Information Processing Systems (2007)
11. Wang, C., Blei, D.M.: Collaborative topic modeling for recommending scientific articles. In: Proceedings of the 17th ACM SIGKDD International Conference on Knowledge Discovery and Data Mining, San Diego, CA, USA, 21–24 August 2011. ACM (2011)

12. Gong, S.: A collaborative filtering recommendation algorithm based on user clustering and item clustering. JSW **5**(7), 745–752 (2010)
13. Liu, Z., Qu, W., Li, H., Xie, C.: A hybrid collaborative filtering recommendation mechanism for P2P networks. Future Gener. Comput. Syst. **26**(8), 1409–1417 (2010)
14. Zhang, S., et al.: Deep learning based recommender system: a survey and new perspectives. ACM Comput. Surv. (CSUR) **52**(1), 5 (2019)
15. Dey, R., Salemt, F.M.: Gate-variants of gated recurrent unit (GRU) neural networks. In: 2017 IEEE 60th International Midwest Symposium on Circuits and Systems (MWSCAS). IEEE (2017)
16. Chung, J., et al.: Empirical evaluation of gated recurrent neural networks on sequence modeling. arXiv preprint arXiv:1412.3555 (2014)
17. Wang, Y., Yin, G., Cai, Z., Dong, Y., Dong, H.: A trust-based probabilistic recommendation model for social networks. J. Netw. Comput. Appl. **55**, 59–67 (2015)
18. Wang, Y., Cai, Z., Tong, X., Gao, Y., Yin, G.: Truthful incentive mechanism with location privacy-preserving for mobile crowdsourcing systems. Comput. Netw. **135**, 32–43 (2018)
19. Wang, Y., Cai, Z., Zhan, Z.-H., Gong, Y., Tong, X.: An optimization and auction based incentive mechanism to maximize social welfare for mobile crowdsourcing. IEEE Trans. Comput. Soc. Syst. Accepted
20. Cai, Z., He, Z.: Trading private range counting over big IoT data. In: The 39th IEEE International Conference on Distributed Computing Systems (ICDCS 2019) (2019)
21. McAuley, J., Targett, C., Shi, Q., Van Den Hengel, A.: Image-based recommendations on styles and substitutes. In: Proceedings of the 38th International ACM SIGIR Conference on Research and Development in Information Retrieval, pp. 43–52. ACM (2015)
22. Qi, L., et al.: Structural balance theory-based e-commerce recommendation over big rating data. IEEE Trans. Big Data **4**(3), 301–312 (2018)
23. Xu, Y., Qi, L., Dou, W., Yu, J.: Privacy-preserving and scalable service recommendation based on SimHash in a distributed cloud environment. Complexity **2017**, 3437854:1–3437854:9 (2017)
24. Xia, X., Yu, J., Zhang, S., Wu, S.: Trusted service scheduling and optimization strategy design of service recommendation. Secur. Commun. Netw. **2017**, 9192084:1–9192084:9 (2017)
25. Lin, Z., Feng, M., Santos, C.N., et al.: A Structured Self-attentive Sentence Embedding. In: International Conference on Learning Representations (2017)

An Efficient and Recoverable Data Sharing Mechanism for Edge Storage

Yuwen Pu[1,2], Ying Wang[1,2], Feihong Yang[1,2], Jin Luo[1,2], Chunqiang Hu[1,2(✉)], and Haibo Hu[1,2]

[1] School of Big Data and Software Engineering,
Chongqing University, Chongqing, China
[2] Key Laboratory of Dependable Service Computing in Cyber Physical Society,
Ministry of Education (Chongqing University), Chongqing, China
{yw.pu,wang,yfh,jin.luo,chu,haibo.hu}@cqu.edu.cn

Abstract. With data growing exponentially, more and more people prefer to share data with others by storing the data in edge servers. However, edge server cannot be deemed completely trustable as the sensitive data my be disclosed. Therefore, in this paper, we propose an efficient and secure data sharing scheme for edge storage by employing Ciphertext-Policy Attribute-Based Encryption (CP-ABE) which can be utilized to conduct fine-grained control. This scheme can not only support data recovery when some edge servers break down by employing Secret Sharing Scheme, but also can support semi-trusted third party authority via employing re-encryption method. That is, the third party authority can not either reveal the private data stored in edge servers. Finally, we analyze security of our scheme to demonstrate that this scheme is resistant to eavesdropping attack and colluding attack. Additionally, relevant experiments results are shown that the scheme is feasibility and efficiency.

1 Introduction

Recent years, with the explosive growth of data, data sharing has been applied in many fields and brings much benefits for us. For example, the educational digital resources can be shared among some universities to improve the quality of education [1]. Medical data of hospitals can also be shared with scientific research institution to assist them in medicine development [2,3]. As the size of shared data grows rapidly, it brings much storage pressure and computation costs. Therefore, data sharing based on edge storage is attracting more and more interests [4].

Although edge storage bring us much convenience, they also bring security and privacy issues [5–7]. Data owners usually upload the data to edge servers, which may make data owners lose the control over data and face privacy leakage risk. That is, a malicious server or an attacker may compromise the data stored in server to disclose privacy information of data owners [8,9]. Therefore, some works on privacy-preserving data sharing have been proposed [5,10,11]. Most of them encrypt the shared data and develop access control policy by employing

© Springer Nature Switzerland AG 2019
E. S. Biagioni et al. (Eds.): WASA 2019, LNCS 11604, pp. 247–259, 2019.
https://doi.org/10.1007/978-3-030-23597-0_20

ciphertext-policy attribute-based encryption(CP-ABE) [12,13]. However, there are still two critical problems to be solved.

- When some edge servers break down, data stored in servers will be lost.
- The third party may be curious about the shared data, which is causing data owners' privacy information leakage.

To address the aforementioned problems, in this paper, an efficient and secure data sharing scheme based on edge storage is proposed. The contributions are summarized as follows:

- First, we construct a data sharing scheme based on Secret Sharing Scheme and Attribute-Based Encryption, which supports distributed storage and file recovery.
- Second, third party authority and edge servers can not reveal the data shared by data owner in our scheme. It should be noted that we do not consider collusion action between them.
- Third, data owners and data users can always communicate with the nearest edge server, which can reduce the communication cost.
- Finally, we present comprehensive security analysis and experiments of our scheme. The security analysis shows our scheme can resist several attacks such as eavesdropping attack, replay attack and so on; the experimental results demonstrate that our scheme is efficient and reduces computation overhead of data owners and data users.

The remainder of this paper is organized as follows. In Sect. 2, we discuss related works. We introduce our system model, attack model and design goals in Sect. 3. In Sect. 4, we introduce Bilinear Map, Bilinear Diffie-Hellman problem(BDH), Rabin cryptosystem, Secret Sharing Scheme and Attribute-Based Encryption. Then, we present our scheme in Sect. 5, which is followed by its security analysis and performance evaluation in Sects. 6 and 7 respectively. Finally, we draw our conclusions in Sect. 8.

2 Related Works

The importance of security of shared data stored in cloud servers and edge servers has attracted much attention from both academy and industry. Many privacy-preserving data sharing schemes have also been proposed [14,15]. In this section, we mainly summarize some state-of-the-art schemes for data sharing privacy preservation.

For instance, Green et al. [16] and Lai et al. [17] propose an efficient CP-ABE scheme with outsourced decryption to reduce computation costs on the user side. Liu et al. [18] propose a multi-owner data sharing system based on CP-ABE which supports dynamically add and remove user without interfering with data sharing. Tian et al. [19] propose a secure and flexible data sharing scheme based on CP-ABE to support fine-grained access control for cloud storage. Wang et al. [20] propose a three-layer privacy preserving cloud storage scheme based on fog computing.

In this paper, we propose an efficient and recoverable data sharing scheme by employing ABE, Rabin encryption, AES encryption, signature mechanism and so on. This scheme can reduce computation costs on the user side and resist many attacks such as replay attack, collusion attack. However, it should be mentioned that we do not consider the collusion action between trusted authority and other entities.

3   System Model, Attack Model, and Design Goals

In this section, we formalize the system model, analyze attack model and present our design goals.

3.1   System Model

In our system model, we mainly focus on how data owner shares data with users via using the privacy-preserving method. There are four entities, including (TA) trusted authority, data owner, data user and edge server. We consider that many people in a certain region intend to share data with some particular persons. Each person can be a data owner and a data user. Besides, there are many edge servers with some computation and storage capacity around people. Data owners uploads encrypted data to the edge servers and data users request data from them. The system model is shown in Fig. 1.

1. *Trustable Authority:* TA is a semi-trustable authority entity, which bootstraps the system by generating and sending system parameters honestly to data owner, data user and edge server in a secure channel. It also assists in user registration. However, it might try to disclose shared privacy data of data owners which are stored in the edge servers.
2. *Data Owner: DO* is an honest entity responsible for uploading data to edge server.
3. *Data User: DU* is an entity who wants to request data shared by *DO*. However, some invalid DU may try to collude to obtain the data stored in edge servers.
4. *Edge Server: ES* is in charge of data storage for data owner and provides data retrieval for data users. Each edge server has some storage space and computation resource.

3.2   Attack Model

We take into consideration the following three types of attack in our system.

1. External Attack: An adversary may eavesdrop, modify or replay the transmitted data during communication among *DO*, *DU*, *TA* and *ES* to reveal users' privacy information. It might also compromise *ES* to disclose the data stored by *DO*.

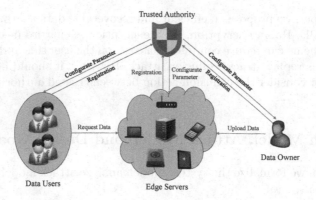

Fig. 1. System model

2. Collusion Attack: For some DUs who do not have the corresponding permission to access data, they may try to disclose the data by colluding together. Moreover, we also consider that some DUs without access permission and ESs collude to achieve this goal. However, it should be mentioned that we do not take into account the collusion between TA and ESs.

3.3 Design Goals

Under the aforementioned system model and attack model, our design concentrates on proposing a privacy-preserving, efficient, flexible, reliable and fault-tolerant data sharing scheme. Specifically, the following three objectives should be achieved:

1. Privacy-Preserving: Secure and privacy is the primary goal of system design. All the transmitted data is encrypted to protect the original data from being revealed, which can guarantee confidentiality, integrity and anti-replay protection. It is very difficult for adversary to compromise DO's privacy by accessing the data stored in ESs.
2. Fault-Tolerant: ES devices may break down sometimes, which may result in losing important data stored in these ESs. Therefore, this scheme should achieve that even if some ESs break down, other ESs can still retrieval all the original data of DO.
3. Efficiency: This scheme should take into account computation and communication efficiency. Specifically, computation overhead of DO and DU, and storage overhead of ES should be reduced. Besides, the communication overhead should be also reduced as much as possible.

4   Preliminaries

In this section, we review the related mathematical concepts for our protocol construction and security analysis.

4.1   Bilinear Map

We assume that $\mathbb{G}_1$ and $\mathbb{G}_2$ are two cyclic groups with the prime order p. We define $e : \mathbb{G}_1 \times \mathbb{G}_1 \longrightarrow \mathbb{G}_2$ as the bilinear map that has the following properties:

1. Bilinear: For all $P, Q \in \mathbb{G}_1$ and $a, b \in \mathbb{Z}_p$, $e = (aP, bQ) = e(P, Q)^{ab}$. Here $\mathbb{Z}_p = 0, 1, ..., p - 1$ is the Galois field of order p.
2. Non-degeneracy: The generator g satisfies $e(g, g) \neq 1$.
3. Computability: There is an efficient algorithm to compute $e(P, Q)$ for $\forall P, Q \in \mathbb{G}_1$.

4.2   Bilinear Diffie-Hellman Problem (BDH)

Given two groups $\mathbb{G}_1$ and $\mathbb{G}_2$ with the same prime order p, let $e : \mathbb{G}_1 \times \mathbb{G}_1 = \mathbb{G}_2$ be a bilinear map and g be a generator of $\mathbb{G}_1$. The objective of BDH is to compute $e(g, g)^{abc}$ in $(\mathbb{G}_1, \mathbb{G}_2, e)$ from the given (g, g^a, g^b, g^c), where $a, b, c \in \mathbb{Z}^p$.

4.3   Rabin Cryptosystem

Rabin cryptosystem is an asymmetric cryptographic technique, whose security is related to the factorization of large prime numbers. The Rabin cryptosystem can shift computation complexity from clients to the server. Therefore, it is efficient for terminal devices with low computing power to implement encryption.

4.4   Access Structure

The description is similar as the definition in [21]. Let $P_1, P_2, ..., P_n$ be a set of parties. A collection $\mathbb{A} \subseteq 2^{\{P_1, P_2, ..., P_n\}}$ is monotone if $\forall B, C$: if $\forall B \in \mathbb{A}$ and $B \subseteq C$ then $C \in \mathbb{A}$. An access structure (respectively,monotone access structure) is a collection (respectively, monotone collection) $\mathbb{A}$ of non-empty subsets of $P_1, P_2, ..., P_n, i.e., \mathbb{A} \subseteq 2^{\{P_1, P_2, ..., P_n\}} \backslash \emptyset$. The sets in $\mathbb{A}$ are called the authorized sets, and the sets not in $\mathbb{A}$ are called the unauthorized sets.

4.5   Ciphertext-Policy Attribute-Base Encryption

In this section, we present an brief introduction of Ciphertext-Policy Attribute-Base Encryption (CP-ABE) by Waters [21]. It can be composed of the following algorithms:

- Setup: It outputs the public parameters PK and a master key MK based on set up algorithm.
- Encrypt($\mathbf{PK}, M, \mathbb{A}$): The encryption algorithm encrypt the message M with the public parameters PK and an access structure $\mathbb{A}$ over the universe of attributes to obtain the ciphertext CT.
- Key Generation($\mathbf{MK}, S$): TA can generate a private key SK by inputting the master key MK and a set of attributes S of user.
- Decrypt($\mathbf{PK}, \mathbf{CT}, \mathbf{SK}$): User can decrypt the CT which contains an access policy $\mathbb{A}$ with public parameters PK and the private key SK.

5   Our Scheme

In this section, we present an efficient privacy-preserving edge storage scheme. In this scheme, we mainly focus on two points. One is how to recover data stored in ESs when some ESs break down. The other is how to protect the stored data from leaking. We assume that there are n ESs which have some computing power and storage capacity in a certain area. DOs can share their data by uploading it to ESs and establishing access policies to permit the valid DUs to access. That is, TA, ESs and invalid DUs can not obtain plaintext of shared data. However, we don't take into account the collusion between ES and TA.

5.1   Initialization

Setup Parameters. For the edge storage system, we assume that *TA* will bootstrap whole system. First, *TA* generates a pair of asymmetrical key(k_{tpu}, k_{tpr}) for itself and setup the corresponding parameters about ABE. It will choose two random exponents $\alpha, \beta \in \mathbb{Z}_p$ and a bilinear group $\mathbb{G}_0$ of prime order p with generator g. The public key will be published as: $PK = \mathbb{G}_0, g, h = g^\beta, e(g, g)^\alpha$. The master key MK is (β, g^α). Moreover, when one system i-th user finishes registration, TA will assign him corresponding attributes set S_i and a pair of asymmetrical key(k_{spu}^i, k_{spr}^i). The system user can be *DO* or *DU*. It should be noted that all the initial keys and parameters are transmitted to the corresponding object by a secure channel, and all the public keys will also be published. Besides, every two *ES*s will be pre-deployed with the same initial symmetrical key and corresponding parameter which is used to update the key. In other words, the i-th ES can communicate with j-th ES by using the same symmetrical key k_{ij} and the corresponding parameter using for updating k_{ij} is φ_{ij}. That is, $k_{ij_n} = H(k_{ij_{n-1}} || \varphi_{ij})$. It should be mentioned that the symmetrical key between two *ES*s is only known by themselves, TA also does not know it. Finally, each *ES* will also generate a pair of key (k_{epu_i}, k_{epr_i}). The public key k_{epu_i} will be published and the private key k_{epr_i} will be hidden secretly.

ABE KeyGen. After assigning system users a set of attributes S, TA outputs a key that identifies with the set. We assume that the i-th system user whose attribute set is S_i requests the ABE private key. TA obtains a set of hash value S_i' on each attribute of S_i. Then, TA chooses a random $r \in \mathbb{Z}_p$, and $r_j \in \mathbb{Z}_p$ for the hash value of each attribute $j \in S_i'$. Then TA computes the key as: $SK = (D = g^{(\alpha+r)/\beta}, \forall j \in S_i' : D_j = g^r \cdot H(j)^{r_j}, D_j' = g^{r_j})$. Finally, SK is transmitted to corresponding system user by a secure channel. It should be noted that once one system user's attribute set has changed, it must request the new ABE private key by transmitting its attribute set to TA.

5.2   Upload Data

When one *DO* wants to share data M with others, it should finish the following three phases: key exchange, encryption and digital signature.

CP-ABE Encryption. In order to share data with others, DO encrypts the shared data M by employing CP-ABE which is proposed by Waters [21]. Firstly, the DO will extract a keyword $keyword$ from M and conduct a hash operation to get $H(keyword)$. Then, DO assigns a tree access structure Γ and the root of Γ is R, the leaf node is the hash value of attribute set. We let Y be the set of leaf nodes of Γ. Moreover, DO will choose polynomial q_x for each node x of Γ and choose a random $s \in \mathbb{Z}_l$. It should be mentioned that $q_R(0) = s$. After above steps, DO can encrypt M under the assigned access policy Γ and get the ciphertext $CT = (\Gamma, \tilde{C} = Me(g,g)^{\alpha s}, C = h^s, \forall y \in Y : C_y = g^{q_y(0)}, C'_y = H(att(y))^{q_y(0)})$.

Digital Signature and Re-encryption. In order to promise the property of data for owner, DO will calculate the signature with his private key k_{spr} which can be denoted as $Sig = E_{k_{spr}}(H(CT)||H(keyword))$. Then, the asymmetrical encryption with the public key of the nearest ES should be computed to get the final ciphertext $FC = E_{k_{epu_i}}(CT||T||H(keyword)||H(CT||T||H(keyword))||Sig)$. Finally, FC will be uploaded to the nearest ES (i-th ES) by DO.

5.3   Distributed Storage

When receiving FC from DO, ES decrypts it with private key k_{epr_i} to get $CT, T, H(CT||T||H(keyword)), Sig, H(keyword)$ at first. ES can also verify whether FC has been replayed, tampered or personated by checking T, $H(CT||T||H(keyword))$ and Sig. After these operations, CT will be divided into n pieces randomly (we assume there are n ESs in a certain area) based on (t, n) threshold scheme proposed by Shamir [22] and $n - 1$ pieces will be transmitted to other ESs. To guarantee adequate security of shared data, we set $t = n/2 + 1$. That is, only more than half of the ESs can recover CT. The detail of distributed storage based on secret sharing scheme can be shown as following. CT will be split into t pieces randomly, and the t pieces will be used as parameters to construct a polynomial. Then, ES will choose n different numbers such as $1, 2, ..., n - 1, n$, and calculate the corresponding result (such as $m_1, m_2, ..., m_n$) based on the constructed polynomial. Finally, ES can obtain n pieces data $CT_1, CT_2, ..., CT_n$ ($CT_1 = (1, m_1), CT_2 = (2, m_2), ..., CT_n = (n, m_n)$). When some ESs break down, other ESs can also recover the data just based on t pieces data.

In order to protect the sensitive data of the data owner, the i-th ES encrypts the piece data with corresponding symmetrical key before transmitting it to other $n - 1$ ESs. We assume that CT has been divided into n pieces ($CT_1, CT_2, ...CT_j..., CT_n, i \neq j$). The i-th ES will encrypt CT_j with the k_{ij} and transmit the ciphertext to the j-th ES, which can be denoted as $C_j = E_{k_{ij}}(CT_j||Sig||H(keyword)||T||H(CT_j||Sig||H(keyword)))$. When receiving C_j, the j-th ES will decrypt it and check whether this message has been tampered or replayed at first. Then, $CT_j, Sig, H(keyword)$ will be stored in the j-th ES.

5.4   Access Data

We assume one DU wants to request data from ESs, it must finish the following two phases.

Request Data. If i-th DU wants to request data from ESs, it should do a hash operation on the *keyword* which it wants to request to obtain $H(keyword)$. Besides, DU will generate a symmetric key K and make a signature based on his private key k_{spr}^i which can be denoted as $DU_{Sig} = E_{k_{spr}^i} H(H(keyword)\|T)$. Moreover, DU will encrypt $H(keyword)$, K, T, DU_{Sig} with public key k_{epu_i} of the nearest ES (i-th ES) NES to get a ciphertext $C_u = E_{k_{epu_i}}(H(keyword)\|K\|DU_{Sig}\|T)$ Finally, C_u will be transmitted to NES.

When receiving C_u from DU, NES decrypts it to obtain $H(keyword)$, K, DU_{Sig}, T and verify integrity, non-replayed by checking the signature DU_{Sig} and the real time T. Then, NES will encrypt DU_{Sig}, $H(keyword)$ and T with symmetric key of each two ESs, which can be denoted as $Req_i = E_{k_{ij}}((H(keyword)\|T\|DU_{Sig})$ and send Req_i to other $n-1$ ESs. When receiving Req_i, the other ESs will check whether this request is from valid DU by checking DU_{Sig}. If it is, the nearest $t-1$(t is the threshold value of recovering CT) ESs for NES will search the requested data based on $H(keyword)$ and transmit the pieces of data to NES.

After receiving $t-1$ pieces of the required data, NES can recover the whole ciphertext CT of original data based on $t-1$ pieces from other ESs and one piece of data stored in itself. The process of data recover is the same as that in "Distributed Storage" phase. After recovering CT, NES will encrypt it with K which is from DU to get the ciphertext $C_r = E_K(CT\|T\|H(CT\|T))$.

Decryption. When receiving C_r from the NES, DU decrypt it to obtain CT, T and $H(CT\|T)$ and verify whether this message have been tampered or replayed by calculating and checking $H(CT\|T)$. If success, DU will decrypt CT with its ABE private key which is generated based on its attributes set to obtain the required data M. The detail of decrypting of ABE can be shown as follows: If the node x is a leaf node, then

$$DecryptNode(CT, SK, x) = \frac{e(D_i, C_x)}{e(D_i', C_x')} = \frac{e(g^r \cdot H(i)^{r_i}, g^{q_x(0)})}{e(g^{r_i}, H(i)^{q_x(0)})} = e(g, g)^{r q_x(0)}$$

$$(1)$$

If the node x is a non-leaf node, then for all nodes z that are children of x, it calls $DecryptNode(CT, SK, z)$ and stores the output as F_z. Let S_x be an arbitrary k_x-sized set of child nodes z. If there is a valid S_x, then

$$F_x = \prod_{z \in S_x} F_z^{\triangle_{i,S'_x}(0)}, where \; i = index(z), S'_x = index(z) : z \in S_x$$

$$= \prod_{z \in S_x} (e(g,g)^{r \cdot q_z(0)})^{\triangle_{i,S'_x}(0)} = \prod_{z \in S_x} e(g,g)^{r \cdot q_x(0)} \tag{2}$$

Therefore, DU can obtain the plaintext of data by computing

$$\tilde{C}/(e(C,D)/e(g,g)^{rs}) = \tilde{C}(e(h^s, g^{(\alpha+r)/\beta})/e(g,g)^{rs}) = M \tag{3}$$

6 Security Analysis

In this section, we analyze security properties of proposed schemes at first. In particular, we focus on how this scheme can resist various attacks and achieve privacy preservation.

6.1 Against Eavesdropping Attack

An attacker may disclose the shared data of DO by eavesdropping the message which are transmitted through the communication channel. However, in our scheme, all the message are encrypted with symmetrical encryption or asymmetric encryption before transmitting. Moreover, only the receiver has corresponding secret key to decrypt it. Therefore, it is impossible for attacker to decrypt and reveal the transmitted data by brute-force with a non-negligible probability.

6.2 Against Colluding Attack

It should be mentioned that we do not consider the collusion between TA and any other entities. We mainly pay attention to the collusion action between ESs and invalid users. We assume that ESs and DUs want to disclose the data stored in ESs by colluding. In our scheme, the data which encrypted by ABE is stored in the ESs as ciphertext. Therefore, even if ESs and invalid user collude to obtain complete ciphertext, they can not decrypt it without corresponding secret key.

7 Performance Evaluation

In this section, we evaluate the computation overheads of proposed scheme. It is well-known for us that computational cost of hash functions and addition operations are much lower than modular exponentiation and multiplication operations. Hence, the cost of hash functions and addition operations can be ignored and only the computational cost incurred by encryption and decryption operations will be considered in this study.

We assume that there are totally n ESs in the edge storage system, the threshold value of recovering data is t. Note that Sha and Rec are the computational costs of data splitting operation and recovery operation based on Secret

Sharing Scheme, respectively. A_e and A_d are the computational costs of an AES encryption operation and an AES decryption operation, respectively. Att_e and Att_d are the computational costs of an Attributed-Based encryption operation and an Attributed-Based decryption operation, respectively. Sig and Ver are the computational costs of an signature operation and an verification operation, respectively. R_e and R_d are the computational costs of an Rabin encryption operation and an Rabin decryption operation, respectively. For one DO, one DU and one ES, we analyze the computational cost in our scheme as follows.

For DO, In the upload data phase, an Attributed-Based encryption operation, a Rabin encryption operation and a signature operation are necessary. Hence, the total computational cost for one DO is $R_e + Att_e + Sig$.

For ES, there are two cases to consider: (i) If ES receives data from DO, a verification operation, an Rabin decryption, an data splitting operation and $n - 1$ AES encryption are required, which can be denoted as $Ver + Sha + (n - 1)A_e + R_d$; (ii) If ES receives request from DU, a verification operation, $n - 1$ AES decryption operation, an AES encryption operation, an Rabin decryption operation, a data recovery operation are required. which can be denoted as $Ver + (n - 1)A_d + nA_e + R_d + Rec$.

For DU, a signature operation and an Rabin encryption are required in request data phase. When receiving the ciphertext of data from ES, an AES decryption and an Attributed-Based decryption operation are required. Hence, the total computational cost for one DU is $Sig + R_e + A_d + Att_d$. Table 1 summaries the computational cost of DO, ES and DU. We conduct the experiments running in python on a 3.7 GHz-processor 16 G-memory computing machine on Windows 10 to study the operation costs. The experimental results indicate that an AES encryption operation with 256-bit key almost costs 0.004 ms, an AES decryption operation with 256-bit key almost costs 0.0039 ms. When the public key of Rabin is 128-bit, an encryption operation costs almost 0.001 ms and an decryption operation costs almost 0.09 ms. An data splitting operation and recovery operation cost respectively almost 14 ms and 5 ms when the threshold is (50,100). An RSA signature operation costs almost 3 ms and an authentication operation also costs almost 0.3 ms. Besides, We conduct Attributed-Based encryption and decryption running in C++ on a 3.2 GHz-processor 8 G-memory computing virtual machine on Ubuntu. The experimental results indicate an Attributed-Based encryption operation on nearly 8 MB file costs almost 69.3 ms and an Attributed-Based decryption operation on nearly 8 MB file costs almost 89.8 ms.

Therefore, on the DO side, the total computational cost of one DO can be denoted as $0.001 + 69.3 + 3 = 72.301$ ms. For ESs, there are two cases. When DO uploading data to ESs, the total computational cost of the nearest ES for DO can be denoted as $0.3 + 14 + 0.004 \times (n - 1) + 0.09 = 0.004 \times n + 14.386$ ms. When DU requesting data to ESs, the total computational cost of the nearest ES for DU can be denoted as $0.3 + 0.0039 \times (n - 1) + 0.004 \times n + 0.09 + 5 = 0.0079 \times n + 5.3861$ ms. On the DU side, the total computational cost of one Du can be denoted as $3 + 0.001 + 0.0039 + 89.8 = 92.8049$ ms. Hence, in the upload

Table 1. Comparisons of functionality

Entities		Computational cost
DO		$R_e + Att_e + Sig$
ES	Case-I	$Ver + Sha + (n-1)A_e + R_d$
	Case-II	$Ver + (n-1)A_d + nA_e + R_d + Rec$
DU		$Sig + R_e + A_d + Att_d$

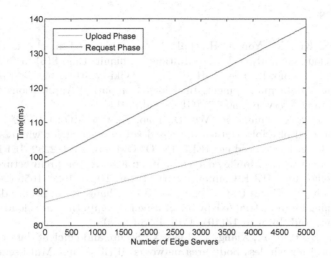

Fig. 2. Total communication costs in upload and request phase

phase, the total computational cost for DO and the nearest ES is $72.301 + 0.004 \times n + 14.386 = 0.004 \times n + 86.687$. In the request phase, the total computational cost for DU and the nearest ES is $92.8049 + 0.0079 \times n + 5.3861 = 0.0079 \times n + 98.191$. As shown in Fig. 2, which illustrates that our scheme is efficient.

8   Conclusion

In this paper, we propose a secure and efficient data sharing scheme for edge storage: The encrypted data are divided into many pieces based on Secret Sharing Scheme and each edge server stores one piece; in this way, just a certain number of pieces can recover integrate data. It voids the stored data lost, and reduce the storage load for edge servers. Moreover, this scheme can resist a variety of attacks such as eavesdropping attack, colluding attack and so on. Furthermore, the experiment result shows that our scheme is efficient and feasible. For the future work, we plan to add attribute revocation mechanism to this scheme and deploy it in real-world data sharing system based on edge servers.

Acknowledgments. This research was partially supported by the National Natural Science Foundation of China under grants 61702062, the National Natural Science Foundation of China with Grant No. U1836114 and the Chongqing Research Program of Basic Research and Frontier Technology with Grant (No. cstc2018jcyjAX0334,cstc2017jcyjB0305), the Fundamental Research Funds for the Central Universities (No. 2019CDQYRJ006), and Overseas Returnees Innovation and Entrepreneurship Support Program of Chongqing(cx2018015).

References

1. Jeong, J.-S., Kim, M., Yoo, K.-H., et al.: A content oriented smart education system based on cloud computing. Int. J. Multimed. Ubiquit. Eng. **8**(6), 313–328 (2013)
2. Li, Y., Wu, C., Guo, L., Lee, C.-H., Guo, Y.: Wiki-health: a big data platform for health sensor data management. In: Cloud Computing Applications for Quality Health Care Delivery, pp. 59–77. IGI Global (2014)
3. Hu, C., Cheng, X., Zhang, F., Wu, D., Liao, X., Chen, D.: OPFKA: secure and efficient ordered-physiological-feature-based key agreement for wireless body area networks. In: 2013 Proceedings IEEE INFOCOM, pp. 2274–2282. IEEE (2013)
4. Mach, P., Becvar, Z.: Mobile edge computing: a survey on architecture and computation offloading. IEEE Commun. Surv. Tutor. **19**(3), 1628–1656 (2017)
5. Fu, J.-S., Liu, Y., Chao, H.-C., Bhargava, B.K., Zhang, Z.-J.: Secure data storage and searching for industrial IoT by integrating fog computing and cloud computing. IEEE Trans. Ind. Inform. **14**(10), 4519–4528 (2018)
6. Hu, C., Li, H., Huo, Y., Xiang, T., Liao, X.: Secure and efficient data communication protocol for wireless body area networks. IEEE Trans. Multi-scale Comput. Syst. **2**(2), 94–107 (2016)
7. He, Z., Cai, Z., Han, Q., Tong, W., Sun, L., Li, Y.: An energy efficient privacy-preserving content sharing scheme in mobile social networks. Pers. Ubiquit. Comput. **20**(5), 833–846 (2016)
8. Zheng, X., Cai, Z., Li, J., Gao, H.: Location-privacy-aware review publication mechanism for local business service systems. In: IEEE INFOCOM 2017-IEEE Conference on Computer Communications, pp. 1–9. IEEE (2017)
9. Alrawais, A., Alhothaily, A., Yu, J., Hu, C., Cheng, X.: SecureGuard: a certificate validation system in public key infrastructure. IEEE Trans. Veh. Technol. **67**(6), 5399–5408 (2018)
10. Hu, C., Li, W., Cheng, X., Yu, J., Wang, S., Bie, R.: A secure and verifiable access control scheme for big data storage in clouds. IEEE Trans. Big Data **4**(3), 341–355 (2018)
11. Zheng, X., Cai, Z., Yu, J., Wang, C., Li, Y.: Follow but no track: privacy preserved profile publishing in cyber-physical social systems. IEEE IoT J. **4**(6), 1868–1878 (2017)
12. Hu, C., Zhang, N., Li, H., Cheng, X., Liao, X.: Body area network security: a fuzzy attribute-based signcryption scheme. IEEE J. Sel. Areas Commun. **31**(9), 37–46 (2013)
13. Varghese, S., Vigila, S.M.C.: A varied approach to attribute based access model for secure storage in cloud. In: 2017 International Conference on Innovations in Information, Embedded and Communication Systems (ICIIECS), pp. 1–4. IEEE (2017)

14. Lyu, M., Li, X., Li, H.: Efficient, verifiable and privacy preserving decentralized attribute-based encryption for mobile cloud computing. In: 2017 IEEE Second International Conference on Data Science in Cyberspace (DSC), pp. 195–204. IEEE (2017)
15. Yang, Y., Chen, X., Chen, H., Xuehui, D.: Improving privacy and security in decentralizing multi-authority attribute-based encryption in cloud computing. IEEE Access **6**, 18009–18021 (2018)
16. Green, M., Hohenberger, S., Waters, B., et al.: Outsourcing the decryption of ABE ciphertexts. In: USENIX Security Symposium, vol. 2011 (2011)
17. Lai, J., Deng, R.H., Guan, C., Weng, J.: Attribute-based encryption with verifiable outsourced decryption. IEEE Trans. Inf. Forensics Secur. **8**(8), 1343–1354 (2013)
18. Liu, X., Zhang, Y., Wang, B., Yan, J.: Mona: secure multi-owner data sharing for dynamic groups in the cloud. IEEE Trans. Parallel Distrib. Syst. **24**(6), 1182–1191 (2013)
19. Tian, W., Xu, H., Komi, M., Zhang, J.: Secure and flexible data sharing via ciphertext retrieval for cloud computing. In 2017 7th IEEE International Conference on Electronics Information and Emergency Communication (ICEIEC), pp. 161–166. IEEE (2017)
20. Wang, T., Zhou, J., Chen, X., Wang, G., Liu, A., Liu, Y.: A three-layer privacy preserving cloud storage scheme based on computational intelligence in fog computing. IEEE Trans. Emerg. Top. Comput. Intell. **2**(1), 3–12 (2018)
21. Bethencourt, J., Sahai, A., Waters, B.: Ciphertext-policy attribute-based encryption. In: 2007 IEEE Symposium on Security and Privacy (SP 2007), pp. 321–334. IEEE (2007)
22. Shamir, A.: How to share a secret. Commun. ACM **22**(11), 612–613 (1979)

Trajectory Comparison in a Vehicular Network II: Eliminating the Redundancy

Letu Qingge[1], Peng Zou[2], Lihui Dai[3], Qing Yang[4], and Binhai Zhu[2]([✉])

[1] College of Computing and Informatics,
University of North Carolina at Charlotte,
Charlotte, NC 28223, USA
letu.qingge@uncc.edu
[2] Gianforte School of Computing, Montana State University,
Bozeman, MT 59717-3880, USA
peng.zou@student.montana.edu, bhz@montana.edu
[3] School of Management, Beijing University of Chinese Medicine,
Beijing 100029, China
wangdlh@189.cn
[4] Department of Computer Science and Engineering,
University of North Texas,
Denton, TX 76207-7102, USA
qing.yang@unt.edu

Abstract. This paper investigates the truthfulness establishment problem between two nodes (vehicles) in a vehicular network. We focus more on the case when no interaction has been conducted and we use the Point of Interests (POIs) visited by the two nodes (vehicles) to establish the initial truthfulness. It turns out that this is a general version of a well-studied problem in computational genomics called CMSR (Complementary Maximal Strip Recovery) in which the letters (similar to POIs) cannot be duplicated, while in our problem POIs could certainly be duplicated. We show that one version (when noisy POIs are deleted all the remaining POIs must be involved in some adjacency), is NP-hard; while the other version (with the adjacency involvement constraint is dropped), is as hard as Set Cover. We then design a practical solution based on local search for the first problem. Simulations with various synthetic data show that the algorithm is very effective.

1 Introduction

While preserving privacy is important in a vehicular network, an even more important problem is that when two vehicles (nodes) communicate, one needs to determine the trustfulness of the other. This security issue must be addressed due to the special safety requirement of vehicular ad hoc networks (VANET), which has a wide range of applications in traffic control, accident avoidance and parking management [15,16].

Almost unique to VANET, false information dissemination and Sybil attacks are some of the critical security issues. The former could be a false information

© Springer Nature Switzerland AG 2019
E. S. Biagioni et al. (Eds.): WASA 2019, LNCS 11604, pp. 260–271, 2019.
https://doi.org/10.1007/978-3-030-23597-0_21

like "parking garage is full" so that the sender can keep away parking competitors. The latter could be a generation of fake identities to completely fail the functioning of the whole system [14,19]. The public-key infrastructure might not be available over a road network; hence, some kind of trust management must be maintained [17,18,20].

One challenge to build such a trust management system is how to build the initial trustfulness between two vehicles while preserving the privacy. Recently a method was proposed to compute the truth-telling probability, which is in turn decided by the opinions of adjacent vehicles [13]. Such information might not be available sometimes, for example, a man who lives remotely and works at home might not have a big chance to connect to a VANET on a regular basis.

The solution we propose is to use the Point of Interests (POIs) visited by each vehicle to establish some level of similarity, which serves as a starting point for determining the trustfulness of vehicles. In this case, to protect privacy, all sensitive information regarding the location of POIs, time a POI is visited, etc, are erased for our computation and comparison. Hence, an example of POIs is "home", "restaurant", "coffee shop", "gym", etc. (See Fig. 1 for a simple example.) Sometimes, we could make POIs slightly more specific without sacrificing privacy, for instance, a restaurant could be more specific, e.g., "Wendy's" or "MacDonalds" could be used.

Fig. 1. The POIs visited by a white-collared professional during a typical working day. If we use A, B, C, and D to represent 'gym', 'office', 'coffee shop', and 'restaurant' respectively, then the trajectory would be represented as a sequence $\langle C, B, D, B, C, B, A \rangle$.

Now suppose that we have the list of POIs visited by two vehicles over some time period, say two weeks. How do we compare these sequences (of POIs)? We adopt a classic concept called *adjacency*, which is used widely in computational genomics [1,7,8]. (We note that in computing genomic maps, this concept of adjacency is only applied on permutations, i.e., each letter appears exact once in the input and in the final solution [21]. This is different for our purpose.) While computing the number of adjacencies between two sequence or two permutations are relatively easy, in our applications (and also in computational genomics applications), a more important and practical problem is to throw away some noisy POIs to obtain the true similarity between two sequence of POIs. A variation of this problem has been studied in the biological community, as the Maximal Strip Recovery (MSR) and Complementary Maximal Strip Recovery (CMSR) problems. (Here a strip is a common substring appears in both sequence, one of which could be in reversed form. For both problem all the remaining letters must be involved in some adjacency.)

The MSR problem was first studied by the Sankoff group at University of Ottawa [5,22]. The MSR problem, and its complement CMSR, have been shown NP-hard [3,4,21]. Late they have been shown to be APX-complete [3,10]. MSR is known to admit a 4-approximation algorithm [4]. (This is achieved by converting the MSR problem to computing the maximum independent set in t-interval graphs, which admits a $2t$-approximation [2].) CMSR have been shown to admit a factor-3 approximation [6], the factor has been improved to 2.33 [11], and the current best approximation factor is 2 [9].

2   Preliminaries

At first, we make some necessary definitions. Given a set Σ of POIs (or just letters), a string P is called *permutation* if each element in Σ appears exactly once in P. We use $c(P)$ to denote the set of elements in permutation P. A string A is called *sequence* if some POIs appear more than once in A, and $c(A)$ denotes all POIs of A, which is a multi-set of elements in Σ. For example, $\Sigma = \{a, b, c, d\}$, $A = abcdacd$, $c(A) = \{a, a, b, c, c, d, d\}$. A substring with k letters (in a sequence A) is called an k-substring, and a 2-substring is also called a *pair*. Throughout this paper, the relative order of the two letters in a pair does not quite matter, i.e., the pair xy is considered to be the same as the pair yx. Given a sequence $A = a_1a_2a_3\cdots a_n$, let $P_A = \{a_1a_2, a_2a_3, \ldots, a_{n-1}a_n\}$ be the set of pairs in A.

Definition 1. *Given two sequences $A = a_1a_2\cdots a_n$ and $B = b_1b_2\cdots b_m$, if $a_ia_{i+1} = b_jb_{j+1}$ (or $a_ia_{i+1} = b_{j+1}b_j$), where $a_ia_{i+1} \in P_A$ and $b_jb_{j+1} \in P_B$, we say that a_ia_{i+1} and b_jb_{j+1} are matched to each other. In a maximum matching of pairs in P_A and P_B, a matched pair is called an **adjacency**, and an unmatched pair is called a **breakpoint** in A and B respectively.*

It follows from the definition that sequences A and B contain the same set of adjacencies but distinct breakpoints. The maximum matched pairs in B (or equally, in A) form the *adjacency set* between A and B, denoted as $a(A, B)$. We use $b_A(A, B)$ and $b_B(A, B)$ to denote the set of breakpoints in A and B respectively. We illustrate the above definitions in Fig. 2.

$$\text{sequence }\ A = \langle c\ b\ c\ e\ d\ a\ b\ a\ \rangle$$
$$\text{sequence }\ B = \langle a\ b\ a\ b\ d\ c \rangle$$
$$P_A = \{cb, bc, ce, ed, da, ab, ba\}$$
$$P_B = \{ab, ba, ab, bd, dc\}$$
$$\text{matched }\ pairs\ :\ (ab \leftrightarrow ba), (ba \leftrightarrow ab)$$
$$a(A, B) = \{ab, ba\}$$
$$b_A(A, B) = \{cb, bc, ce, ed, da\}$$
$$b_B(A, B) = \{ab, bd, dc\}$$

Fig. 2. An example for adjacency, breakpoint and the related definitions.

Note that our breakpoint and adjacency definitions are more general than those for permutations. Let P, Q be permutations over Σ with length n. Let $\tilde{P}$ (resp. $\tilde{Q}$) be the *reversal* of P (resp. Q). Then $|b_P(P,Q)| = |b_Q(P,Q)| = n - 1 - |a(P,Q)|$; moreover, if $|b_P(P,Q)| = |b_Q(P,Q)| = 0$ then either $P = Q$, or $P = \tilde{Q}$. For general sequences, this is not necessarily true. For instance, $A = dabdcba$, $B = dcbabda$, and there is no breakpoint between A and B. But $A \neq B$ and $A \neq \tilde{B}$. Nonetheless, when there are more adjacencies between A and B, they are similar intuitively.

In essence, we need to compare the similarity between A and B when some redundant POIs are deleted. (To start with, any POI family not in A and B at the same time should deleted. Hence we assume that A and B are over the same set of POIs Σ.)

Now, we define the problems we study in this paper formally.

Definition 2. *Redundant POI Deletion (RPD).*

Input: *two sequences A and B of length at most n over a POI set Σ, and two positive integers k, ℓ.*

Question: *Can a total of k letters (POIs) be deleted from A and B to obtain A^* and B^* such that $c(A^*) = c(B^*)$, $|a(A^*, B^*)| \geq \ell$ and all letters in A^* and B^* are involved in some adjacency in $a(A^*, B^*)$?*

If two sequences X and Y are not inherently similar, requiring that the remaining letters in X and Y are all involved in some adjacency might be too much. Hence, we could have a different version of the problem.

Definition 3. *POI Deletion to Maximize the Number of (String) Adjacencies (PD-MNSA).*

Input: *two sequences X and Y of length at most n over a POI set Σ, and two positive integers k, ℓ.*

Question: *Can a total of k letters (POIs) be deleted from X and Y to obtain X^* and Y^* such that $c(X^*) = c(Y^*)$ and $|a(X^*, Y^*)| \geq \ell$?*

We comment that the two problems are very different. As we will show in the next section, the second problem is at least as hard as Set Cover (which cannot be approximated with $C \log n$ unless P=NP), while the first problem can only be shown to be NP-hard at this point and it would be interesting to know whether a constant factor approximation exists.

3 Hardness Results

3.1 RPD Is NP-Complete

Note that in reality we are really interested in the optimization version of the RPD problem, i.e., deleting the minimum number of POIs in the input trajectories A, B to maximize the number of adjacencies between the resulting trajectories A', B' and each letter in A', B' is involved in some adjacency. For the hardness result we simply look at the decision of the RPD problem (RPD for short). This problem is a generalization of the Complementary Maximal Strip Recovery problem in which case no POI can be duplicated in the input T_1, T_2, and even this restricted version of the problem is NP-complete (though the proof is notoriously hard) [21]. Here we give a simple proof.

Theorem 1. *The Redundant POI Deletion problem is NP-complete.*

Proof. It is easy to see that the Redundant POI Deletion (RPD) problem is in NP. We now show that Exact Cover by 3-Sets (X3C) can be reduced to RPD. Given a base set $X = \{x_1, x_2, ..., x_{3q}\}$ and a set $S = \{S_1, S_2, ..., S_m\}$, where $S_i \subseteq X$ and $|S_i| = 3$, the question is whether we could identify q sets in S which collectively cover all the $n = 3q$ elements in X. In our construction, for each x_i we create an x_i'. Let $S_i = \{x_{i1}, x_{i2}, x_{i3}\}$, we construct a string $T_i = x_{i1}x_{i1}'x_{i2}x_{i2}'x_{i3}x_{i3}'$. We construct two trajectories as follows.

$$A = (c_1c_2)^n a_1 b_1 T_1 a_2 b_2 T_2 \cdots a_m b_m T_m a_{m+1} b_{m+1} \#\#,$$

$$B = x_1 x_1' c_1 c_2 x_2 x_2' c_1 c_2 \cdots x_n x_n' c_1 c_2 \cdot \#\# a_1 b_1 a_2 b_2 \cdots a_m b_m a_{m+1} b_{m+1}.$$

Note that in B, all the 2-substrings $c_1 c_2$'s, $x_i x_i'$'s and $a_i b_i$'s (before and after $\#\#$) are already forming $2n + (m+1) + 1 = 2n + m + 2$ adjacencies with the corresponding ones in A. Hence the problem is really to delete letters in T_i's to form new adjacencies in the form $b_j a_{j+1}$. We make the following claim: X3C has a solution of size q iff the RPD problem has a solution of size $\langle 6(m-q), 2n + 2m - q + 2 \rangle$ (i.e., $6(m-q)$ letters can be deleted from A, B to form $2n + 2m - q + 2$ adjacencies and all the remaining letters are in some adjacency). □

We show a simple example for the reduction. $X = \{1, 2, 3, 4, 5, 6, a, b, c, d, e, f\}$. $S_1 = \{1, 2, 3\}$, $S_2 = \{1, 5, a\}$, $S_3 = \{4, 5, 6\}$, $S_4 = \{a, b, c\}$, $S_5 = \{4, b, e\}$, $S_6 = \{d, e, f\}$. Our construction is then

$$A = (c_1c_2)^{12} a_1 b_1 11' 22' 33' \cdot a_2 b_2 11' 55' aa' \cdot a_3 b_3 44' 55' 66' \cdot a_4 b_4 aa' bb' cc' \cdot a_5 b_5 44' bb' ee'$$

$$\cdot a_6 b_6 dd' ee' ff' a_7 b_7 \#\#,$$

$$B = 11' c_1 c_2 \cdot 22' c_1 c_2 \cdot 33' c_1 c_2 \cdot 44' c_1 c_2 \cdot 55' c_1 c_2 \cdot 66' c_1 c_2 \cdot aa' c_1 c_2 \cdot bb' c_1 c_2 \cdot cc' c_1 c_2$$

$$\cdot dd' c_1 c_2 \cdot ee' c_1 c_2 \cdot ff' c_1 c_2 \cdot \#\# \cdot a_1 b_1 \cdot a_2 b_2 \cdot a_3 b_3 \cdot a_4 b_4 \cdot a_5 b_5 \cdot a_6 b_6 \cdot a_7 b_7.$$

As the unique solution for this X3C instance is $\{S_1, S_3, S_4, S_6\}$, we need to delete the 12 letters in T_2 and T_5 from A to obtain A', and notice that $B' = B$.

$$A' = (c_1c_2)^{12} a_1 b_1 11' 22' 33' \cdot a_2 b_2 \cdot a_3 b_3 44' 55' 66' \cdot a_4 b_4 aa' bb' cc' \cdot a_5 b_5$$

$$\cdot a_6 b_6 dd' ee' ff' a_7 b_7 \#\#.$$

The two new adjacencies after T_2, T_5 are deleted are: $b_2 a_3$ and $b_5 a_6$. As there are already $2n + m + 2 = 32$ adjacencies between A and B and the deleted letters are all from A, the total number of adjacencies between A' and B is $2n + 2m - q + 2 = 34$.

Note that the following extensions can be obtained. The problem remains NP-complete when A' and B' must be permutations and when the deletions of letters only occur at one of A and B. This can be done by making all the $c_1 c_2$'s distinct and by changing $\#\#$ to $\#_1 \#_2$.

In the above reduction, notice that all the letters in A' and B' are involved in some adjacency. If we drop this condition, then the problem is much harder.

3.2   PD-MNSA Is as Hard as Set-Cover

We first recall the Set Cover problem. Here the input to set cover is $X = \{x_1, x_2, ..., x_n\}$ and $\mathcal{S} = \{S_1, S_2, ..., S_m\}$, where $S_i \subset X$ and $\cup_i (S_i) = X$. The objective is to find minimum number (say k) of subsets in $\mathcal{S}$ such that they collectively cover X. We consider a special version of Set Cover, in which all S_i's have the same size Δ. We call this version Δ-Set Cover. The following lemma is not hard to obtain.

Lemma 1. Δ-Set Cover is as hard as Set Cover, both in terms of polynomial time approximability and FPT tractability.

Proof. We reduce Set Cover to Δ-Set Cover. Let the input to set cover be $X = \{x_1, x_2, ..., x_n\}$ and $\mathcal{S} = \{S_1, S_2, ..., S_m\}$, where $S_i \subset X$ and $\cup_i (S_i) = X$. Let $\Delta = \max_i |S_i|$.

We construct a set of Δ new elements, $S' = \{y_1, ..., y_{\Delta-1}, z\}$. The instance for Δ-Set Cover is constructed as follows. First set $X' = X \cup S'$, and clearly $|X'| = |X| + \Delta = n + \Delta < 2n$. For all S_i, if $|S_i| < \Delta$, then we take a subset of $\Delta - |S_i|$ elements from $S' - \{z\}$ and union it with S_i to obtain S_i'; otherwise, set $S_i' \leftarrow S_i$. Then, we have $\mathcal{S}' = \{S_1', S_2', ..., S_m', S'\}$. It is obvious that Set Cover has a solution of size k iff Δ-Set Cover has a solution of size $k+1$. We omit the details as the only notice one should pay attention to is that S' must be included in any solution for Δ-Set Cover — as the elements $z \in X'$ is only covered by S'. □

We now reduce Δ-Set Cover to POI Deletion to Maximize the Number of (String) Adjacencies (PD-MNSA).

Theorem 2. *The POI Deletion to Maximize the Number of (String) Adjacencies (PD-MNSA) problem is NP-complete.*

Proof. We reduce Δ-Set Cover to POI Deletion to Maximize the Number of (String) Adjacencies (PD-MNSA). Let the input to Δ-Set Cover be $X = \{e_1, ..., e_n\}$ and $\mathcal{S} = \{S_1, ..., S_m\}$, with $S_i \subseteq X'$ and $|S_i| = \Delta$ for $i = 1..m$. For each e_i, let $f(i)$ be the number of sets in $\mathcal{S}$ which contains e_i.

In the following, i and $\bar{i}$ are all letters (POIs). Let $S_i = \{e_{i,1}, e_{i,2}, ..., e_{i,\Delta}\}$, we build a string $T_i = e_{i,1} e_{i,2} \cdots e_{i,\Delta}$. We construct two permutations: $Y(n) = (2n+1)(2n-1) \cdots 3 \cdot 1 \cdot (2n+2)(2n) \cdots 4 \cdot 2$ and $Z(m, n) = (\overline{2n+1} \cdot \overline{2n-1} \cdots \overline{3} \cdot \overline{1})^m \cdot (\overline{2n+2} \cdot \overline{2n} \cdots \overline{4} \cdot \overline{2})^m$.

We construct two sequences G and H as follows.

$$G = \bar{1}^{m(n+1)}\bar{2}^{m(n+1)}\cdots\overline{2n+2}^{m(n+1)} \cdot a_1 T_1 b_1 \cdot a_2 T_2 b_2 \cdots a_m T_m b_m$$

$$\cdot 1^{n+1} 2^{n+1} \cdots (2n+2)^{n+1},$$

$$H = Y(n) e_1^{f(1)} Y(n) \cdot e_2^{f(2)} Y(n) \cdots e_n^{f(n)} Y(n)$$

$$\cdot a_1 b_1 Z(m,n) \cdot a_2 b_2 Z(m,n) \cdots a_{m-1} b_{m-1} Z(m,n) \cdot a_m b_m Z(m,n).$$

Assuming that $k < n, k < m$, we have the following facts:

Fact 1: To obtain some adjacency in the form of $\bar{i} \cdot \overline{i+1}$ or $i(i+1)$, with $i \neq 2n+1$, one needs to delete at least $n+1$ letters.

Fact 2: To obtain some adjacency in the form of $a_i \bar{j}$ or $b_i \bar{j}$ or $a_i j$ or $b_i j$, with $i \leq m$ and $j \leq 2n+2$, one needs to delete at least $n+1$ letters.

Fact 3: To obtain some adjacency in the form of $e_i \bar{j}$ or $e_i j$, with $i \leq n$ and $j \leq 2n+2$, one needs to delete at least $n+1$ letters.

Fact 4: To obtain some adjacency in the form of $e_i e_j$, with $i, j \leq n$, one needs to delete at least $2n+2$ letters.

Hence, the only possibility to obtain an adjacency in the form $a_i b_i$ is to delete T_i, with is of length $\Delta < n$.

Therefore, we have the following claim: Δ-Set Cover has a solution of size k iff Δk letters are deleted from both G and H to obtain k adjacencies. (Note that to make sure that $c(G') = c(H')$, after each T_i is deleted, we must delete the corresponding e_j's in them from H as well.)   □

Corollary 1. *The optimization version of PD-MNSA does not admit a factor $C \log n$ approximation unless P=NP.*

Proof. The above two reductions in Lemma 1 and Theorem 2 are both L-reductions. As Set Cover cannot be approximated with a factor of $C \log n$ for some constant C (unless $P = NP$) [12], the same claim holds for PD-MNSA.   □

An intriguing problem is whether RPD admits a constant factor approximation. (Recall that the more restricted version of RPD, where the input sequences are permutations, does admit constant factor approximations [6,11].) To solve the problem practically, we will design a practical algorithm in the next section for the RPD problem.

4   A Practical Solution for Redundant POI Deletion

4.1   Algorithm

We first preprocess the data as follows:

1. Given two sequences A and B, we delete elements $x_i \in A$ and $x_i \notin B$ and vice versa, $y_j \in B$ and $y_j \notin A$. This process is safe as such deleted elements x_i or y_j cannot form any adjacency.
2. It is reasonable to delete consecutive elements in either sequence and keep only one copy of them. For example, we would delete three a's from $aaaa$ and keep just one a. This is because in our application we do not count a single POI multiple times if they appear as a substring in the input sequence.

We still call the preprocessed sequences as A and B.

Our idea is very simple: we keep all the existing blocks, then randomly select a block C_i in A and try to extend the block to $C_i x$ by searching for the first letter x to the left or right of C_i in A such that $C_i x$ (or its reverse $\overline{C_i x}$) also appears in B as a subsequence. Note that all the letters between C_i and x, or between x and $\overline{C_i}$, will be deleted. (The case for xC_i is symmetric.) We repeat this enough number of times until no block can be further extended. We call x a *candidate element* for C_i henceforth.

We give some formal definitions first. We define a *block* C as a substring of A with length at least two such that C or its reverse $\overline{C}$ is also a substring in B. Clearly, there are at most $n/2$ blocks in any solution for the RPD problem. Also, note that by keeping all existing blocks we are not guaranteed to have an optimal solution. For example, $A = xabyuv, B = uabvxy$, if we delete ab we have an optimal solution of 2, but if we keep the block ab, we need to delete at least 3 letters, e.g., $\{u, v, x\}$. On the other hand, this algorithm seems to generate a pretty good approximation solution.

Let $s[C_i]$ and $t[C_i]$ be the first and last letter (ending element) of block C_i respectively. If x is a candidate element for block C_i in A, then the distance $d_A(x, C_i)$ is the number of letters between x and $s[C_i]$ (inclusive of $s[C_i]$) if x is to the left of C_i; and if x is to the right of C_i then $d_A(x, C_i)$ is the number of letters between $t[C_i]$ and x (inclusive of x). Then $d_B(x, C_i)$ can be defined similarly (note that C_i could appear in B is reversed form).

Firstly, we compute all the existing blocks in A and B, which gives us potentially an initial solution for the Redundant POI Deletion problem. Secondly, we randomly select a block C_i in A and try to search a neighboring element x for it in both A and B such that $d_A(x, C_i) + d_B(x, C_i) \leq N$, where N is some predefined constant. We repeat this process for $m \leq n/2$ times. The pseudocode of this algorithm is given as Algorithm 1.

4.2　Empirical Results for Simulated Data

We implement our randomized algorithm with Matlab on a PC with an Intel Core 3.40 GHz processor and 16 GB RAM. The data we use are simulated data. The dataset generator builds initial two identity permutations, P_A and P_B, on an alphabet of size M. (In fact $P_A = P_B$, but we use different names on purpose.) Note that for the ease of description here we use integers to represent different POIs, though in practice it is easy to change integers back to POIs.

In the first setting, the sequence A of length L is created by repeating the permutation P_A. For instance, if $L = kM$, then $A = \overbrace{P_A \cdots P_A}^{k}$. The sequence B is obtained by first repeating P_B to have $B \leftarrow \overbrace{P_B \cdots P_B}^{k}$. Then we randomly select a pair of numbers i, j in B and them. We repeat this swapping N times to have the eventual B. Note that if N is small, then we know the optimal solution for RPD (e.g., number of deleted integers) is at most $4N$. We simply calculate the eventual adjacency number n_1 between A' and B', where A' and B are computed by Algorithm 1.

In the second setting, if $L = kM$, then initially we set $A \leftarrow \overbrace{P_A \cdots P_A}^{k}, B \leftarrow \overbrace{P_B \cdots P_B}^{k}$, then we randomly swap integers pairs in A and B. Note that in this case we have no clue what the optimal solution value is. The adjacency number n_2 between A'' and B'' is calculated, where $A'', B/$ are computed by algorithm 1. The second setting is more used on comparing the running times with the first setting.

In Table 1, M represents the alphabet size, L denotes the generated sequence length of A and B. The parameter N has different meanings corresponding to columns n_1 and n_2. When the number of adjacencies n_1 is calculated between A' and B', computed from A and B in the first setting using Algorithm 1, N is the number of pairs of integers swapped in B. The number of adjacencies n_2 is calculated between A'' and B'', again computed from A and B in the second setting using Algorithm 1, N is the maximum of $d_A(x, C_i) + d_B(x, C_i)$ (or, the number of letters scanned to find a candidate element x for a random block C_i).

It can be seen from Table 1 that for the first setting, Algorithm 1 can either find the optimal solutions or find some solutions which are close to the optimal ones. (We could not claim the same for the second setting.) As for the running times, the first setting takes less than 15 s for $L = 1,000$, while the second setting takes less than 180 s for $L = 1,000$. This is not surprising as intuitively the local search should take more time on random shuffled input.

Table 1. In the table, M is the alphabet size, L is the length of A and B. In the first setting, n_1 represents the adjacency number between A' and B' computed by Algorithm 1, where in the input N random swaps are performed to obtain B. In the second setting, n_2 denotes the adjacency number between A'' and B'', again computed using Algorithm 1 on randomly shuffled sequences A and B. In the latter setting, N is the maximum number of letters scanned to find a candidate element (to extend a random block).

M	N	$L = 400$		$L = 600$		$L = 800$		$L = 1000$	
		n_1	n_2	n_1	n_2	n_1	n_2	n_1	n_2
100	5	376.2	56.4	561.8	119.2	761.4	203	945.2	295.6
	10	356.4	64	544	138.4	721	226.2	918.4	326
	15	338.8	72.8	518.2	145	705.2	238.2	884.2	329.2
	20	325.4	72	507.4	139.2	680.4	236.4	853.8	333.4
	25	312	70.8	483.2	147.4	658.8	235.6	836.4	330.8
200	5	383.4	15.8	580.2	33.2	776	65	973.2	100.6
	10	372	20.2	566.4	39.4	750.2	71.2	952	101.6
	15	361.2	25.4	547.4	45	725.8	81.2	928.2	125.6
	20	353.2	20.6	528.6	43.2	713.2	79.6	910.8	133.2
	25	330.8	25	515.8	50.8	692.8	87	885.4	135.6

Algorithm 1 Local Search

Input: sequences A and B

Output: the adjacency number between $A^\star$ and $B^\star$

1: Compute the m existing blocks in A and B;

2: Compute the adjacency number in these blocks, AN;

3: $n \leftarrow 0$;

4: **while** ($n <= m/2$)

5:    Randomly select a block C_ℓ in A;

6:      **for** $i = 1..N$

7:        **for** $j = 1..N - i$

8:          **if** there is a candidate element x for C_ℓ
            such that $d_A(x, C_i) + d_B(x, C_i) \leq i + j$

9:            **then** delete all the letters between x and C_i in both A and B;

10:               AN $\leftarrow$ AN+1;

11:              break;

12:       end for

13:    end for

14:    $n \leftarrow n + 1$;

15: end while

16: Delete all the elements not in any block in A and B and concatenate all the blocks
    in A and B to obtain $A^\star$ and $B^\star$.

---

5 Closing Remarks

In this paper, we considered the redundancy elimination problem in comparing the trajectory of two vehicles. This is a generalized version of the Complementary Maximal Strip Recovery problem in computational genomics, which is NP-hard and admits a constant factor approximation algorithm. The former is inherently the case when each of the trajectories has to be a permutation. We show that this redundancy elimination problem is NP-hard with a much simplified proof and gave an efficient local search algorithm. The algoritm works well for synthetic data generated over a 2-month period. It would be interesting to know whether the RPD problem also admits a constant factor approximation.

Notice that the RPD problem differs from CMSR in several ways. First of all, the letters (gene markers) in CMSR are signed while in RPD they are unsigned. Secondly, we allow letters to repeat in RPD while in CMSR a gene marker cannot repeat itself in one sequence. Consequently, some properties in an optimal solution for CMSR might not hold for the RPD problem. For example, regarding the signed input for CMSR, in an optimal solution of CMSR an existing common adjacency in two input sequences is either kept or deleted. In the RPD problem, it is not necessary the case. For instance, $A = 1234$ and $B = 1324$, the optimal solution for RPD is not to keep 23 in A (resp. 32 in B) or delete 23 in A (resp. 32 in B). Instead, the optimal solution is to delete either 2 or 3 so that two common adjacencies can be obtained. Further investigation along this line is hence necessary.

Acknowledgments. This research was supported by NSF under project CNS-1761641 and by NNSF of China under project 61628207. Peng Zou was also supported by a COE Benjamin PhD Fellowship at Montana State University.

References

1. Angibaud, S., Fertin, G., Rusu, I., Thevenin, A., Vialette, S.: On the approximability of comparing genomes with duplicates. J. Graph Algorithms Appl. **13**(1), 19–53 (2009)
2. Bar-Yehuda, R., Halldórsson, M.M., Naor, J.S., Shachnai, H., Shapira, I.: Scheduling split intervals. SIAM J. Comput. **36**, 1–15 (2006)
3. Bulteau, L., Fertin, G., Rusu, I.: Maximal strip recovery problem with gaps: hardness and approximation algorithms. In: Dong, Y., Du, D.-Z., Ibarra, O. (eds.) ISAAC 2009. LNCS, vol. 5878, pp. 710–719. Springer, Heidelberg (2009). https://doi.org/10.1007/978-3-642-10631-6_72
4. Chen, Z., Fu, B., Jiang, M., Zhu, B.: On recovering syntenic blocks from comparative maps. J. Comb. Optim. **18**, 307–318 (2009)
5. Choi, V., Zheng, C., Zhu, Q., Sankoff, D.: Algorithms for the extraction of synteny blocks from comparative maps. In: Giancarlo, R., Hannenhalli, S. (eds.) WABI 2007. LNCS, vol. 4645, pp. 277–288. Springer, Heidelberg (2007). https://doi.org/10.1007/978-3-540-74126-8_26
6. Jiang, H., Li, Z., Lin, G., Wang, L., Zhu, B.: Exact and approximation algorithms for the complementary maximal strip recovery problem. J. Comb. Optim. **23**(4), 493–506 (2012)

7. Jiang, H., Zhong, F., Zhu, B.: Filling scaffolds with gene repetitions: maximizing the number of adjacencies. In: Giancarlo, R., Manzini, G. (eds.) CPM 2011. LNCS, vol. 6661, pp. 55–64. Springer, Heidelberg (2011). https://doi.org/10.1007/978-3-642-21458-5_7

8. Jiang, H., Zheng, C., Sankoff, D., Zhu, B.: Scaffold filling under the breakpoint and related distances. IEEE/ACM Trans. Comput. Biol. Bioinform. **9**(4), 1220–1229 (2012)

9. Jiang, H., Guo, J., Zhu, D., Zhu, B.: A 2-approximation algorithm for the complementary maximal strip recovery problem. In: Proceedings of the 30th Annual Combinatorial Pattern Matching Symposium (CPM 2019), LIPIcs, vol. 128, pp. 5:1–5:13 (2019)

10. Jiang, M.: Inapproximability of maximal strip recovery. Theor. Comput. Sci. **412**(29), 3759–3774 (2011)

11. Lin, G., Goebel, R., Li, Z., Wang, L.: An improved approximation algorithm for the complementary maximal strip recovery problem. J. Comput. Syst. Sci. **78**(3), 720–730 (2012)

12. Raz, R., Safra, S.: A sub-constant error-probability low-degree test, and sub-constant error-probability PCP characterization of NP. In: Proceedings of the 29th ACM Symposium on Theory of Computing (STOC 1997), pp. 475–484 (1997)

13. Shrestha, R., Nam, S.Y.: Trustworthy event-information dissemination in vehicular ad hoc networks. Mobile Inf. Syst. **9050787**, 1–16 (2017)

14. Douceur, J.R.: The sybil attack. In: Druschel, P., Kaashoek, F., Rowstron, A. (eds.) IPTPS 2002. LNCS, vol. 2429, pp. 251–260. Springer, Heidelberg (2002). https://doi.org/10.1007/3-540-45748-8_24

15. Hartenstein, H., Kenneth, L.: VANET: Vehicular Applications and Internetworking Technologies. Wiley, Hoboken (2009)

16. Papadimitratos, P., et al.: Secure vehicular communication systems: design and architecture. IEEE Commun. Mag. **46**(11), 100–109 (2008)

17. Liu, G., Yang, Q., Wang, H., Lin, X., Wittie, M.: Assessment of multi-hop interpersonal trust in social networks by three-valued subjective logic. In: Proceedings of the INFOCOM 2014, pp. 1698–1706 (2014)

18. Liu, G., Chen, Q., Yang, Q., Zhu, B., Wang, H., Wang, W.: OpinionWalk: an efficient solution to massive trust assessment in online social networks. In: Proceedings of the INFOCOM 2017, pp. 1–9 (2017)

19. Shrestha, R., Djuraev, S., Nam, S.Y.: Sybil attack detection in vehicular network based on received signal strength. In: Proceedings of the 3rd International Conference on Connected Vehicles and Expo (ICCVE 2014), pp. 745–746 (2014)

20. Zhang, J.: A survey on trust management for VANETS. In: Proceedings of 2011 IEEE International Conference on Advanced Information Networking and Applications (AINA 2011), pp. 105–115 (2011)

21. Wang, L., Zhu, B.: On the tractability of maximal strip recovery. J. Comput. Biol. **17**(7), 907–914 (2010)

22. Zheng, C., Zhu, Q., Sankoff, D.: Removing noise and ambiguities from comparative maps in rearrangement analysis. IEEE/ACM Trans. Comput. Biol. Bioinform. **4**, 515–522 (2007)

Differentially Private Event Sequences over Infinite Streams with Relaxed Privacy Guarantee

Xuebin Ren[1]([✉]), Shuyang Wang[1], Xianghua Yao[1], Chia-Mu Yu[2], Wei Yu[3], and Xinyu Yang[1]

[1] School of Electronic and Information Engineering,
Xi'an Jiaotong University, Xi'an, China
{xuebinren,txyao,yxyphd}@mail.xjtu.edu.cn,
wangshuyang@stu.xjtu.edu.cn
[2] Department of Computer Science and Engineering,
National Chung Hsing University, Taichung, Taiwan
chiamuyu@gmail.com
[3] Department of Information Science,
Towson University, Towson, USA
wyu@towson.edu

Abstract. Continuous publication of statistics over user-generated streams can provide timely data monitoring and analysis for various applications. Nonetheless, such published statistics may reveal the details of individuals' sensitive status or activities. To guarantee the privacy for event occurrences in data streams, based on the known privacy standard of ε-differential privacy, w-event privacy has been proposed to hide multiple events occurring at continuous time instances. Nonetheless, the too strict requirement of w-event privacy makes it hard to achieve effective privacy protection with high data utility in many real-world scenarios. To this end, in this paper we propose a novel notion of *average w-event privacy* and the first Lyapunov optimization-based privacy-preserving scheme on infinite streams, aiming to obtain higher data utility while satisfying a relatively stable privacy guarantee for whole streams. In particular, we first formulate both our proposed privacy definition and the utility loss function of statistics publishing in a stream setting. We then design a Lyapunov optimization-based scheme with a detailed algorithm to maximize the publishing data utility under the requirement of our privacy notion. Finally, we conduct extensive experiments on both synthetic and real-world datasets to confirm the effectiveness of our scheme.

Keywords: Differential privacy · Infinite data stream · Data release

1 Introduction

Continuous monitoring of statistics plays an important role in various real-world applications since it can help us better understand the dynamic changes of many

© Springer Nature Switzerland AG 2019
E. S. Biagioni et al. (Eds.): WASA 2019, LNCS 11604, pp. 272–284, 2019.
https://doi.org/10.1007/978-3-030-23597-0_22

phenomenons. For example, real-time traffic data can be continuously aggregated and monitored to show the road congestion and make wiser route plan [1,2]. Infection population of certain disease would be periodically released to timely predict their outbreaks [3]. Nonetheless, the continuous release of statistics could lead to great privacy disclosure risks for individuals [4–6]. In above examples, individuals' locations and healthy status may be sensitive and should be well protected.

Differential privacy (DP) has been the de-facto standard of privacy protection due to its rigorous mathematic proof and flexible composition theorems [7]. In particular, differential privacy can guarantee that the privacy leakage caused by individual's participant or leave in a dataset is bounded by a controllable parameter ε, which is also denoted as the privacy budget. ε-DP is initially introduced in static queries. When it is applied to streaming scenarios, two different definitions: event-level and user-level DP, have been proposed [4,8]. The formal one guarantees the occurrence of a particular event in a sequence is negligible, while the latter one aims to hide the presence of a particular user in the whole sequence, which is impractical to be achieved in infinite streams [9]. To strike a balance between event-level and user-level DP, w-event level DP was proposed to hide the occurrence of events in a sliding window of consecutive w time slots for infinite streams [10]. Two implementations in [10], BD (Budget Distribution) and BA (Budget Absorption), achieve w-event privacy by using a sliding window approach, together with the privacy budget allocation among windows. Nonetheless, either too strict requirement of w-event DP makes the privacy budget cannot be fully utilized, or they only allocate the privacy budget in a heuristic manner, leading to a worse utility.

Contribution. To address the aforementioned issue, in this paper we propose a novel and more flexible privacy model for infinite streams, *average w-event privacy*, which guarantees that the average privacy budget allocated for any event sequence within any window of w time slots is no larger than ε. Then, based on this model, we propose a differentially private algorithm for infinite data streams, which can achieve higher utility than existing algorithms based on w-event privacy. In particular, we model the privacy budget allocation as a dynamic control process and resorted to the drift-plus-penalty algorithm in Lyapunov optimization. Extensive theoretic analysis and experiments validate that our proposed privacy model and privacy-preserving algorithms can better utilize the privacy budget and effectively reduce the average error in the published result of infinite streams.

The remainder of the paper is organized as follows: In Sect. 2, we review the background knowledge about DP and its related work in data streams. In Sect. 3, we define the problem setting in this paper and introduces our new privacy paradigm of average w-event privacy. In Sect. 4, we present our proposed scheme and designed algorithm. In Sect. 5, we demonstrate and analyze the evaluation results of our scheme. Finally, we conclude this paper in Sect. 6.

2   Preliminaries

In this section, we first review the preliminaries about differential privacy and then review the related work of differential privacy on stream data.

2.1   Differential Privacy

Differential privacy is a popular and standard privacy paradigm with rigorous mathematical proof [7]. It limits the possibility of adversaries inferring individuals' privacy from the query output. The formal definition of DP can be given as follows.

Definition 1. *Differential Privacy:* *Given the neighboring datasets D and D' differ at most one data record (i.e., $|D \Delta D'| \leq 1$), a randomized mechanism $\mathcal{M}$ satisfies ε-DP if and only if for any possible output S in the output range of $\mathcal{M}$, there is*

$$P(\mathcal{M}(D) \in S) \leq e^{\varepsilon} P(\mathcal{M}(D') \in S), \tag{1}$$

where the possibility is taken over $\mathcal{M}$'s randomness. Parameter ε is denoted as privacy budget that specifies the tradeoff between privacy and utility, where smaller ε means better privacy, but lower utility.

DP is flexible to many complex mechanisms or queries due to its following compositional properties [11,12].

Theorem 1 *(Sequential Composition). Suppose T randomized mechanisms $\mathcal{M}_1, \ldots, \mathcal{M}_T$ satisfy $\varepsilon_1, \ldots, \varepsilon_T$-DP over a database D, respectively. Then, the whole sequence of $\mathcal{M}_i$ over D will achieve $\sum_i \varepsilon_i$-DP.*

Theorem 2 *(Post-Processing). Denote $\mathcal{M}$ as a randomized mechanism satisfying ε-DP and $f(\cdot)$ as an arbitrary function. Then, $f(\mathcal{M}(\mathcal{D}))$ still satisfies ε-DP.*

2.2   Differential Privacy on Data Streams

Event-Level and User-Level DP: DP is originally proposed for protecting individuals' privacy from statistic query results on static datasets [11,13]. When DP is applied to data streams, two different settings are considered: event-level DP and user-level DP [8]. The event-level DP ensures whether any single event occurs in the stream is probabilistic indistinguishable, while user-level DP promises to hide all the events of any particular user in the stream. Nonetheless, event-level DP only protects the occurrence of any single event, it cannot protect a user's activities in successive timestamps. Besides, user-level DP is mainly considered in finite streams and can not support the algorithms conducted on-the-fly.

w-event Privacy: Thus, in order to strike a balance between event-level and user-level privacy in streaming data, the notion of w-event privacy [10] was proposed to guarantee the occurrence of any event sequence within any window of w timestamps is indistinguishable.

Before giving the definition of w-event ε-DP, we first introduce the notation and definition of w-neighboring, which describes two streams differs in a window of w time slots. For an infinite data stream $S = (D_1, D_2, \ldots)$, we define its stream prefix at timestamp t as $S_t = (D_1, D_2, \ldots, D_t)$.

Definition 2 *(w-neighboring). For any positive integer w, two stream prefixes S_t, S'_t are defined as w-neighboring, if*

1. *for each $S_t[i]$, $S'_t[i]$ such that $i \in [t]$ and $S_t[i] \neq S'_t[i]$, it holds that $S_t[i]$, $S'_t[i]$ are neighboring;*
2. *for each $S_t[i_1]$, $S_t[i_2]$, $S'_t[i_1]$, $S'_t[i_2]$ with $i_1 < i_2$, $S_t[i_1] \neq S'_t[i_1]$ and $S_t[i_2] \neq S'_t[i_2]$, it holds that $i_2 - i_1 + 1 \leq w$.*

Definition 3 *(w-event ε-DP). A mechanism $\mathcal{M}$ is w-event ε-DP, if for the given integer w, all output sets $S \subseteq Range(\mathcal{M})$ and all w-neighboring stream prefixes S_t, S'_t with all t, it satisfies that*

$$Pr[\mathcal{M}(S_t) \in S] \leq e^\varepsilon \cdot Pr[\mathcal{M}(S'_t) \in S]. \tag{2}$$

Notice that w-event privacy will provide generally stronger guarantee than event-level DP and w-event DP will degrade to event-level DP when $w = 1$. Nonetheless, w-event privacy is generally weaker than user-level privacy because it cannot hide all event sequences of a particular user.

Based on the definition of w-event privacy, both BD and BA mechanisms [10] have been proposed for infinite streams to empirically maximize the utility of data publishing by properly allocating privacy budget at each time stamp. In particular, BD mechanism tries to first distribute budget in an exponentially decreasing way and reuse the budget falling outside the current sliding window. While, BA starts by assigning the budget uniformly to all time stamps and absorbs the unused budget at the time stamps where approximation instead of perturbation is chosen for privacy protection.

3   Problem Definition

In this section, we first present the problem settings in this paper and then introduce the average w-event privacy, which is considered as a new privacy definition on infinite data streams.

We consider a system with a curator that aims to publish various events (or locations) associated with a large population of users. At each timestamp i, the curator receives all users' event reports as a two-dimensional matrix D_i with d columns representing the events and n rows representing the users. $D_i(u, e) = 1$ ($D_i(u, e) = 0$) refers to the case that event e of user u has (not) occurred at time i. We assume any user can be involved in exactly one event at a time, that is, every row in D_i contains at most one 1. Then, the curator maintains an infinite stream $S = (D_1, D_2, \ldots)$, where $S[i]$ corresponds D_i at time i. And a stream prefix of S at t can be defined as $S_t = (D_1, D_2, \ldots, D_t)$. Denote $\mathbf{c}_i = f(D_i) = (\mathbf{c}_i[1], \mathbf{c}_i[2], \ldots, \mathbf{c}_i[d])$ as the results of the count query $f : \mathcal{D} \to \mathbf{R}^d$ over all columns of D_i at time i and denote $\mathbf{c}_i[j]$ as the count of 1s in the jth column. Then, at each timestamp i, the curator tends to publish the infinite stream $(\mathbf{c}_1, \mathbf{c}_2, \ldots)$ while collecting S. It is worth noting that the sensitivity of count query $f(\cdot)$ is $\Delta f = 1$. Nonetheless, directly releasing the count results $\mathbf{c}_i$ could leak the privacy of users.

Definition 4 *Denote $\mathcal{M}$ as a mechanism with the input of a stream prefix with arbitrary length and $\mathcal{O}$ as the set of all possible outputs of $\mathcal{M}$. Mechanism $\mathcal{M}$ is said to satisfy average w-event ε-DP (or, simply, average w-event privacy) if for all sets $O \subset \mathcal{O}$, all w-neighboring stream prefix pairs S_τ, S'_τ, and all τ, it satisfies that*

$$\lim_{t \to \infty} \frac{1}{t} \sum_{\tau=1}^{t} \frac{Pr[\mathcal{M}(S_\tau) \in O]}{Pr[\mathcal{M}(S'_\tau) \in O]} \leq e^\varepsilon. \tag{3}$$

Average w-event privacy is a relaxed version of w-event privacy on infinite streams. In particular, unlike w-event privacy strictly requires the privacy budget consumed in a time window of the length w no larger than ε, average w-event privacy allows the privacy budget smaller than ε for some windows or larger than ε for some windows, but the time average privacy budget should be no larger than ε. Obviously, for a sufficient large time window stamp $W \gg w$, average w-privacy can still ensure the total privacy budget allocated on W is no larger than $(W - w)\varepsilon$, which is similar to the requirement of w-event privacy in a long run. With the relax of privacy definition, we aim to leverage better utility for private queries on data streams.

Similar to the sliding window methodology used for w-event privacy in [10], the following theorem can be derived.

Theorem 3. *Suppose an infinite data stream prefix S_t, where $S_t[i] = D_i \in \mathcal{D}$, and denote $\mathcal{M}$ as a mechanism that takes S_t as the input and produces the output transcript as $\mathbf{O} = (o_1, o_2, \ldots, o_t) \in \mathcal{O}$. Suppose the mechanism $\mathcal{M}$ can be decomposed into t mechanisms $\mathcal{M}_1, \mathcal{M}_2, \ldots, \mathcal{M}_t$ such that each mechanism $\mathcal{M}_i(D_i) = \mathbf{O}_i$ is independent with each other and satisfies ε_i-DP. Then, $\mathcal{M}$ satisfies average w-event privacy, if the average value of total privacy guarantees ε_i of $\mathcal{M}_i(D_i)$ in all sliding windows with a length of w is no larger than ε. That is*

$$\lim_{t \to \infty} \frac{1}{t} \sum_{\tau=1}^{t} \sum_{k=\tau-w+1}^{\tau} \varepsilon_k \leq \varepsilon. \tag{4}$$

Proof. The proof of the above theorem follows the proof in [10] directly.

Based on this theorem, we can also view ε as the average privacy budget in a number of sliding windows of size w. Designing an effective mechanism with average w-event privacy on an infinite data stream can be formalized as an optimization problem of allocating privacy budget to the sub mechanisms $\mathcal{M}_1, \mathcal{M}_2, \ldots, \mathcal{M}_t$. In particular, varying privacy budget ε_i will change the noise scale and affect the output accuracy of $\mathcal{M}_i$. Thus, we aim to find an optimized sequence of ε_i to achieve the highest output accuracy for the sequential outputs of $\mathcal{M}_i$ while the whole sequence meets the definition of average w-event privacy. The main challenge is that, in a streaming setting, ε_i must be decided on-the-fly with the arriving data.

Suppose a given privacy budget of ε is uniformly allocated to a window with a fixed length of w, when the length w is larger, privacy budget split at each time stamp will be smaller and the utility will be worse since larger perturbation noise will be added. One effective strategy to reduce the noise addition is to selectively utilize the privacy budget at some key time stamps, which has relatively significant changes, approximating the rest time stamps as the previously perturbed data. The rationale behind this is the existence of temporal correlations and the assumption that query output does not change too much in a stream. Nonetheless, if there are many changes, despite incurring smaller perturbation error, the large allocation gap will still cause larger approximation error. Thus, to minimize the overall error for a privacy-preserving mechanism in a data stream, another challenge is to dynamically seek for an optimal control sequence between perturbation and approximation.

According to the above definition and observations, our problem can be defined as, under the requirement of average w-event privacy in a data stream, how to find an optimal control sequence to not only dynamically choose between approximation and perturbation, but also allocate proper privacy budget for the perturbation operations.

4   Our Approach

4.1   Main Idea

To better utilize the limited privacy budget, inspired by FAST [9] and BD/BA [10], we choose the operations of perturbation or approximation alternatively according to the statistics dynamic of the stream. Different from FAST that allocates the same privacy budget on perturbation (sampling) timestamps, we aim to spend it on perturbation stamps that need it the most. In particular, similar to BD/BA, we also decompose the sub mechanisms $\mathcal{M}_i$ into two phases, i.e., sub mechanism $\mathcal{M}_{i,1}$ at the exploration phase and sub mechanism $\mathcal{M}_{i,2}$ at the exploitation phase, at timestamp i, and leverage $\mathcal{M}_{i,1}$ to identify those key timestamps and $\mathcal{M}_{i,2}$ to allocate proper privacy budget. Nonetheless, contrary to the heuristic mechanisms BD/BA, we aim to further refine the optimization problem in more detail and try to find a theoretically optimal solution. Specifically, we formalize both the perturbation errors and approximation errors in exploitation phase and choose the optimal strategies of allocating privacy budget in our mechanism sequences.

4.2 $\mathcal{M}_{i,1}$: Exploration Phase

The object of exploration phase is to identify the data changes in the stream for wise decision making in exploitation phase. That is, if the current query result is close to the previous result, approximation as the last release should be the privacy economic choice; otherwise, perturbation with proper privacy budget cost is necessary to cover the possible privacy leakage in differences among continuous query results.

We also measure the dissimilarity dis between the current query result $\mathbf{c}_i$ of D_i and the last release result $\mathbf{o}_{i-1}$ by the Manhattan distance at each timestamp. Although dis will not be released, it would still affect the decision made in $\mathcal{M}_{i,2}$ and possibly provide some hints for privacy adversaries. To prevent the adversary inferring the privacy of D_i from dis, some portion β of privacy budget ε should be uniformly allocated for $\mathcal{M}_{i,1}$ in a w-stamp-long window. Thus, since the sensitivity $\Delta dis = 1/d$, at time i, the privacy budget for $\mathcal{M}_{i,1}$ is $\varepsilon_{i,1} = \frac{\varepsilon\beta}{w}$ and the private dissimilarity dis can be computed as

$$dis = \frac{1}{d}\sum_{j=1}^{d} |\mathbf{o}_{i-1}[j] - \mathbf{c}_i[j]| + Lap(\lambda_{i,1}), \text{where } \lambda_{i,1} = \frac{1/d}{\varepsilon_{i,1}} = \frac{w}{\varepsilon\beta d}. \quad (5)$$

Then, the private dissimilarity dis is sent to the second phase as the decision parameter.

4.3 $\mathcal{M}_{i,2}$: Exploitation Phase

With the dissimilarity dis computed by $\mathcal{M}_{i,1}$ in the exploration phase, the $\mathcal{M}_{i,2}$ mechanism in the exploitation phase chooses an actions between perturbation and approximation. As mentioned, if current query result barely changes, i.e., the dissimilarity dis is smaller than a threshold $\lambda_{i,2}$, approximation as the last release $\mathbf{o}_{i-1}$ can be chosen to save privacy budget; otherwise, outputting the result $\mathbf{c}_i$ with some Laplacian perturbation may be necessary to keep data utility. Nonetheless, both approximation and perturbation will cause errors, compared with the true result, described below.

- if $dis < \lambda_{i,2}$, $\mathcal{M}_{i,2}$ will output the last release $\mathbf{o}_{i-1}$ as an approximation, which causes the relative L_2 error $P(t) = \frac{1}{d}\sum_{j=1}^{d} |\mathbf{o}_{i-1}[j] - \mathbf{c}_i[j]|^2$;
- if $dis \geq \lambda_{i,2}$, $\mathcal{M}_{i,2}$ will perturb the result $\mathbf{c}_i$ by adding Laplace noise with privacy budget $\varepsilon_{i,2}$, which causes the relative L_2 error $P(i) = 2(\frac{1}{\varepsilon_{i,2}})^2$;

Thus, we can obtain a utility loss function $P(i)$ as

$$P(i) = \begin{cases} \frac{1}{d}\sum_{j=1}^{d} |\mathbf{o}_{i-1}[j] - \mathbf{c}_i[j]|^2, & dis < \lambda_{i,2}, \\ 2(\frac{1}{\varepsilon_{i,2}})^2, & dis \geq \lambda_{i,2}. \end{cases} \quad (6)$$

The above threshold $\lambda_{i,2}$ is used to check whether the error from the approximation, which equals to dis, is larger than the error incurred by Laplace perturbation with the noise scale $2/\varepsilon_{i,2}$. Thus, the threshold is set as $\lambda_{i,2} = 2/\varepsilon_{i,2}$.

As seen, at each timestamp, the approximation error is fixed with the given query result and the perturbation error varies with the privacy budget $\varepsilon_{i,2}$. Nonetheless, in the long run, both the approximation error and the perturbation error will be affected by different privacy budget $\varepsilon_{i,2}$ allocated at all timestamps. Since a portion β of total privacy budget has been allocated for $\mathcal{M}_{i,1}$, the average privacy budget for $\mathcal{M}_{i,2}$ is $(1 - \beta)\varepsilon$ at most, which is defined as a constraint function

$$Y(i) = \sum_{k=i-w+1}^{i} \varepsilon_{k,2} - (1 - \beta)\varepsilon \leq 0. \tag{7}$$

Then, aiming at maximizing the data utility of published stream $(\mathbf{o}_1, \mathbf{o}_2, \ldots, \mathbf{o}_i, \ldots)$, the design of a mechanism satisfying average w-event privacy can be defined as the following optimization problem.

$$\min \quad \lim_{i \to \infty} \frac{1}{i} \sum_{i \to \infty} P(i), \tag{8}$$

$$\text{s.t.} \quad \lim_{i \to \infty} \frac{1}{i} \sum_{\tau=1}^{i} Y(\tau) \leq 0.$$

Equation (8) is a typical dynamic optimization problem of minimizing time average publishing error subject to time average privacy budget constraint.

4.4 Lya: Lyapunov Optimization-Based Privacy-preserving Infinite Stream Publishing Scheme with Average w-event Privacy

By applying drift plut penalty algorithm [14] to Equation (8), we develop, Lya, a Lyapunov optimization-based privacy-preserving infinite stream publishing scheme with average w-event privacy.

First, we slightly modify the piecewise utility loss function $P(i)$ in Equation (6) to make it a continuous function as

$$P(i) = \frac{1 - \text{sgn}(\varepsilon_{i,2} - \frac{1}{dis})}{2d} \sum_{j=1}^{d} |\mathbf{o}_{i-1}[j] - \mathbf{c}_i[j]|^2 + \frac{1 + \text{sgn}(\varepsilon_{i,2} - \frac{1}{dis})}{2} 2(\frac{1}{\varepsilon_{i,2}})^2, \tag{9}$$

which, unlike Equation (6), has the L_2 error $P(i) = \frac{1}{2d} \sum_{j=1}^{d} |\mathbf{o}_{i-1}[j] - \mathbf{c}_i[j]|^2 + (\frac{1}{\varepsilon_{i,2}})^2$ at the point $dis = \lambda_{i,2}$.

Next, we assume a virtual queue $Q(i)$ to maintain the stability of privacy constraint $Y(i)$ defined in Equation (7) for satisfying average w-event privacy budget as

$$Q(i + 1) = \max[Q(i) + Y(i), 0]. \tag{10}$$

Then, according to the drift plus penalty algorithm in Lyapunov optimization theory, given the defined equations above, the optimization problem in Equation (8) can be solved by greedily choosing a privacy budget $\varepsilon_{i,2}$ to minimize the following drift-plus-penalty expression

$$Q(i)Y(i) + VP(i), \tag{11}$$

where V is a controllable parameter.

5 Performance Evaluation

In this section, we demonstrate the effectiveness of our proposed Lya Algorithm on both synthetic and real-world datasets. We used one synthetic dataset LNS, which is a time-series data with 583 timestamps generated according to a linear model with the variance of $Q = 10^5$ for data fluctuations. In addition, we used one real-world dataset Flu[1], which is part of the weekly flu infection data provided by the Influenza Division of the Center for Disease Control and Prevention. We extracted 791 timestamps as the stream data.

We implemented our proposed algorithm Lya in Matlab for simulating the publishing of data stream based on the above datasets. For comparison, we also implemented the benchmark algorithms Uniform, BD, and BA [10], which all satisfy w-event privacy as well as average w-event privacy. We executed each experiment 100 times, and reported the Mean Average Error (MAE). The average privacy budget for a window is set as $\varepsilon = 1$. Without specific explanation, other parameters are chosen with the best utility.

5.1 Impact of Window Size w

Figure 1 illustrates the publishing error of our proposed scheme Lya versus different window size on both datasets, in comparison with Uniform, BD, and BA. As shown in the figure, the MAE of all schemes increase with the window size w. This is because the fixed privacy budget is allocated on more timestamps and the privacy budget on each timestamp is smaller, which leads to larger perturbations.

In particular, Subfig. 1(a) (in Fig. 1) compares the MAE of all schemes with the increase of w for the LNS dataset. Among the four schemes, our proposed scheme Lya achieves the best utility. It has up to about half the error of BA, 2/3 the error of BD, and nearly 1/4 the error of Uniform in MAE. When w is small, Uniform allocates privacy budget evenly and all budget can be fully utilized. While, BD allocates privacy budget in an exponentially decayed way and will waste some budget. In addition, BA may prefer approximation with larger estimation error since LNS has less fluctuations in a small window. Thus, Uniform can perform better than both BD and BA for smaller w. Nonetheless, for larger

---

[1] http://www.cdc.gov/flu.

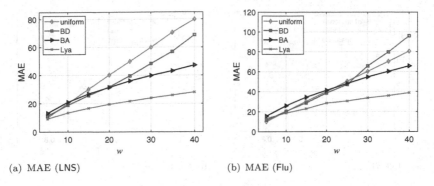

(a) MAE (LNS)   (b) MAE (Flu)

Fig. 1. Error vs. w

w, Uniform incurs the largest error due to no data adaptiveness in privacy budget allocation. BD and BA can save a lot of privacy budget by approximations and lead to much less noise. Compared to greedy minimization in BD and BA, Lya can further exploit the data dynamic of the infinite stream when allocating the privacy budget. Thus, Lya has the least error in all scheme. Subfigure 1(b) (in Fig. 1) illustrates the MAE comparison results on the Flu dataset. Similarly, our scheme Lya has the best performance. As shown in the figure, Lya outperforms BA by up to about 36 % in terms of MAE, and Uniform by up to about 64 %, respectively. BA adapts well to data with large fluctuations on Flu since it can skip some timestamps with approximation but recycle the unused privacy budget. Thus, BD has larger errors but BA shows better performance than Uniform.

5.2 Impact of Privacy Portion β

Figure 2 depicts the publishing error of our proposed Lya with respect to the parameter β, which is the portion of privacy budget reserved for sub mechanism $\mathcal{M}_{i,1}$. As shown in Subfig. 2(a) (in Fig. 2), with the increase of β, the MAE first falls down at around $\beta = 0.4$ and then goes up. It illustrates that either smaller or larger β will cause high errors in the published results. In particular, smaller β means better privacy protection for $\mathcal{M}_{i,1}$, but could lead to larger deviations in dissimilarity computation and unwise decision in $\mathcal{M}_{i,2}$. On the contrary, larger β ensures the effective exploration of similarity between neighbouring timestamps, but causes larger perturbations in $\mathcal{M}_{i,2}$ with less remaining privacy budget. In addition, enlarging w from 20 to 40 with the fixed $\varepsilon = 1$ or decreasing ε from 1 to 0.5 with the fixed $w = 20$ shows the similar trend but causes larger MAE, since privacy budget allocated for each timestamp has been reduced. Subfigure 2(b) (in Fig. 2) demonstrates the similar results on dataset Flu. Nonetheless, MAE on Flu varies greater with β than that on LNS since Flu has larger fluctuations.

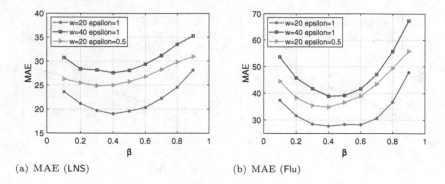

(a) MAE (LNS)   (b) MAE (Flu)

Fig. 2. Error vs. β

5.3 Impact of Parameter V

Figure 3 illustrates the utility changes with the penalty parameter V in our optimization function, on both datasets of LNS and Flu. Parameter V controls the performance balance between the utility loss or the privacy constraint during the dynamic optimization process. According to the optimization Equation (11), larger V means more emphasis on the utility loss; otherwise, smaller V means more requirement of the stability of average w-event privacy.

Subfigures 3(a) and (b) (in Fig. 3) present the MAE of stream publishing result versus parameter V as well as w and ε on both LNS and Flu. Obviously in the figure, MAE in all cases drops with the increase of V. This is because more emphasis on the utility loss and less on privacy constraint during the dynamic optimization. In addition, the MAE falls down nearly exponentially with the increase of V. The reason is that, for smaller V, there will be more emphasis on the average privacy constraint and the privacy budget allocated on each timestamp will be more strictly close to ε/w (i.e., less privacy budget for each timestamp). Consequently, there will be exponentially larger errors in terms of

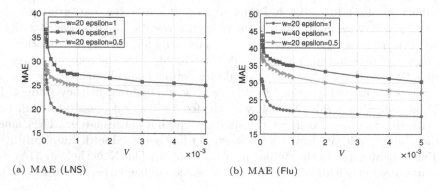

(a) MAE (LNS)   (b) MAE (Flu)

Fig. 3. Error vs. V

$O(\varepsilon/w)$ in the whole published results. Nonetheless, for larger V, there will be less emphasis on the average privacy constraint and the privacy budget on each timestamp changes less with the increase of V. Thus, the MAE then decreases slowly with V. Moreover, enlarging w with the fixed $\varepsilon = 1$ or decreasing ε with the fixed w shows the similar decreasing trend in term of V, however, causing larger overall MAE due to less privacy budget allocated for each timestamp. Similar results can be found in Subfig. 3(b) (in Fig. 3) of dataset Flu. Also, due to larger fluctuations in Flu, the overall MAE on Flu is larger than that in LNS.

6   Final Remark

In this paper, we have addressed the issue of privacy budget insufficient utilization in existing schemes of private infinite stream publishing. To be specific, we first introduced *average w-event privacy*, a new privacy paradigm that guarantees the average privacy budget consumption in a w-timestamp-long window does not exceed a specified value. Then, based on this paradigm, we further proposed Lya, a novel Lyapunov optimization-based privacy-preserving scheme, which can maximize the data utility of data publishing on infinite streams while satisfying average w-event privacy. We formalized the dynamic optimization problem of minimizing utility loss with the constraint of average w-event privacy, and also adopted drift plus penalty algorithm to design an effective solution. Extensive experiments on both synthetic and real-world datasets validated that our proposed scheme are capable of effectively improving the data utility while guaranteeing average w-event privacy for infinite streams.

References

1. Fan, L., Xiong, L., Sunderam, V.: Differentially private multi-dimensional time series release for traffic monitoring. In: Wang, L., Shafiq, B. (eds.) DBSec 2013. LNCS, vol. 7964, pp. 33–48. Springer, Heidelberg (2013). https://doi.org/10.1007/978-3-642-39256-6_3
2. Cai, Z., Zheng, X., Yu, J.: A differential-private framework for urban traffic flows estimation via taxi companies. IEEE Trans. Ind. Inform. (2019, preprint)
3. Lazer, D., Kennedy, R., King, G., Vespignani, A.: The parable of google flu: traps in big data analysis. Science **343**(6176), 1203–1205 (2014)
4. Dwork, C., Naor, M., Pitassi, T., Rothblum, G.: Differential privacy under continual observation. In: Proceedings of ACM STOC, pp. 715–724 (2010)
5. Zahra, F., Liu, Y.: Continuous location statistics sharing algorithm with local differential privacy. In: Proceedings of IEEE Big Data, pp. 5147–5152 (2018)
6. Cai, Z., Zheng, X.: A private and efficient mechanism for data uploading in smart cyber-physical systems. IEEE Trans. Netw. Sci. Eng. (2018, preprint)
7. Dwork, C.: Differential privacy. In: Proceedings of ICALP, pp. 1–12 (2006)
8. Dwork, C.: Differential privacy in new settings. In: Proceedings of ACM-SIAM SODA, pp. 174–183 (2010)
9. Fan, L., Xiong, L.: An adaptive approach to real-time aggregate monitoring with differential privacy. IEEE Trans. Knowl. Data Eng. **26**(9), 2094–2106 (2014)

10. Kellaris, G., Papadopoulos, S., Xiao, X., Papadias, D.: Differentially private event sequences over infinite streams. Proc. VLDB Endow. **7**(12), 1155–1166 (2014)
11. McSherry, F.: Privacy integrated queries: an extensible platform for privacy-preserving data analysis. In: Proceedings of ACM SIGMOD, pp. 19–30 (2009)
12. Dwork, C., Roth, A.: The algorithmic foundations of differential privacy. Found. Trends® Theor. Comput. Sci. **9**(3–4), 211–407 (2014)
13. Cai, Z., He, Z.: Trading private range counting over big IoT data. In: Proceedings of IEEE ICDCS (2019)
14. Neely, M.: Stochastic network optimization with application to communication and queueing systems. Synth. Lect. Commun. Netw. **3**(1), 1–211 (2010)

Performance Investigation of Polar Codes over Nakagami-M Fading and Real Wireless Channel Measurements

Mohammed Sarkhi[1], Abdulsahib Albehadili[2], Osama Hussein[2],
Ahmad Y. Javaid[2(✉)], and Vijay Devabhaktuni[3]

[1] Najaf, Iraq
mo.sarkhi@gmail.com
[2] EECS Department, The University of Toledo, Toledo, OH, USA
{abdulsahib.albehadili,osama.hussein,ahmad.javaid}@utoledo.edu
[3] ECE Department, Purdue University Northwest, Hammond, IN, USA
vjdev@pnw.edu

Abstract. Due to their high performance as well as their low design complexity, polar codes are being considered as a candidate for next generation of mobile and wireless communications. Originally, polar codes were exactly designed over binary erasure channels (BECs) only. Later, polar codes over additive white Gaussian noise (AWGN) channel and fading channels were discussed. Some researches have investigated the performance of polar codes over multipath fading environment characterized by Rayleigh model which, however, fails to accurately predict wireless environments of high frequencies and long distance transmissions. The performance analysis of polar codes over a practical set is rarely addressed. To this end, this paper is devoted to investigate the performance of polar codes over a fading environment characterized by Nakagami-m fading model which demonstrates closer estimates to the measurements of real wireless channels. Then, we investigate the performance of polar codes over real channel measurements collected in an indoor as well as V2V communication environments. The remarkable error rate performance of polar code shows that it will be beneficial to future wireless systems where high data rates and low BERs are necessary.

Keywords: Nakagami-m fading · Polar codes ·
Software-defined Radio (SDR) · Wireless communications

1 Introduction

Polar codes, proposed by Arikan [1], are the first family of codes that achieve the symmetric capacity, $I(W)$, for any binary input discrete memoryless symmetric

M. Sarkhi—Independent Researcher.
This work was funded by Round 2 Award from the Ohio Federal Research Jobs Commission (OFMJC) through Ohio Federal Research Network (OFRN).

E. S. Biagioni et al. (Eds.): WASA 2019, LNCS 11604, pp. 285–296, 2019.
https://doi.org/10.1007/978-3-030-23597-0_23

channel (B-DMC), W, with low complexity. Such characteristics favour polar codes to be one of the key enabling technologies for 5G air interface [2]. A core part of polar codes is the code construction which relies on the concept of channel polarization. Channel polarization comprises two phases, namely; channel combining and channel splitting. Channel combining combines N copies of a B-DMC to produce a vector of polarized channels $\left(W_N^{(j)} : 1 \leq j \leq N \right)$. The N polarized channels would have symmetric capacities that converge either to 0 or 1 as $N \to \infty$. $I(W)$ faction of the resultant channels will be noiseless, while $1 - I(W)$ fraction is completely noisy, where $0 \leq I(W) \leq 1$. Finally, only those good (noiseless) channels are used to send the information bits $K(N \geq K)$, while the remaining noisy channels will be frozen [1]. The basic transformation used to construct a new channel, W_2 is shown in Fig. 1. Here, (U_1, U_2) are two equiprobable bits that are encoded into: $(X_1, X_2) = (U_1 + U_2, U_2)$. (X_1, X_2) are mapped into (Y_1, Y_2). Keeping in mind that the sum capacity of the two virtual channels is preserved and satisfies:

$$I(W^+) + I(W^-) = 2I(W) \tag{1}$$

This process will continue until N polarized synthesized channels are obtained.

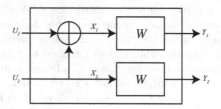

Fig. 1. Synthesized channel

The second step is the channel splitting where the channel vector W_N is split back into N channels, a crucial step for the successive cancellation decoding [1]. The first construction approach, devised by Arikan, was for the binary erasure channel (BEC) [1]. Here, recursive formulas were used to divide the bit-channels into the two extremes, starting by the erasure probability ϵ as the initial state. Let the channel $W : \mathcal{X} \to \mathcal{Y}$ be a B-DMC with binary input alphabet $\mathcal{X} \in \{0,1\}$ and an arbitrary output alphabet $\mathcal{Y}$ with transition probabilities $W(y/x), x \in \mathcal{X}, y \in \mathcal{Y}$. Two important channel parameters were used in [1]: the symmetric capacity $I(W)$ and the Bhattacharyya parameter $Z(W)$ which measure the rate and reliability, respectively:

$$I(W) \triangleq \sum_{y \in Y} \sum_{x \in X} \frac{1}{2} W(y|x) \log \frac{W(y|x)}{\frac{1}{2}W(y|0) + \frac{1}{2}W(y|1)} \tag{2}$$

$$Z(W) \triangleq \sum_{y \in Y} \sqrt{W(y|0)W(y|1)} \tag{3}$$

Based on the Bhattacharyya parameter, recursive equations are given as:

$$Z\left(W_N^{(2j-1)}\right) \leq 2Z\left(W_{N/2}^{(j)}\right) - Z\left(W_{N/2}^{(j)}\right)^2 \tag{4a}$$

$$Z\left(W_N^{(2j)}\right) = Z\left(W_{N/2}^{(j)}\right)^2 \tag{4b}$$

The equality of (4a) is only satisfied for BEC, with $Z\left(W_1^{(1)}\right) = \epsilon$. Another construction was devised in [1], based on a Monte-Carlo simulation. This can be applied to a wide range of channels. However, this algorithm has the highest complexly. Following Arikan's work, a new construction method was devised for *B-DMC* with linear complexity in the blocklength which is based on density evolution algorithm [3]. However, this construction suffers from high computational complexity. A problem that is mitigated in [4] where Gaussian approximation for density evolution is introduced.

1.1   Related Work

Performance investigation of polar codes over AWGN and Rayleigh channels was conducted in [5–15]. In [5], a procedure for obtaining the Bhattacharyya parameters associated to additive Gaussian and Rayleigh channels was presented. The constructed code was tested by transmitting an image, results show better performance compared to low density parity-check codes (LDPC) codes under the same simulation condition. In [6,7], the binary-input fading channel was approximated as combined binary symmetric channels (BSCs). The fading was considered to be flat, i.e., the fading does not change during the symbol transmission (symbol transmission time is less than channel coherence time). However, the extension of this work to a continuous fading channel, such as, Rayleigh is not immediate. In [9], the fading (flat) channel was also modeled as a combined BSCs as in [6] as well as combined binary AWGN with varying channel gain as in [8,15]. The code construction was based on Bhattacharyya parameter. [8] characterized the fading using flat Rayleigh fading channel, where two constructions were studied, one with known channel side information (CSI), and the second with only channel distribution information (CDI) available. Results show that long polar codes are slightly closer to the theoretical limit compared to turbo and LDPC codes. [10] modeled the subchannels induced by the polarizing transformation as Rayleigh fading channels. Error probabilities of these subchannels were used for code construction. It is shown that classical polar codes provide bad performance in the fading channel, while employing the construction with dynamic frozen symbols can improve the performance significantly. The obtained codes are shown to provide significant gain with respect to LDPC codes. In [11], polar lattices for fading channels were constructed. [12] introduced explicit construction for fading channels by matching code polarization with fading polarization. [13] discussed a coded modulation approach for designing polar codes for fading. [14] provided a technique for using polar codes over fading channels with delay and power constraints.

1.2 Contribution

The dynamic behavior of real wireless channels introduces more impairments that the AWGN and Rayleigh models, used in previous studies, fail to characterize. This motives us to investigate the performance of polar codes over more practical environments. The first environment is characterized by Nakagami-m fading model which is found to give closer estimates to real wireless measurements than Rayleigh, log-normal, or Rician models and found to be very good fitting for the mobile radio channel [16,17]. It characterizes fading conditions that are less or more severe than that of Rayleigh, as Rayleigh model, for example, fails to accurately predict wireless environments of high frequencies and long distance transmissions. In addition, Nakagami-m model can include other fading models as a special case; i.e., it can be reduced to one-sided Gaussian, Rayleigh, or Rician-like distributions if the fading parameter found to be $m = 0.5$, $m = 1$, or $m > 1$, respectively; whereas $m = \infty$ indicates a no-fading scenario. To this end, the sum-of-sinusoids (SOS) method is deployed to construct Nakagami-m fading model which is then used to generate the multipath fading effect. This method was introduced in [18], however, in this work the pseudocode of the SOS algorithm is provided to make it available and accessible to fellow researchers, allowing fast reproduction of the results. The second environment is characterized by collecting real channel measurements in three different experiments, i.e, indoor, V2V in parking area, and V2V on main road. To this end, a software-defined radio (SDR) testbed is deployed to collect real wireless measurements. The rest of the paper is organized as follows, in Sect. 2, the system and channels models are described. In Sect. 3, the experiment setups are explained, and results and analysis are presented. In Sect. 4, conclusions and future directions are presented.

2 System and Channel Models

The communication system across the wireless channel can be represented by the complex baseband model:

$$y = hx + n \tag{5}$$

x is the transmitted signal that contains the encoded message, y is the received signal distorted by the channel impairments n and h. Where n is additive Gaussian noise and h is a stochastic process that represents the channel response of a wireless channel that encounters multipath fading. In this work, h is modeled using: (1) Nakagami-m fading model, (2) Real channel measurements collected at three different scenarios as will be discussed in the sequel.

2.1 Sum-of-Sinusoids Nakagami-M Channel Model

Common method used, in literature, for simulating fading channels is based on central theorem which approximates the channel impulse response h as a complex valued Gaussian random process [19]. Such approach, however, does not consider the variation of the number of multipaths M, instead, it assumes high number of multipaths ($M \to \infty$). Also, it does not incorporate the effect of Doppler shift f_d, which is due to relative motion between a transmitter and a receiver. In this paper, instead, Nakagami-m fading is generated using the sum-of-sinusoids (SOS) method. SOS method approximates the multipath fading through the superposition of a finite number of weighted harmonics, each describes one path and represented by amplitude, frequency, and phase values in relation to the Doppler shift f_d [18]. Using the relationship between Nakagami-m, Rayleigh, and Rician fading envelopes [17]:

$$R_{Naka} = R_{Ray}\, e^{1-m} + R_{Ric}\,(1 - e^{1-m}) \tag{6}$$

one can construct Nakagami-m model based on Rayleigh and Rician models. Where m is the Nakagami parameter that characterizes fading severity. To this end, based on Clarke's model [20] and Pop and Beaulieu's modified model [21], Rayleigh and Rician fading envelopes can be defined using the sum-of-sinusoids method [22,23]:

$$R_{Ray}(t) = Y_{re}(t) + jY_{im}(t) \tag{7-a}$$

$$Y_{re}(t) = \frac{1}{\sqrt{M}} \sum_{n_p=1}^{M} cos[w_d t cos(\frac{2\pi\, n_p + \theta_{n_p}}{M}) + \phi_{n_p}]$$

$$Y_{im}(t) = \frac{1}{\sqrt{M}} \sum_{n_p=1}^{M} sin[w_d t cos(\frac{2\pi\, n_p + \theta_{n_p}}{M}) + \phi_{n_p}]$$

$$R_{Ric}(t) = Z_{re}(t) + jZ_{im}(t) \tag{7-b}$$

$$Z_{re}(t) = [Y_{re}(t) + \sqrt{M}cos(w_d t cos\theta_0 + \phi_0)]/\sqrt{1+k}$$

$$Z_{im}(t) = [Y_{im}(t) + \sqrt{M}sin(w_d t cos\theta_0 + \phi_0)]/\sqrt{1+k}$$

where M is the number of multipaths. θ_{n_p} is the angle of arrival and ϕ_{n_p} is the phase delay, which both are uniformly distributed random variables over $[-\pi, \pi]$, w_d is the maximum angular Doppler shift, $Y_{re}(t)$ and $Y_{im}(t)$ are the Non-line-of-sight (NLOS) components. θ_0 (angle of arrival of the line-of-sight (LOS) component) is set to $\pi/4$ [22,23]. k is Rician factor which is defined as the ratio of the specular power to scattered power.

By substituting (7-a & 7-b) in (6), applying Euler's identity, and doing some algebraic manipulation one can find:

$$R_{Naka} = (e^{1-m} + \frac{1 - e^{1-m}}{\sqrt{1+k}})\frac{1}{\sqrt{M}} \sum_{n_p=1}^{M} e^{j(w_d t\psi_{n_p} + \phi_{n_p})} + \frac{1 - e^{1-m}}{\sqrt{1+k}}\sqrt{M}e^{j(w_d t cos\theta_0 + \phi_0)}$$

$$\tag{8}$$

where $\psi_{n_p} = cos((2\pi n_p + \theta_{n_p})/M)$. Now, using the mapping between Rician factor k and Nakagami m parameter [24]:

$$k = \frac{\sqrt{m^2 - m}}{m - \sqrt{m^2 - m}} \tag{9}$$

Nakagami-m envelope can be found as follows:

$$R_{Naka} = (\frac{\beta + e^{1-m}}{\sqrt{M}}) \sum_{n_p=1}^{M} e^{j(w_d t \psi_{n_p} + \phi_{n_p})} + \beta\sqrt{M}e^{j(w_d t cos\theta_0 + \phi_0)} \tag{10}$$

where $\beta = (1 - e^{1-m})\sqrt{1 - \sqrt{1 - m^{-1}}}$. Based on (10), Nakagami-m fading can be generated according to the following pseudocode:

Algorithm 1. Nakagami Fading Generation

$Input = M, N, f_d, T_s, m$
$\beta = (1 - exp(1 - m)) * sqrt(1 - sqrt(1 - m^{-1}))$
$\alpha = (\beta + exp(1 - m))/sqrt(M)$
$n_p = 1 : M$
$\phi_0 = 2 pi (rand - 0.5)$
$\theta_0 = pi/4$
$\theta_{n_p} = (2pi\, n_p + (rand(1, M) - 0.5))/M$
$\phi_{n_p} = 2 pi (rand(1, M) - 0.5)$
$\psi_{n_p} = cos((2 pi\, n_p + \theta_{n_p})/M)$
while $n \leq N$ **do**
  $H = sum(exp(j(2 * pi * f_d * T_s * n * \psi_{n_p} + \phi_{n_p})))$
  $H_N(n) = \alpha * H + \beta * sqrt(M) * exp(j(2 * pi * f_d * Ts * cos\theta_0 + \phi_0))$
$Output = H_N$

Figure 2 shows the simulated PDFs of the fading envelope for two m values; specifically, $m = 1$ (Rayleigh), and $m = 4$ compared to the theoretical PDFs. Simulation parameters are: number of samples generated $N = 10^5$, sampling period $T_s = 0.0001\,$s, $M = 8$, $f_d = 200\,$Hz, θ_{n_p} and $\phi_{n_p} = U(-\pi, \pi)$, $\phi_0 = \pi/4$.

2.2 Software Defined Radio (SDR) Testbed

SDR offers flexible design of entire transceivers for research and development as it implements the PHY and MAC layers entirely by software on General Purpose Processors (GPPs). This work adopts the Ettus Research's Universal Software Radio Peripheral (USRP) B210 platform, Fig. 3, along with the open source GNURadio signal processing framework [25]. GNURadio enables one to develop, simulate, and deploy real-world radio systems. It is a modular and a flowgraph oriented framework that supports DSP development in C++ and Python. It incorporates in-tree DSP libraries that can be readily deployed

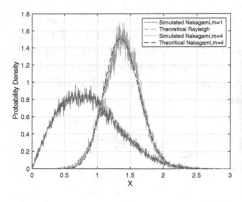

Fig. 2. Analytical vs. simulated PDFs of Nakagami-m fading envelopes

Fig. 3. USRP-based Transceiver Testbed

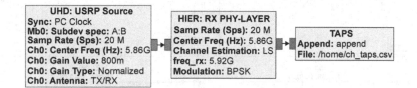

Fig. 4. Receiver flowgraph in GNURadio

in more complex DSP applications, and also supports addition of out-of-tree libraries. Flowgraph stages comprise two types of blocks; basic and/or hierarchical. Basic blocks are where fundamental DSP algorithms can be developed, e.g., fast Fourier transform (FFT). Hierarchical blocks, on the other hand, comprise whole child flowgraphs, e.g., an entire transmitter/receiver flowgraph can be wrapped by one hierarchical block. The receiver flowgraph developed in this work, shown in Fig. 4, consists of three blocks; UHD, HIER, and TAPS. UHD block is the interface between the USRP and the flowgraph. It downstreams received signals as complex baseband IQ samples stream to the flowgraph. HIER block is a hierarchical block that incorporates IEEE 802.11a/g/p receiver [26]. In this block, the OFDM bursts are detected, and the channel response vectors ($\hat{H}$) are estimated. In IEEE802.11p OFDM-based transceiver, adopted in this work, the long training sequence located at the preamble of the OFDM-burst is used to estimate the channel response $\hat{H}$. Upon receiving an OFDM-burst, $\hat{H}$ is estimated as follows [26]:

$$\hat{H}(k) = \frac{Y_1(k) + Y_2(k)}{2X_{LTS}(k)}, \quad k \in \{1, 2, .., 64\} \tag{11}$$

where $Y_1(k) + Y_2(k)$ are the first and second received copies of the pilot sequence, respectively, while X_{LTS} is the original value of the pilot sequence, known by both parties communicating across the wireless channel. $\hat{H}(k)$ contains 64 tones, i.e. $\hat{H}(k) = [h(1), ..., h(64)]$, which captures the effect of frequency-selective multipath fading. Out of 64 subcarriers only 52 are used as one is used as DC subcarrier and 11 subcarriers are used as guard intervals, minimizing delay spread and inter-symbol interference. Once $\hat{H}(k)$ is estimated, it gets downstreamed to TAPS block as vector stream. TAPS extracts $\hat{H}(k)$ to be exported to a file (csv format) to be used later in the simulations.

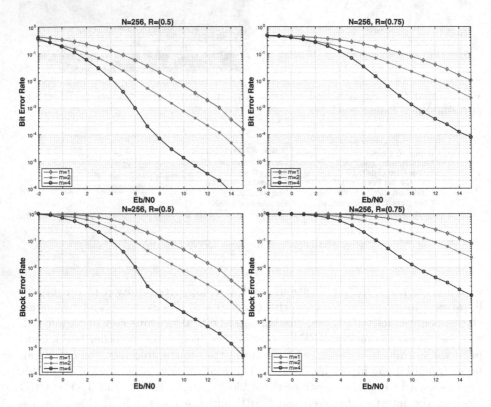

Fig. 5. BER & BLER vs E_b/N_0 for $N = 256$, $f_d = 200\,\text{Hz}$, $M = 8$, #iterations $= 10^6$

3   Experiments, Results, and Analysis

First, we explore the performance of polar codes over various fading scenarios characterized by Nakagami-m model. Thanks to the universality of Nakagami-m model which allows one to characterize different fading conditions, using different values of m. Higher values of m means less fading severity while lower values of m means more fading severity. The simulations are conducted for two blocklengths $N = 256$, and $N = 1024$, each with coding rates of $R = 0.5$, and $R = 0.75$, with 10^6 number of iterations for each case. The fading environment is characterized by maximum Doppler shift of $f_d = 200\,\text{Hz}$ and $M = 8$ multipaths.

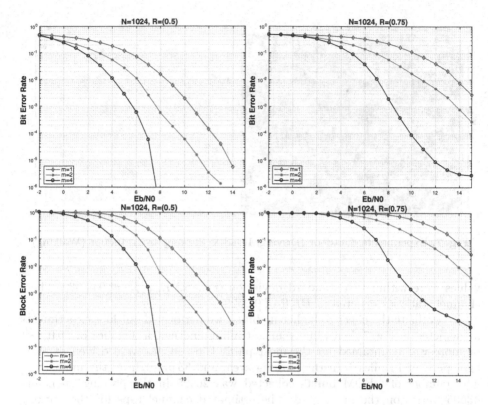

Fig. 6. BER & BLER vs E_b/N_0 for $N = 1024$, $f_d = 200\,\text{Hz}$, $M = 8$, #iterations $= 10^6$

Clearly, m is critical for all cases simulated (Figs. 4 and 5). For higher values of m, the BER and BLER reduce as less fading is encountered. One may also observe that increasing the blocklength from $N = 256$ to $N = 1024$ improves the performance while increasing the code rate from $R = 0.5$ to $R = 0.75$ reduces the performance. Second, we performed three experiments to collect real channel measurements: indoor, outdoor in parking area, and outdoor on main road. In all the experiments, two USRPs and two Dell Precision 5520 laptops (Intel Core i7-7820HQ CPU, 32 GB RAM) were used. Both Laptops run GNURadio on Linux (Ubuntu 18.04.1 LTS) operating system. Operation parameters are summarized in Table 1. The first experiment was conducted in an indoor setting in a hallway of a concrete building with dimensions depicted in Fig. 7. To examine the effect of mobility as well as multipath, the laptops were carried along the hallway in such a way that one trailed another and were separated by a distance of about 22−30 ft. This distance let us encounter NLOS and LOS situations. In this experiment we collected 13275 OFDM bursts. The estimated channel taps had an average signal-to-noise of $SNR_\mu = 5.91\,\text{dB}$, with a standard deviation of $SNR_\sigma = 1.2621\,\text{dB}$, 80.66% of the SNR values were within one standard deviation, i.e., $SNR_{\mu\pm\sigma} = 80.66\%$, and 94.76% of the SNR

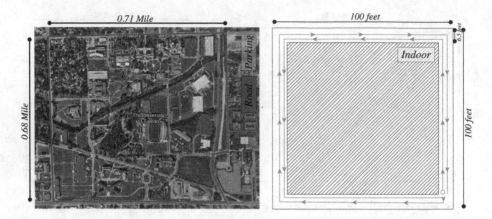

Fig. 7. Experiments: Outdoor (Driving: Road & Parking area), Indoor (Walking)

values were within two standard deviation, i.e., $SNR_{\mu\pm2*\sigma} = 94.76\%$. These channel statistics resulted in BER of 0.0529.

To evaluate the effect of higher mobility, we performed outdoor experiments as depicted in Fig. 7. With one vehicle trailing another, a distance of 65 ft feet or more was maintained for the most part. The vehicles were driven at average speed of 10 miles/h in the parking area, and 35 miles/h on the main road. The number of OFDM bursts collected was 26025 in the parking area, and 43605 bursts on the main road. The estimated channel taps for the parking experiment had: $SNR_{\mu} = 0.6042$ dB, $SNR_{\sigma} = 1.7408$ dB, $SNR_{\mu\pm\sigma} = 74.72\%$, $SNR_{\mu\pm2*\sigma} = 96.58\%$, resulting in $BER = 0.0750$. While for road experiment, $SNR_{\mu} = 0.1582$ dB, $SNR_{\sigma} = 1.6475$ dB, $SNR_{\mu\pm\sigma} = 76.04\%$, $SNR_{\mu\pm2*\sigma} = 96.68\%$, resulting in $BER = 0.0673$.

Table 1. Operation parameters

Frequency/Sampling Rate	5.86 GHZ/20 MSPS
Transmission Mode	Half Duplex
TX Antenna,RX Antenna	TX/RX port(board A), TX/RX port (board B)
Antenna Type	9 dBi
Channel Estimator	Least Squares
Preamble Symbols Modulation	BPSK

4   Conclusions

We investigated the performance of polar codes over various setups. The first setup was characterized by Nakagami-m fading model which has closer estimates to the real wireless channel. The model was built based on the sum-of-sinusoids approach where number of multipaths and effect of mobility (represented by Doppler shift) were taken into consideration. The second setup was characterized by collecting real wireless measurements at three different scenarios, i.e; indoor, outdoor in a parking area, and outdoor on a main road. The low-complexity of the construction, encoding, and decoding operations of polar codes, as well as the superior error-correction performance, make polar codes a candidate for emerging technologies for 5G and other wireless communication systems. While polar codes showed a promising performance in the studied scenarios, the performance over more dynamic channels, such as high traffic and fast speeds on the highways, could be investigated to see whether polar codes can cope with such scenarios.

References

1. Arikan, E.: Channel polarization: a method for constructing capacity-achieving codes for symmetric binary-input memoryless channels. IEEE Trans. Inf. Theory **55**(7), 3051–3073 (2009)
2. Huawei. Up in the air with 5G/cutting edge. http://www-file.huawei.com/-/media/CORPORATE/PDF/publications/communicate/80/15-up-in-the-air-with-5g.pdf. Accessed 23 Nov 23 2018
3. Mori, R., Tanaka, T.: Performance of polar codes with the construction using density evolution. IEEE Commun. Lett. **13**(7), 519–521 (2009)
4. Trifonov, P.: Efficient design and decoding of polar codes. IEEE Trans. Commun. **60**(11), 3221–3227 (2012)
5. Shi, P., Tang, W., Zhao, S., Wang, B.: Performance of polar codes on wireless communication channels. In: 2012 IEEE 14th International Conference on Communication Technology, pp. 1134–1138. IEEE (2012)
6. Si, H., Koyluoglu, O.O., Vishwanath, S.: Polar coding for fading channels. In: IEEE Information Theory Workshop (ITW), pp. 1–5. IEEE (2013)
7. Si, H., Koyluoglu, O.O., Vishwanath, S.: Polar coding for fading channels: binary and exponential channel cases. IEEE Trans. Commun. **62**(8), 2638–2650 (2014)
8. Bravo-Santos, A.: Polar codes for the Rayleigh fading channel. IEEE Commun. Lett. **17**(12), 2352–2355 (2013)
9. Zhang, Y., Liu, A., Pan, K., Gong, C., Yang, S.: A practical construction method for polar codes. IEEE Commun. Lett. **18**(11), 1871–1874 (2014)
10. Trifonov, P.: Design of polar codes for Rayleigh fading channel. In: International Symposium on Wireless Communication Systems (ISWCS), pp. 331–335. IEEE (2015)
11. Liu, L., Ling, C.: Polar codes and polar lattices for independent fading channels. IEEE Trans. Commun. **64**(12), 4923–4935 (2016)
12. Liu, S., Hong, Y., Viterbo, E.: Polar codes for block fading channels. In: IEEE Wireless Communications and Networking Conference Workshops (WCNCW), pp. 1–6. IEEE (2017)
13. Zheng, M., Tao, M., Chen, W., Ling, C.: Polar coding for block fading channels. arXiv preprint arXiv:1701.06111 (2017)
14. Sahasranand, K.R., Deekshith, P.K.: Polar codes over fading channels with power and delay constraints (2017)

15. Islam, M.K., Liu, R.: Polar coding for fading channel. In: 2013 IEEE Third International Conference on Information Science and Technology (ICIST), pp. 1096–1098. IEEE (2013)
16. Suzuki, H.: A statistical model for urban radio propogation. IEEE Trans. Commun. **25**(7), 673–680 (1977)
17. Li, T., Zhu, H.: Analysis and simulation of Nakagami fading channel with MATLAB. In: Conference Proceedings of the Asia-Pacific Conference on Environmental Electromagnetics 2003, CEEM 2003, pp. 490–494 (2003)
18. Albehadili, A., Al Shamaileh, K., Javaid, A., Oluoch, J., Devabhaktuni, V.: An upper bound on PHY-layer key generation for secure communications over a Nakagami-M fading channel with asymmetric additive noise. IEEE Access **6**, 28137–28149 (2018)
19. Viswanathan, M.: Simulation of digital communication systems using MATLAB. Mathuranathan Viswanathan at Smashwords (2013)
20. Clarke, R.H.: A statistical theory of mobile-radio reception. Bell Syst. Tech. J. **47**(6), 957–1000 (1968)
21. Pop, M.F., Beaulieu, N.C.: Design of wide-sense stationary sum-of-sinusoids fading channel simulators. In: Conference Proceedings of the IEEE International Conference on Communications 2002, ICC 2002, vol. 2, pp. 709–716. IEEE (2002)
22. Xiao, C., Zheng, Y.R., Beaulieu, N.C.: Novel sum-of-sinusoids simulation models for Rayleigh and Rician fading channels. IEEE Trans. Wirel. Commun. **5**(12), 3667–3679 (2006)
23. Xiao, C., Zheng, Y.R., Beaulieu, N.C.: Statistical simulation models for Rayleigh and Rician fading. In: Conference Proceedings of the IEEE International Conference on Communications 2003, ICC 2003, vol. 5, pp. 3524–3529. IEEE (2003)
24. Agrawal, D.P., Zeng, Q.-A.: Introduction to Wireless and Mobile Systems. Cengage Learning, Boston (2015)
25. GNUradio. https://www.gnuradio.org. Accessed 12 Dec 2018
26. Bloessl, B., Segata, M., Sommer, C., Dressler, F.: Performance assessment of IEEE 802.11 p with an open source SDR-based prototype. IEEE Trans. Mob. Comput. **17**(5), 1162–1175 (2018)

Optimal Transportation Network Company Vehicle Dispatching via Deep Deterministic Policy Gradient

Dian Shi[1], Xuanheng Li[2], Ming Li[3], Jie Wang[2], Pan Li[4],
and Miao Pan[1(✉)]

[1] University of Houston, Houston, TX 77204, USA
{dshi3,mpan2}@uh.edu
[2] Dalian University of Technology, Dalian, China
{xhli,wangjie}@dlut.edu.cn
[3] University of Texas at Arlington, Arlington, TX 76019, USA
ming.li@uta.edu
[4] Case Western Reserve University, Cleveland, OH 44106, USA
lipan@case.edu

Abstract. With the popularity of smart phones and the maturity of civilian global positioning system (GPS) technology, transportation network company (TNC) services have become a prominent commute mode in many major cities, which can effectively pair the passengers with the TNC vehicles/drivers through mobile applications. However, given the growing number of TNC vehicles, how to efficiently dispatch TNC vehicles poses crucial challenges. In this paper, we propose a novel method for TNC vehicle dispatching in different areas of the city based on deep reinforcement learning (DRL) method with joint consideration of the TNC company, individual TNC vehicle, and customer/passenger. The proposed model optimizes the distribution of vehicles geographically to meet the customers' demands, while improving the drivers' profit. In particular, we consider the high dimensional state and action space in the urban city traffic dynamic environment, and develop a deep deterministic policy gradient, an actor-critic based DRL algorithm for dispatching vacant TNC vehicles. We leverage Didi Chuxing's open data set to evaluate the performance of the proposed approach, and the simulation results show that the proposed approach improves the average income of the driver while satisfying the supply and demand relationship between TNC vehicles and customers/passengers.

Keywords: TNC services · TNC vehicle dispatching ·
Actor-critic algorithm · Deterministic policy gradient

1 Introduction

With the development of the wireless communications and the maturity of civilian global positioning system (GPS) technology, the operating mode of the taxi

© Springer Nature Switzerland AG 2019
E. S. Biagioni et al. (Eds.): WASA 2019, LNCS 11604, pp. 297–309, 2019.
https://doi.org/10.1007/978-3-030-23597-0_24

is also undergoing tremendous changes. From taxi hailing on the street to transportation network company (TNC) service based on mobile applications (e.g., Uber, Lyft, etc.) [5,8], and further to the autonomous TNC service in the future (e.g., Google's Waymo), TNC service is making our daily commute more convenient, and becoming an indispensable part of our life. Beyond solely relying on the TNC drivers' experience to pick up the next customer, it is necessary to intelligently dispatch the TNC vehicles to satisfy the passengers' requirements and reduce the passengers' waiting time while guaranteeing that TNC is profitable. Briefly, to best serve the TNC customers/passengers, the TNC vehicles need more auxiliary information about the traffic conditions throughout the city from service center to learn the recommended so that the passengers can be efficiently and profitably picked up.

TNC service center dispatches TNC vehicles in different areas of the city to match the passengers and vehicles appropriately, and thus providing benefits for both the drivers and passengers. In the urban city, vacant TNC vehicles cannot always find the passengers in one area while passengers cannot always get the TNC vehicles in other areas. This leads to waste of vehicle resources, and thus reduces the income of some drivers and extends the waiting time of passengers. In addition, service center needs to adapt to the more dynamic urban traffic environment today. Especially the TNC autonomous vehicles require more time-sensitive guidance and need to learn knowledge from real-time experience to make decisions. In response to the above issues, it is very appropriate to formulate the framework of deep reinforcement learning to solve the TNC vehicle dispatching problem in system-level, which means considering the dispatching problem from the prospective of the whole city. Compared to the traditional methods, the reinforcement learning methods can adapt to the dynamic traffic environment and adaptive adjustment. The dispatching method based on deep reinforcement learning is not only based on historical data, but it can work intelligently even if new traffic conditions and patterns appear.

Nowadays, deep reinforcement learning (DRL) implements deep neural network for reinforcement learning and has some well-known applications such as Alpha Go [11] or solve communication problem [12]. Recently, many researchers have made tremendous contributions in the field of DRL. Mnih et al. [7] improved Deep Q-Network (DQN) in 2015. Different from DQN, Lillicrap et al. [6] combined DQN with deterministic policy gradient (DPG) [10], and used them in actor-critic framework, which is called deep deterministic policy gradient (DDPG) algorithm. What's more, some researchers have already studied the taxi dispatching problem with reinforcement learning. Verma in [13] used Monte Carlo method to study optimal route planning of cruising taxis, which can provide significant benefits to the drivers. and Han in [3] demonstrated that according to the Q-learning algorithm, we can learn optimal actions for routing autonomous taxis in a real city scenario. Gao et al. [2] also proposed Q-learning algorithm to balance the demands and supplies of taxicabs. Even though these reinforcement learning methods consider dynamic urban environment, they only use a limited number of states and actions which cannot realistically represent

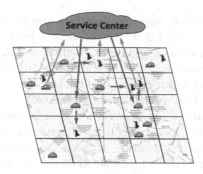

Fig. 1. The description of the dispatching model (Color figure online)

the urban environment. Furthermore, the solutions leak the system level measure, and only from the perspective of the individual driver or vehicle.

In order to solve the deficiencies in the above issues, in this paper we propose an intelligent TNC vehicle dispatching method based on actor-critic deep reinforcement learning dynamic framework for TNC system in urban city with "big" TNC service data. The proposed approach has the potential to balance the supplies and demands between TNC vehicle and passenger appropriately. Moreover, it increases the average long-term profit of drivers. Specifically, our salient contributions are summarized as follows:

- We first model the dispatching issue from the three perspectives, including TNCs, individual vehicle and passengers, which is different from the other existing works which only consider individual vehicle or passengers. Furthermore, we propose two metrics, such as the average profit and vehicle usage measure factor, to measure the performance of the system.
- We formulate the TNC vehicle dispatching problem with the proposed model as a deep reinforcement learning problem. Through considering high-dimensional components of both the action space and state space, our formulation is more in line with city traffic environment.
- We employ deep deterministic policy gradient, where the agent chooses deterministic policy in the learning process according to interacting with the environment. According to learning the urban traffic environment, we can dispatch TNC vehicles from one area to other neighboring areas to increase driver's profit and satisfy customer's requirement.
- We illustrate our proposed dynamic model based on both big real-time data and historical data from real database. In addition, the proposed model can be applied to an actual dynamic urban environment and the future TNC autonomous vehicle issue.

2   System Model

We divide the city into multi-regions, as shown in Fig. 1, and then dispatch the TNC vehicles between the adjacent regions to match the vehicle supplies and passenger demands more appropriate while improving the drivers' average profit in the meantime. In the Fig. 1, the yellow and purple arrows represent the communication between vehicles and service center, and the red arrow represents the dispatching instruction for the vehicle. Assume that the shape of the urban city is a rectangular grid which can be divided into $M \times N$ big cells. The total dispatching process for TNC vehicle is shown below.

In each area there are some vacant TNC vehicles and some potential passengers, the service center can collect this information for future dispatching. In order to consider the consumption of time and distance in the real-world situation, we only dispatch the vehicles between the neighboring area in one dispatching time unit. At any moment, according to the number of TNC vehicles and passengers in each area, the service center dispatches TNC vehicles from one area to another neighboring area, until the ratio of vehicles to passengers in all areas has reached a balance. After taking the passenger to the destination, driver needs to report the revenue for future analyzing to the service center. To formulate the strategy for dispatching TNC vehicles, there are two points that we need to consider: the relationship between vehicle supplies and passenger demands and the average profit of the driver.

In order to satisfy the demands of the passengers, we consider improving the vehicle utilization rate, thereby shortening the waiting time of the passengers. Obviously, it is easier to know that the passenger waiting time and vehicles to passengers ratio are negatively correlated. The higher the proportion of vehicles to passengers, the shorter the waiting time for passengers. Hence, we use vehicles to passengers ratio in the area to measure the problem.

The average vehicles to passengers ratio ρ_b of the whole city can be represented as

$$\rho_b = \frac{\sum_{i=1}^{M} v_i}{\sum_{i=1}^{M} p_i}, \tag{1}$$

where M represents the number of the areas dividing of the city. p_i and v_i are the number of passengers and vehicles in area i. We define the average ratio ρ_b as the baseline standard in the model. If the vehicles to passengers ratio in every area is same and reaches the baseline ρ_b, then the system will have the best performance. On the one hand, from the perspective of the company, we pursue the ratio in every area reaching the baseline to prevent wasting the vehicle resource. On the other hand, ensuring fairness for passengers in different regions is also significant. Fortunately, these two goals are consistent. So the distance between vehicles to passengers ratio in current area i and the baseline ρ_b can be computed as $d(i) = \rho_b - \frac{v_i}{p_i}$.

Then we define the factor $\rho(i)$ to measure the supply and demand relationship in region i, and ρ is the vehicle usage measure factor. $\rho(i)$ can be computed as follow,

$$\rho(i) = \begin{cases} \frac{e^{d(i)} - e^{-d(i)}}{e^{d(i)} + e^{-d(i)}} & d(i) \leq 0 \\ \frac{e^{d(i)} - e^{-d(i)}}{e^{d(i)} + e^{-d(i)}} & d(i) > 0. \end{cases} \tag{2}$$

If the current ratio in area i reach the baseline value, then the vehicle usage measure factor $\rho(i)$ will turn to be 0. If the current ratio has the long distance from the baseline, then the $\rho(i)$ will turn to be the maximum, which is always the bound based on the property of the $tanh$ function. Moreover, the property of the $tanh$ function can also represent the sensitivity of the points near the zero, which means it can measure the small change of the ratio sensitively, and it is suitable for our problem. Totally, from the perspective of TNC and passenger, we want to minimize the vehicle usage measure factor in whole city, and it can be computed by $\rho = \sum_{i=1}^{M} |\rho(i)|$.

Another factor in the TNC vehicle dispatching problem needs to be considered is the driver's profit, which has the most directly impact on driver's enthusiasm. When dispatching the TNC vehicles, we need to optimize the profits of all TNC drivers in the city instead of maximizing individual profit. Therefore, the average profit R_e of each driver in the city can be computed as $R_e = \frac{E-C}{K}$. E and C are the total earnings obtained and costs spent in the city traffic environment, and K is the total number of TNC vehicles in the city. E can be computed as the sum of each single order's benefit, which can be represented as $E = \sum_{k=1}^{K} e(k)$. Based on different ride distances, we define the earning for each order as follows [9]

$$
e(k) = \begin{cases} B & L(k) \leq D_1 \\ B + (L(k) - D_1) * u_1 & D_1 < L(k) \leq D_2 \\ B + (L(k) - D_1) * u_1 + (L(k) - D_2) * u_2 & D_2 < L(k), \end{cases} \quad (3)
$$

where B is the base price, D_1 and D_2 are the distance standards for dividing the earning. $L(k)$ is the distance traveled by the TNC vehicle to drop the passenger k at its final destination, and u_1 and u_2 are dynamic pricing factors which depend on driver's supply and the ride distance.

We define the costs C for all TNC vehicles in the city at one time, including the fuel costs required to dispatch vehicle and deliver passengers as well the TNC company's interest. Thus, C can be computed as

$$
C = \sum_{k=1}^{K} (L(k) \cdot f + p \cdot e(k)) + \sum_{i=1}^{M} K_s(i) \cdot L_s(i) \cdot f, \quad (4)
$$

where f is the price of fuel required per unit distance and p is the percentage of TNC company's interest for each order. $K_s(i)$ and $L_s(i)$ are the number of vehicles mobilized to the i-th area and the distance for dispatching one vehicle. For the TNC driver, the dispatching model we proposed is to maximize the average profit for each vehicle.

3   Problem Formulation

In the dispatching process, when the distribution of vehicles is in one state, TNC service center can guide vehicles move to neighboring area, which will make the distribution of vehicles state to the next state. Therefore, the underlying optimal control problem of TNC vehicle scheduling and dispatching can be formulated as a discrete time Markov decision process (MDP). Since the state transmission probabilities are always unknown in the urban city traffic environment, we can formulate the dispatching problem with model-free reinforcement learning framework.

In this work, the goal of the TNC service center is to learn how to map states and actions in the environment via the learning process, so as to maximize the long term accumulated rewards. Actions will be taken for each state corresponding to each time slot according to the optimal policy. Let s_t be the state of the urban transportation environment, which evolves across time slots $t = \{1, 2, ...\}$, and S donates the state space. The state is the number of vehicles in each area, and $s_t \in S$ can be defined as

$$s_t = (v_1(t), v_2(t), ..., v_M(t)). \tag{5}$$

For the dispatching problem, the TNC service agent will determine how many vehicles should be dispatched from one area to the other adjacent area. Therefore, the action a_t in action space A at time slot t can be represented as

$$a_t = (f_1(t), f_2(t), ..., f_L(t)), \tag{6}$$

where $f_i(t)$ is the number of vehicles dispatched from one area to the neighboring area according to the i-th strategy in the action. For example, if the city can be divided into $a \times b$ areas, then it will have the number of $L = (a-1) \times b + (b-1) \times a$ strategies in each action.

After an action a_t is executed at state s_t, the system will get the immediate reward r_t from the agent interacting with the environment. In order to measure the vehicle usage or fairness of the different regions and the average profit of the drive, the immediate reward can be defined like this

$$r_t = \xi \cdot R_e(t) - \rho(t), \tag{7}$$

where ξ is the trade-off coefficient which balance the fairness and the profit. If the coefficient is larger, then the profit will have a greater impact on immediate reward; otherwise, the vehicle usage measure factor will have a greater impact on immediate reward.

The action space A is high dimensional because there are lots of strategies in each action, so learning the stochastic policy $\pi(a|s) = Pr(a_t = a|s_t = s)$ is not ideal due to the more requirement samples and high computing power. Therefore, based on this situation, we consider a deterministic policy $\mu : S \rightarrow A$, which we directly choose the specific action but not the probability of actions. The reinforcement learning agent can evaluate and improve the policy by computing the value function.

There exists two definition of the value function: the state value function and state-action value function. The expected cumulative reward starting from state s_t and following action a_t is called the state-action value $Q(s_t, a_t)$ or Q value.

The state-action value $Q(s_t, a_t)$ is given by

$$Q(s_t, a_t) = \mathbb{E}[r_t + \gamma r_{t+1} + \gamma^2 r_{t+2} + ...|s_t, a_t] = \mathbb{E}[\sum_{k=0}^{\infty} \gamma^k r_{t+k}|s_t, a_t]. \qquad (8)$$

where γ is the discount factor which can balance the instant reward and the future rewards.

The state-action value function is used to measure the performance of executing the action a at state s. In our application, the state is infinite, and the action space is high dimensional. Thus, it is impractical to compute and save all possible value functions for every state-action value and choose the optimal policy from the value. As for the continuous or the high dimensional problem with the stochastic policy π, the object of the reinforcement learning is to find a policy which can maximize the performance objective function below

$$J(\pi) = \mathbb{E}\{Q^{\pi}(s|a)\} = \int_S d^{\pi}(s) \int_A \pi(a|s)Q^{\pi}(s,a)dads, \qquad (9)$$

where $d^{\pi}(s)$ is the state distribution under the policy π. However, in this work, we adopt the deterministic policy μ, then the performance objective function can be represented as

$$J(\mu) = \mathbb{E}\{Q^{\mu}(s|a)\} = \sum_S \rho(s)Q^{\mu}(s,\mu), \qquad (10)$$

Where $\rho(s)$ is the state distribution under the policy μ. Our goal is to maximize the performance objective as much as possible.

4   Solution with Actor and Critic Algorithm

The actor-critic approach is proposed which combines both the value-based and policy-based method. The actor-critic approach contains two network which can generate (actor) and evaluate (critic) the policy separately. The agent can choose the action according to actor network. After interacting with the environment, the agent receives the immediate reward which can facilitate to evaluate the current policy by critic network. Moreover, temporal difference (TD) error including value function and immediate reward can adjust whether things are getting better or worse to update the parameters of the two networks. In this urban city traffic scenario, we apply one type of the actor-critic approach with DQN and DPG, named deep deterministic policy gradient (DDPG).

4.1   Critic Network

The function of critic part is to measure the performance of the current policy, that is, tell the agent whether the action make things better or worse. As mentioned in Eq. (8), the state-action value function can be used to estimate the policy. In order to represent the Q-value in a high dimension space, we use neural network with the parameter ω as the function approximator to estimate the state-value function. Then the critic network can be shown as $Q(s_t, a_t) = Q^\omega(s_t, a_t)$.

This is similar to DQN algorithm, and we can learn the Q^ω off-line by using some transactions. The TD error represents the error between the approximated one and the real value, and this is always used to update the value function. In DQN, the iterative value function can be defined as

$$Q(s_t, a_t) = Q(s_t, a_t) + \alpha[r_t + \gamma \max_{a_{t+1}} Q(s_{t+1}, a_{t+1}) - Q(s_t, a_t)], \tag{11}$$

where α is the learning rate. Finally, the state-action value will converge to the optimal critic function $Q^*(s_t, a_t)$, and $Q^*(s_t, a_t) = r_t + \gamma \max_{a_{t+1}} Q(s_{t+1}, a_{t+1})$. For learning the optimal critic function, the *Loss* of the critic network in the DQN algorithm can be defined as

$$L(\omega) = \mathbb{E}[y_t - Q^\omega(s_t, a_t)]^2 \tag{12}$$

$$y_t = r_t + \gamma \max_{a_{t+1}} Q^\omega(s_{t+1}, a_{t+1}). \tag{13}$$

The optimal critic function can be found by minimizing the mean square error of the *Loss*. The mini-batch optimization method is applied to optimize the *Loss* by sampling the number of batch size M samples and computing the average *Loss* in these samples.

$$L(\omega) = \frac{1}{M} \sum_{i=1}^{M} (y_i - Q^\omega(s_i, a_i))^2. \tag{14}$$

4.2   Actor Network

In order to choose the action of how to dispatch the vehicles, we define the actor neural network to generate the policy. It is worth mentioning that we directly generate the deterministic policy μ from the actor network but not the stochastic policy. Define θ as the parameter of the actor network, the actor neural network can be defined as $\mu(s_t) = \mu^\theta(s_t)$.

Then we can update the parameters of the actor network by maximizing the objective function defined in Eq. (10) to improve the policy. To maximize the objective function, the gradient of the objective function is described as

$$\nabla_\theta J(\mu^\theta) = \frac{\partial J(\mu^\theta)}{\partial \mu^\theta} \frac{\partial \mu^\theta}{\partial \theta}. \tag{15}$$

The actor is updated by following the applying the chain rule to the expected return, and can be calculated as

$$\nabla_\theta J(\mu^\theta) \approx \int_S \rho(s) \nabla_\theta \mu^\theta(a|s) Q^\mu(s, a) ds = \mathbb{E}_{s \sim \rho}[\nabla_\theta \mu^\theta(a|s) \nabla_a Q^\mu(s, a)|_{a=\mu^\theta(s)}]. \tag{16}$$

Silver et al. [10] proved that this is the policy gradient. For the value function $Q^\mu(s,a)$ in the object, we can replace it by the value function $Q^\omega(s,a)$ we got from the critic network, which always establishes the relationship between the two networks.

4.3 Deep Deterministic Policy Gradient

When applying neural network in RL approach, the samples are always interdependent because they are generated as a sequence, which is always a problem in the neural network training task. We use *experience replay* [7] to solve this problem. Another problem is that the network is unstable and always tends to diverge. Similar to the solution about setting target network in DQN algorithm, Lillicrap et al. [6] modified the target network for actor-critic framework. We set the target network for both the actor network and critic network, as Q' and μ' with weights ω' and θ', and make both the two target networks update their parameters in a more "soft" way:

$$\omega' \leftarrow \tau\omega + (1-\tau)\omega', \theta' \leftarrow \tau\theta + (1-\tau)\theta'. \tag{17}$$

τ is the soft parameter, and this can constrict the target value changing slowly. In DDPG algorithm, we can treat the exploration problem independently from the learning process because it is an off-line policy. Then, we can choose the exploration actions by adding the noise to the actions got from the actor network, as $a_t = \mu^\theta(s_t) + \mathcal{N}_t$. $\mathcal{N}_t$ is the Gaussian noise which can suit the environment.

The total procedure of dispatching TNC vehicle between adjacent regions in the city is shown in Algorithm 1. In state s_t, according to the guidance from the TNC service center, the TNC vehicle can be dispatched to the neighboring regions with action a_t. a_t is chosen from the actor network μ with the randomly noise $\mathcal{N}$. It should be noted that we have to clip the selected actions to suit the real environment. The TNC service center executes an action a_t, receives a reward r_t, and enters into the next state s_{t+1}. After executing action a_t, the TNC service center will store the transition (s_k, a_k, r_k, s_{k+1}) in its memory $\mathbb{M}$. If the relationship between supplies and demands reaches the standard line, episode will end and start a new one; otherwise, the center will continue to dispatch the vehicles. Moreover, this model is better applied for unmanned taxi scenarios.

Further, when the collected transition samples are abundant enough, the TNC center will randomly choose mini-batch size of transitions (s_j, a_j, r_j, s_{j+1}) to train the two neural networks. For the critic part, the service center uses Adaptive Moment Estimation [4] to minimize the mean square errors (MSE) between Q-target and Q-evaluation. The *loss* is shown in Eq. (14). For the actor part, update the online policy network by using sampled policy gradient, and the derivation of the strategy is shown below

$$\nabla_\theta \approx \frac{1}{N}\sum_j \nabla_a Q^\omega(s,a)|_{s=s_j,a=\mu(s_j)} \nabla_\theta\mu^\theta(s)|_{s_j} \tag{18}$$

Finally, update the weights of the network by "soft" way mentioned in Eq. (17).

Algorithm 1. DRL for TNC Vehicle Dispatching Algorithm

Initialization: Randomly initialize the critic network $Q^\omega(s,a)$ and actor network $\mu^\theta(s)$ with parameter ω and θ separately. Initialize the replay memory M and set the parameters of target network Q' and μ' by copying from Q and μ.

Output: the selected action for TNC vehicle.

1: **for** episode $=1,...,N$ **do**
2:     Initialize the noise process $\mathcal{N}$ for action exploration.
3:     The TNC vehicle starts at the state s_1.
4:     **for** $t = 1,...,T$ **do**
5:         Select action $a_t = \mu^\theta(s_t) + \mathcal{N}_t$ according to the evaluation actor network and the noise process.
6:         Clip the action with the actual environment.
7:         The TNC service center executes the action a_t, gets the immediate reward r_t, and observes the next state s_{t+1}.
8:         Store transition (s_t, a_t, r_t, s_{t+1}) in memory M of the center.
9:         Randomly sample mini-batch size of transitions (s_j, a_j, r_j, s_{j+1}) in M.
10:        Set target Q value as r_j, when s_{j+1} is the final state; Otherwise, target Q value is $r_j + \gamma Q'(s_{i+1}, \mu'(s_{i+1}))$.
11:        The TNC center uses Adam to minimize the loss function of the critic network and update w.
12:        The TNC center updates the actor network by sampled policy gradient with the parameter θ.
13:        Update the weights in target networks with "soft" way.
14:     **end for**
15: **end for**

---

5 Performance Evaluation

In this simulation, we employ a real-world public TNC vehicle data [1] from Didi Chuxing, a Chinese TNC. The database concludes all of the orders for a given month (11/2016) in Chengdu, a Chinese city, including the time and locations of boarding and dropping the passengers. In fact, in our model, we only use the data of weekdays, and only consider the time period from 5 to 7 pm.

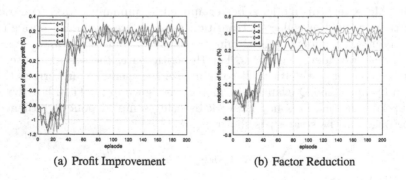

(a) Profit Improvement   (b) Factor Reduction

Fig. 2. Adjust trade-off coefficient ξ

We use the real-world data in Chengdu, for convenience, we select the part of the main urban area of Chengdu as the scope of our scheduling model. Similar to Fig. 1, we consider the main urban area as a square, which can be divided into 5×5 parts, and each cell represents $9 \, km^2$ ($3 \, km \times 3 \, km$). Thus, the action space is 40-dimensional. The parameters of traffic environment are given as follows. For computing the profit of each order, we establish the pricing rules based on real-life situations. The distance standards are defined as $D_1 = 5$ km, $D_2 = 12$ km, base price equals to $B = 9$ CNY and dynamic price factors u_1 and u_2 are $1.6 \, CNY/km$ and $2.4 \, CNY/km$, respectively. The percentage of TNC company's interest for each order p is 10% and unit fuel cost f is $0.5 \, CNY/km$. The number of passengers in each area can be got from the database, and we also randomly set the initial vehicles in each area according to the distribution of passengers to establish the dynamic environment.

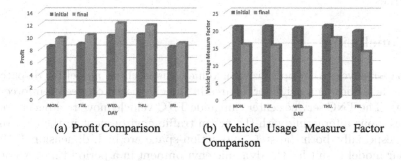

(a) Profit Comparison   (b) Vehicle Usage Measure Factor Comparison

Fig. 3. Final results

In our implementation, we choose a 4-layer full connected feed-forward neural network for actor and critic network, where each hidden layer has 128 nodes. We set the experience replay memory size as $\mathbb{M} = 10000$, and batch size is 64. The parameters of the deep learning and reinforcement learning are got from the parameters tuning. Specifically, the learning rate for both the actor and critic network are 0.001, discount factor γ is 0.9 and "soft" parameter τ is 0.01. Another parameter we need to focus on is the trade-off coefficient ξ in Eq. (7). In order to choose the best value of trade-off coefficient ξ, we evaluate the performance during changing the different value of ξ under a fixed-time urban environment, and the training results can also be gained from the evaluation process.

The definition of the reward includes two parts, i.e., the average profit and the vehicle usage measure factor ξ, respectively. As shown in Fig. 2, to consider the reward efficiently, we compute this two parts separately. The episode of the training process is 200, and each episode have 400 steps. Due to the dynamic environment which means the initial total vehicle number of each episode is different, directly comparing the results is not accurate. Therefore, we measure the performance by computing the improvement of the initial value. Figure 2(a) shows that except $\xi = 4$, the other values have the same impact on the average profit. In the same way, in Fig. 2(b), we can find that when $\xi = 1$, vehicle usage measure factor has the most effective improvement. Thus, we set $\xi = 1$ in our model.

Then we apply our model to a dynamic traffic environment, which means we learn different working day in one month and different time slot in one day. To evaluate the learning performance, we chose the working day data we do not use in the training process, and the results are shown in Fig. 3. In Fig. 3(a), all of the average profit in five working days improve, and the average improvement ratio is 12% comparing to the initial value. Another goal for us is to reduce the vehicle usage measure factor ξ, and the smaller number indicates the better vehicle dispatching results. The Fig. 3(b) shows that ξ for all of the five days decreases dramatically. To sum up, the extensively conducted experiments show that the dynamic TNC vehicle dispatching model improves the driver's average profit dramatically while it meets the supply and demand relationship to guarantee the fairness.

6   Conclusion

This paper develops an optimization vehicle dispatching model for dispatching TNC vehicles between neighboring area in the city based on deep reinforcement learning. The TNC service center can guide TNC vehicle move to adjacent region by continuous interacting with the urban traffic environment in the city. In our model, especially, both the state and action space are high dimensional. Beside this, our model is suit for the dynamic environment in a period time. According to the practical big vehicle data in Chengdu of a Chinese TNC, the evaluation results provide empirical support of the effectiveness of deep deterministic policy gradient for the TNC vehicle dispatching problem. By comparing with the performance of the original commercial system, our dispatching system can significantly optimize the ratio of vehicle supplies and passenger demands in each area, and the average long-term profit of TNC driver also dramatically increase.

Acknowledgement. The work of D. Shi and M. Pan was supported in part by the U.S. National Science Foundation under grants US CNS-1350230 (CAREER), CNS-1646607, CNS-1702850, and CNS-1801925. The work of X. Li was supported in part by the National Natural Science Foundation of China under Grant 61801080, and the Fundamental Research Funds of Dalian University of Technology under Grant DUT18RC(3)012. The work of M. Li was supported by the U.S. National Science Foundation under grants CNS-1566634 and ECCS-1711991. The work of J. Wang was supported in part by the National Natural Science Foundation of China under grant 61671102, Liaoning Province Natural Science Foundation under grant 20180520026, Dalian Science and Technology Innovation Foundation under grant 2018J12GX044. and Dalian High-level Talent Innovation Support Program Project under grant 2017RQ096.

References

1. COMPANY D: Gaia initiative. https://outreach.didichuxing.com/research/opendata/en/. Accessed 4 Apr 2018
2. Gao, Y., Jiang, D., Xu, Y.: Optimize taxi driving strategies based on reinforcement learning. Int. J. Geogr. Inf. Sci. **32**, 1677–1696 (2018)
3. Han, M., Senellart, P., Bressan, S., Wu, H.: Routing an autonomous taxi with reinforcement learning. In: Proceedings of the 25th ACM International on Conference on Information and Knowledge Management (CIKM), Indianapolis, IN, October 2016
4. Kingma, D.P., Ba, J.: Adam: a method for stochastic optimization. arXiv preprint arXiv:1412.6980 (2014)
5. Li, L., Li, Y., Hou, R.: A novel mobile edge computing-based architecture for future cellular vehicular networks. In: 2017 IEEE Wireless Communications and Networking Conference (WCNC), pp. 1–6. IEEE (2017)
6. Lillicrap, T.P., et al.: Continuous control with deep reinforcement learning. arXiv preprint arXiv:1509.02971 (2015)
7. Mnih, V., et al.: Human-level control through deep reinforcement learning. Nature **518**(7540), 529 (2015)
8. Moran, M.: Transportation network companies (2016)
9. Shi, D., et al.: Deep Q-network based route scheduling for TNC vehicles with passengers' location differential privacy. IEEE Internet Things J. (2019)
10. Silver, D., Lever, G., Heess, N., Degris, T., Wierstra, D., Riedmiller, M.: Deterministic policy gradient algorithms. In: International Conference on Machine Learning (ICML), China, June 2014
11. Silver, D., et al.: Mastering the game of go without human knowledge. Nature **550**(7676), 354 (2017)
12. Sun, Y., Peng, M., Mao, S.: Deep reinforcement learning based mode selection and resource management for green fog radio access networks. IEEE Internet Things J. **6**, 1960–1971 (2018)
13. Verma, T., Varakantham, P., Kraus, S., Lau, H.C.: Augmenting decisions of taxi drivers through reinforcement learning for improving revenues (2017)

Fairness-Aware Auction Mechanism for Sustainable Mobile Crowdsensing

Korn Sooksatra[1], Ruinian Li[2], Yingshu Li[1], Xin Guan[3], and Wei Li[1(✉)]

[1] Georgia State University, Atlanta, GA, USA
ksooksatra1@student.gsu.edu, {yili,wli28}@gsu.edu
[2] Bowling Green State University, Bowling Green, OH, USA
lir@bgsu.edu
[3] Heilongjiang University, Harbin, Heilongjiang, China
guanxin.hlju@gmail.com

Abstract. With the proliferation of sensor-embedded mobile devices, mobile crowdsensing has become a paradigm of significant interest. Incentivizing sensory-data providers to keep sustainability in a mobile crowdsensing system is a critical issue nowadays, and auction-based mechanisms have been proposed to motivate providers via monetary rewards. In our work, this sustainability problem is formulated as an optimization problem maximizing providers' proportionally fair utilities with respect to their multi-dimensional fairness factors, and a fairness-aware auction mechanism is designed accordingly. To the best of our knowledge, this is the first work that considers multi-dimensional fairness of providers as the objective in selecting providers for the mobile crowdsensing system. In addition, we present rigorous theoretical analysis proving that our mechanism meets budget feasibility, individual rationality and truthfulness. Finally, simulations are performed to demonstrate the performance of our proposed mechanism.

1 Introduction

Nowadays the number of mobile devices is significantly increased. It is predicted that the number of mobile users will reach 4.68 billion in 2019 [1]. The increasing of mobile users provides an economic way to collect huge amount of information, *e.g.*, companies can hire mobile users to collect data from their mobiles' sensors, such as cameras and accelerometers instead of deploying actual sensors that has a comparable higher cost. Such a mobile crowdsensing system has many practical and valuable usage; for examples, estimate road surface condition [2], detect heat stroke [3], predict traffic condition [4], collect daily weather conditions [5], gather signal and Wi-Fi information at a specific location [6], and maximize influence in location-based social networks [7], etc.

To ensure the performance of mobile crowdsensing, a large number of providers are needed to collect sensory data. But mobile users are often reluctant to serve as providers due to resource limitation (*e.g.*, battery, bandwidth, memory, etc.) and potential privacy leakage [10–13, 24, 25], unless they can gain

© Springer Nature Switzerland AG 2019
E. S. Biagioni et al. (Eds.): WASA 2019, LNCS 11604, pp. 310–321, 2019.
https://doi.org/10.1007/978-3-030-23597-0_25

satisfying rewards as compensation. Another issue in mobile corwdsensing is that some providers submit low-quality data to the system to gain rewards easily, which has a highly negative effect on the applications using the collected data. To solve these issues, many incentive mechanisms have been proposed to select providers to guarantee providers receiving non negative utilities even when there is a big number of providers [14,23].

Most of the existing works mainly focused on monetary-incentive and quality-aware mechanisms motivating mobile users to stay in the mobile crowdsensing system with high-quality sensory data provided in a short term [8,9,15] without caring about long-term sustainability of the system. Notice that in mobile crowdsensing, each provider has different bid price, data quality, and performance history. The system should take these information into consideration, otherwise high-quality providers with higher bids might quit from the system due to lost in multiple rounds. For instance, a provider has lost for 4–5 rounds in the auction and still keep losing due to his high bid price, and he might think that he/she does not have a chance to win in this system. If he loses again, then he might lose interest and leave the system. As a result, eventually the system will have only a few providers who keep winning in many rounds, and these providers can bid any price since there is no competitor anymore, hindering the sustainable development of mobile crowdsensing in a long-term period. Therefore, sustainability should be one critical property of the mobile crowdsensing system for long-term economic and social benefits.

As significant as sustainability is in the mobile corwdsensing system, there are only a few state-of-art works that mentioned how to achieve sustainability [16,18]. There exists a mechanism proposed to maintain sustainability but that mechanism considers only data quality [18]. Motivated by these observation, in this paper, our goal is to develop an incentive mechanism to enhance sustainability by taking multi-dimensional fairness into consideration. To achieve this property, the problem of provider selection is mathematically formulated as an optimization problem with proportional fairness as the objective function, in which the fairness factor is quantified from three aspects, including data quality, lost frequency, and submission time of each provider. Since the optimization problem is NP-Hard, it takes a very long time to obtain the optimal results. Hence, an auction-based greedy algorithm (*i.e.*, our fairness-aware auction mechanism) is utilized to solve the problem. Through rigorous theoretical proofs, we show that our proposed auction mechanism can simultaneously achieve individual rationality, budget feasibility, and truthfulness. Moreover, our simulations validate that our proposed auction mechanism can outperform the existing mechanisms in a long term in terms of sustainability, fairness and data quality. To sum up, the contributions of this paper are as follows:

- To the best of our knowledge, this is the first work to consider multi-dimensional fairness for data provider selection in the mobile crowdsensing system, and such problem is formulated into an optimization problem to achieve proportional fairness.
- A fairness-aware auction mechanism is designed to incentivize providers to stay in the mobile crowdsensing system in a long-term period,

- Theoretical analysis is performed to show that the auction mechanism can guarantee individual rationality, budget feasibility, and truthfulness.
- Comprehensive simulations are conducted to verify the effectiveness of our proposed auction mechanism.

The remainder of this paper is organized as follows. Existing works are briefly describes in Sect. 2. The mobile crowdsensing system model and problem formulation are explained in Sect. 3. The proposed fairness-aware auction mechanism is illustrated in Sect. 4. In addition, the performance evaluation is demonstrated in Sect. 5. Finally, we give a conclusion in Sect. 6.

2   Related Work

Incentive mechanisms are critical for mobile crowdsensing to attract providers and requesters, in which auction has been a widely studied model to motivate users.

Instead of only aiming at attracting mobile users for sensing activities in a short term, recent research have been focusing on how to motivate mobile users to stay in a mobile crowdsensing system for a long term, which is called sustainability. For example, Luo *et al.* [16] surveyed how to make mobile crowdsensing systems sustainable by utilizing three schemes: auctions, lotteries and trust and reputation systems. In [17], Ni *et al.* suggested solutions for fog-based vehicular crowdsensing to reach sustainability. The solutions are that the platform needs to provide security, privacy and fairness to both general users and sensing providers. In addition, Sun *et al.* [18] proposed a mechanism, in which the selection process and payment determination mainly depends on providers' qualities such that the system will be sustainable in a long run with sufficient incentives.

To keep sustainability in mobile crowdsensing systems, fairness is an important factor that has been considered. For instance, in [19], Zhu *et al.* designed an auction-based solution to address free-riding problem and also claimed that the solution can provide fairness for users and improve the quality of works. Huang *et al.* [20] developed a double auction mechanism with considering the fairness among data consumers. Moreover, in [21], Duan *et al.* proposed a mechanism for IoT-based mobile crowdsensing systems considering fairness among providers such that each provider receives a reward with respect to his effort.

Unlike the existing works, this paper is the first one that take into account multi-dimensional fairness of data providers (*i.e.*, mobile users) for auctions in mobile crowdsensing systems, where providers can be selected by considering their data quality, lost frequency, and submission time for sustainability improvement of mobile crowdsensing.

3   System Model and Problem Formulation

Auction Model. The mobile crowdsensing system consisting of a cloud service and a number of mobile users equipped with sensors on their mobile devices.

The cloud service acts as a requester demanding task implementation, and the mobile users act as providers processing tasks, in which there are more providers than tasks. In this paper, we consider a real scenario where auction mechanism is performed in multi-round during a long-term period. In each round, the providers compete for task implementation, and the requester determines the winners and their payments. After collecting sensory data from the winners, the requester records the information of task completion (including data quality, submission time, and others) and uses it for managing auction in the next round.

Assume that there are m providers, denoted by $\Gamma = \{\gamma_1, \gamma_2, ..., \gamma_m\}$, and n tasks, denoted by $\Delta = \{\delta_1, \delta_2, ..., \delta_n\}$. For these n tasks, each provider i ($1 \leq i \leq m$) a bidding profile $b_i^t = \{b_{i1}^t, b_{i2}^t, ..., b_{in}^t\}$ where b_{ij}^t is the bid of provider i for task j ($1 \leq j \leq n$) in round t, and the requester has his value profile $V = \{v_1, v_2, ..., v_n\}$ where v_j is the value of task j. Additionally, the requester has a budget B to purchase task service from the providers. Let p_{ij}^t be the payment paid to provider i for processing task j in round t. Thus, in each round, the total payment paid from the requester cannot exceed B, i.e., $\sum_{i=1}^{m} \sum_{j=1}^{n} x_{ij}^t p_{ij}^t \leq B$, and each provider i's utility is $u_{ij}^t = x_{ij}^t (p_{ij}^t - b_{ij}^t)$, where $x_{ij}^t \in \{0, 1\}$ is the winner determination variable.

Fairness Factor. To keep sustainability of the mobile crowdsensing system, a multi-dimensional fairness factor is quantified from the following three aspects.

(1) *Data Quality.* High-quality data is critical to improve the performance of mobile crowdsensing. The providers who submit higher-quality data should be better considered than the ones with lower-quality data. For example, provider i always measures temperature more accurately than provider j does; hence, provider i deserves to be selected with a higher probability. The data quality of provider i in round t is represented by q_i^t, and the normalized data quality $\overline{q}_i^t$ can be computed as $\overline{q}_i^t = \frac{q_i^t}{max_{i' \in [1,...,m]} \ q_{i'}^t}$.

(2) *Lost Frequency.* A provider may lose interest in mobile crowdsensing if he loses too many times in auctions. Thus, to maintain attractiveness to the providers, the number of losing rounds, denoted by l_i^t, and the number of consecutively losing rounds, denoted by c_i^t, should be taken into account. Accordingly, the normalized number of losing rounds is $\overline{l}_i^t = \frac{l_i^t}{max_{i' \in [1,...,m]} \ l_{i'}^t}$, and the normalized number of consecutively losing rounds is $\overline{c}_i^t = \frac{c_i^t}{max_{i' \in [1,...,m]} \ c_{i'}^t}$.

(3) *Submission Time.* Since some requests may be time-sensitive, submitting data late could cause requester in trouble. For example, the requester would like to know a traffic on a street at a specific time to find a route to go to his destination in time, but if the requester obtains this information late, he has to make a decision by himself without the help of the sensory data. In this case, the received data becomes useless. Therefore, there should be some punishments for the providers who submit data late. Suppose the average late submission of provider i in round t is a_i^t that can be updated

in every round as $a_i^t = \frac{a_i^{t-1}(t-1) + max(0, s_i^t - d_i^t)}{t}$, where s_i^t is the submission time of provider i in round t and d_i^t is the submission deadline assigned to provider i in round t. Moreover, the normalized late submission is $\overline{a}_i^t = 1 - \frac{a_i^t}{max_{i' \in [1,\ldots,m]} a_{i'}^t}$.

By combining the aforementioned aspects, an assignment score for each provider i in round t is computed as $\omega_i^t = \alpha_1 \overline{q}_i^t + \alpha_2 \overline{l}_i^t + \alpha_4 \overline{c}_i^t + \alpha_4 \overline{a}_i^t$, where α_i $(1 \leq i \leq 4)$ indicates the weight of each corresponding aspect, and $\alpha_1 + \alpha_2 + \alpha_3 + \alpha_4 = 1$. To compare all the providers' scores, the fairness factor of provider i in round t can be determined as $f_i^t = \omega_i^t / \sum_{i'=1}^{m} \omega_{i'}^t$.

Optimization Problem. In this paper, our problem can be mathematically expressed in Eq. (1a), (1b), (1c), (1d), (1e) and (1f).

$$\max \quad \sum_{t=1}^{T} \sum_{i=1}^{m} \sum_{j=1}^{n} f_i^t \log(1 + u_{ij}^t); \tag{1a}$$

$$\text{s.t.} \quad \sum_{i=1}^{m} x_{ij}^t \leq 1, 1 \leq j \leq n; \tag{1b}$$

$$\sum_{j=1}^{n} x_{ij}^t \leq 1, 1 \leq i \leq m; \tag{1c}$$

$$\sum_{i=1}^{m} \sum_{j=1}^{n} p_{ij}^t \leq B; \tag{1d}$$

$$x_{ij}^t \in \{0,1\}, 1 \leq i \leq m, 1 \leq j \leq n, 1 \leq t \leq T; \tag{1e}$$

$$p_{ij}^t \geq 0, 1 \leq i \leq m, 1 \leq j \leq n, 1 \leq t \leq T. \tag{1f}$$

In (1a), (1b), (1c), (1d), (1e) and (1f), our objective is to maintain proportional fairness for all the providers in mobile crowdsensing during a long-term period. The constraints in Eqs. (1b) and (1c) respectively mean each task is process by at most one provider and each provider is allowed to carry out at most one task. The budget constraint is indicated by Eq. (1d). The ranges of variables are implied by Eqs. (1e) and (1f).

Furthermore, our auction mechanism based on Eq. (1a), (1b), (1c), (1d), (1e) and (1f) aims to satisfy the following economic properties [14]. (i) *Individual Rationality*: an auction can achieve this property when no provider obtains a negative utility, *i.e.*, $u_{ij}^t \geq 0$. (ii) *Truthfulness*: an auction is truthful when the best strategy for each provider is to report his true bid, *i.e.*, $p_{ij}^t - b_{ij}^t \geq p_{ij}'^t - b_{ij}^t$ where b_{ij}^t is the true bid and $p_{ij}'^t$ is the payment for the untruthful bid $b_{ij}'^t$. (iii) *Budget Feasibility*: the total payment for providers cannot exceed the budget of the requester.

4   Fairness-Aware Auction Mechanism

In this section, our auction mechanism for Eq. (1a), (1b), (1c), (1d), (1e) and (1f) will be detailed, in which the winners are determined by the allocation rule and the payments are calculated by the pricing rule.

4.1   Allocation Rule

The requester selects providers based on the fairness factors, the bids and the budget. Since at first, the providers' payments and utilities are unknown, we estimate the contributions provider i makes to the auction objective using $O_{ij}^t = f_i^t \log(1 + v_j q_i^t)$. Let M be a set of pairs (γ_i, δ_j), where for each pair (γ_i, δ_j) with $b_{ij}^t \neq 0$, $\gamma_i = \arg\max_{\gamma_{i'} \in \Gamma} O_{i'j}^t$. In M, the pairs are sorted in a non-increasing order according to $R_{ij}^t = \frac{O_{ij}^t}{b_{ij}^t}$. The construction of set M is described in line 11 of Algorithm 1. Without lose of generality, we assume that in $M = \{(\gamma_{i^1}, \delta_{j^1}), (\gamma_{i^2}, \delta_{j^2}), \cdots, (\gamma_{i^{|M|}}, \delta_{j^{|M|}})\}$, $R_{i^1 j^1}^t \geq R_{i^2 j^2}^t \geq \cdots \geq R_{i^{|M|} j^{|M|}}^t$.

Let W be the set of pairs of selected providers (i.e., winners) and their assigned tasks. Next, the requester picks pairs from M one by one to W in order until pair $(\gamma_{i^k}, \delta_{j^k})$ cannot satisfy the budget condition:

$$b_{i^k j^k}^t \leq \frac{O_{i^k j^k}^t \cdot B}{O_{i^k j^k}^t + \sum\limits_{(\gamma_{i^w}, \delta_{j^w}) \in W} O_{i^w j^w}^t}. \tag{2}$$

4.2   Pricing Rule

Initially, all the payments are set to be 0. Then, the selected provider i^k assigned to task j^k in set W is paid with the amount according to (3).

$$p_{i^k j^k}^t = \min\{\frac{O_{i^k j^k}^t \cdot B}{\sum\limits_{(\gamma_{i^w}, \delta_{j^w}) \in W} O_{i^w j^w}^t}, \frac{O_{i^k j^k}^t}{R_{i^{|W|} j^{|W|}}^t}\}. \tag{3}$$

where $R_{i^{|W|} j^{|W|}}^t$ is the smallest ratio among the pairs in W.

The pseudo codes of our auction mechanism are presented in Algorithm 1.

4.3   Theoretical Analysis

Lemma 1. *If* $b_{i^k j^k}^t \leq \frac{O_{i^k j^k}^t \cdot B}{\sum\limits_{(\gamma_{i^w}, \delta_{j^w}) \in W} O_{i^w j^w}^t}$, *then* $b_{i^{k-1} j^{k-1}}^t \leq \frac{O_{i^{k-1} j^{k-1}}^t \cdot B}{\sum\limits_{(\gamma_{i^w}, \delta_{j^w}) \in W} O_{i^w j^w}^t}$ *where* $(\gamma_{i^k}, \delta_{j^k}) \in W$ *and* $k \geq 2$.

Proof. This lemma can be proved from the definition of R_{ij}^t and Eq. (2).   □

Lemma 2. *Every pair* $(\gamma_{i^k}, \delta_{j^k})$ *in* W *can satisfy* $b_{i^k j^k}^t \leq \frac{O_{i^k j^k}^t \cdot B}{\sum\limits_{(\gamma_{i^w}, \delta_{j^w}) \in W} O_{i^w j^w}^t}$.

Algorithm 1. Fairness-Aware Auction Mechanism

Require: $\{f_i^t\}, \{b_{ij}^t\}, \Gamma, B, V, \Delta$

 1: **for** $i = 0, 1, 2, ..., m$ **do**
 2:    **for** $j = 0, 1, 2, ..., n$ **do**
 3:       $p_{ij}^t = 0, x_{ij}^t = 0$
 4:       **if** $b_{ij}^t == 0$ **then**
 5:          $\hat{u}_{ij}^t = 0, O_{ij}^t = 0, R_{ij}^t = 0$
 6:       **else**
 7:          $\hat{u}_{ij}^t = v_j \cdot q_i^t, O_{ij}^t = f_i^t \cdot log(1 + \hat{u}_{ij}^t), R_{ij}^t = \frac{O_{ij}^t}{b_{ij}^t}$
 8:       **end if**
 9:    **end for**
10: **end for**
11: $M \leftarrow$ ProviderSelection($\{O_{ij}^t\}, \Gamma, \Delta$), $W \leftarrow \emptyset$, $k = 1$
12: Sort members in M in non-increasing order with respect to R_{ij}^t
13: **while** $k \leq |M|$ **do**
14:    **if** $b_{i_k j_k}^t \leq \dfrac{O_{i_k j_k}^t \cdot B}{O_{i_k j_k}^t + \sum\limits_{(\gamma_i w, \delta_j w) \in W} O_{i_w j_w}^t}$ **then**
15:       $W \leftarrow (\gamma_{i_k}, \delta_{j_k}), x_{i_k j_k}^t = 1$
16:    **else**
17:       break
18:    **end if**
19:    $k = k + 1$
20: **end while**
21: **for** $k = 1$ to $|W|$ **do**
22:    $p_{i_k j_k}^t = min(\dfrac{O_{i_k j_k}^t \cdot B}{\sum\limits_{(\gamma_i w, \delta_j w) \in W} O_{i_w j_w}^t}, \dfrac{O_{i_k j_k}^t}{R_{i|W|j|W|}^t})$
23: **end for**
24: **return** $\{x_{ij}^t\}, \{p_{ij}^t\}$

Proof. This lemma can hold based on Lemma 1 and and Eq. (2).   □

Lemma 3. *Every pair* $(\gamma_{i_k}, \delta_{j_k})$ *in W satisfies* $b_{i_k j_k}^t \leq \dfrac{O_{i_k j_k}^t}{R_{i|W|j|W|}^t} = \dfrac{O_{i_k j_k}^t b_{i|W|j|W|}^t}{O_{i|W|j|W|}^t}$.

Proof. According to Lemma 2, this conclusion can hold.   □

Theorem 1. *Our auction mechanism is individually rational for all providers.*

Proof. According to Lemmas 2 and 3, for any $(\gamma_{i_k}, \delta_{j_k})$ in W, we have $b_{i_k j_k}^t \leq p_{i_k j_k}^t = min(\dfrac{O_{i_k j_k}^t \cdot B}{\sum\limits_{(\gamma_i w, \delta_j w) \in W} O_{i_w j_w}^t}, \dfrac{O_{i_k j_k}^t b_{i|W|j|W|}^t}{O_{i|W|j|W|}^t})$. Therefore, $u_{ij}^t \geq 0$.   □

Lemma 4. *The proposed auction mechanism satisfies monotone allocation.*

Proof. If γ_i wins with b_{ij}^t and submits $b_{ij}'^t < b_{ij}^t$, then γ_i with $b_{ij}'^t$ also wins because $b_{ij}'^t < b_{ij}^t \leq \dfrac{O_{ij}^t \cdot B}{O_{ij}^t + \sum\limits_{(\gamma_{iw},\delta_{jw}) \in W} O_{iwjw}^t}$. □

Lemma 5. *For each provider i, p_{ij}^t is the critical value to process task j.*

Proof. Note that p_{ij}^t is the critical value if and only if γ_i wins when $b_{ij}^t \leq p_{ij}^t$ and loses when $b_{ij}^t > p_{ij}^t$. From the allocation and pricing rules, we have

(i) Case $b_{ij}^t \leq p_{ij}^t$: $b_{ij}^t \leq \dfrac{O_{ij}^t \cdot B}{\sum\limits_{(\gamma_{iw},\delta_{jw}) \in W} O_{iwjw}^t}$, and $\dfrac{O_{ij}^t}{b_{ij}^t} \geq \dfrac{O_{i|W|j|W|}^t}{b_{i|W|j|W|}^t}$; thus, γ_i wins.

(ii) Case $b_{ij}^t > p_{ij}^t$: $b_{ij}^t > \dfrac{O_{ij}^t \cdot B}{\sum\limits_{(\gamma_{iw},\delta_{jw}) \in W} O_{iwjw}^t}$ or $\dfrac{O_{ij}^t}{b_{ij}^t} < \dfrac{O_{i|W|j|W|}^t}{b_{i|W|j|W|}^t}$; thus γ_i loses.

In summary, γ_i has p_{ij}^t as the critical value. □

Theorem 2. *The proposed auction mechanism satisfies truthfulness.*

Proof. According to [22], since the allocation is monotone (Lemma 4) and the payment of each winner is the critical value (Lemma 5), the auction mechanism can guarantee truthfulness. □

Theorem 3. *The auction scheme can meet budget feasibility.*

Proof. From Eq. (3), the total payment is at most $\sum\limits_{(\gamma_i,\delta_j) \in W} p_{ij}^t = \dfrac{\sum_{(\gamma_i,\delta_j) \in W} O_{ij}^t B}{\sum_{(\gamma_i,\delta_j) \in W} O_{ij}^t}$

$= B$. If any γ_i receives payment $\dfrac{O_{ij}^t}{R_{i|W|j|W|}^t}$, then the total payment does not exceed B as $\dfrac{O_{ij}^t}{R_{i|W|j|W|}^t} \leq \dfrac{O_{ij}^t \cdot B}{\sum\limits_{(\gamma_i,\delta_j) \in W} O_{ij}^t}$. Therefore, this mechanism is budget feasible. □

5   Performance Evaluation

5.1   Simulation Setting

To evaluate the performance of our fairness-aware auction mechanism (termed FM), two other auction mechanisms are compared in the simulations, including: (i) Budget Feasible Auction Mechanism (termed BFAM) [23]: this mechanism sets budget feasibility as a constraint of the auction but is not equal to fairness-awareness. (ii) Practical Incentive Mechanism (termed PIM) [21]: this mechanism considers fairness among providers as the objective function such that each provider should gain the benefit according to his work.

In the comparison, the performance metrics contain the number of remaining providers, the average data quality, the providers' cumulative average utilities and total payment. In our setting, each provider has his own range of bids so that in each round, he can randomly pick his bidding price from the range,

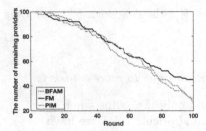

Fig. 1. Number of remaining providers with $B = 200$, $m = 100$, and $n = 60$

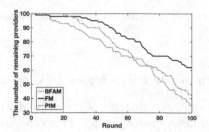

Fig. 2. Number of remaining providers with $B = 1000$, $m = 100$, and $n = 60$

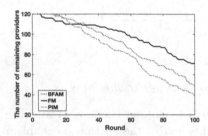

Fig. 3. Number of remaining providers with $B = 1500$, $m = 120$, and $n = 60$

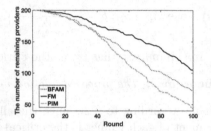

Fig. 4. Number of remaining providers with $B = 1500$, $m = 200$, and $n = 60$

and the fairness factor is updated in every round. At the end of each round, the losers have certain probabilities to quit the mechanism, and the probability of provider i is $\eta_i^t = \frac{\lambda l_i^t + (1 - \lambda)c_i^t}{\lambda L + (1 - \lambda)C}$, where $\lambda \in [0, 1]$ implies the importance of the number of losing rounds compared with the number of consecutive losing rounds, L and C are respectively the maximum number of losing rounds and the maximum number of consecutive losing rounds a provider can tolerate. The system parameters are: $\alpha_1 = 0.2, \alpha_2 = 0.3, \alpha_3 = 0.1$, and $\alpha_4 = 0.4$.

5.2 Simulation Results

The key goal of this paper is to improve sustainability of mobile crowdsensing, which is measured by the number of remaining providers and the fairness index in the long term.

Figures 1 and 2 show the number of remaining providers along with the increasing rounds and different budgets. As can be seen in the figures, when the budget increases, the gap between the number of remaining providers of PIM and that of FM at round 100 becomes wider. Since PIM does not consider fairness, mostly the same providers are selected as winners in each round; hence, many providers happen to lose in many rounds and quit from mobile crowdsensing system. On the other hand, by taking fairness into account, FM provides more chances to providers who have lost for many rounds; thus, those providers

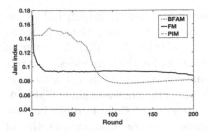

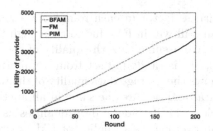

Fig. 5. Jain's index with $B = 1500$, $m = 100$ and $n = 60$

Fig. 6. Cumulative average utility with $B = 1500$, $m = 100$ and $n = 60$

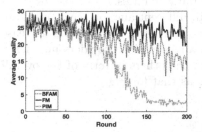

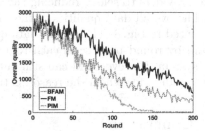

Fig. 7. Average quality of different mechanisms with $B = 1500$, $m = 100$ and $n = 60$

Fig. 8. Overall quality of different mechanisms with $B = 1500$, $m = 100$ and $n = 60$

are still willing to stay in the system. In addition, the increase of budget leads FM to be able to select more providers, and then fewer providers leave.

In Figs. 3 and 4, the number of remaining providers is presented with the increasing rounds and different number of providers (m). As m goes up, the gap between the number of remaining providers of FM and that of PIM in round 100 also becomes bigger. This is because the winners from PIM are mostly the same in every round, the rest of providers rarely have a chance to win; therefore, they give up and quit. In contrast, the providers who lost in prior rounds have more chances to win with their fairness factors in FM.

Jain's index is a factor ranging in $[0, 1]$ and used to measure how fair the mechanisms are for providers; specifically, a larger value of Jain's index indicates a higher degree of fariness. Figure 5 shows the jain's index of different auction mechanisms at each round. At the beginning, BFAM has the higher Jain's index than our proposed mechanism; however, at the certain point, it drops lower than our proposed mechanism because BFAM keeps selecting the same winners. On the other hand, FM outperforms PIM as PIM does not take fairness in the long term into account.

In Fig. 6, the cumulative average utility of providers is shown with the increasing rounds. One can observe that the cumulative average utility from BFAM is the lowest, and the one from FM is the highest. Notice that the number of winners from BFAM is quite constant and in contrary, the one from FM varies with fairness factor in each round. As a result, some providers with high bid prices can still win in FM due to their high fairness factors, obtaining higher utilities.

We assume that the quality of each provider is stable. Initially, the range of quality is randomly set from a uniform distribution for the providers. Figure 7 shows the average data quality of the winners in each round. At first, the average data qualities are the same in all auction mechanisms. However, since FM considers the providers' data qualities as one component of their fairness factors, the average data quality of FM grows up above the average data qualities of BFAM and PIM in the late rounds. Additionally, BFAM and PIM cause many providers to quit from the system; hence, the system does not have many available providers to select, reducing the average data qualities.

The overall data qualities of the winners in different auction mechanism are presented in Fig. 8. The overall data qualities of the three mechanisms decrease round by round because in each round, some high-quality providers may leave the system. However, FM can still outperform the others in term of the overall data quality, for which the reason is the same as that for Fig. 7.

6   Conclusion

We propose a fairness-aware auction mechanism for improving sustainability of mobile crowdsensing systems. Our work is different from state-of-art work as we take multi-dimensional fairness into account to guarantee the incentivized mobile users stay in the system in a long run. Then we perform rigorous theoretical analysis proving that our proposed auction mechanism is budget feasible, individually rational and truthful. Finally, our simulation results clearly demonstrate the improvement of effectiveness compared to the existing works.

Acknowledgment. This work was supported by the U.S. National Science Foundation under Grants SP00013080 and SP00013422, National Science Foundation of China under Grant NSFC 61632010, and Heilongjiang Provincial Natural Science Foundation of China under Grant F2017027.

References

1. https://www.statista.com/statistics/274774/forecast-of-mobile-phone-users-worldwide/
2. Ikeda, Y., Inoue, M.: An estimation of road surface conditions using participatory sensing. In: International Conference on Electronics, Information, and Communication (ICEIC), pp. 1–3, January 2018
3. Ismail, M.Z., Inoue, M.: Map generation to detect heat stroke by using participatory sensing data. In: International Conference on Electronics, Information, and Communication (ICEIC), pp. 1–4, January 2018
4. Waze Mobile. https://www.waze.com
5. WeatherLah, BuUuk Pte Ltd. http://www.weatherlah.com/
6. OpenSignal. http://opensignal.com/

7. Li, J., Cai, Z., Yan, M., Li, Y.: Using crowdsourced data in location-based social networks to explore influence maximization. In: INFOCOM, April 2016
8. Li, J., Cai, Z., Wang, J., Han, M., Li, Y.: Truthful incentive mechanisms for geographical position conflicting mobile crowdsensing systems. IEEE Trans. Comput. Soc. Syst. **5**, 324–334 (2018)
9. Wang, Y., Cai, Z., Zhan, Z., Gong, Y., Tong, X.: An optimization and auction based incentive mechanism to maximize social welfare for mobile crowdsourcing. IEEE Trans. Comput. Soc. Syst. 1–16 (2019, early access)
10. Cai, Z., Zheng, X., Yu, J.: A differential-private framework for urban traffic flows estimation via taxi companies. IEEE Trans. Ind. Inf. (2019, accepted)
11. Cai, Z., Zheng, X.: A private and efficient mechanism for data uploading in smart cyber-physical systems. IEEE Trans. Netw. Sci. Eng. (2018, early access)
12. Wang, Y., Cai, Z., Tong, X., Gao, Y.: Truthful incentive mechanism with location privacy-preserving for mobile crowdsourcing systems. Comput. Netw. **135**, 32–43 (2018)
13. Wang, Y., Cai, Z., Yin, G., Gao, Y., Tong, X., Wu, G.: An incentive mechanism with privacy protection in mobile crowdsourcing systems. Comput. Netw. **102**, 157–171 (2016)
14. Zhang, X., Yang, Z., Liu, Y., Li, J., Ming, Z.: Toward efficient mechanisms for mobile crowdsensing. IEEE Trans. Veh. Technol. **66**, 1760–1771 (2017)
15. Wang, H., Guo, S., Cao, J., Guo, M.: MELODY: a long-term dynamic quality-aware incentive mechanism for crowdsourcing. IEEE Trans. Parallel Distrib. Syst. **29**, 901–914 (2017)
16. Luo, T., Kanhere, S.S., Huang, J., Das, S.K., Wu, F.: Sustainable incentives for mobile crowdsensing: auctions, lotteries, and trust and reputation systems. IEEE Commun. Mag. **55**, 68–74 (2017)
17. Ni, J., Zhang, A., Lin, X., She, X.S.: Security, privacy, and fairness in fog-based vehicular crowdsensing. IEEE Commun. Mag. **55**, 146–162 (2017)
18. Sun, X., Li, J., Zheng, W., Liu, H.: Towards a sustainable incentive mechanism for participatory sensing. In: IEEE First International Conference on Internet-of-Things Design and Implementation (IoTDI), pp. 49–60, April 2016
19. Zhu, X., An, J., Yang, M., Xiang, L., Yang, Q., Gui, X.: A fair incentive mechanism for crowdsourcing in crowd sensing. IEEE Internet Things J. **3**, 1364–1372 (2016)
20. Huang, H., Xin, Y., Sun, Y., Yang, W.: A truthful double auction mechanism for crowdsensing systems with max-min fairness. In: IEEE Wireless Communications and Networking Conference (WCNC), pp. 1–6, March 2017
21. Duan, Z., Tian, L., Yan, M., Cai, Z., Han, Q., Yin, G.: Practical incentive mechanisms for IoT-based mobile crowdsensing systems. IEEE Access **5**, 20383–20392 (2017)
22. Myerson, R.: Optimal auction design. Math. Oper. Res. **6**(1), 58–73 (1981)
23. Singer, Y.: Budget feasible mechanisms. In: IEEE 51st Annual Symposium on Foundations of Computer Science (FOCS), pp. 765–774, October 2010
24. Liu, C.-C., Wang, S., Ma, L., Cheng, X., Bie, R., Yu, J.: Mechanism design games for thwarting malicious behavior in crowdsourcing applications. In: INFOCOM, April 2017
25. Capurso, N., Mei, B., Song, T., Cheng, X., Jiguo, Y.: A survey on key fields of context awareness for mobile devices. J. Netw. Comput. Appl. **118**, 44–60 (2018)

Evolutionary Game Based Gateway Selection Algorithm in Cyber-Physical System

Hao Wang[(✉)]

Heilongjiang University, Harbin 150080, Heilongjiang, China
wanghao@hlju.edu.cn

Abstract. Considering performance and safety of cyber-physical system (CPS), data transmission between devices arranged within the same working area and outside network must be achieved by gateways. Therefore, to guarantee the reliability of the system, one working area is often covered by multiple gateways, and each gateway has limited bandwidth. For its own benefit, each device intends to occupy as much bandwidth as possible. That will occur imbalance and degrade performance of the system. In this paper, we propose an evolutionary game based gateway selection algorithm which can guarantee the fairness among devices in CPS. The load balancing of gateways can also be achieved by using this algorithm. By using evolutionary game theory, we analyze the behaviors of devices when they obtained less bandwidth than the average. The bandwidth allocation model of gateways has been proposed, and we formulate the gateway switching procedure of devices as an evolutionary game. We propose the replicator dynamics of this evolutionary game and analyze the existence and stabilization of the evolutionary equilibrium. Simulation results show that the proposed algorithm converges fast and minimize the maximal difference between any two devices of the same kind.

Keywords: Cyber-physical system · Benefit balancing · Gateway selection · Evolutionary game

1 Introduction

Cyber-physical system(CPS) consists of large number of different kinds of devices, which constitute heterogeneous communication networks [1], and they can be used to control the temperature or monitor wildlife of the designated area [2]. Devices in each heterogeneous network need to send data to external networks [3, 4]. In order to meet the communication and security requirements of the devices arranged in the work area [5, 6], multiple gateways have been placed in the same area to cover these devices collectively, at which point the device in the system can randomly select a gateway to connect and communicate with external network through this gateway.

The bandwidth of the gateway is limited, if there are too many devices have connected to the same gateway, then each device will only obtain a very limited bandwidth, which will seriously degrade the communication performance, and thus reduce the availability of the system. At the same time, if the number of devices connected to a gateway is too small, its bandwidth will be wasted, which can also lead

© Springer Nature Switzerland AG 2019
E. S. Biagioni et al. (Eds.): WASA 2019, LNCS 11604, pp. 322–334, 2019.
https://doi.org/10.1007/978-3-030-23597-0_26

to reduced system performance [7]. As pointed in [8], load balancing can improve the communication capability of the network. If we consider multiple gateways in a zone as multiple different network access points, load balancing can prevent these gateways from generating congestion or decreasing communication performance [9]. Multi-gateway load balancing can be implemented in two ways, one is the network-driven approach [10, 11], the other is the user-driven approach. In a network-driven approach, there is a central controller in the network that assigns all communication resources to each device in the system. In the user-driven way, the gateway selection algorithm is arranged on each device, and the device decides which gateway to choose on their own. Considering the characteristics of the CPS, complex working environment and limited computing ability and energy [12–15], it is obvious that the user-driven method is more suitable. At the same time, to obtain more communication bandwidth, device who gets a lower bandwidth than others will continue switching its connected gateway until the device obtains more bandwidth than or equal to the average bandwidth available for all devices.

Some gateway allocation research focus on increasing the benefit of single user in the system. In [16] the gateway selection mechanism among all candidate gateways as essential component to interconnect MANET and Internet is considered. In [17] a Dynamic DAP Selection Algorithm is proposed for a meter in a smart grid to randomly select Data Aggregation Points (DAPs) from its DAP list and route the packet. This algorithm aims at increasing networking's robustness and resiliency. In [18], authors propose a cooperative traffic transmission algorithm based on fuzzy logic in a joint LTE Advanced-VANET hybrid network architecture where an elected gateway will connect a source vehicle to the LTE advanced infrastructure. These work do not consider the mutual effect between different users and they focus on the problem of how to designate a gateway node among all the users.

This paper utilizes the user-driven method to realize the load balance of the system communication network. We ensure same kind of devices obtains equal communication resources by using dynamic evolutionary game based gateway selection algorithm.

Our contributions in this paper are as follows.

- We propose the problem of benefit balanced gateway selection in CPS. And we formulate the problem as a dynamic evolutionary game.
- We analyze the existence of evolutionary equilibrium of the dynamic evolutionary game, and prove that the evolutionary equilibrium state of the evolutionary game is stable.
- A gateway selection algorithm based on evolutionary game is proposed. And the effectiveness of the algorithm is validated by simulations.

The rest of this paper is organized as follows. We discuss the related work in Sect. 2. Problem statement are given in Sect. 3. In Sect. 4 we formulate the problem as an evolutionary game. In Sect. 5, we discuss the evolutionary equilibrium. We propose a benefit balanced gateway selection algorithm in Sect. 6. Simulation is in Sect. 7. And conclusions are given in Sect. 8.

2 Related Work

Most research are forces on load-balancing or energy-balancing of gateways, such as [19–23]. These work are intended to address the load balancing and net-work life problems of gateways. And the income-balance of devices in the network is not in their concern.

Some studies on network selection have some similarity with our work, but we are focused on different situations. Network selection has been studied using game theory via several models including noncooperative game [24–26]. In [24] the authors propose a study to capture the dynamics among end users and network operators in the pro-cesses of network selection and resource allocation. The authors resort to non-cooperative game theory to model the competition among multiple end users in accessing shared wireless networks. In [25] the authors study the dynamics of network selection in heterogeneous wireless networks. In [26] the authors analyze the conver-gence properties of dynamics of network selection in heterogeneous wireless net-works. All the work mentioned above contribute a lot in investigating the network selection problem using game theory. However, these studies do not consider the benefit balance within the same group and the competition between different groups.

3 Problem Statement

In this paper, we consider there are two different types of devices in an area which has been covered by multiple gateways. All the devices need to connect to the external network through a gateway. The bandwidth available to each device connected to a gateway is determined by the number of connected devices and the bandwidth of the gateway. In the example given in Fig. 1, this area has been covered by 4 gateways, and there are two different types of device A and B in it. Each device needs to connect to one gateways to exchange data with the external network. Devices A and B are equipped with different kinds of wireless communication technology. And the same type of device utilizes orthogonal channels to avoid interference. At the initial stage of the system, each device randomly chooses a gateway to connect. Then, the device investigates the bandwidth available to its same kind of device, and changes the connected gateway to gain more bandwidth.

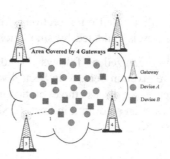

Fig. 1. An example of network model with 4 gateways

Problem Description. Given two kinds of devices A and B, and the gateway G covering them. Each device in A and B are free to select gateways in G to connect. All the devices connected to one gateway share the total bandwidth of it. At the initial stage, each device randomly chooses a gateway to connect. The benefit-balanced gateway selection problem is how each device adjusts its connected gate-way to minimize the maximum bandwidth difference between any two devices of the same kind of devices.

4 Evolutionary Game Formulation

4.1 Games Formulation

We describe a benefit-balanced gateway selection problem as an evolutionary game, and the formulation of benefit-balanced gateway selection game is the following,

- *Players*: devices which can choose a gateway covered the work area.
- *Population*: All devices of the same kind form a population.
- *Strategies*: Gateways that can be chosen by a device.
- *Utilities*: Function U_i for each device.

We denote device's utility gain from gateway i by $f_i = U(w_i)$, where w_i is the bandwidth that a device obtained from gateway i. Considering there two kinds of devices A and B are placed in the same area, we assume that $W_{ai} + W_{bi} = W_i$, where W_{ai} is the bandwidth obtained by device A, and W_{bi} is the bandwidth obtained by device B. W_i is the total available bandwidth of gateway i. The same kind of devices connected to the gateway obtains same bandwidth of the gateway, $w_{ai} = W_{ai}/n_{ai}$ and $w_{bi} = W_{bi}/n_{bi}$. Devices A and B connected to the same gateway will compete for the bandwidth. And if there is only one device connected to the gateway, this device will get the full bandwidth of the gateway. Let $W_{ai}:W_{bi} = n_{ai}:n_{bi}$, and the bandwidth obtained by each device of A is,

$$w_{ai} = \frac{n_{ai} \cdot W_i/(n_{ai} + n_{bi})}{n_{ai}} = \frac{W_i}{n_{ai} + n_{bi}} \tag{1}$$

Let N_a and N_b represent the total number of devices A and B respectively, and x_{ai} and x_{bi} represent the percentage of the devices A and B who connected to gateway i. Such the total benefit of devices A connected to gateway i is,

$$f_{ai}(x) = u_a \cdot \frac{W_i}{N_a \cdot x_{ai} + N_b \cdot x_{bi}} \tag{2}$$

Where x represents the proportion vector of two kinds of device choosing different gateways.

4.2 Replicator Dynamics of Gateway Selection Game

In this paper, we describe the situation that different kinds of device make a competition for bandwidth by connecting different gateways as an evolutionary game, and the gateways available to one device is the strategies it can take. The game is repeated. And we assume that before one device changes its gateway, it has the information about the average gain of the same type of device and the benefit after connecting to a new gateway. Thus, the replicator dynamics is,

$$\dot{x}_{Si} = x_{Si}[f_{Si}(x) - \bar{f}_S(x)] \tag{3}$$

Where x_{Si} is the percentage of device S who have connect to gateway g_i. The average benefit of same kind devices is,

$$\bar{f}_S(x) = \sum x_{Si} f_{Si}(x) \tag{4}$$

According to the replication dynamics of the device, when a gateway can provide more benefit than the average to the device, the proportion of devices selected for this gateway will increase, otherwise the device will leave the gateway. Such each device has the motivation to choose a higher-benefit gateway. At the beginning, each device will randomly connect a gateway, for one kind of device we have $\sum_i x_{Si}(0) = 1$, after time t, devices reconnect to higher-benefit gateways, since the number of device is fixed, and each device must connect to one gateway, we have $\sum_i x_{Si}(t) = 1$ and,

$$\sum_i \dot{x}_{Si} = \sum_i x_{Si}[f_{Si}(x) - \bar{f}_S(x)] = 0 \tag{5}$$

5   Evolutionary Equilibrium and System Stability

5.1   Evolutionary Equilibrium

A stable state in the process of system evolution means the population of the system no longer changes its state. In this case, the strategy set of the strategies adopted by each population is called evolutionary equilibrium. The evolutionary equilibrium of a system can also be defined as a fixed point in the replication dynamics [27], which consists of the proportion of all participants in the population who choose different strategies in each population. In this paper, the evolutionary equalization is considered as the solution of the evolutionary game of gateway selection. The above definition shows that when the system comes to evolutionary equilibrium, the proportion of participants who choose each strategy in the population will no longer change. Thus, we have $\dot{x}_{Si} = 0$. So once the system has evolved into equilibrium, the participants in the population will not change the strategy of their choice, and each participant' benefit will be equal to the average of all the participants in the population, so when the system reaches an evolutionary equilibrium, the fairness of the participants in the population can be satisfied.

By substituting (2) and (4) into (3), and so did devices B, we have,

$$\dot{x}_{ai} = x_{ai}\left[u_a \cdot \frac{W_i}{N_a \cdot x_{ai} + N_b \cdot x_{bi}} - \sum_i x_{ai}f_{ai}(x)\right] \tag{6}$$

$$\dot{x}_{bi} = x_{bi}\left[u_b \cdot \frac{W_i}{N_a \cdot x_{ai} + N_b \cdot x_{bi}} - \sum_i x_{bi}f_{bi}(x)\right] \tag{7}$$

According to the definition of evolutionary equilibrium, the percentage of the total number of participants in the same group who chose different strategies during the evolutionary equalization is the solution x_{ai} and x_{bi} of the equation set, which let (6) and (7) equal to zero respectively. Obviously, there are two kinds of evolution equilibria in this replication dynamic, one is boundary equilibrium, the other is internal equilibrium [28]. Boundary equalization means that all the participants in a group choose the same strategy, in which $x_{ai} = 1$, and $x_{aj} = 0$ when $j \neq i$. Obviously, the boundary equilibrium is unstable, if any participant in the population changes its strategy, the system will never return to the boundary equilibrium. Internal equilibrium means that the participants of a population do not choose the same strategy, in which $0 < x_{ai} < 1$.

5.2 Stability of Evolutionary Equilibrium

Because system state change in evolutionary game can be expressed by system replicator dynamics, the stability of evolutionary equilibrium can be judged by Lyapunov stability criterion. According to Lyapunov first law, when judging the stability of the nonlinear system at the equilibrium point, the eigenvalue of the Jacobian matrix derived from the equilibrium point of the equation of state is needed, and if the eigenvalues have negative real parts, the system is stable. This method can be used to analyze the stability of evolutionary equilibrium state in gateway selection evolutionary game. Next, we will analyze the stability of system evolution equilibrium when there are only two gateways in the system.

Assuming there are two gateways in the system, gateway 1 and gateway 2, then the benefit function of the system can be written as,

$$f_{a1}(x) = u_a \cdot \frac{W_1}{N_a \cdot x_{a1} + N_b \cdot x_{b1}} \tag{8}$$

$$f_{a2}(x) = u_a \cdot \frac{W_2}{N_a \cdot x_{a2} + N_b \cdot x_{b2}} = u_a \cdot \frac{W_2}{N_a(1 - x_{a1}) + N_b(1 - x_{b1})} \tag{9}$$

$$f_{b1}(x) = u_b \cdot \frac{W_1}{N_a \cdot x_{a1} + N_b \cdot x_{b1}} \tag{10}$$

$$f_{b2}(x) = u_b \cdot \frac{W_2}{N_a \cdot x_{a2} + N_b \cdot x_{b2}} = u_b \cdot \frac{W_2}{N_a(1 - x_{a1}) + N_b(1 - x_{b1})} \tag{11}$$

Theorem 1. In a gateway selection evolutionary game with only two gateways and two populations, the internal evolutionary equilibrium is Lyapunov stable.

Proof. If there are only two optional gateways in the system, the replication dynamics of the system can be written as

$$\dot{x}_{a1} = x_{a1}[f_{a1} - \bar{f}_a] = x_{a1}(1 - x_{a1})(f_{a1} - f_{a2}) \tag{12}$$

$$\dot{x}_{b1} = x_{b1}[f_{b1} - \bar{f}_b] = x_{b1}(1 - x_{b1})(f_{b1} - f_{b2}) \tag{13}$$

Since $\sum_i \dot{x}_{Si} = 0$, the replication dynamics of the system can be represented by (12) and (13). Using φ_1 and φ_2 to represent the right part of (12) and (13), and the partial derivatives of (12) are,

$$\frac{\partial \varphi_1}{\partial x_{a1}} = x_{a1}(1 - x_{a1}) \times \left(\frac{\partial f_{a1}}{\partial x_{a1}} - \frac{\partial f_{a2}}{\partial x_{a1}}\right) + (1 - 2x_{a1})(f_{a1} - f_{a2}) \tag{14}$$

$$\frac{\partial \varphi_1}{\partial x_{b1}} = x_{a1}(1 - x_{a1}) \times \left(\frac{\partial f_{a1}}{\partial x_{b1}} - \frac{\partial f_{a2}}{\partial x_{b1}}\right) \tag{15}$$

When the system is in an evolutionary equilibrium, by definition, since $f_{a1} = f_{a2}$ and $f_{b1} = f_{b2}$, we have $(1 - 2x_{a1})(f_{a1} - f_{a2}) = 0$ and $(1 - 2x_{b1})(f_{b1} - f_{b2}) = 0$. Then, we calculate $\partial f_{a1}/\partial x_{a1}$, $\partial f_{a2}/\partial x_{a1}$, $\partial f_{a1}/\partial x_{b1}$, $\partial f_{a2}/\partial x_{b1}$ and $\partial f_{b1}/\partial x_{a1}$, $\partial f_{b2}/\partial x_{a1}$, $\partial f_{b1}/\partial x_{b1}$, $\partial f_{b2}/\partial x_{b1}$. We only list $\partial f_{a1}/\partial x_{a1}$, $\partial f_{a2}/\partial x_{a2}$ for short,

$$\frac{\partial f_{a1}}{\partial x_{a1}} = -u_a \cdot \frac{W_1 \cdot N_a}{(N_a \cdot x_{a1} + N_b \cdot x_{b1})^2} \tag{16}$$

$$\frac{\partial f_{a2}}{\partial x_{a1}} = u_a \cdot \frac{W_2 \cdot N_a}{[N_a(1 - x_{a1}) + N_b(1 - x_{b1})]^2} \tag{17}$$

Thus, for any $x_{a1} \in (0, 1)$ and $x_{b1} \in (0, 1)$, there are $(\partial f_{a1}/\partial x_{a1}) < 0$, $(\partial f_{a2}/\partial x_{a1}) > 0$, $(\partial f_{a1}/\partial x_{b1}) < 0$, $(\partial f_{a2}/\partial x_{b1}) > 0$, $(\partial f_{b2}/\partial x_{b1}) > 0$. Thus, we have, $\partial \varphi_1/\partial x_{a1} < 0$, $\partial \varphi_1/\partial x_{b1} < 0$, $\partial \varphi_2/\partial x_{a1} < 0$, $\partial \varphi_2/\partial x_{b1} < 0$. Let the Jacobian matrix of system replication dynamic at equilibrium point is A, and its eigenvector is λ, thus,

$$|I\lambda - \mathbf{A}| = \left|I\lambda - \frac{\partial \varphi}{\partial x}\right| = \begin{vmatrix} \lambda - \frac{\partial \varphi_1}{\partial x_{a1}} & \frac{\partial \varphi_1}{\partial x_{b1}} \\ \frac{\partial \varphi_2}{\partial x_{a1}} & \lambda - \frac{\partial \varphi_2}{\partial x_{b1}} \end{vmatrix} = \lambda^2 - \left(\frac{\partial \varphi_1}{\partial x_{a1}} + \frac{\partial \varphi_2}{\partial x_{b1}}\right)\lambda = 0 \tag{18}$$

From the above, we have $\lambda_1 = 0$, $\lambda_2 < 0$. Thus, the system at the equilibrium point is Lyapunov stability.   □

Theorem 2. In a gateway selection evolutionary game with only two gateways, if only one kind of devices can change its strategy, the internal evolutionary equilibrium of the system is asymptotically stable.

Proof. Assuming devices A can change their strategies. According to (12), when xa1 is not 0 or 1, the evolutionary game dynamics is,

$$\dot{x}_{a1} = x_{a1}(1 - x_{a1})(f_{a1} - f_{a2}) \tag{19}$$

Since there is only one state equation, the system will be asymptotically stable at the equilibrium point when Jacobian Matrix is negative. Let the left side of (19) be $\varphi(x)$, we have,

$$\frac{\partial \varphi}{\partial x_{a1}} = x_{a1}(1 - x_{a1}) \times \left(\frac{\partial f_{a1}}{\partial x_{a1}} - \frac{\partial f_{a2}}{\partial x_{a1}} \right) + (1 - 2x_{a1})(f_{a1} - f_{a2}) \tag{20}$$

From the procedure of Theorem 1, we know for any $x_{a1} \in (0, 1)$ we have $\partial \varphi_1 / \partial x_{a1} < 0$. So the internal evolutionary equilibrium of the system is asymptotically stable at the equilibrium point.   □

The stability of gateway selection evolutionary game with multiple gateways can be analyzed by above approach, but its calculated amount is huge. Through the simulation, if there is only one kind of device can change its strategy, the system is asymptotically stable with more than two gateways.

6   Gateway Selection Algorithm Based on Evolutionary Game

In the initial state, the participants in the population will randomly select a policy, which is, the device will randomly select a gateway. Then each participant will compare its own earnings with the average earnings of population. And if their own benefit is lower than the average, the participants will change the policy. As the participants in the population constantly adjust their strategies, the system will reach the evolutionary equilibrium.

According to the replication dynamics, this section presents a gateway selection algorithm based on evolutionary game. We assume that there is a cluster-head device in each kind of device, and these devices will transmit the obtained bandwidth and the connected gateway information to the cluster-head. The cluster-head device will calculate the average bandwidth and broadcast the information to each device in its population. The details of this procedure are illustrated in Algorithm 1.

Algorithm 1	*Evolutionary Game Based Gateway Selection Algorithm*
Input:	Set of same kind of device $A=\{a_1, a_2, ..., a_n\}$, Set of gateways $G=\{g_1,g_2,...,g_k\}$
Output:	Strategy of each device, $S=\{s_i=<a_i, g_j>\| 1\leq i\leq n, 1\leq j\leq k\}$
1.	All devices randomly select a gateway in G to connect
2.	Each device transmits the bandwidth it obtains and the connected gateway information to the cluster head device
3.	Wait for the average benefit $\overline{f}_a$ sent by the cluster head device
4.	**for** each device in A
5.	**if** $f_i < \overline{f}_a$ and $f_i < f_j$ when connect to gateway j
6.	device switch gateway from i to j
7.	**end if**
8.	**end for**
9.	**if** there is some device a has changed its gateway
10.	go to step 2
11.	**else**
12.	Return S

7   Simulation Results

This section examines the performance of the gateway selection evolutionary game algorithm, including convergence time of the algorithm, the bandwidth obtained by devices when the system reaches an evolutionary equilibrium, etc. In our simulation, bandwidth of gateways is set to 20 Mbps, and let $u_a = u_b = 1$. In this setting, the two kinds of devices will achieve an evolutionary equilibrium at the same time, so in this chapter of the experiment, only devices A can change its strategy. The number of devices B in the simulation is set to 10. Figures 2 and 3 show the average benefit of devices A when the system reached evolutionary equilibrium in different situations. In Fig. 2, there are 5 gateways and the number of devices A rise from 10 to 20. We can see from Fig. 2, Although the number of device is different, the system all achieve an evolutionary equilibrium after a few switches. As the number of devices increases, the system requires more time to come to a balanced state, since more devices need to adjust their strategy. We can also see from Figs. 2 and 3 that the average benefit of A is not monotonous. This is because sometime in order to increase its own benefit, a device will change its strategy from gateways connected by some device B to those only connected by device A. And sometimes it's the opposite. Figure 4 shows a CDF curve of the time required for the system to achieve an evolutionary equilibrium with the different number of devices. We can see from the diagram, as the number of devices increases, the time required for the system to achieve an evolutionary equilibrium increases significantly. But it's worth note that, in 90% case, it takes no more than one switch per device to reach the equilibrium.

In Figs. 5 and 6, there are 5 gateways, 15 devices *A* and 10 devices *B* in the system. Figure 5 shows the proceeds of devices connected to different gateways along with the evolution of the system. Avg. Benefit of G1 represents the average benefit of devices connected to gateway g1. Figure 6 shows the trajectories of the maximum, minimum, and average benefits of devices A. In this graph, the minimum income of devices A gradually moves towards the average benefit in the process of evolution, and the average benefit is rising meanwhile the maximum benefit of devices is going down. Eventually all the devices proceed the same benefit. Therefore, the gateway selection evolutionary game algorithm has excellent performance in ensuring the fairness of the distribution within the population.

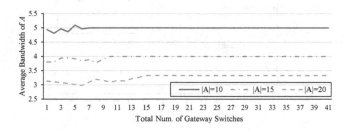

Fig. 2. Convergence of evolutionary gateway selection algorithm ($|G| = 5$)

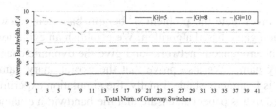

Fig. 3. Convergence of evolutionary gateway selection algorithm ($|A| = 15$)

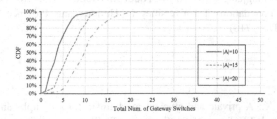

Fig. 4. CDF of time to converge ($|G| = 15$)

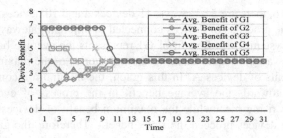

Fig. 5. Trajectories of benefit of different strategies of device A

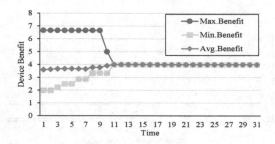

Fig. 6. Trajectories of maximal, minimal and average benefit of device A

8 Conclusions

In this paper, we investigate the problem of benefit balanced gateway selection and propose an evolution game based algorithm. We establish an evolutionary game model for the devices in heterogeneous networks and give the dynamic characteristic formula of the evolutionary game. We also prove that the evolutionary game of two hetero-geneous networks is Lyapunov stable. Finally, the simulation experiment show that the algorithm presented in this paper can ensure that the bandwidth obtained by the devices is balanced, and the evolutionary game converge quickly.

Acknowledgements. This work is supported in part by the Fundamental Research Foundation of Universities in Heilongjiang Province for Youth Innovation Team (RCYJTD201805), Fundamental Research Foundation of Universities in Heilongjiang Province for Research and Innovation (KJCXZD201710).

References

1. Cai, Z., Zheng, X.: A private and efficient mechanism for data uploading in smart cyber-physical systems. IEEE Trans. Netw. Sci. Eng. (TNSE) (Accepted)
2. Yu, J., Wan, S., Cheng, X., Yu, D.: Coverage contribution area based k-coverage for wireless sensor networks. IEEE Trans. Veh. Technol. **66**(9), 8510–8523 (2017)
3. Cai, Z., Chen, Z., Lin, G.: A 3.4713-approximation algorithm for the capacitated multicast tree routing problem. Theor. Comput. Sci. **410**(52), 5415–5424 (2009)

4. Cai, Z., Lin, G., Xue, G.: Improved approximation algorithms for the capacitated multicast routing problem. In: Wang, L. (ed.) COCOON 2005. LNCS, vol. 3595, pp. 136–145. Springer, Heidelberg (2005). https://doi.org/10.1007/11533719_16

5. Cai, Z., He, Z.: Trading private range counting over big IoT data. In: The 39th IEEE International Conference on Distributed Computing Systems (ICDCS 2019). (2019, accepted)

6. Cai, Z., Goebel, R., Lin, G.: Size-constrained tree partitioning: approximating the multicast k-tree routing problem. Theoret. Comput. Sci. 412(3), 240–245 (2011)

7. Cheng, S., Cai, Z., Li, J., Gao, H.: Extracting kernel dataset from big sensory data in wireless sensor networks. IEEE Trans. Knowl. Data Eng. 29(4), 813–827 (2017)

8. Niyato, D., Hossain, E.: Call admission control for QoS provisioning in 4G wireless networks: issues and approaches. IEEE Netw. 19(5), 5–11 (2005)

9. He, Z., Cai, Z., Cheng, S., Wang, X.: Approximate aggregation for tracking quantiles and range countings in wireless sensor networks. Theoret. Comput. Sci. 607, 381–390 (2015)

10. Chu, Y.J., Tseng, C.P., Liao, K.C., et al.: The first order load-balanced algorithm with static fixing scheme for centralized WSN system in outdoor environmental monitoring. Sensors 2009, 1810–1813 (2009)

11. Nandiraju, D., Santhanam, L., Nandiraju, N., Agrawal, D.P.: Achieving load balancing in wireless mesh networks through multiple gateways. In: Proceedings of the 3rd IEEE International Conference on Mobile Adhoc and Sensor Systems, pp. 807–812. IEEE, Vancouver, BC, Canada (2006)

12. Li, J., Cheng, S., Cai, Z., Yu, J., Wang, C., Li, Y.: Approximate holistic aggregation in wireless sensor networks. ACM Trans. Sens. Netw. 13(2), 11 (2017)

13. Cheng, S., Cai, Z., Li, J.: Curve query processing in wireless sensor networks. IEEE Trans. Veh. Technol. 64(11), 5198–5209 (2015)

14. Yu, J., Huang, B., Cheng, X., Atiquzzaman, M.: Shortest link scheduling algorithms in wireless networks under the SINR model. IEEE Trans. Veh. Technol. 66(3), 2643–2657 (2017)

15. Zhang, X., Yu, J., Li, W., Cheng, X., Yu, D., Zhao, F.: Localized algorithms for Yao graph-based spanner construction in wireless networks under SINR. IEEE/ACM Trans. Netw. 25 (4), 2459–2472 (2017)

16. Yan, Y., Ci, L., Wang, Z., He, W.: QoS-based gateway selection in MANET with internet connectivity. In: Proceedings of the 15th International Conference on Advanced Communication Technology, pp. 195–199. IEEE, PyeongChang, South Korea (2013)

17. Okabayashi, V.H., Ribeiro, I.C.G., Passos, D.M., Albuquerque, C.V.N.: A resilient dynamic gateway selection algorithm based on quality aware metrics for smart grids. In: Proceedings of the 18th ACM International Conference on Modeling, Analysis and Simulation of Wireless and Mobile Systems, pp. 91–98. ACM, Cancun, Mexico (2015)

18. El Mouna Zhioua, G., Tabbane, N., Labiod, H., Tabbane, S.: A fuzzy multi-metric QoS-balancing gateway selection algorithm in a clustered VANET to LTE advanced hybrid cellular network. IEEE Trans. Veh. Technol. 64(2), 804–817 (2015)

19. Xu, X., Zhang, X., Khan, M., Dou, W., Xue, S., Yu, S.: A balanced virtual machine scheduling method for energy-performance trade-offs in cyber-physical cloud systems. Future Gener. Comput. Syst. (2017). https://doi.org/10.1016/j.future.2017.08.057

20. Zaman, R.U., Alam, H.M., Reddy, A.V.: Amelioration of load balanced gateway selection protocol in integrated internet-MANET. In: Proceedings of the 2nd International Conference on Contemporary Computing and Informatics, pp. 804–809. IEEE, Noida, India (2016)

21. Mehra, P.S., Doja, M.N., Alam, B.: Energy efficient self organising load balanced clustering scheme for heterogeneous WSN. In: Proceedings of the 2015 International Conference on Energy Economics and Environment, pp. 1–6. IEEE, Noida, India (2015)

22. Abd, M.A., Al-Rubeaai, S.F.M., Singh, B.K., Tepe, K.E., Benlamri, R.: Extending wireless sensor network lifetime with global energy balance. IEEE Sens. J. **15**(9), 5053–5063 (2015)

23. Zhao, M., Yang, Y., Wang, C.: Mobile data gathering with load balanced clustering and dual data uploading in wireless sensor networks. IEEE Trans. Mob. Comput. **14**(4), 770–785 (2015)

24. Malanchini, I., Cesana, M., Gatti, N.: Network selection and resource allocation games for wireless access networks. IEEE Trans. Mob. Comput. **12**(12), 2427–2440 (2013)

25. Keshavarz-Haddad, A., Aryafar, E., Wang, M., Chiang, M.: HetNets selection by clients: convergence, efficiency, and practicality. IEEE/ACM Trans. Networking **25**(1), 406–419 (2017)

26. Monsef, E., Keshavarz-Haddad, A., Aryafar, E., Saniie, J., Chiang, M.: Convergence properties of general network selection games. In: Proceedings of 2015 International Conference on Computer Communications, pp. 1445–1453. IEEE, Hong Kong (2015)

27. Niyato, D., Hossain, E.: Dynamics of network selection in heterogeneous wireless networks: an evolutionary game approach. IEEE Trans. Veh. Technol. **58**(4), 2008–2017 (2009)

28. Semasinghe, P., Hossain, E., Zhu, K.: An evolutionary game for distributed resource allocation in self-organizing small cells. IEEE Trans. Mob. Comput. **14**(2), 274–287 (2015)

Wide and Recurrent Neural Networks for Detection of False Data Injection in Smart Grids

Yawei Wang[1], Donghui Chen[2], Cheng Zhang[1(✉)], Xi Chen[3], Baogui Huang[4], and Xiuzhen Cheng[1]

[1] Department of Computer Science, The George Washington University, Washington DC, USA
{yawei,zhangchengcarl,cheng}@gwu.edu
[2] College of Information and Science Technology, Beijing Normal University, Beijing, People's Republic of China
dh_chen@mail.bnu.edu.cn
[3] GEIRI North America, San Jose, CA, USA
xi.chen@geirina.net
[4] School of Information Science and Engineering, Qufu Normal University, Rizhao, Shandong, People's Republic of China
hjbaogui@163.com

Abstract. A smart grid is a complex system using power transmission and distribution networks to connect electric power generators to consumers across a large geographical area. Due to their heavy dependencies on information and communication technologies, smart grid applications, such as state estimation, are vulnerable to various cyber-attacks. False data injection attacks (FDIA), considered as the most severe threats for state estimation, can bypass conventional bad data detection mechanisms and render a significant threat to smart grids. In this paper, we propose a novel FDIA detection mechanism based on a wide and recurrent neural networks (RNN) model to address the above concerns. Simulations over IEEE 39-bus system indicate that the proposed mechanism can achieve a satisfactory FDIA detection accuracy.

Keywords: Smart grid · False data injection · Deep learning

1 Introduction

As one of the most critical infrastructures of Internet of Things (IoT), smart grid, also called smart electrical/power grid, intelligent grid, or futuregrid, is designed for the next generation power system. Unlike the traditional electrical grids that send electrical power only in one direction, from a power plant to consumers, smart grid improves on the electricity network by using bi-direction flows of electricity and data that provides electrical uses, power interruptions, and instantaneous feedback on system-wide operations back to power plant and

© Springer Nature Switzerland AG 2019
E. S. Biagioni et al. (Eds.): WASA 2019, LNCS 11604, pp. 335–345, 2019.
https://doi.org/10.1007/978-3-030-23597-0_27

regional power grid operators. By utilizing advanced communication and data processing technologies, smart grids are capable of delivering power in more efficient ways and responding to wide-ranging conditions and events. However, the heavy dependence on communication technology and big data highlights the potential vulnerabilities of smart grids to various cyber attacks. Although many communication standards, official guidelines, regulatory laws have been published as countermeasures such as IEC 61850-90-5 and the NISTIR 7628 Guideline [7,11], cyber attack issues still remain in smart grids.

False data injection attacks (FDIA), as a typical type of cyber attacks proposed by Liu *et al.* [20], has been recently identified as one of the most critical malicious behaviours against state estimation in smart grids. In such attacks, the goal of the attackers is to circumvent the conventional bad data detection system and either compromise the communication infrastructures [32] or attack the measurement devices through manipulating system variable measurements. Without effective and robust detection systems, attackers may stealthily launch FDIA multiple times and render a significant threat to smart grids [5].

Therefore, this paper investigates a novel deep learning approach to detect well-constructed FDIA that are not detectable by conventional bad data detection systems in smart grids. In particular, we proposed a wide and recurrent neural networks (RNN) model to learn the state variable measurement data and identify the FDIA. Our wide and RNN model consists of a wide component with a fully connected layer of neural networks and an RNN component with two LSTM layers. Essentially, the wide component can learn the global knowledge and the RNN component can capture the sequential correlations among state variable measurement data. This model integrates the advantages of the wide component and the RNN component resulting in a satisfactory performance in the detection of FDIA. The major research contributions of the paper can be summarized as follows:

- We propose a wide and RNN model to detect FDIA in smart grids. To the best of our knowledge, this paper is among the pioneer studies of using wide and RNN model in FDIA detection research.
- Our model combine the power of memorization of the global knowledge brought by the wide component and generalization of the new temporal knowledge brought by the RNN model.
- We assess the proposed FDIA detection mechanism with existing FDIA patterns on IEEE 39-bus power system test case. The simulation results demonstrate a satisfactory FDIA detection accuracy.

The rest of the paper is organized as follows: Sect. 2 presents an overview on related literature. Our system model is introduced in Sect. 3. Section 4 presents the wide and RNN model for FDIA detection. We then give the simulation settings and results in Sect. 5. Finally, we conclude the paper in Sect. 6.

2   Related Work

A wide range of research focus on the security challenges in smart grids. In this section, we briefly cover two research directions that are mostly related to our work. We first present the existing works for the construction of FDIA. Then, we provide an overview of FDIA detection mechanisms proposed in the literature.

2.1   FDIA in Smart Grids

FDIAs in smart grids were first introduced in 2009 [20] and expanded in [21]. Following these initial work, many researchers tried to investigate more realistic and effective attacks against the state estimation in smart grids. Kosut et al. [14] proposed two regimes of FDIA based on the number of meters that the adversaries can access. In [35], the authors introduced a special type of FDIA focusing on load redistribution (LR) and analyzed the damage to smart grid operation in different time steps with different prior attacking knowledge. An energy deceiving attack proposed by Lin et al. [17] was another type of FDIA that aims to affect the distributed energy routing process. Kim et al. [13] characterized the FDIA problem into a series of linear programs. Moreover, a comprehensive review of the state of the art FDIA methods against modern smart grid systems were presented by Liang et al. [15].

2.2   Detection Mechanisms Against FDIA

At the same time, much research effort has been devoted to devising mechanisms against FDIA using various techniques. Some researchers solved the FDIA detection problem by using different optimization methods. For instance, in [19], according to the sparsity of malicious attacks, the authors formulated the FDIA detection as a sparse matrix optimization problem and solved it by using nuclear norm minimization and low rank matrix factorization methods. Instead of the complex optimization computing, threshold-based comparisons were more commonly utilized to identify the FDIA. The authors of [23] employed the Kalman filter and the Euclidean detector with a selected threshold to detect FDIA in the IEEE 9-bus system. Similarly, by comparing a residual signals with a predefined threshold, a resilient attack detection estimator was proposed in [8] to detect the FDIA in a networked cyber-physical system. However, an increasing number of FDIA can bypass these threshold-based detectors. To combat this challenge, learning-based methods have been utilized to detect FDIA [26]. In [6], the authors proposed a FDIA detector by utilizing the principle component analysis and support vector machine (SVM). In [9], Conditional Deep Belief Network (CDBN) was proposed to reveal attack features, which was then exploited to detect the FDIA on real-time measurements. Motivated by the strengths of these learning-based methods, we propose a FDIA detection mechanism based on a novel wide and recurrent neural network (RNN) model in this paper.

3   System Model

FDIA is considered as one of the most severe malicious behaviours rendering a significant threat to the grid [5]. Well-constructed FDIA can effectively circumvent the conventional residual-based bad data detection mechanism in direct current (DC) state estimation. In this section, we briefly present the state estimation method that is widely employed in power utilities [34], the conventional residual-based bad data detection mechanism [4], and the general patterns of successful FDIA in smart grids.

3.1   State Estimation

State estimation was first proposed by Schweppe and Wilde in 1970 [29–31] as a weighted least-squares (WLS) problem. The goal of state estimation is to estimate the smart grid's operating conditions by using real-time data collected from the measurement units [27]. Typical measurements include bus voltage, active and reactive power injections at each bus, and complex power flows on branches. Based on the DC power flow model, we can construct the relationship between system states $\mathbf{x}$ and measurements $\mathbf{z}$ as a linear model as follows:

$$\mathbf{z} = \mathbf{H}\mathbf{x} + \mathbf{e}, \tag{1}$$

where $\mathbf{x} \in \mathbb{R}^D$ contains the voltage amplitude and voltage phase angle at the buses, $\mathbf{z} \in \mathbb{R}^N$ is the vector of measurements, $\mathbf{H} \in \mathbb{R}^{N \times D}$ is a Jacobian topological matrix that maps the system states to the measurements, $\mathbf{e}$ is the measurement error (additive noise) vector that is commonly modeled by the Gaussian distribution, i.e., $\mathcal{N} \sim (0_{N \times 1}, \mathbf{W}^{-1})$ where $\mathbf{W} \equiv diag\{\mathbb{R}^{-1}\}$ with diagonal elements proportional to variance of each measurement noise. State estimation aims to find an estimated state $\hat{\mathbf{x}}$ that fits the measurement $\mathbf{z}$ the best and minimizes the WLS error [27] defined as follows:

$$\hat{\mathbf{x}} = \arg_x \min(\mathbf{z} - \mathbf{H}\mathbf{x})^T \mathbf{W}(\mathbf{z} - \mathbf{H}\mathbf{x}). \tag{2}$$

In particular, (2) can be solved by using iterative approximation methods such as the Newton-Raphson method [2].

3.2   Conventional Bad Data Detection

In smart grid systems, in order to solve the problem of potential malicious attacks and the sampling error of measurement units, a residual-based bad data detection mechanism was employed to protect state estimations [24]. Given the measurements $\mathbf{z}$, the estimated state vector $\hat{\mathbf{x}}$ can be computed as follows:

$$\hat{\mathbf{x}} = (\mathbf{H}^T \mathbf{W} \mathbf{H})^{-1} \mathbf{H}^T \mathbf{W} \mathbf{z} = \mathbf{Y}\mathbf{z}, \tag{3}$$

where $\mathbf{Y} = \mathbf{H}(\mathbf{H}^T \mathbf{W} \mathbf{H})^{-1} \mathbf{H}^T \mathbf{W}$. Therefore, the residue vector $\mathbf{r} = \mathbf{z} - \hat{\mathbf{z}}$ with threshold γ being calculated using the difference between the observed measurements $\mathbf{z}$ and the measurements inferred by the estimated system state $\hat{\mathbf{z}} = \mathbf{H}\hat{\mathbf{x}}$

for DC power flow model. If $\|\mathbf{r}\|_2 > \gamma$, the estimated state is considered being compromised by bad data; otherwise, the estimated state is trustworthy. According to the threshold test proposed in [33], the value of γ is typically determined by the hypothesis test $Pr\{\|\mathbf{r}\|_2^2 >= \gamma^2\} = \alpha$, where α is the confidence level.

3.3 False Data Injection Attacks

FDIA have been recently identified as a critical malicious data attacks in a smart grid system [14,21,35]. The objective for performing FDIA is to mislead the system operator to treat a compromised state vector $\hat{\mathbf{x}}_{comp} = \hat{\mathbf{x}}+\mathbf{c}$ as the normal estimated system state, where $\mathbf{c} \in \mathbb{R}^n$ is a non-zero vector. To achieve this, the potential attackers aim to change the received measurements to $\mathbf{z_a} = \mathbf{z} + \mathbf{a}$ at the control center, where $\mathbf{a} \in \mathbb{R}^m$ is the injected attack vector which can be constructed as

$$\mathbf{a} = \mathbf{H}(\hat{\mathbf{x}} + \mathbf{c}) - \mathbf{H}\hat{\mathbf{x}}. \tag{4}$$

In order to bypass the bad data detector, the Euclidean norm of the residual $\mathbf{r_a}$ needs to keep unchanged

$$\begin{aligned}
\|\mathbf{r_a}\|_2 &= \|\mathbf{z_a} - \mathbf{H}\hat{\mathbf{x}}\|_2 \\
&= \|\mathbf{z} + \mathbf{a} - \mathbf{H}(\hat{\mathbf{x}} + \mathbf{c})\|_2 \\
&= \|\mathbf{z} - \hat{\mathbf{z}}\|_2 \\
&= \|\mathbf{r}\|_2 ,
\end{aligned} \tag{5}$$

and the detailed injected attack vector construction is discussed in [28]. Therefore, the conventional residual-based bad data detection mechanism in DC state estimation might fail to detect FDIA that are well-constructed by adversaries who have prior knowledge of the gird including network topology $\mathbf{H}$ and estimated states $\hat{\mathbf{x}}$.

4 Proposed Wide and Recurrent Neural Networks for FDIA Detection

In the previous sections, we have shown that well-constructed FDIA can effectively bypass conventional bad data detection mechanisms and render a significant threat to smart grids. In this section, we propose a novel FDIA detection mechanism in DC power flow model based on the wide and deep learning framework [3].

In our approach, we feed the measurements $\mathbf{z}$ into the wide and RNN model consisting of the wide component and the RNN component. We explain them in details as follows.

4.1 Wide Component

The wide component is a fully connected layer of neural networks that is used to learn the global knowledge from the input data with a generalized linear model of the form $\mathbf{y} = \mathbf{w}^T\mathbf{x} + \mathbf{b}$, where y is the output; $\mathbf{x} = [x_1, x_2, ..., x_d]$ is the vector of d features; $\mathbf{w} = [w_1, w_2, ..., w_d]$ are the model parameters, and $\mathbf{b}$ is the bias. Motivated by the previous study [3,16], in the context of FDIA detection, we choose the wide component to learn the frequent co-occurrence of features by memorizing the estimated state estimation data $\hat{\mathbf{x}}$.

To be specific, every neuron in the wide component calculates the prediction score according to the following equation:

$$\mathbf{y_j} = \sum_{i=1}^{n} \mathbf{w}_{i,j}\hat{\mathbf{x}}_i + \mathbf{b}, \tag{6}$$

where $\mathbf{y_j}$ is the output in the jth neuron of the fully connected layer, n is the number of the input data $\hat{\mathbf{x}}$, $\mathbf{w}_{i,j}$ stands for the neuron weight between the ith input value and the jth neuron of the fully connected layer, and $\mathbf{b}$ is the bias. Within each neuron, the activation is given as follows:

$$a_j = f(\mathbf{y_j}) = \begin{cases} 0 & \text{if } \mathbf{y}_j \leq 0 \\ \mathbf{y}_j & \text{otherwise.} \end{cases} \tag{7}$$

where a_j is the output of the activation calculation and $f(\cdot)$ stands for the rectifier linear units (ReLUs) which can effectively prevent overfitting. During the process of backpropagation, the neural network updates the neuron weights $\mathbf{w}_{i,j}$ iteratively based on the loss value sent back from the loss function.

4.2 RNN Component

In our approach, we set the RNN component as a many-to-one RNN model that makes use of sequential information $x_{(1)}, ..., x_{(t)}$ to predict the output. The mathematical model of the RNN is as follows:

$$\mathbf{h}_t = f(\mathbf{h}_{t-1}, \mathbf{x}_t), \tag{8}$$

where $\mathbf{h}_t$ and $\mathbf{h}_{t-1}$ represent the current and previous hidden states, respectively; f stands for a nonlinear function, and $\mathbf{x}_t$ refers to the feature observed at time step t. The constructed RNN mode is composed of two LSTM layers with five LSTM cells each. Each LSTM cell consists of three gates which are forget gate f_t, input layer i_t, and output gate o_t [10]. The information flow of LSTM cell is modeled as follows:

$$f_t = \sigma(W_f \cdot [h_{t-1}, x_t] + b_f), \tag{9}$$
$$i_t = \sigma(W_i \cdot [h_{t-1}, x_t] + b_i), \tag{10}$$
$$\tilde{C}_t = tanh(W_c \cdot [h_{t-1}, x_t] + b_c), \tag{11}$$
$$C_t = f_t \circ C_{t-1} + i_t \circ \tilde{C}_t, \tag{12}$$
$$o_t = \sigma(W_o[h_{t-1}, x_t] + b_o), \tag{13}$$
$$h_t = o_t \circ tanh(C_t), \tag{14}$$

where x_t is the input vector; h_{t-1} is the previous cell output; C_{t-1} is the previous cell memory; h_t is the current cell output; C_t is the current cell memory, $\sigma(\cdot)$ and $tanh(\cdot)$ stand for the sigmoid function and the hyperbolic tangent function respectively, and $\circ$ denotes the element-wise product; W_f, W_c, W_i and W_o represent the weight vectors for forget gate f, candidate c, input gate i, and output gate o, respectively.

After constructing the wide component and the RNN component, we combine them using a weighted sum of their output as hidden features and fed them to a logistic loss function for joint training and prediction. Motivated by the original approach of the wide and deep learning model [3,36], we use backpropagation to train our network. In particular, we set our prediction model as:

$$P(\mathbf{Y} = 1|x) = \delta(\mathbf{W}[\mathbf{x}_{wide}, \mathbf{x}_{RNN}] + \mathbf{b}), \tag{15}$$

where $\mathbf{Y}$ is the binary label which represents that whether there is a FDIA or not in the input data; $\delta(\cdot)$ is the sigmoid function; $\mathbf{W}$ is the joint weights of the combined part of the network; $\mathbf{x}_{wide}$ and $\mathbf{x}_{RNN}$ stand for the features of the wide component and the RNN component, respectively, and $\mathbf{b}$ is the bias.

5 Case Study on IEEE 39-Bus System

In this section, we assess the performance of our proposed FDIA detection mechanism on IEEE 39-bus system, which is shown in Fig. 1, and compare results with those of other existing methods.

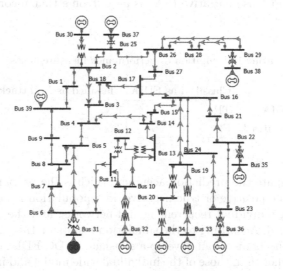

Fig. 1. IEEE 39-Bus system case [1]

5.1   Simulation Settings

The amount of data is critical to the results of neural networks. In this paper, we use DIgSILENT Power System Software [25] to conduct a simulation for generating 150,000 samples. Besides the above normal operational samples, we constructs another 50,000 FDIA samples based on the existing FDIA mechanism introduced in Sect. 3.3 that ensure they can bypass the conventional residual-based bad data detection. The configuration of the test system can be obtained from MATPOWER toolbox [37] including the network topology matrix $\mathbf{H}$. For cross validation, according to the common practice [12], the total 200,000 samples are randomly divided into training data, validation data, and testing data by 6:2:2 ratio. All simulations are conducted on the computer with an Intel Core i7-9700K CPU, an Nvidia RTX 2080 Ti GPU, 64-GB RAM, and 1000 watt power supply. The proposed wide and RNN model is constructed and trained using Tensorflow.

5.2   FDIA Detection Performance Evaluation

In this paper, we use statistical performance matrix to evaluate the proposed FDIA detection mechanism and other existing works. We label a power flow measurement with FDIA as positive class and a normal measurement as negative class. As shown in Table 1, the four measurement instances that we used are defined as follows: True Positive (TP) is an outcome that correctly predicts the positive class, True Negative (TN) is an outcome that correctly predicts the negative class, False Positive (FP) is an outcome that incorrectly predicts the positive class, and False Negative (FN) is an outcome that incorrectly predicts the negative class.

Table 1. Definition of performance measurements

	Classified as FDIA	Classified as No attack
FDIA	TP	FN
No attack	FP	TN

We first calculate the prediction accuracy which is the proportion of correct results, either true positive or true negative, in a population for individual wide neural networks, individual recurrent neural networks, and the wide and RNN model we proposed. According to the simulation results in Table 2, the proposed wide and RNN mechanism can develop a satisfactory DC FDIA detection accuracy which is higher than those of the individual wide model and individual RNN model. Meanwhile, the FP rate and the FN rate of the wide and RNN model are lower than that of the individual ones.

Furthermore, for a complete comparison, we also present the simulation results of the three other DC FDIA detection mechanisms proposed in [6,18,22].

The individual detection accuracy of all the selected detection mechanisms is presented in Table 3. It can be observed that the proposed FDIA detection mechanism can remarkably outperform the previous work. In particular, the detection accuracy is improved from around 70% by [22] to more than 95%.

Table 2. FDIA detection performance of the proposed mechanism

		Wide	RNN	Wide and RNN
Training cases	TP+TN	75.31% (112,965)	92.68% (139,020)	95.39% (143,085)
	FP	14.65% (21,975)	4.85% (7275)	3.75% (5623)
	FN	12.98% (19,476)	4.49% (6735)	3.37% (5048)
Testing cases	TP+TN	75.13% (37,565)	92.58% (46,290)	95.23% (47,615)
	FP	14.78% (7390)	4.92% (2460)	3.78% (1892)
	FN	13.18% (6588)	4.53% (2265)	3.45% (1724)

Table 3. Comparisons of FDIA detection performance

Mechanism	Accuracy
Euclidean detector [22]	72.68%
Sparse Optimization [18]	86.79%
SVM-based [6]	90.06%
Proposed Wide and RNN	95.23%

6   Conclusion

In this paper, we propose a wide and RNN model to detect FDIA in smart grids. In particular, our wide and RNN model consists of the wide component and the RNN component, which takes advantage of memorization of the global knowledge of the input measurements and generalization of the temporal correlation between the measurements at successive time instants. We conduct extensive simulations on IEEE 39-bus system demonstrating the effectiveness and correctness of the proposed mechanism. For future research, we will consider making our FDIA detector adaptive to alternating current (AC) state estimation.

Acknowledgment. This work was partially supported by the US National Science Foundation under grant IIS-1741279, and the National Science Foundation of China under grants 61832012, 61771289, and 61672321.

References

1. Athay, T., Podmore, R., Virmani, S.: A practical method for the direct analysis of transient stability. IEEE Trans. Power Apparatus Syst. **2**, 573–584 (1979)
2. Bertaccini, A., Duduk, B., Paltrinieri, S., Contaldo, N.: Phytoplasmas and phytoplasma diseases: a severe threat to agriculture. Am. J. Plant Sci. **5**(12), 1763 (2014)
3. Cheng, H.T., et al.: Wide & deep learning for recommender systems. In: Proceedings of the 1st Workshop on Deep Learning for Recommender Systems, pp. 7–10. ACM (2016)
4. Deng, R., Xiao, G., Lu, R.: Defending against false data injection attacks on power system state estimation. IEEE Trans. Industr. Inf. **13**(1), 198–207 (2017)
5. Deng, R., Xiao, G., Lu, R., Liang, H., Vasilakos, A.V.: False data injection on state estimation in power systems-attacks, impacts, and defense: a survey. IEEE Trans. Industr. Inf. **13**(2), 411–423 (2017)
6. Esmalifalak, M., Liu, L., Nguyen, N., Zheng, R., Han, Z.: Detecting stealthy false data injection using machine learning in smart grid. IEEE Syst. J. **11**(3), 1644–1652 (2017)
7. Grid, N.S.: Introduction to NISTIR 7628 guidelines for smart grid cyber security. Guideline, September 2010
8. Guan, Y., Ge, X.: Distributed attack detection and secure estimation of networked cyber-physical systems against false data injection attacks and jamming attacks. IEEE Trans. Signal Inf. Process. Over Netw. **4**(1), 48–59 (2018)
9. He, Y., Mendis, G.J., Wei, J.: Real-time detection of false data injection attacks in smart grid: a deep learning-based intelligent mechanism. IEEE Trans. Smart Grid **8**(5), 2505–2516 (2017)
10. Hochreiter, S., Schmidhuber, J.: Long short-term memory. Neural Comput. **9**(8), 1735–1780 (1997)
11. Ikbal, A., Aftab, M.A., Hussain, S.S.: Performance comparison of IEC 61850–90-5 and IEEE C37. 118.2 based wide area PMU communication networks. J. Mod. Power Syst. Clean Energy **4**(3), 487–495 (2016)
12. James, J., Hill, D.J., Lam, A.Y., Gu, J., Li, V.O.: Intelligent time-adaptive transient stability assessment system. IEEE Trans. Power Syst. **33**(1), 1049–1058 (2018)
13. Kim, T.T., Poor, H.V.: Strategic protection against data injection attacks on power grids. IEEE Trans. Smart Grid **2**(2), 326–333 (2011)
14. Kosut, O., Jia, L., Thomas, R.J., Tong, L.: Malicious data attacks on the smart grid. IEEE Trans. Smart Grid **2**(4), 645–658 (2011)
15. Liang, G., Zhao, J., Luo, F., Weller, S.R., Dong, Z.Y.: A review of false data injection attacks against modern power systems. IEEE Trans. Smart Grid **8**(4), 1630–1638 (2017)
16. Liang, Y., Cai, Z., Yu, J., Han, Q., Li, Y.: Deep learning based inference of private information using embedded sensors in smart devices. IEEE Netw. **32**(4), 8–14 (2018)
17. Lin, J., Yu, W., Yang, X., Xu, G., Zhao, W.: On false data injection attacks against distributed energy routing in smart grid. In: Proceedings of the 2012 IEEE/ACM Third International Conference on Cyber-Physical Systems, pp. 183–192. IEEE Computer Society (2012)
18. Liu, L., Esmalifalak, M., Ding, Q., Emesih, V.A., Han, Z.: Detecting false data injection attacks on power grid by sparse optimization. IEEE Trans. Smart Grid **5**(2), 612–621 (2014). https://doi.org/10.1109/TSG.2013.2284438

19. Liu, L., Esmalifalak, M., Ding, Q., Emesih, V.A., Han, Z.: Detecting false data injection attacks on power grid by sparse optimization. IEEE Trans. Smart Grid **5**(2), 612–621 (2014)
20. Liu, Y., Ning, P., Reiter, M.K.: False data injection attacks against state estimation in electric power grids. In: Proceedings of the 16th ACM Conference on Computer and Communications Security, CCS 2009, pp. 21–32. ACM, New York, NY, USA (2009). https://doi.org/10.1145/1653662.1653666, http://doi.acm.org/10.1145/1653662.1653666
21. Liu, Y., Ning, P., Reiter, M.K.: False data injection attacks against state estimation in electric power grids. ACM Trans. Inf. Syst. Secur. (TISSEC) **14**(1), 13 (2011)
22. Manandhar, K., Cao, X., Hu, F., Liu, Y.: Detection of faults and attacks including false data injection attack in smart grid using Kalman filter. IEEE Trans. Control Netw. Syst. **1**(4), 370–379 (2014). https://doi.org/10.1109/TCNS.2014.2357531
23. Manandhar, K., Cao, X., Hu, F., Liu, Y.: Detection of faults and attacks including false data injection attack in smart grid using Kalman filter. IEEE Trans. Control Netw. Syst. **1**(4), 370–379 (2014)
24. Monticelli, A.: Electric power system state estimation. Proc. IEEE **88**(2), 262–282 (2000)
25. PowerFactory-DIgSILENT Germany (2017). https://www.digsilent.de/en/powerfactory.html
26. Ozay, M., Esnaola, I., Vural, F.T.Y., Kulkarni, S.R., Poor, H.V.: Machine learning methods for attack detection in the smart grid. IEEE Trans. Neural Netw. Learn. Syst. **27**(8), 1773–1786 (2016)
27. Phadke, A.G., Thorp, J.S., Karimi, K.: State estimlatjon with phasor measurements. IEEE Transactions on Power Systems **1**(1), 233–238 (1986)
28. Rahman, M.A., Mohsenian-Rad, H.: False data injection attacks against nonlinear state estimation in smart power grids. In: 2013 IEEE Power & Energy Society General Meeting, pp. 1–5. IEEE (2013)
29. Schweppe, F.C.: Power system static-state estimation, Part III: Implementation. IEEE Trans. Power Appar. Syst. **PAS–89**(1), 130–135 (1970)
30. Schweppe, F.C., Rom, D.B.: Power system static-state estimation, Part II: approximate model. IEEE Trans. Power Appar. Syst. **PAS–89**(1), 125–130 (1970)
31. Schweppe, F.C., Wildes, J.: Power system static-state estimation, Part I: exact model. IEEE Trans. Power Appar. Syst. **PAS–89**(1), 120–125 (1970)
32. Ten, C.W., Manimaran, G., Liu, C.C.: Cybersecurity for critical infrastructures: attack and defense modeling. IEEE Trans. Syst. Man Cybern.-Part A: Syst. Hum. **40**(4), 853–865 (2010)
33. Wu, F.F., Liu, W.E.: Detection of topology errors by state estimation (power systems). IEEE Trans. Power Syst. **4**(1), 176–183 (1989). https://doi.org/10.1109/59.32475
34. Wu, F.F.: Power system state estimation: a survey. Int. J. Electr. Power Energy Syst. **12**(2), 80–87 (1990)
35. Yuan, Y., Li, Z., Ren, K.: Modeling load redistribution attacks in power systems. IEEE Trans. Smart Grid **2**(2), 382–390 (2011)
36. Zheng, Z., Yang, Y., Niu, X., Dai, H.N., Zhou, Y.: Wide and deep convolutional neural networks for electricity-theft detection to secure smart grids. IEEE Trans. Industr. Inf. **14**(4), 1606–1615 (2018)
37. Zimmerman, R.D., Murillo-Sanchez, C.E.: Matpower 4.1 user's manual. Power Systems Engineering Research Center, Cornell University, Ithaca, NY (2011)

ONE-Geo: Client-Independent
IP Geolocation Based on Owner
Name Extraction

Yucheng Wang[1,2], Xu Wang[1,2], Hongsong Zhu[1,2(✉)], Hai Zhao[3], Hong Li[1,2],
and Limin Sun[1,2]

[1] School of Cyber Security, University of Chinese Academy of Sciences,
Beijing, China
[2] Beijing Key Laboratory of IOT Information Security Technology,
Institute of Information Engineering, CAS, Beijing, China
zhuhongsong@iie.ac.cn
[3] School of Computer Science and Engineering, Northeastern University,
Shenyang, China

Abstract. Client-independent Internet Protocol address (IP) geolocation is a critical problem in the Internet World, of which the accuracy
is based on highly reliable landmarks. However, most existing methods focus heavily on improving the location estimating method rather
than improving the quality and quantity of landmarks. Without sufficient landmarks of high quality, they face difficulties when attempting
to further improve accuracy. Even though some existing mining based
methods dig massive landmarks from online web resources, most landmarks are of low quality because they do not make full use of these open
resources. In this paper, we propose ONE-Geo, a methodology to mine
highly reliable landmarks as much as possible by extracting the owner
name of web servers. For a given target IP, ONE-Geo extracts the real
owner name from web page information and registration records. Utilizing this clue, ONE-Geo determines the correct location by searching
address information on an organization knowledge graph and conduct
inference. Experimental results show that ONE-Geo achieves a median
error distance of 463 m on 165 web servers and a median error distance
of 7.7 km on 721 nodes that do not host a website. For web servers,
ONE-Geo outperforms existing methods and several commercial tools.
To be specific, 66.1% nodes are geolocated by ONE-Geo with an error less
than 1 km, which is two times as many as Street-level Geolocation(SLG),
which is one of the best existing methods on IP geolocating.

Keywords: IP geolocation · Network measurement ·
Landmark mining

1 Introduction

The ability to determine the geographical location of a networking device is
essential for many location-aware applications, such as content personalization,

© Springer Nature Switzerland AG 2019
E. S. Biagioni et al. (Eds.): WASA 2019, LNCS 11604, pp. 346–357, 2019.
https://doi.org/10.1007/978-3-030-23597-0_28

investigating crimes, and location-based access limitation. Even though existing client-dependent geolocation methods are able to achieve high accuracy on locating client devices based on GPS, cellular or Wi-Fi, the client support is a must, which makes them irrelevant in many applications, such as location-based targeted advertising and location-based access restrictions.

As for client-independent methods, they mainly fall into two categories: (1) data mining-based approaches and (2) network measurement-based geolocation approaches. However, most existing approaches can only guarantee a coarse-grained accuracy at city-level, which can hardly meet the demands mentioned above. In most cases, the low precision of measurement-based methods results from the scarceness of landmarks with high precision location. Even though data mining-based IP geolocation approaches can provide solutions to get massive landmarks, they can only provide landmarks of low quality. Since using cloud hosts is a trend today, previous methods that generate landmarks by directly mapping an address that is revealed on a web page to the web site's IP is no longer reliable anymore. Plus, as the structure of websites is becoming more complicated, it is increasingly difficult to mine address information from web pages.

In this paper, we propose ONE-Geo to mine as many highly reliable landmarks as possible by extracting the owner names of web servers. ONE-Geo is based on three findings. (1) Owner names are more commonly shown on web pages than address information. Almost all web pages explicitly expose indications of the owner of the website, such as organization name in the title, copyright information and logo tag. (2) If a website is hosted on the cloud, the owner name usually appears in WHOIS registration records. Even though the WHOIS database only returns the address of the head office for the whole IP block, the organization name can be utilized as a clue to the location. (3) Given the owner name of an IP, it is easy to narrow down its location to several potential coordinates by using organization-location knowledge graph (OKG).

The main contributions of this paper are summarized as follows:

(1) We propose an efficient method to mine landmarks of high quality without any measurement (ONE-Geo Alpha). Because the structures of websites are more complicated today than they have ever been in the past, it is becoming increasingly difficult to mine address information from web pages. Hence, our highly efficient method can be useful for a variety of IP geolocation efforts.
(2) We propose a universally applicable approach which depends neither on addresses on web pages, nor addresses in IP registration records, but owner names which are common and easy to obtain. So, ONE-Geo is designed to not only mine the locations of web servers that are hosted locally, but also the ones that are hosted on the cloud. As the trend is shifting towards hosting more websites on the cloud, previous methods that generate landmarks by directly mapping an address that revealed on a web page to the web site's IP is increasingly less reliable. ONE-Geo could play a large part in filling this ever-increasing void of location-related information since it can

deduce the location of a data center by using the OKG and the owner name extracted from WHOIS database.

(3) Based on the landmarks mined by ONE-Geo Alpha, we designed a highly fault-tolerant inference algorithm to mine as many landmarks as possible. By this method, we were able to make full use of web resources available to the public.

2   Related Work

Data Mining-Based Methods: GeoTrack [1], DRoP [2], rDNS-Geo [3] and HLOC [4] mine location hints in domain names to geolocate an IP. Structon [5] uses regular expressions to extract location information from web pages. By mapping addresses to the corresponding IPs of the web servers, it generate hundreds of thousands of landmarks. GeoCluster [1] uses the address prefixes in BGP routing tables to cluster IP addresses and then deduce the geographical location of the entire cluster by extracting location information from user registration records in the Hotmail service. Checkin-Geo [6] leverages the location data that users share in location-sharing services and logs of user logins from PCs for IP geolocation. Dan et al. [7] constructs an IP geolocation database by collecting location data from a subset of search engine logs that contain real time global positioning information obtained from mobile devices.

Measurement-Based Methods: GeoPing [1] maps a node to a probe's location based on the measured delays from probes to the node. CBG [8] utilizes measured delays to draw constraints and narrows down the possible region that covers a target to a continuous area. TBG [9] proves that network topology can be effectively used to achieve high geolocation accuracy. Octant [10] takes both positive and negative measurement constraints into account. SLG [11] utilizes zip codes on web pages to generate landmarks. An important contribution of this work lies in introducing a method that indirectly estimates the delay between a target and a landmark by finding the closest common router. Geo-NN [12] and LBG [13] train prediction model to geolocate IPs. SBG [14] uses smartphones as landmarks relying on crowdsourcing principles.

Data mining based methods are widely used in commercial systems due to fast response time and easy deployment. However, they can usually only provide city-level precision because some of them, such as Structon and various domain name mining methods, use the open resources in an inefficient way. Furthermore, methods that use the raw data, such as user registration records, are intrinsically unreliable. As for measurement-based methods, they rely heavily on landmarks. Most of them fail to improve accuracy further because of the lack of high-quality landmarks.

Considering the problems mentioned above, we propose ONE-Geo which relies on owner names which are common and easy to obtain. ONE-Geo is not only a more efficient, convenient and universally applicable approach, compared to previous data mining-based methods, but also an excellent solution to providing a considerable number of landmarks for measurement-based methods.

3   Owner Name Extraction Based Algorithm

Briefly, our geolocation approach consists of three major steps. First, we scan an IP segment and find all IPs that host websites. We crawl homepages and collect their registration records from regional Internet registry databases. For a given IP, we try to extract the owner name from the web pages and the registration records. Second, we use the owner name as a clue to search for potential addresses by an organization knowledge graph (OKG). If there is only one potential address, we directly map it to the IP address and generate a new landmark. Otherwise, by our election based inference algorithm, we infer the correct location from all candidate geographic coordinates. Third, in order to expand the coverage further, we cluster IPs and map every IP in a cluster to the same location.

3.1   Owner Name Extraction

For registration information, we use the application programming interfaces (APIs) provided by WHOIS databases to get the registration records of a given IP and extract the organization name. For homepages, it is more complicated, the details of which are explained in the following section.

Without a context, existing public name entity recognition (NER) tools do not work well on extracting organization names from titles, logo tags, nor copyright information. We tried Stanford NER and Natural Language Toolkit (NLTK). Both of them return false positives in many cases. Take Stanford NER for example, we feed "Palo Alto Research Center Incorporated; © 2018. All Rights Reserved" into the recognition function and it returns "Alto Research Center Incorporated" back, which can lead to huge errors in the next inference process.

Hence, we employ another two strategies to extract organization names: by regular expression (RegEx) and by an organization name dictionary. Since there are some conventions in displaying the copyright information, the RegEx is a good choice for extracting organization names from copyright information. Different from copyright information, website titles and text in logo image tags are usually organized in a variety of styles. In order to extract organization names exactly and not to introduce redundant characters that can lead to negative effects on the inference part, we collect organization names from public semi-structured and structured knowledge databases, e.g. Wikipedia, yellow pages, and recruiting websites. In case we get more than one organization name, we determine the real owner name by scoring according to their position and frequency.

3.2   Election-Based Inference Algorithm

To build our OKG, we first collected a large volume of pointer of interest (POI) data from OpenStreetMap (OSM) [15], Data Center Map [16], and The Real Yellow Pages [17] to generate organization-location links. Then, we crawled Wikipedia [18] for headquarters-subsidiary links. Based on these links, we built an organization knowledge graph for location searching.

Given the owner name of a target IP, we use it as a clue to retrieve all relevant locations of organizations and their subsidiaries from OKG. Before going to the next step, we merge highly clustered locations to a single candidate location (see C^1 on Fig. 1) by calculating their average coordinate. For a given IP, if it has only one owner name and there is only one candidate point for it, we map this IP to the only location and get it into our landmark database. If there is more than one candidate returned, we leave the rest of the job to the next inference process. To our surprise, the number of IPs with only one possible location was substantial (1.2 million of 8 million). In other words, by simply searching for potential locations with the owner name, ONE-Geo got a massive number of landmarks directly without any network measurement. We named the initial ONE-Geo ONE-Geo Alpha. We added the initial landmarks collected by ONE-Geo Alpha to the existing landmark set that were prepared for the next inference part.

As for IPs with multiple candidate locations, we used CBG to filter out points that were far less likely to be the correct location. To determine the possible region of the given IP address, we first measured the network delay time from probes to the target IP by ping. Then, we converted the network delay into a geographical distance. Katz-Bassett et al. [9] and Wang et al. [11] have shown that 4/9 is suitable to be adopted as the converting factor between measured delay and geographical distance. Thus, we also adopted this ratio as the converting factor in our calculations. After estimating the geographical distances, by multilateration, we drew an intersection that covers the target IP. Next, we defined a circular area that covers the intersection area and filters out potential locations that are out of this circular area.

For a given target IP, if there is only one possible location left in the possible area, we map the target IP to this location and add this new landmark to the existing landmark set. If there are still more than one candidate locations, we proposed an election-based inference algorithm to determine the final location.

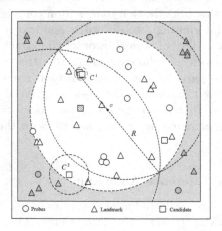

Fig. 1. An election example

As shown in Fig. 1, for a target IP, we draw a circle centered at the centroid of the constrained area, with a radius R' of the maximal error distance. The area bounded by this circle is referred to as the electoral district. In the electoral district, we define an election tuple $E = (t, C, L, P)$ including the target IP t, all candidate locations (squares) C, a set of landmarks (triangles) L, and a set of probes (circles) P. The landmark set not only includes landmarks in the district, but also the ones that are out of the district but still in the vicinity of the candidates. For example, the striped triangle near the candidate C^2 in Fig. 1 is also in the set. All the landmarks in the set were selected from the continuous-expanding landmark set which consists of not only the initial landmarks that were collected by ONE-Geo Alpha but also the ones that were generated in every inference loop.

Probes are used to measure network delays and traceroutes from a probe to a landmark or a target IP. Landmarks, in charge of distributing scores to candidate locations, play the role of a bridge that links IPs to their real locations. To be specific, by basing the measurements on probes, we can estimate the distance from any landmark to a given target IP. The closer a landmark is to the target IP, the higher the score the landmark will get. Also, we can calculate the distance from a landmark to any candidate location by computing the great-circle distance [19] between their coordinates. A location closer to a landmark gets a higher score from that landmark. For each election, the candidate location with the highest score wins the election and gets mapped to the target IP.

The final score of a candidate is defined below:

$$score(c_i) = \sum_{l_j \in L} g(l_j, c_i) s(l_j) \tag{1}$$

In this equation, $s(l_j)$ is the individual score of a landmark l_j and $g(l_j, c_i)$ is a redistributing gate which lets through a proportion of the individual score of the landmark l_j.

As mentioned before, a candidate should get a higher score from a landmark if it is closer to the landmark than the others. Therefore, the redistributing gates are defined below:

$$g(l_j, c_i) = 1 - \frac{e^{dis(c_i, l_j)}}{\sum_{l_k \in L} e^{dis(c_i, l_k)}} \tag{2}$$

Here, c_i represents a candidate, l_i represents a landmark, and $dis(c_i, v_i)$ refers to the great-circle distance between them.

As for the individual score of each landmark, we use the equation below to calculate:

$$s(l_i) = \alpha s_t(l_i) + \beta s_d(l_i) \tag{3}$$

Above, $s_t(l_i)$ represents the score in the topology perspective and $s_d(l_i)$ represents the score in the perspective of pure network delay measurement.

The individual score of a landmark depends on the distance to the targeted node. We estimate the distance by network measurement according to two important insights from previous work: (1) Despite the fact that the direct relationship between the real geographic distance and estimated distance is incredibly weak due to the inevitable circuitous path, queuing and processing delays, the indirect relationship on distance is largely preserved [11]. I.e., the two nearest IP addresses usually have the smallest network delay. (2) For geographically adjacent IP addresses, their network delay measurements resulting from the same probe should be similar [11,20].

In the topology perspective, learning from [11], we manage to calculate the indirect delay distance (IDD) from a landmark to a target IP by doing traceroute measurement and finding the closest common router. Then, we combine IDDs into a delay vector and normalize it. Each element can be calculated by the following equation:

$$s_t(l_i) = 1 - \frac{e^{d(l_i,t)}}{\sum_{l_j \in L} e^{d(l_j,t)}} \tag{4}$$

Here, $d(l_i,t)$ represents the indirect delay time from a landmark to the target IP.

Following this, in the perspective of pure network delay measurement, we measured the pure delay between each probe and every landmark by ping. Then, we embedded all delays into a delay vector. We employ the cosine similarity to estimate the distance. The score of a landmark can be calculated by an equation below:

$$s_d(l_i) = \frac{sim(l_i, t)}{\sum_{l_j \in L} sim(l_j, t)} \tag{5}$$

Above, $sim(l_i, t)$ represents the cosine similarity of a landmark and the target.

Based on the initial landmarks that ONE-Geo Alpha collected, we first deduced the coordinates of the IPs that had two candidate locations. After completing the inference of the two-candidate IPs, we stepped further into the inference of the ones that had three candidate locations. Every time the inference was done, we mapped the target IPs to the estimated locations to generate a batch of new landmarks. Recursively, we added the new landmarks into an existing landmark set and repeat the inference algorithm until no more IPs that could meet the launch condition of a new loop of inferences existed. A new launch is conditional on the credibility of an election being higher than a threshold T. The credibility is defined as shown below where $size(P)$ and $size(L)$ represent the number of the probes and the number of the landmarks separately:

$$c(E_i) = ln(1 + size(P)size(L))^{1/2} \tag{6}$$

3.3 Expanding IP Coverage

We refer to the enhanced ONE-Geo as ONE-Geo Beta. After the inference process, almost 4 million landmarks were generated from 8 million IPs. However, all of them were web servers. Therefore, in order to empower ONE-Geo to geolocate nodes that do not host a website, we must go further to enlarge the IP coverage. Freedman et al. [21] claims that 97% of IPs in the same /24 segment are at nearly the same location with a slight distance from each other. Inspired by this finding, we adopted a /24 clustering method to expand the coverage. Instead of mapping all clustered IPs to the same location, we modified this expanding method a little to avoid introducing errors.

In a /24 IP segment, we cluster existing landmarks and define the largest cluster as the dominant group, which determines the dominant location of this segment. The coordinate of the dominant location is defined as the average coordinate of landmarks in the group. We named the landmarks in the vicinity of the dominant location the followers, and the nearest one the leader. The rest of the dispersed ones are labeled loners.

For the existing landmarks, we did not change their location because the coordinates returned by OKG were very precise. For the rest of the location-unknown IPs, we mapped them to the dominant location of a group, if and only if, they met the requirements to get into the group. We designed 2 rules to evaluate the qualification to join the group. First, we calculated a new node's IDD to the leader, and the IDD between the leader and every single follower. If the IDD of the new IP was less than the IDD of the remotest follower to the leader, it was included in the group. Second, if its IDD to the nearest follower was far less (5 times less in our experiment) than the IDD to any of the loners, it is in the group.

After the addition of the 2 rules mentioned above, a lot of new IPs were selected and clustered into the dominant group. Following this, we mapped the new nodes to the location of the dominant group and got new landmarks. By this method, ONE-Geo expanded the IP coverage even further. We named the fully-fledged ONE-Geo ONE-Geo Epsilon.

4   Evaluation

Our research indicates that, SLG [11] is a typical and one of the best existing IP geolocation methods. Therefore, by primarily focusing on a comparison of ONE-Geo with SLG, we can demonstrate the improvement of ONE-Geo on both web server nodes and Internet of things (IOT) nodes. In addition, we compared ONE-Geo with several commercial tools (ipstack [22], MaxMind's GeoIP2 [23], IPIP [24], and ipinfo [25]) to show ONE-Geo achieves much better estimation precision than popular commercial tools on web servers, and achieves similar precision to them on IOT nodes. In our experiments, we limited our dataset to the US. This choice was made for 3 reasons. First, the time needed to deal with cross-language problems when extracting organization names from web pages made it impractical. Second, analysis of ONE-Geo through the lens of multiple language is not focus of this paper. And third, we can get more ground-truth information from the nodes in the United States.

In order to evaluate the accuracy of our method, we collected ground-truth data from PlanetLab [26] and RIPE Atlas [27]. On these two platforms, nodes with reported coordinates are shared with the public. The PlanetLab data set is a commonly used data set in IP geolocation research (e.g. [9–11]), but the quantity of nodes is limited and are all web servers. To complement this data set, we collected data on IOT nodes from RIPE Atlas. In the end, after filtering out inaccessible nodes, we had 165 web servers and 980 IOT nodes left. As to evaluating coverage and efficiency, we scanned 64.7 million IPs that host websites and crawled 8,283,809 homepages from nodes in the United States.

4.1 Accuracy

As the average error distance is highly influenced by some abnormal errors from a few nodes, the median error is more commonly used to indicate the accuracy of geolocation systems. In the experiment on PlanetLab nodes, the median error distance of ONE-Geo (Beta), SLG, IPIP, ipstack, ipinfo, and Geolite2 are 463 m, 1768 m, 3161 m, 1463 m, 1463 m, and 1272 m respectively. As we can see from Fig. 2 on web servers, both ONE-Geo and SLG perform well; and ONE-Geo performs much better than SLG. An important difference between SLG and ONE-Geo is that SLG tries hard to find the closest locally-hosted node to the target while ONE-Geo tries to find the web server itself by OKG. Therefore, it is easier for ONE-Geo to control the errors within 1 km when geolocating web servers. To be specific, 66.1% of nodes in this experiment were geolocated by ONE-Geo with an error less than 1 km while only 28.8% were geolocated by SLG within the same margin.

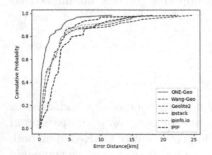 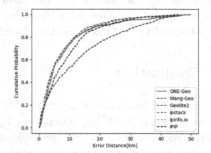

Fig. 2. Comparison of error distance on PlanetLab nodes

Fig. 3. Comparison of error distance on RIPE nodes

ONE-Geo (Epsilon) covers 721 of the 980 IPs after expanding. Even though ONE-Geo can not cover all of them, this number is high enough to evaluate its ability to geolocate nodes that do not host a website. For these 721 nodes, ONE-Geo also performs well (see Fig. 3). This is not a surprise because of the large number of students, teachers, and local community members that live around schools, universities, and research institutions. Since ONE-Geo can cover most nodes that host websites by these organizations, it can also estimate the location of the nodes around the web servers in a precise way. To be specific, the median error distance of ONE-Geo, SLG, IPIP, ipstack, ipinfo, Geolite2 are 7758 m, 14999 m, 8801 m, 5704 m, 6453 m and 6352 m respectively, in which SLG performed the worst (median error 9295 m higher than the leader) while ONE-Geo had a more prominent position in the group (median error 2054 m higher than the leader).

As the main idea of SLG is to associate the target's location with the landmark with the minimum distance and they estimate the distance by the minimum indirect delay, there are 3 reasons that lead to the low precision of SLG on nodes (excluding those with web servers). First, it is not guaranteed to find a common router or the closest common router because of the scarcity of landmarks and probes. Second, the shortest network delay does not always mean the shortest distance [6]. Third, SLG can only utilize local web servers as their landmarks. Since there is a trend to use content delivery network (CDN) to distribute content or use cloud services to store archives, these kinds of local nodes are decreasing, which leads to a lack of high-quality landmarks.

4.2   Coverage

Most existing mining methods, like Structon, focus on utilizing the address information or zip codes on the pages to locate the web servers, like Structon. However, our experiment indicates that these methods can hardly cover most potential landmarks. We used 8 million web pages to estimate the proportion of websites that reveal the addresses and zip codes on their homepage. The results on Table 1 show that the coverage of methods mining address or zip codes are much less than the methods that mine owner names, like ONE-Geo.

Table 1. Comparison of coverage

Clue	Hit	Pages	Ratio
Address	1,037,271	8,283,809	0.125
Zip Code	203,673	8,283,809	0.024
Owner Name	**3,900,443**	**8,283,809**	**0.471**

Table 2. Comparison of efficiency

Methodology	Landmarks	Source	Ratio
Structon	157,407	502,880,364	0.0003
Checkin-Geo	31,634	92,153	0.3432
ONE-Geo	**3,900,443**	**8,283,809**	0.4708

Our research suggests that, the best two landmark mining methods are Structon and Checkin-Geo. In their reports, Structon mines 157K landmarks from 502M web pages and Checkin-Geo mines 31K landmarks from 92K login records. Compared to them, ONE-Geo is a more efficient method, which gets 3.9M landmarks from 8.2M pages (Table 2). Structon spends too much time and computing resources on processing unnecessary pages on the same website. Correspondingly, ONE-Geo can extract the owner names utilizing only the homepage, of which the efficiency is three orders of magnitude higher than Structon. Checkin-Geo has a relatively higher efficiency than Structon. However, Checkin-Geo is not universally applicable because the raw material sources they use are the private data of certain social network companies, which are not open to the public.

5 Conclusion

In this paper, we propose ONE-Geo, a methodology which exploits owner names revealed on homepages and registration records to mine landmarks. Experimental results show ONE-Geo achieves fine-grained precision and large coverage. ONE-Geo Alpha is an efficient method to mine landmarks of high quality without any measurement. By constructing inference, ONE-Geo Beta makes full use of web resources and registration records to mine as many landmarks as possible. It is also a universally applicable approach which depends on neither addresses on web pages nor addresses in IP registration records, but owner names which are common and easy to obtain.

Acknowledgements. This work was supported in part by the National Key R&D Program of China (Grant No. 2018YFB0803402, No. 2017YFB0802804), the Key Program of National Natural Science Foundation of China (Grant No. U1766215), and the National Natural Science Foundation of China (Grant No. 61702503, No. 61702504).

References

1. Padmanabhan, V.N., Subramanian, L.: An investigation of geographic mapping techniques for internet hosts. In: ACM SIGCOMM Computer Communication Review, vol. 31, pp. 173–185. ACM (2001)
2. Huffaker, B., Fomenkov, M., et al.: DRoP: DNS-based router positioning. ACM SIGCOMM Comput. Commun. Rev. **44**(3), 5–13 (2014)
3. Dan, O., Parikh, V., Davison, B.D.: IP geolocation through reverse DNS. arXiv preprint arXiv:1811.04288 (2018)
4. Scheitle, Q., Gasser, O., Sattler, P., Carle, G.: HLOC: hints-based geolocation leveraging multiple measurement frameworks. In: 2017 Network Traffic Measurement and Analysis Conference (TMA), pp. 1–9. IEEE (2017)
5. Guo, C., Liu, Y., Shen, W., Wang, H.J., Yu, Q., Zhang, Y.: Mining the web and the internet for accurate IP address geolocations. In: INFOCOM 2009 IEEE, pp. 2841–2845. IEEE (2009)
6. Liu, H., Zhang, Y., Zhou, Y., Zhang, D., Fu, X., Ramakrishnan, K.: Mining check-ins from location-sharing services for client-independent IP geolocation. In: 2014 Proceedings IEEE INFOCOM, pp. 619–627. IEEE (2014)
7. Dan, O., Parikh, V., Davison, B.D.: Improving IP geolocation using query logs. In: Proceedings of the Ninth ACM International Conference on Web Search and Data Mining, pp. 347–356. ACM (2016)
8. Gueye, B., Ziviani, A., Crovella, M., Fdida, S.: Constraint-based geolocation of internet hosts. IEEE/ACM Trans. Netw. (TON) **14**(6), 1219–1232 (2006)

9. Katz-Bassett, E., John, J.P., Krishnamurthy, A., Wetherall, D., Anderson, T., Chawathe, Y.: Towards IP geolocation using delay and topology measurements. In: Proceedings of the 6th ACM SIGCOMM Conference on Internet Measurement, pp. 71–84. ACM (2006)
10. Wong, B., Stoyanov, I., Sirer, E.G.: Octant: a comprehensive framework for the geolocalization of internet hosts. In: NSDI, vol. 7, pp. 23–23 (2007)
11. Wang, Y., Burgener, D., Flores, M., Kuzmanovic, A., Huang, C.: Towards street-level client-independent IP geolocation. In: NSDI, vol. 11, pp. 27–27 (2011)
12. Jiang, H., Liu, Y., Matthews, J.N.: IP geolocation estimation using neural networks with stable landmarks. In: 2016 IEEE Conference on Computer Communications Workshops (INFOCOM WKSHPS), pp. 170–175. IEEE (2016)
13. Eriksson, B., Barford, P., Sommers, J., Nowak, R.: A learning-based approach for IP geolocation. In: Krishnamurthy, A., Plattner, B. (eds.) PAM 2010. LNCS, vol. 6032, pp. 171–180. Springer, Heidelberg (2010). https://doi.org/10.1007/978-3-642-12334-4_18
14. Ciavarrini, G., Luconi, V., Vecchio, A.: Smartphone-based geolocation of internet hosts. Comput. Netw. **116**, 22–32 (2017)
15. Openstreetmap. https://www.openstreetmap.org/copyright
16. Data center map. https://www.datacentermap.com
17. YP.com. The real yellow pages. https://www.yellowpages.com/
18. Wikipedia. The free encyclopedia. https://www.wikipedia.org/
19. Vincenty, T.: Direct and inverse solutions of geodesics on the ellipsoid with application of nested equations. Surv. Rev. **23**(176), 88–93 (1975)
20. Shue, C.A., Paul, N., Taylor, C.R.: From an IP address to a street address: using wireless signals to locate a target. In: WOOT (2013)
21. Freedman, M.J., Vutukuru, M., Feamster, N., Balakrishnan, H.: Geographic locality of IP prefixes. In: Proceedings of the 5th ACM SIGCOMM conference on Internet Measurement, pp. 13–13. USENIX Association (2005)
22. ipstack - free IP geolocation API. https://ipstack.com/
23. Maxmind GeoIP2. https://www.maxmind.com/en/geoip2-services-and-databases
24. IPIP.NET. https://www.ipip.net
25. IPinfo. https://ipinfo.io
26. PlanetLab. https://www.planet-lab.org/
27. RIPE Atlas. https://atlas.ripe.net

Decentralized Hierarchical Authorized Payment with Online Wallet for Blockchain

Qianwen Wei[1,2], Shujun Li[4], Wei Li[5], Hong Li[1,3], and Mingsheng Wang[1,2(✉)]

[1] School of Cyber Security, University of Chinese Academy of Sciences,
Beijing, China
[2] State Key Laboratory of Information Security,
Institute of Information Engineering, CAS, Beijing, China
{weiqianwen,wangmingsheng}@iie.ac.cn
[3] Beijing Key Laboratory of IoT Information Security Technology,
Institute of Information Engineering, CAS, Beijing, China
lihong@iie.ac.cn
[4] School of Information Engineering, Yancheng Teachers University, Yancheng, China
jojo8086@126.com
[5] Department of Computer Science, Georgia State University, Atlanta, GA, USA
wli28@gsu.edu

Abstract. In Bitcoin, the knowledge of private key equals to the ownership of bitcoin, which occurs two problems: the first problem is that the private key must be kept properly, and the second one is that once the private key is given, it can't be taken back, hence the bitcoin system can only implement the transfer function. In this paper, we first propose a new digital signature algorithm and use it to design an online wallet, which can help the user derive the signature without obtaining the user's private key. Secondly, using our proposed online wallet, we extend the application of private key so that the cryptocurrency system can implement the authorization function. In more detail, we define a new primitive that we call decentralized hierarchical authorized payment scheme (DHAP scheme). We next propose a concrete instantiation and prove its correctness. Finally, we analyze the security and usability of our scheme. For security, we prove our scheme to be secure under the random oracle model. For usability, we examine its performance and compare it with bitcoin's performance.

Keywords: Blockchain · Online wallet ·
Decentralized hierarchical authorized payment scheme

1 Introduction

Since Nakamoto proposed bitcoin [1] in 2008, blockchain technology has been continuously developed [2,3]. As the most well-known decentralized cryptocurrency, as of March 2019, bitcoin's market value has reached $69.1 billion. The

© Springer Nature Switzerland AG 2019
E. S. Biagioni et al. (Eds.): WASA 2019, LNCS 11604, pp. 358–369, 2019.
https://doi.org/10.1007/978-3-030-23597-0_29

foundation of bitcoin is the blockchain, which is an append-only public chain maintained by the bitcoin peers according to the consensus algorithm [4,5]. As a public ledger visible to all nodes, the blockchain records transactions that are verified to be valid by miners. In fact, bitcoins are owned by addresses; an address is simply the hash of a public key. If Alice wants to spend bitcoin in address Y, she must construct a transaction and sign the transaction with the private key y corresponding to Y. Only if the signature is correct, the transaction is valid. After that, Alice broadcasts the transaction to the whole network, then miners in the network verify the signature and add valid transactions to the blockchain. Therefore, the knowledge of private key equals to the ownership of bitcoin, which occurs two problems:

Firstly, the private key must be kept properly. Since 2008, a large number of bitcoins have been lost due to improper storage of private key [6], and the stolen bitcoins' market value has exceeded \$1 billion. The private key can be saved on the local terminal or on the network server. If the private key is stored locally, it is easily lost and can't be used across devices. If the private key is stored on the server, the server may steal the user's cryptocurrency. Secondly, as the transaction is done by signing with a private key, if Alice wants to authorize Bob to spend cryptocurrency in her address, Alice has to give her private key to Bob. However, once the private key is given, there is no way to take it back or limit how it is used, so Alice can't revoke the authorization if it has been given to Bob. Therefore, the functionality of the cryptocurrency system is poor compared to the current financial system. In order to solve this problem, two schemes were proposed: use smart contracts [2,7] or to change the consensus mechanism [8]. But both of them need to make adjustments to the entire system, which is inconvenient.

To solve the problems, we make two improvements.

Firstly, we design an online wallet to manage the user's private key. Using our scheme, the online wallet can help the user generate signature without obtaining the user's private key. At the same time, with the help of wallet, the user only needs to remember the password to complete the transaction. More importantly, during the entire process, the user's private key is encrypted and stored. The attacker can't obtain the user's private key by attacking the local client, the network communication, or even the server. To do this, we first propose a new digital signature algorithm. We make an improvement on Schnorr signature algorithm [18] by introducing a third-party Eve to the traditional two-party digital signature algorithm. Encrypt Alice's private key and send it to Eve, when a transaction need to be signed, Eve generates an encrypted signature with encrypted private key and send it to Alice, then Alice decrypt it to get the correct signature. Then we use the signature algorithm to design an online wallet.

Secondly, using our proposed online wallet, we extend the application of private key so that the cryptocurrency system can implement the authorization function. That is, user A generates private key k', without giving k' to B, A can let user B have access to cryptocurrency in the address corresponding to k', and A can withdraw the authorization given to B at any time. To do this, we first define the abstract functionality and correctness requirements of a new primitive that we call a decentralized hierarchical authorized payment scheme (DHAP scheme). We next propose a concrete instantiation and prove it correct.

Finally, we analyze the security and usability of our scheme. In terms of security, based on two different adversarial models, we respectively prove the security of the scheme under the random oracle model. Based on our proof, it can be stated that even if the adversary can control the server, he still can't forge the user's signature or obtain the user's private key. In terms of usability, the signature algorithm generates a signature with length of 212 bits, which is less than the average 568-bit signature in the bitcoin's signature algorithm. In addition, the signature algorithm requires 246 modular multiplication operations, and modern CPUs can easily achieve it with the help of various acceleration algorithms.

Outline of this Work. The rest of this paper proceeds as follows. In Sect. 2 we introduce the related work about blockchain key management approaches. In Sect. 3 we provide a new digital signature algorithm based on Schnorr signature, and use it to design a new online wallet. Using our proposed online wallet, we extend the application of private key so that the cryptocurrency system can implement the authorization function. In Sect. 4 we formally define the notion of decentralized hierarchical authorized payment scheme and provide correctness requirements for such a system. Finally, in Sect. 5, we analyze the security and usability of our scheme and prove that the scheme is theoretically safe and usable.

2   Related Work

There are four main blockchain key management approaches: keys in local storage, offline storage of keys, password-derived keys and online wallets.

Keys in local storage is the easiest way to store private key. A typical way is to store the private key in a file on a local disk or in a local database [11]. When a transaction needs to be created, the cryptocurrency client software reads the private key, signs the transaction and broadcasts it to the network. In order to improve the security of keys in local storage, the encrypted wallet [12] is proposed. Encrypted wallet encrypt a locally stored wallet with a key derived from a user-chosen password. If the private key is stored locally, the private key is easily stolen by hackers.

In order to against malware attacks, storing private key offline on a portable device [13] was proposed. For example, the private key can be stored on a USB. Unlike general offline storage of keys, Air-gapped [14] is a special offline device that uses private key to generate a signature and output the signature only. If the private key is stored offline, it is inconvenient to use, so it is generally used as a backup.

In 2000, Kaliski proposed password-derived keys [15]. When needed, the user generates a private key via a password. In 2012, Pieter Wuille proposed a new password-based private key generation method [9], which allows generating multiple private keys and corresponding public keys from a master password. The primary drawback of a password-derived wallet is that passwords can be found through exhaustive search.

Another method of private key management is an online wallet, in which case the user's private key is held by the server. The online wallet authenticates the user's identity through a standard web authentication mechanism [16]. After the user is authenticated, the transaction can be completed online. In order to improve security, the protection of the private key with a threshold signature is proposed [17]. This method requires multiple parties to be present at the same time to generate a private key and complete the transaction.

3   Design of Digital Signature and Online Wallet

In this chapter, we propose a new digital signature algorithm and use it to design a cryptocurrency online wallet. Our new digital signature algorithm is actually an improvement of the Schnorr signature algorithm [18]. We introduce a third-party Eve to the traditional two-party digital signature algorithm. (In fact, in the key management approach we proposed, Eve is wallet server that hosts the user's private key).

As shown in Fig. 1, The construction of the scheme is summarized as follows:

Alice's private key is x and the corresponding public key is y. After x is encrypted with password pwd, $\bar{x}$ is obtained and is sent to the Eve. When Alice needs to sign the transaction m, Alice sends m to Eve. Eve uses the $\bar{x}$ to sign the transaction m, generates $\bar{s}$, sends $\bar{s}$ to Alice, then Alice decrypts $\bar{s}$ with the pwd to get the signature s and sends s to Bob. Bob uses public key y to verify whether the signature is correct.

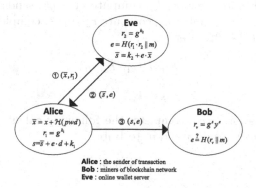

Fig. 1. The construction of the key management scheme

3.1   Notation

For $n \in \mathbb{N}$, let $\mathbb{Z}_n$ be the ring of integers modulo n. We identify $\mathbb{Z}_n$ with the set of integers $\{1, ..., n\}$.

In what follows, we will work on these parameters:

- primes p and q such that $q|(p-1)$, $p \geq 2^{512}$, $q \geq 2^{140}$
- $g \in \mathbb{Z}_p$ with order q, i.e., $g^q = 1 (mod\ p)$, $g \neq 1$
- a one-way hash function $H : \mathbb{Z}_q \cdot \mathbb{Z} \rightarrow \{0, .., 2^t - 1\}$
- a one-way hash function $\mathcal{H} : \mathbb{Z} \rightarrow \mathbb{Z}_p$
- a private key x, and corresponding public key $y = g^x$

3.2 Process of the Scheme

Initiation. The purpose of the initialization is to encrypt Alice's private key x with the password pwd entered by her, and then generate secret data. Explicit security data is then deleted from Alice's device. Given Alice's private key x, public key y, password, and the initiation process can be described as follows:

$$d = \mathcal{H}(pwd)$$

$$\bar{x} = x + d$$

Alice's public key y, the encrypted private key $\bar{x}$ is sent to the Eve, Alice's password pwd and Alice's private key x are deleted from the device, and Alice's private key x is saved offline, in case of emergency.

Signature. In order to get the correct signature s, Alice first needs Eve to sign the message m with the encrypted private key $\bar{x}$, obtain the encrypted signature $\bar{s}$, and then Alice obtains the correct signature s by decrypting $\bar{s}$. The signature process can be described as follows:

1. Alice chooses a random number k_1, compute $r_1 = g^k$, sends r_1 to Eve.
2. Eve chooses a random number k_2, compute $r_2 = g^{k_2}$, completes the following calculation, sends $(\bar{s}, e)$ to user

$$e = H(r_1 \cdot r_2 || m)$$

$$\bar{s} = k_2 - e \cdot \bar{x}$$

3. Alice inputs password pwd, completes the following calculation, obtains the signature $\sigma = (s, e)$, sends σ and m to Bob.

$$d = \mathcal{H}(pwd)$$

$$s = \bar{s} + e \cdot d + k_1$$

Verification. After receiving σ and m, Bob verifies σ using the public key y of Alice.

$$r_v = g^s y^e$$

$$e_v = H(r_v || m)$$

checks whether $e_v = e$, if not, rejects the signature.

3.3   Correctness of the Scheme

Theorem 1. *If Alice uses our proposed scheme to sign the transaction m with her private key x, then Bob can verify the signature using Alice's public key y.*

Proof. The signature that Bob receives is $\sigma = (s, e)$, According to the scheme,

$$s = \bar{s} + e \cdot d + k_1$$
$$= k_2 - e \cdot \bar{x} + e \cdot d + k_1$$
$$= k_1 + k_2 - e \cdot x$$

Let $k = k_1 + k_2$, $r = r_1 \cdot r_2$, then $s = k - e \cdot x$, wherein, $e = H(r\|m)$, Bob computes $r_v = g^s y^e = g^{k-ex} g^e = g^{k-ex} g^{ex} = g^k = r$, because $e_v = H(r_v\|m) = H(r\|m) = e$, Bob can verify that the signature is correct.

4   DHAP Scheme and Its Instantiation

In this chapter, using the online wallet proposed by us, we extend the application of private key so that the cryptocurrency system can implement the authorization function. That is, user A generates private key k', without giving k' to B, A can let user B have access to cryptocurrency in the address corresponding to k', and A can withdraw the authorization given to B at any time. To do this, we first define the abstract functionality and correctness requirements of a new primitive that we call a decentralized hierarchical authorized payment scheme (DHAP scheme). We next propose a concrete instantiation and prove it correct.

4.1   The Definition and Correctness of DHAP

Definition 1 *(Decentralized hierarchical authorized payment scheme): A decentralized hierarchical authorized payment scheme consists of a tuple of possibly randomized algorithms (Authorize, Spend, Verify, Revoke).*

- **Authorize** $(params) \rightarrow (y_i, c)$: On input parameters $params$, output an address y_i and a trapdoor c
- **Spend** $(params, y_i, c, m) \rightarrow s$: On input $params$, y_i, its trapdoor c, and a transaction message m, output a signature s corresponding to y_i
- **Verify** $(params, y_i, c) \rightarrow \{0, 1\}$: On input $params$, y_i, and its signature s, output 1 if s is the correct signature corresponding to y_i, otherwise output 0
- **Revoke** $(params) \rightarrow \{0, 1\}$: On input $params$, output 1 if trapdoor c has been changed, otherwise output 0.

Correctness. Let $(y_i, c) \leftarrow$ Authorize $(params)$, $s \leftarrow$ Spend $(params, y_i, c, m)$. The scheme is correct if the following equality holds with probability $1 - v(\lambda)$, wherein, $v(\lambda)$ represents a negligible function

$$\text{Verify}(c, m, y_i) = 1$$

4.2 The Instantiation of DHAP

By combining the hierarchical deterministic algorithm to generate the private key of the cryptocurrency, with the online wallet private key management scheme proposed in Sect. 3, we next propose a concrete instantiation and prove it secure under standard cryptographic assumptions. The framework of the scheme is illustrated in Fig. 2.

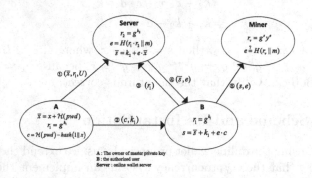

Fig. 2. The construction of DHAP scheme's instantiation

Authorize

Child key Generation. Given a master key pair (x, y) for a user, compute child private key $(x_1, x_2, ...)$ and corresponding public keys $(y_1, y_2, ...)$ as

$$x_i = x + hash(i||x)$$

$$y_i = g^{x_i}$$

Registration. Primary user A registers on the server through a standard web authentication mechanism [16] (such as password or two-factor authentication). In the subsequent process, the information saved in server can be changed only after A's identity is verified. Then, A store $(r_1 = g^{k_1}, \bar{x}, U)$ as the registration information of A.

1. Input A's private key, compute

$$x_1 = x + hash(1||x)$$

$$y_1 = g^{x_1}$$

2. When the primary user A wants to authorize the child user B to spend the cryptocurrency in the address corresponding to the public key y_1, A compute $c = \mathcal{H}(pwd) - hash(1||x)$, send (c, y_1) to B.
3. A sends k_1 to B.

Spend

1. When B wants to spend the cryptocurrency in address corresponding to y_1, B calculates $r_1 = g^{k_1}$, and sends (r_1, m) to the server. Then B requests server to sign the message m with the encrypted private key $\bar{x}$ corresponding to r_1.
2. Server chooses a random number k_2, compute $y_2 = g^{k_2}$, completes the following calculation, sends $(\bar{s}, e)$ to B

$$e = H(r_1 \cdot r_2 \| m)$$

$$\bar{s} = k_2 - e \cdot \bar{x}$$

3. B inputs $c = \mathcal{H}(pwd) - hash(1\|x)$, completes the following calculation, obtains the signature $\sigma = (s, e)$, and sends the signature to miner.

$$s = \bar{s} + e \cdot c + k_1$$

Verify. After receiving σ and m, Bob verifies σ using the public key y of Alice.

$$r_v = g^s y^e$$

$$e_v = H(r_v \| m)$$

checks whether $e_v = e$, if not, rejects the signature.

Revoke. When A wants to revoke the authorization given to B such that B can't spend the cryptocurrency in address corresponding to y_1. A only needs to prove his identity to the server, replace the random number from k_1 to k_3, calculate $r_3 = g^{k_3}$, and store $(r_3, \bar{x}, U)$ as the new registration information of A.

4.3 Correctness of the Scheme

The signature that Bob receives is $\sigma = (s, e)$, According to the scheme,

$$
\begin{aligned}
s &= \bar{s} + k_1 + e \cdot c \\
  &= k_2 - e \cdot \bar{x} + k_1 + e \cdot c \\
  &= k_2 - e \cdot (x + \mathcal{H}(pwd)) + k_1 + e * (\mathcal{H}(pwd) - hash(1\|x)) \\
  &= k_1 + k_2 + e \cdot hash(1\|x + x)
\end{aligned}
$$

Let $r = r_1 + r_2$, $k = k_1 + k_2$, $x_1 = x + hash(1\|x)$, then $s = k + e \cdot x_1$, wherein, $e = H(r\|m)$, Bob computes $r_v = g^s y_1^e = g^{k - e x_1} y_1^e = g^{k - e x_1} g^{e x_1} = g^k = r$, because $e_v = H(r_v \| m) = H(r\|m) = e$, Bob can verify that the signature (s, e) is correct.

5 Security and Usability Analysis

5.1 Security Analysis

We state that the scheme is provably safe under the random oracle model. The random oracle model is based on the standard model, adding a publicly accessible random oracle, idealizing the hash function used in the scheme as a random oracle. Many well-known cryptographic schemes [19,20] are provable secure under the random oracle model.

Adversary Model and System Goals. Based on two adversarial models, we demonstrate the security of the scheme. The first type of adversary model assumes that the adversary can obtain Alice's public key and signature; the second adversary model assumes that the adversary can obtain all the resources on the server. Under random oracle model, adversary can ask oracle $\mathcal{O}_{Alice}$ and $\mathcal{O}_{Server}$. Use q to indicate the number of times the adversary initiated an inquiry to the oracle. A scheme is (q, p) secure if after times q query to oracle, the adversary's probability of success p is negligible.

Security Proof. Let W-schnorr denote the signature scheme proposed in this paper. In the following, the security theorems are given and the security is proved according to the two adversarial models proposed above.

Theorem 2. *There is a probabilistic algorithm F' which on input (F, y) computes $log_g y$. If W-schnorr is not (q, p) secure under the adversary F, which can obtain Alice's public key and signature, then F' can solve the discrete logarithm $log_g y$ with probability p.*

Proof. With the help of F, F' can solve the discrete logarithm $log_g y$ with probability p by using the following steps.

1. F' picks y, obtain the corresponding signature (s, e);
2. F' sends (s, e) to F, gets a forged signature (s', e'), satisfying $r = g^{s'} y^{e'}$, then sends (s', e') to F';
3. F' obtains (s', e'), $log_g y$ can be solved using the following set of equations.

$$r = g^s y^e$$

$$r = g^{s'} y^{e'}$$

4. F' outputs $log_g y = \dfrac{s - s'}{e - e'}$ with a non-negligible probability p.

Theorem 3. *There is a probabilistic algorithm F' which on input (F, r) computes $log_g r$. If W-schnorr is not (q, p) secure under the adversary F, which can control Eve, then F' can solve the discrete logarithm $log_g r$ with probability p.*

Proof. With the help of F, F' can solve the discrete logarithm log_g^r with probability p by using the following steps.

1. F' queries $\mathcal{O}_{start}$, obtain the corresponding $\bar{x}$;
2. F' sends $(\bar{x}, r)$ to F, F queries $\mathcal{O}_{Eve}$ with the input $(\bar{x}, r)$, obtain $(\bar{s}, e)$;
3. F gets the user's signature (s, e) with a non-negligible probability p, sends (s, e) to F';
4. output $\log_g r = s - \bar{s} - e \cdot \mathcal{H}(pwd)$ with a non-negligible probability p.

5.2 Usability Analysis

Time Overhead. The time overhead in the signature phase consist mainly of the computation of g^{k_2} and $e \cdot \bar{x}(mod\ p)$, the former can be fast calculated by the following algorithm, and the latter multiplication can be ignored.

The binary representation of k_2 is $\sum_{i=1}^{l-1} k_{2i} \cdot 2^i$. We can compute g^{k_2} as follows:

Algorithm 1. Compute g^{k_2}

Input: : g and the bits of k_2
Output: res, g to the k_2 power
1: $res \leftarrow 1$
2: **for** each $i \in [l-1, 0]$ **do**
3:     $res \leftarrow g^{k_{2i}} \cdot res^2$
4: **end for**

This computation requires at most $2l$. If half of the bits of k_2 are zero, there are at most $1.5l$ modular multiplication.

The time overhead in signature verification phase consist mainly of the computation of $s = g^s y^e (mod\ p)$. Using the previously mentioned method, we can use m operations on average to get the result. The binary representations of s and e:

$$s = \sum_{i=0}^{l-1} s_i \cdot 2^i$$

$$e = \sum_{i=0}^{t-1} e_i \cdot 2^i$$

we can compute s as follows:

Algorithm 2. Compute $g^s y^e$

Input: : g, y and the bits of s, e
Output: res, the result of $g^s y^e$
1: $res \leftarrow 1$
2: **for** each $i \in [l-1, 0]$ **do**
3:     $res \leftarrow g^{k_{2i}} \cdot res^2$
4: **end for**

This computation requires at most modular multiplication $l + t + \sum_{i=t}^{l} s_i$. If half of the bits s_i with $i > t$ are zero, and $s_i = e_i = 0$ holds for one forth when $i < t$, then there are at most $l + 0.5(l - t) + 0.75t = 1.5l + 0.25t$ modular multiplications.

Overhead of Storage and Communication. The signature consists of (s, e), and the total length of the signature is $l+t$ bits, so each transaction needs bits to store the signature. For $l = 140, t = 72$, it will take 212 bits which is much smaller than the length of signature of bitcoin transaction, meanwhile the transmission overhead is also lower.

6   Conclusion

In the blockchain system, if the private key is stored locally, the private key is easily lose and can't be used across devices. If the private key is stored on the server, the server may steal the user's cryptocurrency. In this paper, we propose a new blockchain online wallet, then using our proposed online wallet and hierarchical key generation scheme, we extend the application of private key so that the cryptocurrency system can implement the authorization function. In more detail, firstly, we design a new signature scheme and use it to design a new online wallet, which is used to manage user's private key. The advantage of the online wallet is that it can help the user derive the signature without obtaining the user's private key. Secondly, we formulate and construct decentralized hierarchical authorized payment schemes (DHAP schemes). A DHAP scheme enables Alice to generate a private key x' from her private key x, without giving x' to Bob, Alice can let Bob have access to currency corresponding to x', and Alice can withdraw the authorization given to Bob at any time. Finally, we demonstrate the security and usability of the scheme and prove that the scheme is theoretically safe and usable.

Acknowledgement. This work is supported by National Key R&D Program of China (No. 2018YFB0803402), National Natural Science Foundation of China (No. 61702503) and National Natural Science Foundation of China (No. 61772516).

References

1. Nakamoto, S.: Bitcoin: A Peer-To-Peer Electronic Cash System (2008). https://bitcoin.org/bitcoin.pdf
2. Eyal, I., Gencer, A.E., Sirer, E.G., et al.: Bitcoin-NG: a scalable blockchain protocol. In: 13th USENIX Symposium on Networked Systems Design and Implementation (NSDI 16), pp. 45–59 (2016)
3. Cachin, C.: Architecture of the hyperledger blockchain fabric. In: Workshop on Distributed Cryptocurrencies and Consensus Ledgers, p. 310 (2016)
4. Garay, J., Kiayias, A., Leonardos, N.: The bitcoin backbone protocol: analysis and applications. In: Oswald, E., Fischlin, M. (eds.) EUROCRYPT 2015. LNCS, vol. 9057, pp. 281–310. Springer, Heidelberg (2015). https://doi.org/10.1007/978-3-662-46803-6_10

5. Yossi, G., Rotem, H., Silvio, M., et al.: Algorand: scaling Byzantine agreements for cryptocurrencies. In: Proceedings of the 26th Symposium on Operating Systems Principles, pp. 51–68. ACM (2017)
6. Zhengtong, T.: Summary of typical token stolen case hacking methods in history. https://www.tokenhand.net/posts/103
7. Kosba, A., Miller, A., Shi, E., et al.: Hawk: the blockchain model of cryptography and privacy-preserving smart contracts. In: 2016 IEEE Symposium on Security and Privacy (SP), pp. 839–858. IEEE (2016). https://doi.org/10.1109/SP.2016.55
8. Zhao, J.L., Fan, S., Yan, J.: Overview of business innovations and research opportunities in blockchain and introduction to the special issue. Financ. Innov. $1(2)$, 28 (2016)
9. Wuille, P.: BIP32: hierarchical deterministic wallets, February 2012. https://github.com/bitcoin/bips/blob/master/bip-0032.mediawiki
10. Gutoski, G., Stebila, D.: Hierarchical deterministic Bitcoin wallets that tolerate key leakage. In: Böhme, R., Okamoto, T. (eds.) FC 2015. LNCS, vol. 8975, pp. 497–504. Springer, Heidelberg (2015). https://doi.org/10.1007/978-3-662-47854-7_31
11. Armory: Armory Secure Wallet. https://bitcoinarmory.com
12. Bitcoin CD: Bitcoin Core. https://bitcoin.org
13. Dmitrienko, A., Noack, D., Yung, M.: In: Proceedings of the 2017 ACM on Asia Conference on Computer and Communications Security, pp. 520–531. ACM (2017)
14. Eskandari, S., Clark, J., Barrera, D., et al.: A first look at the usability of bitcoin key management. preprint arXiv arXiv: 1802.04351 (2018). Journal $2(5)$, 99–110 (2016)
15. Kaliski, B.: PKCS 5: password-based cryptography specification version 2.0. http://www.rfc-editor.org/info/rfc2898
16. Jin, A.T.B., Ling, D.N.C., Goh, A.: Biohashing: two factor authentication featuring fingerprint data and tokenised random number. Pattern Recogn. $11(37)$, 2245–2255 (2004)
17. Gennaro, R., Goldfeder, S., Narayanan, A.: Threshold-optimal DSA/ECDSA signatures and an application to bitcoin wallet security. In: Manulis, M., Sadeghi, A.-R., Schneider, S. (eds.) ACNS 2016. LNCS, vol. 9696, pp. 156–174. Springer, Cham (2016). https://doi.org/10.1007/978-3-319-39555-5_9
18. Schnorr, C.P.: Efficient signature generation by smart cards. J. Cryptol. $3(4)$, 161–174 (1991)
19. Bellare, M., Rogaway, P.: Random oracles are practical-a paradigm for designing efficient protocols. In: Proceedings of the First ACM Conference on Computer and Communications Security, pp. 62–73. ACM (1993)
20. Bellare, M., Rogaway, P.: The exact security of digital signatures-how to sign with RSA and Rabin. In: Maurer, U. (ed.) EUROCRYPT 1996. LNCS, vol. 1070, pp. 399–416. Springer, Heidelberg (1996). https://doi.org/10.1007/3-540-68339-9_34

A Location Predictive Model Based on 2D Angle Data for HAPS Using LSTM

Ke Xiao[1,2]([✉]), Chaofei Li[1], Yunhua He[1], Chao Wang[1], and Wei Cheng[2]

[1] North China University of Technology, Beijing 100144, China
xiaoke@ncut.edu.cn
[2] University of Washington, Tacoma 98402, USA

Abstract. High Altitude Platforms Station (HAPS) is considered to be an effective solution to expand the communication coverage of rural area in the fifth generation (5G) network. However, HAPS is usually in an unstable state because of space airflow. Thus, the inaccurate beamforming performed by the gateway (GW) will result in unnecessary capacity loss of HAPS communication system. To address this issue, a long short-term memory (LSTM)-based location predictive model is proposed to predict next moment location of HAPS by training the current two-dimensional (2D) angle data. Specifically, a novel preprocessing system is introduced to ensure the effectiveness of our model. Moreover, the LSTM-based model with highest predictive accuracy can be saved during the training to realize the real-time prediction. Experimental results reveal that the proposed LSTM-based model is of higher prediction accuracy compared with other two predictive models. Therefore, a more precise beamforming performed by GW can reduce the unnecessary capacity loss and improve the reliability of 5G HAPS communication system.

Keywords: 5G · HAPS · LSTM · DOA estimation

1 Introduction

Facing the growing demand of telecommunications services, the development of new telecommunications infrastructure has become a crucial point in the fifth generation (5G) network. High Altitude Platforms Station (HAPS) is considered to be an important solution to expand the communication coverage, which can offer multiple services on a single platform and provide many advantages over other existing technologies, such as terrestrial and satellite [1]. Therefore, HAPS is widely used in 5G communication system.

In HAPS communication system, whether the beamforming of gateway (GW) is accurate or not will directly affect the reliability of entire communication system. Direction of arrival (DOA) estimation is considered to be an important means to determine the specific location by using the reception of its own signal [2], which makes it possible to be applied to estimate the direction of incoming wave of GW in our scenario. However, HAPS is usually unstable because of the

© Springer Nature Switzerland AG 2019
E. S. Biagioni et al. (Eds.): WASA 2019, LNCS 11604, pp. 370–381, 2019.
https://doi.org/10.1007/978-3-030-23597-0_30

space airflow, the current location estimated by DOA is not enough to ensure the communication between GW and HAPS. In addition, it is worth mentioning that although Global Positioning System (GPS) can locate accurately, only an approximate location can be achieved, so the specific next moment location of HAPS is necessary for better communication. Therefore, a novel method is necessary to be investigated to predict the next moment location of HAPS.

In order to adapt to the characteristics of 2D angle data of HAPS, a neural network with good memory and forgetting ability is necessary to be applied. Long short-term memory (LSTM) can solve the problem of gradient disappearance, and the forgetting gate in it can determine which kind of information to discard based on the state information of past time and current input data [3]. Since HAPS will change the trajectory according to different needs, the input angle data will also be changed. LSTM network can automatically filter through the feedback network, leaving useful information for training next period angle data. Therefore, LSTM network is suitable for 5G HAPS communication system.

Since LSTM has good performance in optimization and prediction, a LSTM-based location predictive model is proposed to predict the specific next moment location of HAPS. First, the DOA estimation is applied to calculate the elevation and horizontal angles of HAPS. Then, a series of complex preprocessing is performed on the calculated angel data, and finally input the data into the LSTM model. In order to improve the prediction effect of proposed model, we design a modified LSTM model for this research scenario, resulting in a more accurate location information of HAPS. Therefore, a more precise beamforming can be performed by GW to reduce the unnecessary capacity loss, so that a more reliable 5G HAPS communication system can be obtained, the contributions of this work are listed as follows.

1. A specific preprocessing system is introduced to meet the characteristics of angle data. Specifically, a data transfer method is applied to combine the elevation and horizontal angles together, which makes the training process of LSTM-based model more effective.
2. To further improve the prediction effect, a specific modified LSTM model for 5G HAPS communication scenario is designed to meet the training process. Experimental results have verified the robustness of the proposed model.
3. The proposed LSTM-based location predictive model can achieve a higher prediction accuracy compared with other two models, and the model with best accuracy can be automatically saved during the training process, thus ensuring the real-time prediction.

The rest of the paper will be organized as follows. Some related works are provided in Sect. 2. In Sect. 3, we introduce the received signal model of DOA estimation and present the basic structure of LSTM model. The specific process of the proposed method is described thoroughly in Sect. 4. Some experimental results and analyses are provided in Sect. 5. Finally, Sect. 6 concludes the paper and presents the future work.

2   Related Work

DOA estimation and beamforming techniques play an important role in wireless communication systems, and the main purpose of DOA estimation is to determine the location of the spatial target. Currently, there are many researches that have applied the DOA estimation to HAPS communication system. In [4], a new hardware architecture was proposed to achieve better performance in real-time computing and DOA estimation accuracy in HAPS communication system. [5] and [6] used a smart antenna array in a high-altitude platform to perform the DOA estimation on mobile railway trains, so that the problem of high-speed data communication links was solved. In above three references, HAPS was considered to be stable so that the DOA estimation can be performed. However, HAPS is usually in an unstable state because of the space airflow. Therefore, the current location estimated by the traditional DOA estimation is not enough to ensure the communication between GW and HAPS, and it is necessary to introduce a new method to predict the next moment location of HAPS, so that a more precise beamforming can be performed by GW.

With the development of deep learning, LSTM has been widely used to solve sequence learning and prediction tasks. Recently, the application of LSTM-based deep learning methods to solve trajectory prediction tasks has attracted much attention. [7] applied LSTM model to build the relationship between pedestrians, so that the current position and movement trend can be learned, thus achieving a more accuracy trajectory prediction. [8] realized the trajectory prediction of pedestrian via a specific social-grid LSTM model, so that the possible collisions can be avoided as early as possible. [9] proposed a novel Antlion optimization (ALO)-LSTM trajectory prediction model to obtain a more quickly and accurately prediction of the flight trajectory.

Since LSTM has good performance in position and trajectory prediction, we propose a LSTM-based location predictive model to predict the specific next moment position of HAPS for better communication. The system model is provided in next section.

3   System Model

The 5G HAPS communication scenario we discussed is shown in Fig. 1, where the triangular antenna array can ensure the efficiency of HAPS communication system. In our scenario, HAPS is located at about 20 km above the sea level, and the Internet provides the network services for GW through the core Network [1]. The coverage area of HAPS at T1 is shown in big gray area, where HAPS is responsible for the communication of entire area. In order to adapt to different communication needs, HAPS will adjust his own flight trajectory in the air. For example, there are almost no users in mountain and sea area during the night, HAPS will shorten the sailing distance to save fuel consumption, and the coverage area at T2 is shown in the blue area. Besides, HAPS will always be affected by the space airflow, so a big offset will occur. Therefore, the two-dimensional (2D) arrival angle is regarded as an effective way to determine the specific location of HAPS. As shown in Fig. 1, HAPS will move to some extent in the vertical and horizontal directions, which is the elevation angle θ and the horizontal angle ϕ respectively. Therefore, current position of HAPS can be determined from the 2D arrival angle estimated by DOA estimation, and then the next moment location of HAPS can be predicted by LSTM-based location predictive model we proposed. For better investigating the DOA estimation, the received signal model is first introduced in part 1, and the detailed discussion is next provided for the LSTM model.

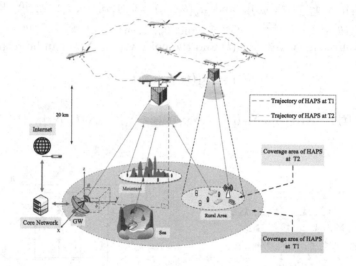

Fig. 1. 5G HAPS communication scenario. (Color figure online)

3.1   Received Signal Model of DOA Estimation Algorithm

The three faces of triangular antenna array we applied are composed of uniform rectangular array (URA) and the height of HAPS is about 20 km, so the high-altitude triangular antenna array can be considered as a point to ignore its own angle. Therefore, the DOA estimation of URA is investigated in this paper, which is shown in Fig. 2 for a better understanding. Suppose that URA is composed of $M \times N$ identical elements, where the distance between adjacent elements in row direction is d_y, and that between neighboring column is d_x. Besides, the squares with arrow represent the elements of the middle sub-arrays. Now we can imagine that there are P uncorrelated signals $S_1(t), ..., S_P(t)$ impacting on URA from directions $(\theta_1, \phi_1), (\theta_2, \phi_2)..., (\theta_P, \phi_P)$ respectively, and θ_i and ϕ_i denote elevation and horizontal angle of the ith signal. In addition, it is assumed that these signals have the same center wavelength λ. Therefore, the output signal of the array can be represented as [10]

$$x(t) = AS(t) + N(t) \tag{1}$$

where $x(t)$ denotes the received signal vector, A is the ideal steering matrix, $S(t)$ and $N(t)$ denote the source signal vector and the noise vector, respectively. For a better understanding, the received signal vector $x(t)$ can also be represented as $x(t) = [x_1(t), ..., x_N(t), x_{N+1}(t), ..., x_{2N}(t), ..., x_{(M-1)N}(t), ..., x_{MN}(t)]^T$, Besides, the ideal steering matrix A can be denoted as

$$A = [a(\theta_1, \phi_1), ..., a(\theta_P, \phi_P)] \tag{2}$$

where $a(\theta_i, \phi_i) = a_x(\theta_1, \phi_1) \otimes a_y(\theta_i, \phi_i), i = 1, ..., P$. Specifically, $a_x(\theta_i, \phi_i) = [1, \beta_x(\theta_i, \phi_i), ..., \beta_x^{M-1}(\theta_i, \phi_i)]$, and $a_y(\theta_i, \phi_i) = [1, \beta_y(\theta_i, \phi_i), ..., \beta_y^{N-1}(\theta_i, \phi_i)]$. Besides, $\beta_x(\theta_i, \phi_i) = e^{j\frac{2\pi d_x}{\lambda} cos\theta_i sin\phi_i}$ and $\beta_y(\theta_i, \phi_i) = e^{j\frac{2\pi d_y}{\lambda} sin\theta_i sin\phi_i}$. In addition, the source signal vector $S(t)$ and the noise vector $N(t)$ can be respectively denoted as

$$S(t) = [S_1(t), ..., S_P(t)]^T \tag{3}$$

$$N(t) = [N_1(t), ..., N_N(t), ..., N_{2N}(t), ..., N_{(M-1)N}(t), N_{MN}(t)]^T \tag{4}$$

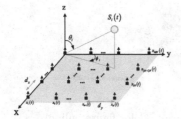   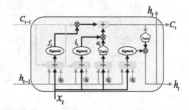

Fig. 2. The specific structure of URA   **Fig. 3.** The basic structure of a LSTM cell

3.2   LSTM Model

In each layer of the LSTM model, there is a set of neurons, each computing for intermediate results is called "gate", and they are called forget, input, output and candidata gate, respectively. We can take a LSTM cell for example, the memory block is used to store the status of the cell so that this status can be transformed to the next time step [11]. The basic structure of a specific LSTM cell is illustrated in Fig. 3, which can also be represented as

$$h_t = o_t * tanh(C_{t-1} * f_t + i_t * a_t) \tag{5}$$

where h_t denotes the hidden state of time step t, C_{t-1} represents the cell state of time step $t-1$, i, f and o are respectively the input gate, forget gate, output gate. Therefore, LSTM can find the optimal solution by finding the loss function, then deriving the partial variable for each variable parameter, and updating the parameters, thus achieving the good effect of learning data with time series.

4   LSTM-Based Location Predictive Model

In this section, we will focus on the prediction process of the LSTM-based model, the learning process is shown in Fig. 4. First, θ and ϕ can be obtained according to DOA estimation of URA. And then, the specific preprocessing system is applied to perform a series of preprocessing on the obtained angle data, thereby achieving the processed new angle data θ' and ϕ'. Finally, the processed angle data is input into the LSTM model as the input layer, and the training model with best prediction performance can be saved to obtain the predicted $\hat{\theta}$ and $\hat{\phi}$.

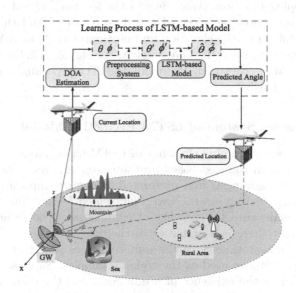

Fig. 4. Learning process of LSTM-based model

4.1   Acquisition of LSTM Model Training Samples

As we discussed above, the received signal vector is shown in Eq. (1), so the covariance matrix of $x(t)$ can be expressed as [12]

$$R_x = E\{x(t)x^H(t)\} = AR_sA^H + \sigma^2 I \tag{6}$$

where R_s represents the source covariance matrix, σ^2 is the common variance, and I denotes a $MN \times MN$ identity matrix. Besides, if the standard subspace method is considered, Eq. (6) can be rewritten to $R_x = \sum_{i=1}^{P} \lambda_i e_i e_i^H + \sum_{i=P+1}^{MN} \lambda_i e_i e_i^H = E_s \Lambda_s E_s^H + \sigma^2 E_n E_n^H$, where $\lambda_1 \geq \lambda_2 \geq \cdots \lambda_P > \lambda_{P+1} = \cdots = \lambda_{MN}$ are the eigenvalues of R_x and $e_1, e_2, ..., e_{MN}$ are the associated eigenvectors of them. The columns of E_s and E_n are the eigenvectors associated with P largest eigenvalues and $MN - P$ smallest eigenvalues respectively.

In addition, the space spanned by $a(\theta_1, \phi_1), ..., a(\theta_P, \phi_P)$ is the same as the signal subspace spanned by E_s, and is orthogonal to the noise subspace spanned by E_n. Thus, we have $\left\| E_n^H a(\theta_i, \phi_i) \right\| = 0, \{i = 1, 2, ..., P\}$, where $\|\cdot\|$ denotes the Kronecker tensor product. Therefore, we can use the multiple signal classification to define following spatial spectrum to estimate the DOA of URA.

$$P(\theta, \phi) = \frac{1}{\left\| E_n^H a(\theta, \phi) \right\|^2} \tag{7}$$

According to the spatial spectrum function we obtained above, two maximum values of the spectrum can be achieved, which means that the angles corresponding to the peak are just the estimated θ and ϕ. In addition, the LSTM-based model is a mapping function. According to the feedback signal of URA, GW can receive the corresponding received signal vector $x(t)$. And then, these two peaks can be obtained as the elevation and horizontal angle of HAPS's current location. It means that once the GW receives the signal, a 2D arrival angle of current moment can be captured. Therefore, the 2D arrival angles of HAPS can be acquired continuously.

4.2   Preprocessing System of LSTM Predictive Model

In order to improve the training efficiency of LSTM-based model, a specific preprocessing system is introduced based on the characteristics of obtained angle data (Fig. 5). Data cleaning is first performed to remove duplicate angle information and correct existing errors. Next, Augmented Dickey-Fuller test (ADF) is performed to make sure the stability of training set. The principle of ADF is to check whether there is a unit root in the data sequence. If it exists, the data sequence is non-stationary; if the unit root does not exist, the sequence is stationary enough to be used as the training samples. Suppose that the null hypothesis of ADF is the existence of a unit root, and the standard is that as long as the test statistic value is less than 1%, the null hypothesis can be rejected significantly, thus determining the stability of data. The experimental results are shown in Table 1, where the test statistic value is much smaller than 1% of the critical statistics. Besides, the probability-value (P-value) of experimental result approaches 0. Therefore, the obtained angel data is considered to be stationary.

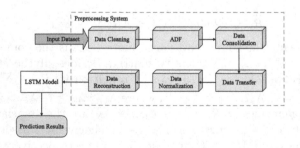

Fig. 5. Flowchart of data preprocessing

Table 1. The experimental result of ADF

Name	Value
Test statistic value	−22.44154
P-value	0
Critical value (1%)	−3.43067
Critical value (5%)	−2.86168
Critical value (10%)	−2.56685

Besides, data consolidation is next applied to collect θ and ϕ of different moments to obtain a complete angle database. In addition, in order to facilitate the training of LSTM model, we imagine the angle data as a point on the coordinate system, where the elevation and horizontal angles are the horizontal and vertical coordinates of the coordinate system, thus converting the two 1D angles into a 2D angle, finishing the process of data transfer. Next, data normalization helps to ensure the convergence speed of program running and data reconstruction helps to make the data more suitable for the structure of LSTM model.

After the processed data is input into the LSTM-based location predictive model, the new angle can be obtained. Therefore, the precise next moment location can be predicted, achieving the goal of location prediction.

4.3   Robustness Analysis of the Proposed LSTM-Based Model

To make sure the robustness of proposed model, we have adjusted a set of LSTM parameters to better adapt to both the data characteristics and the specific 5G HAPS communication scenario, which not only greatly improve the accuracy of LSTM model, but also effectively improve the convergence speed of program running.

Besides, the sliding window method is applied to ensure the real-time prediction. Suppose that the step size of LSTM model is n, then the $(n+1)th$ time node is the angle data that needs to be predicted. In the process of HAPS communication, whenever the latest location data of HAPS is acquired, the angle will merge into the sliding window, and then the oldest data will be automatically deleted, which ensures the real-time updates of the data in the window. In addition, since the input of each moment is a single sample, the data preprocessing and the best predictive model structure have been saved during the training. Therefore, the next moment location of HAPS can be accurately predicted in real time.

5   Experimental Results

In this section, the experimental results are provided through Python to verify the effectiveness of our proposed LSTM-based location predictive model, and the simulation platform is based on HAPS standard parameters provided by International Telecommunication Union (ITU). Besides, the number of training set samples and test set samples are 13570 and 6669, respectively, the step size is defined as 30. In order to obtain the best prediction effect (highest accuracy or lowest MSE), we do a series of experiments by changing the number of hidden nodes, LSTM layers, batch size and learning rate (LR), respectively. The experimental results are shown in Sect. 5.1, and the robustness of proposed model is next verified by comparing three different predictive models in Sect. 5.2.

5.1   Related Parameters of LSTM-Based Location Predictive Model

First, we do a series of experiments by changing the number of LSTM layers and hidden nodes, and the average mean square error (MSE) of training set is shown in Table 2, when hidden nodes exceed 16, the value of MSE tends to be stable and hardly decreases. Therefore, the number of hidden nodes is defined as 16. To further determine LSTM layers, we control the number of hidden nodes to be 16, and only change LSTM layers. The accuracy results are shown in Fig. 6, and only part of the experimental curve is displayed to show the results more clearly. When epoch reaches 490, the experimental curves can be considered to be convergent, especially for 4-layer, 5-layer and 6-layer LSTM models. Since less layers can achieve faster training speed, the 4-layer LSTM model is chosen.

Table 2. MSE of different LSTM network structure

Name	Structure	Training set (average MSE)					
		4	8	12	16	20	24
NET1	1-layer LSTM	0.0014	0.0022	0.0226	0.0008	0.0011	0.0010
NET2	2-layer LSTM	0.0015	0.0084	0.0253	0.0011	0.0013	0.0011
NET3	3-layer LSTM	0.0017	0.0020	0.0247	0.0013	0.0011	0.0013
NET4	4-layer LSTM	0.0023	0.0015	0.0234	0.0015	0.0015	0.0014
NET5	5-layer LSTM	0.0024	0.0020	0.024	0.0017	0.0016	0.0016
NET6	6-layer LSTM	0.0027	0.0020	0.0215	0.0018	0.0018	0.0016

Besides, a suitable batch size is helpful to decrease convergence speed and avoid local optimal situations of our training. Therefore, LSTM layers is determined as 4 with 16 hidden nodes according to above discussion, only the batch size is changed, the experimental results are shown in Fig. 7. When training epoch reaches 200, the experimental curves can be considered to be convergent, and Batch Size-200 (the value of batch size) can achieve the lowest MSE, which means that the stable highest accuracy can be obtained.

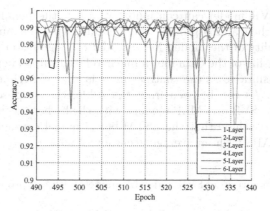

Fig. 6. Accuracy of LSTM-based predictive model under different layers

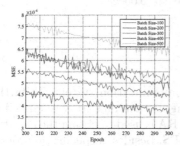

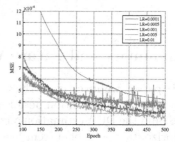

Fig. 7. MSE of different LSTM batch size   **Fig. 8.** MSE of different LSTM LR

In addition, learning rate (LR) is investigated to further increase the convergence speed. According to above discussion, the LSTM network is defined as 4-layer with 16 hidden nodes and 200 batch size, only LR is changed during the experiments. As can be seen from Fig. 8, the lowest MSE can be achieved when LR is 0.005. Therefore, the conclusion can be made that when the number of LSTM layer is 4, the hidden nodes is 16, Batch size-200 is chosen and the LR is 0.005, the LSTM model can get the lowest MSE, which is almost 2.5×10^{-4}, resulting in the highest prediction accuracy with most stable state.

5.2   Performance Comparison

To further verify the reliability of proposed LSTM-based model, we compare our model with two State-of-the-Art models, including Support Vector Regression (SVR) and Multi-Layer Perceptron (MLP) on accuracy and MSE. Traditionally, Autoregressive Integrated Moving Average Model (ARIMA) is the most common type of statistical model. However, ARIMA is only suitable for short-term linear regression training and has good predictive effect on the data with linear relationship. Therefore, SVR and MLP models have been proposed by predecessors to better train a large number of data samples with non-linear relationships.

Specifically, SVR model can continuously adjust the penalty coefficient of the errors during the training process, thereby improving the fault tolerance and generalization ability of the model; MLP model can significantly transform the nonlinear relationship of the data into a linear relationship. Therefore, SVR and MLP models are suitable as the contrast models. The experimental results are shown in Table 3. As can be seen from the table, the proposed LSTM-based model outperforms SVR and MLP models, with the highest accuracy and lowest MSE. So we can conclude that the LSTM-based model can accurately predict the location of HAPS with an average accuracy of 99%.

Table 3. Comparison of SVR and MLP models with our proposed model

Model	SVR	MLP	LSTM
Test accuracy	82%	95%	99%
MSE	0.00143	0.00109	0.00024

6   Summary and Future Work

In this paper, we investigate the 5G HAPS communication system. To further improve the communication performance, triangular antenna array is applied for HAPS, and the DOA estimation algorithm of URA is used to obtain the elevation and horizontal angles of current location of HAPS. Besides, a specific preprocessing system is proposed to process the calculated angle data, and finally the data is input into LSTM-based model as the training sample. The proposed LSTM-based location predictive model has a good performance in training the processed angle data, which makes it possible to accurately predict the next moment location of HAPS. Experimental results show that the LSTM-based model is of high prediction accuracy, and a more precise beamforming performed by GW can reduce the unnecessary capacity loss, so that a more reliable 5G HAPS communication system can be obtained. In the future, the Gated Recurrent Unit (GRU)-based location predictive model will be investigated to further improve the training and prediction speed.

References

1. Lian, Z., Jiang, L., He, C., et al.: A novel channel model for 3-D HAP-MIMO communication systems. In: International Conference on Networking & Network Applications, pp. 1–6. IEEE (2016). https://doi.org/10.1109/NaNA.2016.94
2. Liang, Y., Cai, Z., Han, Q., et al.: Location privacy leakage through sensory data. J. Secur. Commun. Netw. **7576307**, 1–12 (2017)
3. Tolga, E., Suleyman, S.K.: Online training of LSTM networks in distributed systems for variable length data sequences. IEEE Trans. Neural Netw. Learn. Syst., 5159–5165 (2017). https://doi.org/10.1109/TNNLS.2017.2770179

4. Xie, Y., Peng, C., Jiang, X., et al.: Hardware design and implementation of DOA estimation algorithms for spherical array antennas. In: IEEE International Conference on Signal Processing, pp. 219–223. IEEE (2014). https://doi.org/10.1109/ICSPCC.2014.6986186

5. Irma, Z., Suhartono, T., Iskandar, et al.: Sum rate capacity of multiuser MISO designed for HAPS high speed train application. In: International Conference on Electrical Engineering and Informatics, pp. 1–5. IEEE (2011). https://doi.org/10.1109/ICEEI.2011.6021781

6. George, P.W., Yuriy, V.Z.: Data communications to trains from high-altitude platforms. IEEE Trans. Veh. Technol., 2253–2266 (2007). https://doi.org/10.1109/TVT.2007.897185

7. Song, C., Chen, Z., Qi, X., et al.: Human trajectory prediction for automatic guided vehicle with recurrent neural network. J. Eng. **2018**(16), 1574–1578 (2018)

8. Chen, B., Xu, X., Zeng, Y., et al.: Pedestrian trajectory prediction via the Social-Grid LSTM model. J. Eng. **2018**(16), 1468–1474 (2018)

9. Zhang, Z., Yang, R., Fang, Y., et al.: LSTM network based on Antlion optimization and its application in flight trajectory prediction. In: IEEE Advanced Information Management, Communicates, Electronic and Automation Control Conference (IMCEC), pp. 1658–1662. IEEE (2018). https://doi.org/10.1109/IMCEC.2018.8469476

10. Meng, H., Zheng, Z., Yang, Y.: A low-complexity 2-D DOA estimation algorithm for massive MIMO systems. In: IEEE International Conference on Communication in China, pp. 1–5. IEEE (2016). https://doi.org/10.1109/ICCChina.2016.7636811

11. Liang, Y., Cai, Z., Yu, J., et al.: Deep learning based inference of private information using embedded sensors in smart devices. IEEE Netw. Mag. **32**(4), 8–14 (2018). https://doi.org/10.1109/MNET.2018.1700349

12. Mazlout, S., Salah, M.B.B., Samet, A.: Comparative study of two array configurations for 2D-DOA estimation in LS-MIMO systems. In: Sixth International Conference on Communications and Networking, pp. 1–6. IEEE (2018). https://doi.org/10.1109/COMNET.2017.8285597

Cross-Layer Optimization on Charging Strategy for Wireless Sensor Networks Based on Successive Interference Cancellation

Juan Xu[1,2,3], Xingxin Xu[1], Xu Ding[1,2,3(✉)], Lei Shi[1,2,3], and Yang Lu[1,2,3]

[1] School of Computer Science and Information Engineering,
HeFei University of Technology, Hefei, China
dingxu@hfut.edu.cn
[2] Engineering Research Center of Safety Critical Industrial Measurement
and Control Technology, Ministry of Education, Hefei, China
[3] Key Laboratory of Industry Safety and Emergency Technology, Hefei, Anhui, China

Abstract. Communication interference and the energy limitation of nodes seriously hamper the fundamental performance of wireless sensor networks (WSN) such as throughput and network lifetime. In this paper, we focus on the Successive Interference Cancellation (SIC) aiming to realize multi-node concurrency communication and propose a heuristic power control algorithm. To prolong the network lifetime, we consider the scenario of mobile wireless charging equipment (WCE) periodically charging each node's battery wirelessly. Time-slice scheduling scheme and energy consumption optimization protocol are adopted to design an efficient cross-layer charging strategy. Then we use a near-optimal method to transform the original problem into a linear problem which yields identical optimal value. Simulation results demonstrate that adopting SIC and WCE can greatly improve channel utilization ratio and increase network throughput by 200% to 500% while ensuring the network lifetime.

Keywords: Concurrency communication ·
Successive Interference Cancellation · Power control ·
Charging strategy · Cross-layer optimization

1 Introduction

Wireless sensor networks (WSN) are widely applied in military, industry, and agriculture [1]. However, widespread communication interference limits the network throughput, which seriously affects the performance of communications in WSN. And the energy of batteries which power the sensor nodes is severely restricted by the size and cost of the nodes. Thus, communication interference and energy issues seriously affect the performance and development of WSN.

© Springer Nature Switzerland AG 2019
E. S. Biagioni et al. (Eds.): WASA 2019, LNCS 11604, pp. 382–394, 2019.
https://doi.org/10.1007/978-3-030-23597-0_31

In traditional wireless network transmission, collisions occur when multiple nodes transmit data to the same node simultaneously. This affects the efficiency and real-time performance of communication since it leads to the discard or retransmission of conflicting packets. Successive Interference Cancellation (SIC) [2] is one of the most commonly used methods to effectively alleviate interference and achieve concurrency communication. It breaks through the restraint of traditional wireless communication technology for alleviating interference and bringing the increase of channel utilization and network throughput. Consequently, it brings about a large amount of energy consumption for nodes. The increasing demand for energy may cause more significant energy problem.

Solving the energy supply problem relies on two main solutions: energy conservation and energy acquisition. For energy conservation, some previous works are done to save energy to prolong the lifetime of WSN, such as reducing the sensor nodes' energy consumption [3–5]. Energy acquisition is to harvest energy from the environment, such as sunlight, tides and winds. But the energy converter may not be applicable to some specific work scenarios because of its large size. In recent years, Wireless Energy Transmission (WET) technology is a new direction to solve energy issues. A major breakthrough in WET technology based on strongly coupled magnetic resonance provides an improved scheme for long distance wireless transmission [6]. Therefore, some scholars propose that wireless energy supply equipment should be employed to charge nodes in WSN.

The wireless charging equipment (WCE) has already been applied to wireless rechargeable sensor networks (WRSN) in recent years, freely moving inside the networks to charge nodes within its proximity [7–9]. Shi et al. [10] consider employing a mobile charger (MC) with sufficient energy to charge nodes periodically and introduce renewable energy cycle to study the working scheme of MC. As the charging strategy is one of the most important functions of WRSN, it is studied by many researchers in different network scenarios [11–14]. Guo et al. [15] propose a framework of joint wireless energy replenishment and anchor-point with mobile data gathering. Chang et al. [16] firstly introduce the conception and requirements of cyclic energy conservation in conditions of WRSN and enhance the utility of charging achieved by Cuckoo Search. Wei et al. [17] design a Clustering Hierarchical Routing Algorithm for WRSN based on K-means method (K-CHRA) to reduce the energy consumption and the data transmission delay.

The above studies just consider the energy issue and overlook interference management. Therefore, this paper will further study the charging problem on the basis of considering interference management. The introduction of SIC can further improve communication efficiency, but it will also greatly increase the complexity of the original problem. Time-slice scheduling scheme and energy consumption optimization protocol are adopted to solve this complexity. The main contributions of this paper are listed below:

1. We discuss the multi-node concurrency communication conditions in a single-hop WSN and design a heuristic power control algorithm based on SIC to cluster nodes and control their power.

2. By analyzing the working mode of sensor nodes and WCE, we propose a corresponding cross-layer optimization problem with the objective of maximizing the vacation time ratio of WCE.
3. We use a near-optimal method to transform the original problem into a linear problem which yields the same objective value. Subsequently, we obtain the charging strategy and then evaluate the communication performance.

2   Model Construction

2.1   Network Model

The structure model of the single-hop WRSN in this paper is shown in Fig. 1. We consider n sensor nodes randomly distributed over a two-dimensional area and denote the set of nodes as $\mathcal{N} = \{1, 2, 3, \cdots, n\}$. A fixed base station (B) and a fixed service station (S) both with known location are placed in the area [10,13]. B collects data directly from nodes, and S is a place where the WCE is maintained after travelling all nodes and finishing a round of energy replenishment.

Each node is equipped with the same type of wireless rechargeable battery with the maximum capacity of E_{max} and fully charged initially. Denote the minimum energy at a sensor node as E_{min} (for it to be operational). The mobile WCE starts from the service station S and travels all sensor nodes with speed of V (in m/s). When it arrives at a sensor node, say i, it will spend a time of τ_i to charge its battery wirelessly. After τ_i, WCE leaves node i and travels to the next node. Suppose that the power of each node and the charging power of WCE are invariable. WCE has enough energy to recharge all sensor nodes. The communication channel is AWGN channel. The channel capacity between B and nodes is large enough. And the farthest node can communicate with the base station normally.

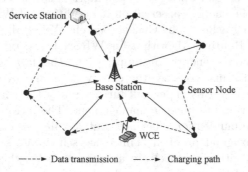

Fig. 1. Structure model of the WRSN with WCE.

2.2   Power Control Model Based on SIC

Basic Idea. SIC technology can be employed by the base station to decode and receive each node's signal according to its power degree. Each transmission power should be configured so that all signals satisfy certain conditions resolved simultaneously. Consequently, this brings about a large amount of energy consumption. We can use WCE to charge nodes for keeping them working properly. The charging time of each node depends on its energy consumption which is related to power in WRSN. The smaller the power, the shorter the charging time. The sending power depends on its transmission rate and the distance from the base station. The minimum sending power of the node can be obtained when the transmission rate and the distance from the base station are known.

Power Control Algorithm. Considering the actual situation that all nodes cannot send data to the base station B simultaneously, only a small proportion of nodes can transmit successfully. So the nodes can be divided into clusters. All nodes in the same cluster can send data to B simultaneously by controlling their power. In this part, the following three points should be taken into consideration.

1. The power of nodes affects energy consumption and further affects charging time. To save the energy of nodes, the power should be as small as possible.
2. The transmitting power of the nodes should be large enough to ensure that the base station successfully detects the signals sent by sensor nodes.
3. Data transmission failure can caused by transmission conflicts when multiple nodes send data to the base station simultaneously. To avoid this situation, the power of each node should satisfy certain constraints.

Compared with the data transmission process, the energy consumption of data collection and processing is negligible. Suppose the data generation rate at node i is f_i $(i \in \mathcal{N})$, and its energy consumption only for transmitting data. The actual sending rate of the node i is R_i which cannot be less than the data generation rate. There is $R_i \geq f_i$. Denote the power of node i as P_i. Therefore,

$$P_i = C_i * R_i \tag{1}$$

where C_i is a power factor indicating the energy consumption rate for transmitting a unit of data from node i to B. Further, $C_i = \psi_1 + \psi_2 \cdot d_{i,B}^\lambda$, where $d_{i,B}$ is the distance between node i and B, λ is the path loss index, ψ_1 is a constant term, and ψ_2 is a coefficient of the distance-dependent term. When node i sends data with the power of P_i, the receiving power at B for node i is $g_i P_i$, where g_i represents the power attenuation between the node i and B when transmitting data. Then, $g_i = a * d_{i,B}^{-\lambda}$ where a is a constant term associated with transmitting antennas. It is normalized to facilitate discussion, $a = 1$.

When multiple nodes send data to B simultaneously, the signal to interference plus noise power ratio of node i $(SINR_i)$ must satisfy the specific constraint to be correctly decoded and received. The constraint can be computed as

$$SINR_i = \frac{g_i P_i}{N_0 + \sum_{g_j P_j < g_i P_i} g_j P_j} \geq \beta \quad (i \neq j; i, j \in \mathcal{N}) \tag{2}$$

where N_0 is noise power, the sum portion indicates the aggregate receiving power of all nodes like node j that transmitting data together with node i simultaneously, but the receiving power is less than the receiving power of node i at B. At this point, if and only if $SINR_i \geq \beta$, the transmitted data can be decoded by B, where β is the threshold of the signal to interference plus noise power ratio. For threshold β, it is required that $\beta > 1$ in most coding and decoding schemes.

Suppose each node sends data with the same channel bandwidth W. If the node i sends data successfully, the channel capacity of node i is $W \log_2(1 + SINR_i)$, where $SINR_i$ can be obtained by Eq. 2. R_i should be less than or equal to the maximum channel capacity during the whole transmission process. Because of $SINR_i \geq \beta$, the channel capacity has the following constraint:

$$W \log_2(1 + \beta) \leq W \log_2(1 + SINR_i) \tag{3}$$

Theorem 1. *Suppose that the distance from node i and node j to the base station B is d_i and d_j, respectively. node i is known to send data to base station at time t with the power of P, and node j sends data to base station simultaneously with the same transmission power as node i. If $d_i \geq d_j$, the data sent by node j must be decoded by B earlier than the data sent by node i, and vice versa.*

Theorem 1 can be proved by contradiction according to Eq. 2. Receiving power at the base station B depends on g_i and P_i, where g_i depends on the distance between the node and B. Thus, we can draw a conclusion from Theorem 1: the decoding order is related to the distance of signal to some degree.

If the receiving power at the base station is sorted according to the value: $g_1 P_1 \leq g_2 P_2 \leq \cdots \leq g_i P_i \leq \cdots \leq g_n P_n$, the relationships between the different receiving power under the SIC conditions are listed as follows.

$$\begin{cases} g_1 P_1 & \geq \beta N_0 \\ g_2 P_2 & \geq \beta(N_0 + g_1 P_1) \geq \beta(N_0 + \beta N_0) = \beta(1 + \beta)N_0 \\ \vdots \\ g_n P_n & \geq \beta(1 + \beta)^{n-1} N_0 \end{cases} \tag{4}$$

To consume as little energy as possible, we consider both minimum sending power in Eq. 1 and minimum received power in Eq. 4. Then taking the minimum power which meets Eqs. 1 and 4 as the actual power. From Eqs. 1–4, the sending power of nodes which communicate with the base station simultaneously can be determined sequentially.

On the premise of the above, a heuristic clustered power control algorithm based on SIC is proposed. Firstly, taking B as the center of the circle, the whole region is divided into circle areas according to different radius sizes. All the nodes can fall in each circle area. Next, the nearest node that has not yet been clustered is searched by traversing each area. If the node satisfies certain conditions, we add it to the cluster and record the real transmission power (calculated by Eqs. 1–4). Otherwise, this round of traversal is terminated. After that, the next cluster is searched according to the same rules during the next round. The algorithm terminates when all nodes are assigned to the clusters. When all the nodes are clustered, the controlled power of each clustered node is also obtained.

If multiple clusters send at the same time, it is likely that conflicts will occur. Therefore, the time-slice scheduling mechanism is adopted in the data link layer. The transmission of each cluster takes up one time slice over a period of T. To make nodes send more data, time slices for each sensor node can be set as

$$t_1 : t_2 : \ldots : t_k = \frac{\sum_{i \in \mathcal{N}_1} R_i}{\sum_{i \in \mathcal{N}} R_i} : \frac{\sum_{i \in \mathcal{N}_2} R_i}{\sum_{i \in \mathcal{N}} R_i} : \ldots : \frac{\sum_{i \in \mathcal{N}_k} R_i}{\sum_{i \in \mathcal{N}} R_i} \qquad (5)$$

where t_k indicates the time slices of the kth cluster, and $\mathcal{N}_k$ is the set of all sensor nodes in the kth cluster.

The heuristic power control algorithm implemented as Algorithm 1 achieves higher throughput with smaller power. However, the demand for energy of sensor nodes is greatly improved. It can be solved by exploiting WCE to charge nodes.

Algorithm 1. Power Control Algorithm Based on SIC

//**input:** the number of areas divided w and related parameters
//**output:** the controlled power of clustered node P_v^k
    Initialize each area lists $AList_u$ $(u = 1, 2, \cdots, w)$
    $interval \leftarrow [max(d_i) - min(d_i)]/w$
    $mindistance \leftarrow min(d_i)$
    while $i \leq N$ **do**
        $u = \lceil (d_i - mindistance)/interval \rceil$
        if $u = 0$ **then**
            Add the node i into the first area list $AList_1$
        else
            Add the node i into the uth area list $AList_u$
        end if
    end while
    while all the area list $AList_u$ are not null **do**
        Construct the kth cluster
        while $AList_u$ is not null and the neatest node meet the conditions of Eq.1– Eq.4
do
            Add the node into the area list $CList_k$, delete this node in $AList_u$ and record
the power as P_v^k. (v represents it is the vth node in $CList_k$)
            Find the next area list $AList_{u+1}$
        end while
        Start constructing the next cluster $CList_{k+1}$
    end while

2.3 Charging Model

The charging cycle is made of three parts: WCE's vacation time τ_{vac}, traversal time τ_p, and charging time for nodes $\Sigma \tau_i$. There are two types of charging cycle:

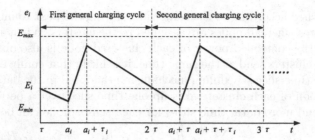

Fig. 2. Complete charging cycle diagram of partially recharged.

the general charging cycle and the initial charging cycle [10]. If the length of the initial charging cycle is τ, the start time of the first general charging cycle is τ and the end time of this cycle is 2τ. This paper just focuses on the general charging cycle which is defined as follows.

Definition 1. *Each node has the same energy curve of its any general charging cycle. The energy level of a sensor node i ($i \in \mathcal{N}$) exhibits a general charging cycle if it meets two conditions: (i) At the end of the general charging cycle, the energy of node i is equal to the energy at the start of the charging cycle over a period of τ; (ii) The dump energy of any time cannot be less than E_{min}.*

Charging cycle of partially recharged is illustrated in Fig. 2. If the periodic working mode can be determined, the rest of the cycles can be regarded as the extension of the first charging cycle. So we only need to consider the case of the first general charging cycle, which is also within $t \in [\tau, 2\tau]$.

Denote D_p the physical distance of path p, so $\tau_p = D_p/V$. τ is computed as

$$\tau = \tau_p + \tau_{vac} + \sum_{i \in \mathcal{N}} \tau_i \tag{6}$$

Denote $\overline{P_i^k}$ the relative power of node i in the kth cluster and P_i^k the real power, then the constraint between them can be written as

$$\overline{P_i^k} = \frac{t_k}{\sum_{m=1}^{k} t_m} \cdot P_i^k \tag{7}$$

In Definition 1, the energy consumed by node i is equal to the energy supplied by WCE. The charging power is U and the charging time is τ_i. Therefore,

$$\tau \cdot \overline{P_i^k} = \tau_i \cdot U \quad (i \in \mathcal{N}) \tag{8}$$

Denote the starting energy of node i as E_i and the energy level at time t as $e_i(t)$, respectively. $e_i(t)$ within $t \in [\tau, 2\tau]$ must satisfy

$$E_{min} \le e_i(a_i) \le e_i(t) \le e_i(a_i + \tau_i) \le E_{max} \quad (\tau \le t \le 2\tau) \tag{9}$$

where $e_i(a_i)$ represents the residual energy of node i when WCE arrives at it. Also, $e_i(a_i + \tau_i)$ represents the residual energy of node i when WCE leaves it.

When the battery energy is charged to E_{max} during the WCE's traversal, the optimal objective maximizing the ratio of the WCE's vacation time over the cycle time is equally good as the battery is partially recharged [10]. Thus, we can only consider the situation of fully recharged. In Fig. 2, $E_i = e_i(2\tau)$. To ensure the second requirement in Definition 1, $e_i(a_i)$ and E_i can be represented as

$$E_i = e_i(a_i + \tau_i) - (2\tau - (a_i + \tau_i)) \cdot \overline{P_i^k} = E_{max} - (2\tau - (a_i + \tau_i)) \cdot \overline{P_i^k} \quad (10)$$

$$e_i(a_i) = E_i - (a_i - \tau) \cdot \overline{P_i^k} = E_{max} - (\tau - \tau_i) \cdot \overline{P_i^k} \geq E_{min} \quad (11)$$

2.4 Cross-Layer Optimization Problem Construction

To make the WCE stay at the service station as long as possible, naturally, taking the percentage of time that WCE takes a vacation over a cycle $\frac{\tau_{vac}}{\tau}$ as the optimization objective. The optimization problem is formulated as follows.

OPT 1

$$max \qquad \frac{\tau_{vac}}{\tau}$$
$$s.t. \qquad (6) \sim (11)$$
$$\tau_i, \tau_p, \tau_{vac}, \tau, P_i^k \geq 0 \quad (i \in \mathcal{N})$$

This problem is a nonlinear optimization problem and cannot be solved directly in polynomial time since it contains nonlinear objective ($\frac{\tau_{vac}}{\tau}$) and product terms in constraints. In the next section, we will discuss how to simplify the formulations and transform the problem OPT 1 into an equivalent linear problem.

3 Model Optimization and Solution

The WCE must move along the shortest Hamiltonian cycle that crosses all the nodes and the service station in an optimal solution with the maximal $\frac{\tau_{vac}}{\tau}$ [10]. Denote D_{TSP} as the total traversal path distance and $\tau_{TSP} = D_{TSP}/V$ as the traversal time. With the optimal traversal path, Eq. 6 is reformulated as

$$\tau = \tau_{TSP} + \tau_{vac} + \sum_{i \in \mathcal{N}} \tau_i \quad (12)$$

Then we use change-of-variable technique to replace the optimization variables to simplify the formulation. For the nonlinear objective $\frac{\tau_{vac}}{\tau}$, we define

$$\eta_{vac} = \frac{\tau_{vac}}{\tau} \quad (13)$$

For Eq. 8, we can remove nonlinear terms $\frac{1}{\tau}$ and $\frac{\tau_i}{\tau}$ by defining

$$\begin{cases} \tau_0 = \tau_{TSP} + \tau_{vac} \\ \eta_0 = \frac{\tau_0}{\tau} \\ \eta_i = \frac{\tau_i}{\tau} \end{cases} \quad (14)$$

Then Eq. 6 is reformulated as

$$\sum_{m=0}^{n} \eta_m = 1 \tag{15}$$

Similarly, Eqs. 8 and 9 can be reformulated (by dividing both sides by τ) as

$$\overline{P_i^k} = U \cdot \eta_i \quad (i \in \mathcal{N}) \tag{16}$$

$$\overline{P_i^k}(1 - \eta_i) \cdot \tau_{TSP} \leq (E_{max} - E_{min})(\eta_0 - \eta_{vac}) \tag{17}$$

By Eqs. 14 and 16, constraint Eq. 17 can be rewritten as

$$\eta_{vac} \leq \eta_0 - \frac{U \cdot \tau_{TSP}}{E_{max} - E_{min}} \cdot \left(\eta_i - \eta_i^2\right) \quad (i \in \mathcal{N}) \tag{18}$$

There is a quadratic term η_i^2 in Eq. 18. An approximate linearization method is adopted to solve this problem, in which the line between two points is used to replace the quadratic curve so that the optimization problem is transformed into a linear programming problem. Specific steps are as follows. Within the η_i definition domain, the chord approximation of a series of points $\{(\frac{k}{m}, \frac{k^2}{m^2})\}$ $(k = 0, 1, 2, \cdots, m)$ on the line $y = \eta_i^2$ characterizes the curve $y = \eta_i^2$. Then any point (η_i, η_i^2) on the curve can find a corresponding point (η_i, γ_i) on the chord. Then we define

$$\eta_i = \mu_{i,k-1} \cdot \frac{k-1}{m} + \mu_{i,k} \cdot \frac{k}{m} \tag{19}$$

$$\gamma_i = \mu_{i,k-1} \cdot \frac{(k-1)^2}{m^2} + \mu_{i,k} \cdot \frac{k^2}{m^2} \tag{20}$$

where $\mu_{i,k-1}$ and $\mu_{i,k}$ are two weights and satisfy the following constraints. And $\mu_{i,k-1} + \mu_{i,k} = 1$, $0 \leq \mu_{i,k-1}, \mu_{i,k} \leq 1$. That is to say, (η_i, γ_i) must be a point on a chord whose endpoints are $(\frac{k-1}{m}, \frac{(k-1)^2}{m^2})$ and $(\frac{k}{m}, \frac{k^2}{m^2})$. Since $y = \eta_i^2$ is a convex function, (η_i, γ_i) must be above (η_i, η_i^2), and $\gamma_i - \eta_i^2 \leq \frac{1}{4m^2}$. The equation can be proved by the maximum value of $\gamma_i - \eta_i^2$, so it is not necessary to elaborate.

Denote $\theta_{i,k}$ $(1 \leq k \leq m, i \in \mathcal{N})$ a binary variable indicating whether η_i falls within the kth segment. (i.e., if $\frac{k-1}{m} \leq \eta_i \leq \frac{k}{m}$, then $\theta_{i,k} = 1$; otherwise, $\theta_{i,k} = 0$). Obviously, $\theta_{i,k}$ can only fall in one of the m segments, so $\theta_{i,k}$ is constrained as

$$\sum_{k=1}^{m} \theta_{i,k} = 1 \tag{21}$$

and (η_i, γ_i) on the kth chord is equivalent to

$$\begin{cases} \mu_{i,0} \leq \theta_{i,1} \\ \mu_{i,k} \leq \theta_{i,k} + \theta_{i,k+1} \quad (1 \leq k < m) \\ \mu_{i,m} \leq \theta_{i,m} \end{cases} \tag{22}$$

Then we have

$$\begin{cases} \eta_i = \sum_{k=0}^{m} \mu_{i,k} \cdot \frac{k}{m} \\ \gamma_i = \sum_{k=0}^{m} \mu_{i,k} \cdot \frac{k^2}{m^2} \\ \sum_{k=0}^{m} \mu_{i,k} = 1 \end{cases} \tag{23}$$

By replacing η_i^2 with γ_i in Eq. 18, we have

$$\eta_{vac} \leq \eta_0 - \frac{U \cdot \tau_{TSP}}{E_{max} - E_{min}} \cdot (\eta_i - \gamma_i) \quad (i \in \mathcal{N}) \tag{24}$$

Now the problem OPT 1 is reformulated as follows.

OPT 2

$max \qquad\qquad \eta_{vac}$

$s.t. \qquad (13) \sim (15), (19) \sim (24)$

$\qquad\qquad 0 \leq \eta_i, \eta_{vac} \leq 1 \quad (i \in \mathcal{N})$

In this problem, $\eta_i, \eta_{vac}, \gamma_i, \mu_{i,k}$ and $\theta_{i,k}$ are optimization variables. P_i^k can be obtained by the power control algorithm. $U, V, E_{max}, E_{min}, \tau_{TSP}$ are constants. And m is an approximate coefficient. $m = \left\lceil \sqrt{\frac{U \cdot \tau_{TSP}}{4\epsilon(E_{max} - E_{min})}} \right\rceil$, where ϵ is the performance gap and is usually required $0 < \epsilon \leq 1$. This can be proved that the solution constructed by the optimal solution of OPT 2 is the ϵ-suboptimal solution of OPT 1 [10]. After reformulation, the optimization problem becomes a linear problem which can now be solved quickly by a solver such as CPLEX.

4   Simulation and Analysis

A $100\,\text{m} \times 100\,\text{m}$ single-hop network is randomly generated. 20 sensor nodes with the data rate randomly generated within $[10, 100]\text{kb/s}$ are deployed over the area,

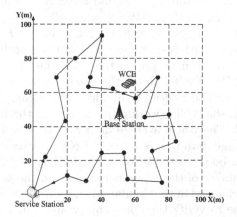

Fig. 3. Optimal traversal path of the WCE.

Table 1. Information and working strategy for nodes in a 20-node network

Cluster	Location	R_i (Kb/s)	Power (J/s)	$\eta_i(\%)$	Cluster	Location	R_i (Kb/s)	Power (J/s)	$\eta_i(\%)$
1	(65, 45)	72	0.0036	0.008	3	(80, 47)	81	0.1064	0.294
	(53, 24)	79	0.0434	0.097		(55, 8)	98	1.0086	2.789
	(69, 25)	39	0.4961	1.109		(31, 8)	35	6.2207	17.20
	(73, 68)	63	3.8444	8.592	4	(19, 43)	44	0.0023	0.005
2	(60, 57)	47	0.0024	0.004		(24, 80)	75	0.0272	0.060
	(40, 24)	27	0.0348	0.065		(20, 12)	55	0.1191	0.260
	(33, 69)	54	0.3551	0.662		(12, 69)	60	0.4918	1.073
	(83, 32)	83	3.0121	5.614		(75, 6)	13	2.2212	4.847
3	(46, 62)	20	0.0010	0.003	5	(7, 22)	22	0.0017	0.002
	(32, 63)	79	0.0136	0.038		(40, 93)	86	0.0069	0.007

Table 2. The simulation results of different networks

Network size	Number of nodes	$\eta_{vac}(\%)$	$\bar{R}$ (Kb/s)	Rate improvement
100 m × 100 m	30	38.47	244.54	435%
200 m × 200 m	30	60.64	192.13	358%
200 m × 200 m	40	32.38	219.08	408%
300 m × 300 m	30	51.83	188.07	374%
300 m × 300 m	40	33.91	193.59	382%
400 m × 400 m	30	53.61	146.15	283%
400 m × 400 m	50	38.43	156.48	305%
500 m × 500 m	30	53.99	146.24	260%
500 m × 500 m	50	58.10	151.65	263%

in which the B is located at $(50\,\text{m}, 45\,\text{m})$ and the S $(0\,\text{m}, 0\,\text{m})$. The parameters are set as follows. $V = 5\,\text{m/s}$, $U = 10\,\text{W}$. $\psi_1 = 5 \times 10^{-8}\,\text{J/b}$, $\psi_2 = 1.3 \times 10^{-15}\,\text{J/}$ (b· m^4), $\lambda = 4$ and $\beta = 3$. $E_{max} = 10800\,\text{J}$, $E_{min} = 0.05 \times E_{max} = 540\,\text{J}$.

The shortest traversal path is shown in Fig. 3. For this optimal cycle, $D_{TSP} = 380\,\text{m}$ and $\tau_{TSP} = 76\,\text{s}$. Then we obtain the cycle time $\tau = 124950\,\text{s}$, and the objective $\eta_{vac} = 57.21\%$. Table 1 shows the power of nodes after adopting the power control strategy. The nodes are divided into 5 clusters. By solving the optimization problem, the WCE's working strategy over the general energy cycle also can be obtained. The whole average data rate is $\bar{R} = 246.62\,\text{Kb/s}$. If SIC not be used, the average data rate is $\bar{R}^* = 56.6\,\text{Kb/s}$. After employing SIC, the average data rate can be increased by about 4.36 times.

To verify the reliability of the experimental results, the network size and the number of nodes are changed in the simulation environment. Several experiments (see Table 2) are done to verify the applicability and scalability of WSN using SIC and wireless energy supply technology. The simulation results with more nodes show that multiple node concurrency communication and wireless energy supply scheme also suit for other broader coverage and denser node deployment networks. In addition, the desired vacation time can be achieved.

In general, the employment of interference management strategy and wireless energy supply technology can greatly improve the network throughput and channel utilization ratio of the WSN, compensate the energy of all sensor nodes and extend the network life cycle.

5   Conclusion

To alleviate the problem of communication interference and energy shortage at nodes in WSN, we proposed a power control algorithm while clustering nodes to achieve concurrency communication, and employed WET to supply energy for sensor nodes. Then we constructed a cross-layer optimization problem and transformed it into a linear problem which yields the same optimization results to get the working strategy. Simulation results show that the channel utilization ratio was greatly improved and network throughput can be increased by 200% to 500%. At the same time, the network lifetime is extended.

Acknowledgment. This research was funded by the National Key Research Development Program of China [No. 2016YFC0801800] and the Nation Nature Science Foundation of China [No. 61806067, No. 61701162].

References

1. Potdar, V., Sharif, A., Chang, E.: Wireless sensor networks: a survey. In: Proceedings of International Conference on Advanced Information Networking and Applications (AINA 2009), Bradford, UK, pp. 636–641, May 2009
2. Kontik, M., Coleri Ergen, S.: Distributed medium access control protocol for successive interference cancellation-based wireless ad hoc networks. IEEE Commun. Lett. **21**(2), 354–357 (2017)
3. Haqbeen, J.A., Ito, T., Arifuzzaman, M., et al.: Joint routing, MAC and physical layer protocol for wireless sensor networks. In: TENCON 2017–2017 IEEE Region 10 Conference, Malaysia, Penang, pp. 935–940 (2017)
4. Zhu, Y., Li, E., Chi, K.: Encoding scheme to reduce energy consumption of delivering data in radio frequency powered battery-free wireless sensor networks. IEEE Trans. Veh. Technol. **67**(4), 3085–3097 (2018)
5. Cai, Z., Zheng, X.: A private and efficient mechanism for data uploading in smart cyber-physical systems. IEEE Trans. Netw. Sci. Eng. (2018, in press). https://doi.org/10.1109/TNSE.2018.2830307
6. Kurs, A., Karalis, A., Moffatt, R., et al.: Wireless power transfer via strongly coupled magnetic resonances. Science **317**(5834), 83–86 (2007)
7. Jiang, G., Lam, S., Sun, Y., et al.: Joint charging tour planning and depot positioning for wireless sensor networks using mobile chargers. IEEE/ACM Trans. Netw. **25**(4), 2250–2266 (2017)
8. Ma, Z., Wu, J., Zhang, S., et al.: Prolonging WSN lifetime with an actual charging model. In: 2018 IEEE Wireless Communications and Networking Conference (WCNC), Barcelona, Spain, pp. 1–6, April 2018

9. Wei, Z., Liu, F., Lyu, Z., Ding, X., Shi, L., Xia, C.: Reinforcement learning for a novel mobile charging strategy in wireless rechargeable sensor networks. In: Chellappan, S., Cheng, W., Li, W. (eds.) WASA 2018. LNCS, vol. 10874, pp. 485–496. Springer, Cham (2018). https://doi.org/10.1007/978-3-319-94268-1_40

10. Shi, Y., Xie, L., Hou, Y.T., et al.: On renewable sensor networks with wireless energy transfer. In: Proceedings of IEEE INFOCOM 2011, Shanghai, China, pp. 1350–1358 (2011)

11. Xie, L., Shi, Y., Hou, Y.T., et al.: Bundling mobile base station and wireless energy transfer: modeling and optimization. In: Proceedings of IEEE INFOCOM 2013, Turin, Italy, pp. 1636–1644 (2013)

12. Xu, W., Liang, W., Ren, X., et al.: On-demand energy replenishment for sensor networks via wireless energy transfer. In: 2014 IEEE 25th Annual International Symposium on Personal, Indoor, and Mobile Radio Communication (PIMRC), Washington, DC, USA, pp. 1269–1273 (2014)

13. Ding, X., Han, J., Shi, L.: The optimization based dynamic and cyclic working strategies for rechargeable wireless sensor networks with multiple base stations and wireless energy transfer devices. Sensors 15(3), 6270–6305 (2015)

14. Xu, J., Yuan, X., Wei, Z., et al.: A wireless sensor network recharging strategy by balancing lifespan of sensor nodes. In: 2017 IEEE Wireless Communications and Networking Conference (WCNC), San Francisco, CA, USA, pp. 1–6 (2017)

15. Guo, S., Wang, C., Yang, Y.: Joint mobile data gathering and energy provisioning in wireless rechargeable sensor networks. IEEE Trans. Mob. Comput. 13(12), 2836–2852 (2014)

16. Chang, H., Feng, J., Duan, C., et al.: Research of recharging scheduling scheme for wireless sensor networks based on cuckoo search. In: 2018 International Joint Conference on Neural Networks (IJCNN), Rio de Janeiro, Brazil, pp. 1–7 (2018)

17. Wei, Z., Liu, F., Ding, X., et al.: K-CHRA: a clustering hierarchical routing algorithm for wireless rechargeable sensor networks. IEEE Access (2018, in press). https://doi.org/10.1109/ACCESS.2018.2885789

An Integrated UAV Platform for Real-Time and Efficient Environmental Monitoring

Linyan Xu[1], Zhangjie Fu[1(✉)], and Liran Ma[2]

[1] School of Computer and Software,
Nanjing University of Information Science and Technology,
Nanjing, China
lillianxu_ly@163.com, fzj@nuist.edu.cn
[2] Department of Computer Science, Texas Christian University,
Fort Worth, TX, USA
l.ma@tcu.edu

Abstract. An important part of environmental monitoring is the collection of meteorological data. In this paper, we develop an integrated data acquisition and transmission platform utilizing unmanned aerial vehicles (UAVs) with an intelligent path planning algorithm to achieve efficient and accurate meteorological data collection in real-time. We adopt the improved traveling salesman problem model to represent the path planning problem. Based on the model, we propose an improved simulated annealing genetic algorithm (ISAGA) to solve the path planning problem. Our proposed ISAGA is able to overcome the deficiencies of the traditional genetic algorithm and simulated annealing algorithm. In addition, we design and implement a mobile application integrated with the path planning algorithm to control UAVs and conduct data exchange to the cloud. Our evaluation results demonstrate that data can be collected and transmitted more efficiently via selecting better paths.

Keywords: Environmental monitoring · UAV path planning · Genetic algorithms

1 Introduction

Environmental monitoring serves a vital role in determining public health and safety issues. A key part of environmental monitoring is the collection of meteorological data. Traditionally, automatic weather stations are installed on fixed ground locations to collect meteorological data. However, ground-based weather stations are suffering from the following problems: (i) The distribution of weather stations cannot be easily changed to match the speed and dynamics of urban development; (ii) Since all the meteorological sensors are mounted to the ground stations, there lacks the ability to perform stereoscopic monitoring; and, (iii) It is inconvenient to add or replace sensors to adapt to the diversity of pollutant types.

© Springer Nature Switzerland AG 2019
E. S. Biagioni et al. (Eds.): WASA 2019, LNCS 11604, pp. 395–406, 2019.
https://doi.org/10.1007/978-3-030-23597-0_32

As a result, the unmanned aerial vehicle (UAV) based environmental monitoring platform emerges as a complementary solution to address the aforementioned problems. To be specific, an UAV can carry a number of sensors, fly to a set of positions, and hang at desired altitudes to perform flexible stereoscopic monitoring. Yet, many existing UAV-based monitoring platforms encounter the following two issues. Firstly, the sensing data needs to be manually downloaded after return, which introduces unnecessary delay and leads to degraded efficiency. Secondly, the route planning is manually done by an operator, which is subject to human errors and poor routes (e.g., time-consuming paths). Although a number of UAV path planning algorithms exist in the literature, they have not been used or tested in real flights.

To address these issues, we develop an integrated UAV platform aiming for real-time and efficient environmental monitoring. Our proposed platform has the following desired features. It is equipped with a wireless communication unit that can transmit sensing data to a base station in real-time. Furthermore, we use an improved traveling salesman problem (ITSP) model and propose a path planning algorithm named improved simulated annealing genetic algorithm (ISAGA). It incorporates the idea of the simulated annealing (SA) [1] into the genetic algorithm (GA) [2] to calculate the optimal or suboptimal safe flight trajectories within a time constraint. Note that the typical battery life of an UAV is up to 30 min. We also design and implement a mobile application integrated with the path planning algorithms to facilitate the control of the UAV platform from a handheld device (e.g., a smartphone). Lastly, our platform is expandable as it can be easily adapted to carry any combination of sensors for security surveillance, wildlife migration tracking, and geographical survey.

Specifically, our developed platform includes a quad-rotor UAV and an onboard computer, which are manufactured by DJI. Different types of sensors can be connected to the onboard computer. In this paper, we mount two kinds of particle pollution (PM) sensors (i.e., PM2.5 and PM10) on the onboard computer for prototyping purposes. Additional, a wireless transceiver module is mounted to the onboard computer, which enables the platform to send collected sensing data to a remote controller or a cloud server in real-time.

Our proposed path planning algorithm is running on the onboard computer. The algorithm is able to calculate the optimal or suboptimal safe flight trajectories that are able to accomplish prearranged tasks within a proper amount of time. Particularly, we design high efficiency genetic operators and control parameters to enhance the global research ability of GA. We also develop a mobile application to ease the control of the UAV and the flight planning process. The application allows a user to select several task points in advance and choose a path planning algorithm to generate the optimal path. Next, the UAV can fly automatically to complete its tasks without user intervention. Moreover, the user can view returned data, flight path, and captured pictures through the application. Evaluation results show that our proposed ISAGA can obtain better travel paths for various scenarios compared with other path optimization algorithms.

The remaining part of this paper is organized as follows. Section 5 reviews current methods based on UAVs for environmental monitoring and existing research on UAV path planning. Section 2 describes the ITSP model, and the deficiencies of GA and SA. Section 3 mainly introduces the ISAGA in detail. Section 4 presents the performances of ISAGA, the design of integrated platform and the results of real-flight experiments. We conclude our paper in Sect. 6.

2 Preliminaries

In this section, we first explain the improved traveling salesman problem (ITSP) model used in our path planning process. Next, we briefly introduce two intelligent algorithms: GA and SA.

2.1 ITSP Model

For our UAV path planning problem, we adopt the ITSP model, which allows the same vertex to be visited for multiple times. This allows UAVs to have the flexibility in vertex selection (i.e., the sequence of visiting the monitoring points) to fit the actual demand. Its mathematical model is given as follows. Let the path of visiting n monitoring points be denoted by U, $U = (u_1, u_2, ..., u_n, u_{n+1})$, and $u_{n+1} = u_1$. The coordinates of u_i are (x_i, y_i, z_i) because UAVs fly in a 3D space. Then the distance between the two visiting points is:

$$d(u_i, u_{i+1}) = \sqrt[3]{(x_{i+1} - x_i)^2 + (y_{i+1} - y_i)^2 + (z_{i+1} - z_i)^2}. \tag{1}$$

The total distance of the access path is shown in (2).

$$D_{ITSP} = \sum_{i=1}^{Q} d(u_i, u_{i+1}), Q \geq n, \tag{2}$$

where $u_{Q+1} = u_1$, Q is an integer greater than or equal to n obtained according to the calculation result, and represents the number of nodes on the path. Our goal is to get the minimum value of (2).

Similar to TSP, ITSP is also an NP-hard problem. As the scale of the problem increases, the computational complexity increases exponentially and it is difficult to obtain an optimal solution. Hence, many existing solutions resort to intelligent algorithms to obtain an approximate optimal solution.

2.2 Intelligent Algorithms

GA and SA are two intelligent algorithms commonly used to solve optimization problems. When the scale of a problem is small, GA is able to search the entire solution space and find the global optimum. When the scale of the problem becomes larger, GA may fall into a local optimum (i.e., premature convergence). Differently, SA uses the Metropolis criterion to accept a less optimal solution with a certain probability to escape from the trap of a local optimum. However, SA's annealing process can be time consuming in the pursuit of the global optimum. Since GA or SA alone cannot achieve the desired outcome, we propose to integrate SA into GA to achieve better results.

3   ISAGA Path Planning Algorithm

The key idea of our proposed ISAGA algorithm is to apply the SA's annealing process in certain stages of GA to avoid being trapped into a local optimum and reduce search time. Next, we explain our proposed ISAGA in detail.

3.1   An Overview

The major components of ISAGA include initialization, fitness function, and genetic operators. An overview of our proposed ISAGA is given in Algorithm 1.

Algorithm 1. ISAGA

Input: P_c: the probability of crossover occurrence; P_m: the probability of mutation occurrence; M: population size; t: evolutionary algebra timer; S: maximum evolutionary algebra; F_i: fitness

Output: the optimal route of flight path

1: *Begin*
2:      Initialize P_m, P_c, M, S, F_i, t and other parameters
3:      Generate the initial population $P_{(0)}$, t=0
4:      Do
5:            Calculate the fitness F_i of each individual in $P_{(t)}$
6:            Initialize the empty population newPop
7:            While $(t < S)$
8:                  Select $P_{(t+1)}$ from $P_{(t)}$
9:                  if $P_c > Random(0, 1)$
10:                       Perform crossover operation
11:                  if $P_m > Random(0, 1)$
12:                       Perform mutation operation
13:                  Evaluate $P_{(t+1)}$
14:         Done
15: End

Firstly, chromosomes are generated randomly using the sequence of the monitoring points to be visited. We use natural number $1, 2, \ldots N$ to represent the N monitoring points. Each chromosome represents an individual flight path. We add "0" (representing the takeoff point) at the head and tail of each chromosome to indicate that the UAV will return to the starting point after completing its mission. The length of each chromosome is Q, where $Q >= N + 2$.

The initial population $P_{(0)}$ is formed by randomly selecting M chromosomes. The subsequent generation population will be generated via applying the previous generation population through the selection, crossover and mutation procedures. To be specific, for each generation, individual chromosomes are selected according to their fitness values. The fitness value F_i of each chromosome is calculated according to the length of the path in generation $P_{(t)}$, where t is the evolutionary algebra timer.

$$F_i = \frac{1}{D_{ITSP}}. \tag{3}$$

Next, crossover and mutation of genetic operations are carried out to generate the next generation population $P_{(t+1)}$. If the evolutionary algebra is smaller than the maximum evolutionary algebra, repeat the selection, crossover, and mutation operations to generate the next generation. Otherwise the evolution ends and the optimal solution is selected from the final population. We explain the selection, crossover, and mutation operations in detail in the following subsections.

3.2 Selection

We adopt roulette wheel selection (RWS) [3] to screen chromosomes. The probability Pi of an individual chromosome C_i is selected to inherit to the next generation population is as follows:

$$Pi = \frac{F_i}{\sum_{i=1}^{M} F_i}. \tag{4}$$

Hence, the cumulative probability of the first i chromosomes q_i is calculated as follows:

$$q_i = \sum_{j=1}^{i} Pi. \tag{5}$$

The chromosome selection threshold r is a random number in the interval $[0, 1]$. To be specific, chromosome C_1 will be selected if $q_1 > r$. Furthermore, chromosome C_k will be selected if $q_{k-1} < r < q_k$.

Note that chromosome selection based on r may result in eliminating chromosomes with high fitness values, which may lead GA not converge to the global optimum. To prevent the loss of highly fitted chromosomes, we add the elitist selection (also known as the elitism strategy) [4]. That is, if the fitness value of an individual chromosome in the previous generation population is larger than that of every individual chromosome in the current generation population, we will add the individual chromosome into the current population. The individual chromosome with the smallest fitness in the current generation population will be eliminated.

3.3 Crossover

GA may fall into a local optimum during the evolution process when the quality of chromosome populations decreases. One major reason for the decrease of diversity is the increased similarity between chromosomes. To remedy this problem, we need to improve the diversity of chromosomes. Since SA can retain individual chromosomes with slightly lesser fitness values with a certain probability, it can be used to enhance the diversity of chromosomes. Therefore, we propose to integrate SA into the crossover operation in GA.

Specifically, the annealing process of SA is initiated before the cross operation. New chromosomes are generated by the crossover operation, where partial-mapped crossover (PMC) is used to cross each chromosome. The detailed steps of PMC are shown in Algorithm 2.

The newly generated chromosomes will be screened by the Metropolis criterion of SA. The Metropolis criterion accepts or rejects chromosomes based on

---

Algorithm 2. PMC

Input: Ci: a chromosome; Ci': the new chromosome;
Output: new individuals
1: *Begin*
2:     Select randomly a chromosome with the same length as the chromosome Ci for crossover
3:     Set two intersections in the individual code string randomly $r_1, r_2 \in [1, Q]$, $r_1 \neq r_2$
4:     Exchange the genes of two chromosomes between the two points
5:     Establish a mapping table
6:     Eliminate gene conflicts according to the mapping table and generate a new chromosome Ci'
7: End

---

the difference of the fitness values between the two generation populations (e.g., Ci and Ci') as shown in (6).

$$\Delta F = F_{Ci'} - F_{Ci}. \tag{6}$$

If Ci' is fitter than Ci (i.e., $\Delta F > 0$), the new chromosomes are accepted. Otherwise, the new chromosomes are accepted with a probability p as shown in (7).

$$p = \begin{cases} 1, & \Delta F > 0 \\ e^{(-\frac{\Delta F}{T})}, & \Delta F \leq 0, \end{cases} \tag{7}$$

where T is the current temperature. Next, the generation-selection process is repeated via the cooling operation of SA. The complete crossover operation in ISAGA is shown in Algorithm 3.

Algorithm 3. Crossover in ISAGA

Input: P_c: the probability of crossover occurrence; F_i: fitness; Ci: a chromosome; Ci': the new chromosome; r: used to control the speed of cooling; T: the temperature of the system, initial state should be in a high temperature; T_{min}: The final temperature.
Output: new generation population
1: *Begin*
2:     Initialize $i = 0$
3:     if $P_c > Random(0, 1)$
4:         Set the initial temperature T and the final temperature T_{min}
5:         Define the cooling schedule $T \rightarrow r * T$
6:         while $(T > T_{min})$
7:             Perform PMC in ISAGA
8:             Calculate $\Delta F = F_{Ci'} - F_{Ci}$
9:             if $\Delta F > 0$ and $e^{(\frac{-\Delta F}{T})} > Random(0, 1)$
10:                $Ci = Ci$
11:            else $Ci = Ci'$
12:            end if
13:        end while
14:     $i + +$
15: End

3.4   Mutation

To further improve chromosome diversity, we also integrate the annealing process of SA into the mutation process. The chromosome is mutated by the simple inversion mutation (SIM) method, which is similar to the operation of the crossover. The detailed mutation procedure is shown in Algorithm 4.

Algorithm 4. Mutation in ISAGA

Input: P_m: the probability of mutation occurrence; F_i: fitness; Cj: a chromosome; Cj': the new chromosome; r: used to control the speed of cooling; T: the temperature of the system, initial state should be in a high temperature; T_{min}: The final temperature.
Output: new generation population
1: *Begin*
2:      if $P_m > Random(0, 1)$
3:          Set initialize the initial temperature T and the final temperature T_{min}
4:          Define the cooling schedule $T \rightarrow r * T$
5:          While $(T > T_{min})$
6:              Cj use SIM to generate a new chromosome Cj'
7:              Calculate $\Delta F = F_{Cj'} - F_{Cj}$
8:              if $\Delta F \geq 0$ and $e^{(\frac{-\Delta F}{T})} > random(0, 1)$
9:              $Cj = Cj$
10:             else $Cj = Cj'$
11:             end if
12:         end While
13:     $j + +$
14: End

---

4   Evaluation

In this section, we evaluate the performance of our proposed ISAGA in both simulation and real flight experiments.

4.1   Simulation Study

We perform a simulation study using MATLAB to compare ISAGA with traditional genetic algorithms with a varying number of monitoring points. For the case of 16 monitoring points, the simulation parameters are as follows: the probability of crossover $P_c = 0.75$, the probability of mutation $P_m = 0.05$, population size $M = 30$, and the maximum evolutionary algebra $S = 500$. The simulation results of 16 and 51 monitoring points are listed in the Table 1. The optimization path and optimization process are shown in the Fig. 2. From these results, we can see that when the number of monitoring points is small, the difference between the paths generated by GA and ISAGA is small. The path obtained by ISAGA is only 6% less than GA. However, through the search process, it can be seen that the convergence rate of ISAGA is obviously faster than that of GA. As a result, a good path can be obtained quickly. In the same time, ISAGA's path is significantly better than GA in general.

Table 1. Path length comparison

Number of points	Path length of ISAGA	Path length of GA
16	584.64	622.02
51	425.61	784.22

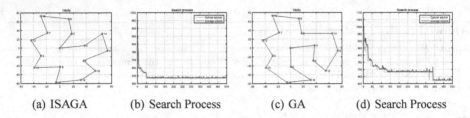

(a) ISAGA   (b) Search Process   (c) GA   (d) Search Process

Fig. 1. 16 monitoring points.

When there are 51 monitoring points being, the parameters are as follows: the probability of crossover $P_c = 0.95$, the probability of mutation $P_m = 0.1$, population size $M = 40$, maximum evolutionary algebra $S = 800$. The optimization path and optimization process are shown in the Fig. 1. From the results of 51 monitoring points, we can see that when the number of monitoring points is large, ISAGA runs much longer than GA. However, the path generated by ISAGA is shorter than that of GA. In the late stage of evolution, GA falls into a local optimum. After incorporating the annealing process of SA, ISAGA is able to escape from the local optimum. This is the reason that path length of ISAGA is 45.7% smaller than the path of GA. Additionally, ISAGA's convergence rate is faster, which makes the path of ISAGA better than that of GA under the same iteration times. It can concluded that, ISAGA is able to escape from local optimal traps and is more efficient for complex problems.

4.2   Real Flight Experiment

We also carry out a number of real flight experiments to evaluate the performance of our proposed ISAGA algorithm.

System Framework. Our environmental monitoring system is composed of an integrated UAV docking platform, a remote control system, and a cloud storage server. The UAV docking platform includes a drone that carries an onboard computer and a number of environmental sensors such as humidity, temperature, and particulate matter (PM2.5). Sensor-collected data is sent to the onboard computer via a serial interface. The onboard computer relays the sensed data to the drone also via a serial interface. Next, the drone will wireless transmit the data to the remote control system, which contains a handheld device (e.g., a smartphone) mounted on a dedicated remote control. An mobile application is running on the handheld device and is in charge of data communication with the cloud server. The overall system design is illustrated in Fig. 3.

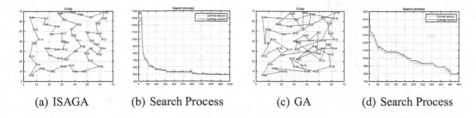

(a) ISAGA   (b) Search Process   (c) GA   (d) Search Process

Fig. 2. 51 monitoring points.

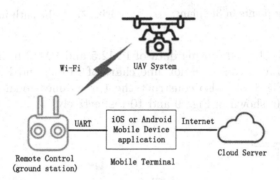

Fig. 3. Framework overview.

UAV Flights. We pick a number of monitoring points on the playground of Nanjing University of Information Science and Technology. The monitoring points are not at the same height. A schematic diagram of the monitoring points selected on the software is shown in Fig. 4. The path planning results by ISAGA is shown in Fig. 5. During the flight experiments, real-time meteorological data (i.e., PM2.5 and PM10) are collected, and the 3D distribution data of PM2.5 and PM10 are obtained. The relative simulated distribution of the monitoring points and flight path are shown in Figs. 6 and 7.

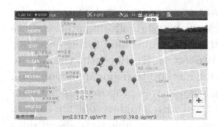

Fig. 4. Monitoring points in 2D plane.

Fig. 5. Flight path in 2D plane.

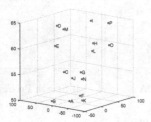
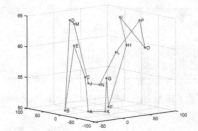

Fig. 6. Monitoring points in 3D plane.　　**Fig. 7.** Flight path in 3D plane.

Based on the collected sensing data of PM2.5 and PM10 from our flights in June 2018, we draw a concentration line chart of PM2.5 and PM10 over time, as is shown in Fig. 8. We also construct the three-dimensional distribution of PM2.5 and PM10, shown in Figs. 9 and 10 respectively.

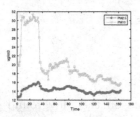
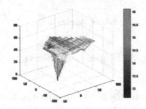
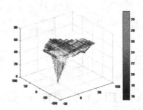

Fig. 8. Concentration of　　**Fig. 9.** PM2.5　　　**Fig. 10.** PM10
PM2.5 and 10 over time

5   Related Work

An air quality monitoring network is important to environmental protection [5]. For example, an environmental protection system based on ground stations was developed in [6]. Yet, it is difficult for traditional ground monitoring methods to meet the pressing needs of environmental protection [7]. Recently, the remote sensing technology has been adopted as a major method to regional air pollution monitoring [8]. A UAV based remote sensing system was proposed for environmental monitoring in [9]. A drone system equipped with a high-resolution camera and a gas monitor was developed in [10]. However, it is not able to transmit data in real time. A UAV based real time data transmission system carrying state estimators and concentration sensors appeared in [11]. An efficient data uploading scheme was proposed in [12] and a data aggregation method was proposed in [13]. A sensor data extraction scheme was proposed in [14]. A 3D model of the atmospheric pollution can be established by UAVs developed in [15].

Due to the similarity between the UAV path planning problem and the traveling salesman problem (TSP) [16], traditional UAV path planning was investigated based on the TSP model. Recently, many intelligent optimization algorithms were applied to address TSP problems, such as simulated annealing algorithm, ant colony optimization algorithm [17], genetic algorithm, neural networks [18], and particle swarm optimization [19].

6   Conclusion

In this paper, we design and develop an integrated UAV platform aiming for real-time and efficient environmental monitoring. The proposed platform can provide intelligent path planning to ensure the efficiency and accuracy of meteorological data collection. Specifically, we adopt an improved traveling salesman problem model to our targeted problem and propose ISAGA to solve the path planning problem. Our proposed ISAGA is able to overcome the deficiencies of the GA and SA algorithms. In addition, we design and implement a mobile application integrated with the path planning to control UAVs and data exchange to the cloud. Our evaluation results demonstrate that data can be collected with little delay via selecting effective paths for UAVs. As part of our future work, we plan to further improve our intelligent algorithms to obtain the shortest path automatically with less time and better accuracy.

Acknowledgment. The work of Zhangjie Fu is partially supported by the National Natural Science Foundation of China (NSFC) under grant U1836110, U1836208, U1536206, 61602253, 61672294; the National Key R&D Program of China under grant 2018YFB1003205; the Jiangsu Basic Research Programs-Natural Science Foundation under grant BK20181407; the Priority Academic Program Development of Jiangsu Higher Education Institutions fund; the Major Program of NSFC (17ZDA092), Qing Lan Project; the Collaborative Innovation Center of Atmospheric Environment and Equipment Technology fund, China; the Opening Project of Guangdong Provincial Key Laboratory of Data Security and Privacy Protection (No. 2017B03031004). The work of Liran Ma is partially supported by the US National Science Foundation (No. OAC1829553).

References

1. Kirkpatrick, S., Gelatt, D., Vecchi, M.: Optimization by simulated annealing. Science **220**(4598), 671–680 (1983)
2. Tsai, C.-F., Tsai, C.-W., Yang, T.: A modified multiple-searching method to genetic algorithms for solving traveling salesman problem. In: IEEE International Conference on Systems, Man and Cybernetics, vol. 3, pp. 6-pp. IEEE (2002)
3. De, J., Kenneth, A.: An Analysis of the Behavior of a Class of Genetic Adaptive Systems (1975)
4. Rudolph, G.: Convergence analysis of canonical genetic algorithms. IEEE Trans. Neural Netw. **5**(1), 96–101 (1994)
5. Wang, Y.: Development and current situation of environmental monitoring system. Technol. Wind **30**(26), 107 (2017)

6. Zhong, L., Zheng, J., Lei, G., Chen, J., Che, W.: Development status and trend analysis of air quality monitoring network. Environ. Monit. China **33**(02), 113–118 (2007)
7. Zhang, Q., Chen, C., Wu, D.: Study on the application of remote sensing technology in environmental monitoring. J. Green Sci. Technol. **6**(03), 235–236 (2015)
8. Huang, Y., Jiangdong, Zhuang, D., Fu, J.: Remote sensing estimation of chlorophyll concentration in lake townsend. J. Nat. Disasters **21**(02), 215–222 (2012)
9. Zhu, J., Xu, G., Liu, J.: Application of UAV remote sensing system in the field of environmental protection. Environ. Prot. Recycl. Econ. **31**(09), 45–48 (2011)
10. Yang, H., Huang, Y.: Remote sensing monitoring of chemical polluted gases by UAV. J. Geo-Inf. Sci. **17**(10), 1269–1274 (2015)
11. Gatsonis, N.A., Demetriou, M.A., Egorova, T.: Real-time prediction of gas contaminant concentration from a ground intruder using a UAV. In: 2015 IEEE International Symposium on Technologies for Homeland Security (HST), pp. 1–6. IEEE (2015)
12. Cai, Z., Zheng, X.: A private and efficient mechanism for data uploading in smart cyber-physical systems. IEEE Trans. Netw. Sci. Eng. (2018)
13. Li, J., Cheng, S., Cai, Z., Yu, J., Wang, C., Li, Y.: Approximate holistic aggregation in wireless sensor networks. ACM Trans. Sen. Netw. **13**(2), 11:1–11:24 (2017)
14. Cheng, S., Cai, Z., Li, J., Gao, H.: Extracting kernel dataset from big sensory data in wireless sensor networks. IEEE Trans. Knowl. Data Eng. **29**(4), 813–827 (2017)
15. Danilov, A., Smirnov, U.D., Pashkevich, M.: The system of the ecological monitoring of environment which is based on the usage of UAV. Russ. J. Ecol. **46**(1), 14–19 (2015)
16. Dantzig, G., Johnson, S.: Solution of a large-scale traveling-salesman problem. Oper. Res. **2**(4), 393–410 (2010)
17. Tsai, C.-F., Tsai, C.-W., Tseng, C.-C.: A new hybrid heuristic approach for solving large traveling salesman problem. Inf. Sci. **166**(1–4), 67–81 (2004)
18. Cochrane, E., Beasley, J.: The co-adaptive neural network approach to the Euclidean travelling salesman problem. Neural Netw. **16**(10), 1499–1525 (2003)
19. Kennedy, J., Eberhart, R.C.: Particle swarm optimization. IEEE (1955)

CXNet-m2: A Deep Model with Visual and Clinical Contexts for Image-Based Detection of Multiple Lesions

Shuaijing Xu[1], Guangzhi Zhang[1], Rongfang Bie[1(✉)], and Anton Kos[2]

[1] Beijing Normal University, Beijing 100875, China
rfbie@bnu.edu.cn
[2] University of Ljubljana, Ljubljana, Slovenia

Abstract. Diagnosing multiple lesions on images is facing with challenges of incomplete and incorrect disease detection. In this paper, we propose a deep model called CXNet-m2 for the detection of multiple lesions on chest X-ray images. In our model, there is a convolutional neural network (CNN) for encoding the images, a recurrent neural network (RNN) for generating the next word (the name of lesion) and an attention mechanism to align the visual contexts with the prediction of words. There are two main contributions of CXNet-m2 to improve the work efficiency and increase the diagnosis accuracy. (1) Inspired by image captioning, CXNet-m2 adapts the classification system to a language model, where Bi-LSTM is used to learn the clinical relationship between lesions. (2) Inspired by attention mechanism, the prediction of possible lesions is guided by visual contexts, where the visual contexts are selected by the previously generated words and chosen visual regions.

The experimental results on Chestx-ray14 show that CXNet-m2 achieves better AUC and the different versions of CXNet-m2 illustrate the importance of pre-training and clinical contexts.

Keywords: Chest X-Rays image · Multi-label classification · Neural network

1 Introduction

Advanced technologies and automated algorithms of image analysis is becoming increasingly important and urgent to support clinical diagnosis and treatment. It is usually formulated as a classification problem and then to identify the abnormalities of images using representation-learning methods such as support vector machine (SVM), random forests (RF) and deep neural networks [1,2]. The traditional shallow methodologies including SVM and RF should build upon hand-crafted image features such as local binary patterns (LBP) and histogram of oriented gradient (HOG), which makes the process complex and difficult [3]. Compared with them, deep neural networks learn more representative image

© Springer Nature Switzerland AG 2019
E. S. Biagioni et al. (Eds.): WASA 2019, LNCS 11604, pp. 407–418, 2019.
https://doi.org/10.1007/978-3-030-23597-0_33

features through automatic back propagation and yield better performances in many fields including medical image analysis [4].

In this paper, we focus on chest X-ray image analysis, one of the most commonly accessible examinations for screening and diagnosis of many lung diseases. Our goal is to detect the multiple lesions of chest X-ray images using the most promising deep neural network methods. In the past decades, the lack of large-scale dataset literally stalls the advancement of chest X-ray image analysis. We therefore choose Chestx-ray14 as our dataset, which was released by reference [5] in 2017. Chestx-ray14 is one of the largest publicly available chest x-ray data set, containing 14 diseases, more than 30,000 patients and 112,120 labeled chest x-ray images. As analysed in reference [4], there are 60361 normal images, 30963 single-lesion images and 20795 muiti-lesion images. Most papers concentrate on multi-class classification problem, where all the abnormal images are classified into 14 categories. Reference [5] fine-tuned four standard CNN architectures (AlexNet, VGGNet, GoogLeNet and ResNet) and ResNet achieved the best result [6–9]. Reference [10] utilized a 121-layer DenseNet architecture and made little modification on it [11]. Reference [12] presented a model that simultaneously performed disease classification and localization based on Resnet and a simple recognition network. All of them made use of fine-tuning pre-trained networks, a good choice when the number of training examples is limited. However, they mixed multi-lesion images and single-lesion images together when training and testing, and they did not focus on multi-lesion detection specially. Reference [13] is the only work to classify multi-label images on this data set, found on arXiv. they combined DenseNet and Longshort Term Memory Networks (LSTM), and illustrated the necessaries of exploiting the dependencies between abnormalities. Although their method is just a simple combination of CNN and RNN, they offer a thought of using the clinical contexts.

Therefore, we present CXNet-m2 taking advantage of fine-tuning existing deep convolutional neural networks and learning interdependencies between lesions, and made some improvements on it. (1) In the first improvement, we adapt the multi-label classification problem to an image-captioning problem, where the names of lesions are generated from a Bi-LSTM decoder. Compared with LSTM, Bi-LSTM makes the prediction of the lesion under the information of both previously and lately generated lesions. Bi-LSTM can make better use of clinical contexts because there are not exact causal relationships between lesions. For example, studies have suggested that a chest x-ray image containing cardiomegaly is more likely to contain pulmonary edema because of the left ventricular failure and chronic nasopharyngeal obstruction [14,15]. In this case, the sequential order of prediction is not fixed and the lately predicted word may give some information for the generation of the previous words. (2) In the second improvement, we add visual contexts for generating the possible lesions by attention mechanism, which means we can make better use of the encoded image features. Different from the common attention mechanism, the visual contexts are selected according to not only the weight function, but also the previously generated words and previously chosen visual regions.

2   Related Work

Convolutional Neural Networks. As a deep-learning method, deep convolutional neural networks (CNN) is wisely used to image analysis because of the local connectivity and shared weights. These two features not only keep the affine invariance of CNN, but also reduce the number of parameters, which ensures that CNN can be widely used in the learning and processing of complex data. The basic architecture of CNN contains convolutional layers, pooling layers and fully connected layers. Convolutional layers are stacked to detect local conjunctions of features from the previous layer, pooling layers behind are designed to reduce computational complexity, and fully connected layers in the end are used to output the classification result. Some researchers replace the fully connected layers with convolutional layers to input test images on different scales. Many robust CNN frameworks have been designed including VGGnet, Resnet and Densenet [7,9,11].

Recurrent Neural Networks. In the traditional neural network model, information is passed from the input layer to the hidden layer and then to the output layer. The layers are connected to each other, the nodes between each layer are not connected. This structure can not model data with timing sequence. For example, it is generally necessary to use the information of the previous and subsequent words to predict the next word of a sentence, because the words before and after in a sentence are semantically linked. Recurrent Neural Networks models sequence data, where the current output of a sequence is also related to the previous output [16]. All RNNs have a chain of a repetitive neural network module. In a standard RNN, this duplicate module has only a very simple structure, such as a tanh layer, while duplicate module of LSTM has a complex structure. The structure of LSTM solves the problem of long-term dependencies, which RNN loses the ability to learn [17]. GRU, a variant of LSTM, replaces the forgetting gate and inputting gate the updating gate, reducing the computational complexity of LSTM [18]. In some problems, the output of the current moment is not only related to the previous state, but also related to the state after it. At this time, a two-way RNN (Bi-RNN) is needed, where there is a combination of two unidirectional RNNs [19].

Attention Mechanism. Attention is a brain signal processing mechanism unique to human vision. Human vision captures the target area that needs to be focused on by quickly scanning the global image, suppressing other useless information [20]. In deep learning method, most of the current attention models are attached to the Encoder-Decoder framework. There are two common attention-based models, global attentional model and local attentional model [22]. The idea of a global attentional model is to consider all the hidden states of the encoder when deriving the context vector, where it has to attend to all words on the source side for each target word. A local attentional mechanism can choose to focus only on a small subset of the source positions per target word.

Image Captioning. The recent progress on image captioning has greatly proved that it is possible to describe the images with accurate and meaningful sentences or words. In most cases, there are a CNN and a RNN or other advanced versions of them to understand images. CNN is used to encode images and RNN are used to decode and output the words. Several methods used lexical representations instead of visual representations. Reference [23] first used multiple instance learning to train a word detector. Reference [24] minimized a joint objective learning from these diverse data sources and leverage distributional semantic embeddings, enabling the model to describe novel objects outside of training data sets. Other methods used visual representations instead of lexical representations.Reference [25] proposed a multimodal Recurrent Neural Network (m-RNN) architecture to fuse text information and visual features extracted on the whole image. Reference [26] formulate a discriminative bimodal neural network, which can be trained by a classifier with extensive use of negative samples.

3   CheXray-m2

3.1   Image-Caption Model

Our model for detection of multiple lesions on chest X-ray images is composed of the following components: a pre-trained CNN encoder that extracts visual feature representation and an LSTM-based neural network that models the attention dynamics of focusing on those regions and generating sequentially labels. We describe in detail each of the components.

Encoder: Image Representation. Our model takes a single raw image and generates a sequence of encoded words which denote different lesions. Convolutional neural networks (CNN) has gained popularity in recent years due to their ability to learn representative image features through automatic back propagation. Many robust convolutional neural network frameworks have been designed including VGGnet, Resnet, Inception-Resnet and Densenet [6–9,11]. They have been trained on ImageNet, containing 1.3 million natural images [6]. It is promising to fine tune these existing deep networks due to the limit of data size, labeling and computer hardware. However, it may lead to low transfer efficiency, over-fitting and other problems when medical image data set is totally different from the source dataset and the number of training examples are quite limited. We therefore propose an encoder based on the advantage of CNN while taking into account the peculiarity of the chest X-ray image at hand. There are three main improvements.

Firstly, the proposed encoder should be much thinner in network depth and smaller in parameter number. Models using hundreds of layers, such as DenseNet, typically require hundreds of thousands to millions of examples to train and they are more likely to over-fitting with one tenth the training data. Based on VGGNet and ResNet, we reduce some repetitive convolutional layers and

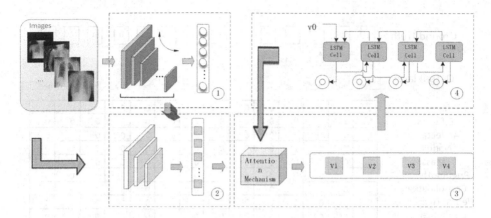

Fig. 1. The architectural diagram of our CheXray-m2 model. Parameters of pre-trained CNN model (modified from Vggnet or Resnet) are first trained on images as a 14-label classification problem, as shown in ①. Image Features are then extracted from a relatively low layer of the CNN model trained in ①, as shown in ②. The visual feature vectors are then fed into a Bi-LSTM network which predicts both the sequence of concentrated visual contexts and the sequence of generating words based on attention mechanism, shown in ③ and ④.

pooling layers behind randomly. Our framework can be easily extended to any other advanced CNN models and modified to be a proper encoder.

Secondly, parameters of the proposed encoder should not be the same as those pre-trained on ImageNet. There are ample evidences suggesting the transfer learning from natural images to chest x-ray images without training again is not a good choice [4,5]. As shown in Fig. 1, we therefore train the modified convolutional neural network by changing to a new classification layer and minimizing the multi-label loss function. The last layer has 14 output ports and each of them denotes a kind of lesion. Sigmoid layer turn the input into probability value between 0 and 1. If an output of this layer is larger than the threshold (here is 0.5), the model classify the image into this category. Figure 2 shows the coding rule of the ground truth and an example. If the label of a training image is infiltration, effusion and atelectasis, the label should be encoded as 11100000000000.

Thirdly, features should be extracted from a lower convolutional layer of the proposed encoder, which is unlike previous work. Extracting relatively low-level feature vectors allows the decoder to selectively focus on certain parts of an image by using the attention model to weight the vectors. As shown in (1), the encoder extracts L vectors, each of which is a D-dimensional representation corresponding to a part of the image.

$$A = \{a_1, ..., a_M\}, a_i \in R^N \tag{1}$$

| Ground Truth: | 1 | 1 | 1 | 0 | 0 | 0 | 0 | 0 | 0 | 0 | 0 | 0 | 0 | 0 |

0.81   0.56   0.74   0.43   0.34   0.01   0.45   0.28   0.19   0.23   0.09   0.33   0.25   0.08

Output layer: ◯◯◯◯◯◯◯◯◯◯◯◯◯◯

Infiltration:	1	0	0	0	0	0	0	0	0	0	0	0	0	0
Effusion:	0	1	0	0	0	0	0	0	0	0	0	0	0	0
Atelectasis:	0	0	1	0	0	0	0	0	0	0	0	0	0	0
Nodule:	0	0	0	1	0	0	0	0	0	0	0	0	0	0
Mass:	0	0	0	0	1	0	0	0	0	0	0	0	0	0
Pneumothorax:	0	0	0	0	0	1	0	0	0	0	0	0	0	0
Consolidation:	0	0	0	0	0	0	1	0	0	0	0	0	0	0
Pleural Thickening:	0	0	0	0	0	0	0	1	0	0	0	0	0	0
Cardiomegaly:	0	0	0	0	0	0	0	0	1	0	0	0	0	0
Emphysema:	0	0	0	0	0	0	0	0	0	1	0	0	0	0
Edema:	0	0	0	0	0	0	0	0	0	0	1	0	0	0
Fibrosis:	0	0	0	0	0	0	0	0	0	0	0	1	0	0
Pneumonia:	0	0	0	0	0	0	0	0	0	0	0	0	1	0
Hernia:	0	0	0	0	0	0	0	0	0	0	0	0	0	1

Fig. 2. The coding rule of the ground truth. If an image contains infiltration, effusion and atelectasis, the label should be encoded as 11100000000000.

Decoder: Attention-Based Bi-LSTM. Recurrent Neural Networks (RNN) is a kind of neural network that models the dynamic temporal behavior of sequences through connections between the units. The t in the lower right corner of these elements represents the state at time t. Current hidden states h_t is updated as (2), where x is the input, h is the hidden layer unit, wo is the output word, and V, W, and U are weights.

$$h_t = tanh(Ww_t + Uh_{t-1} + b) \qquad (2)$$

Current output o_t is updated as (3):

$$wo_t = Vh_t + c \qquad (3)$$

Current hidden states h_t is generated by the previous hidden state h_{t-1} and the current word w_t. The recurrent transition makes h_t also contain information of the previously generated words and states h_{t-2}, h_{t-3}, h_{t-4}, ...

LSTM extends RNN by adding three gates to a RNN neuron: a forget gate f to control whether to forget the current state; an input gate i to indicate if it should read the input; an output gate o to control whether to output the state. We use a long short-term memory (LSTM) network that inspired by reference [27] where i_t^1, f_t^1, o_t^1, c_t^1 and h_t^1 represent the outputs of the input, forget, output gates, memory cell and hidden state of the LSTM respectively. (4), (5) and (6) show how those variables are related, where T is a properly defined affine transformation, σ is the logistic sigmoid function, $tanh$ is the hyperbolic tangent function and $\odot$ is element-wise multiplication.

$$\begin{pmatrix} i_t^1 \\ f_t^1 \\ o_t^1 \\ g_t^1 \end{pmatrix} = \begin{pmatrix} \sigma \\ \sigma \\ \sigma \\ tanh \end{pmatrix} T \begin{pmatrix} w_{t-1} \\ h_{t-1} \\ v_t \end{pmatrix} \qquad (4)$$

$$c_t^1 = f_t^1 \odot c_{t-1}^1 + i_t^1 \odot g_t^1 \qquad (5)$$

$$h_t^1 = o_t^1 \odot tanh(c_t^1) \qquad (6)$$

Different from common LSTM, there is a context vector v_t, a dynamic representation of the relevant part of the image input at time t. There are two steps to computes v_t from the vectors $A = \{a_1, ..., a_M\}, a_i \in R^N$. Firstly, we compute the probability α_i of focusing on the ith location by an attention model f_{att}, as shown in (7). The inputs to the model is the extracted features from the ith visual element, the hidden state h_{t-1} and the previously generated word w_{t-1}. We believe that they can help us to find a proper v_t because of the association of lung lesions. Then, we use weighted sum to update the visual context vector v_t, as shown in (8).

$$\alpha_{it} = \frac{exp(f_{att}(a_i, h_{t-1}, w_{t-1}))}{\sum_{k=1}^{M} exp(f_{att}(a_k, h_{t-1}, w_{t-1}))} \qquad (7)$$

$$v_t = \sum_i \alpha_{it} a_i \qquad (8)$$

The next word w_t can be updated conditioning on the previously generated word w_{t-1}, the context vector v_t, and the decoder state h_t, as shown in (9) and (10):

$$p_{wt} = f_{softmax}(w_{t-1}, h_t^1, vt) \qquad (9)$$

$$w_t = f_w(p_{wt}) \qquad (10)$$

In order to make better use of the interdependency of lesions, we believe that w_{t+1} and h_{t+1} can also contribute to the update of h_t and the generation of the current word. We therefore define $i_t^2, f_t^2, o_t^2, c_t^2$ and h_t^2 in (11), (12) and (13):

$$\begin{pmatrix} i_t^2 \\ f_t^2 \\ o_t^2 \\ g_t^2 \end{pmatrix} = \begin{pmatrix} \sigma \\ \sigma \\ \sigma \\ tanh \end{pmatrix} T \begin{pmatrix} w_{t+1} \\ h_{t+1} \\ v_t \end{pmatrix} \qquad (11)$$

$$c_t^2 = f_t^2 \odot c_{t+1}^2 + i_t^2 \odot g_t^2 \qquad (12)$$

$$h_t^2 = o_t^2 \odot tanh(c_t^2) \qquad (13)$$

The word w_t can be updated as (14) and (15):

$$p_{wt}^{new} = f_{softmax}(w_{t-1}, w_{t+1}, [h_t^1, h_t^2], vt) \qquad (14)$$

$$w_t^{new} = f_w(p_{wt}^{new}) \qquad (15)$$

3.2   Training

There are two steps of training. Firstly, we see the modified CNN as a model for multi-label classification and roughly train it on the whole Chest x-ray14 data set. The purpose of this step is to increase the transfer efficiency as medical images are quite different from natural images, which were used to train Vggnet and Resnet. We use binary cross entropy loss function to learn, defined as (16):

$$loss_1 = -\frac{1}{n}\sum_i [y_i ln p_i + (1 - y_i)ln(1 - p_i)] \tag{16}$$

Where y_i is the ground truth and $p_i \in [0, 1]$ is the output of the sigmoid layer.

After that, we extract image features from a lower-level layer and feed them into decoder as our purpose is to train the decoder under the help of clinical contexts and visual contexts. We train our network on 16637 of 20796 training images (setting aside 2079 for validation and 2080 for test) on Chest x-ray14 data set. The length of Bi-LSTM is $T = 4$ as most images contain less than 4 lesions. The scale of the vocabulary is $C = 14$ as the number of lesions is 14 in this data set. The loss function is also a binary cross entropy loss function, shown as (17):

$$loss_2 = -\frac{1}{n}\frac{1}{T}\sum_{t=1}^{T}\sum_{i=1}^{|C|} [y_{ti} ln p_{ti} + (1 - y_{ti})ln(1 - p_{ti})] \tag{17}$$

As for some setups, the experimental environment is an ubuntu linux server with 2 GeForce GTX 1080 Ti GPUs and the model is implemented using Tensorflow. Due to the limit of GPU memory, the batch size $= 8$ is set as a constant. According to experience and the validation results, we finally chose stochastic gradient descent (SGD) and the learning rate is decayed from 0.01.

4   Experiment

4.1   Dataset

To verify the efficacy of CXNet-m2 in medical diagnosis on chest x-ray images, we conduct experiments on Chestx-ray14 introduced in reference [5]. It contains more than 30,000 patients, 112,000 labeled chest x-ray images and 14 kinds abnormal images including Infiltration, Effusion, Atelectasis, Nodule, Mass, Pneumothorax, Consolidation, Pleural Thickening, Cardiomegaly, Emphysema, Edema, Fibrosis, Pneumonia and Hernia. Among them, there are 20795 muitilesion images where the number of labels ranges from 2 to 14.

4.2 Metrics

AUC[28]. There are 4 quantities and the specific definitions shown in Table 1. The ROC curve has typically horizontal axis as specificity and vertical axis as sensitivity, where sensitivity is computed as $TP/(TP + FN)$ and specificity is defined as $TN/(TN + FP)$. AUC is the Area Under the ROC Curve, and using AUC to evaluate the result is more clear and direct than ROC. In order to compare our model with other models, we use AUC as one of the metric because it is widely used in many references to measure experimental results. We did not consider the clinical relevance to compute AUC as it is intractable to compute with equation (17).

BLEU[29]. BLEU is a popular metric of machine translation including image captioning that analyzes the co-occurrences of n-grams between the result and ground truth. It computes a corpus-level clipped n-gram precision between sentences.

ROUGE-L[30]. ROUGE is a set of evaluation metrics designed to evaluate text summarization algorithms. Given the length of Longest Common Subsequence (LCS) between a pair of sentences, ROUGE-L is found by computing recall and precision of LCS.

Table 1. 4 Evaluation results and corresponding symbols

Quantities	Descriptions
TP	The prediction is 1 with ground truth 1
TN	The prediction is 0 with ground truth 0
FP	The prediction is 1 with ground truth 0
FN	The prediction is 0 with ground truth 1

4.3 Results

The AUC per abnormality is shown in Table 2, compared with the result of Reference [5] and Reference [13] including average AUC. It can be found that the total AUC of our model is better, despite of the lower value of cardiomegaly, edema and hernia than those of Reference [13]. In fact, the structure of our CNN encoder is similar with that in Reference [5]. The main reason of higher AUC may be that we use larger training set and there is patient-wise overlap between training and test sets for learning more distinguishable features. The basic structure of Reference [13] is Densenet, which we used but did not get the best average result. The BLEU and ROUGE-L are compared in Table 3, where there are three versions of CXNet-m2. CXNet-m2-a is the basic model with considering the visual and clinical contexts by LSTM, CXNet-m2-b is trained by attention-based LSTM with pre-training in Fig. 1① and CXNet-m2-c is trained by attention-based Bi-LSTM with pre-training in Fig. 1①. It can be found that the pre-training step in Fig. 1① is important to improve the performance of the model and using more clinical information helps learn the pattern accurately.

Table 2. Result evaluation by AUC

Abnormality	Reference [5]	Reference [13]	CXNet-m2
Atelectasis	0.716	0.772	**0.788**
Cardiomegaly	0.807	**0.904**	0.848
Effusion	0.784	0.859	**0.865**
Infiltration	0.609	0.695	**0.702**
Mass	0.706	0.792	**0.793**
Nodule	0.671	0.717	**0.732**
Pneumonia	0.633	0.713	**0.719**
Pneumothorax	0.806	0.841	**0.861**
Consolidation	0.708	0.788	**0.792**
Edema	0.835	**0.882**	0.869
Emphysema	0.815	0.829	**0.853**
Fibrosis	0.769	0.767	**0.781**
PT	0.708	0.765	**0.774**
Hernia	0.767	**0.914**	0.853
A.V.G	0.738	0.798	**0.802**

Table 3. Result evaluation by BLEU and ROUGE-L

Models	BLEU-1	ROUGE-L
CXNet-m2-a	0.632	0.636
CXNet-m2-b	0.724	0.713
CXNet-m2-c	0.739	0.741

5 Conclusion

Chest X-ray is the most popular mean to detect lung lesion and deep learning is a good tool to assist the diagnosis. For detecting multiple lesions on a chest x-ray image, the common approach is to see it as a multi-label classification problem and break the multi-label classification problem into independent binary classification problems. It takes advantage of a rich body of work on binary classification but suffers from ignoring the interdependencies between labels. To avoid this problem, we propose an unified model that extracts the image features with a modified CNN encoder and predicts multiple lesions with an attention-based Bi-LSTM decoder by making use of visual and clinical contexts. Inspired by image captioning and attention mechanism, we adapt the multi-label classification problem into an image understanding problem as researches have proved there are relationships between lesions. Quantitative and qualitative results demonstrate that our method significantly outperforms the state-of-the-art algorithm.

In the future, we will continue to explore the dependencies between lesions on chest x-ray images from a perspective of association mining. How to take advantage of clinical contexts to predict multiple lesions on chest x-ray images is still the emphasis of our further research.

Acknowledgements. This research is sponsored by Fundamental Research Funds for the Central Universities (No. 2016NT14), National Natural Science Foundation of China (No. 61601033, No. 61571049) and Inter-discipline Research Funds of Beijing Normal University (BNUXKJC1825).

References

1. Ari, S., Hembram, K., Saha, G.: Detection of cardiac abnormality from PCG signal using LMS based least square SVM classifier. Expert Syst. Appl. **37**(12), 8019–8026 (2010)
2. Niu, D., Li, Y., Dai, S., et al.: Sustainability evaluation of power grid construction projects using improved TOPSIS and least square support vector machine with modified fly optimization algorithm. Sustainability **10**(1), 231 (2018)
3. Hu, Z., Tang, J., Zhang, P., et al.: Identification of bruised apples using a 3-D multi-order local binary patterns based feature extraction algorithm. IEEE Access **6**, 34846–34862 (2018)
4. Xu, S., Hao, W., Bie, R.: CXNet-m1: anomaly detection on chest X-Rays with image-based deep learning. IEEE Access **7**, 4466–4477 (2019)
5. Wang, X., Peng, Y., Lu, L., et al.: Chestx-ray8: hospital-scale chest x-ray database and benchmarks on weakly-supervised classification and localization of common thorax diseases. In: 2017 IEEE Conference on Computer Vision and Pattern Recognition (CVPR), pp. 3462–3471. IEEE (2017)
6. Krizhevsky, A., Sutskever, I., Hinton, G.E.: ImageNet classification with deep convolutional neural networks. In: Advances in Neural Information Processing Systems, pp. 1097–1105 (2012)
7. Simonyan, K., Zisserman, A.: Very deep convolutional networks for large-scale image recognition. arXiv preprint arXiv:1409.1556 (2014)
8. Szegedy, C., Liu, W., Jia, Y., et al.: Going deeper with convolutions. In: CVPR (2015)
9. He, K., Zhang, X., Ren, S., et al.: Deep residual learning for image recognition. In: Proceedings of the IEEE Conference on Computer Vision and Pattern Recognition, pp. 770–778 (2016)
10. Rajpurkar, P., Irvin, J., Zhu, K., et al.: CheXNet: radiologist-level pneumonia detection on chest X-Rays with deep learning. arXiv preprint arXiv: 1711.05225 (2017)
11. Huang, G., Liu, Z., Weinberger, K.Q., et al.: Densely connected convolutional networks. In: Proceedings of the IEEE Conference on Computer Vision and Pattern Recognition, vol. 1, no. 2, p. 3 (2017)
12. Li, Z., et al.: Thoracic disease identification and localization with limited supervision. In: Proceedings of the IEEE Conference on Computer Vision and Pattern Recognition (2018)
13. Yao, L., Poblenz, E., Dagunts, D., et al.: Learning to diagnose from scratch by exploiting dependencies among labels. arXiv preprint arXiv:1710.10501 (2017)

14. Luke, M.J., et al.: Chronic nasopharyngeal obstruction as a cause of cardiomegaly, cor pulmonale, and pulmonary edema. Pediatrics **37**(5), 762–768 (1966)
15. Dodek, A., Kassebaum, D.G., Bristow, J.D.: Pulmonary edema in coronary-artery disease without cardiomegaly: paradox of the stiff heart. N. Engl. J. Med. **286**(25), 1347–1350 (1972)
16. Castrejon, L., Kundu, K., Urtasun, R., et al.: Annotating object instances with a polygon-RNN. In: CVPR, vol. 1, p. 2 (2017)
17. Williams, R.J., Zipser, D.: A learning algorithm for continually running fully recurrent neural networks. Neural Comput. **1**(2), 270–280 (1989)
18. Chung, J., Gulcehre, C., Cho, K., et al.: Gated feedback recurrent neural networks. In: International Conference on Machine Learning, pp. 2067–2075 (2015)
19. Schuster, M., Paliwal, K.K.: Bidirectional recurrent neural networks. IEEE Trans. Signal Process. **45**(11), 2673–2681 (1997)
20. Yantis, S.: Control of visual attention. Attention **1**(1), 223–256 (1998)
21. Ha, T.L., Niehues, J., Waibel, A.: Effective strategies in zero-shot neural machine translation. arXiv preprint arXiv:1711.07893 (2017)
22. Rush, A.M., Chopra, S., Weston, J.: A neural attention model for abstractive sentence summarization. arXiv preprint arXiv:1509.00685 (2015)
23. Fang, H., et al.: From captions to visual concepts and back. In: Proceedings of IEEE Computer Vision and Pattern Recognition, pp. 1473–1482 (2015)
24. Venugopalan, S., Hendricks, L.A., Rohrbach, M., et al.: Captioning images with diverse objects. arXiv preprint arXiv:1606.07770, vol. 1, no. 3 (2016)
25. Mao, J., Xu, W., Yang, Y., et al.: Explain images with multimodal recurrent neural networks. arXiv preprint arXiv:1410.1090 (2014)
26. Zhang, Y., Yuan, L., Guo, Y., et al.: Discriminative bimodal networks for visual localization and detection with natural language queries. In: Proceedings of the IEEE Conference on Computer Vision and Pattern Recognition (CVPR) (2017)
27. Fu, K., et al.: Aligning where to see and what to tell: image captioning with region-based attention and scene-specific contexts. IEEE Trans. Pattern Anal. Mach. Intell. **39**(12), 2321–2334 (2017)
28. Lobo, J.M., Jiménez-Valverde, A., Real, R.: AUC: a misleading measure of the performance of predictive distribution models. Glob. Ecol. Biogeogr. **17**(2), 145–151 (2008)
29. Papineni, K., Roukos, S., Ward, T., Zhu, W.-J.: BLEU: a method for automatic evaluation of machine translation. In: ACL (2002)
30. Lin, C.-Y.: Rouge: a package for automatic evaluation of summaries. In: ACL Workshop (2004)

OWLS: Opportunistic Wireless Link Scheduling with SINR Constraints

Xiaohua Xu[1]([✉]), Yuanfang Chen[2], Shuibing He[3], and Patrick Otoo Bobbie[1]

[1] Department of Computer Science, Kennesaw State University, Kennesaw, USA
xxu6@kennesaw.edu
[2] School of Cyberspace, Hangzhou Dianzi University, Hangzhou, China
[3] College of Computer Science and Technology, Zhejiang University,
Hangzhou, China

Abstract. We study a classical opportunistic wireless link scheduling problem in cognitive radio networks with Signal to Interference plus Noise Ratio (SINR) constraints. Consider a collection of communication links, assume that each link has a channel state. The state transitions follow a transition rule. The exact state information of each link is not available due to the uncertainty of primary users' activities. The expected channel state is predicted probabilistically by investigating its history and feedbacks when the channels are used. The objective is to pick communication links sequentially over a long time horizon to maximize the average reward. To the best of our knowledge, no prior work can satisfyingly provide solutions for the opportunistic wireless link scheduling problem when considering SINR constraints. In this work, we adopt the robust paradigm of restless multi-armed bandit for the problem and design an efficient algorithm. We analyze the performance via Lyapunov potential function and demonstrate that the proposed algorithm can achieve an approximation bound.

Keywords: Restless multi-armed bandit ·
Opportunistic wireless link scheduling ·
Signal to Interference Plus Noise Ratio

1 Introduction

The pressing issues such as spectrum scarcity and low spectrum utilization have motivated the study on Cognitive radio networks (CRNs) [17]. In CRNs, a cognitive radio can be programmed and configured sophisticatedly to explore the available spectrum opportunities. A CRN consists of two types of users, *i.e.*, primary users and secondary users. Primary users such as big corporations have guaranteed quality of service while secondary users must accept interference from primary users. Secondary users can detect available channels to allow more transmissions. A secondary user can transmit successfully only when its transmission does not conflict with any active primary user and other active secondary users.

© Springer Nature Switzerland AG 2019
E. S. Biagioni et al. (Eds.): WASA 2019, LNCS 11604, pp. 419–431, 2019.
https://doi.org/10.1007/978-3-030-23597-0_34

In cognitive radio networks, Opportunistic Wireless Link Scheduling problem (noted as **OWLS**) is a well-formulated problem in the literature [14]. In the problem **OWLS**, we assume there is a collection of communication links, each of them has a demand to transmit. For simplicity, we assume all nodes lie in a two-dimensional plane. Every communication link has a channel state to indicate whether the link is occupied by a primary user or not. In a discrete version, the channel state can be either occupied (busy) or idle (free). The channel state of a link will change according to some rules. The evolving process belongs to a Markov chain. Each link's channel state evolves independently. The problem **OWLS** aim to pick communication links sequentially over a long time horizon to achieve a maximum expected reward.

In a CRN, for each link, the true channel state is unknown unless we schedule it to transmit. This is due to unpredictable primary user activities. Thus, we have to predict the channel states by investigating their history and feedbacks when the channels are actually used. Let us use the channel state of a communication link to indicate the probability that the channel is free for that link. Thus, the channel state of a link directly reflects the throughput along the link or the link quality. We use a reward proportional to a link's channel state to denote the expected reward when the link is selected to transmit. In this work, we assume multiple communication links may transmit simultaneously subject to wireless constraints. Along with channel state predictions, we need to optimize the scheduling decision policy for the problem **OWLS**.

The problem **OWLS** has been studied extensively. However, most of the existing work simply assumes the protocol interference model [10] or an even simpler model. The protocol interference model can only capture the binary interference. In other words, if one communication link is transmitting, does another link conflict with this link? Generally, we can use a binary conflict graph to model the protocol interference model. However, the physical inter-ference model [28,29] is well-accepted as it captures wireless interference more accurately. Under this model, the interference cause a cumulative effect on data transmissions. Thus, we have to take care of multiple signal to interference and noise ratio (SINR) constraints.

In this work, we consider the problem **OWLS** with SINR constraints. As observed in [7] and subsequent works, there is a gap between these two inter-ference models. Generally, an algorithm under the protocol interference model does not imply any similar solution for another model. Even worse, the dif-ficulty of scheduling problems may suddenly increase when considering SINR constraints. For example, maximum weighted independent set (MWIS) [19] is well-known and fundamental wireless scheduling problem. Such a problem under the protocol interference model was addressed extensively, and now one focus has been designing simple and fast algorithms [19] instead of deriving improving the approximation bounds. However, whether the counterpart under the physi-cal interference model admits a constant approximation is still open. The only positive results under the physical interference model exist in some restricted settings of the MWIS problem such as monotone power control or linear power control settings.

We address the problem **OWLS** subject the SINR constraints. We consider the problem **OWLS** with the paradigm of Restless Multi-Armed Bandit (abbreviated to Restless MAB, Restless Bandit, or RMAB in the literature) [6]. The Restless MAB paradigm models sequential constrained resource allocations among several competing arms. The traditional MAB [6] focuses on the conflict of allocating constrained resources between arms that yield high current rewards and ones with better future rewards. However, we consider restless MAB which means that the state evolution of unprocessed arms. In other words, the arms selected are allowed to changes its state, at the same time, the rest of the arms are also allowed to change states instead of remaining frozen. Corresponding to the problem **OWLS** setting, this means that passive links (links that did not transmit last time) are also allowed to change channel states. Restless MAB theory has been applied to the problem **OWLS** in single-hop cognitive radio networks [14]. However, the existing work in the literature on Restless MAB does not consider the SINR constraints.

In this work, we design an efficient scheduling algorithm with an approximation guarantee for the opportunistic wireless link scheduling problem with SINR constraints. The proposed algorithm is low-complexity by using the *divide and conquer* paradigm. This paradigm only applies to the condition that the length of each link is at most $(1 - \epsilon)$ fraction of the maximum link length where ϵ is a arbitrarily small constant. We first divide the whole plane into small cells and use a double partition and coloring scheme to ensure the links scheduled each time are well seperated. We then solve the problem **OWLS** in each cell and combine the individual solutions to obtain a feasible transmission schedule for the whole plane. The approximation ratio of this algorithm is bounded under an arbitrary setting. Under the length-monotone power control setting, the approximation bound is a constant. For each small cell, based on a semi-infinite programming and Lyapunov analysis which are challenging for the opportunistic wireless link scheduling problem even without interference constraint. we show the algorithm can achieve a solution with low time complexity.

The remaining of the paper is organized as follows. Section 2 formulates the problem **OWLS** under the physical interference model. Section 3 presents an approximation algorithm under the physical interference model. Section 4 details the performance analysis. Section 5 presents the related work on Restless MAB and cognitive radio scheduling. Section 6 outlines the conclusion and the future work.

2   Network Model

Given a collection $L = \{\ell_1, \ell_2, \cdots, \ell_N\}$ of communication links. Each communication link consists of a sender node and a receiver node. The Euclidean distance between two nodes u and v is denoted by $\|\vec{uv}\|$. Assume all nodes lie in a two-dimensional Euclidean plane.

Table 1. Notations

$\overrightarrow{uv}$	A link from node u to node v
$\|\overrightarrow{uv}\|$	Link length, Euclidean distance, of link $\overrightarrow{uv}$
L	Set of all links
P	Maximum power for a node
η	Reference path loss factor
κ	Path loss exponent
ξ	Noise power
σ	SINR threshold for successful reception

Under the physical interference model [28,29], each node u has a transmission power P_u upper-bounded by P. When a signal is sent from u to v over a Euclidean distance ℓ, there is a path loss of $\eta\ell^{-\kappa}$. Here η is called the *reference loss factor* and κ is called the *path loss exponent*. Let ξ be the background noise power. Let σ be the SINR threshold for successful reception. Let S_u be the set of other simultaneous senders with sender u. A transmission $\overrightarrow{uv}$ is able to occur successfully if and only if the following constraint (*i.e.*, Eq. (1)) is satisfied.

$$\frac{P_u \cdot \eta\ell^{-\kappa}}{\xi + \sum_{w \in S_u} P_w \cdot \|\overrightarrow{wv}\|^{-\kappa}} \geq \sigma. \tag{1}$$

Table 1 lists major notations of the physical interference model.

Given a collection of links L, a subset I of links in L is said to be interference free if and only if all links in I transmit without interference under the physical interference model.

Suppose each communication link has a channel state for transmitting along that channel. The channel state space for all links is {idle or good, busy or bad}. The channel state of each link will evolve independently across time. The states are evolving according to the probability transition matrix in Table 2.

In Table 2, α_i and β_i are defined in the Gilbert-Elliot channel model [5]. Specifically, α_i and β_i are associated with link i. α_i denotes the probability for link i to transit from busy state to idle state. β_i denotes the probability to transit from idle state to busy state. For simplicity, we only consider that for each link, the probability that each channel state remains the same is greater than the probability that the channel state jump to the other one. In this scenario, the state evolution is called positive correlated [14]. The scenario of a positive auto-correlation occurs when $\alpha_i + \beta_i < 1$ for each i.

Table 2. The state transition of link i is shown by a 2×2 probability transition matrix.

Begin	End	
	Idle	Busy
Idle	$1 - \beta_i$	β_i
Busy	α_i	$1 - \alpha_i$

Let r_i be the expected reward of the channel for a link i. We assume there is a communication request along the link all the time. Suppose a communication link transmits without any conflict along a channel which is in an idle state, a reward of r_i is obtained.

The complete state information of each channel is not known due to unpredictable activities of primary users. To address this difficulty, we estimate the channel state by researching the history and feedback from the activated links. Assume time is divided equally into time-slots. The scheduler maintains a parameter $\pi_i[T]$ for each communication link. $\pi_i[T]$ means the probability that link i's channel state is idle at time-slot T.

At each time-slot, we select a collection of links to sense and transmit. The accurate channel state is revealed via *Acknowledgement/Negative Acknowledgement (ACK/NACK)* feedbacks. Here ACK/NACK messages are generated only after the data are transmitted according to the *Automatic Repeat Request (ARQ)* mechanism. The value of $\pi_i[T]$ represents the expected reward collected if the link i is scheduled in time-slot T.

For simplicity, we assume that the the time horizon starts from slot $T = 0$. At the time-slot 0, we assume an arbitrary initial channel state for each communication link.

We define a scheduling algorithm as selecting a collection of links to transmit at each time-slot. For an algorithm, let $a_i[T]$ denote whether link i is scheduled ($a_i[T] = 1$) or not ($a_i[T] = 0$) at time-slot T. The problem **OWLS** aims to design an algorithm that maximizes the average reward over the long time horizon, *i.e.*,

$$\lim_{T \to +\infty} E\left\{ \frac{\sum_{T=0}^{T} \sum_{i=0}^{N} a_i[T] \cdot \pi_i[T] \cdot r_i}{T} \right\}.$$

The system is subject to SINR constraints such that the selected communication links at each time-slot do not cause any conflict.

We introduce a set of variables as defined in [9]. For any link i, let $u_i(t)$ be the probability that the channel remains in an idle state after t time-slots; let $v_i(t)$ be the probability that the channel moves to an idle state from a busy state after t time-slots. Both $u_i(t)$ and $v_i(t)$ have monotone properties. In other words, as t increases, $u_i(t)$ strictly decreases and $v_i(t)$ strictly increases.

For any algorithm, we define a performance measure $\{I_i(t), O_i(t)\}$ of link $i, i = 1, 2, \cdots, N$ as follows. $I_i(t)$ denotes the probability that the last time of selecting the link i is t time-slots ago, its last observed state is idle state, and link i is selected in the current slot. Note that the three events are independent from each other. Similar we define $O_i(t)$ denotes the probability that the last time of selecting the link i is t time-slots ago, its last observed state is busy state, and link i is selected in the current slot. Here, $I_i(t), O_i(t)$ take expected values and can capture the time distribution of different channel states of each link when executing an algorithm.

3   Algorithm Design

3.1   Seperating Links via Partition and Coloring

Under the condition that each link has a length at most $(1 - \epsilon)\mathbf{r}$ where ϵ is a small constant, we design a fast and simple algorithm for the problem **OWLS** in the following. Our main idea is inspired by the fact that if transmissions are well-separated geographically, the interference on each link is bounded. After observing this geometric property, we schedule communication links such that at each time step, we use the well seperated links distributed in the plane.

From Eq. (1), if no other link is transmitting concurrently, *i.e.*, S_u is empty, the SINR is reduced to *signal to noise ratio* (SNR): $\frac{P_u \cdot (\eta \cdot \|uv\|^{-\kappa})}{\xi} \geq \sigma$, thus, we have $\|uv\| \leq \sqrt[\kappa]{\frac{\eta P_u}{\sigma \xi}} \leq \sqrt[\kappa]{\frac{\eta P}{\sigma \xi}}$. Let $\mathbf{r} = \sqrt[\kappa]{\frac{\eta P}{\sigma \xi}}$ be the *maximum transmission radius*.

The plane is partitioned into a grid, where each cell has a diagonal length of $\mathbf{r}$. Let $\gamma = \mathbf{r}/\sqrt{2}$ denote the side length of a cell. Let $\mathbb{Z}$ represent the integer set. We use the vertical line segments $\{x = i \cdot \gamma : i \in \mathbb{Z}\}$ and horizontal line segments $\{y = j \cdot \gamma : j \in \mathbb{Z}\}$ to partition the plane. After the partition, the plane consists of half-open, half-closed grids of side length γ: $[i\gamma, (i+1)\gamma) \times [j\gamma, (j+1)\gamma) : i, j \in \mathbb{Z}$. We call the plane area $[i\gamma, (i+1)\gamma) \times [j\gamma, (j+1)\gamma)$ as cell $g_{i,j}$. In other words, the plane is partitioned into square cells $g_{i,j}$ for $i, j \in \mathbb{Z}$, with side length γ. After this partition of the plane, we define a large-block as a square which consists of $(K+1) \times (K+1)$ cells. The value of K is set as follows to based on the parameters of the physical interference model.

$$K = \left\lceil \sqrt{2} \left((4\tau)^{-1} (\sigma^{-1} - \xi(\eta)^{-1} R^{\kappa - \beta}) \right)^{-1/\kappa} + \sqrt{2} \right\rceil \tag{2}$$

For each cell, we first derive an upper bound on the number of links that transmit concurrently without interference. Based on the parameters of the SINR constraints, this upper bound is $\omega = \lceil \frac{2^\kappa P}{\sigma^2 \xi} + 1 \rceil$.

3.2   Decouple Links in a Cell via Lagrange Relaxation

We then consider the problem **OWLS** in a cell c. We formulate the restricted version of the problem **OWLS** as a Whittle's Linear Programming (LP) [25]. Consider one cell c, let L' be the collections of communication links in this single cell. We have the following LP.

$$\max \sum_{i \in L'} \sum_{t \geq 1} r_i I_i(t)$$

$$s.t. \sum_{i \in L'} \sum_{t \geq 1} \big(I_i(t) + O_i(t)\big) \leq \omega \qquad (3)$$

$$\sum_{t \geq 1} t\big(I_i(t) + O_i(t)\big) \leq 1, \forall i$$

$$\sum_{t \geq 1} O_i(t) v_i(t) = \sum_{t \geq 1} I_i(t)(1 - u_i(t)), \forall i$$

$$I_i(t), O_i(t) \geq 0, \forall i, t \geq 1$$

The maximum value of the above LP, OPT, is greater than or equal to the maximum value for the problem **OWLS** in the cell c under the physical interference model.

For any $\lambda_c \geq 0$, the Lagrange relaxation of the LP in Eq. (3) is as follows.

$$\max \sum_{i \in L'} \sum_{t \geq 1} r_i I_i(t)$$

$$+ \lambda_c \Big(\omega - \sum_{i \in L'} \sum_{t \geq 1} \big(I_i(t) + O_i(t)\big) \Big)$$

$$= \max \ \omega \lambda_c + \sum_{i \in L'} \sum_{t \geq 1} \Big(r_i I_i(t) - \lambda_c(I_i(t) + O_i(t)) \Big) \qquad (4)$$

In the Lagrange relaxation, the links are decoupled. Thus, we decouple an $|L'|$-dimensional LP to a collection of one-dimensional LPs. Moreover, these one-dimensional LP are not interleaved and can be solved independently.

3.3 Semi-infinite Programming of Each Link Independently

For each link in the cell c, we identify the Semi-Infinite Program (SIP) as follows.

$$\text{SIP}_i^{\lambda_c} : \quad \max \sum_{t \geq 1} \Big(r_i I_i(t) - \lambda_c(I_i(t) + O_i(t)) \Big) \qquad (5)$$

$$s.t. \sum_{t \geq 1} t\big(I_i(t) + O_i(t)\big) \leq 1$$

$$\sum_{t \geq 1} O_i(t) v_i(t) = \sum_{t \geq 1} I_i(t)(1 - u_i(t))$$

$$I_i(t), O_i(t) \geq 0, t \geq 1.$$

For $\text{SIP}_i^{\lambda_c}$ with a Lagrange multiplier λ_c, the maximum value of $\text{SIP}_i^{\lambda_c}$ is

$$H_i^{\lambda_c} = \frac{(r_i - \lambda_c) v_i(t_i) - \lambda_c \beta_i}{v_i(t_i) + t_i \beta_i}, \quad t_i = \arg\max_t \frac{(r_i - \lambda_c) v_i(t) - \lambda_c \beta_i}{v_i(t) + t \beta_i}.$$

Since we have $\forall \lambda_c \geq 0 \ \omega \lambda_c + \sum_i H_i^{\lambda_c} \geq OPT$, and $H_i^{\lambda_c}$ decreases with λ_c, there is a λ_c such that $\lambda_c = \sum_i H_i^{\lambda_c} \geq \frac{OPT}{\omega + 1}$.

Algorithm 1. Divide and Conquer Algorithm for the problem **OWLS** with SINR Constraints

---

Input   : Set of links L.

Compute the value of K under the physical interference model;

Implement the cell partition and coloring scheme;

for *each cell* **do**

> Find the links restricted to the cell and formulate the problem as Whittle's LP;
>
> Calculate the Lagrange relaxation of Whittle's LP;
>
> Solve the decoupled SIP for each link in the cell;
>
> Let $H_i^{\lambda_c} \leq 0$ be the maximum value for link i and let t_i be the corresponding t such that $H_i^{\lambda_c}$ is achieved;
>
> Remove any link i with $H_i^{\lambda_c} \leq 0$;

For each color k, let R_k denote the summation of rewards of all cells with color index k;

We return the largest reward $R_{k'}$ with a color k';

$t \leftarrow 0$;

while *TRUE* **do**

> $t \longrightarrow t + 1$;
>
> **for** $i, j \in \mathbb{Z}$ *and the cell* $g_{i,j}$ *contains links from* L ; **do**
>
> > **if** *the cell* $g_{i,j}$ *has a color* k' **then**
> >
> > > Find the links whose sender lies within $g_{i,j}$, assume they form $L_{i,j}$;
> > >
> > > We select a link from $L_{i,j}$ based on the following priority: if there is a link last observed in idle state, then we select it for this time-slot;
> > >
> > > Else, we select a link last observed in busy state $t \geq t_i$ time-slots ago;
> > >
> > > If we cannot find any link, we skip the selection for this cell.
> >
> > All the selected links among all cells form a set S_t;

if $S_t \neq \emptyset$ **then**

> Transmit all links in S_t at time-slot t;

return $S_1, S_2, \cdots, S_t : t \to \infty$.

3.4   Overall Algorithm

The proposed algorithm is described in Algorithm 1. At each time, a link with (g, t) is called *idle ready*. A link with $(b, t), t \geq t_i$ is called *busy ready*. Here, R_k is the summation of rewards of all cells with color index k. At the initial time-slot, we simply assume that the initial states are all busy for all links. This assumption will not modify the long term's average reward.

4   Performance Analysis

We first prove the correctness of Algorithm 1. Then, we compute its approximation ratio. The analysis is based on a carefully defined Lyapunov potential function.

Theorem 1. *Algorithm 1 outputs an independent set of links at each time-slot.*

Proof. For all $i, j \in \mathbb{Z}$, let L_{ij} be the set of links in L whose senders lie in cell $g_{i,j}$. For each large block, I contains up to one link from the cell of the same color. As each link set S_T contains well-separated links, the link set is an independent set according to the selection of K. This proof is similar to Theorem 1 of [26].

Next, we derive the approximation bound of Algorithm 1. The main idea of the proof is that at each time-slot, the scenario of collecting rewards may be different. We employ a potential function to derive the total reward. The average reward is derived by dividing the total reward by the total time used.

Theorem 2. *Algorithm 1 achieves a $(K+1)^2 \cdot (\omega+1)$ approximation bound for the problem **OWLS** subject to SINR constraints.*

Proof. For a cell of the color k', assume L' consists of links in the cell. We first define a potential function for each link $i \in L'$. At time-slot T, if link i moved to busy channel state y time-slots ago, the potential $\phi_i^T = H_i^{\lambda_c}\left(\min(y, t_i) - 1\right)$. If link i was last observed at idle channel state, the potential $\phi_i^T = \frac{\lambda_c + t_i H_i^{\lambda_c}}{v_i(t)}$. When a link is observed in a busy state, after that, the link will become blocked if the link has not been selected to transmit for more than t_i time-slots.

Let r_i^T denote the expected reward (throughput) accrued from link i until time T.

$$\Delta\phi_i^T = \phi_i^{T+1} - \phi_i^T, \quad \Delta r_i^T = r_i^{T+1} - r_i^T.$$

Next, we consider a link i at any time-slot $T+1$. Based on whether the link is blocked or not, we have the following cases:

If the link i has been observed in a busy channel state for consecutive $t < t_i$ time-slots, the potential function is increased by $H_i^{\lambda_c}$ at this time-slot, the reward obtained by this link is zero, and we have

$$E[\Delta r_i^T + \Delta\phi_i^T] = H_i^{\lambda_c}$$

If the link i is selected and the link is last observed in busy channel state, assume the link is last observed y time-slots ago, then $y \geq t_i$. Since $v_i(t)$ is monotonically increasing with t, with probability $q \geq v_i(t_i)$, the observed channel state is idle and the reward $\Delta r_i^T = r_i$ and the change of potential is $\frac{\lambda_c + t_i H_i^{\lambda_c}}{v_i(t)} - H_i^{\lambda_c}(t_i - 1)$. With probability $1 - q$ the observed channel state is busy and the change of potential is $H_i^{\lambda_c}(t_i - 1)$ and the reward remains the same. Since we have $q \geq v_i(t_i)$ and $\frac{\lambda_c + t_i H_i^{\lambda_c}}{v_i(t)} \geq 0$, we have

$$E[\Delta r_i^T + \Delta\phi_i^T] = q\left(r_i + \frac{\lambda_c + t_i H_i^{\lambda_c}}{v_i(t)}\right) - H_i^{\lambda_c}(t_i - 1) \geq \lambda_c + H_i^{\lambda_c}$$

If the link i's last observed state is idle, then the link is selected at last time-slot. There are two cases. The first case is that the reward is increased by r_i

and the potential remains the same. The probability of the first case is $1 - \beta_i$. The second case is that the potential function is decreased by $\frac{\lambda_c + t_i H_i^{\lambda_c}}{v_i(t)}$. The probability of the second case is β_i. We have

$$E[\Delta r_i^T + \Delta \phi_i^T] = (1 - \beta_i)r_i - \beta_i \frac{\lambda_c + t_i H_i^{\lambda_c}}{v_i(t)} \geq \lambda_c + H_i^{\lambda_c}$$

If link i is blocked, then the reward from this link is zero, and the potential function of the link is not changed, i.e., $\phi_i^T = \phi_i^{T+1} = H_i^{\lambda_c}(t_i - 1)$. Then we have $E[\Delta r_i^T + \Delta \phi_i^T] = 0$.

For all of the four cases, we have obtained the expected reward of a link. Next we consider the links in the cell together at time T. Let $\Phi_T = \sum_{i \in L'} \phi_i^T$.

We use $R_T = \sum_{i \in L'} r_i^T$ to denote the total reward collected from the begining to the time-slot T.

$$\Delta \Phi_T = \Phi_{T+1} - \Phi_T = \sum_{i \in L'} \Delta \phi_i^T, \quad \Delta R_T = R_T - R_{T-1} = \sum_{i \in L'} \Delta \phi_i^T.$$

The following equality holds no matter whether blocked links exist or not. $E[\Delta R_T + \Delta \Phi_T | \Phi_T] \geq \frac{OPT}{\omega + 1}$

In the first scenario, there exists blocked link(s). A link is blocked because of some other link in the same cell. The total reward of the selected links at this time-slot is λ_c. Note that the values of $\Delta r_i^T + \Delta \phi_i^T$ of other selected links are non-negative.

$$E[\Delta r_i^T + \Delta \phi_i^T] \geq \frac{OPT}{\omega + 1}$$

If no link is blocked, then each link is either last observed $t < t_i$ time-slots ago or selected. In either case, we have

$$E[\Delta r_i^T + \Delta \phi_i^T] \geq H_{\lambda_c}^i.$$

To sum up, for all N links, we have

$$E[\Delta R_T + \Delta \Phi_T | \Phi_T] \geq \sum_{i \in L'} H_{\lambda_c}^i \geq \frac{OPT}{\omega + 1}.$$

Thus, no matter whether there is a link blocked or not, at each time-slot we have

$$E[\Delta R_T + \Delta \Phi_T | \Phi_T] \geq \frac{OPT}{\omega + 1}$$

Since we have $\Phi_T = \sum_{i \in L'} H_i^{\lambda_c}(\min(y, t_i) - 1 \leq \sum_{i \in L'} H_i^{\lambda_c}(t_i - 1)$, the value of Φ_T is bounded. We have

$$\lim_{t \to \infty} \frac{R_T}{T} \geq \frac{OPT}{\omega + 1}$$

Note that there is one cell with color k' among every $(K+1)^2$ cells. Based on the definition of R_k and the fact that k' corresponds to the largest reward $R_{k'}$ among all $(K+1)^2$ colors, Algorithm 1 outputs a $(K+1)^2 \cdot (\omega+1)$ approximation solution.

5   Related Work

MAB can be classified into three categories, *i.e.*, stochastic bandits, adversarial bandits, and restless MAB. Here we only conduct the literature review for the third class *i.e.*, restless MAB, which is the focus of this paper. **Index Structure:** In [25], the pioneer work of Whittle suggested extending the multi-armed bandit [6,12] to a restless version, where an arm not selected to be active can also change its state. The investigation on Restless MAB has led to "Whittle's index" policies or algorithms. In such policies, an index called Whittle's index which is a mapping from a channel state to a real value is computed, each time we simply select the channels whose indices are above some threshold. In [14], Liu and Zhao studied the optimality of Whittle's index policy for multiple channels scheduling and computed a closed form of Whittle's index.

Myopic Algorithms: Ahmad *et al.* [2] proposed a myopic algorithm for stochastically identical and independent channels. They assume that one arm is activated. In [1], the myopic algorithm was extended to select multiple channels each time. Wang *et al.* [21–24] addressed the Restless MAB from the perspective of myopic algorithm for both two and multiple state Restless MAB. Comprehensive surveys on Restless MAB are available in [4,15,16]. However, their work either cannot provide a performance guarantee for opportunistic wireless scheduling or simply assume all links have the same transition probabilities.

Approximation Algorithm Perspective: Guha and Munagala [8,9] initiated the study on the Restless MAB problem from an approximation algorithm perspective. Wan and Xu [20] designed two approximation algorithms for Restless MAB. They considered both a weighted version and a multiple constrained version of the problem respectively. In [27], Xu and Song focused on the protocol interference model and proposed an interference-aware approximation algorithm for Restless MAB. The difference between their work and this study is that they either did not address wireless interference or use a over-simplified graph-based interference model.

In terms of the applications, the restless MAB has been applied to opportunistic downlink fading channel scheduling [18,20], network utility maximization [13], unmanned aerial vehicle routing [11], and energy harvesting [3].

6   Conclusion

We designed an efficient scheduling algorithm with an approximation guarantee for opportunistic link scheduling problem with SINR constraints. Some questions are left open in this area. The first one is to design a simple algorithm with idle performance guarantees for the simple but common case where all links have the same state transition matrix. The second one is to explore the connection between the opportunistic wireless link scheduling problem and the well studied maximum weighted independent set problem. The third one is that the state transition dynamics may be unknown. Under such a setting, it is critical to take a learning approach to estimate the state transition dynamics and design a scheduling policy. Thus, how to optimize the performance through learning is the key.

Acknowledgements. The research of authors is supported in part by KSU OVPR grant, NSFC Grant No. 61802097 and No. 61572377, and the Project of Qianjiang Talent (Grant No. QJD1802020).

References

1. Ahmad, S., Liu, M.: Multi-channel opportunistic access: a case of restless bandits with multiple plays. In: Allerton, pp. 1361–1368 (2009)
2. Ahmad, S.H.A., Liu, M., Javidi, T., Zhao, Q., Krishnamachari, B.: Optimality of myopic sensing in multichannel opportunistic access. IEEE Trans. Inf. Theory **55**(9), 4040–4050 (2009)
3. Blasco, P., Gündüz, D.: Multi-access communications with energy harvesting: a multi-armed bandit model and the optimality of the myopic policy. IEEE JSAC **33**(3), 585–597 (2015)
4. Bubeck, S., Cesa-Bianchi, N., et al.: Regret analysis of stochastic and nonstochastic multi-armed bandit problems. Found. Trends Mach. Learn. **5**(1), 1–122 (2012)
5. Gilbert, E., et al.: Capacity of a burst-noise channel. Bell Syst. Tech. J **39**(9), 1253–1265 (1960)
6. Gittins, J., Glazebrook, K., Weber, R.: Multi-armed Bandit Allocation Indices. Wiley, Hoboken (2011)
7. Goussevskaia, O., Wattenhofer, R., Halldórsson, M.M., Welzl, E.: Capacity of arbitrary wireless networks. In: IEEE INFOCOM, pp. 1872–1880 (2009)
8. Guha, S., Munagala, K.: Approximation algorithms for partial-information based stochastic control with Markovian rewards. In: IEEE FOCS, pp. 483–493 (2007)
9. Guha, S., Munagala, K., Shi, P.: Approximation algorithms for restless bandit problems. J. ACM (JACM) **58**(1), 3 (2010)
10. Gupta, P., Kumar, P.R.: The capacity of wireless networks. IEEE Trans. Inf. Theory **46**(2), 388–404 (2000)
11. Le Ny, J., Dahleh, M., Feron, E.: Multi-UAV dynamic routing with partial observations using restless bandit allocation indices. In: American Control Conference, pp. 4220–4225. IEEE (2008)
12. Li, B., Yang, P., Li, X.-Y., Tang, S., Liu, Y., Wu, Q.: Almost optimal dynamically-ordered multi-channel accessing for cognitive networks. In: IEEE INFOCOM, pp. 3081–3085. IEEE (2012)
13. Li, C.-P., Neely, M.J.: Network utility maximization over partially observable markovian channels. Perform. Eval. **70**(7), 528–548 (2013)
14. Liu, K., Zhao, Q.: Indexability of restless bandit problems and optimality of whittle index for dynamic multichannel access. IEEE Trans. Inf. Theory **56**(11), 5547–5567 (2010)
15. Lunden, J., Koivunen, V., Poor, H.V.: Spectrum exploration and exploitation for cognitive radio: recent advances. IEEE Signal Process. Mag. **32**(3), 123–140 (2015)
16. Mahajan, A., Teneketzis, D.: Multi-armed bandit problems. Found. Appl. Sens. Manag., 121–151 (2008)
17. Mitola, J., Maguire, G.Q., et al.: Cognitive radio: making software radios more personal. IEEE Pers. Commun. **6**(4), 13–18 (1999)

18. Ouyang, W., Murugesan, S., Eryilmaz, A., Shroff, N.B.: Exploiting channel memory for joint estimation and scheduling in downlink networks–a Whittle's indexability analysis. IEEE Trans. Inf. Theory **61**(4), 1702–1719 (2015)
19. Wan, P.-J., Jia, X., Dai, G., Du, H., Frieder, O.: Fast and simple approximation algorithms for maximum weighted independent set of links. In: IEEE INFOCOM, pp. 1653–1661 (2014)
20. Wan, P.-J., Xu, X.: Weighted restless bandit and its applications. In: IEEE ICDCS, pp. 507–516 (2015)
21. Wang, K., Chen, L.: On optimality of myopic policy for restless multi-armed bandit problem: an axiomatic approach. IEEE Trans. Signal Process. **60**(1), 300–309 (2012)
22. Wang, K., Chen, L., Liu, Q., Wang, W., Li, F.: One step beyond myopic probing policy: a heuristic lookahead policy for multi-channel opportunistic access. IEEE Trans. Wirel. Commun. **14**(2), 759–769 (2015)
23. Wang, K., Chen, L., Yu, J., Zhang, D.: Optimality of myopic policy for multistate channel access. IEEE Commun. Lett. **20**(2), 300–303 (2016)
24. Wang, K., Liu, Q., Li, F., Chen, L., Ma, X.: Myopic policy for opportunistic access in cognitive radio networks by exploiting primary user feedbacks. IET Commun. **9**(7), 1017–1025 (2015)
25. Whittle, P.: Restless bandits: activity allocation in a changing world. J. Appl. Probab. **25**, 287–298 (1988)
26. Xu, X., Li, X.-Y., Song, M.: Efficient aggregation scheduling in multihop wireless sensor networks with SINR constraints. IEEE Trans. Mob. Comput. **12**(12), 2518–2528 (2013)
27. Xu, X., Song, M.: Approximation algorithms for wireless opportunistic spectrum scheduling in cognitive radio networks. In: IEEE INFOCOM (2016)
28. Yu, D., Ning, L., Zou, Y., Yu, J., Cheng, X., Lau, F.C.: Distributed spanner construction with physical interference: constant stretch and linear sparseness. IEEE/ACM Trans. Netw. **25**(4), 2138–2151 (2017)
29. Yu, J., Huang, B., Cheng, X., Atiquzzaman, M.: Shortest link scheduling algorithms in wireless networks under the SINR model. IEEE Trans. Veh. Technol. **66**(3), 2643–2657 (2017)

Distributed Real-Time Data Aggregation Scheduling in Duty-Cycled Multi-hop Sensor Networks

Xiaohua Xu[1]([✉]), Yi Zhao[2], Dongfang Zhao[3], Lei Yang[4], and Spiridon Bakiras[5]

[1] Department of Computer Science,
Kennesaw State University, Kennesaw, USA
xxu6@kennesaw.edu
[2] Department of Computer Science and Technology,
Tsinghua University, Beijing, China
[3] Department of Computer Science and Engineering,
University of Nevada, Reno, USA
[4] School of Software Engineering,
South China University of Technology, Guangzhou, China
[5] College of Science and Engineering,
Hamad Bin Khalifa University, Doha, Qatar

Abstract. Wireless sensor network (WSN) systems often need to support real time periodic queries of physical environments. In this work, we focus on periodic queries with sufficiently long time horizon in duty-cycled sensor networks. For each periodic query issued by a control center in a WSN, after the source sensors produced the sensory data, the data are to be sent to the sink via multi-hop data aggregation timely in a periodic fashion. To this end, we propose efficient and effective data aggregation algorithms subject to quality of service constraints such as deadline requirements and interference constraints. We decompose these into three sequential operations: (1) aggregation tree construction (2) node and link-level scheduling and (3) packet scheduling. Inspired by the scheduling algorithms, we identify both sufficient conditions and necessary conditions for scheduling multiple queries. The schedulability analysis under various interference models demonstrate that the proposed algorithms achieve an approximate proportion of the maximum possible load.

Keywords: Real time scheduling · Duty cycle · Data aggregation · Interference

1 Introduction

In numerous applications of wireless sensor networks (WSNs), we often need to support queries (*e.g.* habitat monitoring, structural health monitoring, queries for assessment of potential damages for earthquakes) formed in a Structured

© Springer Nature Switzerland AG 2019
E. S. Biagioni et al. (Eds.): WASA 2019, LNCS 11604, pp. 432–444, 2019.
https://doi.org/10.1007/978-3-030-23597-0_35

Query Language (SQL). After a user queries regarding a data report, the sensors cooperate to generate a convincing response with the help of in-network aggregation. Data aggregation allows data compressing where the data from different source nodes may be correlated. Thus, data aggregation is recommended for answering queries via using an aggregation function, *e.g.*, max, min, average, associated with each query. As an example, when computing the summation of all data in the network, instead of transmitting all raw data to the sink, we only need to transmit the sum result from corresponding children nodes to the sink. Therefore, this feature of in-network data processing potentially allows energy efficient information delivery, compared to the raw data collection. This is because an outgoing packet size possibly becomes smaller during the data aggregation process.

In this work, we concentrate on satisfying a set of aggregation queries (*i.e.*, queries for monitoring light, temperature, acoustic and ammonia). Given a sink node and a collection of sensor nodes, assume that a control center releases multiple queries. Some query may ask for average ammonia concentration in certain wastewater processing tank and some query may ask for the temperature data in certain area. Each query has a period and a release time and the data from all source nodes are expected to be aggregated to the sink node for each period. Each query also has an end-to-end latency requirement for getting the answer, thus there is an expected deferred deadline for each instance of the query. Given a query set and a wireless interference model, the objective is to design an efficient aggregation tree and an interference-aware schedule of node, link, and packet-level activities for each query.

We study the problem in a duty-cycled scenario. Duty-cycled is originally proposed to save energy. Nowadays, most WSNs are duty-cycled. Under the uncoordinated duty-cycled model, we assume that the time horizon is divided equally into time-slots. In a single time-slot, a node is allowed to transmit data at any time-slot while the node is only able to receive data at some pre-defined time-slot(s) of every period.

Related Work: Job scheduling has been well studied in the literature for both single node case and multi-nodes case [13,14]. Considering a group communication pattern of the job scheduling where multiple nodes need to cooperate together to finish a job or task, Chipara *et al.* [5] studied the real time query scheduling in wireless network by assuming that the routing tree is pregiven. Xu *et al.* [21] considered the real time data aggregation scheduling with a bounded end-to-end delay performance. However, the proposed scheduling method is centralized and the method does not consider the duty-cycled constraints. Later on, [19,22] studied the real time data collection and multicast scheduling respectively. On the other hand, one-shot data aggregation scheduling has received a lot of research interests such as [2,3,9,12,16]. However, only a few [4,8,10,11,17,18,23,24] studied fast data aggregation scheduling in duty-cycled scenario.

Our main contributions in this paper are on the efficient duty-cycled scheduling algorithms and schedulability test for periodic data aggregation queries. We design routing and scheduling algorithms for data aggregation queries. Inspired by the proposed algorithms, we present sufficient conditions for scheduling multiple queries in a duty-cycled sensor network. We also identify necessary conditions. The schedulability analysis under various interference models demonstrate that the proposed algorithms achieve an approximate proportion of the maximum possible load.

We organize the remaining of the paper as follows. Section 2 presents the system model and the questions to be studied. Section 3 presents scheduling algorithms for data aggregation queries under variant interference models. Section 4 presents schedulability results queries. Section 5 presents the conclusion and the future work.

2   System Model

Let $G = (V, E, v_s)$ be an aggregation graph that models a WSN where V consists of all nodes, E consists of all communication links, and the node $v_s \in V$ is the distinguished sink node. Suppose all nodes have a uniform communication radius. There is a communication link between two nodes if and only if (iff) their distance is at most the communication radius.

We assume a duty-cycling scenario. Each node i has a period $\mathbf{P}$, and an active time-slot in a period of $\mathbf{P}$ consecutive time-slots. In a duty-cycling network, for any node v, suppose its active time-slot is $k(0 \leq k < \mathbf{P})$, then the node v is active and ready for data reception at time t iff $t \equiv k \mod \mathbf{P}$. We assume that a node u can send a data packet to node v at time t, if and only if $\overrightarrow{uv} \in G$ and the receiver node v is active at time-slot t. In this case, node u should already have the data ready before time t and has been waiting for node v to be active.

Considering that multiple link transmissions may occur simultaneously and possibly cause interference, we address extensively several commonly used interference models.

Protocol Interference Model (PrIM) [7]: Each node has a transmission range of one and an *interference range* ρ. A node u can transmit to another node v iff $\|uv\| \leq 1$ and the distance between v and any other sender node is greater than ρ.

RTS/CTS Model [1]: A node u can transmit to another node v iff $\|uv\| \leq 1$ and both nodes u and v are not interfered. Here a node is interfered if the distance between the node and any other sender node or receiver node is at most one.

Physical Interference Model (PhyIM) [25,26]: A receiver node v can receive the data from a sender u iff the signal to interference plus noise ratio is above a threshold value β, *i.e.*,

$$SINR = \frac{P \cdot \|uv\|^{-\kappa}}{N_0 + \sum_{w \in I} P \cdot \|wv\|^{-\kappa}} \geq \beta.$$

Here P is node u's transmission power and we assume that all nodes have the same power. $\kappa > 2$ is the path loss exponent, $\|wv\|$ is the distance between w and

v, $N_0 > 0$ is the background noise, and I is the set of concurrent transmitting nodes.

Query Model: Assume source nodes generate data reports periodically for some applications (*e.g.* temperature monitoring, assessment of potential damages for earthquakes). In a connected network $G = (V, E)$ with $v_s \in V$ as the sink node, the control center issues a query set $\mathcal{Q} = \{\mathbf{q}_1, \mathbf{q}_2, \cdots, \mathbf{q}_N\}$. For each query $\mathbf{q}_i$, let $\mathcal{S}_i \subseteq V$ be a collection of source nodes that have data to report. The size of a data unit for a source node $v \in \mathcal{S}_i$ is ℓ_i and χ_i is the time needed to transmit ℓ_i data over a communication link. The data need to be convergecasted to the distinguished sink v_s to answer query $\mathbf{q}_i$ periodically.

The period of each query $\mathbf{q}_i \in \mathcal{Q}$ is $\mathbf{p}_i$. Each query $\mathbf{q}_i$ has a release time $\mathbf{a}_i$, thus, the release time of the query's t-th instance is $\mathbf{a}_i + (t-1) \cdot \mathbf{p}_i$. Each query also has an end-to-end latency requirement $\mathbf{d}_i$ for getting the answer, thus the expected time for the data from all source nodes to be aggregated is $\mathbf{a}_i + (t-1) \cdot \mathbf{p}_i + \mathbf{d}_i$ for the t-th instance. Note that due to the network delay and duty-cycled constraints, the latency requirement $\mathbf{d}_i$ is usually in the order of $O(R \cdot \mathbf{P})$ for each query. Here R is the radius of the graph G.

Given a query set $\mathcal{Q} = \{\mathbf{q}_1, \mathbf{q}_2, \cdots, \mathbf{q}_N\}$ for data aggregation, we mainly address two questions. The first question is to design periodic data aggregation scheduling to answer queries. The second question is to determine whether all queries can be satisfied or not. The sufficient condition and necessary condition are used to test whether a given query set for data aggregation is schedulable. A query set is schedulable *iff* they can be answered.

3 Distributed Duty-Cycled Aggregation Query Scheduling

We assume for each query, the data aggregation routing tree that is used can be varied, *i.e.*, for different queries or different instants of a single query, different routing trees can be used. Under this general assumption, we develop effective routing algorithms, node, link, and packet scheduling to avoid interference, and answer all queries.

3.1 Overall Approach

The proposed scheduling of queries for aggregation consists of four phases:

Phase I: For each query, construct a routing tree in the network.

Given a network with the communication graph G, we first build a Connected Dominating Set (CDS) based spanning tree $\mathbf{T}_{CDS}$. The construction of a CDS is in [6]. Then using a *pruning* method, we can derive a data aggregation routing tree $\mathbf{T}_i$ for each query $\mathbf{q}_i \in \mathcal{Q}$. Note that any data aggregation routing tree $\mathbf{T}_i$ is a Steiner tree connecting $\mathcal{S}_i \cup \{v_s\}$ with node $v_s \in V$ as the sink node. In addition, $\mathbf{T}_i$ is a subtree of $\mathbf{T}_{CDS}$.

Phase II: Identify the load of each node in real time which specifies the data packets to transmit for each node.

Given a data aggregation routing tree $\mathbf{T}_i$, for each node u not in dominating set, its original data first are aggregated to a dominator (a neighbor in dominating set) periodically. After that, all data in the G_{CDS} are routed to the sink periodically. Using this routing method, for each query $\mathbf{q}_i \in \mathcal{Q}$, first every leaf node (must be a source node) of the tree $\mathbf{T}_i$ adds packets to its load for each period, then every non-leaf node u in the tree $\mathbf{T}_i$ adds *one* packet to its load upon receiving all packets from its children in $\mathbf{T}_i$ for the query $\mathbf{q}_i$. Note that node u may receive several packets but generates only one packet by computing an aggregation function on data received possibly with its own data. After processing for all queries, we get a load of each node.

Phase III: Allocate transmission time to cells and nodes in proportion to their load.

For a query set $\mathcal{Q}$ and a set of data aggregation routing trees, under the duty-cycled model, a node u's load is defined as $\mathcal{L}_{G,\mathcal{Q}}(u) = \sum_{u \in \mathbf{T}_i} \frac{\chi_i}{\mathbf{P}_i} \cdot \mathbf{P}$.

We partition the plane into cells. We define the load of a cell g as the summation of the loads of all nodes in the cell, *i.e.*, $\mathcal{L}_{G,\mathcal{Q}}(g_{v,h}) = \sum_{u \in V(g)} \mathcal{L}_{G,\mathcal{Q}}(u)$. Here $V(g) \subseteq V$ consists of all nodes lying in cell g. Thus, the load also accounts for routing data.

Based on the definition of load, a cell or node with more packets (thus more load) need to be allocated with more time to transmit.

Phase IV: Prioritize data packets to transmit when it is a node u's allocated time. We use *rate monotonic (RM)* [14] or *earliest-deadline first (EDF)* method in this phase. Note that both methods are effective to ensure that every packet can catch its deadline.

3.2   Constructing CDS-based Routing Trees

The construction for data aggregation routing trees relies on selecting a CDS G_{CDS} of G first. For every node not in the CDS, we connect it to its neighboring dominator. For a query, the corresponding source nodes may be only a subset of the node set. Thus, for query $\mathbf{q}_i \in \mathcal{Q}$, we prune every node $u \in V$ and the corresponding link $\vec{uv}$ in $\mathbf{T}_{CDS}$ that does not have any source node in the subtree of $\mathbf{T}_{CDS}$ rooted at u. Thus we can get a data aggregation routing tree $\mathbf{T}_i$ for $\mathbf{q}_i$. Here CDS's sparsity property can ensure that the size of CDS in a cell is bounded by a constant times the area of the cell.

For physical interference model, let $\mathbf{r} = \sqrt[\kappa]{\frac{P}{N_0 \beta}}$ be the maximum transmission radius. If a communication link's length is approaching $\mathbf{r}$ in practice, the SINR of the link cannot exceed the threshold with high probability (*w.h.p.*), then the transmission probably fails. Therefore, a link of length close to $\mathbf{r}$ is prevented from transmissions in this work. Given a parameter δ, we only focus on links of length at most $\delta\mathbf{r}$ in the network as in [20]. We can obtain a parameterized reduced graph, denoted as $G(V, \delta\mathbf{r})$. If $G(V, \delta\mathbf{r})$ is connected, we can perform data transmissions in this subgraph instead. Therefore, under physical interference model, we construct data aggregation trees in a parameterized graph $G(V, \delta\mathbf{r})$.

3.3   Identifying Load of Each Node According to Routing Trees

Before constructing a load of a node, we need to determine which queries the node is involved with. If a node participates in a query $\mathbf{q}_i$, the node adds a packet (either original packet or aggregated one in the corresponding data aggregation routing tree $\mathbf{T}_i$) periodically for $\mathbf{q}_i$ to its load. We store the load of each node in the node's buffer. The details are shown in Algorithm 1. Here, we use $[N]$ to denote $\{1, 2, \cdots, N\}$.

3.4   Allocate Time to Node in Proportion to Load

After we identify loads, each node may store some packets in its load. The next phase is to allocate time to each node in proportion to its load.

We employ a cell partition and coloring to ensure that only nodes far apart could possibly be allocated the same time to transmit. We use vertical lines $a_v : x = v \cdot l(\mathcal{M})$ where $v \in \mathbb{Z}$ and horizontal lines $b_h : y = h \cdot l(\mathcal{M})$ where $h \in \mathbb{Z}$ to partition the plane into cells. Here $\mathbb{Z}$ is the set of all integers. Under the protocol interference model, we set $l(\mathcal{M}) = \rho + 1$; Under the CTS/RTS model, we set $l(\mathcal{M}) = 3$. The above values of $l(\mathcal{M})$ can ensure that any two senders of a mutual distance $l(\mathcal{M})$ do not cause any interference. Under the physical interference model, we set the cell length $l(\mathcal{M}) = \mathbf{r}$.

After cell partition, we allocate time to cells. We color all cells such that every neighboring cells of the same color are separated apart by exactly $\sqrt{c_2(\mathcal{M})} - 1$ cells. Thus, the number of cell colors used is $c_2(\mathcal{M})$. The value of $c_2(\mathcal{M})$ is given in Lemma 5. After cell coloring, we allocate time to each cell in proportion to its load. Due to the duty-cycled constraints, we set the time allocated to a cell as the load of the cell multiplied by the cycling period.

Then, we allocate time to a node from a selected cell to transmit. Suppose a cell is allocated with a time period T, we allocate each node u in a cell g with transmission time $T \cdot \frac{\mathcal{L}_{G,\varrho}(u)}{\mathcal{L}_{G,\varrho}(g_{v,h})}$.

Note that we can implement the proposed algorithms in a distributed manner as we do not require global coordination for each cell. Another benefit of cell partition is the increasing adaptivity of our method, thus we may allow the network to be more dynamic.

3.5   Packet-Level Scheduling

When it is the transmission time for a node, we determine the packet(s) to transmit from the node's load. We use a *rate monotonic* [15] method for packet scheduling and satisfy the duty-cycled constraints at the same time.

Algorithm 1. Identifying Load of Each Node According to Routing Trees

---

Input : A network $G = (V, E, v_s)$, a set of queries $\mathcal{Q} = \{q_i : i \in [N]\}$, a set of routing
trees $\{T_i : i \in [N]\}$.

Output: The load of each node: a set of packets for each node.

1 $t \longleftarrow 1$;
2 **while** *TRUE* **do**
3 | **for** *each query* $q_i \in \mathcal{Q}$ **do**
4 | **for** *each node* $u \in T_i$ **do**
5 | **if** *u is a leaf node in* T_i **then**
6 | add the original packet for t-th instance of query q_i to node u's load;
7 | **else**
8 | **if** *u receives a packet for* q_i **then**
9 | store the packet to its buffer;
10 | **if** *u has received packets for* t-th instance of query q_i *from all children in* T_i **then**
11 | aggregate all packets to be one packet;
12 | add the packet to node u's load;
13 | $t \longleftarrow t + 1$;
14 **return** *packets for each node for each period.*

---

1. A packet of current instance has a lower priority than that of any previous instance.
2. A packet of current instance for a query with a shorter period should be scheduled later than any the packet of current instance for a query with a longer period. Similarly, a packet of previous instance for a query with a shorter period should be scheduled later than any packet of previous instance for a query with a longer period. Ties are broken randomly.

As proved in [15], the rate monotonic method achieves maximum performance for each packet to be transmitted before deadline if each node has a load of at most 0.69.

We can also use EDF scheduling instead if each node has a load of at most one. The details of EDF scheduling are shown in Algorithm 3.

4 Schedulability Analysis

First, we derive **sufficient conditions** for schedulability of queries for data aggregation. Then, we propose **necessary conditions** for schedulability. We verify the schedulability of a given query set by comparing the sufficient conditions and necessary conditions.

4.1 Sufficient Condition on Schedulability

In Sect. 3, we proposed algorithms to schedule periodic queries for data aggregation. We prove that the proposed algorithms are *feasible*. Here we call an

---

Algorithm 2. Allocate Time to Node in Proportion to Load

Input : The load of each node.
Output: Allocated time to nodes.

1 Perform cell partition and coloring;
2 Allocate time to each cell in proportion to its load and only cells with the
  same color can be allocated to the same time;
3 **while** *TRUE* **do**
4   **for** $i \in [c_2(\mathcal{M})]$ **do**
5   **for** *each cell* $g_{v,h}, v, h \in \mathbb{Z}$ *with the i-th color* **do**
6   **for** *each node u in the cell* $g_{g,h}$ **do**
7   allocate u's transmission time as: $T \cdot \frac{\mathcal{L}_{G,\mathcal{Q}}(u)}{\mathcal{L}_{G,\mathcal{Q}}(g_{v,h})}$;

8 **return** *allocated transmission time for each node.*

Algorithm 3. EDF-Based Packet Scheduling of Each Node

Input : A node u.
Output: A packet scheduling.

1 **while** *TRUE* **do**
2   **if** *node u is to transmit* **then**
3   select a packet from u's load with the earliest deadline, assume the packet
         is for query $\mathbf{q}_i$;
4   node u transmits the packet to its parent in $\mathbf{T}_i$ at its parent's active
         time-slot under the duty-cycled model;

---

algorithm is feasible for a query set iff by using the algorithm, we can both avoid
interference and answer all queries under the duty-cycled model.

Lemma 1. *The proposed algorithms in Sect. 3 are interference-free.*

Proof. In Algorithm 2, when allocating transmission time to nodes, each time
we only select one node from only cells with the same color. By the definition
of $c_2(\mathcal{M})$ which is the number of cell colors used for cell coloring, the proposed
algorithms can avoid interference under various interference models.

Lemma 2. *The proposed algorithms in Sect. 3 answer all data aggregation
queries.*

Proof. From Algorithm 2, each cell has $1/c_2(\mathcal{M})$ fraction of time to be active.
At the same time, the load of each cell is at most $0.69/c_2(\mathcal{M})$. Considering the
ratio of the node's load to the fraction of time the node is allocated to, note that
each node's relative load is at most one. By using linear time allocation, we can
allocate time to each node to transmit as long as each node has enough buffer.
Therefore, we can answer the given set of data aggregation queries in time as
long as the latency requirement is large enough.

The feasibility verification (Lemmas 1, 2) implies schedulability of queries by using the proposed algorithms in Sect. 3. To sum up, we present a sufficient condition on which a query set is schedulable.

Theorem 1. *There exist scheduling algorithms to satisfy a data aggregation query set $\mathcal{Q}$ under an interference model $\mathcal{M}$, if*

$$
\begin{cases}
\mathcal{L}_{G,\mathcal{Q}}(g_{v,h}) & \leq \frac{0.69}{c_2(\mathcal{M}) \cdot \boldsymbol{P}}, \ \forall g_{v,h} \\
\sum_{\boldsymbol{q}_i \in \mathcal{Q}} \frac{\chi_i}{\boldsymbol{p}_i} & \leq \frac{0.69}{\boldsymbol{P}}
\end{cases}
\tag{1}
$$

Here $\mathcal{L}_{G,\mathcal{Q}}(g_{v,h})$ is the load of cell $g_{v,h}$ and $c_2(\mathcal{M})$ is the number of cell colors. The value of $c_2(\mathcal{M})$ is provided in Lemma 5.

4.2 Necessary Condition on Schedulability

Consider the communication graph $G = (V, E)$ and a query set $\mathcal{Q}$, we define the source load of a node $u \in V$ as $\ell_{G,\mathcal{Q}}(u) = \sum_{u \in \mathcal{S}_i \cap \boldsymbol{q}_i \in \mathcal{Q}} \frac{\chi_i}{\boldsymbol{p}_i}$. The source load of a cell g is defined as the summation of the source loads of all nodes in the cell: $\ell_{G,\mathcal{Q}}(g_{v,h}) = \sum_{u \in V(g)} \ell_{G,\mathcal{Q}}(u)$ where $V(g)$ is the set of nodes from V lying inside the cell g.

To schedule nodes' transmissions in the worst case, for every set of clique nodes where no two nodes can transmit concurrently, the total load of all nodes can not exceed 1 in duty-cycled networks. Generally, for a cell $g_{v,h}$, in which the maximum number of sender nodes in $g_{v,h}$ that can transmit without interference is $c_1(\mathcal{M})$, the source load of the cell is at most $c_1(\mathcal{M})$.

Moreover, for a query $\boldsymbol{q}_i \in \mathcal{Q}$, the sink node ($v_s \in V$) needs to receive at least one packet for data aggregation during every period $\boldsymbol{p}_i$, which takes time χ_i. Given a query set $\mathcal{Q}$, the amount of data received at sink v_s, given by $\sum_{\boldsymbol{q}_i \in \mathcal{Q}} \frac{\chi_i}{\boldsymbol{P}_i}$, is at most one if $\mathcal{Q}$ can be answered.

To sum up, we present a necessary condition for a query set to be schedulable in Theorem 2.

Theorem 2. *A set of aggregation queries $\mathcal{Q} = \{\boldsymbol{q}_i : i \in [N]\}$ in a duty-cycled model are schedulable if the following conditions are satisfied.*

$$
\begin{cases}
\ell_{G,\mathcal{Q}}(g_{v,h}) & \leq c_1(\mathcal{M}), \ \forall g_{v,h} \\
\sum_{\boldsymbol{q}_i \in \mathcal{Q}} \frac{\chi_i}{\boldsymbol{p}_i} & \leq 1
\end{cases}
\tag{2}
$$

Here $\ell_{G,\mathcal{Q}}(g_{v,h})$ is the source load of an cell $g_{v,h}$. $c_1(\mathcal{M}) \geq 1$ is the maximum possible number of nodes that can transmit currently in a cell. The value of $c_1(\mathcal{M})$ is provided in Lemma 5.

4.3 Sufficiency vs Necessity

In Theorems 1 and 2, we present sufficient conditions and necessary conditions on scheduling queries for data aggregation respectively. Despite of a constant ratio difference for the sink's requirement, their main gap lies in that we use different terms for schedulability. In Theorem 2, we use the term *source load* of a cell to test schedulability, as the routing structure is unknown when testing schedulability, we cannot compute the load of a cell; while in Theorem 1, we use another term *load* to guarantee schedulability. Note that different routing structures (a set of data processing trees) for the query set have vast impact on the load of a cell, even if the source load of the cell is fixed.

To capture the exact difference between necessary and sufficient conditions on schedulability, we need to unify the terms used for comparing. We address the questions for two cases: (1) all nodes are source nodes for all queries, (2) only a subset are source nodes for every query.

Queries on All Nodes. When all nodes have data, every node needs to report a packet during each period of a query $\mathbf{q}_i \in \mathcal{Q}$. Then the source load of each node is $\sum_{\mathbf{q}_i \in \mathcal{Q}} \frac{\chi_i}{\mathbf{P}_i}$. On the other hand, for data aggregation, each node only needs one transmission during a period of a given query $\mathbf{q}_i$. Then the load of a node is at most $\sum_{\mathbf{q}_i \in \mathcal{Q}} \frac{\chi_i}{\mathbf{P}_i}$ despite the routing structure used. Thus the source load of a node is the same as the load of the node when all nodes have data for all queries. As a corollary, for each cell, the load is the same the source load.

Lemma 3. *When all nodes have data, given an aggregation query set $\mathcal{Q}$ with any interference model $\mathcal{M}$, for each cell, the load is the same as the source load.*

Using Lemma 3, we prove that the gap between necessary and sufficient conditions is a constant.

Theorem 3. *When all nodes have data, we can achieve a constant approximation ratio of $c_1(\mathcal{M}) \cdot c_2(\mathcal{M}) \cdot \mathbf{P}/0.69$ for scheduling an aggregation query set $\mathcal{Q}$ under various interference models.*

Proof. By Lemma 3, the sufficient conditions on schedulability given in Theorem 1 is equivalent to

$$\begin{cases} \ell_{G,\mathcal{Q}}(g_{v,h}) & \leq \frac{0.69}{c_2(\mathcal{M}) \cdot \mathbf{P}}, \ \forall g_{v,h} \\ \sum_{\mathbf{q}_i \in \mathcal{Q}} \frac{\chi_i}{\mathbf{P}_i} & \leq \frac{0.69}{\mathbf{P}} \end{cases}$$

At the same time, a necessary condition on schedulability given in Theorem 2 is:

$$\begin{cases} \ell_{G,\mathcal{Q}}(g_{v,h}) & \leq c_1(\mathcal{M}), \ \forall g_{v,h} \\ \sum_{\mathbf{q}_i \in \mathcal{Q}} \frac{\chi_i}{\mathbf{P}_i} & \leq 1 \end{cases}$$

By comparing the difference, we can see that the maximum load is at most $c_1(\mathcal{M}) c_2(\mathcal{M}) \cdot \mathbf{P}/0.69$ times of the load we can schedule for each cell and the sink. Thus we can achieve an approximation ratio of $c_1(\mathcal{M}) \cdot c_2(\mathcal{M}) \cdot \mathbf{P}/0.69$ for schedulability. Therefore the proof is done.

Queries on Subset of Nodes. When a subset of nodes have data for each query, the load can differ from the source load of a cell. In an extreme case, the load may be very large while the source load is zero. We compare necessary and sufficient conditions on schedulability from another perspective.

Lemma 4. *Given an interference model $\mathcal{M}$ and an aggregation query set $\mathcal{Q}$, by using our routing algorithms in Sect. 3,*

$$\begin{cases} \ell_{G,\mathcal{Q}}(g_{v,h}) & \leq 0.69/\left(2 \cdot c_2(\mathcal{M})\boldsymbol{P}\right), \forall g_{v,h} \\ \sum_{q_i \in \mathcal{Q}} \frac{\chi_i}{\boldsymbol{p}_i} & \leq \frac{0.69}{2 \cdot c_2(\mathcal{M}) \cdot (c_3(\mathcal{M}) - 1) \cdot \boldsymbol{P}} \end{cases} \tag{3}$$

implies:

$$\begin{cases} \mathcal{L}_{G,\mathcal{Q}}(g_{v,h}) & \leq \frac{0.69}{c_2(\mathcal{M}) \cdot \boldsymbol{P}}, \forall g_{v,h} \\ \sum_{q_i \in \mathcal{Q}} \frac{\chi_i}{\boldsymbol{p}_i} & \leq \frac{0.69}{\boldsymbol{P}} \end{cases}$$

Here $\boldsymbol{P}$ is the cycling period, $c_2(\mathcal{M})$ is the number of cell colors used, and $c_3(\mathcal{M}) > 1$ is the maximum size of a CDS in a cell plus one. The values of $c_2(\mathcal{M})$ and $c_3(\mathcal{M})$ are provided in Lemma 5.

Corollary 1. *Given a query set $\mathcal{Q}$ with $\mathcal{M}$, Eq. (3) is a sufficient condition on schedulability.*

Theorem 4. *When a subset of nodes have data for each query, we can achieve an approximation ratio of $\max\{2c_1(\mathcal{M})c_2(\mathcal{M})\boldsymbol{P}/0.69, \frac{2 \cdot c_2(\mathcal{M}) \cdot (c_3(\mathcal{M}) - 1) \cdot \boldsymbol{P}}{0.69}\}$ on schedulability of an aggregation query set $\mathcal{Q}$ under various interference models.*

Proof. By Lemma 4, the sufficient conditions on schedulability in Theorem 1 is Eq. (3),

$$\begin{cases} \ell_{G,\mathcal{Q}}(g_{v,h}) & \leq \frac{0.69}{(2 \cdot c_2(\mathcal{M}))\boldsymbol{P}}, \forall g_{v,h} \\ \sum_{q_i \in \mathcal{Q}} \frac{\chi_i}{\boldsymbol{p}_i} & \leq \frac{0.69}{2 \cdot c_2(\mathcal{M}) \cdot (c_3(\mathcal{M}) - 1) \cdot \boldsymbol{P}} \end{cases}$$

while a necessary condition on schedulability is:

$$\begin{cases} \ell_{G,\mathcal{Q}}(g_{v,h}) & \leq c_1(\mathcal{M}), \forall g_{v,h} \\ \sum_{q_i \in \mathcal{Q}} \frac{\chi_i}{\boldsymbol{p}_i} & \leq 1 \end{cases}$$

By comparing the difference, the approximation ratio is $\max\{2c_1(\mathcal{M}) \cdot c_2(\mathcal{M}) \cdot \boldsymbol{P}/0.69, \frac{2 \cdot c_2(\mathcal{M}) \cdot (c_3(\mathcal{M}) - 1) \cdot \boldsymbol{P}}{0.69}\}$.

Last, we provide the values of $c_1(\mathcal{M}), c_2(\mathcal{M})$, and $c_3(\mathcal{M})$ in Lemma 5 and summarize the notations in Table 1.

Lemma 5 [19]. *The values of $c_1(\mathcal{M}), c_2(\mathcal{M}), c_3(\mathcal{M})$ under various interference models are as follows.*

$$c_1(\mathcal{M}) = \begin{cases} \frac{16 \cdot \rho^2}{(\rho - 1)^2} \\ 36 \\ \lfloor \frac{2^\kappa \cdot P}{N_0 \beta^2} \rfloor \end{cases} \qquad c_2(\mathcal{M}) = \begin{cases} 4 \\ 4 \\ O(1) \end{cases} \qquad c_3(\mathcal{M}) = \begin{cases} 8 \cdot (\rho + 4)^2 & under\ PrIM \\ 200 & RTS/CTS \\ 200 & under\ PhyIM \end{cases}$$

Table 1. Notations

$\ell_{G,\mathcal{Q}}(u)$	source load of a node u	$\ell_{G,\mathcal{Q}}(g_{v,h})$	source load of a cell
$\mathcal{L}_{G,\mathcal{Q}}(u)$	load of a node u	$\mathcal{L}_{G,\mathcal{Q}}(g_{v,h})$	load of a cell
l	cell side-length	$\mathcal{S}_i$	the set of source nodes for query i
$\mathbf{T}_i$	routing tree for query i	ℓ_i	size of data unit of query i
$\mathbf{P}$	duty cycling period	χ_i	transmission time of data unit of query i
v_s	sink node	$c_1(\mathcal{M})$	max # of senders transmitting in a cell
$\mathcal{Q}$	query set	$c_2(\mathcal{M})$	# of cell colors
$\mathbf{q}_i$	query i	$c_3(\mathcal{M})$	maximum size of CDS in a cell plus one

5   Conclusions

We designed real-time aggregation scheduling algorithms in duty-cycled sensor networks under various interference models. The proposed algorithms achieve constant approximation bound in terms of schedulability.

Some interesting questions are left for future research. The first one is to consider the aggregation latency of the proposed algorithms. The second one is to consider each query may have multiple sink nodes and the sink nodes of different queries could be different. The last one is to extend the proposed algorithms to deal with a more duty-cycled model. For example, the cycling periods of different nodes may be different.

References

1. Alicherry, M., Bhatia, R., Li, L.: Joint channel assignment and routing for throughput optimization in multi-radio wireless mesh networks. In: ACM MobiCom , p. 72 (2005)
2. Chen, K., Gao, H., Cai, Z., Chen, Q., Li, J.: Distributed energy-adaptive aggregation scheduling with coverage guarantee for battery-free wireless sensor networks. In: IEEE INFOCOM (2019)
3. Chen, Q., Gao, H., Cai, Z., Cheng, L., Li, J.: Energy-collision aware data aggregation scheduling for energy harvesting sensor networks. In: IEEE INFOCOM, pp. 117–125 (2018)
4. Chen, Q., Gao, H., Cheng, S., Li, J., Cai, Z. Distributed non-structure based data aggregation for duty-cycle wireless sensor networks. In: IEEE INFOCOM, pp. 1–9 (2017)
5. Chipara, O., Lu, C., Roman, G.: Real-time query scheduling for wireless sensor networks. In: IEEE RTSS (2007)
6. Du, D.-Z., Wan, P.-J.: Weighted CDS in unit disk graph. In: Du, D.-Z., Wan, P.-J. (eds.) Connected Dominating Set: Theory and Applications, pp. 77–104. Springer, New York (2013). https://doi.org/10.1007/978-1-4614-5242-3_5
7. Gupta, P., Kumar, P.: The capacity of wireless networks. IEEE Trans. Inf. Theory **46**(2), 388–404 (2000)
8. Ha, N.P.K., Zalyubovskiy, V., Choo, H.: Delay-efficient data aggregation scheduling in duty-cycled wireless sensor networks. In: ACM RACS, pp. 203–208 (2012)

9. He, Z., Cai, Z., Cheng, S., Wang, X.: Approximate aggregation for tracking quantiles and range countings in wireless sensor networks. Theor. Comput. Sci. **607**, 381–390 (2015)

10. Jiao, X., Lou, W., Feng, X., Wang, X., Yang, L., Chen, G.: Delay efficient data aggregation scheduling in multi-channel duty-cycled WSNs. In: IEEE MASS, pp. 326–334 (2018)

11. Jiao, X., Lou, W., Wang, X., Cao, J., Xu, M., Zhou, X.: Data aggregation scheduling in uncoordinated duty-cycled wireless sensor networks under protocol interference model. Ad Hoc Sens. Wirel. Netw. **15**(2–4), 315–338 (2012)

12. Li, J., Cheng, S., Cai, Z., Yu, J., Wang, C., Li, Y.: Approximate holistic aggregation in wireless sensor networks. ACM Trans. Sens. Netw. **13**(2), 11 (2017)

13. Liu, C.L., Layland, J.W.: Scheduling algorithms for multiprogramming in a hard-real-time environment. J. ACM **20**(1), 46–61 (1973)

14. Liu, J.: Real-Time Systems. Prentice Hall, Upper Saddle River (2000)

15. Shih, W., Liu, J., Liu, C.: Modified rate-monotonic algorithm for scheduling periodic jobs with deferred deadlines. IEEE Trans. Softw. Eng. **19**(12), 1171–1179 (1993)

16. Wan, P.-J., Huang, S.C.-H., Wang, L., Wan, Z., Jia, X.: Minimum-latency aggregation scheduling in multihop wireless networks. In: ACM MobiHoc (2009)

17. Xiao, S., Huang, J., Pan, L., Cheng, Y., Liu, J.: On centralized and distributed algorithms for minimizing data aggregation time in duty-cycled wireless sensor networks. Wirel. Netw. **20**, 1729–1741 (2014)

18. Xu, X., Cao, J., Wan, P.-J.: Fast group communication scheduling in duty-cycled multihop wireless sensor networks. In: Wang, X., Zheng, R., Jing, T., Xing, K. (eds.) WASA 2012. LNCS, vol. 7405, pp. 197–205. Springer, Heidelberg (2012). https://doi.org/10.1007/978-3-642-31869-6_17

19. Xu, X., Li, X.-Y., Song, M.: Distributed scheduling for real-time data collection in wireless sensor networks. In: IEEE GLOBECOM, pp. 426–431 (2013)

20. Xu, X., Li, X.-Y., Song, M.: Efficient aggregation scheduling in multihop wireless sensor networks with sinr constraints. IEEE Trans. Mob. Comput. **12**(12), 2518–2528 (2013)

21. Xu, X., Li, X.-Y., Wan, P.-J., Tang, S.: Efficient scheduling for periodic aggregation queries in multihop sensor networks. IEEE/ACM Trans. Netw. **20**(3), 690–698 (2012)

22. Xu, X., Song, M.: Delay efficient real-time multicast scheduling in multi-hop wireless sensor networks. In: IEEE GLOBECOM, pp. 1–6 (2015)

23. Yan, X., Du, H., Ye, Q., Song, G.: Minimum-delay data aggregation schedule in duty-cycled sensor networks. In: Yang, Q., Yu, W., Challal, Y. (eds.) WASA 2016. LNCS, vol. 9798, pp. 305–317. Springer, Cham (2016). https://doi.org/10.1007/978-3-319-42836-9_28

24. Yu, B., Li, J.-Z.: Minimum-time aggregation scheduling in duty-cycled wireless sensor networks. J. Comput. Sci. Technol. **26**(6), 962–970 (2011)

25. Yu, D., Ning, L., Zou, Y., Yu, J., Cheng, X., Lau, F.C.: Distributed spanner construction with physical interference: constant stretch and linear sparseness. IEEE/ACM Trans. Netw. **25**(4), 2138–2151 (2017)

26. Yu, J., Huang, B., Cheng, X., Atiquzzaman, M.: Shortest link scheduling algorithms in wireless networks under the sinr model. IEEE Trans. Veh. Technol. **66**(3), 2643–2657 (2017)

Building Trustful Crowdsensing Service on the Edge

Biao Yu[1], Yingwen Chen[1(✉)], Shaojing Fu[1], Wanrong Yu[1], and Xiaoli Guo[2]

[1] College of Computer, National University of Defense Technology,
Changsha 410073, China
ywch@nudt.edu.cn
[2] Foreign Studies College, Hunan Normal University,
Changsha 410081, China

Abstract. Edge computing enables the data to be processed in the edge of networks in order to decrease the latency of crowdsensing services. However, due to the distributed environment and vulnerability of edges, it is difficult for different edges to reach consistency to provide the same service and protect the data from tampering at the same time. To solve these problems, the Blockchain, a credible and natural decentralized technique, is considered as a suitable tool. In this paper, we proposed a Blockchain-based edge crowdsensing service system in which the edge runs a changeable auction algorithm for every task that the users request to find a winner who can provide corresponding sensing data. Specifically, based on PBFT algorithm, we proposed a consensus algorithm named Leader Stable Practical Byzantine Fault Tolerance (LS-PBFT). This algorithm enables all edges to collaboratively maintain an updated, consistent and credible ledger in Blockchain. Furthermore, the data generated in this process are constructed as a multi-transaction, which can be packaged into a block and stored in the block. Simulation results reveal that the proposed system is not only efficient in generating and storing blocks but also feasible in resisting attacks of malicious users and edges. Our experiments also show that LS-PBFT takes less than 50% of the time cost by PBFT to reach consensus.

Keywords: Edge computing · Crowdsensing · Blockchain · Trustworthy

1 Introduction

Recently, edge computing has became a hot topic in Internet of Things (IoT) because of its friendliness to the heterogeneous devices for sensing, computation and communication [1]. This new model of computation has been applied to many fields, *e.g.*, cloud offloading, smart home [2], mobile big data analytics [3], smart transportation [4,5,16], *etc.* Specially, cloud service offloading is always the main direction to apply edge computing to reduce latency [6].

© Springer Nature Switzerland AG 2019
E. S. Biagioni et al. (Eds.): WASA 2019, LNCS 11604, pp. 445–457, 2019.
https://doi.org/10.1007/978-3-030-23597-0_36

As we all know, crowdsensing service based on cloud has been studied for several years [7, 8]. Nevertheless, the latency between sensors and cloud is always the bottleneck of application [9]. To decrease service latency, the edge that provides computing, storage and network source between data resource and cloud centre is a good middleware [10, 17]. Therefore, in order to offload crowdsensing service from cloud to edges, the most important thing is to collaborate different edges in an efficient way. Moreover, because of their vulnerability, how to protect the data from being tampered in the edges is another big problem.

With all these in mind, Blockchain is considered as a feasible tool to deal with the problems. The consensus in Blockchain can be applied in edges to solve the collaboration problem among edges and the high security and reliability of Blockchain guarantee the property of data tamper-proofing [11–14]. Moreover, communication between nodes is encrypted, which protects against eavesdropping. Specifically, to offload crowdsensing service, we proposed a new system for edge crowdsensing service based on blockchain. Further more, the edge might be crashed caused by devices' damage or become compromised as a result of hacker attack. In order to better adapt to this scenario, we proposed a consensus algorithm named LS-PBFT based on PBFT algorithm for the proposed system [14]. The contributions of this paper can be summarized as follows:

(1) We proposed a new decentralized system for the edge in crowdsensing service based on Blockchain technology, which not only enables all edges to work together to provide crowdsensing service but also stores the interacted information between users and edges.
(2) We show the details of this system, which contain a light weight auction and reputation model and consensus algorithm. Further more, the format of multi-transaction block and transaction verification design details are also included.
(3) We conduct the simulation to show that our proposed consensus algorithm is efficient in Blockchain-based edge crowdsensing service.

The rest of the paper is organized as follows: A Blockchain-based system for crowdsensing service in the edge is briefly introduced in Sect. 2. Detailed design of the proposed system is discussed in Sect. 3. In Sect. 4, we give the performance evaluation. Section 5 reviews the related work. Finally, Sect. 6 concludes this paper.

2 Framework of the System

As illustrated in Fig. 1, the overall framework of the Blockchain-based edge crowdsensing service system is summarized as follows:

Users: The user can be devices or individuals who need specific data of some events beyond their sensing range. Then they send requests to the local edge for these specific data. For a certain task about the same event, there may be

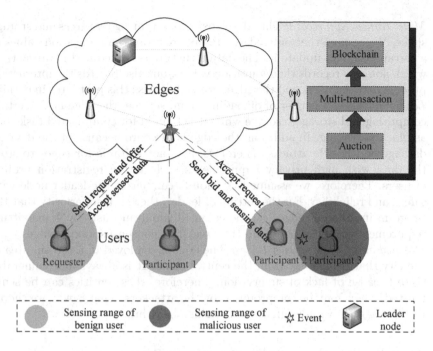

Fig. 1. System model of Blockchain-based edge crowdsensing service

multiple participants. Thus the auction procedure is needed in edges to select the winner. Since the sending of requests, the transmission of participants' feedback, or the delivery of the sensed data, they all need to go through the edge. Consequently, the edge will record and store this kind of interactive information.

Sometimes a number of malicious users may exist in the network. In order to prevent these users, we have added reputation values in the system to limit the compromised users. Both auction and reputation model will be showed in the next part.

Edges: The edges provide resources and capabilities to execute the tasks from users and record the interactive information between users and edges. The functions of edges are introduced as follows:

(a) *Auction procedure:* After receiving the sensing request about some events from users, the edge will broadcast the request (task) to the participants in its jurisdiction. Each participant will evaluate whether he can complete this task. If it can be completed, he will accept the task and give his feedback to the edge. The edge execute an auction procedure to generate the winner, who gets the permission to send his own sensing data to the requester and get rewarded. In order to motivate users and prevent malicious users, we mainly consider the bid given by the participants and the reputation values of these participants in the auction procedure.

(b) *Multi-transaction record:* The edge provides computing resources and storage space. We assume that only edges are able to store the reputation values of a certain user and update it. The data structure is named multi-transaction, which not only records the reputation values, but also records the interaction process between users and the edge. We will discuss this part later in details.

(c) *Leader node:* As a carrier of offloading cloud service, the edge has a certain computing and storage resource while it is limited for complicated task such as block packaging. In addition, the edge is insecure because of the devices' damage and hostile attacks. Therefore, it is not suitable for edges to store the data with high privacy requirements such as the registration profiles of users. Therefore, we assume the "cloud" can act as the leader node with safety and reliability. For the setting of leader, there is a superiority that the program in different edges can be changed simultaneously by transmitting requirement to leader node and then reaching consensus among edges.

(d) *Crashed and Compromised Edges:* The edge is deployed in a certain area of the city that is far away from the central cloud. It is always in a vulnerable state because of lack of supervision. Therefore, these entities can be semi-trusted, which may be compromised by the attackers. That is why we choose PBFT algorithm to design our consensus algorithm.

3   Detailed Design of the Proposed System

As illustrated in Fig. 2, the design details of Blockchain based edge crowdsensing service can be divided into the following parts: (1) Auction, *i.e.*, winner selection and trust management, (2) Format of multi-transaction block and transaction verification process, (3) LS-PBFT consensus algorithm and theoretical analysis.

3.1   A Lightweight Auction and Reputation Model for Crowdsensing Service

Before starting the auction program, we need to know the available information collected by the edge. The first step is the requester's request T, followed by the number of participants P_T and the corresponding bid price B_T, and the participant's reputation value information R_T is the last one. For convenience, we use P, B, R represent P_T, B_T, R_T respectively. Table 1 presents the notation used in the following algorithms and formulas.

The auction aims at selecting one winner out of P participants. Algorithm 1 shows the pseudocode of the auction program. In our model, we first consider defining the reputation bids B_R, as shown in the fourth line of Algorithm 1. Then, a reputation bid standard s is defined according to the adjustable reputation threshold τ, as defined by the first line in Algorithm 1. The reputation bid standard guarantees that the participants' bid cannot be too high and their reputation values need to meet a certain level. In the algorithm, we select the winner in two steps. The first step is to select the candidate set P' by comparing

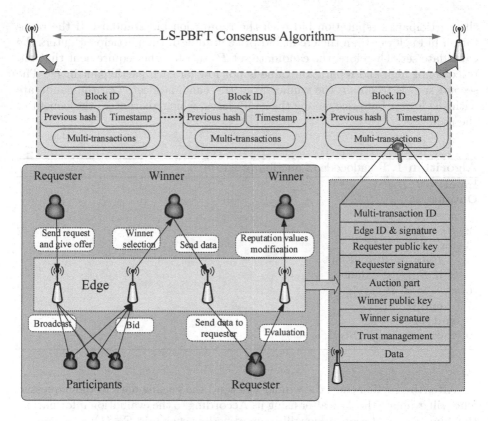

Fig. 2. System design details of Blockchain-based edge crowdsensing service

Table 1. Notation used in this paper.

Notation	Explanation
T	Request or task
o	Offer of requester
P_T, P	Set of participants
B_T, B	Bid list of participants
$B(p)$	Bid of participant p
R_T, R	Reputation value list of participants
$R(p)$	Reputation value of participant p, $R(p) \in [0,1]$
B_R	Reputation bid list
$B_R(p)$	Reputation bid of participant p
w	Winner, $w \in P$
τ	Threshold of reputation value, $\tau \in [0,1]$
E	Evaluation of winner
r	Reward

the participant's reputation bid with the reputation bid standard. If the reputation bid is lower than the credit bid price standard, the participant enters the candidate set. Therefore, the candidate set P' satisfies the requirement that bid price is not high and reputation value is not low for each participant in P'. The second step is to obtain the winner from the candidate set, *i.e.*, the candidate with the lowest bid price among the candidates, which guarantees the benefit of the requester.

Algorithm 1. Pseudocode of auction program

Input: o, P, B, R, τ;
Output: w;
1: $s \Leftarrow o/\tau$;
2: $P' \Leftarrow \phi$;
3: **for all** $p \in P$ **do**
4:     $B_R(p) \Leftarrow B(p)/R(p)$;
5:     **if** $B_R(p) < s$ **then**
6:         $P' \Leftarrow P' \cup \{p\}$;
7:     **end if**
8: **end for**
9: $w \Leftarrow \arg\min_{p \in P'}\{B(p)\}$;

After the auction ends, the winner will send the sensing data to the requester, who will evaluate the data after using it. According to the evaluation information, the winner's reputation value will be modified as shown in Eq. (1):

$$R^{new}(w) = \alpha R(w) + (1 - \alpha)(2 + \frac{4}{e - 1})(\frac{1}{1 + (\frac{1}{e})^E} - \frac{1}{2}), \alpha \in [0, 1] \quad (1)$$

where E is the evaluation information and α is an adjustable parameter. E meets the restriction $E \in [0, 1]$, which indicates that the closer E is to 1, the worse the evaluation is. For the parameter α, the greater the value of α is, the more contribution the previous reputation makes, and vice verse.

Additionally, we also need to provide reward to the winner, which is calculated by Eq. (2):

$$r = \min(o, B(w)) + R(w)|o - B(w)| \quad (2)$$

where o is the offer; $B(w)$ is the bid of the winner; and $R(w)$ is the reputation value of the winner. It should be noted that $R(w)$ is the reputation value before modification, not the value $R^{new}(w)$, thus preventing the requester always from giving bad evaluation of the winner.

3.2   Multi-transaction Block and Transaction Verification

This part introduces the format of multi-transaction and the transaction verification to provide a detailed architecture of Blockchain used in this system.

Multi-transaction Block: The format of block includes two parts, the head and body. The head stores three pieces of information, *i.e.*, block ID, previous hash, and generating time of the block. The hash of previous block is used to chain this block to the existing Blockchain. The body contains the list of multi-transaction.

The structure of a multi-transaction is shown in Fig. 3, which can be divided into six parts. The first part is basic information of the multi-transaction, which contains the transaction ID, edge ID, and the signature of the edge. And the second part is the public key and signature of requester. This is followed by the auction part, which record the auction process. The data set $\{o, P, R, B, \tau, w\}$ is contained in this part. The following public key and signature of winner is recorded for winner verification. The fifth part is the transfer and trust management, which includes the reward, evaluation and the new reputation value of winner. The last data part records the data used in crowdsensing service, such as hash of request, hash of sensing data, and hash of auction program.

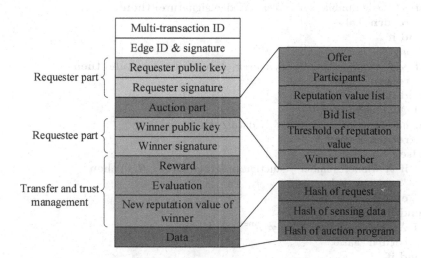

Fig. 3. Format of multi-transaction

Transaction Verification: The edge must validate each new block it receives from the leader node to chain it to Blockchain. To validates a block, the edge first validates the signature of leader node by using the public key of leader. It is assumed that only the leader node has the right to package the block. Next, each individual multi-transaction in the block is verified. If all the multi-transactions contained in the block are valid, the block is considered to be valid.

Algorithm 2 outlines the procedure for verifying an individual multi-transaction (X). The verifier (*i.e.* edges) first confirms the validity of transaction generator, by using the public key (queried by edge ID), which is known by every edge (line 1–3). Following this, the requester signature is verified (also called redeemed) using its public key in X (line 4–6). Afterward, the auction process need to be verified, which can be divided into three parts. Firstly, the verifier checks the consistency of auction program by comparing the hash of auction program with the third item of data part of transaction (line 7–8). If the auction program is valid, the validity of winner selection is confirmed (line 10–13) by rerunning the program. Finally, the new reputation value of the winner must be also verified (line 14–15). In the last step of multi-transaction verification, the edge verify the signature of winner by using its public key in X. With the steps completed successfully, X is verified.

Algorithm 2. Transaction verification

Input: Multi-transaction(X);
Output: True or False;
    Edge verification:
 1: **if** $\sim$(X.edge_public_key *redeem* X.edge_signature) **then**
 2:    **return** False;
 3: **end if**
    Requester verification:
 4: **if** $\sim$(X.requester_public_key *redeem* X.requester_signature) **then**
 5:    **return** False;
 6: **end if**
    Auction verification:
 7: **if** hash(auction_program) $\neq$ X.data[2] **then**
 8:    **return** False;
 9: **else**
10:    **if** X.winner_number $\neq$ auction_program(o, P, B, R, τ) **then**
11:      **return** False;
12:    **end if**
13: **end if**
14: **if** X.new_reputation_value $\neq$ $R^{new}(w)$ **then**
15:    **return** False;
16: **end if**
    Winner verification:
17: **if** $\sim$(X.winner_public_key *redeem* X.winner_signature) **then**
18:    **return** False;
19: **end if**
20: **return** True

3.3 LS-PBFT Consensus Algorithm

As proposed in our system, the edge can provide cloud offloading crowdsensing service. While how to ensure the consistency of different edges to guarantee the same service is the key point of the system. To solve this problem, we proposed

LS-PBFT consensus based on PBFT algorithm. Further more, the data tamper-proofing property of LS-PBFT also guarantees the security of data stored in Blockchain. The Algorithm 3 shows the procedure of this algorithm.

Algorithm 3. Procedure of LS-PBFT

1: After packaging multi-transactions, the leader node automatically generates the request of chaining the block to Blockchain;
2: The leader node multicasts the request to the edge. The edge performs the pre-preparation phase, the preparation phase, and the commit phase step by step once receiving the request.
3: Edges execute the request and send a reply to the leader node.
4: When the leader node receives f results from f different edges and the results are the same as leader node's, the consensus is completed and the block is chained successfully.

In order to facilitate the narrative, we assume that the total number of node is $N = 3f + 1$, which is consistent with the one represented in the PBFT algorithm. And we also have the assumption that the leader node is always credible. Once the leader node receives f replies, which are the same as leader node's, the process of LS-PBFT is completed. For LS-PBFT consensus, the most important part of the algorithm is its three phases, *i.e.* pre-prepare, prepare and commit, which are the same as PBFT algorithm.

4   Performance Evaluation

In order to evaluate the efficiency and feasibility of this system, performance evaluations are conducted. We use a laptop with Intel i5-4210H CPU @ 2.90 GHz and 8.00 GB RAM to run our experiments. Meanwhile, the operating system is Windows 8.1 and the programming language is Python 3.6.3. The simulation results can be divided into two parts. The first part discusses the effectiveness of auction model for resisting malicious users. The comparison of running time between PBFT and LS-PBFT is provided in the second part.

4.1   Effectiveness of Auction Model for Resisting Malicious Users

This part mainly shows the procedure from auction to evaluation, and from evaluation to reputation values calculation. The initial configuration of parameters is shown in follows: We set o, P, and τ equal 5, 100, 0.5 respectively. The initial value of reputation is 0.5 for every participant in P. The bid prices of participants are assumed as normal distribution. And we also give a warning threshold, which equals 0.25.

The relationship between percentage of malicious users and average auction times is shown in Fig. 4. We have tested six values of parameter α for the calculation of reputation value based on algorithm 1 and Eq. 1. The percentage of malicious users decreases gradually with the increase of average auction times, which indicates the availability of auction model for resisting malicious users' attacks. Furthermore, the value of α has remarkable effects on calculation of reputation value. For example, the red line shows the percentage of malicious users when the previous reputation values of users are not taken into consideration ($\alpha = 0$). From the result, we know that the best setting of α is $\alpha \in [0.3, 0.7]$.

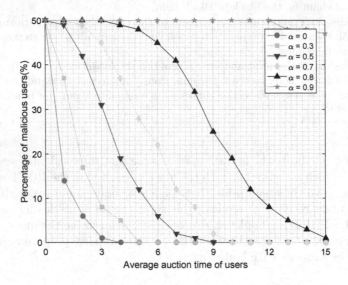

Fig. 4. Ratio of malicious users versus average auction time

4.2   Running Time to Reach Consensus

After the accomplishment of auction process, the edges try to record the data as a multi-transaction and transmit the transaction to the leader node, which packages the transaction to a block. The block will be chained into Blockchain once the consensus is reached between different edges. Therefore, the running time to reach consensus T is mainly influenced by the number of edges. Figure 5 shows that the running time rises with the increase of edge number N. As the theoretical analysis section presented, the exact relationship between T and N is $T \sim O(N^2)$. our simulation result of curvilinear trend also holds this analytic consequence.

To make a comparison, the running time to reach consensus based on PBFT algorithm is also evaluated. As we can see in Fig. 5, compared with the PBFT, the proposed consensus algorithm LS-PBFT saves one half of the running time, which is a significant promotion. The reduction of transmission times among edges are the main reason for this promotion, which is caused by the setting of the leader node.

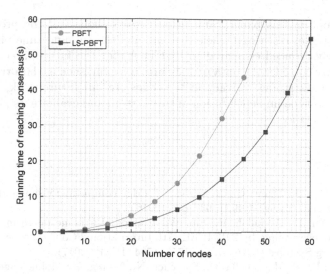

Fig. 5. Running time of reaching consensus

5 Related Work

Blockchain has drawn an increasing attention in the edge of IoT. For example, Dorri *et al.* proposed a Lightweight Scalable Blockchain (LSB) in smart home to ensure data security and privacy of IoT [15]. LSB achieves these by forming an overlay network where high resource devices jointly manage a public Blockchain and by associating the security with privacy nature of Blockchain. Blockchain is also applied to data management. In [5], Yang *et al.* presented a decentralized trust management in vehicular network based on blockchain. In this system, the information of vehicles such as the register ID, trust values, value of offsets is stored in Blockchain, which provides trust environment in vehicular network. The most important part of Blockchain is the consensus algorithm, which has always occupied the focus of academic research [11,13,14]. A kind of Byzantine fault tolerance called Practical Byzantine Fault Tolerance (PBFT) proposed by Castro and Liskov [14] was used for Hyperledger Fabric, which is a famous Blockchain platform that has been used by many enterprises such as IBM.

6 Conclusion

In this paper, we proposed a Blockchain based edge crowdsensing service system, which enables users to get the corresponding sensing data they want or participate the auction procedure to get reward by supplying sensed data. The multi-transaction records the data generated in this process. By using LS-PBFT consensus algorithm, all edges work together to maintain a consistent and tamper-proof database. In order to evaluate the performance of this system, simulations are carried out in this paper. Simulation results show that the proposed system is effective in resisting malicious users and the running time of LS-PBFT is significantly reduced compared to PBFT. As for the future direction of this work, one may consider the data privacy preservation, such as data transmission privacy and data storage privacy in the edges. In our future work, we plan to develop a prototype implementation of this system and evaluate its performance in real-world settings.

References

1. Shi, W., Cao, J., Zhang, Q., Li, Y., Xu, L.: Edge computing: vision and challenges. IEEE Internet Things J. **3**(5), 637–646 (2016)
2. Cao, J., Xu, L., Abdallah, R., Shi, W.: Edgeos_h: a home operating system for internet of everything. In: 2017 IEEE 37th International Conference on Distributed Computing Systems (ICDCS), pp. 1756–1764. IEEE (2017)
3. Hu, Y.C., Patel, M., Sabella, D., Sprecher, N., Young, V.: Mobile edge computing a key technology towards 5G. ETSI White Paper **11**(11), 1–16 (2015)
4. Zhang, Q., et al.: OpenVDAP: an open vehicular data analytics platform for CAVs. In: 2017 IEEE 38th International Conference on Distributed Computing Systems (ICDCS). IEEE (2018)
5. Yang, Z., Yang, K., Lei, L., Zheng, K., Leung, V.C.: Blockchain-based decentralized trust management in vehicular networks. IEEE Internet Things J. (2018)
6. Teerapittayanon, S., McDanel, B., Kung, H.: Distributed deep neural networks over the cloud, the edge and end devices. In: 2017 IEEE 37th International Conference on Distributed Computing Systems (ICDCS), pp. 328–339. IEEE (2017)
7. Sheng, X., Tang, J., Xiao, X., Xue, G.: Sensing as a service: challenges, solutions and future directions. IEEE Sens. J. **13**(10), 3733–3741 (2013)
8. Pouryazdan, M., Kantarci, B., Soyata, T., Song, H.: Anchor-assisted and vote-based trustworthiness assurance in smart city crowdsensing. IEEE Access **4**, 529–541 (2016)
9. Bonomi, F., Milito, R., Zhu, J., Addepalli, S.: Fog computing and its role in the internet of things. In: Proceedings of the First Edition of the MCC Workshop on Mobile Cloud Computing, pp. 13–16. ACM (2012)
10. Shi, W., Dustdar, S.: The promise of edge computing. Computer **49**(5), 78–81 (2016)
11. Nguyen, G.T., Kim, K.: A survey about consensus algorithms used in blockchain. J. Inf. Process. Syst. **14**(1), 101–128 (2018)
12. Yang, Z., Zheng, K., Yang, K., Leung, V.C.: A blockchain-based reputation system for data credibility assessment in vehicular networks. In: 2017 IEEE 28th Annual International Symposium on Personal, Indoor, and Mobile Radio Communications (PIMRC), pp. 1–5. IEEE (2017)
13. Wood, G.: Ethereum: A secure decentralised generalised transaction ledger. Ethereum Project Yellow Paper **151**, 1–32 (2014)
14. Castro, M., Liskov, B., et al.: Practical byzantine fault tolerance. In: OSDI, vol. 99, pp. 173–186 (1999)
15. Dorri, A., Kanhere, S.S., Jurdak, R., Gauravaram, P.: LSB: a lightweight scalable blockchain for IoT security and privacy. arXiv preprint arXiv:1712.02969 (2017)

16. Chen, Y., Ming, X., Yu, G., Pei, L., Lei, S., Xiao, X.: Empirical study on spatial and temporal features for vehicular wireless communications. EURASIP J. Wirel. Commun. Netw. **2014**(1), 180 (2014)
17. Yeting, G., Fang, L., Zhiping, C., Nong, X., Ziming, Z.: Edge-based efficient search over encrypted data mobile cloud storage. Sensors **18**(4), 1189 (2018)

User Identity De-anonymization Based on Attributes

Cheng Zhang[1], Honglu Jiang[1,2(✉)], Yawei Wang[1], Qin Hu[1], Jiguo Yu[2,3,4], and Xiuzhen Cheng[1]

[1] The George Washington University, Washington, DC, USA
{zhangchengcarl,hljiang0720,yawei,qinhu,cheng}@gwu.edu
[2] Qufu Normal University, Rizhao, China
[3] Qilu University of Technology (Shandong Academy of Sciences), Jinan, China
jiguoyu@sina.com
[4] Shandong Computer Science Center (National Supercomputer Center in Jinan), Jinan, China

Abstract. Online social networks provide platforms for people to interact with each other and share moments of their daily life. The online social network data are valuable for both academic and business studies, and are usually processed by anonymization methods before being published to third parties. However, several existing de-anonymization techniques can re-identify the users in anonymized networks. In light of this, we explore the impact of user attributes in social network de-anonymization in this paper. More specifically, we first quantify the significance of attributes in a social network, based on which we propose an attribute-based similarity measure; then we design an algorithm by exploiting attribute-based similarity to de-anonymize social network data; finally we employ a real-world dataset collected from Sina Weibo to conduct experiments, which demonstrate that our design can significantly improve the de-anonymization accuracy compared with a well-known baseline algorithm.

Keywords: Social network · De-anonymizaion · Attribute similarity

1 Introduction

As an innovation of Web 2.0 technology, Online Social Networking (OSN) has been transforming our daily lives. OSN apps such as Facebook, Instagram, and Sina Weibo, provide platforms for individuals and organizations to share their generated original contents such as posts, pictures, and short videos. People who use OSNs enjoy sharing their life and interacting with online friends. Nevertheless, both the contents generated by users and the social relationships among them are valuable for business and academic studies. In order to protect users' privacy, service providers (i.e., data publishers) usually *anonymize* these data before releasing to third parties. Existing anonymization approaches

© Springer Nature Switzerland AG 2019
E. S. Biagioni et al. (Eds.): WASA 2019, LNCS 11604, pp. 458–469, 2019.
https://doi.org/10.1007/978-3-030-23597-0_37

can be generally categorized into six classes, i.e., naive identity removal, edge randomization [8,20], k-anonymity [4,11,21,22], clustering [7,17], differential privacy [3,5,9,19], and random walk [12], which can partially perturb the network structure and attributes, and simultaneously preserve a high level of data utility.

However, there exist a series of structure-based de-anonymization algorithms that are used to re-identify users from anonymized network data [2,14,16,18]. De-anonymization refers to the process of mapping a node from the anonymized graph to a node in the original social network graph (called reference graph). Backstrom *et al.* presented passive attacks and active attacks in [1], in which attackers who are users of the original social network first find their own entities in the anonymized network and then de-anonymize others connected with them (passive attacks), or before publishing the data first fake a number of dummy "Sybil" users and then link them to the victims to create special structures, which can be easily discovered in the anonymized network and used to identify the victims (active attacks). Since active attacks are not scalable, Narayanan *et al.* [14] developed a de-anonymization algorithm based on network structure without involving any dummy "Sybil" users. In [15], a community-enhanced de-anonymization algorithm was proposed, which divides the whole network into smaller communities that can be first mapped (community mapping), then de-anonymizes the users within each community, and finally maps the remaining users in the entire graph. Besides the structural features as mentioned above, user attributes are also employed to improve the accuracy of de-anonymization. In [10], Li *et al.* analyzed the following two major limitations of the structure-based de-anonymization algorithms: structure-based algorithms cannot distinguish two users with similar friends in the anonymized social networks, and a specific user with a few common friends in two social networks can affect the de-anonymization accuracy. To overcome these limitations, the authors introduced an enhanced structure-based de-anonymization scheme leveraging structural transformation similarity in social networks.

Inspired by the structural transformation employed in [10], we notice that the attributes of users could also be used to improve identity de-anonymization in OSNs. Therefore, we examine the attributes of 20 popular OSNs, including 10 OSNs in the USA and 10 OSNs in China, and made the following key observations: (1) the types of attributes obtained during user registration are very similar for all the 20 OSNs; (2) each attribute implies a different amount of discriminatory information for de-anonymization. For example, given a dataset of undergraduate students who are Facebook users from University of Maryland, the attribute *age* may not provide much discriminatory information as *home address* does; and a fine-grained address, such as a detailed postal address, if available, is more valuable for user identification than an address only specifying the state of residency; likewise, the value of attribute *sex*, i.e., female or male, is not as important as sex ratio. Based on the above observations, we propose an attribute-based de-anonymization algorithm in this paper to re-identify users by quantifying the significance values of their attributes and measuring attribute

similarities between user pairs from the reference and the anonymized social
network graphs. Our contributions of the paper can be summarized as follows:

- Based on the finding stating that attributes in a social graph are not equally
  important in de-anonymization, we propose a quantification approach to
  quantify the *significance value* of each attribute.
- Using the significance values of the attributes, we present an attribute-based
  de-anonymization algorithm to re-identify user identities in a social graph.
- With the help of a real-world social network dataset collected from the Sina
  Weibo, we evaluate the performance of our algorithm; and the experimental
  results show that our proposed attribute-based de-anonymization approach
  can achieve a better performance compared to a well-known baseline algorithm.

The rest of the paper is organized as follows. In Sect. 2, we present the basic
social network model and the corresponding definitions. In Sect. 3, we introduce the existing structure-based de-anonymization methods and the motivation of our study. In Sect. 4, we quantify the significance values of the attributes
in a social graph and propose an attribute-based de-anonymization algorithm.
Experimental results are reported in Sect. 5. Conclusions and future work are
summarized in Sect. 6.

Table 1. Notations

Symbol	Semantics
G	Undirected graph
V	User set
E	Edge set
A	Attribute set
u_i	The ith user in V
A_{u_i}	The attribute set of the ith user
a_k	The kth attribute in A
$v_{a_k}^j$	The jth value of attribute a_k
k_n	The number of attribute values of a_k
$v_{i_{a_k}}$	The value of attribute a_k at user u_i
S_{a_k}	The set of users in V that possess the attribute $a_k \in A$
$S_{a_k}^j$	The set of users possessing the value of $v_{a_k}^j$

2   Social Network Model

Given a social network, we build a corresponding undirected graph $G(V, E, A)$,
with vertex (user) set $V = \{u_1, u_2, ..., u_i, ...\}$, edge (friendship relations) set

$E = \{e_{i,j} = (u_i, u_j) | u_i, u_j \in V, i \neq j\}$, and attribute set $A = \{a_1, a_2, ..., a_k, ...\}$. Each user u_i has a set of attributes A_{u_i}, including identity, gender, province, city, etc. We denote a_k as the kth attribute in A, $v_{a_k}^j$ as the jth value of attribute $a_k{}^1$, and k_n as the number of attribute values of a_k. Meanwhile, let v_{ia_k} be the value of attribute a_k for user u_i, $S_{a_k}^j$ be the set of users possessing the value of $v_{a_k}^j$, and S_{a_k} be the set of users in V that possess the attribute $a_k \in A$. We summarize the notations and their semantic meanings in Table 1.

Figure 1(a) presents a reference social graph $G_r(V_r, E_r, A_r)$ with real identities and the anonymized social graph $G_a(V_a, E_a, A_a)$ shown in Fig. 1(b) is obtained by perturbing G_r. In V_a, the identities (e.g., name) that can be used to uniquely identify a vertex are replaced with random characters. Other attributes in A_r, such as address and occupation, are preserved for research and business purposes. The edge set E_a is partially modified by adding or deleting edges from E_r where the red dashed lines in Fig. 1(b) are removed edges and the red solid lines are added fake ones. Once adversaries obtain the knowledge of G_a and G_r, they can launch de-anonymization attacks by mapping the users in G_a to those in G_r.

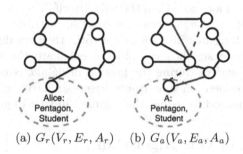

(a) $G_r(V_r, E_r, A_r)$ (b) $G_a(V_a, E_a, A_a)$

Fig. 1. Social network model and anonymization process. (Color figure online)

3 Background and Motivation

Structure-based de-anonymization attacks generally involve two phases. The first phase is called *seed identification*, where a small number of "seed" vertices in both the anonymized network and the reference network are identified and mapped to each other. The second is the *propagation* phase, in which the algorithm randomly selects an unmapped user u_a in V_a and computes the similarity value for each unmapped node u_r in V_r at each iteration. The similarity values are usually calculated according to the topology information such as vertex degree of both networks. Moreover, eccentricity [10,13,14] is generally employed to measure

---

[1] We assume all attribute values are discrete or categorical for simplicity.

how much a candidate vertex u_r "stands out" from the others, which is defined as

$$ecc(S) = \frac{Max_1(S) - Max_2(S)}{\sigma(S)}, \tag{1}$$

where S is the set of similarity values between u_a and candidate vertices in V_r, $Max_1(\cdot)$ and $Max_2(\cdot)$ are the two highest similarity values in S, and σ denotes the standard deviation of the values in S. User u_a is mapped to u_r if $ecc(S)$ is above some threshold and the similarity value of u_a and u_r equals $Max_1(S)$.

Structure-based de-anonymization attacks rely heavily on the similarity of typologies between the reference graph and the anonymized graph. Existing research considered mainly the topology structure of the graphs, ignoring the rich information carried by the node attributes. In this paper, we intend to exploit node attribute values to facilitate de-anonymization and enhance the de-anonymization success rate for perturbed graphs, which are obtained by adding edges into or removing edges from the corresponding reference graphs. Based on our study, we notice that in a social network dataset, different attributes and different values of the same attribute contribute an unequal amount of discriminatory information to de-anonymization; and the distribution of the attribute values may illustrate a lot more than the value itself. Therefore, we first present a method to quantify the *significance value* of an attribute, which can reflect the importance of attributes in a social network; then we design a mechanism based on the attribute significance value to calculate the similarities among unmapped users u_a and u_r during the process of de-anonymization; finally, we implement the above-mentioned attribute-based similarity measurement in the de-anonymization method to reduce the negative impact of graph perturbation.

4   The Design of Our Algorithm

4.1   Significance Values of Attributes

Intuitively, a widely-distributed attribute with diverse values in a social graph has great importance. This observation motivates the definition of attribute significance values. We first define $\sigma'_{a_k} = J_{a_k} / J^u_{a_k}$, which approximates the distribution information of attribute a_k in the graph of a social network. As shown in (2), J_{a_k} is defined as the ratio of edges between two nodes sharing the same attribute value of a_k to the total number of edges plus that of the nodes possessing the attribute a_k to the total number of nodes in the social graph. In this case, a large J_{a_k} implies that a_k is widely-distributed in the social graph, and accordingly, a large number of users possess this attribute. $J^u_{a_k}$ shown in (3) approximates the fraction of edges and nodes for attribute a_k when the attribute values are placed randomly. A small $J^u_{a_k}$ means that attribute a_k has more diverse attribute values.

$$J_{a_k} = \frac{|\{e = (u_i, u_j) \in E : (u_i \in S_{a_k}) \wedge (u_j \in S_{a_k}) \wedge (v_{ia_k} = v_{ja_k})\}|}{|E|} + \frac{|S_{a_k}|}{|V|}. \tag{2}$$

$$J_{a_k}^u = \frac{\sum_{j=1}^{k_n} |S_{a_k}^j|^2}{(\sum_{j=1}^{k_n} |S_{a_k}^j|)^2}. \tag{3}$$

With the calculated distribution information σ'_{a_k}, we define the *significance value* σ_{a_k} of an attribute a_k as follows,

$$\sigma_{a_k} = \begin{cases} \sigma'_{a_k}, & \text{if } \sigma'_{a_k} \geq 1, \\ 1, & \text{if } \sigma'_{a_k} < 1. \end{cases} \tag{4}$$

Therefore, σ_{a_k} quantifies how important a_k is in G compared with the scenario where the values of a_k are randomly placed. Note that σ_{a_k} is in the range of $[1, |V|]$, and a larger value indicates that a_k plays a more significant role. For example, let a_k refer to the address attribute, and then if coarse-grained address values of the users are given, such as states or countries, then σ_{a_k} should be close to 1, while when fine-grained addresses are provided, e.g., the detailed postal address, σ_{a_k} should be close to $|V|$.

User	SSN	State
u1	1001	Virginia
u2	1002	Virginia
u3	1003	Maryland

Fig. 2. Example of calculating significance value of attributes.

Next, we present an example to illustrate how to calculate the *significance value* of an attribute in a social graph. As shown in Fig. 2, we assume that there is an undirected social graph with three vertices and three edges. Each user has two attributes: *SSN* (Social Security Number) and *State*, where *SSN* is unique for each user while *State* can be the place where a lot of users live in. Intuitively, *SSN* is more important than *State*. Based on the *significance value* defined above, we can calculate the corresponding value of each attribute as follows,

- For *SSN*: $S_{a_{SSN}} = \{u_1, u_2, u_3\}$; $S_{a_{SSN}}^{1001} = 1$; $S_{a_{SSN}}^{1002} = 1$; $S_{a_{SSN}}^{1003} = 1$. Since three users have different *SSN*, we have $J_{a_{SSN}} = 1$, $J_{a_{SSN}}^u = 1/3$, and $\sigma'_{a_{SSN}} = J_{a_{SSN}}/J_{a_{SSN}}^u = 3 > 1$. Thus, the *significance value* of *SSN* is $\sigma_{a_{SSN}} = 3$.
- For *State*: $S_{a_{State}} = \{u_1, u_2, u_3\}$; $S_{a_{State}}^{Virginia} = 2$; $S_{a_{State}}^{Maryland} = 1$. Since u1 and u2 both live in "Virginia", we can calculate $J_{a_{State}} = 4/3$, $J_{a_{State}}^u = 5/9$, and $\sigma'_{a_{State}} = J_{a_{State}}/J_{a_{State}}^u = 2.4 > 1$. Finally, the *significance value* of *State* is $\sigma_{a_{State}} = 2.4$.

The above calculation results indicate that the attribute *SSN* has a larger significance value than *State* in this example, and SSN is more crucial for identifying users. Next, we leverage the significance values of the attributes in a social graph to design an attribute-based similarity measurement, which will be further exploited to improve the performance of social graph de-anonymization.

4.2 Attribute-Based Similarity Measurement

In this section, we employ the significance values of attributes proposed in the above subsection to measure the similarity value between two vertices. The basic idea of is straightforward: for any pair of users, the more number of same attribute values they have, the more similar they are; moreover, the higher the significance values of the attributes between two users, the higher the similarity.

More specifically, given $G_a(V_a, E_a, A_a)$ and $G_r(V_r, E_r, A_r)$ as the anonymized graph and the reference one with true user identities, respectively, we can compute the *significance value* σ_{a_k} for each attribute a_k based on the information provided by G_r. For a vertex u_a in V_a and a vertex u_r in V_r, let $\{a'_1, a'_2, ..., a'_n\}$ be the set of their common attributes; then their attribute-based similarity value $d_{(u_a, u_r)}$ can be calculated as follows: we initially set $d_{(u_a, u_r)} = 1$; then for each common attribute a'_k, if two vertices have the same attribute value (i.e., $v_{ia'_k} = v_{ja'_k}$), we define $d_{(u_a, u_r)} = d_{(u_a, u_r)} \times \sigma_{a'_k}$; otherwise, we set $d_{(u_a, u_r)} = d_{(u_a, u_r)} \times \frac{1}{\sigma_{a'_k}}$. Note that the term $\frac{1}{\sigma_{a'_k}}$ indicates that two nodes that have the same attribute but the corresponding attribute values are different have small similarity values.

4.3 Design of De-anonymization Algorithm

Based on the concepts presented in the previous subsections, we propose a de-anonymization algorithm for a social graph where each vertex has several attributes. Our algorithm takes advantage of the existing structure-based algorithms with two phases: *seed identification* and *propagation*.

Seed Identification. In this phase, we identify a few "seed" pairs of users (u_a, u_r) between G_a and G_r. To achieve this goal, several seeding methods such as k-clique, matching top nodes, and random selection discussed in [6], can be employed. The next propagation phase starts from these "seed" pairs, and newly mapped user pairs will become new "seeds".

Propagation. In this phase, starting from the identified "seeds", the de-anonymization algorithm iteratively maps each unmapped vertex u_a in G_a to an unmapped vertex u_r in G_r. We use $S = \{(u, u')|u \in V_a, u' \in V_r\}$ to denote the already mapped "seed" pairs, and calculate significance values $\{\sigma_{a_k}\}$ for all attributes in A_r of the reference graph $G_r(V_r, E_r, A_r)$. At each iteration, we pick an arbitrary unmapped user u_a who has a successfully mapped neighbor from anonymized social graph $G_a(V_a, E_a, A_a)$, and calculate its similarity values with all unmapped nodes in V_r who possess at least one successfully mapped neighbor. This process is detailed in Algorihtm 1 whose inputs include G_a, G_r, significance values $\{\sigma_{a_k}\}$, u_a, and "seed" pairs S. We first initialize V_{map} to be the collection of seed vertices in V_r and D to be the empty set. Then we pick up a u_r who is not in V_r but has a seed neighbor in V_r (Lines 3 and 4), and calculate the attribute-based similarity value between u_a and u_r (Lines 6–13) based on the similarity parameter $d_{(u_a,u_r)}$ defined in Sect. 4.2. Finally we select the u_r (i.e., the u'_r in Algorithm 1) based on the eccentricity measure defined in (1) as the mapping of u_a. This newly mapped vertex pair (u_a, u'_r) is inserted into S as a new seed pair for the next round of iteration (the next execution of Algorithm 1).

Algorithm 1. Attribute-based Similarity Calculation

> **Input** : Two social graphs: $G_a(V_a, E_a, A_a)$ and $G_r(V_r, E_r, A_r)$
> Unmapped users: $u_a \in V_a$
> Significance values of attributes: σ_{a_k}
> Seed pairs: $S = \{(u, u')|u \in V_a \text{ and } u' \in V_r\}$
> **Output:** the newly mapped pair (u_a, u'_r) with $u'_r \in V_r$

1   Set $V_{map} = \{u'|u' \in V_r \text{ and } \exists(u, u') \in S\}$
2   set $D = \emptyset$
3   **for** *each* $u' \in V_{map}$ *and* $(u', u_r) \in E_r$ **do**
4   **if** $u_r \notin V_{map}$ **then**
5   Set attribute-based similarity value: $d_{(u_a,u_r)} = 1$
6   **for** *each common attribute* $a'_k \in A_{u_a} \cap A_{u_r}$ **do**
7   // $v_{a'_k}(\cdot)$: attribute value of a'_k
8   **if** $v_{a'_k}(u_a) = v_{a'_k}(u_r)$ **then**
9          $d_{(u_a,u_r)} = d_{(u_a,u_r)} \times \sigma_{a'_k}$
10   **else**
11          $d_{(u_a,u_r)} = d_{(u_a,u_r)} \times \frac{1}{\sigma_{a'_k}}$
12   **end**
13   **end**
14       $D = D \cup d_{(u_a,u_r)}$
15   **end**
16   **end**
17   Calculate $ecc(D)$ based on (1) and select the node u'_r with the highest $d_{(u_a,u'_r)}$ if $ecc(D)$ is above a threshold
18   Set $S = S \cup (u_a, u'_r)$
19   return (u_a, u'_r)

---

5   Experiments

In this section, we use a dataset collected from Sina Weibo, a popular social media in China, to evaluate the performance of the proposed algorithm. The Weibo social network is based on "following" relationships among users. Our dataset includes 5663 nodes and 10000 edges. We convert this dataset into an undirected graph/network with an average degree of 3.5317. Each vertex (user) in the network has three attributes: province, city, and gender. We duplicate the network to get an anonymized version and apply Random Add/Del or Random Switch, which are edge randomization methods proposed in [20], to add noise. For comparison, we also implement the most influential de-anonymization method proposed in [14] to obtain experimental results that can serve as the baseline. In the seed identification phase, we randomly select nodes from 3-cliques in the reference graph and employ the corresponding nodes in the anonymized network as the matching seeds. In other words, there is no error in seed mapping. This consideration makes us focus on the performance of the propagation phase of the de-anonymization algorithm.

The performance metric is the de-anonymization accuracy, which is the ratio of the number of nodes correctly de-anonymized over the total number of nodes in the whole network. The reported results in the following subsections are the average of 50 trials.

5.1   Impact of the Number of Seeds

At first, we evaluate the impact of the number of seeds on de-anonymization accuracy. In this experiment, no noise is added, the eccentricity threshold is set to 0.1, and the number of seeds varies from 10 to 90. As shown in Fig. 3, when the number of seeds is increased from 10 to 90, the percentage of vertices correctly de-anonymized is increased, and our algorithm can correctly de-anonymize more vertices than the baseline algorithm. More particularly, when the number of seeds is 10, the results of baseline algorithm and our algorithm are respectively 0.0219 and 0.5890; when the number of seeds is increased to 90, the results are increased to 0.1636 and 0.7864, respectively.

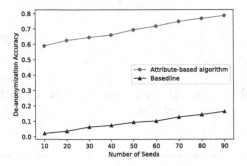

Fig. 3. Impact of the number of seeds on the de-annoynimization accuracy.

5.2   Impact of Noise

Next, we add noises into the anonymized network with two edge randomization methods. The first one is Random Add/Del, which randomly removes certain number of edges from a network and then randomly adds the same amount of edges back into the network. The second one is called Random Switch, which removes two randomly chosen edges $e_{m,n}$ and $e_{a,b}$ from a network and creates two new edges $e_{m,a}$ and $e_{n,b}$ back into the network. The *noise ratio* is defined to be the ratio of the number of newly added and deleted edges over the total number of edges in the network. In this evaluation, the noise ratio is increased from 0 to 0.3 at an interval of 0.05, the number of seeds is fixed to 90, and the eccentricity threshold is set to 0.1.

Figure 4 presents the accuracy of de-anonymization in the network processed by Random Add/Del. Since adding or removing edges changes the degrees of the vertices in the anonymized network, both de-anonymization algorithms are negatively affected, compared to the case when no noise is added. Nevertheless, our algorithm has better performance than the baseline. More specifically, when the noise ratio increases from 0 to 0.3, the result of our algorithm decreases from 0.7864 to 0.5285; while that of the baseline algorithm decreases from 0.1636 to 0.0340.

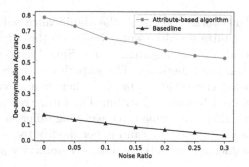

Fig. 4. Impact of noise on the de-annoynimization accuracy in the Random Add/Del annonymized graph.

Figure 5 demonstrates the result of de-anonymization in the network processed by Random Switch. From the result we can see that Random Switch has a little impact on the baseline algorithm but noticeably impacts on our algorithm. This is because the similarity calculation of the baseline algorithm is based on the local structure similarity between two nodes, while that of our algorithm is based on the attribute similarity between two vertices. Random Switch does not change the degree of vertices, but it disturbs the structure of the network, and more severely affects the attribute similarity between two vertices. As shown in Fig. 5, when the noise ratio is increased from 0 to 0.3, the result of our algorithm drops from 0.7864 to 0.3880, while that of the baseline algorithm drops from 0.1636 to 0.1399. Despite this, our algorithm is still more efficient than the baseline one.

6   Conclusion and Future Work

In this paper, we investigate the impact of attributes on social network de-anonymization and propose a method to quantify the significance values of the

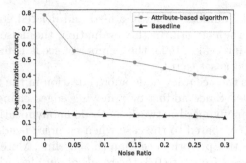

Fig. 5. Impact of noise on the de-annoynimization accuracy in the Random Switch annonymized graph.

attributes in social networks. Based on the significance values, we design an algorithm to de-anonymize social networks based on the attribute similarity of users. Finally, we evaluate our algorithm on a Sina Weibo dataset processed by two edge randomization methods. The experimental results indicate that the proposed algorithm can achieve a much higher de-anonymization accuracy compared to the selected baseline algorithm. For future research, we can refine the definition of the significance value by considering different value scopes, such as a continuous space. Moreover, we can further modify the similarity definition of two nodes by considering both attribute-based similarity and local structure similarity.

Acknowledgment. This work was partially supported by the US National Science Foundation under grants CNS-1704397, CNS-1704287, and CNS-1704274, and the National Science Foundation of China under grants 61832012, 61771289, and 61672321.

References

1. Backstrom, L., Dwork, C., Kleinberg, J.: Wherefore art thou R3579x?: anonymized social networks, hidden patterns, and structural steganography. In: Proceedings of the 16th International Conference on World Wide Web, pp. 181–190. ACM (2007)
2. Cai, Z., He, Z., Guan, X., Li, Y.: Collective data-sanitization for preventing sensitive information inference attacks in social networks. IEEE Trans. Dependable Secure Comput. **15**(4), 577–590 (2018)
3. Chen, S., Zhou, S.: Recursive mechanism: towards node differential privacy and unrestricted joins. In: Proceedings of the 2013 ACM SIGMOD International Conference on Management of Data, pp. 653–664. ACM (2013)
4. Cheng, J., Fu, A.W.C., Liu, J.: K-isomorphism: privacy preserving network publication against structural attacks. In: Proceedings of the 2010 ACM SIGMOD International Conference on Management of Data, pp. 459–470. ACM (2010)
5. Day, W.Y., Li, N., Lyu, M.: Publishing graph degree distribution with node differential privacy. In: Proceedings of the 2016 International Conference on Management of Data, pp. 123–138. ACM (2016)

6. Gulyás, G.G., Imre, S.: Measuring importance of seeding for structural de-anonymization attacks in social networks. In: 2014 IEEE International Conference on Pervasive Computing and Communication Workshops (PERCOM WORKSHOPS), pp. 610–615. IEEE (2014)
7. Hay, M., Miklau, G., Jensen, D., Towsley, D., Weis, P.: Resisting structural re-identification in anonymized social networks. Proc. VLDB Endow. 1(1), 102–114 (2008)
8. He, Z., Cai, Z., Yu, J.: Latent-data privacy preserving with customized data utility for social network data. IEEE Trans. Veh. Technol. 67(1), 665–673 (2018)
9. Li, C., Hay, M., Miklau, G., Wang, Y.: A data-and workload-aware algorithm for range queries under differential privacy. Proc. VLDB Endow. 7(5), 341–352 (2014)
10. Li, H., Zhang, C., He, Y., Cheng, X., Liu, Y., Sun, L.: An enhanced structure-based de-anonymization of online social networks. In: Yang, Q., Yu, W., Challal, Y. (eds.) WASA 2016. LNCS, vol. 9798, pp. 331–342. Springer, Cham (2016). https://doi.org/10.1007/978-3-319-42836-9_30
11. Liu, K., Terzi, E.: Towards identity anonymization on graphs. In: Proceedings of the 2008 ACM SIGMOD International Conference on Management of Data, pp. 93–106. ACM (2008)
12. Liu, Y., Ji, S., Mittal, P.: SmartWalk: enhancing social network security via adaptive random walks. In: Proceedings of the 2016 ACM SIGSAC Conference on Computer and Communications Security, pp. 492–503. ACM (2016)
13. Narayanan, A., Shmatikov, V.: Robust de-anonymization of large sparse datasets. In: 2008 IEEE Symposium on Security and Privacy, pp. 111–125. IEEE (2008)
14. Narayanan, A., Shmatikov, V.: De-anonymizing social networks. arXiv preprint arXiv:0903.3276 (2009)
15. Nilizadeh, S., Kapadia, A., Ahn, Y.Y.: Community-enhanced de-anonymization of online social networks. In: Proceedings of the 2014 ACM SIGSAC Conference on Computer and Communications Security, pp. 537–548. ACM (2014)
16. Qian, J., Li, X.Y., Zhang, C., Chen, L., Jung, T., Han, J.: Social network de-anonymization and privacy inference with knowledge graph model. IEEE Trans. Dependable Secure Comput. (2017)
17. Thompson, B., Yao, D.: The union-split algorithm and cluster-based anonymization of social networks. In: Proceedings of the 4th International Symposium on Information, Computer, and Communications Security, pp. 218–227. ACM (2009)
18. Tian, W., Mao, J., Jiang, J., He, Z., Zhou, Z., Liu, J.: Deeply understanding structure-based social network de-anonymization. Procedia Comput. Sci. 129, 52–58 (2018)
19. Wang, Q., Zhang, Y., Lu, X., Wang, Z., Qin, Z., Ren, K.: Real-time and spatio-temporal crowd-sourced social network data publishing with differential privacy. IEEE Trans. Dependable Secure Comput. 15(4), 591–606 (2018)
20. Ying, X., Wu, X.: Randomizing social networks: a spectrum preserving approach. In: Proceedings of the 2008 SIAM International Conference on Data Mining, pp. 739–750. SIAM (2008)
21. Zhou, B., Pei, J.: Preserving privacy in social networks against neighborhood attacks (2008)
22. Zou, L., Chen, L., Özsu, M.T.: K-automorphism: a general framework for privacy preserving network publication. Proc. VLDB Endow. 2(1), 946–957 (2009)

Detecting Anomalies in Communication Packet Streams Based on Generative Adversarial Networks

Di Zhang[1]([✉]), Qiang Niu[2], and Xingbao Qiu[3]

[1] School of Computer Science, Communication University of China,
Beijing 100024, People's Republic of China
di.zhang@cuc.edu.cn
[2] Department of Mathematical Sciences, Xi'an Jiaotong-Liverpool University,
Suzhou 215123, People's Republic of China
qiang.niu@xjtlu.edu.cn
[3] China Mobile Communications Corporation,
Beijing 100032, People's Republic of China
qiuxingbao@sn.chinamobile.com

Abstract. The fault diagnosis in a modern communication system is traditionally supposed to be difficult, or even impractical for a purely data-driven machine learning approach, for it is a humanmade system of intensive knowledge. A few labeled raw packet streams extracted from fault archive can hardly be sufficient to deduce the intricate logic of underlying protocols. In this paper, we supplement these limited samples with two inexhaustible data sources: the unlabeled records probed from a system in service, and the labeled data simulated in an emulation environment. To transfer their inherent knowledge to the target domain, we construct a directed information flow graph, whose nodes are neural network components consisting of two generators, three discriminators and one classifier, and whose every forward path represents a pair of adversarial optimization goals, in accord with the semi-supervised and transfer learning demands. The multi-headed network can be trained in an alternative approach, at each iteration of which we select one target to update the weights along the path upstream, and refresh the residual layer-wisely to all outputs downstream. The actual results show that it can achieve comparable accuracy on classifying Transmission Control Protocol (TCP) streams without deliberate expert features. The solution has relieved operation engineers from massive works of understanding and maintaining rules, and provided a quick solution independent of specific protocols.

The work is supported by Jiangsu Science and Technology Basic Research Programme (BK20171237, BK20150373), Key Program Special Fund in XJTLU (KSF-E-21, KSF-A-01), Research Enhance Fund of XJTLU (REF-18-01-04).

E. S. Biagioni et al. (Eds.): WASA 2019, LNCS 11604, pp. 470–481, 2019.
https://doi.org/10.1007/978-3-030-23597-0_38

1   Introduction

A telecommunications network is a collection of distributed devices, entirely designed and manufactured by humans for a variety of transmission, control and management tasks, striving to provide a transparent channel between external terminals, via an actual internal relay process node by node. As a typical conversation in the style of client and server, the two linked nodes send their messages in the form of packets, encapsulated the load with miscellaneous attributes in headers to ensure the correctness, consistency, and smoothness of the entire process. A typical header includes packet sequence number, source and destination addresses, control bits, error detection codes, etc.

The large-scale network cannot always work ideally, due to its inherent complexity inside massive devices and their interactions. When there is a malfunction of a device, either caused by the traffic overload, or software bugs, or hardware misconfiguration, or malicious attacks, it will be reflected on the packet streams that pass through, such as packet loss, timeout, out of order, etc. System administrators captured those suspicious streams and sent back to the service center for cautious offline analysis, which is time-consuming and domain-specific.

The primary challenge of automatic diagnosis is that, it is almost impossible to formalize all the logic inside the system and make them available to artificial intelligence. A typical modern communication system consists of tens of thousands devices end-to-end and runs based on a list of hundreds of protocols layer-by-layer (Fall and Stevens 2011). If we could figure out the latent states of protocols by constructing specific features from raw bytes, the subsequent classification tasks would be quite straightforward and easy to implement. For instance, the Transmission Control Protocol (TCP) relies on sequence numbers to judge the receiving order of packets, which may be just big integers roughly linearly growing from the view of machine learning models. Another example is a few critical control bits may reside among much more useless bits, such as checksum codes, which is harmful noises for models. Even if we have the patience to dive into all the industrial protocols and build up an exhausted feature library; eventually, we will fail again to achieve the target of automation, one of the main advantages of the modern data-driven approach.

Another difficulty is scarcity of labeled samples. In spite of the fact there are seemingly numerous packet flows running through the Internet all the time, the real valid faults occur at random and occupy only a tiny portion of whole traffic volume. The actual labeled data are usually collected from the archive of fault cases, which is hard to have enough samples for all possible categories, or cannot at least cover them completely.

The previous works on this issue mainly follow two technical routes: (1) a traditional two-phase framework, using expert features and some general-propose classifiers (Bhuyan et al. 2014); (2) an end-to-end approach based on deep learning for automatic feature extraction (Javaid et al. 2016). All these prior arts seldom use generative models, which is usually more promising for expressing structural relationship among random variables. They may fuse 1–2 data sources in semi-supervised setting (Javaid et al. 2016), but not scale to even more data sources.

In this paper, we resort to a generative model to mimic the messages in a terminal's conversation and enrich the target data domain from two abundant but different information sources: labeled but from simulation, and genuine but unlabeled. The transfer and semi-supervised demands are integrated into an intuitive framework, composed of a connected graph of multiple simple Generative Adversarial Networks (GANs)' components, trained in an alternative optimization approach. The contribution of this paper includes: (1) combine three kinds of data sources in a generative approach, to solve the small-sample problem with a simulation environment; (2) extend the two players in usual GANs to a system of multiple ones, still keeping its merit of end-to-end training; (3) verify its effect on our practice problem of packet sequence classification.

The left of paper is organized as below: first, we introduce the previous work selectively in network anomaly detection and the research frontier in the generative neural network. Next, we present the model and algorithm in detail with feature design at different levels. The results of experiments are followed in Sect. 4. Finally, we conclude the whole article.

2   Related Work

The anomaly detection in communication packets has been long-term studied, either for the Quality of Service (QoS) management or instruction detection. Bhuyan et al. (2014) summarized the past works based on their applied technologies, which almost cover all popular machine learning methods before 2012. The works after that are surveyed by ourselves. Dondo and Treurniet (2004) started to train neural networks (NN) on labeled data to build models for more categories of anomalies than hard-coded rules, with an expert feature library and three-layer perceptron classifiers. Later, Amini et al. 2006 verified the feasibility of Self Organizing Map (SOM) in an unsupervised scenario, where the unexpected packets were automatically saved for analyzers. Lee and Heinbuch (2001) used the self-taught learning to enrich the dataset from unlabeled live stream, and build up a comprehensive feature space for embedding. The enhancement can be observed even using a simple K-Nearest-Neighbors. Yin et al. (2017) used Recurrent Neural Network (RNN) on classifying 5 categories of packet flows, and achieved obviously better results than models ignoring the temporal orders. Tang et al. (2016) designed an NN with 6-dimensional manual feature vectors and 3 hidden layers for inherent mapping as input and claimed accuracy improvements after testing. Javaid et al. (2016) also used self-taught learning, similar to Lee and Heinbuch (2001), but with more sophisticated models. It extracted features automatically from unlabeled data by a sparse auto-encoder, and classify them by a single hidden layer perceptron. To our best knowledge, it is the first time we employ generative neural networks for the semi-supervised and transfer learning simultaneously on this problem.

The classical GANs are composed of two neural components contesting with each other in a zero-sum game (Goodfellow et al. 2014). It can be extended to more components for the following purposes (but not limited to): (1) reflecting the relationship between multiple random variables. Odena et al. (2016) employed a conditional GAN to generate multi-class images. Li et al. (2017) solved the multi-class classification by adding an extra classifier to denote the conditional probability $p(y|X)$. The newly classifier can shift the burden of predicting labels from identifying fake samples, which is blended in the previous Salimans et al. (2016). This triple-player formulation makes the model even clearer and brings more stableness during training. In multi-view learning, Chen and Denoyer (2016) defined one discriminator for each view and enabled the distribution estimation over all possible output y if any subset of view on a particular input X is fixed. (2) Enhancing the training process. Hoang et al. (2017) addressed the mode collapse problem in GANs by training many generators, which envisions to discriminate itself to an additional classifier and fool the original discriminator meanwhile. It improved the steadiness of training significantly. Instead, Durugkar et al. (2016) used multiple discriminators to ensemble a more powerful one; on the other hand, the training process is retarded by a predefined function (similar to soft-max) on the top of them to match the generator's capability better. In this paper, we only focus the former purpose.

3   Solution

3.1   Problem Definition and Levels of Features

The packet stream in reality is a sequence of attributed events $\{(t_i, \{a_{i,j}\})|i \in N, j \in N\}$, where t_i is the timestamp sealed by the receiver, and $a_{i,j}$ is a tuple of key-value parsed from packet headers. The label c of event sequences can be K classes of anomalies containing 1 special class for normality. To focus the main aspect of our problem, we prefer to simplify it by two assumptions: (1) anomalies can only happen at one side of the communication, such as server side, to prevent the number of possible situations from blowing up to K^2. It seldom happens that, both terminals have problems simultaneously and produce a complicated interaction that can fully not be diagnosed by a one-sided model. In fact, we can train two individual models for both sides, and thus the records from client side can be removed from the train set in experiments. (2) The continuous valued (or fine-grained in 10^{-6} s) timestamps are ignored, while only their ascending index is kept, from 1 to T. We insert dummy packets, which replicate sequence id from the previous one and fill all other fields with 0, to denote an occurrence of timeout between two consecutive items. The overall number of dummy packets is informative to models since it indicates how many periods the opposite side has not responded. It is justified because most protocols are indifferent to the exact time intervals during sending/receiving unless they exceed the predefined timeout threshold.

The available content of attributes depends on how much effort we want to pay for an accurate inspection of packet headers. The clearer we want to know about the states of every system running, the much we should know about the details of a given protocol. There are 3 levels of feature engineering: (1) raw bytes of headers, which needs little effort; (2) the numerical values (sequence index, integer or Boolean) parsed by a data scheme indicating their positions and necessity; (3) the latent states defined in protocols, based on complete domain knowledge and Finite-State Machine (FSM) -driven analysis. For instance, a packet at level 1 may be only a binary sequence, like $1001 \ldots 1000$, which is unreadable for humans. At level 2 (Fig. 1a), it turns to be a data structure with proper data types, but without semantics defined by the protocol draft. The array of structures can further be arranged into a multi-dimensional vector. At level 3 (Fig. 1b), the inherent states are explicitly parsed out, and the sequence finally achieves its most compact representation – a categorical vector. NN can digest all levels above, though an extra effort is needed for discrete values at level 3, discussed later in Sect. 3.2.

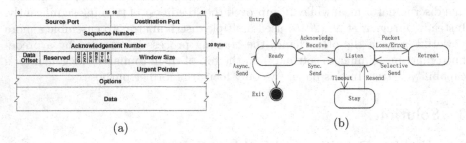

(a)   (b)

Fig. 1. (a) The format of TCP header. Every attribute occupies a segment at a fixed position. (b) A simplified version of FSM for a sender during TCP's transmission phase. In the typical situation, the sender shuttles between the Ready and Listen state. When there is some error occurred in the direction that data goes, the system will retreat to a previous position and resend the datum; when the acknowledge packet loses in the coming direction, a timeout will be triggered, and the system will resend the last piece of data. In practice, these states are implicitly encoded in the headers, and the computer program has to analyze them based on TCP protocol.

3.2   NN Design

Optimization Goal. Assume that the N-dimensional sequence $\mathbf{Y} = \{\mathbf{y}_t : t \in T\}$ is generated from repetitive application of a function $\mathbf{G}$ on a latent M-dimensional vector $\mathbf{z}$:

$$\mathbf{y}_t = \mathbf{G}^{(t)}(\mathbf{z}, c; \boldsymbol{\theta}), \tag{1}$$

where c is a categorical variable to switch between the types of anomalies, and $\boldsymbol{\theta}$ is the parameters of $\mathbf{G}$. We assume that, if $\mathbf{z} \sim \mathcal{N}(0, \sigma^2)$ and $c \sim \mathcal{C}at(\boldsymbol{\pi})$, the resulted $\mathbf{Y}$ will conform to a distribution where our observations $\hat{\mathbf{Y}}$ come from. In the adversary approach, we guide the training of $\mathbf{G}$ by minimizing the distance (cross entropy) between the $p(\mathbf{Y}, c)$ and observed $\hat{p}(\mathbf{Y}, c)$, via the transformation of an extra binary discriminator D_r:

$$\boldsymbol{\theta}^{(\mathbf{G})*} = \underset{\boldsymbol{\theta}^{(\mathbf{G})}}{\operatorname{argmin}} \max_{\boldsymbol{\theta}^{(D_r)}} L_r \tag{2}$$

$$L_r = H(p(D_r(\mathbf{G}(\mathbf{z})), c), \hat{p}(D_r(\mathbf{Y}), c)), \tag{3}$$

where H is the cross entropy between two distributions. Similarly, we define a function $\mathbf{G_s}$ that transforms $\mathbf{Y}$ to its correspondence $\mathbf{Y_s}$ in the simulation world, and a function D_s to discriminate them from real simulation data:

$$\boldsymbol{\theta}^{(\mathbf{G},\mathbf{G_s})*} = \operatorname*{argmin}_{\theta^{(\mathbf{G},\mathbf{G_s})}} \max_{\theta^{(D_s)}} L_s \tag{4}$$

$$L_s = H(p(D_s(\mathbf{G_s}(\mathbf{G}(\mathbf{z}))), c), \hat{p}(D_s(\mathbf{Y_s}), c)). \tag{5}$$

For the unlabeled data, we define a D_c to distinguish them from the generated samples without labels c:

$$\boldsymbol{\theta}^{(\mathbf{G})*} = \operatorname*{argmin}_{\theta^{(\mathbf{G})}} \max_{\theta^{(D_u)}} L_u \tag{6}$$

$$L_u = H(p(D_u(\mathbf{G}(\mathbf{z})), \cdot), \hat{p}(D_u(\mathbf{Y}), \cdot)). \tag{7}$$

The overall optimization goal is a convex combination of Eqs. 3, 5 and 7:

$$L = L_r + \lambda_s L_s + \lambda_c L_c, \tag{8}$$

where λ_s, λ_c is the coefficients to adjust the importance of targets. Once we obtain the $p(\mathbf{Y}, c)$ in the implicit form of $\mathbf{G}$, the classifier output probability $p(c|\mathbf{Y})$ can be derived with the marginal distribution $p(c)$ according to the Bayes rule.

Layout of GANs. The neural components and their connections are shown in Fig. 2. There are 3 information sinks in Fig. 2(a), each of which connects to exact 2 data sources and corresponds to one part of loss function in Eq. 8; minimizing them concurrently, is equivalent to make the data come from different paths look the same with the best effort. Note that the graph $\mathcal{G}$ is connected, directed and acyclic, which makes any topological order (must exist based on graph theory) of nodes viable to a gradient descent approach. It provides a convenience for the design of optimization heuristic in Sect. 3.2. The trained G will be frozen in a secondary training process in Fig. 2(b), to consistently offer the classifier C its pseudo-samples with labels until convergence.

The neural blocks in Fig. 2 can be built from even more fine-grained modules: ① an input layer concatenating a vector of $\mathbf{z}$ (or $\mathbf{y}$) and an optional one-hot vector for c; ② a Long Short-Term Memory (LSTM) layer mapping a sequence to a vector; ③ a LSTM layer reversely mapping a vector to a sequence; ④ a fully connected layer; ⑤ a sigmoid (or softmax) layer classifying real/fake samples (or outputting labels). The generator G is built by ①+③, and G_s is ②+③, and C is ②+⑤; all D, D_s, D_u share a same structure, which is ②+①+⑤. The modules ②, ③ and ④ are kept as one single hidden layer here, after the multi-layer structures have been tried in practice and their improvement was found to be negligible. For the discrete state sequence at feature level 3, it is feasible to map its discrete values into continuous vector globally by Word2vec during preprocessing, since the C is what we finally interested for diagnosis and the intermediate results are not visible to end users indeed.

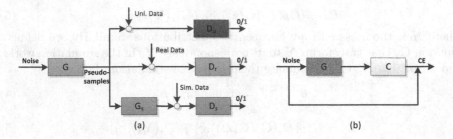

Fig. 2. The layout of building blocks in our solution. The arrows denote for the information flow among blocks, and they are connected as three forward paths in (a), representing real, simulated and unlabeled information sources colored as orange, green, and blue. The noises driven the whole process is assumed to be sampled from two independent sources, $\mathbf{z} \sim \mathcal{N}(0, \sigma^2)$ and $c \sim \mathcal{C}\text{at}(\boldsymbol{\pi})$. The $\boldsymbol{\pi}$ are estimated directly based on real labeled data. In (b), the white block C is trained with a fixed $\mathbf{G}$, colored with shading. (Color figure online)

Algorithm. We need a heuristics to guide the whole optimization process of G, depicted in Algorithm 1. During every mini-batch iteration of training, every time we select a forward path whose loss function contributes most in the Eq. 8, weighted by λs, and update the $\boldsymbol{\theta}$ of blocks on the way in the form of gradient descent. The all three sub-loss functions will be updated after G has been modified. Once the process has found a selected target that does not contribute to the overall goal, the update will be rolled back, and the algorithm will switch to others. The failure record for any target will not bring into next batch. For individual blocks, RMSprop is preferred for components containing a recurrent layer, including G, G_s and C, while all discriminators use Adam instead.

4   Experiments

4.1   Data

The real labeled data are collected from the archive of fault cases, probed at the core section of a wireless telecom site in service. It locates in a western province of China and serves more than 250 million users with nearly 80k base stations. The problematic TCP streams have four categories: (1) uplink packet loss at random, (2) downlink packet loss at random, (3) packet loss periodically when load exceeds capacity, (4) checksum error at random, (5) healthy but falsely alarmed. The faults in the connection establishment and release phase are not considered here. In the historical records, all we have are 58 samples, unevenly distributed from category 1–5, which are 16, 22, 10, 3, and 7.

The unlabeled data are captured from the same site, having 2000 real samples sufficient for training propose. Though its size is much larger than the labeled ones, it can hardly contain valid anomalies by an arbitrary, short-term collection. It provides a reference for the average condition of service quality for a

```
   Input: forward path set {P} of G
 1  initialize a masking vector m = (0, 0, 0);
 2  while #n ≤ #batch do
 3  │   // select one path
 4  │   {P} ← filter {P} by m;
 5  │   {P} ← sort {P} by λL descendingly;
 6  │   // back propagation
 7  │   for v ∈ {P₀} do
 8  │   │   θ⁽ᵛ⁾ ← θ⁽ᵛ⁾ − η∇L(θ⁽ᵛ⁾);
 9  │   end
10  │   // forward update
11  │   for Pᵢ ∈ {P} do
12  │   │   for v ∈ Pᵢ do
13  │   │   │   update L(θᵛ);
14  │   │   end
15  │   end
16  │   // check process
17  │   update L, ΔL;
18  │   if ΔL > threshold then
19  │   │   m = 0;
20  │   │   roll back {θ⁽ᵛ⁾|v ∈ G};
21  │   else
22  │   │   m_{P₀} = 1
23  │   end
24  end
```

Algorithm 1. The main procedure of optimization of G guided by heuristic.

specific site. The simulation is conducted from a mirror environment in labs, with a similar or maybe simplified configuration. The 5 types of anomalies are generated in equal ratio, and each of them has 2000 records. The phenomenon of occurring errors here is much more evident than reality: (1) for uplink and (2) downlink packets, the probability of loss is 50%, (3) the stream have 50% of time transmitting over the limit of throughput; (4) the probability of checksum error is 50%. The sequence lengths of all synthetic data are all fixed to 500.

The data preprocessing on the TCP header is based on different levels discussed in Sect. 3.1, where the latent states of TCP include normal, resend, and timeout, distilled from 7 useful attributes, and also from 24 bytes of raw binary records. A simple FSM is defined to compress the attributes to several states, according to TCP's standard logic. All sequences are split into the size of 500, and the ones shorter than that are padded by 0.

4.2 Setup

The performance of our multi-class problem is evaluated by the accuracy $Acc = N_{correct}/N$, which is the only metric cared by operation engineers. They rank all the possible causes descendingly based on the model's output and take the whole list as a recommendation, which acts as a shortcut leading them to the underlying causes much more quickly, especially compared to their existing manual-based approach. We measure two variations of accuracy: averaging on samples as above, and averaging on class, i.e., $\sum_{c=1}^{K} \frac{N}{N_c} Acc_c$, to emphasize the performance on minor-classes. 3-fold cross-validation is used for the set of real labeled data, with all other 2 datasets always assisting the train partition for every fold. The program is based on Keras[1] and a GAN library[2]. The one-to-many recurrent layer of Keras is implemented merely in the form of many-to-many, by repeating the input as a vector of equal length as output. The dimension of noise z is set to 20, and hidden dimension of LSTM is 10 with L2 regularization. The learning rates of all components are configured to 10^{-3}. All other parameters are kept by default.

4.3 Comparison Result

We have two kinds of factors to combine into a workable model: feature levels as described in Sect. 3.1 and data sources, shown in Table 1. The solution in Fig. 2(a) can be trimmed based on available data sources. In the group 1 of Table 1, we give two referential models for comparison, one (Line 1) is the dummy model which always give the most frequent class as prediction, and the other (Line 2) is the result if we only use the simulation data both for train and test with one standalone classifier. With the deliberately amplified anomalies and evenly distributed classes, the performance can be quite ideal, and to some extent be an empirical upper limit of diagnosis. It can be observed in group 4–5 that, the simulation data are crucial for substantial enhancement by adding more typical anomalies, while the unlabeled contributes slightly via only supplying normal samples. The improvements in weighted accuracy are more obvious, which is more than twice that of dummy model.

On the other hand, the features still act an essential role in our problem. The level 3 feature can always perform better than the rest two levels, while the level 1 can especially not produce any meaningful results. The level 2 can approximate the best performance with the help of massive data, offering an always worse but still acceptable accuracy, without the effort of understanding protocols.

---

[1] https://keras.io/.
[2] https://github.com/bstriner/keras-adversarial.

Table 1. The comparison of performance on 3×4 combinations of data and features. The meaningful improvements are colored as green, and referential models are colored as blue.

Group	Data			Feature			Accuracy	
	Lab.	Unl.	Sim.	1	2	3	average	weighted
1	X				\		0.388	0.200
			X			X	0.766	0.876
2	X			X			0.279	0.208
	X				X		0.300	0.182
	X					X	0.367	0.230
3	X	X		X			0.307	0.169
	X	X			X		0.386	0.235
	X	X				X	0.425	0.271
4	X		X	X			0.374	0.214
	X		X		X		0.538	0.381
	X		X			X	0.584	0.419
5	X	X	X	X			0.363	0.199
	X	X	X		X		**0.558**	**0.432**
	X	X	X			X	**0.599**	**0.490**

4.4 Training

The evolution of losses of 3 discriminators is demonstrated in Fig. 3(a), and the classifier is shown in Fig. 3(b). All loss curves of GANs' components converge to their roughly horizontal limits, with more or less mutually influenced fluctuations, caused by the continuous attempts to seek for a better equilibrium in every batch. However, these efforts seem to merely make the overall loss tremble, instead of moving to lower places. The variances of simulated data are obviously much smaller than real data, which may be ascribed to the sufficient size of data and evenly distribution among classes, whereas the real data are of imbalance, and have few samples to validate the improvements during training. We terminated the whole process at iteration 10^4, and use the trained G to gain a corresponding C, which is much easier to train as the loss goes steadily to its convergence level, shown in Fig. 3(b).

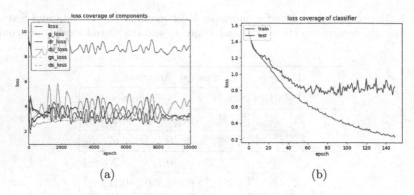

Fig. 3. the convergence of overall loss during the training of G (left) and C (right). The dashed lines denote the simulation data.

5   Conclusion

In this paper, the widely used semi-supervised and transfer learning requirements have been implemented in an integrated way, via a system of cooperative or adversarial neural blocks. Its effectiveness has been verified in our application of packet flow classification, and it is hopeful to be a widely adopted method in this specific domain. The work also prompts us that, complex machine learning tasks and their compound loss functions can be directly mapped into connected networks, and their optimization process can be designed over an entire graph, rather than each individual's hierarchical layers. In future work, we may study how to apply this approach to even larger scale tasks, and make a theoretical analysis of the existence of equilibrium and why we can always reach it.

References

Amini, M., Jalili, R., Shahriari, H.R.: RT-UNNID: a practical solution to real-time network-based intrusion detection using unsupervised neural networks. Comput. Secur. **25**(6), 459–468 (2006)

Bhuyan, M.H., Bhattacharyya, D.K., Kalita, J.K.: Network anomaly detection: methods, systems and tools. IEEE Commun. Surv. Tutor. **16**(1), 303–336 (2014)

Cannady, J.: Applying CMAC-based online learning to intrusion detection. In: Proceedings of the IEEE-INNS-ENNS International Joint Conference on Neural Networks, IJCNN 2000, vol. 5, pp. 405–410. IEEE (2000)

Chen, M., Denoyer, L.: Multi-view generative adversarial networks. arXiv preprint arXiv:1611.02019 (2016)

Dondo, M., Treurniet, J.: Investigation of a neural network implementation of a TCP packet anomaly detection system. Technical report, Defence Research and Development Canada Ottawa (Ontario) (2004)

Durugkar, I., Gemp, I., Mahadevan, S.: Generative multi-adversarial networks. arXiv preprint arXiv:1611.01673 (2016)

Fall, K.R., Stevens, W.R.: TCP/IP Illustrated: The Protocols, vol. 1. Addison-Wesley, Boston (2011)

Goodfellow, I., et al.: Generative adversarial nets. In: Advances in Neural Information Processing Systems, pp. 2672–2680 (2014)

Hoang, Q., Nguyen, T.D., Le, T., Phung, D.: Multi-generator generative adversarial nets. arXiv preprint arXiv:1708.02556 (2017)

Javaid, A., Niyaz, Q., Sun, W., Alam, M.: A deep learning approach for network intrusion detection system. In: Proceedings of the 9th EAI International Conference on Bio-inspired Information and Communications Technologies (formerly BIONETICS), pp. 21–26. ICST (Institute for Computer Sciences, Social-Informatics and Telecommunications Engineering) (2016)

Lee, S.C., Heinbuch, D.V.: Training a neural-network based intrusion detector to recognize novel attacks. IEEE Trans. Syst. Man Cybern. Part A: Syst. Hum. **31**(4), 294–299 (2001)

Li, C., Xu, K., Zhu, J., Zhang, B.: Triple generative adversarial nets. arXiv preprint arXiv:1703.02291 (2017)

Odena, A., Olah, C., Shlens, J.: Conditional image synthesis with auxiliary classifier GANs. arXiv preprint arXiv:1610.09585 (2016)

Salimans, T., Goodfellow, I., Zaremba, W., Cheung, V., Radford, A., Chen, X.: Improved techniques for training GANs. In: Advances in Neural Information Processing Systems, pp. 2234–2242 (2016)

Tang, T.A., Mhamdi, L., McLernon, D., Zaidi, S.A. R., Ghogho, M.: Deep learning approach for network intrusion detection in software defined networking. In: 2016 International Conference on Wireless Networks and Mobile Communications (WINCOM), pp. 258–263. IEEE (2016)

Yin, C., Zhu, Y., Fei, J., He, X.: A deep learning approach for intrusion detection using recurrent neural networks. IEEE Access **5**, 21954–21961 (2017)

Multi-hop Wireless Recharging Sensor Networks Optimization with Successive Interference Cancellation

Peng Zhang[1,2], Xu Ding[1,2], Jing Wang[1,2], and Juan Xu[1(✉)]

[1] School of Computer Science and Information Engineering,
HeFei University of Technology, Hefei, China
xujuan@hfut.edu.cn
[2] Institute of Industry and Equipment Technology,
HeFei University of Technology, Hefei, China

Abstract. Wireless sensor networks (WSNs) are constrained by limited battery energy and channel utilization. Thus, ephemeral network lifetime and low channel utilization are widely regarded as the performance bottlenecks. In this paper, we investigate the operation of multi-hop recharging sensor wireless networks (WRSNs) with successive interference cancellation (SIC) technique. In WRSNs, the power of the sensor nodes are not constants, but the receiving power of nodes need to be sorted. To solve the problem, we first establish a minimum energy routing, unify nodes transmission rate for determining the power of transmitting and time Schedule scheme. Then, we analyze an optimization problem with objective of maximizing the mobile charger's (MC) vacation time over the cycle time. Subsequently, we develop a near-optimal solution and verify its feasible performance. Simulation results show that SIC can achieve better throughput (about increasing 350%–550% compared with inference avoid) and no extra energy consumption in multi-hop WRSNs.

Keywords: Network lifetime · Successive interference cancellation · Multi-hop sensor wireless network · Interference Management

1 Introduction

With the rapid development of modern wireless communication technology and advanced sensor manufacturing technology, Wireless sensor networks (WSNs) have attracted more and more attention in theory and application research [1]. However, the battery energy of the sensor node is severely limited, it remains the bottleneck of a WSN that hinder sensor nodes wide hide deployment. Simultaneously, the communication interference will increase in WSNs and the channel utilization will decrease. And as the deployment scope of WSN expands, there

Supported by National Natural Science Foundation of China with grant number [61701162].

will be more and more interference in the network, and the throughput will be greatly reduced.

The breakthrough in the area of wireless charging technique (WCT) [2] has opened up a revolution for wireless sensor nodes lifetime. Their work shows a technique called *magnetic resonance*, furthermore, they have experimentally showed WCT is both feasible and practical.

In WSNs, a sensed curve derivation algorithm to support curve query processing in WSNs is proposed to achieve continuous sensed data [3]. In the multicast k-tree routing problem, Cai et al. [4] and [5] presented some approximation algorithms along the line, and then, the ratio achieved by the algorithm is less than 3.4713. The amount of sensory data manifests an explosive growth due to the increasing popularity of WSNs. E-Kernel Dataset [6] has been presented to solve the problem, which is a small data subset and can represent the vast information carried by big sensory data with the information loss rate being less than E. It is not difficult to find that the data sent by sensors is increasing.

In the terms of communication interference, fortunately, novel techniques called Interference Management (IM) [7] give us opportunities for solving this problem. IM is not a single technology, but a collective for many techniques, such as interference coordination [8] and interference alignment [9], etc. The core idea of IM is to enable the receiver to receive the desired information from multiple signals. For example, if a receiver uses successive interference cancellation (SIC) [10], then when it receives a set of data from several transmitting nodes, it will decode the strongest signal in turn according to the strength of the signal in the combined data. For instance, Jiang et al. [11] proposed a cross-layer optimization framework for multi-hop wireless network with SIC. and showed that the network throughput increased about 47%. Liu et al. [12] proposed a heuristic algorithm for routing in multi-hop wireless network, and presented a bandwidth-aware high-throughput protocol with SIC. In [13], the authors used SIC technique in a special wireless network, they showed an analytical framework for studying the performance of SIC in the Device-to-Device cellular network, and showed some general expressions for the transmission probabilities in SIC. In [14], the authors eliminated loop interference in multiple-input multiple-output(MIMO) relay system with SIC technique.

In this paper, we analyze the sensor node's work model with SIC in multi-hop single base station WRSNs. Unlike the other SIC schemes with fixed and identical transmit power, we formulate network model and constraints by the energy consumption pattern of each sensor node, and introduce a lemma for defining SIC constraints under dynamic power. Then based on the energy consumption pattern, we propose a optimization problem that maximizes the vacation time ratio of MC. Subsequently, we transform the original problem into a linear model, then we develop a feasible near-optimal solution within desired level of error.

The remainder of this paper is organized as follows. In Sect. 2, we describe the scope of the problem for a multi-hop WRSNs with SIC. In Sect. 3, we give the mathematical and optimization model for SIC multi-hop wireless sensor networks. Section 4 shows the problem formulation and a near-option solution. In

Sect. 5, we present numerical results to demonstrate the performance under our solution. Section 6, concludes this paper.

2   Problem Description

In this section, we will introduce the principle of SIC, the multi-hop network scenario and the model of sensor nodes power consumption and supply.

Multi-hop Network Scenario with SIC. Within the WRSN (see Fig. 1), there are a fixed base station (B), which is the sink node for all sensor nodes. Consider a set of nodes $\mathcal{N}$ distributed over a two-dimensional area. Define E_{min} as the threshold of the node keeps from malfunctioning. The data rate is generated by each node i is R_i (in b/s, $i \in \mathcal{N}$). Define R_{ij} as the data rate from node i to node j and R_{iB} the data rate from node i to B.

With increasing the number of nodes in WSNs, the interference is also greatly increasing, which has a negative effect on the throughput. SIC is a powerful physical technique based on signal processing, which can decode signals in order according to the signal strength. Thus, we use SIC to mitigate some interference in WSNs and increase the efficiency of the network.

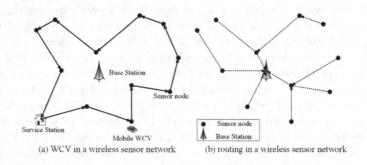

(a) WCV in a wireless sensor network   (b) routing in a wireless sensor network

Fig. 1. A wireless sensor network with a wireless charging vehicle

Sensor Power Supply Model. To recharge the nodes, we employed a mobile charger (MC) in WSNs. The MC traverses all sensor nodes with the speed of V (in m/s) from the service station (S) to the nodes and finally returns to S for preparing for the next trip. Denote τ as the time for a recharging cycle of MC and τ_{vac} as the vacation time of MC, respectively. When MC arrives at node i, it will take τ_i to charge node i. We assume that the MC has enough energy to charge all nodes within a single trip.

This paper aims to discuss the SIC multi-hop WSNs scenario and design a recharging cycle for MC to obtain more vacation time. In other words, it is to maximize the vacation percentage in a recharging cycle (i.e., $\frac{\tau_{vac}}{\tau}$).

3   The Mathematical and Optimization Model for SIC Multi-hop Wireless Networks

In this section, we will show the energy consumption model of each sensor node and time schedule scheme for the SIC multi-hop WSN. From these two points we can determine the communication model and the energy consumption model, which are sufficient conditions for the later recharging model.

The Mathematical Model for SIC Multi-hop Wireless Networks. In the physical layer, we employ SIC technique, meanwhile, in the link layer, we consider time schedule scheme to improve the throughput in the network. Suppose a schedule time divided into l time slices equally. Define x_{ij}^k (or x_{iB}^k) as a binary variable, if node i sends data to node j (or to base station), x_{ij}^k (or x_{iB}^k) = 1, otherwise x_{ij}^k (or x_{iB}^k) is 0. In each time slot t_k, node i can transmit to at most one node (or base station), then we have

$$\sum_{j \in I_i} x_{ij}^k + x_{iB}^k \leq 1 \quad (i \in \mathcal{N}, 1 \leq k \leq l). \tag{1}$$

In half-duplex model, the node i can't transmit or receive simultaneously:

$$\frac{\sum_{h \in I_i} x_{hi}^k}{|I_i|} + \sum_{j \in I_i} x_{ij}^k + x_{iB}^k \leq 1 \quad (i \in \mathcal{N}, 1 \leq k \leq l), \tag{2}$$

where I_i is a set of all neighbors nodes within the transmission range of node i.

With SIC, the receiver can receive and decode multiple signals sequentially. During the SIC decoding process, node j (or B) tries to decode the signal in time slot k, it will receive and eliminate the strongest signal in turn. Denote the channel loss function $g = \alpha d_{i,j}^{-\lambda}$, where d is the distance between two nodes and α generally is equal to 1. Denote N_0 as the noise power. If the SINR of this signal is no less than the threshold β, the transmission is successful. Then we have the constraint of SIC as follow,

$$SINR_{ij}^k = \frac{g_{ij}p_{ij}}{\sum_{\substack{l \neq i}}^{g_{lj}p_{lj} \leq g_{ij}p_{ij}} \left(g_{lj}p_{lj} \sum_{l \in T_m} x_{ml}^k \right) + N_0} \geq \beta \quad (x_{ij}^k = 1), \tag{3}$$

Where p_{ij} is the power of node i send data to node j. If node m transmits data to the other node in time slot k, $\sum_{l \in T_m} x_{ml}^k = 1$, otherwise, $\sum_{l \in T_m} x_{ml}^k = 0$. We suppose $x_{ij} = 1$ (or $x_{iB} = 1$), because $x_{ij} = 0$ (or $x_{iB} = 0$) means node i does not transmit any data to node j (or B) at the time slot.

With the time schedule scheme, the flow balance constraint at node i as

$$\sum_{h \in T_i} \sum_{k=0}^{l} R_{hi} \cdot x_{hi}^k + k \cdot R_i = \sum_{j \in T_i} \sum_{k=0}^{l} R_{ij} \cdot x_{ij}^k + \sum_{k=0}^{l} R_{iB} \cdot x_{iB}^k \quad (i \in \mathcal{N}). \tag{4}$$

Each node consumes energy for transmitting and receiving data, denote P_i^k as the power of node i. The energy consumption model as follow [15],

$$P_i^k = c \sum_{h \in \mathcal{N}}^{h \neq i} R_{hi} \cdot x_{hi}^k + \sum_{j \in \mathcal{N}}^{j \neq i} C_{ij} \cdot R_{ij} \cdot x_{ij}^k + C_{iB} R_{iB} \cdot x_{iB}^k \qquad (i \in \mathcal{N}), \qquad (5)$$

where c is the rate of energy consumption for receiving a unit of data rate. Additionally, $C_{ij} = \chi_1 + \chi_2 \cdot d_{ij}^\lambda$, where d_{ij} represents the distance between node i and node j, λ is the path loss index, χ_1 is constant, which is independent of distance, χ_2 is a coefficient of the distance-dependent constant term.

We can find that R_{ij} and R_{iB} are optimization variables, that is, p_{ij} is also a optimization variable and $g_{ij} p_{ij}$ can't be sorted in the optimization problem, that means SINR can't be calculated. Simultaneously, among the above constraints, x_{ij}^k and x_{iB}^k are binary variables, that is, the problem is a mixed integer problem, which is NP-hard in general and cannot be solved efficiently.

Optimization for SIC Multi-hop Wireless Networks. In last subsection, there are binary variables (such problems are usually NP-hard problems) and the problem of sorting optimization variables. In other words, this will be a great challenge to find an optimal solution for SIC multi-hop wireless network. In the section, we are ready to calculate the SINR, x_{ij}^k and x_{iB}^k by using minimum energy routing and two lemmas.

Due to the unknown data rate, we can't the get the power of each node. However, Lemma 1 can determine the energy consumption of the node only requiring the power formula instead of the exact power.

Lemma 1. *The total energy consumption of a node is only related to the amount of data receiving and transmitting.*

Proof. Note P_i^k is the power of node i (ignore the other energy consumption), and total energy consumption is $\sum_{k=0}^{l} P_i^k$ over a schedule time. Thus, we have

$$\sum_{k=0}^{l} P_i^k \cdot t_k = c \sum_{h \in \mathcal{N}}^{h \neq i} \sum_{k=0}^{l} R_{hi} \cdot x_{hi}^k t_k + \sum_{j \in \mathcal{N}}^{j \neq i} \sum_{k=0}^{l} C_{ij} \cdot R_{ij} \cdot x_{ij}^k t_k + \sum_{k=0}^{l} C_{iB} R_{iB} \cdot x_{iB}^k t_k,$$

where $\sum_{j \in \mathcal{N}}^{j \neq i} \sum_{k=0}^{l} R_{ij} \cdot x_{ij}^k$ is the amount of data that node i sends to node j during a schedule time. The three items on the right side of the equation are the energy consumption of the node receiving data by other nodes, sending to the other node or B.

In a determinate routing, each node only wants to transmit the data to B or forward the data, the amount of data is a constant in the route.

Therefore, the total energy consumption of a node is only related to the amount of data receiving and transmitting, regardless of the rate of transmission. This completes the proof.

Based on Lemma 1, We unite all R_{ij} to the same value R, so that $P'_{ij} = \sum_{j \in \mathcal{N}}^{j \neq i} C_{ij} \cdot R \cdot x_{ij}^k + C_{iB} \cdot R \cdot x_{iB}^k$. After determining P'_{ij}, we can successfully calculate the $SINR_{ij}^k$. If $x_{ij}^k = 1$, then $SINR_{ij}^k \geq \beta$. If $x_{iB}^k = 1$, then $SINR_{iB}^k \geq \beta$.

To reduce complexity, we are ready to calculate the upper bound of the number of signals that can be successfully decoded by a node or the base station. Denote B_j as an upper bound of the number of signals that node j can decode successfully.

Lemma 2. *The number of successfully decoded signals at node j is no more than $B_j = min\{1 + log_{\beta+1}\left(\frac{P_j^{max}}{\beta N_0}\right), |I_j|\}$, where P_j^{max} is the strongest desired signal in the received power at node j.*

Proof. Make $g_{1i}p_{1i} \leq g_{2i}p_{2i} \leq \cdots \leq g_{ki}p_{ki}$ be the set of powers of signals successfully at node j, it is easy to find that $g_{ki}p_{ki} \leq P_j^{max}$. With $g_{ki}p_{ki} \leq \beta(1+\beta)^{k-1} N_0$, we have

$$k \leq \beta(1+\beta)^{k-1} N_0 = B_j,$$

since $|I_j|$ is the number of neighbor nodes of receiver j, $B_j = min\{|I_j|, 1 + log_{\beta+1}\left(\frac{P_j^{max}}{\beta N_0}\right)\}$ is the upper bound of the number of signals which receiver j can decode. This completes the proof.

With Lemmas 1 and 2, we use the minimum energy routing to get a minimal energy consumption in transmission. Simultaneously, through the above constraints we can get the appropriate time schedule scheme.

4   The Mathematical Model for Charging Cycle

In this section, we will focus on building the model of charging cycle, then simplify the formulation through change-of-variable technique, finally get a near-optimal solution. The charging cycle can be divided into three parts: the traversal time τ_{tsp}, the sum of the charging time $\sum \tau_i$ and the vacation time τ_{vac}.

The Mathematical Formulation. In the last section, we introduce some lemmas and constrains for solving the problem of the dynamic power of nodes in SIC multi-hop WSNs. that is, nodes' energy consumption model has been completed, and then it is time for analyzing the energy recharging model.

Note sensor node i will have the same energy consumption curve during different charging cycles. Each node must meet the following restrictions on energy: (i) it stars and ends with the same energy, (ii) it is never less than E_{min}.

Denote $\Psi = \{\psi_1, \cdots, \psi_n\}$ as a set of locations of nodes and the location of service station as ψ_0. Denote $d_{\psi_i, \psi_{(i+1)}}$ as Euclidean distance between i and $(i+1)$. Under the charging cycle, the MC arrival time a_i at node i is as $a_{\psi_i} = \tau + \sum_{l=0}^{i-1} \frac{d_{\psi_l, \psi_{l+1}}}{V} + \sum_{l=1}^{i-1} \tau_l$.

Denote D_{tsp} the distance of the shortest Hamiltonian cycle over one charging cycle, then $\tau_{tsp} = \frac{D_{tsp}}{V}$. For a whole recharging cycle τ,

$$\tau = \tau_{tsp} + \tau_{vac} + \sum_{i \in \mathcal{N}} \tau_i \tag{6}$$

We use the average power $\overline{P}_i = \frac{\int_{k\tau}^{(k+1)\tau} P_i}{\tau} (k \in N)$ to analyzing the node power consumption. The amount of power consumed by the node i during τ is equal to the amount of supply power in τ_i. We have

$$\tau \cdot \overline{P}_i = \tau_i \cdot U \qquad (i \in \mathcal{N}) \tag{7}$$

Note when the MC reaches node i at time a_i, there are two options: (i) the MC recharging the battery to E_{max}, and (ii) the MC leave when node don't fully recharged. The results of the two options are the same, the proof shows in [16]. For convenience, we choose the fully charging. It is easy to find that after the introduction of $\overline{P}_i$, the energy level has only two approximate slope within a cycle $[k\tau, (k+1)\tau]$: one slope of $(u - \overline{P}_i)$ when the MC is charing this node at a rate of u during charging period, the other slope of $(-\overline{P}_i)$ when MC do not charge for this node. The residual energy relationship of the node i can be written as $E_{min} \le e_i(a_i) \le e_i(t) \le e_i(a_i + \tau_i) \le E_{max}$. For a cycle, $E_i = e_i(2\tau) = e_i(a_i + \tau_i) - (2\tau - (a_i + \tau_i)) \cdot \overline{P}_i = E_{max} - (2\tau - (a_i + \tau_i)) \cdot \overline{P}_i$. Then we have $e_i(a_i) = E_i - (a_i - \tau) \cdot \overline{P}_i = E_{max} - (2\tau - (a_i + \tau_i)) \cdot \overline{P}_i - (a_i - \tau) \cdot \overline{P}_i$. Then,

$$E_{max} - (\tau - \tau_i) \cdot \overline{P}_i \ge E_{min} \quad (i \in \mathcal{N}) \tag{8}$$

Summarizing all the constraints and the objective in the model, we formulate the problem as OPT shown as follows,

$$\max \frac{\tau_{vac}}{\tau}$$
$$\text{s.t.} \quad (4), (5), (6), (7), (8)$$
$$\tau_i, \tau_{vac}, \tau \ge 0 \qquad (i \in \mathcal{N}).$$

In OPT, τ_i, τ_{vac} and τ are optimization variables. $\overline{P}_i$, R, R_i, c, C_{ij}, C_{iB}, u, E_{min}, E_{max} and τ_{tsp} are constants. There is a nonlinear objective $\left(\frac{\tau_{vac}}{\tau}\right)$.

Reformulation. We simplify the formulation by change-of-variable technique. For the nonlinear objective $\frac{\tau_{vac}}{\tau}$, we define $\eta_{vac} = \frac{\tau_{vac}}{\tau}$.

For constraint (6), we divide the sides of equation by τ and get $1 = \frac{\tau_{tsp}}{\tau} + \eta_{vac} + \sum_{i \in \mathcal{N}} \frac{\tau_i}{\tau}$. With transforming the nonlinear terms $\frac{1}{\tau}$ and $\frac{\tau_i}{\tau}$, we define $\eta_{vac} = \frac{\tau_i}{\tau}$, $\eta_0 = \frac{1}{\tau}$, respectively. Constraint (6) is reformulated as $\eta_0 = \frac{1 - \sum_{i \in \mathcal{N}} \eta_i - \tau_{vac}}{\tau_{tsp}}$. Similarly, (7) and (8) can be rewritten as $\overline{P}_i = u \cdot \eta_i$, $(1 - \eta_i) \cdot \overline{P}_i \le (E_{max} - E_{min}) \cdot \eta_0$ $(i \in \mathcal{N})$.

Then, we have $\eta_{vac} \le 1 - \sum_{l \in \mathcal{N}} \eta_l - \frac{u \cdot \tau_{tsp}}{E_{max} - E_{min}} \cdot \eta_i \cdot (1 - \eta_i)$ $(i \in \mathcal{N})$. Meanwhile, constraint (2) can be reformulated as $c \sum_{h \in \mathcal{N}}^{h \ne i} \sum_{k=0}^{l} (R \cdot x_{hi}^k) + \sum_{j \in \mathcal{N}}^{j \ne i} \sum_{k=0}^{l} (R \cdot x_{ij}^k) + C_{iB} \sum_{k=0}^{l} (R \cdot x_{iB}^k) - u \cdot \eta_i = 0$.

The constrains become linear except through reformulation, in which we have a second order term (η_i^2). In the next section, we show how to approximate the second order term with an efficient technique. Then, we present an near-optimal solution to OPT within a presetting error.

A Near-Optimal Solution. In this section, we use piecewise straight lines instead of the quadratic curves (η_i^2) in reformulation. The approximation make the corresponding nonlinear constraints become linear constrains, and the solution can be quickly found by some solvers such as GUROBI. Base on the solution, we construct a feasible solution to original problem OPT. At the end, we prove the near-optimality of the solution from GUROBI.

Note that the only one nonlinear term in the OPT-R is η_i^2, and it lies in a very small interval ([0,1]). This is the reason why we employ a piecewise linear approximation for η_i^2.

The core idea set m piecewise linear segments to replace the quadratic curve. For curve $f(\eta_i) = \eta_i^2 (0 \leq \eta_i \leq 1)$, we construct a piecewise linear approximation $f(\gamma_i) = \gamma_i$ by connecting points $(\frac{s}{m}, \frac{s^2}{m^2})$ where s = $0,1,\cdots, m$. The specific value of m will be given in the next section.

Now, we show how to mathematically represent the piecewise linear curve. For $s = 0, 1, \cdots, m$, all point $f(\gamma_i) = \gamma_i$ on the piecewise linear curve within sth segment can be represented by $\eta_i = \lambda_{i,s-1} \cdot \frac{s-1}{m} + \lambda_{i,s} \cdot \frac{s}{m}$, $\gamma_i = \lambda_{i,s-1} \cdot \frac{(s-1)^2}{m^2} + \lambda_{i,s} \cdot \frac{s^2}{m^2}$, where $\lambda_{i,s-1}$ and $\lambda_{i,s}$ are two weights and should satisfy constraint as $\lambda_{i,s-1} + \lambda_{i,s} = 1, 0 \leq \lambda_{i,s-1}, \lambda_{i,s} \leq 1$.

Because $f(x) = x^2$ is a convex function, the piecewise linear approximation curve $f(\gamma_i) = \gamma_i$ always lies above the curve $f(\eta_i) = \eta_i^2$. The Lemma 3 can quantify the upper bound of error when $\gamma - \eta^2$ is divided into m. Its proof can be found in [16].

Lemma 3. $\gamma_i - \eta_i^2 \leq \frac{1}{4m^2} (i \in \mathcal{N})$.

Note that the mathematical representation of λ_{is} is for a given sth segment. We now show a general mathematical formulation for the whole piecewise linear curve. Define $l_{is} (1 \leq s \leq m)$ as one binary variable indicating whether η_i lies in the sth segment, that is, if $\frac{s-1}{m} \leq \eta_i < \frac{s}{m}$, then $l_{is} = 1$, otherwise, $l_{is} = 0$.

Since each η_i only falls into one interval of the m segment, we have,

$$\sum_{s=1}^{m} l_{is} = 1, \tag{9}$$

with the definition of $l_{is} (1 \leq s \leq m)$, we will reformulate mathematical representation of λ_{is} for the whole piecewise linear curve. First, we show the relationship between λ_{is} and $l_{is} (1 \leq s \leq m)$. Then base on the last reformulation, we can get $\lambda_{i,s-1}$ and $\lambda_{i,s}$ positive only while any other $\lambda_{i,j} (j \neq s-1, s)$ be all zero, when η_i falls in the sth segment, i.e., $\lambda_{i0} > 0$ only if $l_{i1} = 1$, $\lambda_{is} > 0$ only if $l_{is} = 1$ or $l_{i,s+1} = 1 (1 \leq s \leq m)$, and $\lambda_{im} > 0$ only if $l_{im} = 1$. These relationships can be expressed as

$$\lambda_{i0} \leq l_{i1}, \tag{10}$$

$$\lambda_{is} \leq l_{is} + l_{i,s+1}, \tag{11}$$

$$\lambda_{im} \leq l_{im}, \tag{12}$$

The above three constrains indicate that there are up to two adjacent positive λ_{ik} for each η_i. Now we can rewrite the mathematical representation for the whole piecewise linear curve as follow,

$$\eta_i = \sum_{s=0}^{m} \lambda_{is} \cdot \frac{s}{m}, \tag{13}$$

$$\gamma_i = \sum_{s=0}^{m} \lambda_{is} \cdot \frac{s^2}{m^2}, \tag{14}$$

$$\sum_{s=0}^{m} \lambda_{is} = 1. \tag{15}$$

Now we replace η_i^2 with γ_i in $\eta_{vac} \leq 1 - \sum_{l \in \mathcal{N}} \eta_l - \frac{u \cdot \tau_{tsp}}{E_{max} - E_{min}} \cdot \eta_i \cdot (1 - \eta_i)$, i.e.,

$$\eta_{vac} = 1 - \sum_{l \in \mathcal{N}} \eta_l - \frac{u \cdot \tau_{tsp}}{E_{max} - E_{min}} \cdot (\eta_i - \gamma_i) \qquad (i \in \mathcal{N}) \tag{16}$$

By formulating some constraints, we have the following linear relaxed formulation called OPT-L as follow.

$$
\begin{aligned}
\max\ & \eta_{vac} \\
\text{s.t.}\ & (7), (16), (10) \sim (15) \\
& 0 \leq \eta_i, \eta_{vac}, \gamma_i \leq 1 \quad (i, j \in \mathcal{N}, i \neq j) \\
& l_{ik} \in \{0, 1\} \quad\quad\quad (i \in \mathcal{N}, 1 \leq s \leq m) \\
& 0 \leq \lambda_{ik} \leq 1 \quad\quad\quad (i \in \mathcal{N}, 0 \leq s \leq m).
\end{aligned} \tag{17}
$$

Where γ_i, η_i, η_{vac}, l_{is}, λ_{ik} are optimization variables, η_{tsp}, E_{min}, E_{max}, u, C_{ij}, C_{iB}, c, x_{ij}^k, x_{iB}^k, R and R_i are constants. Now, the new formulation can be solved easily by some solvers such as GUROBI.

The solution of problem OPT-L looks like an infeasible solution of OPT. However, by its solution, we can construct a feasible solution to OPT. Suppose $\Pi' = (\eta_i', \eta_{vac}', l_{is}', \lambda_{is}', \gamma_i')$ is the solution of problem OPT-L. We find that (η_i', η_{vac}') satisfies all constraints about the reformulation. To construct a feasible solution $\Pi = (\eta_i, \eta_{vac})$ to the reformulation, we make $\eta_i = \eta_i'$. To satisfy constraint (16) in the reformulation, we define η_{vac} as $\min_{i \in \mathcal{N}}\{1 - \sum_{l \in \mathcal{N}} \eta_l' - \frac{u \cdot \tau_{tsp}}{E_{max} - E_{min}} \cdot \eta_i' \cdot (1 - \eta_i')\}$. It can be verified that the solution of the newly constructed solution Π satisfies all the constraints of the reformulation. After getting the solution to the reformulation, we can easily find a feasible solution for OPT in the next section.

Proof of Near-Optimality. In this section, we quantify the gap between the optimal objective (η_{vac}') and the objective (η_{vac}) obtained by the feasible solution

Π. We expect this performance error to be related to m, i.e., the number of segments of the piecewise linear approximation. With this result, we can reverse the calculation of the m by the given target error ξ $(0 < \xi \ll 1)$.

Lemma 4. $\eta'_{vac} - \eta_{vac} \leq \frac{u \cdot T_{tsp}}{4(E_{max}-E_{min})} \cdot \frac{1}{m^2}$, where η_{vac} is the objective value for the feasible solution Π.

Proof. Note η'_{vac} is the objective value for the solution Π' of the relaxed linear problem OPT-L. Because problem OPT-L is a relaxation of problem reformulation, η'_{vac} is an upper bound of η_{vac} (i.e., $\eta_{vac} \leq \eta'_{vac}$). Thus, we have
$\eta'_{vac} - \eta_{vac} \leq \eta'_{vac} - \eta_{vac} = [1 - \sum_{l \in \mathcal{N}} \eta'_l - \frac{u \cdot T_{tsp}}{E_{max}-E_{min}} \cdot \eta'_i \cdot (1-\eta'_i)] - [1 - \sum_{l \in \mathcal{N}} \eta'_l - \frac{u \cdot T_{tsp}}{E_{max}-E_{min}} \cdot \eta_{max} \cdot (1-\eta_{max})] = \frac{u \cdot T_{tsp}}{E_{max}-E_{min}} (\gamma_{max} - \eta^2_{max}) \leq \frac{u \cdot T_{tsp}}{4(E_{max}-E_{min})} \cdot \frac{1}{m^2}$,
where the second equality holds by lemmas in [16], and the fourth inequality holds by Lemma 1. This completes the proof.

With Lemma 4, we will introduce the Theorem 1 and show how to set m to make $\eta'_{vac} - \eta_{vac} \leq \xi$ by a presetting target error $\xi(0 < \xi \ll 1)$.

Theorem 1. *For one given error ξ $(0 < \xi \ll 1)$, if $m = \lceil \sqrt{\frac{u \cdot T_{tsp}}{4\xi(E_{max}-E_{min})}} \rceil$, then $\eta'_{vac} - \eta_{vac} \leq \xi$.*

Proof. Lemma 4 shows that the gap is $\eta'_{vac} - \eta_{vac} \leq \frac{u \cdot T_{tsp}}{4(E_{max}-E_{min})} \cdot \frac{1}{m^2}$. Thus, if we set $m = \lceil \sqrt{\frac{u \cdot T_{tsp}}{4\xi(E_{max}-E_{min})}} \rceil$, then we have $\eta'_{vac} - \eta_{vac} \leq \frac{u \cdot T_{tsp}}{4(E_{max}-E_{min})} \cdot \frac{1}{m^2} \leq \frac{u \cdot T_{tsp}}{4(E_{max}-E_{min})} \cdot \frac{4\xi(E_{max}-E_{min})}{u \cdot T_{tsp}} = \xi$. This completes the proof.

With Theorem 1, we present the complete problem-solving process on how to calculate the solution of OPT as follow,

1. Given a feasible error ξ.
2. Let $m = \lceil \sqrt{\frac{u \cdot T_{tsp}}{4\xi(E_{max}-E_{min})}} \rceil$.
3. Solve the optimization problem OPT-L with m segments by GUROBI, then obtain its solution $\Pi' = (\eta'_{vac}, \eta'_i, l'_{ik}, \lambda'_{ik}, \gamma'_i)$.
4. Establish one feasible solution $\Pi = (\eta_{vac}, \eta_i)$ for linear relaxed problem OPT-S by letting $\eta_{vac} = \eta'_{vac}$, $\eta_i = \eta'_i$ and $\eta_{vac} = \min_{i \in \mathcal{N}} \{1 - \sum_{l \in \mathcal{N}} \eta'_l - \frac{u \cdot T_{tsp}}{E_{max}-E_{min}} \cdot \eta'_i \cdot (1-\eta'_i)\}$.
5. Obtain one near-optimal solution $(\tau_{vac}, \tau, \tau_i)$ to primeval optimization problem OPT.

5   Simulation

In this section, we give some numerical results to show how our solution can get infinite lifetime WRSNs and we also compare the throughput of SIC and interference avoid to show the advantage of SIC.

Simulation Setting. Consider WRSNs with 40 and 50 nodes generated randomly in a square region of $0.8\,\text{km}\times0.8\,\text{km}$ and $1\,\text{km}\times1\,\text{km}$. Additionally, consider WSN with 10 nodes generated randomly in a square region of $0.8\,\text{km}\times0.8\,\text{km}$. The data generation rate R_i is randomly generated within $[1,20]\,\text{kb/s}$ and data transmission rate R is twice the maximum R_i, equaling to $40\,\text{kb/s}$. The service station for MC is assumed to be located at origin. The speed of the MC is $V = 5\,\text{m/s}$.

For the battery at each node, we choose a regular battery and we have $E_{max} = 10.8\,\text{KJ}$. Let $E_{min} = 0.05 \cdot E_{max} = 540\,\text{J}$. The coefficients of power consumption are $c = 50\,\text{nJ/b}$, $\chi_1 = 50\,\text{nJ/b}$, $\chi_2 = 0.0013\,\text{pJ/(b}\cdot\text{m}^4)$, $\lambda = 4$.

Set the feasible error $\xi = 0.01$, i.e., the solution is up to 1% from the optimum.

Result. Consider a WSN in Fig. 2. The coordinates and the data generation rate R_i are shown in Table 1. Simultaneously, the base station's coordinate is $(400, 400)$. With SIC, the total amount of data received by the base station increase by 550% compared with interference avoid.

Table 1. The coordinates (in m) and the R_i (in kb/s) of each node in the network.

i	Coordinates	R_i	i	Coordinates	R_i	i	Coordinates	R_i	i	Coordinates	R_i
1	$(235, 635)$	4	2	$(580, 130)$	9	3	$(311, 354)$	16	4	$(708, 240)$	5
5	$(268, 6)$	14	6	$(432, 160)$	17	7	$(509, 93)$	19	8	$(775, 454)$	13
9	$(149, 312)$	13	10	$(461, 247)$	16						

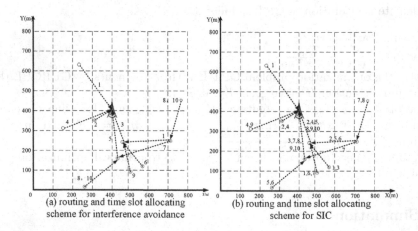

(a) routing and time slot allocating scheme for interference avoidance

(b) routing and time slot allocating scheme for SIC

Fig. 2. The 10-node 1-base-station network and schemes in the two different techniques.

We employ Concorde solver generating the shortest Hamiltonian cycle, and get $m = \left\lceil \sqrt{\dfrac{u \cdot \tau_{tsp}}{4\xi(E_{max} - E_{min})}} \right\rceil = 4$, a small number, by the error $\xi = 0.01$. Table 2 illustrate the numerical results in four different WRSNs, in which the throughput is greatly increased, while no increasing in the objective η_{vac}.

Table 2. The numerical results in the four different networks.

The size of square	B	$|\mathcal{N}|$	η_{vac}	The increasing in throughput
800 * 800	$(400, 400)$	40	89.06%	540.01%
800 * 800	$(400, 400)$	50	88.01%	434.78%
1000 * 1000	$(500, 500)$	40	67.85%	364.78%
1000 * 1000	$(500, 500)$	50	69.89%	353.34%

6   Conclusion

We study the problem of throughput and node lifetime in WRSNs. We employ the SIC technique to increase the throughput of the network and WCT technique to prolong lifetime of sensor node. We study a practical optimization problem with the objective of maximizing the percentage of MC's vacation time over the cycle time, which is non-linear. Then, we show a feasible near-optimal solution for both cycle time and charging time at each node. Simulation results demonstrated that SIC can increase the throughput obviously and cause no increasing on energy consumption comparing with interference avoid scheme.

References

1. Antonio, P., Grimaccia, F., Mussetta, M.: Architecture and methods for innovative heterogeneous wireless sensor network applications. Remote Sens. **4**(5), 1146–1161 (2012)
2. Kurs, A., Karalis, A., Moffatt, R., Joannopoulos, J.D., Fisher, P., Soljacic, M.: Wireless power transfer via strongly coupled magnetic resonances. Science **317**(5834), 83–86 (2007)
3. Cheng, S., Cai, Z., Li, J.: Curve query processing in wireless sensor networks. IEEE Trans. Veh. Technol. **64**(11), 5198–5209 (2015)
4. Cai, Z., Goebel, R., Lin, G.: Size-constrained tree partitioning: approximating the multicast k-tree routing problem. Theor. Comput. Sci. **412**(3), 240–245 (IF: 1.085) (2011)
5. Cai, Z., Cheng, Z., Lin, G.: A 3.4713-approximation algorithm for the capacitated multicast tree routing problem. Theor. Comput. Sci. **410**(52), 5415–5424 (2009)
6. Cheng, S., Cai, Z., Li, J., Gao, H.: Extracting kernel dataset from big sensory data in wireless sensor networks. IEEE Trans. Knowl. Data Eng. **29**(4), 813–827 (2017)
7. Noura, M., Nordin, R.: A survey on interference management for device-to-device (D2D) communication and its challenges in 5G networks. J. Netw. Comput. Appl. **71**, 130–150 (2016)

8. Ma, J., Zhang, S., Li, H., Zhao, N., Leung, V.C.M.: Interference-alignment and soft-space-reuse based cooperative transmission for multi-cell massive MIMO networks. IEEE Trans. Wirel. Commun. **3**, 1907–1922 (2018)
9. Gupta, V.K., Nambiar, A., Kasbekar, G.S.: Complexity analysis, potential game characterization and algorithms for the inter cell interference coordination with fixed transmit power problem. IEEE Trans. Veh. Technol. **4**, 3054–3068 (2018)
10. Weber, S.P., Andrews, J.G., Yang, X., Veciana, G.D.: Transmission capacity of wireless ad hoc networks with successive interference cancellation. IEEE Trans. Inf. Theory **8**, 2799–2814 (2007)
11. Jiang, C., et al.: Cross-layer optimization for multi-hop wireless networks with successive interference cancellation. IEEE Trans. Wirel. Commun **8**, 5819–5831 (2016)
12. Liu, R., Shi, Y., Liu, K.S., Shen, M., Wang, Y., Li, Y.: Bandwith-aware high-throughput routing with successive interference cancelation in multihop wireless networks. IEEE Trans. Vel. Technol **12**, 5866–5877 (2015)
13. Ma, C., Wu, W., Cui, Y., Wang, X.: On the performance of successive interference cancellation in D2D-enabled cellular networks. In: Proceedings of IEEE Conference on Computer Communications, vol. 8, pp. 37–45 (2015)
14. Lin, C.T., Tseng, F.S., Wu, W.R., Jheng, F.J.: Joint precodeers design for full-duplex MIMO relay systems with QR-SIC detector. IEEE Glob. Commun. Conf **7**, 1–6 (2015)
15. Hou, Y.T., Shi, Y., Sherali, H.D.: Rate allocation and network lifetime problems for wireless sensor networks. IEEE/ACM Trans. Netw. **16**(2), 1–6 (2015)
16. Shi, Y., Xie, L., Hou, Y.T., Sherali, H.D.: On renewable sensor networks with wireless energy transfer. Technical report, The Bradley Department of Electrical and Computer Engineering, Virginia Tech, Blacksburg, VA, July 2010. http://filebox.vt.edu/users/yshi/papers/charging.pdf

Deep Neural Model for Point-of-Interest Recommendation Fused with Graph Embedding Representation

Jinghua Zhu[✉] and Xu Guo

School of Computer Science and Technology, Heilongjiang University,
Harbin 150080, Heilongjiang, China
zhujinghua@hlju.edu.cn

Abstract. With the rapid popularity of smart mobile devices and the rapid development of location-based social networks (LBSNs), location-based recommendation has become an important method to help people find the attractive point-of-interest (POI). However, due to the sparsity of user-POI check-in data, the traditional recommendation model based on collaborative filtering cannot be well applied to the POI recommendation problem. In addition, location-based social networks are different from other recommendation scenarios, and users' POI check-ins are closely related to social relations and geographical factors. Therefore, this paper proposes a neural networks POI recommendation model fused with social and geographical graph embedding representation(SG-NeuRec). Our model organically combines social and geographical graph embedding representations with user-POI interaction representation, and captures the latent interactions between users and POIs under the neural networks framework. Meanwhile, in order to improve the accuracy of POI recommendation, the relevance between users' accessing time pattern and POI is modeled by the designed shallow network and unified under the same framework. Extensive experiments on two real location-based social networks datasets demonstrate the effectiveness of the proposed model.

Keywords: POI recommendation · Neural networks ·
Graph embedding · Deep learning · LBSNs

1 Introduction

With the rapid development of mobile Internet, location-based social networks applications are becoming more and more abundant, such as Foursquare, yelp, facebook, etc. Many researches have discussed the hot topics of LBSNs and cloud service, such as recommendation [5,10,11], privacy protection [1,8,13] and crowdsourcing [8,9,13]. The POI Recommendation system brings considerable business value to service providers and users in LBSNs also tend to share their

Supported by Chinese National Natural Science Foundation (61602159).

favorite point-of-interest with friends. So in recent years, POI recommendation has attracted extensive attention in both academia and industry. However, in the scenarios of location-based social networks, traditional methods such as collaborative filtering cannot be well applied to POI recommendation problems. The main problems are as follows: first of all, the check-in behavior records of users on LBSNs only contain implicit feedback information, which makes it difficult to capture users' interest and preference. Secondly, data sparsity problem exists in users' check-in data. Thirdly, different from e-commerce recommendation task, in the scenarios of LBSNs, there are great constraint factors in the user's accessing activity, such as the user's social relationship, geographical restrictions, and accessing time restrictions. In recent years, one of the latest trends in recommendation system research is utilizing deep neural networks instead of traditional collaborative filtering method. The research shows that in the case of behavior data sparsity, the deep neural networks model can better learn the user-item latent interaction representation.

Therefore, this paper proposes a neural networks POI recommendation model fused with social and geographical graph embedding(SG-NeuRec), which integrates users' social relationship networks, POIs' geographical networks and user-POI check-in interactions into a neural networks recommendation framework. Specifically, we embed each user and each POI into a low-dimensional latent space, which is similar to the latent factors for users and items in traditional matrix factorization method. In order to capture users' social relationship information and POIs' geographical information, we model users' social relationship and POIs' geographical relationship in the LBSNs as unweighted graphs, and use an unsupervised autoencoder learning technology to obtain the graph embedding representations of users and POIs. Then, the latent low-dimensional representations of users and POIs is combined with graph embedding representations to learn the latent interaction representation of user-POI under the deep neural networks model of multi-layer perceptron. At the same time, considering that users' check-in behaviors have obvious time preference, we utilize a shallow network to learn the relevance representation between the time patterns of users' check-ins and POIs under the same framework. Finally, we take the check-in behavior of users as a positive sample of binary classification and train our model with cross entropy loss. The main contributions of this paper include:

1. We propose a deep neural networks recommendation model that integrates users' social relationship and POIs' geographical relationship. It integrates the graph embedding representations of users and POIs, and models the latent interactions between users and POIs under a multi-layer perceptron structure.
2. In order to obtain better recommendation performance, under the model framework of this paper, we integrate the time pattern of users' accessing behaviors and design a shallow network structure to simulate the relevance between the time patterns of users' check-ins and POIs.
3. Extensive experiments are conducted on two real world datasets. Compared with other recommendation models, the results show that the recommenda-

tion model proposed in this paper has better performance in terms of recommendation accuracy and ranking quality.

2   Related Work

In recent years, with the development of LBSNs, POI location recommendation has been widely studied. Traditional recommendation algorithms utilize users' historical implicit feedback data or rating data to provide recommendations to users based on collaborative filtering method. Many researches, such as [16], have widely explored utilizing social factors, geographical factors, temporal factors to enhance POI recommendation performance. Lian et al. [3] incorporated spatial clustering caused by geographical influence into the weighted matrix factorization framework to solve the challenges brought by matrix sparsity. Yuan et al. [15] included the time cycle information into the user-based collaborative filtering framework for the time-aware POI recommendation.

Utilizing deep neural network methods to extract features or model interactions between users and items has become a trend in the field of recommendation system research. For example, [2] regarded the latent interaction between the user and the item as a binary classification and proposed a neural networks recommendation model. It is oriented to the user's implicit feedback behavior and utilizes the multi-layer perceptron to model the latent interaction between the user and the item. [14] proposed a POI recommendation model based on neural networks, which integrates context factors and collaborative filtering methods. It integrates user preferences and context into a semi-supervised learning framework and utilize neural networks to model user-POI interaction.

3   SG-NeuRec Model

3.1   Problem Definition

A POI is defined as a specific location that is uniquely identified. A POI has two attributes: identification number p and geographical coordinate l. The geographical coordinate of each POI is given by the corresponding latitude and longitude. A check-in activity is generated by user's accessing to POI, and each check-in activity consists of a triple (u, p, t), representing user u who accessed POI p in the time stamp t. Given user set U, POI set P, users social graph G_U and POI geographical graph G_P, our POI recommendation task is to recommend the POIs that user u is interested in when he is in the time stamp t according to the users' historical check-in behavior records.

3.2   Graph Embedding Representation

In this paper, social relationship information and geographical information is modeled as unweighted graphs, which are described by adjacency matrix. In the matrix of user social graph, if there is a social relationship between any two users, the corresponding edge weight between them is 1, otherwise is 0. In the matrix of POI geographical graph, if the distance between any two POIs is not greater than δ, the corresponding edge weight between them is 1, otherwise is 0.

Inspired by SDNE model [7] (Structural Deep Network Embedding), we adopt the unsupervised autoencoder to learn the embedding representation of the node in the graph networks. The model is shown in Fig. 1.

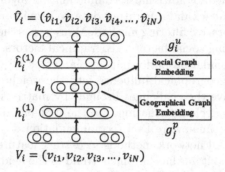

Fig. 1. Graph embedding representation.

In the adjacency matrix of unweighted graph with N nodes, for node i, $V_i = (v_{i1}, v_{i2}, v_{i3}, ..., v_{iN})$ represents the node vector composed of the weights of the joining edges. V_i is fed into the encoder as the input vector. The expressions of the two hidden layers of the encoder are as follows:

$$h_i^{(1)} = (W_1 V_i + b_1) \tag{1}$$

$$h_i = \sigma \left(W_2 h_i^{(1)} + b_2 \right) \tag{2}$$

The expressions of the two hidden layers of the decoder are as follows:

$$\widehat{h}_i^{(1)} = \sigma \left(\widehat{W}_1 h_i + \widehat{b}_1 \right) \tag{3}$$

$$\widehat{V}_i = \sigma \left(\widehat{W}_2 \widehat{h}_i^{(1)} + \widehat{b}_2 \right) \tag{4}$$

where W_*, b_*, $\widehat{W}_*$, $\widehat{b}_*$ denote the parameters of the layers in the encoder and decoder. σ represents the nonlinear activation function of hidden layers. The output vector h_i of the encoder is the graph embedding representation vector of node i. Through the decoder, we obtain the node vector reconstruction representation $\widehat{V}_i = (\widehat{v}_{i1}, \widehat{v}_{i2}, \widehat{v}_{i3}, ..., \widehat{v}_{iN})$.

The optimization goal of the graph embedding representation model is to minimize the error between the original input and the reconstruction output of the node, and to make the graph embedding representations of the connected nodes close to each other. Therefore, for the unweighted graph embedding model in this paper, the loss function is:

$$L_{GE} = - \sum_{i,j=1}^{N} [v_{ij} \log \widehat{v}_{ij} + (1 - v_{ij}) \log (1 - \widehat{v}_{ij})] + \alpha \sum_{i,j=1}^{N} v_{ij} \|h_i - h_j\|^2 \quad (5)$$

where α is the hyperparameter. Through the graph embedding representation model, we obtain graph embedding representation vector of user u_i and POI p_j in low-dimensional latent space, respectively denoted as g_i^u and g_j^p. The representation vectors contain users' social relationship information and POIs' geographical information.

3.3 User-POI Interaction Representation

In our model, we adopt the stacking multi-layer structure to learn the interaction representation between the user and POI. The overview of the model is shown in Fig. 2. Next, we will explain these layers in details.

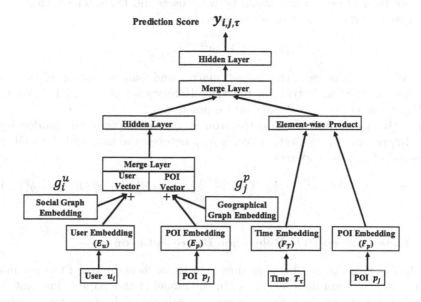

Fig. 2. The SG-NeuRec model.

Input Layer: the input layer receives user-POI pair (u_i, p_j), and both the user and POI are represented in the form of one-hot encoding vector.

Embedding Layer: The Embedding layer makes users and POIs one-hot encoding mapped into dense latent embedding vectors. Through the Embedding layers, we obtain the latent factor matrixs of users and POIs $E_u \in \mathbb{R}^{N \times D}, E_p \in \mathbb{R}^{M \times D}$ respectively, where N represents the total number of users, M represents the total number of POIs, D denotes latent factor dimension of the users and POIs. When using u_i, p_j to represent the users and POIs one-hot encoding input vector, $E_u^T u_i$, $E_p^T p_j$ represent embedding vector of user u_i and POI p_j respectively.

Merge Layers: in the merge layers, we add social graph embedding g_i^u to $E_u^T u_i$, and add geographical graph embedding g_j^p to $E_p^T p_j$, to generate user vector and POI vector respectively. Then these two vectors are concatenated and served as the input vector z of subsequent hidden layer. The expression of the Merge layer is as follows:

$$z = \left[E_u^T u_i + g_i^u ; E_p^T p_j + g_j^p \right] \tag{6}$$

Hidden Layer: the hidden layer uses a stacking multi-layer perceptron to learn the latent interaction representation between users and POIs. The output of the hidden layer of the K-th layer is expressed as:

$$h^K(z) = a \left(W^K h^{K-1}(z) + b^K \right) \tag{7}$$

where W^K, b^K represent the weight matrix and bias vector of K-th layer, a denotes a nonlinear activation function. Here we adopt rectified linear unit $ReLU(x) = max(0, x)$ as the activation function.

We take the output of the perceptron at the last layer of the hidden layer as the interaction representation vector $h_{u,p}$ between the user and the POI. the expression of $h_{u,p}$ is as follows:

$$h_{u,p} = h^K \left(h^{K-1} \left(...h^1(z) \right) \right) = h^K \left(h^{K-1} \left(...h^1 \left(\left[E_u^T u_i + g_i^u ; E_p^T p_j + g_j^p \right] \right) \right) \right) \tag{8}$$

3.4   Time Pattern-POI Relevance Representation

Establishing the relevance between time patterns of check-ins and POIs can make POI recommendation more accurate. In the model of this paper, time slots are divided as follows: the 24 h in one day are evenly divided into 24 time periods, and the 7 days in one week are evenly divided into 7 time periods. In this way, the one-week time cycle is divided into 168 time slots as the time pattern of users' check-ins. We adopt the embedding layer design similar to the user-POI interaction representation part. The time pattern of user's check-in t_τ and POI p_j are embedded respectively, and we obtain the embedding vector of time pattern $F_t^T t_\tau$ and the embedding vector of POI $F_p^T p_j$. F_t, F_p denote latent factor matrixs of time patterns and POIs respectively. We adopt a shallow network modeling the relevance between POI and time pattern, and take the element-wise product of the two embedding vectors to obtain the relevance representation $h_{t,p}$ between the time pattern and POI, expression is as follows:

$$h_{t,p} = F_t^T t_\tau \odot F_p^T p_j \tag{9}$$

where $\odot$ denotes the element-wise product of the vectors.

3.5 Model Training

After obtaining the interaction representation $h_{u,p}$ between users and POIs, and the relevance representation $h_{t,p}$ between time patterns and POIs, we concatenate these two vectors in the merge layer and feed it into subsequent hidden layer, and the latent representation $h_{u,p,t}$ among users, POIs and time patterns can be obtained through a single hidden layer, expression is as follows:

$$h_{u,p,t} = ReLU\left(W\left[h_{u,p}; h_{t,p}\right] + b\right) \tag{10}$$

where W, b respectively represent the weight matrix and bias vector of the hidden layer. In the prediction output layer, the interaction prediction score of user u_i and p_j on timestamp t_τ is obtained, expression is as follows:

$$\widehat{y}_{i,j,\tau} = \sigma\left(H^T h_{u,p,t}\right) \tag{11}$$

where H is the connection weight of the prediction output layer and σ is the sigmoid activation function, which is defined as $\sigma(x) = 1/(1 + e^{-x})$. It maps the interaction score into the interval of [0,1].

Considering the implicit feedback of the users' check-ins, whether the user interacts with the POI can be regarded as a binary classification problem. The sigmoid activation function acts on the output layer of the model so that the output of the model represents the probability score of the user's interaction with the POI. Assuming that Y represents the set of POIs which are accessed by users in dataset, Y^- represents the set of POIs which are not accessed by users in dataset, then we can obtain the target likelihood function:

$$P\left(Y, Y^- | \Theta\right) = \prod_{(i,j,\tau) \in Y} \widehat{y}_{i,j,\tau} \prod_{(i,j,\tau) \in Y^-} \left(1 - \widehat{y}_{i,j,\tau}\right) \tag{12}$$

where Θ is the model parameters. Taking the negative logarithm of the likelihood function, we obtain the objective function:

$$L_{predict} = -\sum_{(i,j,\tau) \in Y} \log \widehat{y}_{i,j,\tau} - \sum_{(i,j,\tau) \in Y^-} \log \left(1 - \widehat{y}_{i,j,\tau}\right) \tag{13}$$

In the graph embedding representation, we obtain the loss function of the user social graph embedding and the loss function of the POI geographical graph embedding, denoted as L_U and L_P respectively. In this way, we can obtain the objective function that we need to minimize of the whole model, namely:

$$L = L_{predict} + \lambda_U L_U + \lambda_P L_P \tag{14}$$

where λ_U and λ_P are the hyperparameters, which represent the weight of loss in the user graph embedding and POI graph embedding respectively.

4 Experiments and Analyses

4.1 Experimental Settings

We evaluate the proposed model on two real-world datasets, Gowalla and Yelp. Each check-in record in the datasets contains a timestamp, a user ID, a POI ID, the latitude and longitude of the POI. The statistics of datasets are given in Table 1.

Table 1. The statistics of datasets.

Datasets	User	POI	check-ins	Density
Gowalla	43,071	46,234	1,720,082	0.0500%
Yelp	30,887	18,995	860,888	0.1399%

For performance evaluation, we take Hit Ratio (HR) and Mean Reciprocal Rank (MRR) as the performance metrics and adopt the leave-one-out method. For each user, we use their recent interactions as the test sets and the rest of the behavior records as the training set. And we randomly select 100 POIs that are not accessed by users as negative samples, and the test POI is arranged in these 100 POIs by calculating the interaction prediction scores. We obtain HR and MRR value for each test user and calculate the average scores as result.

In the geographical graph embedding model of POIs, if the distance between any two POIs is within 1 km, we set the edge weight to 1, otherwise set the edge weight to 0. And we set the hyperparameter α in the loss function of the graph embedding representation to 0.1. We set the learning rate to 0.0001, use gaussian distribution random to initialize the model weights (mean value is 0, standard deviation is 0.01), set batch size as 256, and select Adam optimization method. The dropout ratio was set to 0.2. The ratio of negative samples to positive samples is 4. In the part of time pattern-POI relevance representation, we set the embedding dimension of POIs and time patterns to 16. In the part of user-POI interaction representation, we set the embedding dimension of users and POIs to 32, and the number of hidden layers to 3, using a tower structure. The dimension of the latter layer is half of the previous one, that is, the dimension of each layer is 64, 32, 16, respectively. In Sect. 4.3, we will analyze the impact of the dimension and number of hidden layers on the performance of the recommendation model through comparative experiments. For the objective function of the model, we will also make a comparative analyses on the setting of hyperparameter λ_U and λ_P in the following experimental analyses, so as to select the optimal parameters for the model.

Comparative Baselines: The comparative algorithms used in our experiments includes the traditional recommendation method based on collaborative filtering, the recommendation methods integrating geographical factor and social factor, and the latest recommendation methods based on neural networks.

- **BPR-MF** [6]: a recommendation model based on bayesian personalized ranking, which optimizes the matrix factorization model by using the pair-wise loss.
- **SoRec** [4]: a social recommendation algorithm which models users and items by decomposing social relationship matrix and rating matrix and sharing users' latent feature matrix.
- **GE** [12]: a POI recommendation model based on graph embedding, which joinly embeds bipartite graphs of POIs, time, regions and behaviors in latent space.
- **NeuMF** [2]: a recommendation model based on neural networks, which utilizes the multi-layer perceptron to model the latent interaction between the user and the item.
- **PACE** [14]: a POI recommendation model based on neural networks, which integrates context factors and collaborative filtering method into a semi-supervised learning framework.

4.2 Performance Comparison

According to the statistical results of the comparison experiments on the two datasets in Tables 2 and 3, our proposed model is greatly improved in terms of prediction accuracy and ranking quality, which proves the effectiveness of the proposed method. In addition, it can be seen that GE and SoRec are superior to BPR-MF, which shows the effectiveness of integrating geographical factors and social factors. NeuMF also outperforms GE, SoRec, and BPR-MF methods, demonstrating that neural networks method offers significant advantages in modeling latent interactions between users and POIs. When compared with NeuMF, it can be seen that the HR of PACE is close to NeuMF, but PACE's MRR is better. It indicates that PACE integrating the context information improve the ranking quality of recommendation. And Comparing with the PACE method, the recommendation accuracy and ranking performance of our proposed model SG-NeuRec are improved to a certain extent.

Table 2. Experimental results on the Gowalla dataset.

Method	HR@5	HR@10	HR@20	MRR@20
BPR-MF	0.3018	0.3364	0.4039	0.0986
SoRec	0.376	0.4217	0.4836	0.1103
GE	0.4221	0.4782	0.5103	0.1409
NeuMF	0.5139	0.5787	0.6394	0.1749
PACE	0.5208	0.5914	0.643	0.203
SG-NeuRec	**0.5521**	**0.6203**	**0.763**	**0.2541**

Table 3. Experimental results on the Yelp dataset.

Method	HR@5	HR@10	HR@20	MRR@20
BPR-MF	0.258	0.3116	0.3904	0.103
SoRec	0.335	0.4382	0.4701	0.1309
GE	0.3696	0.4501	0.5113	0.1607
NeuMF	0.4119	0.5118	0.6128	0.1617
PACE	0.4299	0.521	0.6209	0.181
SG-NeuRec	**0.5023**	**0.589**	**0.7156**	**0.2159**

4.3   Model Analyses

Balance Parameters Settings: In the objective function of our model, there are two balance parameters, λ_U and λ_P, controlling the loss weight of social graph embedding and geographical graph embedding respectively. In the experiment, we fixed one parameter and change the value of another parameter to evaluate the impact of parameter on recommendation performance, so as to select the optimal model parameters. Figure 3 shows the change curves of MRR@20 that vary with λ_U and λ_P on the two datasets. We set λ_P fixed to 0.2 and 0.1 in Gowalla dataset and Yelp dataset respectively. The MRR@20 achieves the maximum on the two datasets when λ_U is 0.15. And we set λ_U fixed to 0.15 on Gowalla dataset and Yelp dataset.The MRR@20 achieves the maximum on Gowalla dataset when λ_P is 0.2, and the MRR@20 achieves the maximum on Yelp dataset when λ_P is 0.1. This may have something to do with the fact that the number of POIs in Gowalla dataset is larger than Yelp, and that the geographical factor of POIs plays a bigger role.

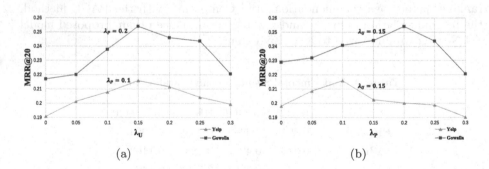

(a)   (b)

Fig. 3. Impact of balance parameters on recommendation performance of MRR@20.

Hide Layer Settings: By changing the number of hidden layers and the dimensional capacity of each hidden layer, we explore the impact of the different design of hidden layers on recommendation performance. In the experiment, we change the embedding dimension size of users and POIs, and then change the dimension capacity of the hidden layers accordingly. For example, if the embedding dimension of users and POIs is 32 and the number of hidden layers is 3, the dimension of the each hidden layer will be 64, 32, 16. As shown in Tables 4 and 5, when the embedding dimension of users and POIs is 32 and the number of hidden layers is 3, the MRR@20 of the recommendation model achieves maximal value.

Table 4. MRR@20 results of different hidden layers on Gowalla dataset.

Dimension	Layer = 0	Layer = 1	Layer = 2	Layer = 3	Layer = 4
8	0.211	0.2219	—	—	—
16	0.2127	0.2368	0.2513	—	—
32	0.2183	0.2424	0.2522	**0.2541**	—
64	0.229	0.2437	0.2528	0.2532	0.2528

Table 5. MRR@20 results of different hidden layers on Yelp dataset.

Dimension	Layer = 0	Layer = 1	Layer = 2	Layer = 3	Layer = 4
8	0.1823	0.2076	—	—	—
16	0.1964	0.2083	0.212	—	—
32	0.1973	0.2089	0.2136	**0.2159**	—
64	0.1987	0.2102	0.2117	0.2142	0.2137

5 Conclusion and Future Work

In this paper, we propose a neural networks POI recommendation model named SG-NeuRec. Our model integrates the users' social relationship information and the POIs' geographical information. Under the framework of a neural networks model, the multi-layer perceptron is utilized to learn the latent representation of interactions between users and POIs. We also design a shallow network to model the relevance between users' accessing time patterns and POIs. We unified user-POI interaction representation and time pattern-POI relevance representation under the same framework to improve the performance of POI recommendation. Finally, extensive experiments on two real world datasets show the effectiveness of the proposed model. In the future, we will consider extracting the features of users' comments on POIs to further model users' emotional preferences for their check-ins.

References

1. Cai, Z., He, Z.: Trading private range counting over big IoT data. In: The 39th IEEE International Conference on Distributed Computing Systems (ICDCS 2019) (2019)
2. He, X., Liao, L., Zhang, H., Nie, L., Hu, X., Chua, T.S.: Neural collaborative filtering. In: Proceedings of the 26th International Conference on World Wide Web, pp. 173–182. ACM (2017)
3. Lian, D., Zhao, C., Xie, X., Sun, G., Chen, E., Rui, Y.: GeoMF: joint geographical modeling and matrix factorization for point-of-interest recommendation. In: Proceedings of the 20th ACM SIGKDD International Conference on Knowledge Discovery and Data Mining, pp. 831–840. ACM (2014)
4. Ma, H., Yang, H., Lyu, M.R., King, I.: SoRec: social recommendation using probabilistic matrix factorization. In: Proceedings of the 17th ACM Conference on Information and Knowledge Management, pp. 931–940. ACM (2008)
5. Qi, L., et al.: Structural balance theory-based e-commerce recommendation over big rating data. IEEE Trans. Big Data 4(3), 301–312 (2018)
6. Rendle, S., Freudenthaler, C., Gantner, Z., Schmidt-Thieme, L.: BPR: Bayesian personalized ranking from implicit feedback. In: Proceedings of the 25th Conference on Uncertainty in Artificial Intelligence (2009)
7. Wang, D., Cui, P., Zhu, W.: Structural deep network embedding. In: Proceedings of the 22nd ACM SIGKDD International Conference on Knowledge Discovery and Data Mining, pp. 1225–1234. ACM (2016)
8. Wang, Y., Cai, Z., Tong, X., Gao, Y., Yin, G.: Truthful incentive mechanism with location privacy-preserving for mobile crowdsourcing systems. Comput. Netw. 135, 32–43 (2018)
9. Wang, Y., Cai, Z., Zhan, Z., Gong, Y., Tong, X.: An optimization and auction based incentive mechanism to maximize social welfare for mobile crowdsourcing. IEEE Trans. Comput. Soc. Syst. (2019)
10. Wang, Y., Yin, G., Cai, Z., Dong, Y., Dong, H.: A trust-based probabilistic recommendation model for social networks. J. Netw. Comput. Appl. 55, 59–67 (2015)
11. Xia, X., Yu, J., Zhang, S., et al.: Trusted service scheduling and optimization strategy design of service recommendation. Secur. Commun. Netw. 2017, 1–9 (2017)
12. Xie, M., Yin, H., Wang, H., Xu, F., Chen, W., Wang, S.: Learning graph-based poi embedding for location-based recommendation. In: Proceedings of the 25th ACM International on Conference on Information and Knowledge Management, pp. 15–24. ACM (2016)
13. Yanwei, X., Lianyong, Q., Wanchun, D., et al.: Privacy-preserving and scalable service recommendation based on simhash in a distributed cloud environment. Complexity 2017, 1–9 (2017)
14. Yang, C., Bai, L., Zhang, C., Yuan, Q., Han, J.: Bridging collaborative filtering and semi-supervised learning: a neural approach for poi recommendation. In: Proceedings of the 23rd ACM SIGKDD International Conference on Knowledge Discovery and Data Mining, pp. 1245–1254. ACM (2017)
15. Yuan, Q., Cong, G., Ma, Z., Sun, A., Thalmann, N.M.: Time-aware point-of-interest recommendation. In: Proceedings of the 36th International ACM SIGIR Conference on Research and Development in Information Retrieval, pp. 363–372. ACM (2013)
16. Zhang, J.D., Chow, C.Y.: GeoSoCa: exploiting geographical, social and categorical correlations for point-of-interest recommendations. In: Proceedings of the 38th International ACM SIGIR Conference on Research and Development in Information Retrieval, pp. 443–452. ACM (2015)

A Hybrid Approach for Recognizing Web Crawlers

Weiping Zhu[1]([envelope]), Hang Gao[1], Zongjian He[2], Jiangbo Qin[1], and Bo Han[1]

[1] School of Computer Science, Wuhan University, Wuhan, People's Republic of China
{wpzhu,gaohangcs,qinjiangbo,bhan}@whu.edu.cn
[2] Center for eResearch, University of Auckland, Auckland, New Zealand
jason.he@auckland.ac.nz

Abstract. In recent years, web crawlers have been widely used for collecting data from the Internet. Accurately recognizing web crawlers can help to better utilize friendly crawlers while stopping malicious ones. Existing web crawler recognition researches have difficulties in handling new crawlers, such as distributed crawlers, proxy based crawlers, and browser engine based crawlers. Moreover, it is non-trivial to achieve both high identification accuracy and high response time simultaneously. To tackle these issues, we propose a novel approach to web crawler recognition which combines real-time recognition methods based on heuristic rules and offline recognition methods based on machine learning. The aforementioned problems are well solved in this approach. The advantage of this approach is that both accuracy and efficiency are improved. We build a website and analyze its web access log using the proposed method. According to the results, the proposed approach achieves desirable performance in both accuracy and efficiency.

Keywords: Web crawler recognition · Machine learning ·
Hybrid approach

1 Introduction

In the last decade, data collection becomes increasingly important for many fields in our work and daily life. A web crawler is a computer program used to acquire data from different websites. It has been widely used in many applications such as search engine [1], software testing [2], and data analysis systems [3,4].

Web crawlers offer convenience for data collection, however, cause new problems. These problems mainly include QoS degrading, inaccuracy of data analysis, and business concerns. First, without proper restrictions, crawling behaviors generate additional work load at the server, therefore affecting the QoS of normal visits. It is reported that 40%–60% traffic on the Internet comes from web crawlers [5]. Second, web crawlers deteriorate the data analysis results based on the visit of websites. Most data analysis assumed that the visits of websites are from normal users, which is not hold when many of them are from web crawlers.

© Springer Nature Switzerland AG 2019
E. S. Biagioni et al. (Eds.): WASA 2019, LNCS 11604, pp. 507–519, 2019.
https://doi.org/10.1007/978-3-030-23597-0_41

Third, some data in the websites are of important commercial usage, and prohibited to be collected and used for any other purpose. Therefore, it is highly demanded that an approach can be developed to recognize web crawlers and block their access if needed. We call such technology web crawler recognition.

Compared with rapid development of web crawlers, few researches have been done on crawler identification. Existing web crawler recognition researches can be mainly classified into two categories: heuristic rules based, and machine learning based. The first category utilizes the rules (e.g., whether users request the *robots.txt* file) to recognize web crawlers, while the second category utilizes machine learning methods [7]. Although these excellent approaches perform in a satisfactory manner in their target scenarios, they encounter difficulties to recognize web crawlers using new techniques, such as distributed web crawlers, web crawlers based on proxy servers, and web crawlers based on PhantomJS, which is a web browser engine that can be invoked by programs. Moreover, they cannot achieve high identification accuracy. The heuristic rules based approach misses recognizing complex web crawlers due to the limited number of rules, and the machine learning based approach requires much time to train and update the classification model.

In this paper, we propose a hybrid system that uses both heuristic rules and machine learning to recognize the visit of web crawlers. The proposed heuristic rules can effectively detect the visits of web crawlers using proxy servers and PhantomJS. The proposed machine learning approach has several advantages, including handling the behaviors of distributed web crawlers, automatic labeling of sample data, and extracting nine effective features for web crawler recognition. We combine these heuristic rules and machine learning technology to achieve better identification accuracy and low latency. A real dataset is used to validate the proposed approach and the results show the approach achieve desirable performance. In summary, this paper offers the following contributions.

- We proposed two new heuristic rules for web crawler recognizing. These rules can effectively detect the visits of web crawlers using proxy servers and using PhantomJS.
- We proposed a machine learning approach for web crawler recognizing. The key techniques in it including distributed access handling and automatic labeling method can also be used in other web log analysis.
- We proposed a hybrid method combining heuristic rules and machine learning to recognize the visit of web crawlers. This approach achieves better identification accuracy and less latency.

2   Related Works

Significant progress has been made on crawler identification technology. They are mainly be classified into categories, heuristic rules based approaches and machine learning based approaches.

Heuristic rules based approaches recognize the web crawlers based on predefined features. Chan proposed an web crawler recognition approach based on website traffic [8]. Fan et al. recognized crawlers based on trap technique [9]. They use trap URLs to track the behaviors of human users and web crawlers, and then analyze the difference of these two kinds of behaviors. Doran et al. made a comparison between human users and web crawlers when access network resources [10]. They found out that human users tend to visit image resources and crawlers tend to visit html text resources. In addition, human users are less frequent to trigger 404 errors than crawlers. Jacob et al. proposed a method of crawler detection based on the difference of human users traffic and crawlers traffic, even though the web crawler visits are through proxies [11].

For machine learning based approaches, Jacob et al. firstly proposed the solution to distributed crawlers and used large scale real dataset to evaluate their methods [11]. Wan used heuristic rules for train samples in machine learning to detect web crawlers, by using SVM techniques [12]. They detected the web crawlers on the early stage and then restrained the crawlers. Suchacka et al. applied Bayesian methods to crawler detection based on the features of user session [13]. Their experimental results showed that the classification model based on cluster analysis achieved high accuracy.

Both the above two categories of approaches have advantages and disadvantages. Heuristic rules outperform machine learning in response time, while machine learning technology can get more accurate results than heuristic rules. Some crawler recognition technologies achieve good result in certain environments, however, due to the development of crawlers, some new web crawlers cannot be identified. At present, very little research has been conducted on combining machine learning technology with heuristic rules for crawler recognition. The work [12] tried to combined to them, but requires to add URL marker in the part of website preprocessing. This paper investigates the web crawler recognition based on both heuristic rules and machine learning technology.

In our system, we combines heuristic rules based approach and machine learning based approach to achieve better results.

3   Proposed Crawler Recognition Approach

The crawler recognition approach proposed in this study combines the real-time recognition based on heuristic rules and off-line recognition based on machine learning. By using heuristic rules, we can obtain good real-time performance and help labeling the sessions for machine learning based approach. By using machine learning, we can find out hidden web crawlers, such as distributed web crawlers, and hence improve the recognition accuracy. Moreover, the results of machine learning can be further used to improve the accuracy of heuristic rules. Compared with solutions using only a single approach, heuristic rules and machine learning based approach compensate each other in hybrid approach and thus achieve better results. In the following subsections, we illustrate heuristic rules processing and machine learning based processing in details.

3.1 Heuristic Rules Based Recognition

Heuristic rules are predefined conditions that can distinguish the web visits of humans from web crawlers. Using heuristic rules for web crawler recognition can achieve real time performance. In this paper, we adopt the following heuristic rules:

- *Whether the user request visits the robots.txt file.* Generally speaking, human users do not visit the *robots.txt* file, but web crawlers often visit this file to determine which parts of a website meet their requirements.
- *Whether the user request is from proxy servers.* Some web crawlers use a proxy to hide themselves. There are three types of proxy, transparent proxy, anonymous proxy, and high anonymous proxy. The using of transparent proxy and anonymous proxy can be detected by analyzing the headers of the requests. For the requests using high anonymous proxy, the headers are removed, so it is difficult to distinguish it from the visits of human users. We builds a database to store known proxy servers, and compare the web visits with this database to determine the web crawlers.
- *Whether the user request has a known crawler user-agent.* There is a list[1] of all open-source crawlers' user-agent. By checking the visits with this list, web crawlers could be detected in real-time.
- *Whether the user request uses PhantomJS.* PhantomJS is a headless web content engine scriptable with a JavaScript API [14]. It can be used to simulate the behaviors of web browsers and hence make the visits quite similar with human's visits. We propose a method to identify the visits of web crawlers using PhantomJS. We first write a Javascript and embed it into web pages. If the requests are from PhantomJS, this Javascript will be triggered and our system is notified.
- *Whether the user request visits the trap URLs.* We can detect web crawlers by placing some trap URLs in the web sites. Once the web crawler sends request via trap URLs, the system recognize them immediately.

It is noted that the rules to handle high anonymous proxy, PhantomJS, and using trap URLs are developed by us, while the others are from existing works. We do not use more rules in this module because we want to achieve a quick response. More complex processing are left for the machine learning recognition module.

3.2 Machine Learning Based Recognition

Although using heuristic rules can recognize web crawlers in real-time, it has difficulties to recognize the hidden web crawlers. Machine learning technology can be used to solve this problem. By utilizing supervised learning, we label some visits of web sites as either from humans or from web crawlers, and then train a classification model. Compared with a typical process of supervised learning, our

---

[1] https://github.com/monperrus/crawler-user-agents.

Table 1. Improved results of session segmentation

Segmentation method	Number of split sessions	Number of real sessions	Precision rate	Recall rate
SD ($\theta = 25$)	223	109	48.879%	80.147%
SD ($\theta = 30$)	215	118	54.884%	86.765%
SD ($\theta = 10$)	247	103	41.700%	75.735%
SD ($\theta = 12$)	236	94	39.830%	69.118%
AI	466	80	17.167%	58.824%

approach has several differences. First, we propose an improved session segment approach. Second, we propose an automatic labeling method for the web site visits. Third, we determine nine features for the web crawler recognition problem. We then illustrate our approaches in details.

Session Segmentation. Session is an important concept in web analytics. A session is a unit of measurement of a user's actions taken within a period of time or with regard to completion of a task. Session segmentation is to split an access log of a web site into proper sessions [15]. Existing works of session segmentation first group the access records by their source IP addresses, and then split each of them based on time-oriented criterions such as fixed time interval between requests [16–18], adaptive time interval between requests [19], or duration of a session [20, 21]. These approaches have problems when the web crawler runs in distributed environment. Because the requests have different source IP addresses, they might be incorrectly split into different sessions.

We further show the problem with access logs from America National Philosophical Counseling Association (NPCA for short) [22]. The logs span from July 18, 2011 to January 10, 2014 with a total of 580,123 access records. Table 1 shows the results of existing approaches where FI denotes the approach based on fixed time interval between requests, AI denotes the approach based on adaptive time interval between requests, SD denotes the approach based on session duration, and θ denotes the threshold in corresponding approaches.

In order to recognize the sessions of distributed web crawlers, we proposes an improved approach. We found out that the requests from distributed web crawlers tend to have the same user agents and the same first two IP address segments. Although these access records have different IP addresses, the access time is completely coherent, and the user agents for each request are exactly the same. Therefore, it can be judged that these access requests come from the same source. Based on this, when the web log is processed, the requests with the same user agent and the first two IP segment can be grouped into the same session. Algorithm 1 shows the pseudocode of the improved method.

According to Table 1, the approach based on session duration and a threshold of 30 min achieved the best results, with the precision rate and recall rate of

54.884% and 86.765% respectively. So we perform session segmentation based on session duration (threshold is set to 30) in our approach.

Algorithm 1. Improved session segmentation algorithm

Input: *requests* - http requests
Output: *sessions* - http session segments
  request_dict = MERGEIP(*requests*)
  for *requests* **in** *request_dict.values* **do**
    sessions.add(SESSIONIZE(*requests*))
  end for

  function SESSIONIZE(*requests*)
    for *request* **in** *requests* **do**
      for *session* **in** *active_sessions* **do**
        if *request.time − session.firstTime > theta* **then**
          session.close()
        else
          session = **new** *Session*()
          session.add(*request*)
        end if
      end for
    end for
  end function

  function MERGEIP(*requests*)
    for *request* **in** *requests* **do**
      if *prefix_list.contains*(GETPREFIX(*request*)) **and**
        user_agent_dict[GETPREFIX(*request*)] == *request.userAgent* **then**
      requests_dict[GETPREFIX(*request*)].*add*(*request*)
      else
        prefix_list.add(*request*)
        user_agent_dict.add(GETPREFIX(*request*), *request.userAgent*)
      end if
    end for
  end function

  function GETPREFIX(*request*)
    ip = *request.ip*
    fragment_list = *ip*.split(".")
    return *fragment_list*[0].append(".").append.*fragment_list*[1])
  end function

Session Labeling. After converting the web logs into sessions, we need to label the sessions by either from humans or from web crawlers. Typically, the number of sessions could be extremely huge, we cannot label them manually. We propose a heuristic rule based labeling method for solving this problem. The basic logic of this method is to first determine whether the access record in this session has been marked as a web crawler before. If so, this session will be marked as a web crawler; otherwise the next discrimination will be carried out. Second, determine whether the access record in this session belongs to the IP of the known web crawler or not. If so, the session will be marked as a web crawler. Then, determine whether the access record in this session belongs to the user agent of the known web crawler. If so, the session will be marked as a web crawler. Finally, determine whether the access record in this session accesses the robots.txt file. If so, the session will be marked as a web crawler; otherwise, the session will be marked as a normal user. Three heuristic rules are used to label these sessions, and the last condition is used to check if the session has been recognized as a web crawler previously in case of inconsistency.

Feature Extraction. Based on the study of behaviors of human beings and web crawlers [10], we choose nine features for our classification model to distinguish web crawlers from humans. We illustrate them in detail as follows.

- *Percentage of requests with error codes.* The main difference between the behaviors of a human and a web crawler is that a web crawler can more easily access some non-existent links because of exploratory behaviors, and thus generates erroneous requests and responses. Therefore, web crawlers incur more requests with error codes such as 40X and 50X.
- *Percentage of requests with HEAD method.* HEAD method of HTTP request is used to get the header information of a response. It is used to obtain the length of the content in advance for later processing, which is commonly used for crawlers to determine and adjust their crawling strategies. Therefore, higher percentage of requests with HEAD method indicates higher possibilities of web crawlers.
- *Percentage of requests for HTML files.* Requests from humans always access the HMTL file and the resource file as well. For some web crawlers, the useful information only exists in HTML files, so they choose not to access the resource files but only the HTML files.
- *Percentage of requests for image files.* For the web crawlers aiming to collect image files, the only thing they care about is image files. Therefore, higher percentage of requests for image files indicates the access of web crawlers.
- *Percentage of requests for binary files.* Same as the previous feature, some web crawlers focus on the binary files such as PDF files, PhotoShop files and so on. Therefore, higher percentage of requests for binary files indicates higher possibilities of web crawlers.
- *Percentage of requests without referrer.* Requests without referrer indicates a direct access rather than jumped from other web pages. Normal humans usually browser a web page while a web crawler is often designed to directly access a web page according to the URL queue generated by the web crawler. Therefore, higher percentage of requests without referrer indicates the access of web crawlers.

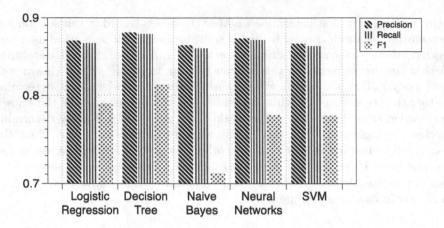

Fig. 1. Precision and Recall of different machine learning models.

- *Percentage of requests at night.* During night time (2:00am–8:00am), requests are more likely sent by web crawlers than humans, since people are usually asleep.
- *Deviation of time between two requests.* Interval between two requests is used to measure the stability of the requests. The difference between behaviors of a web crawler and a normal human is that a normal human access web pages more randomly, therefore the interval between two requests is greater than a web crawler.
- *Number of requests in one session.* The number of requests in one session is also called the length of the session. By studying the behaviors of web crawlers and human beings, we know that the session of a web crawler lasts longer than human beings. Therefore larger number of requests in one session indicates the access of web crawlers.

Model Training. Through previous steps, we build a labeled dataset for model training. There are several machine learning predictive models can be used for our purpose including logistic regression, decision tree, neural networks, naive Bayes and SVM (Support Vector Machine). In this paper, we use a java machine learning library—Weka[2] for model training.

For choosing a proper model for our problem, we compare the performance of each model with the labeled dataset by conducting 5 groups of experiments. 10-fold cross-validation method is used on this dataset to evaluate the performance. Figure 1 shows the precision and recall rate of each machine learning model. According to Fig. 1, decision tree has the largest precision and recall.

Taking training time, precision and recall into account, we choose decision tree as our system model, because it has the greatest precision and recall, and

---

[2] Weka is a collection of machine learning algorithms for data mining tasks. Its website is https://www.cs.waikato.ac.nz/ml/weka/.

Table 2. Results of heuristic rule based approach

	Predicted:Human	Predicted:Robot
Actual:Human	317	13
Actual:Robot	310	63

Table 3. Results of machine learning approach

	Predicted:Human	Predicted:Robot
Actual:Human	209	121
Actual:Robot	67	306

relatively short training time. Another reason for choosing decision tree model is that it is more interpretive than other models.

4 Performance Evaluation

We build a website for testing and recording users' behaviors. We use the access log data of it to evaluate our proposed approach. The time spans from July 29, 2018 to September 4, 2018. A total of 35679 access requests and 703 independent IP addresses are recorded. In addition to comparing heuristic rule approach, machine learning approach and hybrid approach, we also compared Markov chain model and Adaboost algorithm.

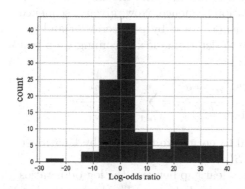
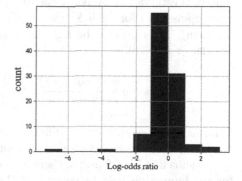

Fig. 2. Log-odds ratio of human   **Fig. 3.** Log-odds ratio of crawler

4.1 Comparison Experiment

Markov Chain Model. We used the Markov chain model to test the test set. We use the status code returned from the page as the state, and divide the data

Table 4. Results of hybrid approach

	Predicted:Human	Predicted:Robot
Actual:Human	207	123
Actual:Robot	36	337

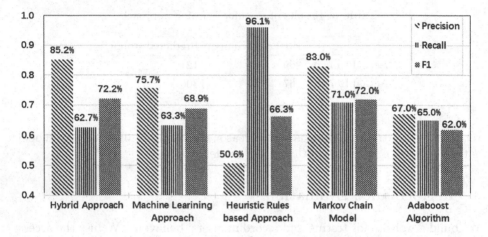

Fig. 4. Comparison between different approaches.

set into training set and test set (30% test set). Then, the crawler in the test set is separated from the user's normal access, and the respective visiting sequence is used to establish the respective observation sequence, and the state transition matrix is established by using the observation sequence. Now, given a sequence x, compute p(x) for each Markov chain, denote these by p(x | crawler) and p(x | human). Then we use the log-odds ratio to determine if x is coming from real crawler or not [23].

$$S(x) = log\frac{p(x|crawler)}{p(x|human)} = log\frac{\prod_{i=0}^{n} a_{xix_{i+1}}^{crawler}}{\prod_{i=0}^{n} a_{xix_{i+1}}^{human}} = \sum_{i=1}^{n} log\frac{a_{xix_{i+1}}^{crawler}}{a_{xix_{i+1}}^{human}}$$

Lengths of the sequences are different and to normalize this ratio by length, we used length-normalized log-odds ratio of $S(x)/|x|$.

As shown in Figs. 2 and 3, there exists a clear gap between the log-odds ratios for the human visiting behavior and the crawler behavior. The higher the log-odds score, the higher the probability that a given sequence is from the human visiting behavior. We have calculated a threshold score for our test data set to conclude the type of a given sequence. Further we have applied the methodology another new data set. Threshold score to differentiate crawler behavior from the human visiting behavior varies from site to site.

Adaboost Algorithm. We used the Adaboost algorithm to test the test set. We used the request method returned from the page, the response status code, the number of bytes sent, and the user agent as the state, and divided the data set into a training set and a test set (30% test set), where the test set was used not only as an adjustment parameter but also to measure how good the model was. For a given parameter, we start with a wide range of coarse tuning parameters, and then fine tuning with a small range. Here, we select the maximum number of iterations of the weak learner, n_estimators, as 50.

4.2 Precision, Recall, F_1 Measure

The performance of different approaches are shown in Tables 2, 3 and 4 and Fig. 4 where the first three table are the detailed results of heuristic rules based approach, machine learning approach, and our hybrid approach, and the last figure compares these approaches and the two approaches of the comparison experiment in terms of *Precision rate, Recall rate* and F_1 *measure*. It can be seen that the precision of the hybrid approach is 85.2%, which is greater than the machine learning approach, heuristic rules based approach and Markov chain model. The recall of hybrid approach is 62.7%, which is less than machine learning approach, heuristic rules based approach and Markov chain model. The indicator used to measure the overall performance of a system is the F1 value. Because the F1 value takes into account the accuracy and recall rate, it can effectively reflect the overall performance of the system. It can be seen that the F1 value of the web crawler recognition system is 72.2%, which is the best compared to several other methods. Considering these indicators, the hybrid method combining machine learning approach with heuristic rules can find web crawlers more effectively.

5 Conclusion

In this paper, we propose a novel web crawler recognition approach which combines heuristic rules and machine learning. We proposed two new heuristic rules for web crawler recognizing. These rules can effectively detect the visits of web crawlers using proxy servers and using PhantomJS. We also implemented machine learning approach for web crawler recognizing and illustrate adequate details in it including behaviors of distributed access handling, automatic labeling of sample data, and extracting nine effective features of web crawler visits. By combining the heuristic rules and machine learning, this approach achieves better identification accuracy.

Acknowledgments. This research is supported in part by National Key R&D Program of China No. 2018YFC1604000, Chutian Scholars Program of Hubei, Luojia Young Scholar Funds of Wuhan University No. 1503/600400001, 2018 Science and Technology Transformation Project of Grain Administration of Hubei Province "Grain and Oil Quality & Safety Assurance System Research", and Applied Basic Research Program of WuHan City, China No. 2017010201010117.

References

1. da Silva, A.S., Veloso, E.A., Golgher, P.B., Ribeiro-Neto, B., Laender, A.H.F., Ziviani, N.: Cobweb-a crawler for the Brazilian web. In: 6th International Symposium on String Processing and Information Retrieval, pp. 184–191 (1999)
2. Raina, S., Agarwal, A.P.: How crawlers aid regression testing in web applications: the state of the art. Int. J. Comput. Appl. **68**(14), 33–38 (2014)
3. Lau, C.H., Tao, X., Tjondronegoro, D., Li, Y.: Retrieving information from microblog using pattern mining and relevance feedback. In: Xiang, Y., Pathan, M., Tao, X., Wang, H. (eds.) ICDKE 2012. LNCS, vol. 7696, pp. 152–160. Springer, Heidelberg (2012). https://doi.org/10.1007/978-3-642-34679-8_15
4. Cai, R., Yang, J.-M., Lai, W., Wang, Y., Zhang, L.: irobot: An intelligent crawler for web forums. In: Proceedings of the 17th International Conference on World Wide Web, pp. 447–456. ACM, New York (2008)
5. Lu, P.: Bring you into the world of crawler and anti-crawler. Softw. Integr. Circ. **12**, 12–13 (2016)
6. CtripTech: This is enough for anti-crawler technology, June 2016. https://segmentfault.com/a/1190000005840672
7. Friesel, R.: PhantomJS cookbook over 70 recipes to help boost the productivity of your applications using real-world testing with PhantomJS (2014)
8. Chan, L.: Anti crawler technology in the era of big data. Comput. Inf. Technol. **24**(6), 2016
9. Fan, C., Yuan, B., Yu, Z., Xu, L.: Spider detection based on trap techniques. J. Comput. Appl. **30**(7), 1782–1784 (2010)
10. Doran, D., Morillo, K., Gokhale, S.S.: A comparison of web robot and human requests. In: Proceedigs of IEEE/ACM International Conference on Advances in Social Networks Analysis and Mining, pp. 1374–1380 (2013)
11. Jacob, G., Kirda, E., Kruegel, C., Vigna, G.: PUBCRAWL: protecting users and businesses from CRAWLers. In: Proceedings of USENIX Conference on Security Symposium, p. 25 (2013)
12. Wan, S., Li, Y., Sun, K.: Protecting web contents against persistent distributed crawlers. In: Proceedings of IEEE International Conference on Communications (2017)
13. Suchacka, G., Sobków, M.: Detection of internet robots using a Bayesian approach. In: Proceedings of IEEE International Conference on Cybernetics, pp. 365–370 (2015)
14. phantomjs.org: Full web stack, no browser required, March 2018. http://phantomjs.org/
15. Stassopoulou, A., Dikaiakos, M.D.: Web robot detection: a probabilistic reasoning approach. Comput. Netw. **53**(3), 265–278 (2009)
16. Lalani, A.S.: Data mining of web access logs. In: Hybrid Intelligent Systems (2003)
17. Tan, P.N., Kumar, V.: Discovery of web robot sessions based on their navigational patterns. Data Min. Knowl. Discov. **6**, 9–35 (2002)
18. Srivastava, J., Cooley, R., Deshpande, M., Tan, P.N.: Web usage mining: discovery and applications of usage patterns from web data. ACM SIGKDD Explor. Newsl. **1**(2), 12–23 (2000)
19. Zhuang, L., Kou, Z., Zhang, C.: Session identification based on time interval in web log mining. J. Tsinghua Univ. **163**, 389–396 (2004)
20. Spiliopoulou, M., Mobasher, B., Berendt, B., Nakagawa, M.: A framework for the evaluation of session reconstruction heuristics in web-usage analysis. Informs J. Comput. **15**(2), 171–190 (2003)

21. Catledge, L.D., Pitkow, J.E.: Characterizing browsing strategies in the world-wide web. In: Proceedings of the Third International World-Wide Web Conference on Technology, Tools and Applications, pp. 1065–1073 (1995)
22. npcassoc.org, July 2011. http://npcassoc.org/log/access.log
23. Algiryage, N.: Distinguishing real web crawlers from fakes: Googlebot example. In: 2018 Moratuwa Engineering Research Conference (MERCon), pp. 13–18 (2018)

Contextual Combinatorial Cascading Thompson Sampling

Zhenyu Zhu, Liusheng Huang$^{(\boxtimes)}$, and Hongli Xu

University of Science and Technology of China, Hefei, China
zzy7758@mail.ustc.edu.cn, {lshuang,honglixu}@ustc.edu.cn

Abstract. We design and analyze contextual combinatorial cascading Thompson sampling (C^3-TS). C^3-TS is a Bayesian heuristic to balance the exploration-exploitation tradeoff in the cascading bandit model. And it incorporates the linear structure to share information among different items. These two important features allow us to prove an expected cumulative regret bound of the form $\tilde{O}(d\sqrt{KT})$, where d and K are the dimension of the feature space and the length of the chosen list respectively, and T is the number of time steps. This regret bound matches the regret bounds for the state-of-the-art UCB-based algorithms. More importantly, it is the first theoretical guarantee on a contextual Thompson sampling algorithm for cascading bandit problem. Empirical results demonstrate the advantage of C^3-TS over existing UCB-based algorithms and non-contextual TS in terms of both the cumulative reward and time complexity.

1 Introduction

Most recommendation systems recommend an ordered list of candidate items due to the limited space. The user examines the list in a sequential manner and clicks on the first attractive item. The recommendation system observes the feedback of the user, but it can only obtain partial information. The feedback reveals that the items before the clicked item are not attractive and the items after the clicked item are unexamined. This kind of interaction is often formulated as the cascade model [9]. The key assumption in the cascade model is that the probability of the user clicking on each item is independent. Under this assumption, the optimal list that maximizes the click-through rate is the ordered list of the most attractive items. The cascade model is intuitive but effective in characterizing user behaviors.

In this paper, we consider the contextual cascading bandit model. In the contextual cascading bandit [12,16], the expected reward of an item is assumed to be the inner product between the contextual vector of the item and a stationary but unknown user parameter vector. At each time step, the learning agent recommends an ordered list of items to the user and adjusts its recommendation strategy according to the user feedbacks. The goal of the learning agent is to maximize the cumulative rewards after T rounds. This requires to balance

© Springer Nature Switzerland AG 2019
E. S. Biagioni et al. (Eds.): WASA 2019, LNCS 11604, pp. 520–532, 2019.
https://doi.org/10.1007/978-3-030-23597-0_42

the tradeoff between exploiting the current information to maximize immediate reward and exploring new information that may improve future performance.

Two popular approaches have been introduced to balance the exploration-exploitation tradeoff: the Upper Confidence Bound (UCB) [10] and Thompson Sampling (TS) [3]. UCB utilizes the optimism in the face of uncertainty principle and evaluates the items by their highest possible reward. While Thompson sampling is a Bayesian heuristic and selects an item corresponding to its probability of being optimal. In this paper, we mainly focus on the design and analysis of Thompson sampling algorithm because of its advantage over UCB in both empirical performance [4, 14] and computational efficiency [15]. In the decision-making process, our algorithm estimates the expected reward of all items based on the historical feedbacks and the contextual information and selects a list to recommend according to its probability of being the optimal solution.

Although the regret bound of UCB-based cascading algorithm has been thoroughly studied [12, 16], the randomness of Thompson sampling brings about new challenges. The main challenge is to control the variance of reward estimator of each item. The variance represents the uncertainty of the learning agent and is used to balance the exploration-exploitation tradeoff in most bandit algorithms. Under some reasonable assumptions, we use the matrix martingale theory and existing analysis techniques for contextual bandits to analyze the regret bound of C^3-TS. We prove an upper bound of $\tilde{O}(d\sqrt{TK})$ for the expected cumulative regret, where d is the dimension of feature space, T is the number of the time step, and K is the number of recommended items. This bound matches the regret bounds for state-of-the-art UCB-based algorithms. And it is the first theoretical analysis on a contextual Thompson sampling algorithm for stochastic combinatorial cascading bandit problem. We also experiment on two real-world datasets to demonstrate the advantage of our model and algorithm over existing algorithms. The empirical results show that our algorithm outperforms UCB-based algorithms and non-contextual cascading TS [5] in terms of both the prediction accuracy and the time complexity.

The rest of this paper is organized as follows. Section 2 introduces the basic notations and assumptions and provides a detailed description of C^3-TS algorithm. Section 3 provides the theoretical analysis of its cumulative regret bound and the technique Lemmas used in the proof. Section 4 reports the experimental results on the real-world dataset to demonstrate the empirical performance of C^3-TS. Section 5 concludes this paper.

2   Preliminaries

2.1   Problem Settings

We consider the stochastic linear cascading bandit model. We assume that the user preference is encoded by a fixed but unknown user vector $\theta \in \mathbb{R}^d$. Let $\mathcal{X} \subset \mathbb{R}^d$ be the set of items. When an item $x \in \mathcal{X}$ is recommended to the user, the expected reward $[r(x)]$ of this item x is generated by a linear function $\mathbb{E}[r(x)] = x^T \theta$.

In the cascading model, at each round t, the algorithm selects an ordered list of items $\mathcal{X}_t = X_{t,1}, X_{t,2}, ..., X_{t,K}$ to recommend to the user. The user checks the items in the recommended list from the first item to the last, clicks on the first satisfying item and stops checking the rest items. We assume that the observed payoff $r(x)$ of an item x is generated by sampling from a Bernoulli distribution with mean $x^T\theta$. The observed payoff of the recommended list X_t is the index of the clicked item C_t. It indicates that the payoffs of the first $C_t - 1$ recommended items are all 0 and the payoff of the C_t-th recommended item is 1; the rest recommended items are not checked by the user. If no recommended item is clicked, the observed payoff will be $C_t = \infty$.

An item list X is evaluated by its expected reward $E[r(X)]$. The expected reward of X is defined as:

$$\mathbb{E}[r(X)] = 1 - \prod_{x \in X}(1 - x^T\theta) \tag{1}$$

It is worth noting that the expected reward of a list does not depend on the order of its items.

We denote the optimal item list X^* by

$$X^* = \arg\max_{X \subset \mathcal{X}} \mathbb{E}[r(X)]. \tag{2}$$

The expected regret $R(t)$ at round t is defined as the gap between the expected reward of the optimal item list and the recommended item list. The objective of the algorithm is to minimize the expected cumulative regret up to a time horizon T,

$$\mathbb{E}[\mathcal{R}(T)] = \mathbb{E}[\sum_{t=1}^{T}(r(X^*) - r(X_t))], \tag{3}$$

where the expectation is taken over the randomness in selecting the recommended list X_t and the noise.

2.2   Contextual Combinatorial Cascading Thompson Sampling

The Thompson sampling algorithm selects the recommended list according to its posterior probability of being optimal. At every round t, the algorithm generates a sample $\tilde{\theta}_t$ from its posterior distribution $\mathcal{N}(\hat{\theta}_{t-1}, V_{t-1}^{-1})$. It then selects the list of items by the value of $\tilde{\theta}_t$. More specifically, it selects the list that maximizes $X_t = \arg\max_{X \subset \mathcal{X}} 1 - \prod_{x \in X}(1 - x^T\tilde{\theta}_t)$.

Let $(X_1, X_2, ..., X_t) \in \mathcal{X}^t$ be the sequence of the selected item lists and $(C_1, C_2, ..., C_t)$ be the observed rewards. The posterior distribution of parameter θ at round $t+1$ is $\mathcal{N}(\hat{\theta}_t, V_t^{-1})$, where

$$V_t = \lambda I + \sum_{s=1}^{t}\sum_{j=1}^{C_t} X_{s,j}X_{s,j}^T \qquad \hat{\theta}_t = V_t^{-1}\sum_{s=1}^{t}\sum_{j=1}^{C_t} X_{s,j}\mathbb{I}(j = C_t) \tag{4}$$

Algorithm 1. Contextual Combinatorial Cascading Thompson Sampling

> **Input:** Set of items $\mathcal{X}$, Regularization parameter λ
> **Init:** $f_0 = 0_d$, $V_0 = \lambda I_d$, $\hat{\theta}_0 = V_0^{-1} f_0$, $T_0 = 0$.
> **for** $t = 1, 2, 3, ..., T$ **do**
> > Sample $\tilde{\theta}_t$ from its posterior distribution $\mathcal{N}(\hat{\theta}_{t-1}, V_{t-1}^{-1})$
> > **for** $k \in [K]$ **do**
> > > Extract $X_{t,k} = \arg\max_{x \in \mathcal{X} \setminus \{X_{t,1}, X_{t,2}, ... X_{t,k-1}\}} x^T \tilde{\theta}_t$
> > **end for**
> > Recommend the item list X_t and observe the payoff C_t
> > Update f_t, V_t, $\hat{\theta}_t$ as follows:
> > $$f_t = f_{t-1} + \sum_{j=1}^{C_t} X_{t,j} \mathbb{I}\{j = C_t\}$$
> > $$V_t = V_{t-1} + \sum_{j=1}^{C_t} X_{t,j} X_{t,j}^T$$
> > $$\hat{\theta}_t = V_t^{-1} f_t$$
> > $$T_t = T_{t-1} + C_t$$
> **end for**

Theorem 1. *For the stochastic contextual cascading bandit problem, the cumulative expected regret for C^3-Thompson Sampling algorithm in time T is bounded by*

$$R(T) = \tilde{O}(d\sqrt{KT}), \tag{5}$$

where the notation $\tilde{O}$ ignores only the logarithmic factors.

Our regret bound does not depend on the number of items and can be applied to the case of infinite items.

2.3 Notations

We use $\|x\|_p$ to denote the p-norm of $x \in \mathbb{R}^d$. We denote by $\|x\|_M = \sqrt{x^T M x}$ the weighted norm of x. We use $\lambda_{min}(M)$ and $\lambda_{max}(M)$ to denote the minimal and the maximal eigenvalue of matrix M respectively. We use $\lambda_i(M)$ for $i \in [d]$ to denote the i-th largest eigenvalues of matrix M.

Assumption 1 (Noise). The random noise ϵ is conditionally R-sub-Gaussian for some constant $R \geq 0$,

$$\forall \alpha \in \mathbb{R}, \mathbb{E}[e^{\alpha \epsilon} | \mathcal{F}_t^x] \leq \exp^{\alpha^2 R^2 / 2}$$

This assumption is satisfied whenever the actual reward is bounded.

Assumption 2 (Contextual vector and parameter). The contextual vector and the user parameter are bounded in a closed subset of $\mathbb{R}^d$ such that $0 < \|x\|_2^2 \leq 1$. This assumption is required so that the regret bound does not depend on the scale of the vectors. If $0 < \|x\|_2^2 \leq L$, our regret bounds would increase by a factor of L.

Assumption 3 (Eigenvalues). At each time step t, the items in the recommended list X_t are drawn independently from a distribution with mean $\mathbb{E}[x_t x_t^T]$, where $\mathbb{E}[x_t x_t^T]$ is a full rank matrix and all its eigenvalues satisfy $\lambda_{min} \leq \lambda_i(\mathbb{E}[x_t x_t^T]) \leq \lambda_{max}$ for some constant λ_{min} and λ_{max}.

Assumption 3 facilitates the generalization of Bayes gap to the contextual setting [8] and is in accordance with [6]. It allows us to bound the eigenvalues of the cumulative matrix $V_t = \lambda I + \sum_{s=1}^{t} \sum_{j=1}^{C_t} X_{s,j} X_{s,j}^T$, which allows us to qualify the variance of an item and is crucial to our theoretical analysis.

In standard contextual bandit algorithms, this assumption of the eigenvalue is often violated. After enough rounds, the probability of selecting the optimal item will be almost 1. Thus the smallest eigenvalue will be $\lambda_{min}(\mathbb{E}[x_t x_t^T]) = \lambda_{min}(x^* x^{*T}) = 0$. But in cascading settings, if the expected reward of the optimal item is smaller than 1, then the suboptimal items will be checked by the user with at least constant probability, thus $\lambda_{min}(\mathbb{E}[x_t x_t^T]) > \lambda_{min}$ is a reasonable assumption.

3 Regret Analysis

3.1 Challenges and Proof Outline

In analyzing the C^3-Thompson sampling algorithm, the main challenge is to control the variance of reward estimator of each item. The variance plays a central role in bandit algorithms. It represents the uncertainty of the reward estimator and is used to balance the exploration-exploitation tradeoff. In the basic multi-armed bandit problem, the variance of the reward estimator is inversely proportional to the number of plays of an item at round t. Thus, each time a suboptimal item is selected, the algorithm will accumulate more information about its true value. The trade-off between regret and information can be precisely quantified. Existing researches rely on this observation to upper bound the regret of basic MAB and non-contextual cascade bandits. In linear cascading bandit, however, the covariance of the parameter θ is the inverse of the cumulative matrix $V_t = \lambda I + \sum_{s=1}^{t} \sum_{j}^{C_t} X_{s,j} X_{s,j}^T$ and the variance of reward estimator is $\|x\|_{V_t^{-1}}^2$. The precise tradeoff between the regret and the variance has not been thoroughly studied. Thus the techniques used in analyzing basic MAB cannot be directly applied in the analysis of contextual cascading bandit.

We follow three steps to bound the expected cumulative regret up to time horizon T. First, we define event $F_{t,k} = \{$the k-th item of X_t is examined$\}$ for time step t and $k \in [K]$, and decompose the expected regret at round t as:

$$\mathbb{E}[R(t)] \leq \mathbb{E}[\sum_{k=1}^{K} \mathbb{I}(F_k)(r(x_k^*) - r(x_k))] \qquad (6)$$

After decomposing, the instantaneous regret can be bounded by the difference between expected rewards of optimal items and checked items.

Second, we define events $E^\theta(t)$ and $E^\mu(t)$, which indicate that for all $x \in \mathcal{X}$, its empirical value $x^T \hat\theta_t$ and sampled value $x^T \tilde\theta_t$ are both concentrated around their respective mean. Under events $E^\theta(t)$ and $E^\mu(t)$, which holds with high probability, the instantaneous regret can be bounded by

$$\mathbb{E}[R(t)] \leq \mathbb{E}[\sum_{k=1}^{K} \mathbb{I}(F_k)(\alpha_t + \beta_t)(s^* + s_t)] \tag{7}$$

Where α_t and β_t are the variables defined in $E^\theta(t)$ and $E^\mu(t)$.

Finally, we show that under Assumption 3, the eigenvalues of the matrix V_t grows linearly with the number of items the user has observed, which is referred to as T_{t-1} in the algorithm. Using this result, we can prove that the sum of the cumulative variance $\sum_{t=1}^{T} \sum_{k=1}^{C_t} s_t^*$ is of order $\sqrt{dKT \ln KT}$. Then, using this result along with Lemma 1, we obtain the desired expected cumulative regret bound.

3.2   Formal Proof

Following the previous works [9, 11], we rearrange the position of the items in the optimal list X^* to satisfy that if an item appears in both the optimal list X^* and the recommended list X_t, it is placed at the same position. Under this rearrangement,

$$\forall k \in [K], \qquad X_{t,k}^{*T}\theta \geq X_{t,k}^{T}\theta \quad and \quad X_{t,k}^{*T}\tilde\theta_t \leq X_{t,k}^{T}\tilde\theta_t.$$

During the iterations, we update $\hat\theta$ such that it approaches the real parameter θ gradually. To do so, we select a set X_t according to the order of expected reward $x^T \hat\theta$ at each time step. Hence, if $x^T \hat\theta$, $x^T \tilde\theta$ and $x^T \theta$ are close enough, we are likely to select the optimal set. This intuition lead to the definition of two events.

Definition 1. *Define* $\mathbb{E}^\mu(t)$ *and* $\mathbb{E}^\theta(t)$ *as the events that* $x^T\tilde\theta_t$ *and* $\hat\theta_t$ *are concentrated around* $x^T\hat\theta_t$ *and* θ *respectively. More precisely, define* $\mathbb{E}^\mu(t)$ *and* $\mathbb{E}^\theta(t)$ *as the event that*

$$Event \quad \mathbb{E}^\mu(t) : \forall x \in \mathcal{X} : |x^T\tilde\theta_t - x^T\hat\theta_t| \leq \beta_t s_t(x)$$

$$Event \quad \mathbb{E}^\theta(t) : |\hat\theta_t - \theta|_{V_{t-1}} \leq \alpha_t$$

where $\beta_t = \sqrt{d \ln \frac{4t}{\delta}}$, $s_t(x) = \|x\|_{V_{t-1}^{-1}}$ *and* $\alpha_t = \sqrt{d \ln(\frac{4 + 4T_{t-1}}{\delta})} + \sqrt{\lambda}$.

We can prove that both events happen with probability at least $1 - \frac{\delta}{4t^2}$. The proof is similar to the proof of Lemma 1 in [3]. The probability bound for $\mathbb{E}^\mu(t)$ is proven by using the concentration inequality of Gaussian random variables as stated in [2]. The probability bound for $\mathbb{E}^\theta(t)$ is proven by using the concentration inequality given by [1].

We decompose the expected regret $\mathbb{E}[R(t)]$ of round t. If events $\mathbb{E}^\mu(t)$ and $\mathbb{E}^\theta(t)$ are both true, the instantaneous expected regret can be bounded as:

$$
\begin{aligned}
\mathbb{E}[R(t)] &= \mathbb{E}[r(X^*) - r(X_t)] \\
&= \mathbb{E}[\prod_{k \in [K]}(1 - r(X_k^*)) - \prod_{k \in [K]}(1 - r(X_{t,k}))] \\
&\leq \mathbb{E}[\sum_{k=1}^{K}[\prod_{j=1}^{k-1}(1 - r(X_{t,j}))](r(X_k^*) - r(X_{t,k}))] \\
&\leq \mathbb{E}[\sum_{k=1}^{K}\mathbb{I}(F_{t,k})(r(X_k^*) - r(X_{t,k}))] \\
&\leq \mathbb{E}[\sum_{k=1}^{K}\mathbb{I}(F_{t,k})(\alpha_t + \beta_t)(s_t(X_k^*) + s_t(X_{t,k}))] \qquad (*)
\end{aligned}
$$

Where $F_{t,k}$ is the event that $X_{t,k}$ is checked by the user at round t. α_t and β_t are defined as in the definition of the events $\mathbb{E}^\theta(t)$ and $\mathbb{E}^\mu(t)$.

The inequality $(*)$ is by

$$
\begin{aligned}
(x^{*T} - x^T)\theta &\leq (x^{*T} - x^T)\tilde{\theta}_t + (\alpha_t + \beta_t)(\|x\|_{V_{t-1}^{-1}} + \|x^*\|_{V_{t-1}^{-1}}) \\
&\leq (\alpha_t + \beta_t)(\|x\|_{V_{t-1}^{-1}} + \|x^*\|_{V_{t-1}^{-1}}).
\end{aligned}
$$

Definition 2. *Define event $\mathbb{E}^\lambda(t)$ as the event the eigenvalues of V_t grows linearly with T_t, where T_t is the number of examined items after round t. More precisely, define $\mathbb{E}^\lambda(t)$ as the event that*

$$
\lambda_{min}(V_t) \geq 1/2 T_t \cdot \lambda_{min}, \quad \forall T_t \geq \frac{32(1 - \lambda_{min})}{\lambda_{min}^2} \ln \frac{4dt^2}{\delta}
$$

We prove that event $\mathbb{E}^\lambda(t)$ happens with probability at least $1 - \frac{\delta}{4t^2}$ by Lemma 2.

The expected cumulative regret for C^3-TS can be decomposed as

$$
\begin{aligned}
\mathbb{E}[R(T)] &= \sum_{t=1}^{T}\mathbb{E}[R(t)] \\
&\leq \sum_{t=1}^{T}\mathbb{E}[\sum_{k=1}^{K}\mathbb{I}(F_{t,k})(\alpha_t + \beta_t)(s_t(X_{t,k}^*) + s_t(X_{t,k}))] \\
&\leq (\alpha_T + \beta_T)\sum_{t=1}^{T}\mathbb{E}[\sum_{k=1}^{K}\mathbb{I}(F_{t,k})(s_t(X_{t,k}^*) + s_t(X_{t,k}))] \\
&\leq (\alpha_T + \beta_T)\sum_{t=1}^{T}\mathbb{E}[\sum_{k=1}^{C_t}s_t(X_{t,k}^*) + \mathbb{E}[\sum_{k=1}^{C_t}s_t(X_{t,k})] \\
&\leq (\alpha_T + \beta_T)(\sqrt{\frac{dTK}{\lambda_{min}}(K + \ln(1 + TK)} + \sqrt{2dTK\ln(1 + \frac{KT}{\lambda d})}) \qquad (**)
\end{aligned}
$$

The inequality $(**)$ follows from Lemma 1 and the fact that if event $E^\lambda(t)$ is true, then $\lambda_{min}(V_{t-1}) \geq 1/2 T_{t-1}\lambda_{min}$. It implies that for any item $\|x\|^2 \leq 1$, $\|x\|_{V_{t-1}^{-1}} \leq \sqrt{\frac{2d}{T_{t-1}\lambda_{min}}}$. Thus

$$\sum_{t=1}^{T} \mathbb{E}[\sum_{k=1}^{C_t} s_t(X_{t,k}^*)] \leq \sum_{t=1}^{T} C_t \sqrt{\frac{2d}{\sum_{j=1}^{t-1} C_j \lambda_{min}}}$$

$$\leq \sqrt{\frac{2d}{\lambda_{min}}} \sqrt{(\sum_{t=1}^{T} C_t) \sum_{t=1}^{T} \frac{C_t}{\sum_{j=1}^{t-1} C_j}}$$

$$\leq \sqrt{\frac{2dTK}{\lambda_{min}} \ln(1 + KT)}$$

Substituting above in $\mathbb{E}[R(T)]$, we obtain that

$$R(T) = O(d\sqrt{TK \ln KT}), \tag{8}$$

which completes the proof.

Lemma 1 *(Sum of standard deviation). Let $\lambda > 1$, for any sequence $(X_1, X_2, ..., X_T)$, let V_t be the cumulative matrix defined in Equation (4), then*

$$\sum_{t=1}^{T} \sum_{k=1}^{C_t} \|X_{t,k}\|_{V_{t-1}^{-1}} = O(\sqrt{dTK \ln(1 + \frac{TK}{\lambda d})}) \tag{9}$$

Proof. This Lemma is by Lemma 6 of [12].

Lemma 2 *(Lower bound and upper bound on the i-th largest eigenvalue of sum of Hermitian matrices). Let $(x_t : t \geq 1)$ be a sequence generated from random distribution $x \in \mathbb{R}^d$. Assume all the assumptions hold, $\mathbb{E}[x_t x_t^T]$ is full rank Herimitian matrix with $\lambda_{min} \leq \lambda_i(\mathbb{E}[x_t x_t^T]) \leq \lambda_{max}$. Let $V_t = \sum_t x_t x_t^T$.*

Then for any $t \geq \frac{32(1-\lambda_{min})^2}{\lambda_{min}^2} \ln \frac{d}{\delta}$, event $1/2t\lambda_{min} \leq \lambda_i(V_t)$ happens with probability at least $1 - \delta$.

And for any $t \geq \frac{32(1-\lambda_{min})^2}{\lambda_{max}^2} \ln \frac{d}{\delta}$, event $\lambda_i(V_t) \leq 3/2t \cdot \lambda_{max}$ happens with probability at least $1 - \delta$.

Proof. We first define a matrix martingale process:

$$X_t = x_t x_t^T - \mathbb{E}[x_t x_t^T]$$

$$Y_t = \sum_{k=1}^{t} X_k = \sum_{k=1}^{t} x_k x_k^T - \sum_{k=1}^{t} \mathbb{E}[x_k x_k^T]$$

It is obvious that Y_t is a matrix martingale process and X_t is the difference sequence.

Let $A_k^2 = (1 - \lambda_{min})^2 I$ and we prove that

$$X_k^2 \preceq A_k^2 \quad \text{for any } k \in [1:t].$$

Note that for any X, $X = xx^T - \mathbb{E}[xx^T]$, we apply the Weyl's theorem for eigenvalues and get that $\lambda_{max}(X) \leq L - \lambda_{min}$. Suppose that $\lambda \leq 1 - \lambda_{min}$ is an eigenvalue of X and v is the eigenvector. $(A^2 - X^2)v = ((1 - \lambda_{min})^2 - \lambda^2)v$, then $((1 - \lambda_{min})^2 - \lambda^2) \geq 0$ is the eigenvalue of $A^2 - X^2$, thus $X^2 \preceq A^2$ for any X.

We then define $\sigma^2 := \|\sum_{i=1}^t A_i^2\|$, where σ^2 is the spectral norm of $\sum_t A_t^2$. By definition, $\sigma^2 := \|\sum_{i=1}^t A^2\| = \|t(L - \lambda_{min})^2 I\| = t(L - \lambda_{min})^2$.

Substituting $\sigma^2 = t(L - \lambda_{min})^2$ into martrix Azuma [17], we get

$$\mathbb{P}(\lambda_{min}(Y_t) \leq m) \leq d \cdot e^{-m^2/8t(1-\lambda_{min})^2}$$

$$\mathbb{P}(\lambda_{max}(Y_t) \geq n) \leq d \cdot e^{-n^2/8t(1-\lambda_{min})^2}.$$

Note that $V_t = Y_t + \mathbb{E}[V_t]$, by the Weyl's theorem [13], we have $\lambda_{min}(Y_t) + \lambda_i(\mathbb{E}[V_t]) \leq \lambda_i(V_t) \leq \lambda_{max}(Y_t) + \lambda_i(\mathbb{E}[V_t])$. We substitute this inequality, and we get that for any $m \leq 0$ and $n \geq 0$:

$$\mathbb{P}(\lambda_i(V_t) - \lambda_i(\mathbb{E}[V]) \leq m) \leq \mathbb{P}(\lambda_{min}(Y_t) \leq m) \leq d \cdot e^{-m^2/8t(1-\lambda_{min})^2}$$

$$\mathbb{P}(\lambda_i(V_t) - \lambda_i(\mathbb{E}[V]) \geq n) \leq \mathbb{P}(\lambda_{max}(Y_t) \geq n) \leq d \cdot e^{-n^2/8t(1-\lambda_{min})^2}$$

Note that $\lambda_i(\mathbb{E}[V]) = \lambda_i(\sum_{k=1}^t \mathbb{E}[x_k x_k^T])$. We substitute that $m = -1/2t \cdot \lambda_{min}$ and $n = 1/2t \cdot \lambda_{max}$ into previous inequality, and we obtain

$$\mathbb{P}(\lambda_i(V_t) \leq 1/2t \cdot \lambda_{min}) \leq d \cdot e^{-t\lambda_{min}^2/32(1-\lambda_{min})^2}$$

$$\mathbb{P}(\lambda_i(V_t) \geq 3/2t \cdot \lambda_{max}) \leq d \cdot e^{-t\lambda_{max}^2/32(1-\lambda_{min})^2},$$

which completes the proof.

4   Experiment

We evaluate our algorithm, C^3-TS on two real-world datasets. Its performance is compared with C^3-UCB, Cascade-UCB and Cascade-TS, which are the most related algorithms. The results demonstrate the advantage of using Bayesian heuristic and contextual information.

4.1   Movielen Dataset

In this experiment, we evaluate C^3-TS on the MovieLens dataset [7]. The learning problem is formulated as follows. All the records are summarized in a sparse matrix $A \in \{0, 1\}^{N_1 \times N_2}$ where $A(i, j) = 1$ denotes that the user i has watched movie j. We splitted A into two matrix $H + F$ by randomly assign an entry to either matrix. We then use the matrix H to generate feature vectors with $d = 15$ for all movies using singular-value decomposition (SVD). The other matrix F is used to represent the real weight of movie j. For this experiment, we randomly choose $L = 200$ movies and recommend $K = 2, 4, 6$ movies at each time. The results are shown in Fig. 1.

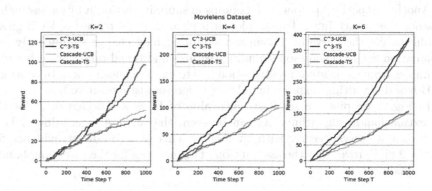

Fig. 1. These figures compare C^3-TS with C^3-UCB, Cascade-UCB and Cascade-TS on Movielens dataset. Plots reporting the cummulative reward over time step T. The basic setting is that there are 200 movies and the dimension of feature space is 15. Left: $K = 2$; Middle:$K = 4$; Right: $K = 6$.

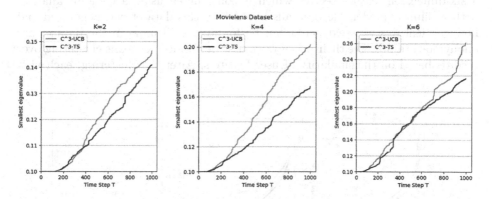

Fig. 2. These figures plot the smallest eigenvalue of V_t over time step T for C^3-TS and C^3-UCB on Movielens dataset. The basic setting is that there are 200 movies and the dimension of feature space is 15. Left: $K = 2$; Middle:$K = 4$; Right: $K = 6$.

In Fig. 1, we plot the cumulative reward as a function of T for C^3-TS, C^3-UCB, Cascade-UCB and Cascade-TS when $N_{movie} = 200$, $d = 15$ and $K = \{2, 4, 6\}$. It is clear that our algorithm outperforms the other algorithms in all settings. We then compare the performance of Thompson sampling and UCB-based algorithm. It can be seen that all Thompson sampling algorithms achieve higher reward than UCB algorithms. Next, we compare the performance of contextual algorithms and the non-contextual algorithm. It can be seen that the contextual algorithms significantly outperform those algorithms without contextual information, which demonstrate the advantage of utilizing contextual information in real-world applications.

Another important property of Thompson sampling is that it often has higher variance than UCB. In the left subplot, it is clear that the reward of UCB grows steadily while the curve of Thompson sampling may change significantly. An explanation is that Thompson sampling requires additional randomness because it samples from the posterior distribution of θ to explore information. In contrast, UCB-based algorithms explore by adding a deterministic positive bias.

In Fig. 2, we plot the smallest eigenvalue of V_t as a function of T for the contextual bandit algorithms. As can be seen, the smallest eigenvalue of V_t is small, but it grows linearly with time step. This result is direct evidence for Lemma 2 and proves that the assumption of eigenvalues for the cascading bandit is reasonable.

4.2   Yahoo! Dataset

The second dataset we used to evaluate C^3-TS was the Yahoo! front page today module dataset. This dataset was provided for the "ICML 2012 Exploration & Exploitation Challenge" by Yahoo!. It contains the records of over 45 million user visit to the Today Module. The articles in the dataset are represented by a six-dimension feature vector, which is constructed using a conjoint analysis with a bilinear model. More details about how this dataset was generated and how the features were extracted can be found. As all users in the dataset are anonymous to preserve their privacy, we first performed K-means clustering over records based on the similarity of user features. After the clustering, each visit

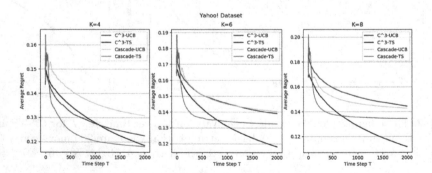

Fig. 3. These figures compare C^3-TS with C^3-UCB, Cascade-UCB and Cascade-TS on Yahoo! dataset. Plots reporting the average regret over time step T. The regret is averaged over 100 users. Left: $K = 4$; Middle: $K = 6$; Right: $K = 8$

record was assigned to a cluster, and these clusters were then treated as users in our experiment.

In Fig. 3, we plot the average regret as a function of T for C^3-TS, C^3-UCB, Cascade-UCB and Cascade-TS when $N_{user} = 100$, $N_{article} = 50$, $d = 6$ and $K = \{4, 6, 8\}$. As can be seen, C^3-TS receives smaller average regret than the other algorithms. It is also clear that the average regret $R(T)/T$ for our algorithm behaves as $O(\frac{1}{\sqrt{t}})$, which implies that the empirical performance on time step T matches the upper bound derived in our proof. In contrast, the total regret is decreasing in K while our regret bound is $O(\sqrt{K})$. It reveals that our upper bound may not match the information theoretic lower bound in contextual cascading settings.

5 Conclusion

We designed and analyzed C^3-Thompson Sampling for the stochastic cascading bandit with linear payoffs. We proved that its regret bound matches the regret bound of UCB-based algorithms. And the experiments demonstrated the advantage of our algorithm over most related works. Further investigations include deriving the lower regret bound and the frequentist upper bound for the contextual cascading bandit algorithm.

Acknowledgments. This paper is supported by the National Science Foundation of China under Grant 61472385 and Grant U1709217.

References

1. Abbasi-Yadkori, Y., Pál, D., Szepesvári, C.: Improved algorithms for linear stochastic bandits. In: Advances in Neural Information Processing Systems, pp. 2312–2320 (2011)
2. Abramowitz, M., Stegun, I.: Handbook of Mathematical Functions with Formulas, Graphs, and Mathematical Tables. Applied Mathematics Series, vol. 55. National Bureau of Standards, Washington, DC (1964)
3. Agrawal, S., Goyal, N.: Thompson sampling for contextual bandits with linear payoffs. In: International Conference on Machine Learning, pp. 127–135 (2013)
4. Chapelle, O., Li, L.: An empirical evaluation of Thompson sampling. In: Advances in Neural Information Processing Systems, pp. 2249–2257 (2011)
5. Cheung, W.C., Tan, V.Y.F., Zhong, Z.: Thompson sampling for cascading bandits (2018)
6. Deshmukh, A.A., Sharma, S., Cutler, J.W., Moldwin, M., Scott, C.: Simple regret minimization for contextual bandits. arXiv preprint arXiv:1810.07371 (2018)
7. Harper, F.M., Konstan, J.A.: The movielens datasets: history and context. ACM Trans. Interact. Intell. Syst. (TIIS) **5**(4), 19 (2016)
8. Hoffman, M., Shahriari, B., Freitas, N.: On correlation and budget constraints in model-based bandit optimization with application to automatic machine learning. In: Artificial Intelligence and Statistics, pp. 365–374 (2014)
9. Kveton, B., Szepesv, C., Wen, Z., Ashkan, A.: Cascading bandits: learning to rank in the cascade model (2015)

10. Lattimore, T., Szepesvári, C.: Bandit algorithms (2018, preprint)
11. Li, S., Karatzoglou, A., Gentile, C.: Collaborative filtering bandits. In: Proceedings of the 39th International ACM SIGIR Conference on Research and Development in Information Retrieval, pp. 539–548. ACM (2016)
12. Li, S., Zhang, S.: Online clustering of contextual cascading bandits (2018)
13. Polya, G.: Remark on Weyl's note "inequalities between the two kinds of eigenvalues of a linear transformation". Proc. Natl. Acad. Sci. **36**(1), 49–51 (1950)
14. Russo, D., Van Roy, B.: Learning to optimize via posterior sampling. Math. Oper. Res. **39**(4), 1221–1243 (2014)
15. Russo, D., Van Roy, B.: An information-theoretic analysis of Thompson sampling. J. Mach. Learn. Res. **17**(1), 2442–2471 (2016)
16. Shi, Z., Hao, N., Sung, K., Nan, R.K., Kveton, B.: Cascading bandits for large-scale recommendation problems. In: Conference on Uncertainty in Artificial Intelligence (2016)
17. Tropp, J.A., et al.: An introduction to matrix concentration inequalities. Found. Trends® Mach. Learn. **8**(1–2), 1–230 (2015)

Trajectory Comparison in a Vehicular Network I: Computing a Consensus Trajectory

Peng Zou[1], Letu Qingge[2], Qing Yang[3], and Binhai Zhu[1(✉)]

[1] Gianforte School of Computing, Montana State University,
Bozeman, MT 59717-3880, USA
peng.zou@student.montana.edu, bhz@montana.edu
[2] College of Computing and Informatics, University of North Carolina at Charlotte,
Charlotte, NC 28223, USA
letu.qingge@uncc.edu
[3] Department of Computer Science and Engineering, University of North Texas,
Denton, TX 76207-7102, USA
qing.yang@unt.edu

Abstract. In this paper, we investigate the problem of computing a consensus trajectory of a vehicle giving the history of Points of Interest (POIs) visited by the vehicle over certain period of time. The problem originates from building the social connection between two vehicles in a vehicular network. Formally, given a set of m trajectories (sequences S_i's over a given alphabet Σ, each with length at most $O(n)$, with $n = |\Sigma|$), the problem is to compute a target (median) sequence T over Σ such that the sum of similarity measure (i.e., number of adjacencies) between T and all S_i's is maximized. For this version, we show that the problem is NP-hard and we present a simple factor-2 approximation. If T has to be a permutation, then we show that the problem is still NP-hard but the approximation factor can be improved to 1.5. We implement the greedy algorithm and a variation of it which is based on a more natural greedy search. Using simulated data over two months (e.g., $m = 60$) and variants of $|S_i|$ and Σ (e.g., $30 \leq |S_i| \leq 100$ and $30 \leq |\Sigma| \leq 60$), the empirical results are very promising and with the local adjustment algorithm the actual approximation factor is between 1.5 and 1.6 for all the cases.

1 Introduction

In a vehicular network, before two vehicles (nodes) communicate useful information, they need to determine the trustfulness among them while preserving their privacy. (This problem is getting more important with the advent of autonomous driving.) This security issue must be addressed due to the special safety requirement of vehicular ad hoc networks (VANET), which has a wide range of applications in traffic control, accident avoidance and parking management [5,11].

Unique to VANET, false information dissemination and Sybil attacks are some of the critical security issues. The former could be a false information like

© Springer Nature Switzerland AG 2019
E. S. Biagioni et al. (Eds.): WASA 2019, LNCS 11604, pp. 533–544, 2019.
https://doi.org/10.1007/978-3-030-23597-0_43

"parking garage is full" so that the sender can turn away parking competitors. The latter could be a generation of fake identities to falter the functioning of the whole system [3,14]. The public-key infrastructure might not be available over a road network; hence, some kind of trust management must be maintained [8,9,16].

To build the initial trustfulness, the solution we propose is to use the Point of Interests (POIs) visited by each vehicle to establish some level of similarity, which serves as a starting point for determining the trustfulness of vehicles. (Later, the trustfulness computation can be enhanced using some other methods [8,9], or simply some standard method in game theory.) In this case, to protect privacy, all sensitive information regarding the location of POIs, time a POI is visited, etc, are erased for our computation and comparison. Hence, an example of POIs is "office", "restaurant", "coffee shop", "gym", etc. (See Fig. 1 for a simple example.) Certainly, we could make POIs slightly more specific without sacrificing privacy, for instance, a restaurant could be more specific, e.g., "Wendy's" or "MacDonalds" could be used.

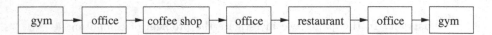

Fig. 1. The POIs visited by a white-collared professional during a typical working day. If we use A, B, C, and D to represent 'gym', 'office', 'coffee shop', and 'restaurant' respectively, then the trajectory would be represented as a sequence $\langle A, B, C, B, D, B, A \rangle$.

Now suppose that we have two list of POIs, S_1 and S_2, visited by two vehicles over some time period, say two months. How do we compare these sequences (of POIs)? We adopt a classic concept called *adjacency*, which is commonly used in computational genomics [1,6,7]. Our idea is to compute two consensus trajectories, T_1 and T_2, for each vehicle and then compare T_1 and T_2 directly. (The latter comparison could be done naively by counting the number of adjacencies between T_1 and T_2; of course, to make the computation more accurate, we could delete some redundant POIs—the latter research will be presented in a companion paper.)

Computing the consensus trajectory (sequence) is a traditional problem in computational biology, under different distance measures. For instance, given a set of DNA sequences $\{S_1, S_2, ..., S_m\}$, computing a median sequence T of length L such that $\sum_i d_H(T, S_i)$ is minimized—where $d_H()$ is the Hamming distance, is an important problem in computing conserved regions in many molecular biology problems [10]. When the input sequences are genomes and the distance measure is the *breakpoint* distance, then we have the breakpoint median problem [2,12,15]. It is not surprising that all these problems are NP-hard; in fact, for the breakpoint-median problem it is NP-hard even if there are only three input genomes [2]. Note that this problem is different from ours. For example, if we have three permutations $A_1 = 1234$, $A_2 = 2431$, $A_3 = 3241$ then any permutation median like $M = 1234$ could contribute at most 5 adjacencies between M and

A_i's. On the other hand, if the median does not have to be a permutation, as in our case, then $M' = 2342$ would contribute 6 adjacencies.

As what has just been shown, the problem we investigate in this paper, while similar in some sense to these previous works, are different in several aspects. First of all, the similarity measure we use is not a distance measure; instead, it is a similarity measure featuring "the more similar, the more number of adjacencies". Secondly, the alphabet (i.e., set of POIs) we use is not necessarily a small constant and POIs are allowed to repeat in any input sequence. Thirdly, the length of the median trajectory is bounded (as otherwise the problem becomes trivial to solve) and the median trajectory is in general not a permutation. These make the design of algorithms more challenging.

The paper is organized as follows. In Sect. 2, we give necessary definitions and define the corresponding problems. In Sect. 3, we give NP-hardness proofs for these problems. In Sect. 4, we present two approximation algorithms for these problems, with approximation factor 2 and 1.5 respectively. In Sect. 5, we implement two methods based on one of these approximation algorithms and show the corresponding empirical results. In Sect. 6, we conclude the paper with several open questions.

2   Preliminaries

At first, we make some necessary definitions. Given a set Σ of POIs (or just letters or nodes), a string P is called *permutation* if each element in Σ appears exactly once in P. We use $c(P)$ to denote the set of elements in permutation P. A string A is called *sequence* if some POIs appear more than once in A, and $c(A)$, which is a multi-set of elements in Σ, denotes POIs of A. (Throughout this paper, we will mix the use of sequences and trajectories, with the understanding that consecutive identical letters will always be preprocessed as a single letter. For instance $A = abcdddab$ would be preprocessed as $A = abcdab$.) For example, $\Sigma = \{a, b, c, d\}$, $A = abcdacd$, $c(A) = \{a, a, b, c, c, d, d\}$. A substring with k letters (in a sequence A) is called an k-*substring*, and a 2-substring is also called a *pair*. The relative order of the two letters of a pair does not matter, i.e., the pair xy is equal to the pair yx. Given a sequence $A = a_1 a_2 \cdots a_n$, let $P_A = \{a_1 a_2, a_2 a_3, \ldots, a_{n-1} a_n\}$ be the set of pairs in A.

Definition 1. *Given two sequences $A = a_1 a_2 \cdots a_n$ and $B = b_1 b_2 \cdots b_m$, if $a_i a_{i+1} = b_j b_{j+1}$ (or $a_i a_{i+1} = b_{j+1} b_j$), where $a_i a_{i+1} \in P_A$ and $b_j b_{j+1} \in P_B$, we say that $a_i a_{i+1}$ and $b_j b_{j+1}$ are matched to each other. In a maximum matching of pairs in P_A and P_B, a matched pair is called an **adjacency**, and an unmatched pair is called a **breakpoint** in A and B respectively.*

It follows from the definition that sequences (trajectories) A and B contain the same set of adjacencies but distinct breakpoints. The maximum matched pairs in B (or equally, in A) form the *adjacency set* between A and B, denoted as $a(A, B)$. We illustrate the above definitions in Fig. 2.

$$\text{sequence} \quad A = \langle a\ b\ a\ e\ c\ a\ b\ d \rangle$$
$$\text{sequence} \quad B = \langle c\ b\ d\ a\ b\ a\ d \rangle$$
$$P_A = \{ab, ba, ae, ec, ca, ab, bd\}$$
$$P_B = \{cb, bd, da, ab, ba, ad\}$$
$$\text{matched pairs} : \ (ab \leftrightarrow ab), (ba \leftrightarrow ab), (bd \leftrightarrow bd)$$
$$a(A, B) = \{ab, ba, bd\}$$
$$b_A(A, B) = \{ae, ec, ca, ab\}$$
$$b_B(A, B) = \{cb, da, ad\}$$

Fig. 2. An example for adjacency, breakpoint and the related definitions.

We now define the problems to be studied in this paper. We use the decision versions in the definition, though in designing approximation algorithms we will focus on the corresponding optimization versions.

Definition 2. *Median Trajectory Problem.*
Input: *A set of m sequences/trajectories S_i's, $i = 1..m$, over a POI set Σ (with $|\Sigma| = n$), and two positive integers k and ℓ.*
Question: *Can a trajectory T with ℓ elements over Σ be computed such that $\sum_i |a(T, S_i)| \geq k$?*

T is typically called a *median trajectory*. When the median trajectory is restricted to be a permutation. We have a variation of the problem.

Definition 3. *Median Permutation Problem.*
Input: *A set of m sequences/trajectories S_i's, $i = 1..m$, over a POI set Σ (with $|\Sigma| = n$), and a positive integers k.*
Question: *Can a permutation M (with n elements) over Σ be computed such that $\sum_i |a(M, S_i)| \geq k$?*

When the median trajectory must cover a superset of (all the POIs in) Σ, but some POIs could appear multiple times, we have the following problem.

Definition 4. *Median Canonical Trajectory Problem.*
Input: *A set of m sequences/trajectories S_i's, $i = 1..m$, over a POI set Σ (with $|\Sigma| = n$), and two positive integers k and $\ell > n$.*
Question: *Can a trajectory Z with ℓ elements over Σ be computed such that $\sum_i |a(Z, S_i)| \geq k$ and $c(Z) \supseteq \Sigma$?*

3   Hardness Results

In this section we prove that all the three problems are NP-hard. As the proofs are in general similar (certainly with some twist), for the first one we give all the details and for the second and third one we only give the most important ideas. The details will be given in the full version of this paper.

Theorem 1. *The decision version of the Median Trajectory problem is NP-complete.*

Proof. We reduce the Hamiltonian Path problem to the Median Trajectory with a bounded length $3n$. WLOG, let $G = (V, E)$ be an undirected graph with vertex degree $deg(u) \geq 2$ for $u \in V$. For each vertex $u \in V$, let $u^1, u^2, \cdots, u^{deg(v)}$ be the list of vertices adjacent to u ordered by their indices. We define $L_1(u)$ as follows:

$$L_1(u) = \#_u^1 \cdot uu^1 \#_u^2 \cdot uu^2 \cdot \#_u^3 \cdot .... \cdot \#_u^{deg(u)} \cdot uu^{deg(u)}.$$

Then, we define

$$L_j(u) = u\$_u u,$$

for $j = 2, 3, 4$. Finally, we define

$$L(u) = \{L_1(u), L_2(u), L_3(u), L_4(u)\}.$$

Let $V = \{v_1, v_2, ..., v_n\}$, and we write $\#_{v_i}^k$ and $\$_{v_i}$ simply as $\#_i^k$ and $\$_i$ respectively. Note that $\#_i^k$ are POIs which occur only once in all trajectories. Then we construct $4n$ trajectories as

$$L = L(v_1) \cup L(v_2) \cup L(v_3) \cup \cdots \cup L(v_n).$$

Notice that $\Sigma = V \cup \{\$_v | v \in V\} \cup \{\#_i^j | i = 1..n, j = 1..deg(v_i)\}$.

Let $P(V) = \langle v_{\pi(1)}, v_{\pi(2)}, \cdots, v_{\pi(n)} \rangle$ be a permutation of V. We claim the following: $P(V)$ is a Hamiltonian path for G if and only if

$$T = \langle v_{\pi(1)}, \$_{\pi(1)}, v_{\pi(1)}, v_{\pi(2)}, \$_{\pi(2)}, v_{\pi(2)}, \cdots, v_{\pi(n)}, \$_{\pi(n)}, v_{\pi(n)} \rangle,$$

which is of $\ell = 3n$ elements, is a median trajectory with a total of $8n - 2$ adjacencies between T and L.

"If part": If $P(V)$ is a Hamiltonian path, then in T each 3-substring $v_{\pi(i)}\$v_{\pi(i)}v_{\pi(i)}, i = 1..n$, contributes 6 adjacencies with $L_2(v_\pi(i))$, $L_3(v_\pi(i))$ and $L_4(v_\pi(i))$ in $L(v_\pi(i))$ (containing 4 trajectories). Moreover, each 2-substring $v_{\pi(i)}v_{\pi(i+1)}, i = 1..n-1$, contributes 2 adjacencies (one with $L_1(v_{\pi(i)})$, the other with $L_1(v_{\pi(i+1)})$. This gives us a total of $6n + 2(n-1) = 8n - 2$ adjacencies between T all the trajectories in L.

"Only-if part" If T is a median trajectory of length $3n$ for L forming a total of $8n - 2$ adjacencies from T to $L(i)$'s, the first thing to notice is that T has length $3n$, hence to form $8n - 2$ adjacencies we cannot use any POI $\#_i^k$ as $\#_i^k v_i$ or $v_j \#_i^k$ in T each could form only one adjacency with trajectories in L. Hence, to maximize the number of adjacencies between T and L, we must only use POIs in $V \cup \{\$_v | v \in V\}$. As $v_{\pi(i)}\$v_{\pi(i)}v_{\pi(i)}$ contributes 6 adjacencies with $L(v_\pi(i))$, including all of them in the median trajectory naturally gives us $6n$ adjacencies. Now, to increase the total adjacencies between T and L to $8n - 2$, we must make use of the $2(n-1)$ adjacencies in the form of $v_{\pi(i)}v_{\pi(i+1)}$—which implies that $v_{\pi(i)}v_{\pi(i+1)}$ must form an edge of G, hence the 2 adjacencies are formed with $L_1(v_\pi(i))$ and $L_1(v_\pi(i+1))$ respectively. Obviously, the order of such $v_{\pi(i)}v_{\pi(i+1)}$'s gives us a Hamiltonian path for G.

The reduction takes $O(|V| + |E|)$ time. Hence the theorem is proven. $\qquad \square$

Theorem 2. *The decision version of the Median Permutation problem is NP-complete.*

Proof. Again, we reduce the Hamiltonian Path problem to the Median Permutation problem, this time with a bounded length $2n$. WLOG, let $G = (V, E)$ be an undirected graph with vertex degree $deg(u) \geq 2$ for $u \in V$. For each vertex $u \in V$, we define $L_1(u) = L_2(u) = uu'$. For each edge $e = (u, w) \in E$, we define $L_3(e) = u'w$ and $L_4(e) = uw'$. L contains $2|V| + 2|E|$ trajectories. Let $\pi(i)$ be a permutation on $[1..n]$, then for $V = \{v_1, v_2, \cdots, v_n\}$, $M = \langle v_{\pi(1)}, v_{\pi(2)}, \cdots, v_{\pi(n)} \rangle$ is a permutation on V. We claim the following: G admits a Hamiltonian path M if and only if T is a median permutation for L in one of the two forms:

1. $T = \langle v_{\pi(1)}, v'_{\pi(1)}, v_{\pi(2)}, v'_{\pi(2)}, \cdots, v_{\pi(n)}, v'_{\pi(n)} \rangle$, or
2. $T = \langle v'_{\pi(1)}, v_{\pi(1)}, v'_{\pi(2)}, v_{\pi(2)}, \cdots, v'_{\pi(n)}, v_{\pi(n)} \rangle$.

We leave the detailed arguments as an exercise for the readers. The reduction obviously takes $O(|V| + |E|)$ time. Hence the theorem is proven. □

Theorem 3. *The decision version of the Median Canonical Trajectory problem is NP-complete.*

Proof. The reduction is slightly different from the previous two. We will reduce the Hamiltonian Cycle problem to the Median Canonical Trajectory problem. Given an undirected graph $G = (V, E)$, WLOG, we want to compute a Hamiltonian Cycle starting from some vertex v_1. For each edge $e = (v_i, v_j)$, we construct a trajectory

$$L(e) = v_i v_j.$$

For v_1, we construct two trajectories

$$L_1(v_1) = L_2(v_1) = \langle \$_s, \#_1, \#_2, \cdots, \#_\gamma, v_1, \#_\gamma, \#_{\gamma-1}, \cdots, \#_1, \$_t \rangle.$$

Let $L = \{L(e)|e \in E\} \cup \{L_1(v_1), L_2(v_1)\}$. Then we have $m = |E| + 2$ trajectories, with $|\Sigma| = n + \gamma + 2$.

Let $\pi(i)$ be a permutation on $[n]$, with $\pi(1) = 1$. We claim the following: G has a Hamiltonian Cycle if and only if T (of $\ell = n + 2\gamma + 3$ elements) is a median canonical trajectory for L in one of the two forms:

1. $T = \langle \$_s, \#_1, \#_2, \cdots, \#_\gamma, v_1, v_{\pi(2)}, \cdots, v_{\pi(n)}, v_1, \#_\gamma, \#_{\gamma-1}, \cdots, \#_1, \$_t \rangle$, or
2. $T = \langle \$_t, \#_1, \#_2, \cdots, \#_\gamma, v_1, v_{\pi(2)}, \cdots, v_{\pi(n)}, v_1, \#_\gamma, \#_{\gamma-1}, \cdots, \#_1, \$_s \rangle$;

moreover, there are $n + 4\gamma + 4$ adjacencies between T and L.

Again, we leave the detailed arguments as an exercise for the readers. The reduction obviously takes $O(|V| + |E|)$ time. Hence we have the theorem. □

4   Approximation Algorithms

In this section we present two simple approximation algorithms for the median trajectory and the median permutation problems respectively. It is open whether a constant factor approximation for the median canonical trajectory problem can be designed.

4.1   A 2-Approximation for the Median Trajectory Problem

Given a set of m trajectories $\mathcal{S} = \{S_1, S_2, \cdots, S_m\}$ over the same alphabet Σ, we need to compute a median trajectory T^* with ℓ nodes such that $\sum_{i=1..m} |a(T^*, S_i)|$ is maximized.

We use a greedy method to select $\lfloor \ell/2 \rfloor$ edges uv as follows: select uv that appear in $\mathcal{S}$ the maximum number of times, then subtract one copy of the edge uv (or vu) from the corresponding S_i's that uv or vu appears, update S_i's and then repeat until $\lfloor \ell/2 \rfloor$ edges are selected. We then concatenate these edge arbitrarily into a trajectory T. If ℓ is odd, then we arbitrarily concatenate another POI at the end of T.

As a POI could appear in T (and in T^*) multiple times, by the greedy search, the selected $\lfloor \ell/2 \rfloor$ edges form the maximum number of adjacencies with $\mathcal{S}$. This in turns implies that $\sum_{i=1..m} |a(T, S_i)|$ is greater than or equal to the adjacencies formed between any $\lfloor \ell/2 \rfloor$ edges in T^* with the trajectories in $\mathcal{S}$. Hence, $\sum_{i=1..m} |a(T, S_i)| \geq \frac{1}{2} \sum_{i=1..m} |a(T^*, S_i)|$. We thus have the following theorem.

Theorem 4. *The Median Trajectory problem admits a factor-2 polynomial-time approximation.*

4.2   A 1.5-Approximation for the Median Permutation Problem

Given a set of m trajectories $\mathcal{S} = \{S_1, S_2, \cdots, S_m\}$ over the same alphabet Σ, we need to compute a median permutation M^* with $n = |\Sigma|$ nodes such that $\sum_{i=1..m} a(M^*, S_i)$ is maximized. For this problem we are able to give a factor-1.5 approximation, the details will be given in the full version of this paper.

Theorem 5. *The Median Permutation problem admits a factor-1.5 polynomial-time approximation.*

We comment that the median permutation problem is mainly of theoretical meaning only: in practice, it is hardly the case that the median trajectory must be a permutation. In the next section, we present a practical solution, based on the greedy 2-approximation algorithm, for the median trajectory problem.

5   Empirical Results

5.1   Heuristic Method for the Median Trajectory Problem

The 2-approximation algorithm presented in the previous section is probably not practical. We present a slightly different heuristic method based on the 2-approximation algorithm. Later, we compare the performance of these two algorithms using simulated data over a 2-month period.

To make the presentation more clear, we formally define the concept of *adjacency map* as follows. Let ab be a 2-substring which appears in some $S_i, 1 \leq i \leq m$. The *adjacency map* of ab, denoted as $AM(ab)$, is a vector

$$AM(ab) = \langle w_1(ab), w_2(ab), \cdots, w_q(ab) \rangle$$

$$sequence \quad S_1 = \langle a\ b\ a\ e\ c\ a\ b\ d\ \rangle$$
$$sequence \quad S_2 = \langle c\ b\ d\ a\ b\ a\ d \rangle$$
$$sequence \quad S_3 = \langle a\ b\ e\ c\ a\ b\ c\ a\ f \rangle$$
$$AM(ab) = \langle 3, 3, 1 \rangle$$
$$AM(ac) = \langle 2, 1 \rangle$$

Fig. 3. An example for the adjacency map, with $m = 3$ and $\Sigma = \{a, b, c, d, e, f\}$. If $\ell = 6$, the 2-approximation would return $T = ab \cdot ab \cdot ac$, which incurs a total of 9 adjacencies with S_i's. The optimal solution would be $abacbd$, which incurs 12 adjacencies.

with $w_1(ab) \geq w_2(ab) \geq \cdots \geq w_q(ab) > 0$ and $w_0(ab) = 0$, such that $w_i(ab)$ is the number of S_i's that contains either ab or ba as a 2-substring after $w_{i-1}(ab)$ number of 2-substrings in the form of ab or ba have been removed from each of these S_i's. In Fig. 3, we show an example for this definition.

With this concept, the original 2-approximation is simply a greedy search in the space (of adjacency maps) $\mathcal{M} = \{w_i(ab)|i > 0, ab$ is a 2-substring in some $S_i\}$. More precisely, the algorithm repeatedly selects 2-substrings ab without replacement such that $w_i(ab)$ is the current maximum; moreover, when ab is selected the corresponding $w_i(ab)$ is deleted from the search space. Our new heuristic method is based on this greedy search, and searches more carefully by possibly extending existing solutions.

We first present the one-step implementation of this greedy search method, named as *Greedy1*, which is a subroutine used in the final algorithm. This implementation is mainly used for the comparison purpose.

Algorithm 1. Greedy1

Input: adjacency map $\mathcal{M}$, temporary solution T

Output: adjacency map $\mathcal{M}$, temporary solution T, integer $k > 0$

1: find a 2-substring ab with the maximum $k = w_i(ab)$ in $\mathcal{M}$.
2: put ab in T.
3: remove $w_i(ab)$ from $\mathcal{M}$.

To improve the simple greedy search method, which adds a 2-substring to the solution at each round, we make the following observations. In general, the final solution T is a concatenation of *maximal* substrings $T_1, T_2, \cdots, T_q$ such that breakpoints only exist between T_i and T_{i+1}. More precisely, let $T_i = \langle T_i[1], T_i[2], \cdots, T_i[|T_i|]\rangle$, then $w_x(T_i[|T_i|]T_{i+1}[1]) = 0$ for any x—in other words, $T_i[|T_i|]T_{i+1}[1]$ does not even exist in $\mathcal{M}$. (For convenience, we will also use $left(T_i)$ and $right(T_i)$ to represent $T_i[1]$ and $T_i[|T_i|]$ respectively.) With this observation in mind, if ab is first selected with Greedy1 and uv would be selected next with Greedy1, then we could select cd instead if $w_1(bc) + w_1(cd) > w_1(uv)$. Naturally, this means if we could extend ab into $abcd$, then it is better than $ab \cdot uv$, where $b \cdot u$ could be a breakpoint.

We are now ready to give the heuristic algorithm based on Greedy1 and Greedy2.

Algorithm 2. Greedy2

   Input: adjacency map $\mathcal{M}$, temporary solution T

   Output: adjacency map $\mathcal{M}$, temporary solution T, integer $k > 0$

1: **for** a maximal substring S in the temporary solution T **do**
2:     find a 2-substring ab s.t. $L = w_i(ab) + w_j(\langle b, left(S) \rangle)$ is maximum.
3:     find a 2-substring cd s.t. $R = w_{i'}(\langle right(S), c \rangle) + w_{j'}(cd)$ is maximum.
4:     update $temp \leftarrow \max(L, R)$.
5:     update $k \leftarrow \max(k, temp)$.
6: **end for**
7: update $S \leftarrow ab \circ S$ if $temp = L$, and update $S \leftarrow S \circ cd$ if $temp = R$.
8: remove $w_i(ab)$ and $w_j(\langle b, left(S) \rangle)$ from $\mathcal{M}$ if $temp = L$.
9: remove $w_{i'}(\langle right(S), c \rangle)$ and $w_{j'}(cd)$ from $\mathcal{M}$ if $temp = R$.

Algorithm 3. The Heuristic Algorithm

   Input: sequences $S_i (i = 1..m)$, integer ℓ

   Output: sequence T with ℓ nodes, number r of adjacencies between T and S_i's.

1: $T \leftarrow \varepsilon$, $r \leftarrow 0$.
2: compute the adjacency map $\mathcal{M}$ from S_i's.
3: $(\mathcal{M}, T, r) \leftarrow \text{Greedy1}(\mathcal{M}, T)$
4: $\ell \leftarrow \ell - 2$
5: **while** $\ell \geq 2$ **do**
6:     **if** $\text{Greedy1}(\mathcal{M}, T).r > \text{Greedy2}(\mathcal{M}, T).r$ **then**
7:       $(\mathcal{M}, T, r) \leftarrow \text{Greedy1}(\mathcal{M}, T)$
8:     **else**
9:       $(\mathcal{M}, T, r) \leftarrow \text{Greedy2}(\mathcal{M}, T)$
10:    **end if**
11:    $\ell \leftarrow \ell - 2$
12: **end while**
13: **if** $\ell > 0$ **then**
14:     extend a maximal substring S of T by a new node x such that $temp1 = \max(w_i(\langle x, left(S) \rangle), w_j(\langle right(S), x \rangle))$ is maximized over all S and x.
15:     update $r \leftarrow r + temp1$.
16:     update $S \leftarrow x \circ S$ if $temp1 = w_i(\langle x, left(S) \rangle)$.
17:     update $S \leftarrow S \circ x$ if $temp1 = w_j(\langle right(S), x \rangle)$.
18: **end if**

Note that as the heuristic algorithm subsumes the 2-approximation algorithm, it provides a performance guarantee of at most 2 as well. Unfortunately, this is the best we could say regarding its theoretical performance. We show next that with randomly generated simulated data, the actual performance (approximation factor) is always between 1.5 and 1.6.

5.2   Empirical Results

For the empirical results, we first generate 60 sequences randomly (presumably for 60 days or 2 months), each with a length in the range $[1.5|\Sigma| - 5, 1.5|\Sigma| + 5]$. Then for different target length ℓ, we run the 2-approximation algorithm and the heuristic algorithm to obtain the median trajectories T_1 and T_2 respectively. We run this 10 times to obtain the average of the maximum *appearance* (the maximum number of time a node, or POI, appearing in any sequence S_i), and the averages of T_1 and T_2—the last two being rounded to the largest integers below. The result is summarized in Table 1.

We also obtain the following Table 2, using some variations to the simulated data. With the 2-approximation algorithm, we have $App_1 \geq Opt/2$, or equivalently, $Opt \leq 2 \cdot App_1$. (For practical reason, here we can take App_1 roughly the same as $|T_1|$.) Hence, the actual performance (aka. approximation factor) can be bounded from above by

$$\mathcal{R} = \frac{|T_2|}{2 \cdot |T_1|} \leq \frac{|T_2|}{Opt},$$

which is always between 1.5 and 1.6 for the data in both tables.

Table 1. Results for $|S_i| \in [1.5|\Sigma| - 5, 1.5|\Sigma| + 5]$, averaged over 10 tries.

$|\Sigma|$	ℓ	Avg. of max appearance	$|T_1|$ (2-App)	$|T_2|$ (Heuristic)	$\mathcal{R}$
30	40	6.7	295	381	1.55
30	45	6.6	332	424	1.57
30	50	6.4	368	469	1.60
40	55	7.2	341	446	1.53
40	60	7.0	375	487	1.54
40	65	7.1	416	525	1.58
50	70	7.0	381	507	1.50
50	75	7.1	413	537	1.54
50	80	6.9	434	572	1.52
60	85	6.9	425	564	1.51
60	90	7.5	454	588	1.54
60	95	7.6	471	618	1.52

Table 2. Results for $|S_i| \in [1.5|\Sigma| - 10, 1.5|\Sigma| + 10]$, averaged over 10 tries.

$|\Sigma|$	ℓ	Avg. of max appearance	$|\mathcal{T}_1|$ (2-App)	$|\mathcal{T}_2|$ (Heuristic)	$\mathcal{R}$
30	35	6.8	258	336	1.54
30	40	7.1	302	382	1.58
30	45	6.9	339	427	1.59
30	50	7.0	370	469	1.58
30	55	6.4	394	503	1.57
40	50	6.8	313	405	1.55
40	55	6.8	352	451	1.56
40	60	7.1	372	488	1.52
40	65	6.6	414	522	1.59
40	70	6.6	429	560	1.53
50	65	6.7	358	468	1.53
50	70	6.7	383	504	1.52
50	75	7.0	407	536	1.52
50	80	7.3	434	569	1.53
50	85	7.1	463	602	1.54
60	80	7.4	400	525	1.52
60	85	6.9	419	553	1.52
60	90	7.1	443	585	1.51
60	95	7.2	472	620	1.52
60	100	7.1	495	645	1.53

6   Concluding Remarks

Using the concept of adjacency from computational genomics, we try to compare the similarity of trajectories from a vehicular network, which we propose to use as the first step to build trustfulness in vehicular networks. Here, a trajectory is a sequence of POIs visited by a vehicle in one day. This paper focuses on computing a consensus trajectory given a set of such trajectories, the objective being maximizing the total number of adjacencies between the consensus trajectory and the input trajectories. We consider three versions of the problem: Median Trajectory, Median Permutation and Median Canonical Trajectory, which are all NP-hard. We also give factor-2 and factor-1.5 approximation algorithms for the first two problems. For the Median Trajectory problem, we also design a heuristic algorithm which greatly outperforms the 2-approximation algorithm using simulated data articulately generated. The actual approximation factor is in the range $[1.5, 1.6]$, even though in theory it is 2 in the worst case.

There are still many open questions along this line. Theoretically, does Median Canonical Trajectory admit a constant factor approximation? Can the approximation factor for Median Trajectory be improved to be below 2? These questions definitely need further research.

Acknowledgments. This research was supported by NSF under project CNS-1761641 and by NNSF of China under project 61628207. Peng Zou was also supported by a COE Benjamin PhD Fellowship at Montana State University.

References

1. Angibaud, S., Fertin, G., Rusu, I., Thevenin, A., Vialette, S.: On the approximability of comparing genomes with duplicates. J. Graph Algorithms Appl. **13**(1), 19–53 (2009)
2. Bryant, D.: The complexity of the breakpoint median problem. Technical report CRM-2579. Centre de Recherches en Mathématiques, Université de Montréal (1998)
3. Doucer, J.: The sybil attack. In: Proceedings of IPTPS 2001 Revised Papers from the First International Workshop on Peer-to-Peer Systems, pp. 251–260 (2002)
4. Edmonds, J., Johnson, E.: Matching: a well-solved class of integer linear programs. In: Combinatorial Structures and Their Applications, Gordon and Breach, New York, pp. 89–92 (1969)
5. Hartenstein, H., Kenneth, L.: VANET: Vehicular Applications and Internetworking Technologies. Wiley, Hoboken (2009)
6. Jiang, H., Zhong, F., Zhu, B.: Filling scaffolds with gene repetitions: maximizing the number of adjacencies. In: Giancarlo, R., Manzini, G. (eds.) CPM 2011. LNCS, vol. 6661, pp. 55–64. Springer, Heidelberg (2011). https://doi.org/10.1007/978-3-642-21458-5_7
7. Jiang, H., Zheng, C., Sankoff, D., Zhu, B.: Scaffold filling under the breakpoint and related distances. IEEE/ACM Trans. Comput. Biol. Bioinform. **9**(4), 1220–1229 (2012)
8. Liu, G., Yang, Q., Wang, H., Lin, X., Wittie, M.: Assessment of multi-hop interpersonal trust in social networks by three-valued subjective logic. In: Proceedings of INFOCOM 2014, pp. 1698–1706 (2014)
9. Liu, G., Chen, Q., Yang, Q., Zhu, B., Wang, H., Wang, W.: OpinionWalk: an efficient solution to massive trust assessment in online social networks. In: Proceedings of INFOCOM 2017, pp. 1–9 (2017)
10. Li, M., Ma, B., Wang, L.: Finding similar regions in many sequences. J. Comput. Sys. Sci. **65**(1), 73–96 (2002)
11. Papadimitratos, P., et al.: Secure vehicular communication systems: design and architecture. IEEE Commun. Mag. **46**(11), 100–109 (2008)
12. Pe'er, I., Shamir, R.: The median problems for breakpoints are NP-complete. Elec. Colloq. Comput. Complex. TR-98-071 (1998)
13. Shiloach, Y.: Another look at the degree constrained subgraph problem. Inf. Process. Lett. **12**(2), 89–92 (1981)
14. Shrestha, R., Djuraev, S., Nam, S.Y.: Sybil attack detection in vehicular network based on received signal strength. In: Proceedings of 3rd International Conference on Connected Vehicles and Expo (ICCVE 2014), pp. 745–746 (2014)
15. Tannier, E., Zheng, C., Sankoff, D.: Multichromosomal median and halving problems under different genomic distances. BMC Bioinform. **10**, 120 (2009)
16. Zhang, J.: A survey on trust management for VANETS. In: Proceedings of 2011 IEEE International Conference on Advanced Information Networking and Applications (AINA 2011), pp. 105–115 (2011)

Short Papers

Utility Aware Task Offloading for Mobile Edge Computing

Ran Bi[1]([✉]), Jiankang Ren[1]([✉]), Hao Wang[2]([✉]), Qian Liu[1]([✉]),
and Xiuyuan Yang[1]([✉])

[1] School of Computer Science and Technology, Dalian University of Technology,
Dalian 116024, China
{biran,rjk,qianliu}@dlut.edu.cn, yxy815754134@mail.dlut.edu.cn
[2] Department of Computer Science and Technology, Heilongjiang University,
Harbin 150080, China
wanghao@hlju.edu.cn

Abstract. Mobile edge computing (MEC) casts the computation-intensive and delay-sensitive applications of mobiles on the network edges. Task offloading incurs extra communication latency and energy cost, and extensive efforts have been focused on the offloading scheme. To achieve satisfactory quality of experience, many metrics of the system utility are defined. However, most existing works overlook the balancing between the throughput and fairness. This paper investigates the problem of seeking optimal offloading scheme and the objective of the optimization is to maximize the system utility for leveraging between throughput and fairness. Based on KKT condition, we analyze the expectation of time complexity for deriving the optimal scheme. We provide an increment based greedy approximation algorithm with $1 + \frac{1}{e-1}$ ratio. Experimental results show that the proposed algorithm has better performance.

1 Introduction

With the advancement in wireless communication and cloud computing, MEC bridges the gap between the intensely computational requirements and the restricted capability of individual devices [1,2]. MEC leverages the physical proximity to mobile devices. By offloading part of the tasks to nearby MEC cloud [3], computation latency and energy consumption can be significantly decreased [4].

Since offloading incurs extra communication latency and energy cost, the offloading decision becomes a critical issue for both mobile cloud and MEC systems [5]. To achieve satisfactory quality of experience (QoE) [6,7], researchers propose many metrics of the system utility [8,9]. In [10], the utility measures the improvement in delay and energy consumption by offloading compared with local execution. Tao et al. [11] study the performance guaranteed scheme, which minimizes the energy consumption for mobiles. Optimal offloading decision is formalized as a latency-constrained energy minimization problem in [12,13].

© Springer Nature Switzerland AG 2019
E. S. Biagioni et al. (Eds.): WASA 2019, LNCS 11604, pp. 547–555, 2019.
https://doi.org/10.1007/978-3-030-23597-0_44

However, most existing works on MEC has overlooked the balancing between the throughput and fairness. The computing tasks cast different requirement, such as, data size, the number of CPU cycles, the deadline of completion time, and the constraint for the energy consumption. In short of the consideration for fairness, the offloading scheme will look down on some type of computation task, that leads to significant reduction in QoE. The computation capability is always given in advance. The relation between the requirements of computing tasks and the computation capability of server is neglected.

The aforementioned observation motivates us to investigate the problem of finding optimal offloading scheme, which maximizes the system utility balancing the throughput and fairness. We present the formal formulation for the above optimization problem. Based on KKT condition, we prove the expectation of time complexity for deriving the optimal scheme. For given precision parameter, a $(1 + \frac{1}{e-1})$-approximation algorithm is provided based on the greedy. Its time complexity and space complexity are $O\left(\frac{N^4 \tau}{c_{\min}}\right)$ and $O(N^3)$ respectively, where N is the number of computing tasks, τ is the computation constraint of server, and c_{min} is the number of CPU circles of task i.

The rest of this paper is organized as follows. In Sect. 2, the optimization problem is defined, and the computation complexity is analyzed. Section 3 proposes an approximate greedy algorithm, and the approximation ratio bound is proved. Performance evaluation is illustrated in Sect. 4, and Sect. 5 concludes this paper.

2   System Model and Problem Formulation

In this section, the problem of finding optimal offloading scheme with different computational requirements is defined, and is formalized as a general optimization problem. Based on KKT condition, expectation of time complexity is proved to be $O(4^N)$.

2.1   System Model

We consider that the system consists of a base station and N devices, which can include IoT and mobile devices. The devices can access the station resources through a wireless channel, and each device is endowed with different computing and communication capabilities, such as smart meters, tablets, and laptops. The system operates with a slotted structure. Let $\mathcal{N} = \{1, 2, ..., N\}$ denote the index set for N devices.

Definition 1. *(Computing task): A computing task $\mathcal{T}_i$ is represented by a tuple (d_i, c_i, t_i, e_i). d_i describes the data size of task of device i. c_i is the total number of CPU cycles required to accomplish the computation task. t_i denotes the deadline of completion time for the task. e_i is the upperbound of energy consumption, which includes the energy cost for wireless transmission and local computation.*

For the uplink transmission, the data rate of device i can be written as [10]

$$r_i = W \log_2 \left(1 + \frac{p_i h_i}{N_0}\right) \tag{1}$$

where W is the bandwidth, and p_i represents the transmission power of device i. We assume that the system bandwidth is B, thus there are no more than $M = B/W$ devices allowed to transmit at the same time.

2.2   Task Offloading Model

Based on the communication model, the task duration of offloading consists of time consumption by two parts, i.e., (i) communication time consumed by uplink transmission, (ii) execution time consumed by edge server. The task delay incurred by offloading can be denoted as $t_i^{off} = \frac{d_i}{r_i} + \frac{c_i}{f_e} = \frac{d_i}{W \log_2 \left(1 + p_i h_i N_0^{-1}\right)} + \frac{c_i}{f_e}$, where f_e is the computation capability of edge server in terms of instructions per second. In the procedure of task offloading, we only consider the energy cost of the upload. Therefore, the energy consumption depends on the data size of the task. If device i offloads a task to edge server, The energy consumption of device i for uplink transmission can be denoted as $e_i^{off} = \frac{d_i}{r_i} \times p_i = \frac{d_i p_i}{W \log_2 \left(1 + p_i h_i N_0^{-1}\right)}$.

2.3   Local Computation

For local task computing, let f_i denote the CPU computing capability of device i. The local execution time of the task can be obtained as $t_i^{loc} = \frac{c_i}{f_i}$. The energy cost of CPU is a superlinear function of computation frequency. We denote p_i^{loc} as the power consumption per CPU cycle. For task $\mathcal{T}_i$, the energy cost of locally processing can be written as $e_i^{loc} = p_i^{loc} \times c_i$.

2.4   Problem Formulation

For each task $\mathcal{T}_i$, we consider the task completion time and energy consumption simultaneously. Let λ_i denotes the fraction of offloading task for device i. The task delay consists of offloading and local computation,

$$\lambda_i \times t_i^{off} + (1 - \lambda_i) \times t_i^{loc} = \frac{\lambda_i d_i}{r_i} + \frac{\lambda_i c_i}{f_e} + (1 - \lambda_i) \times \frac{c_i}{f_i}. \tag{2}$$

Similarly, the energy consumption of each device i includes the uplink communication and local computation as following,

$$\lambda_i \times e_i^{off} + (1 - \lambda_i) \times e_i^{loc} = \frac{\lambda_i d_i p_i}{r_i} + (1 - \lambda_i) \times p_i^{loc} c_i. \tag{3}$$

In our model, a set of tasks arrive and seek for the derived computing service. We adopt an economic point to measure the utility for edge server performing a computing task. The nonlinear value function in this paper is similar as that in [14], based on the law of diminishing marginal utility [15]. The utility of the edge server by serving task $\mathcal{T}_i$ can be written as,

$$u_i = \log(1 + \lambda_i d_i). \tag{4}$$

Let C denote the total CPU computation capability, which can be seen as the maximum instructions per second. For given a set of computation tasks $\{\mathcal{T}_1, \mathcal{T}_2, ..., \mathcal{T}_N\}$, the computation capability of the server satisfies that $\sum_{i=1}^{N} c_i \leq \tau$. That is, the service can not enable each task to be computed at the BS. In this paper, we aim at maximizing the sum of the utility for the given tasks. The optimization problem can be formulated as follows,

$$\max_{\lambda} \sum_{i=1}^{N} \log(1 + \lambda_i d_i) \tag{5}$$

$$s.t. \ \frac{\lambda_i d_i}{r_i} + \frac{\lambda_i c_i}{f_e} + (1 - \lambda_i) \times \frac{c_i}{f_i} \leq t_i, \ \forall i \in \mathcal{N} \tag{6}$$

$$\frac{\lambda_i d_i p_i}{r_i} + (1 - \lambda_i) \times p_i^{loc} c_i \leq e_i, \ \forall i \in \mathcal{N} \tag{7}$$

$$\sum_{i=1}^{N} \lambda_i c_i \leq \tau \tag{8}$$

$$0 \leq \lambda_i \leq 1, \ \forall i \in \mathcal{N} \tag{9}$$

2.5   Computation Complexity Analysis

Lemma 1. *The objective function of optimization problem (5) is strictly concave.*

For any given i, we know that the inequality constraints of the problem are convex function, regarding to λ_i. We can apply *Karush-Kuhn-Tucker* (KKT) condition to obtain the optimal solutions for the proposed problem (5). For simplification, we introduce notations D_i and E_i, such that

$$U(\lambda) = \sum_{i=1}^{N} \log(1 + \lambda_i d_i), C(\lambda) = \sum_{i=1}^{N} \lambda_i c_i - \tau$$

$$T_i(\lambda_i) = \frac{\lambda_i d_i}{r_i} + \frac{\lambda_i c_i}{f_e} + (1 - \lambda_i) \times \frac{c_i}{f_i} - t_i \tag{10}$$

$$E_i(\lambda_i) = \frac{\lambda_i d_i p_i}{r_i} + (1 - \lambda_i) \times p_i^{loc} c_i - e_i$$

$$\forall i \in \{1, 2, ..., N\} \tag{11}$$

Theorem 1. *We assume that $\lambda_1^*, \lambda_2^*, ..., \lambda_N^*$ are the optimal solutions to problem (5), then there must exist $\alpha_1^*, ..., \alpha_N^*, \beta_1^*, ..., \beta_N^*$ and ξ^*, satisfies the following,*

$$\nabla U(\boldsymbol{\lambda}^*) - \sum_{j=1}^{N} \alpha_i^* \nabla T_i(\lambda_i^*) - \sum_{k=1}^{N} \beta_k^* \nabla E_k(\lambda_k^*) - \xi^* \nabla C(\boldsymbol{\lambda}^*) = 0 \quad (12)$$

$$\alpha_i^* E_i(\lambda_i^*) = 0, \ \beta_i^* E_i(\lambda_i^*) = 0, \ \forall i \in \{1, 2, ..., N\} \quad (13)$$

$$\xi^* C(\boldsymbol{\lambda}^*) = 0 \quad (14)$$

$$T_i(\lambda_i^*) \leq 0, \ E_i(\lambda_i^*) \leq 0, \ C(\boldsymbol{\lambda}^*) \leq 0, \ \forall i \in \{1, 2, ..., N\} \quad (15)$$

$$\xi^* \geq 0, \ 0 \leq \lambda_i^* \leq 1, \ \alpha_i^* \geq 0, \ \beta_i^* \geq 0, \ \forall i \in \{1, 2, ..., N\} \quad (16)$$

We define the Lagrangian function as following,

$$L(\boldsymbol{\lambda}, \boldsymbol{\alpha}, \boldsymbol{\beta}, \xi) = \sum_{i=1}^{N} \log(1 + \lambda_i d_i) + \sum_{i=1}^{N} \alpha_i (0 - T_i(\lambda_i))$$
$$+ \sum_{i=1}^{N} \beta_i (0 - E_i(\lambda_i)) + \xi (0 - C(\boldsymbol{\lambda})) \quad (17)$$

Based on Theorem 1, we need to solve $(3N+1)$ equations, that is, Eqs. (12)–(14). And then we check if the solutions satisfy the constraints (15)–(16). For given $i \in \{1, ..., N\}$, we obtain the optimal solutions by dealing with the equations.

$$\begin{cases} \frac{\partial L}{\partial \lambda_i^*} = \frac{d_i}{(1 + \lambda_i^* d_i) \ln 2} + \alpha_i^* \left(\frac{c_i}{f_i} - \frac{d_i}{r_i} - \frac{c_i}{f_e} \right) + \beta_i^* \left(p_i^{loc} c_i - \frac{d_i p_i}{r_i} \right) - \xi^* c_i = 0 & (18a) \\ \alpha_i^* \left(\frac{\lambda_i^* d_i}{r_i} + \frac{\lambda_i^* c_i}{f_e} + (1 - \lambda_i^*) \times \frac{c_i}{f_i} - t_i \right) = 0 & (18b) \\ \beta_i^* \left(\frac{\lambda_i^* d_i p_i}{r_i} + (1 - \lambda_i^*) \times p_i^{loc} c_i - e_i \right) = 0 & (18c) \\ \xi^* \left(\sum_{i=1}^{N} \lambda_i^* c_i - \tau \right) = 0 & (18d) \end{cases}$$

Lemma 2. *Without the constraint of (18d), there exist 4 cases to check the feasibility of the solutions derived by the above equations.*

Theorem 2. *For given N tasks, the expectation of time complexity for deriving the optimal points is $O(4^N)$.*

3 Increment Based Approximation Algorithm

There is no exact algorithm with polynomial time overhead for optimal deployment scheme, due to the *NP-Complete*. In this section, we prove that the objective function of *OEDQ* problem is increasing and submodular. And we provide a greedy polynomial time algorithm with approximation ratio bound $1 + \frac{1}{e-1}$. In the following, we propose an increment per cost based greedy algorithm, and the approximation ratio is analyzed.

Step 1. We enumerates all feasible solutions of cardinality 2.

Step 2. For each feasible solution, we find the offloading task with the largest increment per cost. We let the corresponding λ is increased by 10^{-k}, until the constraints (6)–(9) are not be satisfied. And k is the input parameter for precision, which can be defined by the users.

Step 3. At last, the algorithm returns the offloading scheme with the largest utility among all the schemes derived from step 2, and returns it as the final result.

Based on the above analysis, Fig. 1 presents the pseudo-code of calculating the feasible offloading scheme.

Algorithm 1 Increment based Approximation Algorithm for Offloading Scheme

---

Input: $k, W, C, f_e, \mathcal{T}_i = <d_i, c_i, t_i, e_i, p_i, p_i^{loc}>$, for $i = 1, ..., N$
Output: $\lambda_1, \lambda_2, ..., \lambda_N$

1: Initialization, let $\lambda_i = 0$ for $i \in \{1, 2, ..., N\}$.
2: Enumerates all feasible solutions of cardinality 3, as the initial scheme set $S_3 = \{\lambda(1), \lambda(2), ..., \lambda(M)\}$. Such that for each scheme $\lambda(j) = \{\lambda_1(j), \lambda_2(j), ..., \lambda_N(j)\}, \sum_{i=1}^{N} \lambda_i(j) \leq 3 \times 10^{-k}$, and the constraints are satisfied, **i.e.** $\forall i \in \{1, ..., N\}, T_i(\lambda_i(j)) \leq 0, E_i(\lambda_i(j)) \leq 0$ and $\sum_{i=1}^{N} \lambda_i(j)c_i \leq \tau$.
3: $U_{max} = \max\{U(\lambda(j))|j \in \{1, 2, ..., M\}\}$;
4: **for** $j = 1$ to M **do**
5:     **while** $\sum_{i=1}^{N} \lambda_i(j)c_i + 10^{-k} * \min\{c_1, .., c_N\} \leq \tau$ **do**
6:         **for** $h = 1$ to N **do**
7:             $\varepsilon_h(j) = 0$;
8:             $\lambda_h(j) = \lambda_h(j) + 10^{-k}$;
9:             **if** $\frac{\lambda_h(j)d_h}{r_h} + \frac{\lambda_h(j)c_h}{f_e} + (1 - \lambda_h(j)) \times \frac{c_h}{f_h} \leq t_h \wedge \frac{\lambda_h(j)d_h p_h}{r_h} + (1 - \lambda_h(j)) \times p_h^{loc} c_h \leq e_h$ **then**
10:                 **if** $\sum_{i=1}^{N} \lambda_i(j)c_i + 10^{-k} * c_h \leq \tau$ **then**
11:                     $\varepsilon_h(j) = \{U(\lambda(j) + I(k, h)) - U(\lambda(j))\}/10^{-k}c_h$
12:         $g = \arg\max\{\varepsilon_h(j)|h \in \{1, 2, ..., N\}\}$;
13:         $\lambda(j) = \lambda(j) + I(k, g)$;
14:     $U_{max} = \max(U_{max}, U(\lambda(j)))$
15: **return** U_{max} and the corresponding offloading scheme.

Theorem 3. *The objective function of problem (5) is submodular.*

Corollary 1. *For given precision parameter k, let $Q_{OPT}(k)$ denote the utility of the optimal solutions of problem (5). And we denote the utility derived from the solution of Algorithm 1 as $Q_{GAA}(k)$. Then the approximation ratio $r = \frac{Q_{OPT}(k)}{Q_{GAA}(k)}$ satisfies the following:*

$$r \leq 1 + \frac{1}{e - 1}. \tag{19}$$

There exist N^3 feasible schemes, such that $\sum_{i=1}^{N} \lambda_i \leq 3 * 10^{-k}$. According to Fig. 1, the time complexity for enumerating all feasible solutions of cardinality 3 is $O(N^3)$. For each feasible scheme $\lambda(h)$, the complexity for greedily increasing $\lambda_i(h)$ by 10^{-k} is $O\left(\min\left\{\frac{N\tau}{c_{min}}, 10^k\right\}\right)$, where $c_{min} = \min\{c_i|i = 1, 2, ..., N\}$. Then the cost is $O\left(\frac{N^4 \tau}{c_{min}}\right)$ from line 4 to 14. Based on the above analysis, the computation complexity is $O\left(\frac{N^4 \tau}{c_{min}}\right)$. And the space complexity is $O(N^3)$. In conclusion, the proposed algorithm can be implemented in time complexity of $O\left(\frac{N^4 \tau}{c_{min}}\right)$ and space complexity of $O(N^3)$.

4   Performance Evaluation

In this section, a series of experiments have been carried out to evaluate the performance of **I**ncrement based **A**pproximation **A**lgorithm for **O**ffloading **S**cheme (IAAOS). We compare the performance of IAAOS with the exact solutions, which are calculated by convex optimisation matlab toolbox. In the simulation, the number of offloading task is set to be 20, the mobile CPU ability is randomly from $\{1, 1.1, ..., 2\}$. The size of the task follows uniform distribution over $(0, 2)$ MB. We set the channel bandwidth $B = 10$ MHz. The transmitting power is uniformly distributed $(0, 1)$ W. For each i, t_i and t_i are randomly generated. The first group of experiments is to investigate the utility of the proposed algorithm, when the computation capability of server varies. From Fig. 1(a), the utility increases when the server computation is enhanced. Since the objective function is concave, the increment of the is falter with larger computation capability. Due to the limited bandwidth, the increasing is not obvious, even if the server computation is more than the total number of CPU circles.

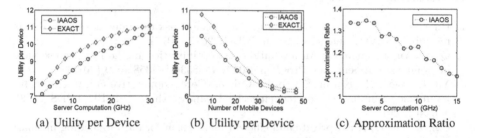

(a) Utility per Device   (b) Utility per Device   (c) Approximation Ratio

Fig. 1. Utility and approximation raito

Figure 1(b) plots the number of mobile devices and the utility of the proposed approximation algorithm. Since the computation capability of server is given, the utility per device is decreased with larger number of devices. Due to the concave, the data size of offloading will more fair, when the number of mobile devices become larger. Thus the difference between the utility of approximation algorithm and that of the exact algorithm is smaller.

The third group of experiments is to investigate the computing performance of IAAOS and the correctness of the approximation ratio is verified. In the experiments, approximation ratio(AR) is the ratio of generated by the solutions of exact approach to that of the approximated solutions output by IAAOS. Figure 1(c) demonstrates the relationships between the approximation ratio and the server computation, where precision parameter $k = 3$. Experimental results show that the utility value of approximation results returned by IAAOS are very close to that of the optimal ones. And the proposed approximation algorithms can achieve high accuracy.

5   Conclusion

By offloading part of the tasks to nearby MEC cloud, MEC can bring down the computation latency and energy cost by optimizing task offloading and resource allocation policies. Many factors make offloading decision challenging. To maximize the system utility, the problem of finding optimal offloading scheme is defined. We study the expectation of time complexity for deriving the optimal scheme based on KKT condition. We provide an greedy based polynomial-time algorithm with $(1 + \frac{1}{e-1})$-approximation ratio. Simulation results show that the proposed algorithms have better performance for system utility.

Acknowledgments. This work is supported in part by the National Natural Science Foundation of China (61602084, 61602080, 61772112, 61761136019), the Post-Doctoral Science Foundation of China (2016M600202), the Doctoral Scientific Research Foundation of Liaoning Province (201601041), the Fundamental Research Funds for the Central Universities (DUT19JC53).

References

1. Duan, Z., Li, W., Cai, Z.: Distributed auctions for task assignment and scheduling in mobile crowdsensing systems. In: ICDCS 2017 (2017)
2. Qi, L., Yu, J., Zhou, Z.: An invocation cost optimization method for web services in cloud environment. Sci. Program. **2017**, 4358536:1–4358536:9 (2017)
3. Yu, L., Shen, H., Karan, S., Ye, L., Cai, Z.: Core: cooperative end-to-end traffic redundancy elimination for reducing cloud bandwidth cost. IEEE TPDS **28**(2), 446–461 (2017)
4. Cai, Z., Zheng, X.: A private and efficient mechanism for data uploading in smart cyber-physical systems. IEEE Trans. Netw. Sci. Eng. (accepted)
5. Xu, Y., Qi, L., Dou, W., Yu, J.: Privacy-preserving and scalable service recommendation based on simhash in a distributed cloud environment. Complexity **2017**, 3437854:1–3437854:9 (2017)
6. Hu, C., Li, W., Cheng, X., Yu, J., Wang, S., Bie, R.: A secure and verifiable access control scheme for big data storage in clouds. IEEE Trans. Big Data **4**(3), 341–355 (2018)
7. Yu, L., Chen, L., Cai, Z., Shen, H., Liang, Y., Pan, Y.: Stochastic load balancing for virtual resource management in datacenters. IEEE Tran. Cloud Comput. (accepted)
8. Duan, Z., Li, W., Zheng, X., Cai, Z.: Mutual-preference driven truthful auction mechanism in mobile crowdsensing. In: ICDCS 2019 (accepted)
9. Yu, L., Cai, Z.: Dynamic scaling of virtualized networks with bandwidth guarantees in cloud datacenters. In: INFOCOM 2016 (2016)
10. Lyu, X., Tian, H., Sengul, C., et al.: Multiuser joint task offloading and resource optimization in proximate clouds. IEEE Trans. Veh. Technol. **66**(4), 3435–3447 (2017)
11. Tao, X., Ota, K., Dong, M.: Performance guaranteed computation offloading for mobile-edge cloud computing. IEEE Wirel. Commun. Lett. **6**(6), 774–777 (2017)
12. Wang, F., Xu, J., Wang, X.: Joint offloading and computing optimization in wireless powered mobile-edge computing systems. IEEE Trans. Wirel. Commun. **17**(3), 1784–1797 (2018)

13. Zhu, T., Shi, T., Li, J., Cai, Z., Zhou, X.: Task scheduling in deadline-aware mobile edge computing systems. IEEE Internet Things J. (accepted)
14. Tang, L., Chen, H.: Joint pricing and capacity planning in the IaaS cloud market. IEEE Trans. Cloud Comput. **5**(1), 57–70 (2017)
15. Liu, F., Zhou, Z., Jin, H., et al.: On arbitrating the power-performance tradeoff in SaaS clouds. IEEE Trans. Parallel Distrib. Syst. **25**(10), 2648–2658 (2014)

Analysis of Best Network Routing Structure for IoT

Shasha Chen[1], Shengling Wang[1(✉)], and Jianghui Huang[2]

[1] The College of Information Science and Technology, Beijing Normal University,
Beijing 100875, China
chenshasha@mail.bnu.edu.cn, wangshengling@bnu.edu.cn
[2] The Institute of Computing Technology, Chinese Academy of Sciences,
Beijing 100190, China
huangjianhui@ict.ac.cn

Abstract. The internet of things (IoT) enables physical objects to sense the world and hence perform specific tasks, winning a great market success. Routing bears significant importance to IoT since punctual and reliable information delivery is indispensable for most IoT applications. The start-of-the-art work on IoT routing mainly focuses on designing algorithms to select efficient relays according to a given topology for improving routing performance. In this paper, we take a dramatically different viewpoint to study the routing in IoT. In detail, we figure out the best IoT network structure to attain the best message transmission. We have proved that IoT with small-world properties can achieve better routing performance when the probability of long-range connections obeys Lévy distribution. Furthermore, we deduce the upper and lower bound of the average number of message transmission steps respectively. Finally, we do extensive experiments to validate our analysis.

Keywords: IoT · Small-world properties · Lévy distribution · Routing

1 Introduction

Last decade witnessed IoT has stepped out of its infancy with the development of wireless/mobile computing [1,3] and micro-electronics technologies [2,4]. IoT enables physical objects, ranging from simple devices (e.g., sensors and meters) to smart equipments (such as robots and vehicles), to sense the world and hence perform specific tasks. IoT plays a remarkable role to change the way in which we are acting and improve the quality of our lives, winning a great market success. It is predicted that the number of connected physical objects has grown 300% over the last 5 years and will reach 212 billion by the end of 2020 [5].

In many IoT applications, data may need to be disseminated to interconnect objects embedded communication capability. Hence, routing bears significant importance since punctual and reliable information delivery is indispensable for most IoT applications. The state-of-the-art work on IoT routing [6] focuses on

© Springer Nature Switzerland AG 2019
E. S. Biagioni et al. (Eds.): WASA 2019, LNCS 11604, pp. 556–563, 2019.
https://doi.org/10.1007/978-3-030-23597-0_45

designing algorithms to select efficient relays according to a given topology for improving transmission delay and delivery success probability.

In this paper, we take a dramatically different viewpoint to study the routing in IoT. In detail, we will figure out the best IoT network structure to attain the best performance of message transmission. The difference between the start-of-the-art work and ours lies in that the former tries to understand IoT, aiming to improve the performance of existing IoT networks, while the latter strives to change IoT through designing a new IoT network to achieve some perfect performance. The start-of-the-art work is a bottom-up idea but it can not fundamentally make up the defects of IoT networks, and may even intensify its chaotic situation. Our study is a top-down solution with the aim of optimizing IoT networks systematically.

Regarding on designing a network structure for enhancing routing efficiency, there were some studies [7,8] on small-world networks with the features that rich in short-range connections and poor in long-range connections. Although most IoT networks have the traits of small-world networks, the assumption in the existing work that the probability of long-range connections obeys power-law probability distribution is not practical. This is because the links of many IoT networks, such as mobile opportunity networks [9–11] and wildlife networks [12], are formed depending on human walk or animals movement. That is, the physical objects are often carried by people or animals whose contacts driven by their movements forming the links of IoT networks. Researches have shown that Lévy mobility rather than power-law probability distribution can closely mimic human walk [13] and animal species searching target [14].

As mentioned above, since most IoT networks have the properties of small-world networks with rich short-range connections and poor long-range connections, in this paper, we find a network structure based on small-world networks for IoT applications to optimize the data delivery. And we have proved that small-world networks can achieve better routing performance when the probability of long-range connections obeys Lévy distribution. The details are as follows:

1. We have shown that the average number of message transmission steps is $\Lambda \leq \beta\sqrt{n}$, where n denotes the number of short-range connections and β is a constant depending on the cluster parameter of Lévy distribution c and the mean parameter of Lévy distribution μ but independent of n. Our small-world network structure can attain shorter delivery time than which Kleinberg has proposed in present small-world network scale [7].
2. And we have shown that the average number of message transmission steps is $\Lambda \geq \beta_c n^{1/2-c}$ where β_c is a constant depending on c and μ but independent of n and c is the cluster parameter of Lévy distribution when $0 < c < 1/2$ and $\Lambda \geq \beta_c n^{c-1/2}$ when $1/2 < c < 1$.

The rest of the paper is organized as follows. Section 2 introduces small-world networks and Lévy distribution. The transmission method adopted in our analysis is in Sect. 3. Section 4 reveals the upper bound and lower bound of average number of message transmission steps in small-world networks respectively. This paper is concluded by Sect. 6.

2   Our Model

Usually, an IoT network is composed of thousands of or even more nodes, and each node can directly communicate with several other nodes. Such a network should have small-world properties. The small-world phenomenon shows that most of us are linked by short chains of acquaintances [7].

In this paper, we use $n \times n$ lattice to represent the small-world network [7]. Each vertex in the lattice represents a node in small-world networks, in which edges of the network are divided into short-range connections and long-range ones. The connections between vertexes and their neighbors are called short-range connections and otherwise, connections are long-range ones. In Fig. 1, each vertex represents a node in small-world networks which has k short-range connections and m long-range connections. As we can see in Fig. 1, each vertex in the lattice is connected to four neighboring nodes, e.g., node S has four short-range connections and the number of its long-range connections is 2. As for node V, k is 4 and m is 3. In this paper, we assume that m is 1.

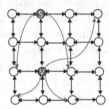

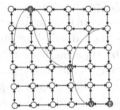

Fig. 1. A 4×4 two-dimensional lattice represents the small-world network

Fig. 2.   The   transmission   method adopted in our analysis

In our analysis, every node has a probability of reaching message. i.e., the network does not need to percolate. Thus, the distribution of long-range connections is the critical factor because it influences short paths.

We adopt Lévy distribution to describe the probability of small-world networks long-range connections in this paper because of the advantage of Lévy distribution that we have mentioned in the previous section. To better study the navigation in small-world networks, and secondly, we give a short introduction of Lévy Distribution.

The probability density function (PDF) of Lévy distribution $f(x, c, \mu)$ is $\sqrt{\frac{c}{2\pi}} \frac{e^{-\frac{c}{2(x-\mu)}}}{(x-\mu)^{3/2}}$ where c is cluster parameter and μ is mean parameter.

3   The Transmission Method Adopted in Our Analysis

In this section, we seek a network structure for IoT with small-world properties. However, the best network structure depends on different transmission methods. In this paper, we adopt a conventional transmission method [7], which is described as follows.

To formulate the transmission method, s and t are denoted as the source node and target one. And phase j is the moment that the distance to the target lattice distance is from 2^j to 2^{j+1}. Therefore, the maximum value of j is $logn$. And $P_r(w, v)$ be the probability of long-range connection between nodes w and v. In order to normalize the probability, the probability that node w chooses node v as long-range connection is $P_r(w, v)/\sum_{w \neq v} P_r(w, v)$ [7].

Since we assume that the probability $P_r(w, v)$ of any two vertices w and v in the network obeys to Lévy distribution, we have $P_r(w, v) = f(r, c, \mu) \cdot 1$ where r is the lattice distance between w and v because the lattice distance is a positive integer. The probability $P_r(w, v)$ of connection between two vertices is smaller when the distance gets larger. The lattice distance starts from 1. Therefore, the maximum probability density of the Lévy distribution is obtained in this paper. And this point is fixed in 1.

The transmission method adopted in our analysis is as follows. Firstly, we choose a source s and a target t from two-dimension lattice randomly (see Fig. 2). Node w represents current message holder. Node v denotes the next node that w chooses to transmit a message which is the nearest node to target. In Fig. 2, node s chooses w to transmit a message because w is the nearest node to target t. And node v is the nearest node to target among nodes linking to w. Thus w chooses v as the next message holder.

4   Theoretical Analysis

Based on the transmission method in Sect. 3, we adopt Lévy distribution to describe small-world networks node links. And we analysed the upper bound and lower bound of average message transmission steps.

4.1   Upper Bound

Theorem 1. *When the probability of long-range connections in $n \times n$ two-dimensional lattice obeys Lévy distribution, there exists a constant β depending on c and μ but independent of n makes the average number of message transmission steps $\Lambda \leq \beta\sqrt{n}$.*

Proof. In order to analyse the average number of message transmission steps in a small-world network, we divide the network into different transmission areas according to distance on target. And the average number of message transmission steps is the sum of average message steps spending in different transmission areas which depends on the probability of message entering this area. While the probability of message entering a specific transmission area depends on links probability. In this paper, we divide all nodes in a small-world network into different set $A_j(j = 1, 2, ..., logn)$ which is the set of nodes whose distance to the target is from 2^j to 2^{j+1}. E_j denotes average steps spending in set A_j. X denotes average number of message transmission steps. Based on the above analysis and notations, thus the analysis process is divided into four steps. The first step is to calculate the link probability of any two nodes which obeys Lévy distribution. And then the probability that message enters set A_j can be attained. Thirdly, the average number of message transmission steps EX_j in set A_j can be calculated. In the last, the result X (the average total number of message transmission steps) can be gotten by summing EX_j [7].

According to the analysis process, we need to calculate link probability of any two nodes. The probability that node w chooses node v as long-range connection is $P_r(w,v)/\sum_{w \neq v} P_r(w,v)$. In order to figure out the probability of connection between node w and v, we calculate $\sum_{w \neq v} P_r(w,v)$ and $P_r(w,v)/\sum_{w \neq v} P_r(w,v)$. Since $k = 4$ and $m = 1$, each node w in the network is connected to its four neighbors (two or three neighbors in the case of nodes on the boundary) and has only one long-range connection v. The lattice distance ranges from 1 to $2n - 2$. Thus, we have $\sum_{w \neq v} P_r(w,v) \leq 4\sqrt{\frac{c}{2\pi}}(2\sqrt{2n - 2 - \mu} - 2\sqrt{1 - \mu} + \sum_{i=2}^{\infty} c_i)$.

Where c_i is a constant and $c_i = (-1)^i \frac{c^i}{2^{i-1} \cdot i! \cdot (1-\mu)^{(2i-3)/2}} \left[\frac{1}{2i-3} - \frac{\mu}{(2i-1)(1-\mu)} \right]$. c_i depends on c and μ but is independent of n. c_i is convergent when c ranges from 0 to 2.

Therefore the probability of long-range connections between node w and node v is at least $P_r(w,v)/\sum_{w \neq v} P_r(w,v)$. Hence, $P_r(w,v)/\sum_{w \neq v} P_r(w,v)$ is $[4\sqrt{\frac{c}{2\pi}}(2\sqrt{2n - 2 - \mu} - 2\sqrt{1 - \mu} + \sum_{i=2}^{\infty} c_i)P_r(w,v)]^{-1}$.

The strategy of achieving best message transmission is defined as follows: at any phase, the current message holder w chooses the node which is nearer target t as much as possible to transmit message. In phase j, the distance of current message holder w to target t is from 2^j to 2^{j+1}.

The second step is to calculate the probability of message entering specific transmission area (e.g., A_j). In order to attain the probability of message entering A_j, we calculate the probability of current message holder choosing any node in set A_j to transmit message P_r and the node number N_j of set A_j. Thus the probability of message entering A_j is $P_j = N \cdot P_r$, i.e., P_j.

We assume that the current message holder is w. Since the probability of connections drops when lattice distance between two nodes increases, the probability of w choosing any node in set A_j to transmit message P_r is at least

$$\frac{1}{4(2\sqrt{2n-2-\mu}-2\sqrt{1-\mu}+\sum_{i=2}^{\infty} c_i)} \frac{e^{-\frac{c}{2(2^{j+1}-\mu)}}}{(2^{j+1}-\mu)^{3/2}}.$$

The node number N_j of set A_j is at least 2^{2j-1}.

Thus the probability that message transmission enters set A_j is at least

$$P_j \geq \frac{(2^{j+1}-\mu)^{1/2} \cdot e^{-\frac{c}{2(2^{j+1}-\mu)}}}{32(2\sqrt{2n-2-\mu}-2\sqrt{1-\mu}+\sum_{i=2}^{\infty} c_i)}.$$

Based on the second step, the third step is to analyse the average number of message transmission steps in a specific transmission area. i.e. A_j. X_j is the total number of steps spent in set A_j and EX_j denote the average number of steps spending in set A_j. Hence, we have $EX_j = \sum_{i=1}^{\infty} P_r(X_j \geq i) \leq 32(2\sqrt{2n - 2 - \mu} - 2\sqrt{1 - \mu} + \sum_{i=2}^{\infty} c_i)(2^{j+1} - \mu)^{-1/2} e^{\frac{c}{2(2^{j+1}-\mu)}}$.

In the last, we can attain the average message transmission steps X by summing EX_j. X denotes the average total number of message transmission steps from source s to target t. Thus we have $X = \sum_{j=0}^{logn} EX_j \leq \beta\sqrt{n}$.

Where β is a parameter which is related to c_i and μ. Thus we can draw a conclusion that the upper bound of average number of transmission steps is proportional to $\sqrt{n}$ where n is lattice scale.

4.2   Lower Bound

Theorem 2. *When the probability of long-range connections in $n \times n$ two-dimensional lattice obeys Lévy distribution, there exists a constant β_c depending on c and μ but independent of n makes the average number of message transmission steps $\Lambda \geq \beta_c n^{1/2-c}$ where $0 < c < 1/2$ and $\Lambda \geq \beta_c n^{c-1/2}$ where $1/2 < c < 1$.*

Proof. As we defined, the probability of long-range contact between w and v is $P_r(w,v)/\sum_{w \neq v} P_r(w,v)$ where $0 < c < 1/2$. The analysis is similar when $1/2 < c < 1$. Thus we analyse the average number of message transmission steps when $0 < c < 1/2$ in the next part.

Similar to the analysis of upper bound, the analysis of lower bound is divided into four steps.

5   Numerical Analysis

Based on the previous analysis, we do extensive experiments on our upper bound and lower bound. Firstly, we compare the upper bound of Lévy distribution which is proposed in this paper and that of inverse square distribution $P \sim r^{-2}$ where r denotes the distance between two nodes [7] in Fig. 3. Figure 3 shows that the upper bound grows with the increase of lattice scale n whether small-world networks display a Lévy distribution or an inverse square distribution in their node links. However, the upper bound is lower when small-world networks node links obey Lévy distribution where n is less than 40000.

In this section, we compare the navigation performance in small-world networks by varying the cluster parameter c of Lévy distribution. Since we fix the point of maximum probability density to be 1, the mean parameter μ is $1 - (c/3)^{2/5}$. The following is the impact of c on message transmission steps. Figure 4 illustrates the average number of message transmission steps by varying cluster parameter c where $0 < c < 1/2$. As shown in Fig. 4, we observed the message transmission steps dropped when we varied cluster parameter c from $1/32$ to $1/2$.

Figure 5 shows the impact of c on the average number of message transmission steps when $1/2 < c < 1$. As showed in Fig. 5, a higher c value leads to more steps spent in message transmission from source s to target t where $1/2 < c < 1$. While a higher c value leads to fewer steps spent where $0 < c < 1/2$ in Fig. 4. We can draw a conclusion that the average number of message transmission steps is the least when cluster parameter c is $1/2$. Simulation parameters where $1/2 < c < 1$ are that parameter c is $\frac{1}{2} + 2^i$ where i ranges from -5 to -1.

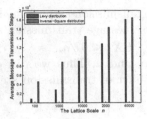

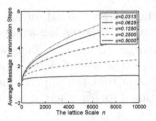

Fig. 3. The upper bound of Lévy distribution and inverse square distribution

Fig. 4. The performance of the message transmission steps where $0 < c < 1/2$

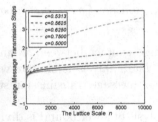

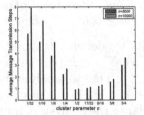

Fig. 5. The performance of the message transmission steps where $1/2 < c < 1$

Fig. 6. Impacts of c on the navigation

Figure 6 shows the impact of c on navigation in small-world networks navigation. It illustrates how the average transmission steps changes with cluster c when n is fixed. It indicates that a higher c value leads to fewer steps spent where $0 < c < 1/2$. However, a higher c value leads to more steps spent where $1/2 < c < 1$. Because we can find a better networks structure to achieve a better navigation like less average transmission steps.

6 Conclusion

In this paper, we aim to find the best network routing structure for IoT with small-world properties where the probability of long-range connections obeys Lévy distribution. We deduce the upper and lower bound of average transmission steps of IoT. In detail, the average number of message transmission steps is proportional to the square root of network scale where proportional coefficient depends on the cluster and mean parameters of Lévy distribution; the average message number of transmission steps depends on not only the network scale but also cluster parameters. Our analysis is practical because Lévy distribution perfectly fit small-world properties and is the most efficient routing strategy. We also do extensive simulations to validate our results. Simulations show that our results match the theoretical analysis very well.

Acknowledgment. This work has been supported by the National Natural Science Foundation of China (No. 61772080).

References

1. Chen, S., et al.: Mobility-driven networks (MDN): from evolution to visions of mobility management. IEEE Netw. **28**(4), 66–73 (2014)
2. Atzori, L., Iera, A., Morabito, G.: The internet of things: a survey. Comput. Netw. J. **54**, 2787–2805 (2010)
3. Zheng, X., Cai, Z., Li, Y.: Data linkage in smart IoT systems: a consideration from privacy perspective. IEEE Commun. Mag. **56**(9), 55–61 (2018)
4. Cai, Z., He, Z.: Trading private range counting over big IoT data. In: The 39th IEEE International Conference on Distributed Computing Systems (ICDCS) (2019)
5. Gantz, J., Reinsel, D.: The digital universe in 2020: big data, bigger digital shadows, and biggest growth in the far east. IDC iView: IDC Anal. Future **2007**, 1–16 (2012)
6. Bakshi, A., et al.: EMIT: an efficient MAC paradigm for the Internet of Things. In: The 36th IEEE Conference on Computer Communications (INFOCOM) (2016)
7. Kleinberg, J.: The small-world phenomenon: an algorithmic perspective. In: The 32nd Annual ACM Symposium on Theory of Computing (STOC) (2000)
8. Watts, D.J., Strogatz, S.H.: Collective dynamics of 'small-world' networks. Nature **393**(6684), 440–442 (1998)
9. Wang, S., et al.: Analyzing the potential of mobile opportunistic networks for big data applications. IEEE Netw. **29**(5), 57–63 (2015)
10. Wang, S., et al.: Opportunistic routing in intermittently connected mobile P2P networks. IEEE J. Sel. Areas Commun. **31**(9), 369–378 (2013)
11. Wang, S., Liu, M., Cheng, X., Song, M.: Routing in pocket switched networks. IEEE Wirel. Commun. **19**(2), 67–73 (2012)
12. Rushmore, J., Caillaud, D., Matamba, L., et al.: Social network analysis of wild chimpanzees provides insights for predicting infectious disease risk. J. Anim. Ecol. **82**(5), 976–986 (2013)
13. Wang, S., et al.: The tempo-spatial information dissemination properties of mobile opportunistic networks with levy mobility. In: The 34th International Conference Distributed Computing Systems (ICDCS) (2014)
14. Hu, C., et al.: A multi-verse optimizer with levy flights for numerical optimization and its application in test scheduling for network-on-chip. PloS ONE **11**(12), e0167341 (2016)

Parallel Multicast Information Propagation Based on Social Influence

Yuqi Fan[1(✉)], Liming Wang[1], Lei Shi[1], and Dingzhu Du[2]

[1] School of Computer Science and Information Engineering,
Hefei University of Technology, Hefei 230601, Anhui, China
{yuqi.fan,shilei}@hfut.edu.cn, wlm1018@mail.hfut.edu.cn
[2] Department of Computer Science,
University of Texas at Dallas, Richardson 75080, USA
dzdu@utdallas.edu

Abstract. Most research on information propagation in social networks does not consider how to find information dissemination paths from the information source node to a set of influential nodes. In this paper, we introduce a multicast information propagation model which disseminates information from the information source node to a set of designated influential nodes in social networks, and formulate the problem with the objective to maximize the social influence on the information propagation paths. We then propose a Parallel Multicast information Propagation algorithm (PMP), which concurrently constructs a subgraph for each influential node, joins all the subgraphs into a merge graph, and finds the information propagation paths with the maximum social influence in the merge graph. The simulation results demonstrate that the proposed algorithm can achieve competitive performance in terms of the social influence on the information propagation paths.

Keywords: Information propagation · Opinion leader ·
Social influence

1 Introduction

The information dissemination in social networks starts with a node who spreads the information to the neighbors of the node, and some of the neighbors can further spread the information to their neighbors in the networks. The social influence of the nodes triggers a cascade of information propagation [1]. Two models were proposed in [2] to measure how to activate the neighbors, i.e., the LT model and the IC model. A heterogeneous network based epidemic model was proposed to block rumors at influential users and spread truth to clarify

This work was partly supported by the National Natural Science Foundation of China (61701162), the Anhui Provincial Natural Science Foundation (1608085MF142), and the open project of State Key Laboratory of Complex Electromagnetic Environment Effects on Electronics and Information System (CEMEE2018Z0102B).

E. S. Biagioni et al. (Eds.): WASA 2019, LNCS 11604, pp. 564–572, 2019.
https://doi.org/10.1007/978-3-030-23597-0_46

rumors [3]. An information propagation model was proposed to incorporate the real-time optimization strategy, the pulse spreading truth and the continuous blocking rumor strategy to describe rumor spreading [4]. A model was proposed to deal with the dynamic attitudes changing problem on the basis of people's social structures, which considered median process that explained how people's attitudes would change [5].

Some individuals who have a wide influence to share the information are called opinion leaders. The problem of influence maximization aims to identify a set of opinion leaders from a network so that the influence propagation invoked by these nodes is maximized. There exist four types of influence maximization algorithms: approximation algorithms [6], heuristic-based algorithms [7], greedy-based algorithms [8] and other algorithms [9].

It is also important to make the opinion leaders receive and accept the information from the information source node, such that the opinion leaders will forward the information to a large number of users in the social network. To the best of our knowledge, very little attention in literature has ever been paid on information diffusion from a source node to a set of opinion leaders based on social influence in social networks. In this paper, we will deal with the problem of searching for information propagation paths from a node to a set of designated influential nodes with an objective to maximize the social influence on the information propagation paths.

The main contributions of this paper are as follows. We introduce a multicast information propagation model which depicts the phenomenon that an information source node disseminates information to a set of opinion leaders, and formulate the problem with the objective to maximize the social influence on the information propagation paths. We then propose a Parallel Multicast information Propagation algorithm (PMP), which concurrently constructs a subgraph for each influential node, joins all the subgraphs into a merge graph, and finds the information propagation paths with the maximum social influence. The experimental results on real-world and artificial network datasets demonstrate the proposed algorithm can achieve competitive performance in terms of the social influence on the information propagation paths.

The rest of the paper is organized as follows. The problem formulation is presented in Sect. 2. In Sect. 3, we introduce some related definitions and then propose an efficient algorithm PMP. The performance evaluation of the proposed algorithm is given in Sect. 4, and the conclusions are detailed in Sect. 5.

2   Problem Formulation

We model a social network as a directed graph $G = (V, E)$, where V is the set of nodes, and E is the set of directed edges representing the relationship between the nodes in the network. The notations used in the paper are listed in Table 1.

There is an information source node s and a set of influential nodes L. The source node needs to diffuse the information to all the nodes in L. The information propagation starts from the information source node and the information dissemination paths form a tree. We want to maximize the social influence of the

Table 1. Table of notations

Notation	Definition
L	The set of opinion leader nodes
T	Terminal node set consisting of information source node s and all the nodes in L
u, v	Nodes u and v in social network G
t, r	Nodes t and r in terminal node set T
$e_{u,v}$	Directed edge from node u to node v, representing node u has an influence on node v
$w_{u,v}$	Social influence on edge $e_{u,v}$
$c_{u,v}$	Cost of information propagation on edge $e_{u,v}$ $(= \frac{1}{w_{u,v}})$
$p(u, v)$	The shortest path from node u to node v
$c^p(u, v)$	The information propagation cost of path $p(u, v)$; if $u = v$, $c^p(u, v) = 0$

information dissemination tree so that the nodes in influential node set L will admit the information. We define the cost of the information propagation cost $c_{u,v}$ on directed edge $e_{u,v}$ as $c_{u,v} = \frac{1}{w_{u,v}}$. The greater the social influence, the smaller the information dissemination cost. That is, we want to find the tree from source node s to all the influential nodes in set L with the objective to minimize the information propagation cost. The problem is formulated as follows.

Objective to:

$$min \sum_{\forall t \in L} c^p(s, t) \qquad (1)$$

Subject to:

$$p(s, t) \subseteq G, \quad \forall t \in T \qquad (2)$$

Equation (2) ensures the shortest path from information source node s to opinion leader node t in L is a subgraph of network G.

3   Algorithm

In this section, we give some related definitions, and then propose a Parallel Multicast information Propagation (PMP) algorithm to find the minimum cost tree.

Definition 1. *For terminal node t, node set V_c^t is the set of nodes containing terminal node t and some other nodes in graph G, such that terminal node t has no greater cost to each node u in V_c^t than all the other terminal nodes in T to u, that is*

$$V_c^t = \{u | c^p(t, u), \forall t \in T, \forall u \in V\} \qquad (3)$$

Definition 2. *For terminal node t and node set V_c^t, node set V_p^t is a set of nodes including all the nodes on the shortest paths from t to all the other nodes in V_c^t.*

Definition 3. *For terminal node t, node set V^t is the union of V_c^t and V_p^t, that is*

$$V^t = V_c^t \cup V_p^t \qquad (4)$$

Definition 4. *For terminal node t, edge set E^t is a subset of edge set E such that each edge in E^t connects 2 nodes in V^t, that is*

$$E^t = \{e_{u,v} | u, v \in V^t, e_{u,v} \in E\} \tag{5}$$

Definition 5. *For terminal node t, subgraph H^t is defined as*

$$H^t = \{V^t, E^t\} \tag{6}$$

Definition 6. *Subgraphs H^t and H^r are adjacent, if they can be connected by an edge.*

Definition 7. *Bridge path $p^b(t, r)$ is the shortest path connecting adjacent subgraphs H^t and H^r.*

Definition 8. *Merge graph H^m is the union of all subgraphs H^t for each $t \in T$, that is*

$$H^m = \bigcup_{t \in T} H^t \tag{7}$$

Definition 9. *Information propagation tree P is a subset of edges in H^m such that each edge in P is on the shortest paths from source node s to all the nodes in L.*

Algorithm 1. *PMP algorithm*

Input: $G = (V, E)$, source node s, terminal node set T.
Output: Information propagation tree P.
1: Cobegin
2: Each terminal node $t \in T$ forms a subgraph H^t;
3: For each terminal node t, calculate the minimum path cost from t to all other nodes in G;
4: Coend
5: Put all the path cost into non-descending order list l and remove the duplicated path cost;
6: **for** $i = 1$ to l **do**
7:     **for** each terminal node $t \in T$ **do**
8:         **for** each node $u \in V$ **do**
9:             **if** $c^p(t, u) = l[i]$ and $u \notin$ any subgraph **then**
10:                 Add u into V^t, add all the edges in path $p(t, u)$ into edge set E^t;
11:             **end if**
12:         **end for**
13:     **end for**
14: **end for**
15: Search for the bridge paths for all adjacent subgraphs and calculate the bridge path cost;
16: Connect all the subgraphs into merge graph H^m via the bridge paths to get the H^m;
17: Find information propagation tree P by searching the shortest paths from information source node s to all the opinion leader nodes in merge graph H^m;
18: **return** the information propagation tree P.

Algorithm PMP shown in Algorithm 1 consists of six steps.

Step 1: Each terminal node $t \in T$ forms a subgraph H^t in parallel and calculates concurrently the minimum cost path from terminal node t to all the other nodes in graph G (lines 1–4).

Step 2: Put all path costs in non-descending order list l and remove the duplicated path costs (line 5).

Step 3: Construct subgraphs iteratively. Within the $i - th$ iteration, for each $t \in T$, we check whether there is a node $u \in V$ that has not been added to any subgraph, and path cost $c^p(t, u)$ equals to path cost $l[i]$. If such node u is found, we put node u and $p(t, u)$ into subgraph H^t (lines 6–14).

Step 4: Search for the bridge paths for all the adjacent subgraphs and calculate the bridge path cost (line 15).

Step 5: Connect all the subgraphs into merge graph H^m via the bridge paths to get merge graph H^m (line 16).

Step 6: Find information propagation tree P in H^m by searching the shortest paths from node s to all the opinion leader nodes (line 17).

4   Performance Evaluation

4.1   Performance Evaluation of the Proposed Algorithm in Real-World Datasets

We evaluate the proposed algorithm PMP against the Serial Unicast information Propagation (SUP) algorithm, where algorithm SUP propagates information by one-to-one dissemination from the source node to each of the opinion leaders. We use the real-world datasets [10], i.e. Dolphin social network and Zachary's karate network, and vary the number of terminal nodes, i.e. $|T| \in \{3, 6, 9, 12, 15\}$. We run the simulations by changing the source node 30 times in each network and take the average value as the final result.

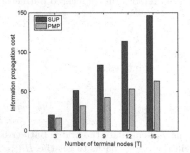
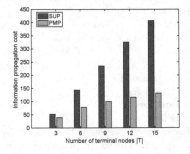
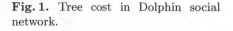

Fig. 1. Tree cost in Dolphin social network.

Fig. 2. Tree cost in Zachary's karate club.

Figures 1 and 2 show the performance of the tree cost with different number of terminal nodes in Dolphin social network and Zachary's karate network, respectively. The information propagation cost increases as the number of terminal nodes, $|T|$, increases for both of the algorithms. With more terminal nodes, the algorithms need to find more edges to spread information, which increases the cost. As $|T|$ increases, algorithm PMP performs increasingly better than algorithm SUP. Algorithm SUP disseminates information from the source node to each opinion leader independently. Therefore, the bigger number of the opinion leader nodes, the more edges used for information propagation. Algorithm PMP uses a tree to disseminate information and the information is transmitted on each edge at most once, which enables algorithm PMP to reduce the tree cost significantly.

4.2 Performance Evaluation of the Proposed Algorithm in Artificial Networks

We evaluate the impact of average degree, network density and average path length on the performance of algorithm PMP in generated artificial networks. We construct 16 networks via SNAP [10], and the parameters of the networks are shown in Table 2.

Table 2. 16 generated artificial networks

Network id	Number of nodes	Number of edges	Average degree	Network density	Average path length
network1	50	100	2	0.0816	5.294
network2	100	200	2	0.0404	8.301
network3	150	300	2	0.0268	9.705
network4	200	400	2	0.0201	11.788
network5	50	150	3	0.1224	4.016
network6	100	300	3	0.0606	7.126
network7	150	450	3	0.0402	7.136
network8	200	600	3	0.0301	9.472
network9	50	200	4	0.1632	3.131
network10	100	400	4	0.0808	4.977
network11	150	600	4	0.0536	6.467
network12	200	800	4	0.0402	7.500
network13	50	250	5	0.2040	2.694
network14	100	500	5	0.1010	4.287
network15	150	750	5	0.0671	4.541
network16	200	1000	5	0.0502	5.042

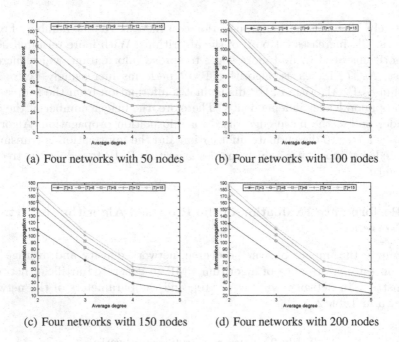

(a) Four networks with 50 nodes   (b) Four networks with 100 nodes

(c) Four networks with 150 nodes   (d) Four networks with 200 nodes

Fig. 3. Information propagation cost with different average degrees.

Impact of Average Degree: Figure 3 shows that the tree cost decreases with the increase of average degree. With a high average degree, the nodes have a good opportunity to find low cost edges for information propagation, and hence the tree cost is reduced. Figure 3 depicts that the tree cost increases with the increasing number of terminal nodes. The algorithm needs a large number of edges to disseminate the information to a big number of terminal nodes, which increases the tree cost. It can be observed from Fig. 3(a)–(d) that the networks with a big number of nodes have a high tree cost. In a large network, the information potentially needs to go through more nodes to reach the influential nodes, and thus the tree cost is increased.

Impact of Network Density: We study the impact of network density on the performance of the proposed algorithm, assuming the average degree is 4. Figure 4 shows that the tree cost decreases with the increase of network density. With a high network density, each node can potentially choose the low-cost edges to spread information, and hence the tree cost is reduced. In general, a big number of terminal nodes results in a big tree cost, which is consistent with the observation in Fig. 3.

Impact of Average Path Length: Figure 5 shows the impact of average path length on algorithm PMP, supposing the average degree is 4. In general, the information propagation cost increases with the increasing average path lengths. The

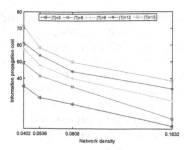   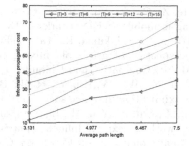

Fig. 4. Information propagation cost with different network densities.

Fig. 5. Information propagation cost with different average path lengths.

information potentially needs more hops to travel from the information source to the destination nodes, as the average path length increases. More terminal nodes lead to a bigger tree cost, since more edges are needed for information propagation, which is consistent to the results in Fig. 3.

5   Conclusions

Few research on information propagation in social networks considered how to find information dissemination paths from the information source node to a set of influential nodes. In this paper, we introduced a multicast information propagation model which depicts the phenomenon that an information source node disseminates information to a set of opinion leaders, and formulated the problem with the objective to maximize the social influence on the information propagation paths. We then proposed algorithm PMP, which concurrently constructs a subgraph for each influential node, joins all the subgraphs into a merge graph, and finds the information propagation paths with the maximum social influence in the merge graph. The experiments demonstrated that the proposed algorithm can achieve competitive performance in terms of the social influence on the information propagation paths.

References

1. Peng, S., Zhou, Y., Cao, L., et al.: Influence analysis in social networks: a survey. J. Netw. Comput. Appl. **106**(2018), 17–32 (2018)
2. Kempe, D., Kleinberg, J., Tardos, E.: Maximizing the spread of influence through a social network. In: Proceedings of the Ninth ACM SIGKDD International Conference on Knowledge Discovery and Data Mining. Washington, D.C., pp. 137–146 (2003)
3. He, Z., Cai, Z., Wang, X.: Modeling propagation dynamics and developing optimized countermeasures for rumor spreading in online social networks. In: 2015 IEEE 35th International Conference on Distributed Computing Systems, Columbus, USA, pp. 205–214 (2015)

4. He, Z., Cai, Z., Yu, J., et al.: Cost-efficient strategies for restraining rumor spreading in mobile social networks. IEEE Trans. Veh. Technol. **66**(3), 2789–2800 (2017)
5. Wang, Z., Shinkuma, R., Takahashi, T.: Dynamic social influence modeling from perspective of gray-scale mixing process. In: 9th International Conference on Mobile Computing and Ubiquitous Network, Hakodate, Japan, pp. 1–6 (2015)
6. Zhu, Y., Wu, W., Bi, Y., et al.: Better approximation algorithms for influence maximization in online social networks. J. Comb. Optim. **30**(1), 97–108 (2015)
7. Li, J., Cai, Z., Yan, M., Li, Y.: Using crowdsourced data in location-based social networks to explore influence maximization. In: The 35th Annual IEEE International Conference on Computer Communications, San Francisco, USA, pp. 1–9 (2016)
8. Tong, G., Wu, W., Tang, S., et al.: Adaptive influence maximization in dynamic social networks. IEEE/ACM Trans. Netw. **25**(1), 112–125 (2017)
9. Dinh, T., Nguyen, H., Ghosh, P., et al.: Social influence spectrum with guarantees: computing more in less time. In: International Conference on Computational Social Networks, Beijing, China, pp. 84–103 (2015)
10. Leskovec, J., Sosic, R.: SNAP: a general-purpose network analysis and graph-mining library. ACM Trans. Intell. Syst. Technol. **8**(1), 1 (2016)

Research on Physical Layer Security
Scheme Based on OAM

Modulation for Wireless Communications

Weiqing Huang[1,2], Yan Li[1,2], Dong Wei[1,2(✉)], and Qiaoyu Zhang[1,2]

[1] Institute of Information Engineering, Chinese Academy of Sciences,
Beijing 100093, China
{huangweiqing,liyan,weidong,zhangqiaoyu}@iie.ac.cn
[2] University of Chinese Academy of Sciences, Beijing 100049, China

Abstract. Aiming at the physical layer information security risk in wireless communication system, a physical layer security transmission technology based on OAM (Orbital angular momentum) modulation is proposed in this paper. Through introducing the OAM state as an information bearing parameter, the modulated electromagnetic (EM) wave will have a helical transverse phase structure, which means that the phase front varies linearly with azimuthal angle. In such case, the modulated signal will present the direction-dependent characteristic; in addition, since the OAM state becomes very weak beyond a certain distance, utilizing this characteristic, the effective communication distance can be limited. Therefore, the communication range can be accurately limited by OAM modulation. Furthermore, an OAM pre-compensation algorithm is proposed to improve the QoS of legitimate users. The simulation results show that the proposed scheme can effectively prevent eavesdroppers from detecting OAM modulated signals.

Keywords: Physical layer security · OAM modulation ·
Wireless communication

1 Introduction

Currently, the wireless communication's security mainly relays on the cryptographic techniques in the link and application layer, but there is little protection on the physical layer. Without physical layer security measures, the wireless communication has the risk of being intercepted or jammed. To address such problem, the researches on physical layer security are necessary [1].

So far, the physical layer security techniques can be classified into two categories. One category uses a key to encrypt the modulation parameters, such as the low interception probability [2] and constellation encryption techniques [3]. However, the above techniques depend on the secret key security, once the key is cracked, the communiqion will be intercepted. The other category uses the randomness characteristics of the wireless channel to increase difference between the legal channel and the eavesdropping channel [4], such as cross-layer key generation technology [5] and

© Springer Nature Switzerland AG 2019
E. S. Biagioni et al. (Eds.): WASA 2019, LNCS 11604, pp. 573–586, 2019.
https://doi.org/10.1007/978-3-030-23597-0_47

keyless physical layer secure transmission technology [6]. However, if the channel is invariant-quasi-static, these techniques will be less effective.

Recently, the directional modulation technique [7] has been proposed as a promising technique to address those physical layer security problems, and this technique needs neither key nor the randomness of channel. Depending on antenna's spatial characteristics, the directional modulation technique is capable of protecting digitally modulated information signals in the pre-specified spatial direction, and it can simultaneously distort the constellation formats of the same signals in all other directions, thus directional modulation can lower the possibility of interception.

In this paper, we proposed an orbital angular momentum (OAM) modulation scheme, which is different from the above directional modulation researches and the spectrum efficient researches on OAM multiplexing techniques [8–10]. The purpose of this paper is to accurately restrict the communication direction and distance through using OAM states to carry information. The basic ideas of the proposed scheme are as follows: through OAM modulation, the traditional plane electromagnetic wave will be transferred to spiral wave, which has a helical transverse phase structure, to correctly recover the OAM states from the spiral wave, and the prerequisite is both the transmitting and receiving antennas are facing each other perfectly on the same axis in free space, so the OAM modulated signal presents strong direction-dependent characteristic; moreover, OAM states with different order presents different sensitivity to transmission distance, and in general, when the distance exceeds a certain range, the OAM state will become very weak. Utilizing this property, the effective communication distance can be limited through selecting specific OAM states to bear information. Above all, it can be found that the communication range can be accurately restricted through OAM modulation, that is, the proposed scheme can effectively prevent the eavesdroppers to receive the OAM modulated signal. Furthermore, to reduce the Qos (quality of service) degradation resulted from the imperfect receiving direction, an OAM pre-compensation algorithm is proposed this algorithm can guarantee the communication QoS of the legitimate users when the transmitting and receiving antennas are not parallel.

The remainder of the paper is organized as follows. Section 2 introduces the system model. The physical layer security scheme based on OAM modulation is presented in Sect. 3. The OAM pre-compensation algorithm is illustrated in Sect. 4. Some simulations and comparisons are given in Sect. 5. Finally, we conclude this paper in Sect. 6.

2   The Secure Communication Model Based on OAM Modulation

The secure communication system model is depicted in Fig. 1. Let us consider three users, Alice, Bob and Eve, and two wireless MIMO channels, HAB, and HAE. Alice and Bob are legitimate users, and Eve is the eavesdropper. The confidential messages are carried by OAM states, and transmitted through channel H_{AB} between Alice and Bob. The Time-Division Duplex (TDD) method is adopted, according to the channel reciprocity in TDD system, H_{AB} can be acquired by Alice and Bob. Through channel H_{AE}, the OAM modulated signal transmitted by Alice can be received by Eve, but the channel information H_{AE} is unknown to Eve. Likewise, such channel information is also unknown to Alice and Bob.

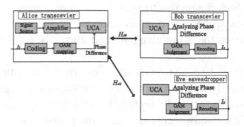

Fig. 1. The secure communication system model

In this paper, the uniform circular array (UCA) antenna is used to generate vortex electromagnetic waves with different OAM mode and achieve the OAM modulation. As shown in Fig. 2, the UCA is composed of N array elements, and the elements are evenly arranged on the circumference of the radius R. In order to generate a vortex electromagnetic wave carrying the l order OAM state, an equal-amplitude feed is required for each antenna element, and also the phase difference between two adjacent antenna elements is set as $\Delta\phi = \frac{2\pi l}{N}(-\frac{N}{2} \leq l \leq \frac{N}{2})$ [9]. Based on such OAM generating method, the OAM modulation can be achieved by controlling the feed phase of each element according to the transmitting information. For convenience, the phases of elements are defined as phase vector, each phase vector corresponding an OAM state. The concrete process is as follows:

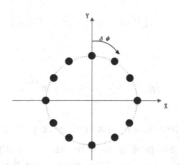

Fig. 2. Uniform circular array (UCA)

When Alice sends confidential messages I_C to Bob, I_C is encoded to the digital sequence consisting of "0" and "1", then through OAM mapping, the digital sequence is mapped to the phase vector according to the modulation order. For example, when the modulation order is 2, "00" corresponds to phase vector $\overrightarrow{P_1}$, "01" corresponds to phase vector $\overrightarrow{P_2}$, "10" corresponds to phase vector $\overrightarrow{P_3}$, "11" corresponds to phase vector $\overrightarrow{P_4}$. According to phase vector, adjusting the feeding phase of UCA array elements, the vortex electromagnetic wave with specific order OAM is generated and such wave bears the information I_C.

To receive the vortex electromagnetic wave, the same configuration of the UCA is adopted by Bob, and both the transmitting and receiving antennas are facing each other on the same axis in free space. Based on the channel information, Bob can estimate the phase difference between the array elements and correctly identifies the OAM order, then I_C is decoded.

For the eavesdropper Eve, the UCA deviates from the central axis of the transmitting antenna array and the direction cannot be completely aligned, the OAM states received by the Eve will be severely degraded, and since the channel information H_{AE} cannot be obtained, Eve cannot recognize the correct mode value and get the message I_C.

3 The Physical Layer Security Scheme Based on OAM Modulation

In this section, the physical layer security scheme based on OAM modulation is illustrated, also the direction-dependent and distance sensitive characteristics are analyzed.

If we assume the UCA is adopted by Alice, Eve and Bob, and the UCA is composed of N array elements, the channel can be expressed as:

$$H = \begin{bmatrix} h_{1,1} & h_{1,2} & \cdots & h_{1,N} \\ h_{2,1} & h_{2,2} & \cdots & h_{2,N} \\ \vdots & \vdots & \ddots & \vdots \\ h_{N,1} & h_{N,2} & \cdots & h_{N,N} \end{bmatrix} \tag{1}$$

where

$$h(d_{ij}) = \frac{\beta\lambda}{4\pi d_{ij}} exp(-j2\pi\frac{d_{ij}}{\lambda}) \tag{2}$$

where $\frac{\lambda}{4\pi d_{ij}}$ represents the free space loss, complex exponential term represents the additional phase rotation due to propagation distance, d_{ij} is the distance between the jth transmitting element and the ith receiving element, and β is the attenuation constant.

As shown in Fig. 3, we assume that both the UCAs of Alice and Bob are facing each other on the same axis, and the two arrays are parallel. We define θ is the angle between received antenna element n_{RX} and transmitted antenna element n_{TX}, and $d(\theta)$ is the linear distance between n_{RX} and n_{TX}, which can be expressed as

$$d(\theta_{n_{RX},n_{tx}}) = [D^2 + R_{TX}^2 + R_{RX}^2 - 2R_{TX}R_{RX}\cos\theta_{n_{RX},n_{tx}}]^{1/2}$$
$$= [D^2 + 2R^2(1 - \cos\theta_{n_{RX},n_{tx}})]^{1/2} \tag{3}$$

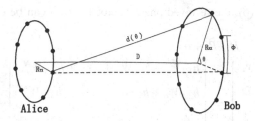

Fig. 3. Model of the channel between Alice and Bob

where R_{RX} and R_{TX} are the radius of the transmitting arrays and the receiving arrays, In order to simplify the calculation, we make $R_{RX} = R_{TX} = R$. D is the linear distance between the two antenna arrays, ϕ is the angle between the first elements in the two antenna arrays; and θ is:

$$\theta(n_{RX}, n_{TX}) = \frac{2\pi(n_{RX} - n_{TX})}{N} + \phi \tag{4}$$

According to (2) and (3), the channel function $h(n_{RX}, n_{tx})$ between n_{RX} and n_{TX} is given as

$$h(n_{RX}, n_{tx}) = \frac{\beta\lambda}{4\pi d(n_{RX}, n_{tx})} \cdot \exp\left(-j2\pi\frac{d(n_{RX}, n_{tx})}{\lambda}\right) \tag{5}$$

Therefore, the channel matrix H_{AB} between Alice and Bod can be expressed as

$$H_{AB} = \begin{bmatrix} h_{1,1} & h_{1,2} & \cdots & h_{1,N} \\ h_{2,1} & h_{2,2} & \cdots & h_{2,N} \\ \vdots & \vdots & \ddots & \vdots \\ h_{N,1} & h_{N,2} & \cdots & h_{N,N} \end{bmatrix} \tag{6}$$

The OAM state transmitted by Alice can be expressed as the phase vector

$$\overrightarrow{P_l} = \begin{bmatrix} p_1 \\ p_2 \\ \vdots \\ p_N \end{bmatrix} \tag{7}$$

where $p_n = (e^{\frac{j2\pi l}{N}})^n = e^{\frac{j2\pi n l}{N}}$.

Combined with (6), the received phase vector by Bob can be expressed as

$$\overrightarrow{Y_{AB}} = H_{AB}\overrightarrow{P_l} + \vec{n}$$

$$= \begin{bmatrix} y_1 \\ y_2 \\ \vdots \\ y_N \end{bmatrix} = \begin{bmatrix} h_{1,1}W_q + h_{1,2}W_q^2 + \cdots + h_{1,N}W_q^N \\ h_{2,N}W_q + h_{2,2}W_q^2 + \cdots + h_{2,N}W_q^N \\ \cdots \\ h_{N,1}W_q + h_{N,2}W_q^2 + \cdots + h_{N,N}W_q^N \end{bmatrix} + \vec{n} \tag{8}$$

where y_i represents the ith element of $\overrightarrow{Y_{AB}}$, which $i \in [1,N]$, $W_q = \exp(j\frac{2\pi l}{N})$, and $\vec{n} \sim N(\vec{0}, \sigma_n^2 \vec{I}_N)$.

Each element in $\overrightarrow{Y_{AB}}$ represents the phase received by each element, and the received OAM state can be obtained according to the phase difference between adjacent array elements, which can be expressed as

$$\exp(j\frac{2\pi \overrightarrow{l_{Bob}}}{N}) = \frac{y_{i+1}}{y_i} \tag{9}$$

where $\overrightarrow{l_{Bob}}$ represents the OAM state received by Bob. Since the channel matrix H_{AB} is known to Bob, and through (9), $\overrightarrow{l_{Bob}}$ can be recovered correctly.

However, as shown in Fig. 4, the channel matrix H_{AE} between Alice and Eve is expressed as

$$H_{AE} = \begin{bmatrix} h'_{1,1} & h'_{1,2} & \cdots & h'_{1,N} \\ h'_{2,1} & h'_{2,2} & \cdots & h'_{2,N} \\ \vdots & \vdots & \ddots & \vdots \\ h'_{N,1} & h'_{N,2} & \cdots & h'_{N,N} \end{bmatrix} \tag{10}$$

if we assume the UCA of Eve is not at the same axis between Alice and Bob, and d_1 is the distance offset on the axis. Additionally, there is an oblique angle between the UCAs of Alice and Eve, which is defined as α.

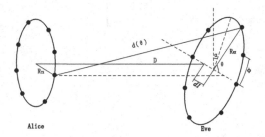

Fig. 4. Model of the channel between Alice and Eve

The distance $d'(\theta, d_1, \alpha)$ between n_{RX} and n_{TX} can be expressed as

$$
\begin{aligned}
d'(\theta_{n_{RX},n_{tx}}, d_1, \alpha) = [D^2 + (R - d_1)^2 + R^2(\cos^2 \theta_{n_{RX},n_{tx}} \\
+ \sin^2 \theta_{n_{RX},n_{tx}} \cos^2 \alpha) + 2DR \sin^2 \theta_{n_{RX},n_{tx}} \sin^2 \alpha \\
- 2R(R - d_1) \cos \theta_{n_{RX},n_{tx}}]^{1/2}
\end{aligned}
\tag{11}
$$

According to (5), the channel function $h'(n_{RX}, n_{tx}, d_1, \alpha)$ between n_{RX} and n_{TX} is given as

$$
h'(n_{RX}, n_{tx}, \alpha) = \frac{\beta\lambda}{4\pi d'(\theta_{n_{RX},n_{tx}}, d_1, \alpha)} \cdot \exp(-j2\pi \frac{d'(\theta_{n_{RX},n_{tx}}, d_1, \alpha)}{\lambda})
\tag{12}
$$

Combined with (7), the received phase vector by Eve can be expressed as

$$
\overrightarrow{Y_{AE}} = H_{AE}\overrightarrow{P_l} + \vec{n}
$$

$$
\begin{aligned}
= \begin{bmatrix} y'_1 \\ y'_2 \\ \vdots \\ y'_N \end{bmatrix} &= \begin{bmatrix} \sum_{j=1}^{N} h'_{1,j} W_q^j \\ \sum_{j=1}^{N} h'_{2,j} W_q^j \\ \cdots \\ \sum_{j=1}^{N} h'_{N,j} W_q^j \end{bmatrix} + \vec{n} \\
\\
&= \begin{bmatrix} \sum_{j=1}^{N} \frac{\beta\lambda}{4\pi d'(\theta_{1,j}, d_1, \alpha)} \exp(-j2\pi \frac{d'(\theta_{1,j}, d_1, \alpha)}{\lambda}) W_q^j \\ \sum_{j=1}^{N} \frac{\beta\lambda}{4\pi d'(\theta_{2,j}, d_1, \alpha)} \exp(-j2\pi \frac{d'(\theta_{2,j}, d_1, \alpha)}{\lambda}) W_q^j \\ \cdots \\ \sum_{j=1}^{N} \frac{\beta\lambda}{4\pi d'(\theta_{N,j}, d_1, \alpha)} \exp(-j2\pi \frac{d'(\theta_{N,j}, d_1, \alpha)}{\lambda}) W_q^j \end{bmatrix} \\
&+ \vec{n}
\end{aligned}
\tag{13}
$$

where y'_i represents the ith element of $\overrightarrow{Y_{AE}}$, which $i \in [1, N], W_q = \exp(j\frac{2\pi l}{N})$ and $\vec{n} \sim N(\vec{0}, \sigma_n^2 \vec{I}_N)$.

Each element in $\overrightarrow{Y_{AE}}$ represents the phase received by each element, and the received OAM state can be obtained according to the phase difference between adjacent array elements, which can be expressed as

$$\exp(j\frac{2\pi \overrightarrow{l_{Eve}}}{N}) = \frac{y'_{i+1}}{y'_i} \tag{14}$$

where $\overrightarrow{l_{Eve}}$ represents the OAM state received by Eve, and such state is related to the oblique angle α, the distance offset d_1 and the transmitting OAM state.

Through calculation, we find that when α is within a certain range centered on $\pi/2$, the value of received OAM state $\overrightarrow{l_{Eve}}$ will vibrate sharply, especially when the transmitted OAM state is relatively large. Furthermore, when d_1 is farther than a certain distance range, the value of received OAM state $\overrightarrow{l_{Eve}}$ will vibrate sharply, especially, for the larger transmitted OAM state, this certain range is smaller. Since the channel matrix H_{AE} is unknown to Eve, $\overrightarrow{l_{Eve}}$ cannot be recovered correctly.

4 OAM Pre-compensation Algorithm

According to Sect. 3, when the oblique angle α exists, the received OAM state will be affected. However, in actual communication system, it is difficult for both sides to ensure the UCAs are parallel (as shown in Fig. 5). The QoS of communication will be effect if the oblique angle exists, as a result, we propose an OAM pre-compensation algorithm to solve such problem.

If we assume the transmitting OAM state is $\vec{l}_1$, when $\alpha = 0$, the channel matrix H_{AB} can be expressed as (6), and the received OAM state is $\vec{l}_2$.

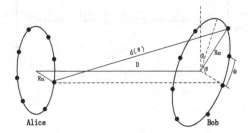

Fig. 5. Model of actual communication system between Alice and Bob

When $\alpha \neq 0$, the distance between n_{RX} and n_{TX} can be expressed as

$$\begin{aligned}
d'_{AB}(\theta_{n_{RX},n_{tx}},\alpha) = [D^2 + R^2 + R^2(\cos^2\theta_{n_{RX},n_{tx}} \\
+ \sin^2\theta_{n_{RX},n_{tx}}\cos^2\alpha) + 2DR\sin^2\theta_{n_{RX},n_{tx}}\sin^2\alpha \\
- 2R^2\cos\theta_{n_{RX},n_{tx}}]^{1/2}
\end{aligned} \tag{15}$$

The corresponding channel function $h'_{AB}(n_{RX}, n_{tx}, \alpha)$ between n_{RX} and n_{TX} is given as

$$h'_{AB}(n_{RX}, n_{tx}, \alpha) = \frac{\beta\lambda}{4\pi d'_{AB}(\theta_{n_{RX},n_{tx}}, \alpha)}$$
$$\cdot \exp(-j2\pi\frac{d'_{AB}(\theta_{n_{RX},n_{tx}}, \alpha)}{\lambda})$$

(16)

Therefore, the channel matrix H'_{AB} between Alice and Bob can be expressed as

$$H'_{AB} = \begin{bmatrix} h'_{AB(1,1)} & h'_{AB(1,2)} & \cdots & h'_{AB(1,N)} \\ h'_{AB(2,1)} & h'_{AB(2,2)} & \cdots & h'_{AB(2,N)} \\ \vdots & \vdots & \ddots & \vdots \\ h'_{AB(N,1)} & h'_{AB(N,2)} & \cdots & h'_{AB(N,N)} \end{bmatrix}$$

(17)

Through the channel matrix H'_{AB}, the received OAM state is $\vec{l}_3$.

To get the correct OAM state, our target is finding an OAM state $\vec{l}^*$, which can minimize the difference between $\vec{l}_2$ and $\vec{l}_3$, i.e.

$$\vec{l}^* = \min_{\vec{l}_1}\left|(H'_{AB})^{-1}.\vec{l}_3 - (H_{AB})^{-1}.\vec{l}_2\right|$$

(18)

To achieve this target, we can perform the OAM pre-compensation at the Alice side, and the pre-compensation vector is

$$\Delta\vec{l} = \vec{l}^* - \vec{l}_1 = \min_{\vec{l}_1}\left|(H'_{AB})^{-1}.\vec{l}_3 - (H_{AB})^{-1}.\vec{l}_2\right| - \vec{l}_1$$

(19)

5 Simulations

In this section, simulations are performed to evaluate the physical layer security performance of the proposed OAM modulation scheme.

5.1 The Effect of Linear Distance, Distance Offset and Oblique Angle on Received OAM State

Under the different transmitted states, the curves in Fig. 6 represent the trend of the received OAM states as the linear distance between the two UCAs increases. In our simulation, the UCAs are composed of 10 array elements, $\lambda = 125\,\text{mm}$, the radii of both UCAs are equal to λ, and the SNR is 30 dB.

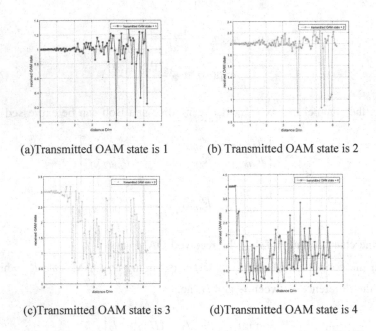

(a)Transmitted OAM state is 1   (b) Transmitted OAM state is 2

(c)Transmitted OAM state is 3   (d)Transmitted OAM state is 4

Fig. 6. Relationship between the received OAM states and the linear distance between the two UCAs

According to the curves, we found that when transmitted OAM state is 1, as the linear distance between the two UCAs increases, initially the received state is 1, then a small range fluctuation occurs around 1; when the distance reaches 4.2 m, the received OAM state changes drastically and attenuates. When transmitted OAM state is 2, the trend of received OAM state is similar to that of the transmitted state is 1, and the only difference is the point where the curve changes drastically at the distance of 3.8 m. Similarly, when transmitted state is 3 and 4, this point is at the distance of 1.5 m and 0.5 m respectively.

Through analysis, we found that with the increase of transmitted OAM state, the range of linear distance which could be recovered correctly decreases.

Under the different transmitted states, when the distance offset the axis between Alice and Bob increases, the curves in Fig. 7 represent the trend of the received OAM states. In our simulation, the UCAs are composed of 10 array elements, $\lambda = 125$ mm, the radii of both UCAs are equal to λ, the linear distance between the two UCAs is 1.25 m, and the SNR is 30 dB.

According to the curves, we found that when transmitted OAM state is 1, as the distance offset increases, initially the received state is 1, then a small range fluctuation occurs around 1; when the distance reaches 18 m, the received OAM state changes drastically and attenuates. When the transmitted OAM state is 2, the trend of received OAM state is similar to that of the transmitted state is 1, and the only difference is the point where the curve changes drastically at the distance of 13 m. Similarly, when transmitted state is 3 and 4, this point is at the distance of 8 m and 3 m respectively.

Through analysis, we found that with the increase of transmitted OAM state, the range of distance offset which could be recovered correctly decreases. This conclusion is consistent with Sect. 3.

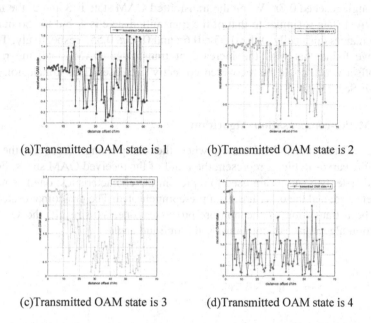

(a)Transmitted OAM state is 1   (b)Transmitted OAM state is 2

(c)Transmitted OAM state is 3   (d)Transmitted OAM state is 4

Fig. 7. Relationship between the received OAM states and the distance offset between the two UCAs

Under the different transmitted states, when the oblique angle between the UCAs increases, the curves in Fig. 8 represent the trend of the received OAM states. In our simulation, the UCAs are composed of 10 array elements, $\lambda = 125$ mm, the radii of both UCAs are equal to λ, the linear distance between the two UCAs is 2 m, and the SNR is 30 dB.

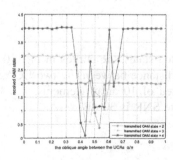

Fig. 8. Relationship between the received OAM state and the oblique angle between the UCAs.

According to the curves, we found that when transmitted OAM state is 4, as the oblique angle increases, initially the received state is 4, then a small range fluctuation occurs around 4; when the angle reaches $\pi/3$, the received OAM state changes drastically and attenuates, and then restore the small range fluctuation occurs around 4 when the angle reached 0.7π. When the transmitted OAM state is 3 and 2, the trend of received OAM state is similar to that of the transmitted state is 4, but the points where the curve changes drastically at the 0.35π, 0.6π and 0.45π, 0.55π respectively. Through analysis, we found that with the increase of transmitted OAM state, the range of distance offset which could be recovered correctly decreases. This conclusion is consistent with Sect. 3.

5.2 OAM Pre-compensation Algorithm

Under the different transmitted states, when the oblique angle between the UCAs increases, the curves in Fig. 9 represent the trend of the received OAM states. For each transmitted state, two curves are used to represent the characteristics; one has not been pre-compensated, and the other has been pre-compensated. The pre-compensated curve seems to be a translation of the non-pre-processed one, as a result, the OAM pre-compensation algorithm can compensate the oblique angle.

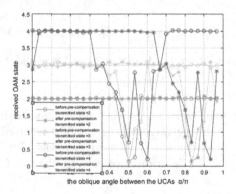

Fig. 9. Relationship between the received OAM states and the linear distance between the two UCAs (before pre-compensation and after pre-compensation)

5.3 BER of Bob and Eve

Under the different transmitted states, the curves in Fig. 10 represent the trend of the received BER as the linear distance between the two UCAs increases. In our simulation, the UCAs are composed of 10 array elements, $\lambda = 125$ mm, the radii of both UCAs are equal to λ, and the SNR is 30 dB.

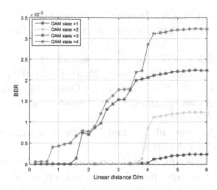

Fig. 10. Relationship between the received BER and the linear distance.

According to the curves, we found that when the transmitted OAM state is 4, as the linear distance increases, the BER curve rises slowly at the beginning, and then the curve rises sharply at the distance of about 0.5 m; when the transmitted OAM state is 3, 2 and 1, the trend of received BER is similar to that of the transmitted state is 4, but the points where the curve changes drastically at the distance of 1.5 m, 3.8 m and 4.2 m respectively.

Through analysis, we found that if Eve is controlled beyond a certain distance, Eve's bit error rate will be much higher than Bob's.

6 Conclusions

In this paper, a physical layer security transmission technology based on OAM modulation is proposed. Through introducing OAM as information bearing parameter, the communication range can be accurately controlled. Moreover, an OAM precompensation algorithm is proposed to adjust the communication direction, so the communication QoS of legitimate users can be guaranteed. The simulation results show that the proposed OAM modulation scheme can effectively prevent the eavesdropper to intercept the communication.

References

1. Liu, Y., Chen, H.H., Wang, L.: Physical layer security for next generation wireless networks: theories, technologies, and challenges. IEEE Commun. Surv. Tutor. **PP**(99), 1 (2016)
2. Zhao, L., Wang, L., Bi, G., Zhang, L., Zhang, H.: Robust frequency hopping spectrum estimation based on sparse bayesian method. IEEE Trans. Wirel. Commun. **14**(2), 781–793 (2015)
3. Ma, R., Dai, L., Wang, Z., Wang, J.: Secure communication in TDS-OFDM system using constellation rotation and noise insertion. IEEE Trans. Consum. Electron. **56**(3), 1328–1332 (2010)

4. Mukherjee, A., Fakoorian, S.A.A., Huang, J., Swindlehurst, A.L.: Principles of physical layer security in multiuser wireless networks: a survey. IEEE Commun. Surv. Tutor. **16**(3), 1550–1573 (2014)
5. Wang, T., Liu, Y., Vasilakos, A.V.: Survey on channel reciprocity based key establishment techniques for wireless systems. Wirel. Netw. **21**(6), 1–12 (2015)
6. Liao, W.C., Chang, T.H., Ma, W.K., Chi, C.Y.: Qos-based transmit beamforming in the presence of eavesdroppers: an optimized artificial-noise-aided approach. IEEE Trans. Signal Process. **59**(3), 1202–1216 (2011)
7. Ding, Y., Fusco, V.: A review of directional modulation technology. Int. J. Microwave Wirel. Technol. **8**(7), 981–993 (2016)
8. Tamburini, F., Mari, E., Sponselli, A., et al.: Encoding many channels on the same frequency through radio vorticity: first experimental test. New J. Phys. **14**(3), 003–005 (2012)
9. Mohammadi, S.M., Daldorff, L.K.S., Bergman, J.E.S., et al.: Orbital angular momentum in radio—a system study. IEEE Trans. Antennas Propag. **58**(2), 565–572 (2010)
10. Edfors, O., Johansson, A.J.: Is orbital angular momentum (OAM) based radio communication an unexploited area. IEEE Trans. Antennas Propag. **60**(2), 1126–1131 (2012)

Optimal Routing of Tight Optimal Bidirectional Double-Loop Networks

Liu Hui[1,2] and Shengling Wang[1(✉)]

[1] Beijing Normal University, Beijing 100875, China
wangshengling@bnu.edu.cn
[2] An Hui University of Technology, Maanshan 243002, China

Abstract. Double-loop networks are widely used in computer networks for its simplicity, symmetry and scalability. In this paper, we focus on optimal routing of Bidirectional Double-loop Network (BDLN) using coordinates embedding and transforming. First, we get the lower bound both of diameter and average distance of BDLN by embedding BDLN into Cartesian coordinates. Then, we find nodes distribution regularity on the embedding graph of tight optimal BDLNs that achieve the lower bound both in diameter and average distance. On the basis of nodes distribution regularity in tight optimal BDLNs, we present on demand optimal message routing algorithms which do not require routing tables and are highly efficient requiring very little computation.

Keywords: Bidirectional Double-loop Networks · Diameter · Average distance · Lower bound · Routing

1 Introduction

A double-loop network (DLN) is a widely used topology in computer networks, parallel and distributed computing, for its simplicity, symmetry and scalability [1]. There are two types of DLN: unidirectional double-loop network (UDLN) and bidirectional double-loop network (BDLN). A UDLN $G(N; r, s)$ has N vertices 0, 1..., N − 1, for each node $i(0 < i < N)$, there are two unidirectional edges: $i \rightarrow i + r(modN)$, $i \rightarrow i + s(modN)$, $1 \leq r < s < N$. It is strongly connected if and only if N, r and s are relatively prime. Unlike a UDLN, For each node i in BDLN $G(N; \pm r, \pm s)$, there are four unidirectional edges: $i \rightarrow i + r(modN)$, $i \rightarrow i + s(modN)$, $i \rightarrow i - r(modN)$, $i \rightarrow i - s(modN)$, noted as [+r], [+s], [−r], [−s] edge, respectively. Compared with a unidirectional double-loop network (UDLN), a BDLN can use both positive and negative links to send messages. Thus, it has a higher bandwidth, a smaller diameter, and is more resilient to node or link failures [2].

One common way to improve the performance of a network is to increase its connectivity and decrease its diameter. As diameter represents the maximum delay in a network between two nodes, average distance means the average delay. It is noted that these two parameters are both important for BDLN in measurement of delay of messages transmission. Take optimal BDLN [2] whose diameter gets the lower bound for an example, average distance of optimal BDLN is not sure to be the minimum. Some optimal BDLN may has bigger average distance than non-optimal one, when this

© Springer Nature Switzerland AG 2019
E. S. Biagioni et al. (Eds.): WASA 2019, LNCS 11604, pp. 587–595, 2019.
https://doi.org/10.1007/978-3-030-23597-0_48

happens, the overall efficiency of transmission performs worse. Special attention has been paid to network properties of BDLN such as diameter [3], fault tolerance [4], however, little work has been concerned with the average distance.

Concerning the method to research double-loop networks, L-shaped Title Method (the Minimum Distance Diagram of UDLN is like L-shaped title) is widely used in UDLN which requires only four parameters to describe [5]. This method, however, does not work well in BDLNs due to the complexity of Minimum Distance Diagram of BDLN. Some alternative structure such as spiral ring [6] or tree [7] have been proposed to calculate diameter and find the optimal BDLNs. Compared with the simplicity and intuition of L-shape Title Method, both spiral ring and tree are difficult to construct.

It's overt that the tight optimal BDLN has better performance compared with other BDLNs, such as smallest delay, powerful ability to route messages easily with minimum diameter and average distance.

In this paper, we study the optimal routing of BDLN by using a simple and efficient method based on coordinates embedding and transforming since routing has been a general yet important problem in networks [8–11]. We present an on demand optimal message routing algorithm for the tight optimal BDLN. The algorithms presented do not require routing tables and are highly efficient in real time.

The rest of this paper is organized as follows: In Sect. 2, we provide a brief embedding description of BDLN in Cartesian coordinates and we get the lower bound both of diameter and average distance of BDLN based on embedding graph. In Sect. 3, we introduce tight optimal BDLNs that achieve the lower bound both in diameter and average distance, we find nodes distribution regularity on the embedding graph of tight optimal BDLNs by coordinate embedding and transforming. Then, we present on demand optimal message routing algorithms which do not require routing tables and are highly efficient in real time in Sect. 4 based on nodes distribution regularity. At last, we summarize our results and make some concluding remarks.

2   Coordinates Embedding of BDLN

When a message is routed in a BDLN $G(N; \pm r, \pm s)$, it traverses a series of r and s links to reach the destination. Suppose a message traverses from node i to node j, the routing may be signed as: $x_1[+r] + x_2[-r] + y_1[+s] + y_2[-s]$, where x_1, x_2, y_1, y_2, are number of [+r] edges, [−r] edges, [+s] edges, [−s] edges. The optimal routing between x_1 and x_2 includes four cases: [+r], [+s]; [−r], [+s]; [+r], [−s]; [−r], [−s]. Thus, a BDLN has a tabular representation where X axis is represented by "r links" and Y axis is represented by "s links." Without loss of generality, source node 0 is considered to be the origin because of the high symmetry of BDLN.

Definition 2.1. Visiting nodes of $G(N; \pm r, \pm s)$ in Cartesian coordinates in the order of node distance: $(0, 0), (1, 0), (0, 1), (−1, 0), (0, −1)\ldots$. The location(x, y) on the plane is occupied by node of k, where $k \in \{0, 1, \ldots N − 1\}$. Each number k, represented by corresponding grid in Cartesian coordinates, fills the tabular cell by turns if the number has not been visited previously. Such embedding graph is called $CG(N; \pm r, \pm s)$ in this paper.

Figure 1 shows BDLN $G(8; \pm 2, \pm 3)$, Fig. 2 shows the coordinate embedding graph of $G(13; \pm 2, \pm 3)$ in Cartesian coordinates named $CG(13; \pm 2, \pm 3)$.

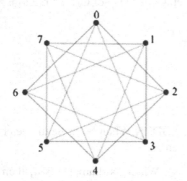

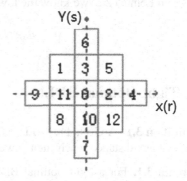

Fig. 1. BDLN $G(8; \pm 2, \pm 3)$

Fig. 2. $CG(13; \pm 2, \pm 3)$

Example 1. For the second layer, nodes are visited under order: $(2, 0), (1, 1), (0, 2), (-1, 1), (-2, 0), (-1, -1), (0, -2), (1, -1)$, corresponding nodes are: $4, 5, 6, 1, 9, 8, 7, 12$.

Let d denote the diameter of $G(N; \pm r, \pm s)$. From Definition 2.1, it is easy to find that the maximum layer of the embedding graph is the diameter.

Definition 2.2. The average distance of BDLN is $avgd(N; \pm r, \pm s) = \frac{1}{N-1} \sum_{i=1}^{N-1} d_i$
d_i is the shortest distance from node 0 to node i.

Property 2.1. In $CG(N; \pm r, \pm s)$, $1 \le u_i \le 4i(1 \le i \le d)$, where u_i is the number of nodes in each layer i.

Lemma 2.1. $2d \le N \le 2d^2 + 2d + 1$.

Proof. From Definition 2.1, $N = 1 + \sum_{i=1}^{d} u_i$

From Property 2.1, $N \le 1 + 4 \sum_{i=1}^{d} i$, then we get: $N \le 2d^2 + 2d + 1$.

The worst condition is that all nodes are on X axis or Y axis, if N is even, then $N = 2d$; or if N odd, then $N = 2d + 1$, $G(N; \pm r, \pm s)$ is degenerated to ring network.

If $N = 2d^2 + 2d + 1$, vertices are closely located on the embedding graph layer by layer, just like Fig. 2. both the diameter and average distance of $G(N; \pm r, \pm s)$ reach their lower bound.

From Lemma 2.1, we know the lower bound of diameter of BDLN $G(N; \pm r, \pm s)$ is:

$lb(N) = \lceil (\sqrt{(2N - 1)} - 1)/2 \rceil$, here $\lceil X \rceil$ is the minimum integer which is greater than X. Thus, we certify the lower bound of diameter of BDLN presented by Boesch and Wang [12].

Lemma 2.2. $avgd(N; \pm r, \pm s) \ge 2d(d + 1)(2d + 1)/3(N - 1)$.

Proof. From Definitions 2.1 and 2.2, $avgd(N; \pm r, \pm s) \geq \frac{4}{N-1} \sum_{i=1}^{d} i^2$, So we get:
$avgd(N; \pm r, \pm s) \geq 2d(d+1)(2d+1)/3(N-1)$

From Lemma 2.2, we know the lower bound of average distance of $G(N; \pm r, \pm s)$ is:

$$lba(N) = \sqrt{(2N-1)/3}$$

3   Tight Optimal BDLN

Definition 3.1. A $G(N; \pm r, \pm s)$ is called tight optimal BDLN When both the diameter and average distance reach their lower bound for given N.

Lemma 3.1. For a tight optimal BDLN $G(N; \pm r, \pm s)$, When its diameter is d, then $N = 2d^2 + 2d + 1$, average distance is $(2d + 1)/3$.

Proof. For a tight optimal BDLN $G(N; \pm r, \pm s)$, $N = 1 + 4\sum_{i=1}^{d} i = 2d^2 + 2d + 1$

Put this into Lemma 2.2, we get average distance of a tight optimal BDLN is $(2d + 1)/3$.

When $r = d$, $s = d + 1$, the corresponding tight optimal BDLN is $G(N; \pm d, \pm(d+1))$. Since network structure of this kind of tight optimal BDLN is relatively more stabilized and well-regulated, we pay more attention to it in the following sections. Without loss of generality, tight optimal BDLN is mainly referred to this kind, simply noted as G_d with diameter d.

3.1   Coordinates Transforming of Tight Optimal BDLN

Since a BDLN is vertex transitive, any node can be easily relocated in the coordinates. Take node 0 for an example, it can be located in the first quadrant (d, d + 1) and the fourth quadrant (d + 1, −d). Define $\vec{p}$ and $\vec{\sigma}$ as vectors from the origin to the copies of node 0 at (d, d + 1) and (d + 1, −d). here e $\vec{p} = d\vec{x} + (d+1)\vec{y}$, $\vec{\sigma} = (d+1)\vec{x} - d\vec{y}$. Thus, vectors from any node to its copies can be made respectively with $\vec{p}$, $\vec{\sigma}$ or combination of them. By means of coordinates transforming, any node can be relocated (Fig. 3).

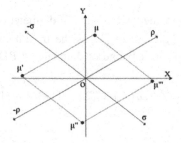

Fig. 3.   Vectors of copies of node 0

We first generate the relocation matrix of the source node 0, and then use it to determine the position of optimal copy of the destination node u. Let u' be one copy of node u (x_0, y_0) such that u' can be reached from u by placing vector $\vec{\sigma}$ at u, therefore, coordinates of u' are $(x_0 + d + 1, y_0 - d)$.

3.2 Nodes Distribution Regularity on the Embedding Graph

In particular, vertices are located according to the order of number sequence on line: $y = -x + a$ $(-d \le a \le d)$ on the embedding graph in the coordinates. Without loss of generality, following lemmas and theorems are restricted for use in the embedding graph of G_d.

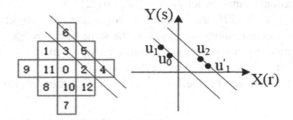

Fig. 4. Number sequence on line $y = -x + a$

Lemma 3.2. Nodes are distributed successively on the same line: $y = -x + a$, according to the order of number sequence.

Proof. Suppose vertex $u_0(x_0, y_0)$ on line: $y = -x + a$, $u_1(x_1, y_1)$ is the adjacent vertex on the same line, $x_1 = x_0 - 1$, as shown in Fig. 4, thus we have:

$$f(x_0) = y_0 = -x_0 + a, \text{ then } u_0 = f(x_0) = -x_0 d + (-x_0 + a)(d + 1)(\text{mod } N)$$
$$f(x_0 - 1) = y_1 = -x_0 + 1 + a, \text{ then: } u_1 = f(x_0 - 1) = (-x_0 + 1)d + (-x_0 + 1 + a)(d + 1)(\text{mod } N)$$

Thus, $f(x_0 - 1) - f(x_0) = 1(\text{mod } N)$

Therefore, the adjacent vertices are distributed successively on the same line: $y = -x + a$.

Lemma 3.3. Suppose vertex u_1 (x_1, y_1) on line: $y = -x + a$, one copy of u_1 is on the adjacent line: $y = -x + a + 1$.

Proof. Let u_1' be one copy of node u_1 (x_1, y_1) such that u_1' can be reached from u_1 (x_1, y_1) by placing vector $\vec{\sigma}$ at u_1, as shown in Fig. 4, therefore, coordinates of u_1' are $(x_1 + d + 1, y_1 - d)$. Suppose u_1' is on line: $y = -x + b$.

$$u_1 = -x_1 d + (-x_1 + a)(d + 1)(\text{mod } N)$$
$$u_1' = -x_1 d + (-x_1 + a)(d + 1)(\text{mod } N)$$

Since $u_1 = u_1'$, then we have: $b = a + 1$. Hence, one copy of u_1 is on the adjacent line: $y = -x + a + 1$.

Lemma 3.4. Coordinates of maximum node on the line: $y = -x + a$ in the embedding graph of BDLN are $(-k, a + k)$ and the minimum node with coordinates $(a + k, -k)$, here $k = -\lfloor (d - a)/2 \rfloor$. Note that $\lfloor x \rfloor$ is the maximum integer which is not greater than x.

Proof. Assume the maximum number $u_1(x_1, y_1)$ on line: $y = -x + a$ in the embedding graph of BDLN, where $0 \leq a < d$. X coordinate of the copy of node u_1 is $x_1 + d + 1$, thus X coordinate of the upper left node u_2 is $x_1 + d$, as shown in Fig. 4 Since u_2 is in the MDD area, Then: $x_1 + d \leq d$, Thus $x_1 \leq 0$

$|x_1| + |y_1| \leq d$, so $|x_1| + |-x_1 + a| \leq d$, so $x_1 \geq (a - d)/2$.

To get the maximum number, let $x_1 = -\lfloor (d - a)/2 \rfloor$

Suppose $k = -\lfloor (d - a)/2 \rfloor$, then coordinates of u_1 are $(-k, a + k)$.

Assume the minimum number $u_0(x_0, y_0)$ on the same line: $y = -x + a$, right below the maximum number u_1. Suppose $x_0 = a + m$, then $y_0 = -m$.

$|x_0| + |y_0| \leq d$, $|a + m| + |-m| \leq d$, so $m \leq (a - d)/2$.

To get the maximum number, let $m = -\lfloor (d - a)/2 \rfloor$, then coordinates of u_0 are $(a + k, -k)$.

Lemma 3.5. Number of nodes are distributed as $d + 1$, d, $d + 1$, d...on line $y = -x + d$, $y = -x + d - 1$, $y = -x + d - 2$, $y = -x + d - 3$... in the embedding graph of BDLN.

Proof. From Lemma 3.4, the number of nodes on the line: $y = -x + a$ in the embedding graph of BDLN is $2k + a$. When $a = d$, $2k + a = d + 1$; $a = d - 1$, $2k + a = d$; $a = d - 2$, $2k + a = d + 1$.... So, we get this Lemma.

We can now summarize in the form of the following theorem of distribution regularities of nodes in the embedding graph of BDLN.

Theorem 3.1. Nodes are distributed successively on the line: $y = -x + a$ $(-d \leq a \leq d)$ in the embedding graph of G_d by their number order.

Proof.

(1) From Lemma 3.2, we know that nodes are distributed successively on the same line: $y = -x + a$.
(2) From Lemma 3.3, the copy of any node on the line: $y = -x + a$ is located on the adjacent line: $y = -x + a + 1$.

Assume maximum number $u_1(-k, a + k)$ on line: $y = -x + a$, where $k = -\lfloor (d - a)/2 \rfloor$, $-d < a < d$. Suppose u_1' is the copy of node u_1 on the adjacent line $y = -x + a + 1$ with coordinates $(-k + d + 1, a + k - d)$, u_2 is the left above node, on the same line $y = -x + a + 1$, nearest to u_1, as shown in Fig. 4, Then, the coordinates of u_2 are $(-k + d, a + k - d + 1)$.

We now proof that u_2 is the minimum number on line: $y = -x + a + 1$ in the embedding graph of G_d.

① If $d - a = 2$ m, then $k = (a - d)/2$, $-k + d = (a + d)/2 = -\lfloor (d - a - 1)/2 \rfloor + a + 1$

② If d-a $<>$ 2 m, then $k = (a + 1 - d)/2$, $-k + d = (a + d + 1)/2 = -\lfloor (d - a - 1)/2 \rfloor + a + 1$

Similar proof to the Y coordinate of $u_1 = -\lfloor (d - a - 1)/2 \rfloor$.

From Lemma 3.4, we know that u_2 is the minimum number on line: $y = -x + a + 1$ in the embedding graph of BDLN.

We can now summarize above two cases in the form of the successive distribution of nodes in the embedding graph of G_d by their number order.

4 Optimal Routing of Tight Optimal BDLN

When a message is routed in BDLN $G(N; \pm r, \pm s)$, it traverses a series of r and s links to reach the destination. The cost of the route is $x + y$, where x, y are the number of r and s links in the route, respectively. When the cost of the route from the source to the destination is minimum, it is called an optimal route. Therefore, the optimal route of the node in the embedding graph can be expressed with its coordinates. As in G_3, the shortest path of the destination node 31 in the embedding graph $(-3, 2)$ is: $3[-r] + 2$ [+s], which means a message can be transferred from 0 to node 31 through taking $3[-r]$ edges and $2[+s]$ edges in any order (Fig. 5).

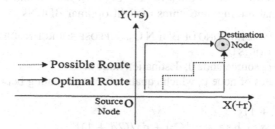

Fig. 5. Optimal routing of BDLN

Lemma 4.1. Node u(x, y) is in the embedding graph of G_d. Suppose
$0 \leq u \leq d(d + 1)$, then $x = a(d + 1) - u$, $y = -x + a$, Here, $a = \lfloor (2u + d)/(2d + 1) \rfloor$.

Proof. Assume node u(x, y) is on the line: $y = -x + a$, where $0 \leq a \leq d$, the maximum number is Max, the Minimum number is Min, $k = \lfloor (d - a)/2 \rfloor$, Then, we have these equations:

$$u = \text{Min} + \lambda(\text{Max} - \text{Min}), \lambda \in [0, 1], \text{Min} = (a + k)d - k(d + 1),$$
$$\text{Max} = -kd + (a + k)(d + 1)$$

Based on equations above, we get the range of a:

$$a \in \left[\frac{2u - d}{2d + 1}, \frac{2u + d}{2d + 1} \right]$$

Here a is a positive integer, $-d \leq a \leq d$. Since the difference value between the lower and upper bound is less than 1, a is positive integer, therefore we have:
$a = \lfloor (2u + d)/(2d + 1) \rfloor$, Given a, d, u, then $x = a(d + 1) - u$, $y = -x + a$.

Using Lemma 4.1, we can give formulas of coordinates of some special nodes, such as node 1, node 2 quickly:

(1) Node 1.

$$a = \lfloor (2 + d)/(2d + 1) = 0 \rfloor$$

Thus, coordinates of node 1 are $(-1, 1)$.

(2) Node 2.

$$a = \lfloor (4 + d)/(2d + 1) \rfloor$$

When $d < 4$, $a = 1$, coordinates of node 2 are $(d - 1, -d + 2)$, when $d \geq 4$, $a = 0$, coordinates of node 2 are $(-2, +2)$.

Since BDLN is vertex-transitive, the problem of optimal routing between any two nodes can be transformed into optimal routing between node 0 and another node. We now give the optimal routing algorithms of tight optimal BDLNs.

ALGORITHM: OPTIMAL ROUTING OF BDLN G_D, SUPPOSE SOURCE NODE IS 0, DESTINATION NODE IS U.

input: diameter d, source node 0, destination node u.

output: coordinates of node u, which equals to optimal routing between node 0 and node u.

if $0 \leq u \leq d(d + 1)$

x=a(d+1)-u, y=-x+a, here $a = \lfloor (2u + d)/(2d + 1) \rfloor$.

else

u=N-u, here $N = 2d^2 + 2d + 1$

x=u-a(d+1), y=x-a, $a = \lfloor (2u + d)/(2d + 1) \rfloor$.

end

Example 2. Optimal Routing Between node 5 and node 0

① G_2, BDLN $G(13; \pm2, \pm3)$

d = 2, u = 5, a = 2, so coordinates of node 5 are $(1, 0)$, the shortest path is $1[+2]$.

② G_3, BDLN $G(25; \pm3, \pm4)$

d = 3, v = 5, a = 1, coordinates of node 5 are $(-1, 2)$, the shortest path is $1[-3] + 2[+ 4]$.

5 Conclusion

In this paper, we present an on demand optimal message routing algorithm for the tight optimal BDLN by coordinate embedding and transforming. The algorithm presented does not require routing tables and are efficient requiring very little computational overhead.

Because of the minimum of both diameter and average distance, it's obvious that the tight optimal-BDLNs have the better performance compared with other BDLNs. By coordinate embedding and transforming in the coordinate system, each node of BDLN can be located precisely and this makes related research become easy, such as message routing, fault tolerances analysis etc.

Acknowledgment. This work has been supported by the National Natural Science Foundation of China (No. 61772080).

References

1. Chen, Y., Li, Y., Chen, T.: Optimal fault-tolerant routing algorithm and fault-tolerant diameter in directed double-loop networks. Theoret. Comput. Sci. **468**, 50–58 (2013)
2. Dharmasen, H.P., Yan, X.: An optimal fault-tolerant routing algorithm for weighted bidirectional double-loop networks. IEEE Trans. Parallel Distrib. Syst. **16**(9), 841–952 (2005)
3. Zhou, J.Q., Xu, X.R.: On infinite families of optimal double-loop networks with non-unit steps. Ars Combinatoria **97**(10), 81–95 (2010)
4. Mukhopadhyaya, K., Sinha, B.P.: Fault-tolerant routing in distributed loop networks. IEEE Trans. Comput. **44**, 1452–1456 (1995)
5. Wong, C.K., Coppersmith, D.: A combinatorial problem related to multi-module memory organizations. Assoc. Comput. Mach. **21**, 392–402 (1974)
6. Fang, M., Zhao, B.: Method to calculate the diameter of undirected double-loop networks G (N; ± 1, ± s). J. Commun. **28**(2), 124–129 (2007)
7. Li, Y., Chen, Y.: The algorithm to calculate the diameter of undirected double-loop networks G(N; ± r, ± s) based on tree. J. Huazhong Univ. Sci. Technol. (Nat. Sci. Ed.) **37**(6), 8–11 (2009)
8. Lu, J., Cai, Z., Wang, X., Zhang, L., Li, P., He, Z.: User social activity based routing for cognitive radio networks. Pers. Ubiquit. Comput. **22**(3), 471–487 (2018)
9. Cai, Z., Goebel, R., Lin, G.: Size-constrained tree partitioning: approximating the multicast k-tree routing problem. Theoret. Comput. Sci. **412**(3), 240–245 (2011)
10. Cai, Z., Chen, Z., Lin, G.: A 3.4713-approximation algorithm for the capacitated multicast tree routing problem. Theoret. Comput. Sci. **410**(52), 5415–5424 (2009)
11. Cai, Z., Lin, G., Xue, G.: Improved approximation algorithms for the capacitated multicast routing problem. In: Wang, L. (ed.) COCOON 2005. LNCS, vol. 3595, pp. 136–145. Springer, Heidelberg (2005). https://doi.org/10.1007/11533719_16
12. Boesch, F.T., Wang, J.F.: Reliable circulant networks with minimum transmission delay. IEEE Trans. Circuits Syst. **32**(12), 1286–1291 (1985)

DDSEIR: A Dynamic Rumor Spreading Model in Online Social Networks

Li Li[1,2], Hui Xia[1,2(✉)], Rui Zhang[1,2], and Ye Li[2]

[1] College of Computer Science and Technology, Qingdao University,
Qingdao 266000, Shandong, China
xiahui@qdu.edu.cn
[2] Shandong Provincial Key Laboratory of Computer Networks,
Shandong Computer Science Center (National Supercomputer Center in Jinan),
Qilu University of Technology (Shandong Academy of Sciences),
Jinan 250014, Shandong, China

Abstract. Online Social Network (OSN) has become an indispensable part of our daily life. Analyzing influence factors and propagation rules for rumor spreading in OSN is of great significance to the guidance and prediction of social public opinion. This paper proposes a dynamic information propagation model, Disseminate & Discriminate-Spread-Exposed-Ignorant-Recover (i.e., DDSEIR) based on user's dissemination capacity and discriminant ability. First, this paper introduces a hierarchical mechanism based on degree centrality theory to roughly categorize Internet users according to user's dissemination capacity. And subsequently, user's discriminant ability can be evaluated by sender's identity and information attributes. Finally, experimental results prove that the DDSEIR not only delays the time of rumor spreading but also reduces the scale of rumor propagation.

Keywords: Online Social Network · Rumor spreading · DDSEIR · Dissemination capacity · Discriminant ability

1 Introduction

Online social network (OSN) has become one of the most important communication tools. OSN can be seen as an internet-based service, which allows internet users to generate and share information quickly [1,17]. However, as OSN has brought us many conveniences, it also poses serious problems for our future [18]. One of the biggest problems is rumor spreading. OSN users don't have to take on responsibility for spreading fake news due to the incomplete law and related regulations. And they can spread information at a relatively low cost anonymously. The wide spread of rumors can cause public panic, social unrest and harm public order. Analyzing the influence factors and propagation rules for rumor spreading is of great value to the guidance and prediction of public opinion.

The rumor spreading correlation models are mainly divided into four categories: the models derived from the classical Susceptible Infected Recovered

© Springer Nature Switzerland AG 2019
E. S. Biagioni et al. (Eds.): WASA 2019, LNCS 11604, pp. 596–604, 2019.
https://doi.org/10.1007/978-3-030-23597-0_49

Model (i.e., SIR) [2,3,12–15], combination mechanisms of human behaviors and the SIR [4,5], combination model of Game Theory and the SIR [6,7], and four-state improved models of SIR [8,9]. All categories did not consider the differences on different user's dissemination capacity and discriminant ability, which can also influence the process of rumor spreading. To solve the above mentioned problems, the main contributions of this paper include:

(1) This paper proposes a dynamic information propagation model, Disseminate & Discriminate-Spread-Exposed-Ignorant-Recover (i.e., DDSEIR) based on user's dissemination capacity and discriminant ability. It includes different kinds of influence factors, not only about user's behavior attributes, but also information attributes.
(2) Since users' dissemination capacities are in proportional to the scale of information transmission, a hierarchical mechanism based on the degree centrality theory is introduced to divide the users in a fuzzy way. For instance, the users can be divided into advanced users and common users.
(3) User's discriminant ability can be evaluated by spreader's identities and information attributes. One user can decide whether to continue to spread the information or not according to the evaluation result.
(4) This paper uses Netlogo platform to verify the effectiveness of DDSEIR. The experimental results prove that the DDSEIR performs better than the other relevant models.

2   Related Work

Rumor spreading in OSN has been a hot spot for research in recent years. The process of rumor spreading is similar to that of infectious diseases.

The First Category: In the 1960s, Daley and Kendal [2] proposed the DK model, which was the first model to apply the epidemics model to rumor propagation. In Ref [14], the authors applied the SIR model into DTN. Matsubara et al. [12] put forward a new model, named SPIKEM, which is applicable to the detection of rising and falling peaks in all propagation processes. Zheng et al. [13] divided information propagation into two parts: popular perception and consciousness diffusion. Basaras et al. [15] proposed that fighting the key nodes near the source of misinformation under could block the propagation of malicious information dynamically. He et al. [16] designed two cost-efficient strategies to restrain rumors in MSN. Xu et al. [3] studied the process of epidemic information dissemination in mobile social networks, and proposed two new elements (i.e., pre-immunity and immunity) to indicate the changes of nodes' interests. The aspects considered in the above research are relatively simple, and the propagation probability is fixed. Meanwhile, they ignore the influence of some behavior characteristics and information attributes on rumor propagation.

The Second Category: Researchers [4,5] noticed the role of another two factors (i.e., human behaviors and different mechanisms) in rumor spreading. The spatial and temporal characteristics of information propagation are explored in [4]. Han *et al.* [5] found that the influence of power-law distribution on information propagation is also related to the audience size. These studies just considered the influence of human behaviors on rumor propagation, while ignored the influence of information attributes.

The Three Category: The Ref. [6] proposed a simulation model based on evolutionary game theory, which takes user decision-making and socio-economic interaction into consideration. Xiao *et al.* [7] combined evolutionary game theory with the SIR. This research shows that the changes of user's willingness to participate in hot topics are affected by user popularity and interaction. All of the abovementioned models are based on the SIR. However, the state of consideration is not comprehensive enough, which is inconsistent with actual situation.

The Four Category: Taking the characteristics of human behaviors into account, Zhao *et al.* [8] proposed a Susceptible-Infected-Hibernator-Removed model (i.e., SIHR). They introduced a new hibernator status and premeditate the forgetting mechanism and memory mechanism into this model. Xia *et al.* [9] proposed a new information propagation model, Susceptible-exposed-Infected-Removed (i.e., SEIR), which came up with a new state E-state (i.e., exposed state) compared to the SIR. As mentioned above, the improved models of the SIR did not consider the important factors, e.g., node's different influence level and discriminant ability. SEIR [9] considers more factors compared with other advanced models. This paper aims to improve and extend the SEIR model.

3   Model Construction

This paper proposes a dynamic information diffusion model, named disseminate & discriminate-spread-exposed-ignorant-recover (DDSEIR), based on user's dissemination capacity and discriminant ability.

3.1   Definition of Model

Assume N is the total number of users in an OSN. This paper uses undirected graph to simulate users' social relationships. Lines in the graph refer to the relationships between users and the nodes refer to the users. Similar to the SIR, this paper categorizes users' different status in the process of rumor spreading into four groups:

Definition 1. *Ignorant status (I): users who have never received information.*

Definition 2. *Exposed status (E): users who heard rumors but didn't take any actions. Virus is concealed for a period of time and then may burst.*

Definition 3. *Spreader status (S): users who are interested in rumors and regard it as valuable information to spread.*

Definition 4. *Stifler status (R): users who heard the rumor and are not interested in it. They refuse to spread the rumor.*

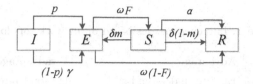

Fig. 1. The DDSEIR propagation process.

The DDSEIR's rumor spreading process is illustrated in Fig. 1 and propagation rules are as follows:

(1) Assume the proportion of advanced user is p and $1-p$ is the common user. When an ignorant node meets with a rumor spreader, if the spreader is an advanced user, this ignorant node will then directly turn into exposed status. If the spreader is a common user, this ignorant node will turn into the exposed status with γ probability.

(2) An exposed node (E status) will assess the authenticity and value of the information and then decide whether to become a spreader. With ϖF probability, it will become a spreader. If they regard information as rumor, nodes will turn into stifler status with $\varpi(1-F)$ probability.

(3) If a spreader changes its status, it will go on different directions in two ways. One is that this spreader meets with those who have received the information (E, R, S status) and turns into the stifler status with α probability, because the user assess the information as of no value. Another situation is that under the influence of self-defense mechanism, the spreader forgets its motive to transmit the information. And if the information disguise itself so well and make it difficult for user to make the decision whether to transmit or not, the spreader will turn into exposed node with δm probability and continue the process in rule (2), otherwise it will turn into stifler status with $\delta(1-m)$ probability.

3.2   Differences in User's Dissemination Capability

Most research on rumor spreading didn't take user's dissemination capability into account. If a user has big influence on an OSN, it means it has strong transmission ability. Han *et al.* [10] has introduced multiple measurement methods for node's influence, the advantages and disadvantages are listed in Table 1.

A spreader sends messages to its neighbors and this whole process cannot be completed without neighbors' help. The measurement based on degree centrality is easy to calculate, which can visually reflect the number of neighbors. It demonstrates that the amount of neighbors is proportional to node's influence.

3.3　Calculation of User's Discriminant Ability

People with different levels of discriminant ability may have different opinions with the same information. Judgment can be affected by two factors: the resource and attribute of this message. Information attribute can be evaluated by its popularity and the level of digital steganography.

Table 1. Influence metrics based on network topology.

Indicator	Advantage	Disadvantage
Degree	Easy to understand and calculate	Ignorant integral features
Clustering coefficient	Valuing relationship between nodes	Unable to find influential nodes
Betweenness	Easy to find nodes with high load capacity	Limited scope of applicability
Closeness	Able to calculate node's direct influence	High computational complexity
PageRank	Large-scale network, high sorting accuracy	Sorting result not unique
LeaderRank	Unique sorting result, anti-noise capability	Unapplicable to undirected networks

Calculation of Judgment for Information Resource. After a user with I status receives an information, he will decide whether to believe the information based on how close their relationship is. That means the higher multiplicity of their neighbors, the more similar they are to each other. This paper uses below equation to calculate the similarity between two users:

$$Frisim(AB) = \frac{|C_{AB}|}{|K_A + K_B - C_{AB} + 1|} \tag{1}$$

C_{AB} is the number of mutual friends of A and B. K_A, K_B separately refer to the number of A, B's followers.

Calculation of Information Popularity. If an information is a hot topic in an OSN, users with E status will simply parrot others to attract attentions and will turn into S status with a high probability. Besides, if the spreaders are influential users, the popularity of this information will increase.

$$Inf_A(t) = \frac{Geg(A)}{Sn} \tag{2}$$

Which refers to the influence of node A on the whole network. $Geg(A)$ refers to total user number that A influences. Sn refers to total number of users on Internet.

$$CInf_s(t) = \frac{\sum\limits_{n \in Speader} Inf_n(t)}{Sn} \tag{3}$$

$CInf_s(t)$ refers to spreaders' influence at time t in the networks. $Speader$ refers to the set of spreaders at time t in the networks.

$$\varpi = 1 + CInf_s(t) \tag{4}$$

ϖ refers to the popularity of information at time t.

Integrated Computation of User's Discriminant Ability. User's discriminant ability means the ability to integrate information popularity and the resource of information. The equation is shown in Eq. (5). The baseline represents an assessment for the whole society to judge whether this information is true or false. If $\varpi \times Fridsim$ is lower than baseline, which means that the information is unreliable, user with E status will turn into R status with $\varpi \times (1 - Fridsim)$ probability. If $\varpi \times Fridsim$ is higher than baseline, which means that the information is reliable, the user will turn into spreader with $\varpi \times Fridsim$ probability. This indicates that the more the two users trust each other, more probable it is that they will help to transmit the information.

$$Judabiliy_A = \begin{cases} \varpi \times Fridsim, \varpi \times Fridsim \geq baseline \\ \varpi \times (1 - Fridsim), \varpi \times Fridsim < baseline \end{cases} \tag{5}$$

4   Simulation Results

To analyze the influence that user's dissemination capacity and discriminant ability bring to the rumor spreading process in an OSN, this paper uses Net-Logo [11] platform to simulate. In the following simulation, our study assumes $N = 5000$, rewiring probability $\rho = 0.3$, $<k> = 6$, and randomly choose a spreader from network. And we get the average value of 200 times result of simulation. (a), (b), (c), (d) in Fig. 2 describe proportion changes of different nodes with different models. S0 refers to the SEIR [9] model. S1 refers to the improved SEIR model with user's discriminant ability factor. S2 refers to the DDSEIR model.

Comparing (a) and (d), we can see that S1 and S2 has both postponed rumor spreading process, which gives us more time to notice the rumor and deal with it. Comparing S1 and S2, we can see that S2 propagations information in a faster pace. The reason behind is that S2 has more advanced users whose diffusion capacity is high.

Comparing (a) and (d), S1 and S2 have a much higher proportion of ignorant nodes than S0 and have a lower rumor scale than S0 as system become stable. The reason is that users in S1 and S2 will evaluate the information to see if it is true or false. As S0 doesn't include this evaluation process, most of the

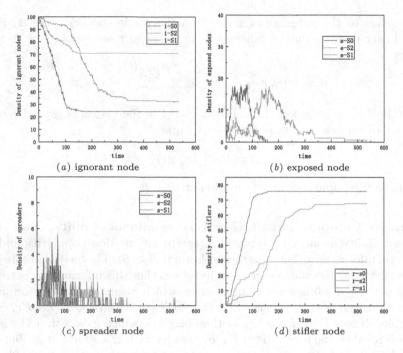

(a) ignorant node

(b) exposed node

(c) spreader node

(d) stifler node

Fig. 2. Assume $\gamma = 0.3, \alpha = 0.1, \delta = 0.6, \beta = 0.2$, m $= 0.7$, p $= 0.1$, baseline $= 0.2$, different nodes' variation in different models.

exposed nodes that should turn into stifler nodes become spreader nodes in the end. Therefore rumor spreading scale in S0 is bigger than S1 and S2. Comparing S1 with S2, S2 has advanced users, once an advanced user becomes a stifler node, some of its followers will lose the chance to hear this information forever if advanced user choose not to believe the information. Thus S2 has a smaller rumor spreading scale.

From (b) and (c), we can see that no matter if the node is in exposed status or infected status, proportion value in S2 are lower than that of S0 and S1 and stay relatively stable. S2 provides an environment that makes it easy to control the resource of rumor as soon as possible and control the nodes to stop them from continuing to spread the message.

5   Conclusion and Future Work

This paper proposes a new rumor spreading model (i.e., DDSEIR) based on user's diffusion capacity and discriminant ability. User's discriminant ability can decide the proportion of ignorant nodes that turn into exposed nodes. At the same time, a use's discriminant ability is evaluated after this user heard the information, which can decide whether to continue to spread the information. Simulation results indicate that user's diffusion capacity and discriminant ability are two important influence factors in rumor spreading. Besides, user's evaluation value changes with the popularity of the information. Next step is to further divide users into proper groups referring to transmission ability level. And we will further explore other influence factors to construct an accurate model.

Acknowledgment. This research is supported by the National Natural Science Foundation of China (NSFC) under Grant Nos. 61872205, the Shandong Provincial Natural Science Foundation No. ZR2019MF018, the Project of Shandong Province Higher Educational Science and Technology Program under Grant No. J16LN06, the Source Innovation Program of Qingdao under Grant No. 18-2-2-56-jch, the Open Research Fund from Shandong Provincial Key Laboratory of Computer Networks under Grant No. SDKLCN-2018-07 and the State Foundation of China for Studying Abroad to Visit the United States as a 'Visiting Scholar'.

References

1. He, Z., Cai, Z., Wang, X.: Modeling propagation dynamics and developing optimized countermeasures for rumor spreading in online social networks. In: 2015 IEEE 35th International Conference on Distributed Computing Systems, pp. 205–214. IEEE (2015)
2. Daley, D.J., Kendall, D.G.: Epidemics and rumours. Nature **204**(4963), 1118 (1964)
3. Xu, Q., Su, Z., Zhang, K., et al.: Epidemic information dissemination in mobile social networks with opportunistic links. IEEE Trans. Emerg. Top. Comput. **3**(3), 399–409 (2015)
4. Wang, F., Wang, H., Xu, K., et al.: Characterizing information diffusion in online social networks with linear diffusive model. In: 2013 IEEE 33rd International Conference on Distributed Computing Systems (ICDCS), pp. 307–316. IEEE (2013)
5. Han, S.C., Liu, Y., Chen, H.L., et al.: Influence model of user behavior characteristics on information dissemination. Int. J. Comput. Commun. Control **11**(2), 209–223 (2016)
6. Jiang, C., Chen, Y., Liu, K.J.R.: Evolutionary dynamics of information diffusion over social networks. IEEE Trans. Signal Process. **62**(17), 4573–4586 (2014)
7. Xiao, Y., Song, C., Liu, Y.: Social hotspot propagation dynamics model based on multidimensional attributes and evolutionary games. Commun. Nonlinear Sci. Numer. Simul. **67**, 13–25 (2019)
8. Zhao, L., Qiu, X., Wang, X., et al.: Rumor spreading model considering forgetting and remembering mechanisms in inhomogeneous networks. Phys. Stat. Mech. Appl. **392**(4), 987–994 (2013)
9. Xia, L.L., Jiang, G.P., Song, B., et al.: Rumor spreading model considering hesitating mechanism in complex social networks. Phys. Stat. Mech. Appl. **437**, 295–303 (2015)
10. Han, Z.M., Chen, Y., et al.: Research on node influence analysis in social networks. J. Softw. **28**(1), 84–104 (2017)
11. Wilensky, U.: Netlogo. http://ccl.northwestern.edu/netlogo/
12. Matsubara, Y., Sakurai, Y., et al.: Nonlinear dynamics of information diffusion in social networks. ACM Trans. Web (TWEB) **11**(2), 11 (2017)
13. Zheng, C., Xia, C., Guo, Q., et al.: Interplay between SIR-based disease spreading and awareness diffusion on multiplex networks. J. Parallel Distrib. Comput. **115**, 20–28 (2018)

14. De Abreu, C.S., Salles, R.M.: Modeling message diffusion in epidemical DTN. Ad Hoc Netw. **16**, 197–209 (2014)
15. Basaras, P., Katsaros, D., Tassiulas, L.: Dynamically blocking contagions in complex networks by cutting vital connections. In: 2015 IEEE International Conference on Communications (ICC), pp. 1170–1175. IEEE (2015)
16. He, Z., Cai, Z., Yu, J., et al.: Cost-efficient strategies for restraining rumor spreading in mobile social networks. IEEE Trans. Veh. Technol. **66**(3), 2789–2800 (2017)
17. Xia, H., Hu, C., Xiao, F., et al.: An efficient social-like semantic-aware service discovery mechanism for large-scale Internet of Things. Comput. Netw. **152**, 210–220 (2019)
18. Hu, C., Li, W., Cheng, X., et al.: A secure and verifiable access control scheme for big data storage in clouds. IEEE Trans. Big Data **4**(3), 341–355 (2018)

Data Forwarding and Caching Strategy for RSU Aided V-NDN

Zhenchun Wei[1,2], Jie Pan[1], Kangkang Wang[1], Lei Shi[1,2(✉)],
Zengwei Lyu[1(✉)], and Lin Feng[1]

[1] School of Computer Science and Information Engineering,
Hefei University of Technology, Hefei, China
thunder10@163.com, lvzengwei@mail.hfut.edu.cn
[2] Engineering Research Center of Safety Critical Industrial Measurement
and Control Technology, Ministry of Education, Hefei, China

Abstract. Vehicular Named Data Networking (V-NDN) is an Vehicular Ad-hoc Network (VANET) using Named Data Network (NDN). Interest packet forwarding and data packet caching strategy are two key issues in the field. This paper focus on the data distribution and caching strategy of V-NDN in urban road environment. First, we propose a RSU-assisted strategy for interest packet and data packet forwarding. Secondly, it is the first time to use the method of decision tree prediction to guide the data packet cache, and uses a cache replacement policy based on popularity and request cost to store data due to the memory limit of RSU. Finally, the simulation results show that the proposed strategy and method effectively improve quality of service (QoS) of network.

Keywords: NDN · VANET · Forwarding strategy · Caching strategy ·
Decision tree

1 Introduction

Vehicle ad-hoc Network (VANET) is a kind of special mobile ad-hoc network consist of vehicles to achieve communication between vehicles (V2V) or vehicles and infrastructure (V2I) [1]. Due to the frequent changes in network topology, VANET with IP network architecture cannot maintain the stability of link in end-to-end communication, and the network load will change greatly along with traffic density changes, so the traditional IP network is unable to work well in VANET [2, 3]. Instead of host-based on end-to-end communication, NDN communication looks for data in network by name. When requestor needs to obtain data, it sends the interest packet of data name to the network, and the data will return from the network as a data packet. Because NDN is more concerned with the data itself, NDN network is more suitable for VANET than IP network [4]. In recent years, the application of NDN to VANET's vehicle named data network become a research hotpot.

© Springer Nature Switzerland AG 2019
E. S. Biagioni et al. (Eds.): WASA 2019, LNCS 11604, pp. 605–612, 2019.
https://doi.org/10.1007/978-3-030-23597-0_50

2 Related Work

To improve the quality of service, the existing researches mainly improve packet forwarding strategy, and introduces some mechanisms to make the forwarding of the interest packet as efficient or directional as possible. In Ref. [5], the author sets a maximum forwarding limit to reduce the flooding of the interest package in the free channel, and deploy the electronic map to expand the broadcast range. Reference [6] proposed a push data transmission method to reduce the safety data transmission delay. Reference [7] forward route packet according to the road to make the packet forwarding directional. Reference [8] and [9] provide effective data uploading methods which could be used in VANET to improve security.

Based on the actual situation, this paper improves the traditional V-NDN network model and makes use of RSUs. In addition, this paper also considers the RSUs' memory limit, and deploy machine learning in data packets caching strategy. The constructed decision tree model is used to predict which packets are likely to be requested next and to guide which RSUs are cached on that basis. The main contributions of this study can be summarized as follows:

1. We proposed a RSU assisted V-NDN network model, which can help to solve the communication between different regions due to discontinuous of vehicle stream.
2. The method of machine learning is applied in V-NDN packet caching strategy to predict the data that is more likely to be requested, so as to reduce the average request delay of the network.
3. The network performance of RSU aided V-NDN, traditional V-NDN and cellular aided V-NDN under the same scenario is analyzed through experimental simulation, which verifies the superiority of the proposed strategy.

3 Network Model

To improve the QoS of the network, this paper proposes an RSU-aided V-NDN network model. In this model, RSU can be used as a forwarding node to assist vehicle communication. This paper also takes into account the heavily load of RSU and limited memory, then proposes a data cache strategy based on decision tree and a data replacement strategy based on attention and cost of request for buffering data packet. Figure 1 describe two situations in RSU-assisted V-NDN network model.

As shown in Fig. 1(a), the RSUs are set in different connected regions. The requester C_1 sends an interest packet I_s to request the resource S from P_2, I_s is forwarded to roadside unit RSU_1 via F_1, and RSU_1 forwards I_s to the roadside unit RSU_2 nearest to the position of S's name. Then, RSU_2 sends I_s to nearby vehicles through wireless channel, and P_2 returns corresponding data after gets interest packets. In Fig. 1(b), the RSU assists communication between distant vehicles in same connected region, and the assistance of the RSU reduces the hops of forwarding packet during the communication from C_1 to P_2.

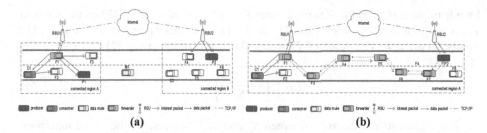

(a)   **(b)**

Fig. 1. Network model of RSU aided V-NDN

4 Data Forwarding Strategy

The RSU-aided V-NDN data forwarding strategy can be divided into two parts: interest packet forwarding and data packet forwarding.

4.1 Forwarding Strategy for Interest Packet

To use the fewer hops to forward the interest packet farther, the vehicle farthest from C will be selected as the forwarder next. If a vehicle once processed I_s, when I_s is received again, it will be ignored. When roadside unit R_s receives I_s, R_s will forward I_s to the roadside unit R_n nearest to the destination of data S using TCP/IP protocol. After R_n receives I_s, it broadcasts the interest packet I_s to the wireless channel.

Vehicle Node Forwards Interest Package. According to the above, the vehicle which is farthest from C in the vehicles that receive I_s will be selected as the forwarder. The process of the vehicle nodes forwarding the interest package is as shown in Fig. 2. First, S_1 broadcasts interest packets. Since S_4 is the farthest from S_1, the second forwarding is performed by S_4. In the same way, next forwarded are S_{10} and S_{11}, finally forwarded by S_7 and S_{13}.

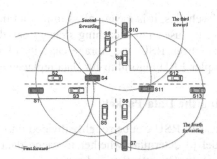

Fig. 2. Interest packet forwarding process of vehicle nodes

To select farthest vehicle from the sender as a forwarder, this paper uses a method of timing forwarding. For each data request, when any vehicle node S_a receives a broadcast interest packet I_i, it starts a timer Tr_i with a duration of T_d. When the value of Tr_i is reduced to 0, S_b deletes the Tr_i firstly, then records S_b and decrease the TTL, finally forwards I_i. The value of T_d is calculated according to Eq. (1).

$$T_d = \left\lfloor \frac{R - D_{ab}}{S} \right\rfloor T_m \tag{1}$$

D_{ab} represents the distance between S_a and S_b, R represents the maximum communication distance of the DSRC, and S is the step size, and T_m is the maximum time for any two vehicles to communicate in one hop.

RSU Node Forwards Interest Package. The interest packet forwarding process between the RSU and the vehicle could be described as follows. After the roadside unit RSU_1 receives the interest package from C_2, it matches RSU_2 according to the target position. Then, RSU_2 broadcasts interest packets to nearby vehicles.

4.2   Forwarding Strategy for Data Packet

The forwarding process of data packet is basically the same as the NDN. According to the request record in pending interest table (PIT), the data packet is returned to the data requester along the reverse path of the interest packet.

5   Caching Strategy for Data Packet

In the network model proposed in this paper, vehicle nodes use probabilistic caching strategies to cache data packets and use least recently used strategy (LRU) to replace data packets. The RSU apply decision tree to caching packets, and the data replacement algorithm uses an alternative strategy based on data attention and request cost.

5.1   Vehicle Node Caching the Data Packet

Due to the high speed of vehicles, it is meaningless to predict the data packet caching of vehicles. Therefore, we the uses a data caching strategy based on probability which is denoted as P_v. Different from RSU, the storage capacity of vehicle nodes is large enough, so we use a simpler LRU algorithm for data replacement in vehicle nodes.

5.2   RSU Node Caching the Data Packet

The packet caching process of RSU can be roughly divided into two steps: (1) Using a cache decision tree model to determine whether to cache data packets; (2) Using a replacement strategy based on data attention and request cost to store data packets. We apply machine learning method in predict the request for interest packet because of the characteristics of packets. Due to the weak computing power of RSU, we use the decision tree method to reduce the cost of prediction.

Decision Tree Based Data Caching Strategy. Owing to the memory limit of RSU, the RSU cannot cache all packets. So the data packet caching strategy will greatly affect hit ratio of interest packets. To improve the hit rate, we proposes a decision tree caching strategy to predict which data should be cached. The generation process of the cache decision tree model can be divided into the following three steps: sample extraction, feature calculation, construction of decision tree and pruning optimization.

Sample Extraction. By analyzing the interest packets RSU received, it is easy to count the last N requested data packets and their requested times. $S = \{s_0, s_1, \ldots, s_{n-1}\}$ denote the set of data packets, I_j indicates the interest packet corresponding to the packet s_j. During Δt period, the requested times of I_j can be expressed as q_j, and the time gap between interest packet i-th and (i + 1)-th request can be expressed as t_{ji}. The average requested times of data packet S is as follows.

$$\overline{Q} = \frac{1}{n}\sum_{i=0}^{n-1} q_i \tag{2}$$

Assign $S_0 = \{s_i|q_i < \overline{Q}, 0 \leq i < n-1\}$, $S_1 = \{s_i|q_i \geq \overline{Q}, 0 \leq i < n-1\}$, then the sample set can be represented as follows.

$$D_0 = \{(s_i, 0)|s_i \in S_0\} \cup \{(s_i, 1)|s_i \in S_1\} \tag{3}$$

In Eq. (3), $(s_i, 0)$ indicates that s_i should be cached, $(s_i, 1)$ indicates that s_i should not be cached.

Feature Calculation. The active time and location of different types of resources in the network will be different, and the requests for traffic information of vehicles near the RSU are related to the location of the RSU, so we should choose features from message. The feature attribute collection for this paper is $A = \{F_{mt}, F_d, F_t, F_\tau\}$, where F_{mt} represents the type of resource, F_d indicates the distance between the resource and location of RSU, F_t represents the time attribute of the resource, and F_τ indicates the age of the data, that is the time the packet was generated.

Construction of Decision Tree and Pruning Optimization. This paper builds a decision tree with reference to the C4.5 decision tree generation algorithm [10]. We firstly discretize the continuous attributes F_d, F_t, F_τ, and then select the information gain ratio as a criterion for building a complete decision tree. This paper uses the dichotomy method to discretize continuous attributes. We also use the post-pruning strategy to prune the decision tree to reduce the risk of overfitting.

Data Substitution Strategy. This article considers the data attention and request cost to determine whether a data packet should be retained. When the RSU needs to store a new data packet to the content store (CS), it firstly sorts the data packets according to the comprehensive weights, and then deletes the data packets from the lowest comprehensive weight. The definition of attention, request cost, and comprehensive weight are described below.

The data attention degree is related to the frequency and freshness of recent data requests. The frequency refers to the times of the data be requested during the time Δt. The freshness can be measured by the time gap between the latest request time and the current time. For any data s_j, the degree of attention is defined as follows.

$$R_i(j) = \sum_{k=1}^{n} F(t_c - t_{jk}) \tag{4}$$

t_{jk} represents the time of the k-th request data s_j, and t_c represents the current time. $F(x)$ is a weight function used to adjust the importance of frequency and freshness, $F(x) = 2^{-\lambda x}$, $\lambda \in (0, 1)$. The λ more near to 0, the more important frequency be. Conversely, the λ more near to 1, the more important freshness be.

The request cost C_i of packet s_i is the times of packet that has passed from the data provider to the current node. In summary, the comprehensive weight P_i of data s_i attention and request costs is expressed as Eq. (5). ω_1 and ω_2 indicates the weight of unit attention weight of the unit request cost, respectively.

$$P_i = R_i(j) \cdot \omega_1 + C_i \cdot \omega_2 \tag{5}$$

Cache Process of Data Packet in RSU Node. The RSU updates its own cache decision tree every Δt time. When RSU receives the data packet, it firstly predicts whether it should cache packet. The data packets which are not be stored will directly forward according to the PIT. For the packet data to be cached, it will be forward according to the data substitution strategy based on attention and request cost.

6 Simulation and Analysis

To generate a more realistic vehicle trajectory, this paper uses the urban traffic simulator SUMO. We set five data providers and data requester vehicles respectively, and they randomly collects the environmental information and generates data packets. The data requester requests the data packet 5 times per second. Also, the vehicles randomly generate the weather information for the last 5 days per hour and 1,000 news information. For the sake of performance of our strategy, we tested the traditional V-NDN and cellular network-assisted NDN at the same simulation.

6.1 Average Request Delay and Data Request Success Rate

As shown in Fig. 3(a), as the number of vehicles increases, the average delay of the three network strategies has a downward trend. This is because the increase in the number of vehicles leads to an increase in vehicle density, and consumer vehicles can acquire data from nearby vehicles. Cellular Aided V-NDN strategy has the largest delay, because it will use the cellular network to broadcast interest packets when data requests are unresponsive, so that all nodes that have data copy data to surrounding vehicles and then tries again to request data.

The curves of the obtained data success rate with the number of vehicles are shown in Fig. 3(b), both the Cellular aided V-NDN and the RSU aided V-NDN have better performance. RSU aided V-NDN enables vehicles in different connected regions to communicate, so it has a higher data request success rate than traditional V-NDN. Figure 4(a) shows the curve of the hit rate of interest packet as the number of vehicles. In summary, it can be seen that the strategy proposed in this paper has better performance for improving QoS.

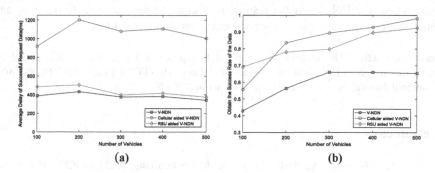

(a)   (b)

Fig. 3. The average delay of successful request data varies with the number of vehicles and obtain the success rate of the data with the curve of the number of vehicles

6.2   RSU Aided V-NDN Performance

In RSU aided V-NDN, because of the limit of storage space of RSU, we use a data packet cache strategy based on decision tree and compared it with probabilistic cache strategy. In Fig. 4(b), the cache hit rate of the RSU using the decision tree is higher than that of the RSU using the probabilistic cache strategy under the same cache capacity. With the increase of RSU capacity, the gap between them is also increasing.

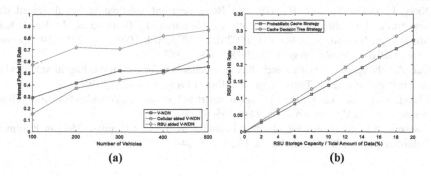

(a)   (b)

Fig. 4. Interest packet hit rate with the number of vehicles curve and RSU cache hit rate with RSU cache capacity curve

7 Conclusions

In this paper, the naming data network and RSU are applied in vehicular ad-hoc network, and it is well adapted to the frequent changes of vehicular ad-hoc network. We designed a data forwarding and caching strategy based on RSU aided vehicle naming data network. The decision tree is firstly applied to the packet caching decision of the NDN network, which solves the problem of limited RSU storage capacity. To verify the effectiveness of our method, we compared with traditional V-NDN and cellular aided V-NDN. From the results, it is clear to see the data forwarding and caching strategy in this paper has a good effect on improving QoS.

Acknowledgements. The material presented in this paper is based upon work funded by National Key Research Development Program of China (2016YFC0801405, 2016YFC0801804) and National Natural Science Foundation of China (61806067).

References

1. Zhang, L., Afanasyev, A., Burke, J.: Named data networking. ACM SIGCOMM Comput. Commun. Rev. **44**(3), 66–73 (2014)
2. Xian, Y., Wang, H.: A survey of VANET oriented NDN research. Electron. World **1**(6), 11–13 (2017)
3. Cai, Z., He, Z., Guan, X., Li, Y.: Collective data-sanitization for preventing sensitive information inference attacks in social networks. IEEE Trans. Dependable Secure Comput. **15**(4), 577–590 (2018)
4. Cai, Z., He, Z.: Trading private range counting over big IoT data. In: The 39th IEEE International Conference on Distributed Computing Systems, Dallas, p. 1
5. Grassi, G., Pesavento, D., Pau, G., Vuyyuru, R., Wakikawa, R., Zhang, L.: VANET via named data networking. In: The 33rd IEEE Conference on Computer Communications Workshops, Toronto, pp. 410–415
6. Majeed, M.F., Ahmed, S.H., Dailey, M.N.: Enabling push-based critical data forwarding in vehicular named data networks. IEEE Commun. Lett. **21**(4), 873–876 (2017)
7. Xiao, J., Deng, J., Cao, H., Wu, W.: Road segment information based named data networking for vehicular environments. In: Carretero, J., Garcia-Blas, J., Ko, R.K.L., Mueller, P., Nakano, K. (eds.) ICA3PP 2016. LNCS, vol. 10048, pp. 245–259. Springer, Cham (2016). https://doi.org/10.1007/978-3-319-49583-5_19
8. Cai, Z., Zheng, X.: A private and efficient mechanism for data uploading in smart cyber-physical systems. IEEE Trans. Netw. Sci. Eng. **129**(5), 423–429 (2019)
9. Zheng, X., Cai, Z., Li, Y.: Data linkage in smart IoT systems: a consideration from privacy perspective. IEEE Commun. Mag. **56**(9), 55–61 (2018)
10. Salzberg, S.L.: Programs for Machine Learning by J. Ross Quinlan. Morgan Kaufmann Publishers, Inc., 1993. Mach. Learn. **16**(3), 235–240 (1994)

Lightweight IoT Malware Visualization Analysis via Two-Bits Networks

Hui Wen[1,2], Weidong Zhang[1,2], Yan Hu[4], Qing Hu[3], Hongsong Zhu[1,2(✉)],
and Limin Sun[1,2]

[1] Beijing Key Laboratory of IOT Information Security Technology,
Institute of Information Engineering, CAS, Beijing, China
`zhuhongsong@iie.ac.cn`
[2] University of Chinese Academy of Sciences, Beijing, China
[3] School of Aerospace Engineering, Beijing Institute of Technology, Beijing, China
[4] School of Computer and Communication Engineering,
University of Science and Technology Beijing, Beijing, China

Abstract. Internet of Things (IoT) devices are typically resource constrained micro-computers for domain-specific computations. Most of
them use low-cost embedded system that lacked basic security monitoring and protection mechanisms. Consequently, IoT-specific malwares are
made to target at these vulnerable devices for deep infection and utilization, such as Mirai and Brickerbot, which poses tremendous threats to
the security of IoT. In this issue, we present a novel approach for detecting malware in IoT environments. The proposed method firstly extract
one-channel gray-scale image sequence that converted from the disassem-
bled malware binaries. Then we utilize a Two-Bits Convolutional Neural
Network (TBN) for detecting IoT malware families, which can encode
the network edge weights with two bits. Experimental results conducted
on the collected dataset show that our approach can reduce the memory
usage and improve computational efficiency significantly while achieving
a considerable performance in terms of malware detection accuracy.

Keywords: Internet of Things · Malware detection ·
Lightweight analysis · Two-bits convolutional neural network

1 Introduction

The Internet of Things (IoT) is an extension of the traditional networks, which
allows a very large of smart devices to connect each other to share information
for a specific work flow. Traditional networks devices are typically only able to
perform function-specific tasks based on pre-defined rules, such as many kinds of
sensors and controllers. Different from traditional micro devices, IoT devices have
more powerful computation to solve complex tasks with smarter micro-system.
Nevertheless, it imply more vulnerabilities, due to the complexity in hardware
and software, with more chances for potential adversaries to threaten them. In

© Springer Nature Switzerland AG 2019
E. S. Biagioni et al. (Eds.): WASA 2019, LNCS 11604, pp. 613–621, 2019.
https://doi.org/10.1007/978-3-030-23597-0_51

recent years, IoT-specific malwares are made to target at these vulnerabilities for deep infection and utilization, such as Mirai and Brickerbot. And IoT devices still lack sufficient computational resources to be able to use existing security solutions to protect themselves.

Despite the requirements of the lightweight security solutions, malware detection still faces many difficulties and challenges. The particularly challenge is the exponential growth of uncovering malware variants. Millions of variants captured by honeypot or other technologies bring a large amount of work to security experts. Specifically, when a new variant of malware is acquired, experts commonly use static or dynamic method to analyze the sample manually because the knowledge about the functions of malware is necessary for its removal or detection [1]. Such manual analysis requires several hours to several weeks, depending on the malware complexity [2]. To reduce the workload of human analysts, powerful methods based on machine learning use the specific feature of malware families to detect uncover malwares or their variants automatically [3]. Moreover, these traditional feature based methods also demonstrate low efficiency when exposed to packed or obfuscated malware in IoT environments.

Recently, rather than focusing on nonvisible features for malware classification, visualization-based approaches [5–7] have been proposed to directly analyze malware binaries for classification, which further improves the efficiency of malware analysis because no in-depth analysis is required. It assumes that most of variants have some similarity in binary code by reusing some important modules, and can be well represented by an image binaries sequence. Nataraj et al. [7] visualized malwares as gray images and found that image textures of the same families are particularly similar, and there is a big difference between different families. Kirat et al. [10] proposed another image-based classification method and demonstrated that the method shows higher accuracy than methods using n-gram feature and methods based on control flow graphs against obfuscated binary samples.

Reportedly, deep learning based method demonstrated a better classification performance than others in malware detection. The deep learning is based on the structure of convolutional neural networks (CNN), which consist of multiple layers of various types and hundreds to thousands of neurons in each layer. Raff et al. [11] used raw byte sequences as inputs of deep learning. In their work, they noted that detection from raw bytes presents a sequence problem with over two million time steps. Yue et al. [12] utilized convolutional neural network for malware family classification and achieve a considerable performance. However, a typical CNN has millions of parameters and perform billions of arithmetic operations for each inference. It shows that traditional deep learning model can not fit the resource-constrained IoT environments. Actually, it is intuitive to implement a reduced-size deep learning model with negligible accuracy loss. Hence the removal of redundant parameters in the deep learning models, if performed properly, will produce similar overall accuracy as the original models.

To solve above mentioned problems, this paper offered the following contributions:

(1) we proposed a method to extract visualized byte sequences peculiar to the malware family from the malware binaries automatically. Then we use an imbalanced sampling method to make sure that the trained model is not biased towards the class that has more data.
(2) we proposed a novel method for detecting malware variants based on a two-bits convolutional neural network, which represent a considerable performance with low computation resources.
(3) we constructed a IoT malware dataset that collected in real world, which contains 2387 samples with 10 families.

The rest of this paper is organized as follows. Section 2 provides an overview of our approach. Section 3 describes the malware visualization method and the malware classification model based on Two-Bits Convolutional Neural Network. Section 4 shows the results and analysis of malware visualization and classification. Finally, the conclusions are presented in Sect. 5.

2 Overview

The proposed method contains two steps work for training a lightweight malware classification model, which can detect malwares with limited resources (Fig. 1).

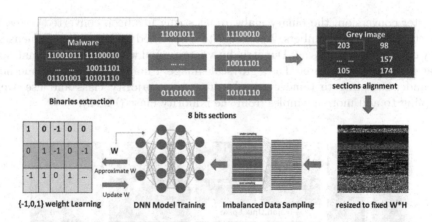

Fig. 1. Overview of proposed method.

(1) *Malware Visualization & Imbalanced Data Sampling*
In this step, the proposed method visualized a malware to a gray image. It reads each byte of the binary data of the target malware and transformed to a numeric array that range from 0 to 255 and convert the numeric array

to a gray image with determined image size. Then it resamples data by removing samples from the majority class and adding more examples from the minority class.

(2) *Two-bits Network Learning*

CNN model can be used to learn the feature from higher levels of the hierarchy formed by the composition of lower level features. To reduce the complexity of CNN model, our approach use a Two-Bits Network (TBN) to compress model by constraining weights to +1, 0, −1. The proposed method minimizes the Euclidian distance between origin weights and two-bits weights along with a scaling factor. And the results show that the model size can be largely compressed while achieving a considerable performance in terms of malware classification accuracy.

3 Approach

3.1 Malware Visualization and Imbalanced Data Sampling

Firstly, the proposed method convert malware bit string into a number of that are 8 bits in length. Each substrings can be considered as a pixel that values ranged from 0 to 255. For instances, a series binary number that extracted form malware would split into a 8 dimension vector $[b_0, b_1, b_2, b_3, b_4, b_5, b_6, b_7]$. And values in vector can be joint into a decimal number as follows:

$$I = b_0 * 2^0 + b_1 * 2^1 + b_2 * 2^2 + b_3 * 2^3 + b_4 * 2^4 + b_5 * 2^5 + b_6 * 2^6 + b_7 * 2^7 \quad (1)$$

After conversion, the binary malware bit string has been converted into a 1-D vector of decimal numbers. According to a specified width, this 1-Dimension array can be stretched as a 2-D matrix by a determined width. Then, the malware binaries matrix is interpreted as a grayscale image. Finally, the proposed method use under-sampling to remove samples from the majority class and use over-sampling to add more examples from the minority class (Fig. 2).

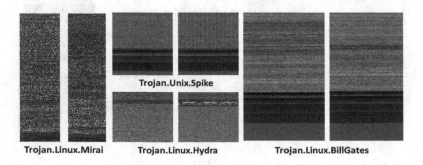

Trojan.Unix.Spike

Trojan.Linux.Mirai   Trojan.Linux.Hydra   Trojan.Linux.BillGates

Fig. 2. Illustration of malware images.

3.2 Malware Classification Using Two-Bits Networks

Problem Formulation. The core problem of Two-Bits Networks is to minimize the Euclidian distance between CNN weights W and two-bits weights W^b with a nonnegative factor α. The optimization problem can be formulated as follows:

$$f(W, \alpha) = \underset{\alpha, W^b}{argmin} ||W - \alpha * W^b||^2$$

$$s.t. \quad \alpha > 0 \tag{2}$$

$$W_i^b = \{-1, 0, 1\}, i = 1, 2, ..., n.$$

where n is the size of the matrix W, W_i is the i-th value of W^b, and W^b is the approximation weight that only have two bits values $\{-1, 0, 1\}$. With the approximation $W = \alpha W^b$, the convolution operation of deep learning can be approximated as follows:

$$I * W \approx I * (\alpha W^b) = (\alpha I) \oplus W^b \tag{3}$$

Where I is the matrix of the image, and $*$ is the convolution operation or an inner product operation. $\oplus$ indicates a special convolution operation or an inner product without any multiplication, because of bitwise operation that can be used with approximated two-bits values of W^b.

Optimization Solution. It assumes that a threshold λ can divide W_i into a proper value in $\{-1, 0, 1\}$. The process of converting W_i to W_i^b can be expressed as a segmented function:

$$W_i^b = \begin{cases} +1, & if & W_i > \lambda \\ 0, & if & |W_i| \leq \lambda \\ -1, & if & W_i < -\lambda \end{cases} \tag{4}$$

In this condition, the cost function of original optimization problem can be transformed to another formulation:

$$\begin{aligned} J(W) &= ||W - \alpha * W^b||^2 \\ &= \sum_{|W_i|>\lambda} (|W_i| - \alpha * |W_i^b|)^2 + \sum_{|W_i|\leq\lambda} |W_i|^2 \\ &= \sum_{|W_i|>\lambda} \alpha^2 - 2 \sum_{|W_i|>\lambda} \alpha |W_i| + C \end{aligned} \tag{5}$$

Where C represent a constant value. Then we take the derivative with regard to α for minimal cost function $J(W)$, and get the optimal parameter α^*:

$$\alpha^* = \frac{1}{m} \sum_{|W_i|>\lambda} |W_i| \tag{6}$$

Where m is the number of elements in $\{i||W_i| > \lambda\}$. By substituting α^* int formula (5), the optimal λ^* can be computed as follows:

$$\lambda^* = \underset{\lambda>0}{argmin}(-\frac{1}{m}\sum_{|W_i|>\lambda}|W_i|^2) \qquad (7)$$

Model Training. The Two-Bits Network are based on Deep Convolutional Neural Network (DNN). It can be trained by stochastic gradient descent (SGD) method. Firtstly, Given the input, compute the unit activations layer by layer. Then, given the target, compute the training objective's gradient with regard to each layer's activations. Finally, compute the gradient with regard to each layer's parameters and then update the parameters using their computed gradients and their previous values.

4   Experiment and Analysis

In this section, we present our evaluation of the effectiveness of TBN. We employed the framework *pytorch* to create and train a Two-Bits Network model. Then we conducted many scientific experiments on our IoT malware dataset. 80% of them are used for training and the rest for validation.

4.1   Dataset Preparation

We collect IoT malwares in real world for making the experimental result more convincing. The dataset contains 2387 samples from 10 families. The details of malware samples are shown in Table 1.

Table 1. Illustration of IoT malware dataset.

Family	Trojan.Hydra	Trojan.Mirai	Trojan.Spike	Trojan.Tsunami	Trojan.Xorddos
Numbers	38	137	31	429	77
Family	Trojan.BillGates	Trojan.Ddostf	Backdoor.Dofloo	Trojan.Gafgyt	DDoS.Lightaidra
Numbers	62	93	55	1293	172

4.2   Experimental Setting

The malware binaries is interpreted as a grayscale image. For simplicity, the width of the image is fixed, and the height of the image varies depending on the size of the file. Table 2 presents some converted image widths for various file sizes, based on empirical observations from literature [8].

Table 2. Image width for various file sizes.

File size range	Image width	File size range	Image width
<10 kB	32	100 kB−200 kB	384
10 kB−30 kB	64	200 kB−500 kB	512
30 kB−60 kB	128	500 kB−1000 kB	768
60 kB−100 kB	256	>1000 kB	1024

4.3   Model Compression and Run Time Usage

In the process of malware classification, the scaling factor α could be transformed to the inputs according to the function (3). Thus, we only need to keep the two bits valued weights and the scaling factors for deployment. This would results up to a high model compression rate for run time usage compared with the float precision based model. And the experimental results show a considerable performance while compared with several typical deep learning model, such as AlexNet, LeNet5, ResNet. As Figs. 3 and 4 presents, our approach TBN generated smallest model size and presented fastest classification speed.

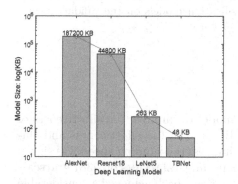

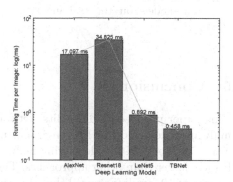

Fig. 3. The comparison of model size   **Fig. 4.** The comparison of run-time

4.4   Classification Results

We compare the results of our proposed approach with the outcomes of other typical deep learning methods for malware classification. Figures 5 and 6 shows classification performance obtained from the experiments. Figure 5 shows the loss curve, for which the results of the three methods were similar. The loss of ResNet method was not as good as others, perhaps because training samples may not be sufficient to fit learning problem. Figure 6 shows the performance of the different classification models on the validation set. The performance of the LeNet5 method was the best. The others also achieved a good result with respect to accuracy.

From the above, it was confirmed that the automatically acquired features in the deep learning model are useful for classification, as described in Sect. 3. Overall, the performance of the proposed method is verified. These observations justify that the visualized malware feature obtained from TBN model can well characterize the target malware families. Moreover, TBN have approximated performance while comparing with the other deep learning model.

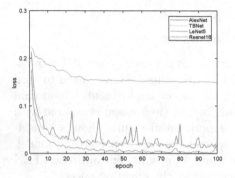

Fig. 5. Performance of different classification models on the training set (Loss)

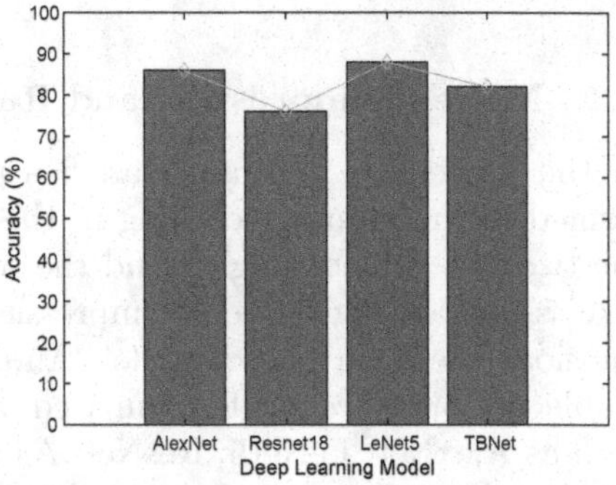

Fig. 6. Performance of different classification models on the validation set (Accuracy)

5   Conclusion

This paper proposed a Two-Bits Network model to improve the effectiveness of malware recognition in IoT environment. Because of the effectiveness and efficiency of the TBN for identifying malware images, the running speed was significantly faster than other approaches. The experimental results on 2387 grayscale images of 10 families showed that the proposed approach achieved a considerable performance with a high model compression rate and low computation cost.

Acknowledgement. This work was partially supported by the National Key R&D Program of China (2018YFC1201102), National Natural Science Foundation of China (61802016, U1636120), China Postdoctoral Science Foundation (2018M641198), and the National Social Science Foundation of China (17ZDA331).

References

1. Moser, A., Kruegel, C., Kirda, E.: Exploring multiple execution paths for malware analysis. In: Proceedings of the IEEE Symposium on Security and Privacy (2007)
2. Anderson, B., Storlie, C., Yates, M., Mcphall, A.: Automating reverse engineering with machine learning techniques (2014)

3. Ahmadi, M., Giacinto, G., Ulyanov, D., Semenov, S., Trofimov, M.: Novel feature extraction, selection and fusion for effective malware family classification. In: ACM Conference on Data and Application Security and Privacy (2016)
4. Su, J., Vargas, D.V., Prasad, S., Sgandurra, D., Feng, Y., Sakurai, K.: Lightweight classification of IOT malware based on image recognition (2018)
5. Zhang, J., Zheng, Q., Hui, Y., Lu, O., Hu, Y.: Malware variant detection using opcode image recognition with small training sets. In: International Conference on Computer Communication and Networks (2016)
6. Liu, L., Wang, B.: Malware classification using gray-scale images and ensemble learning. In: International Conference on Systems and Informatics (2017)
7. Han, K.S., Lim, J.H., Kang, B., Im, E.G.: Malware analysis using visualized images and entropy graphs. Int. J. Inf. Secur. **14**(1), 1–14 (2015)
8. Nataraj, L., Yegneswaran, V., Porras, P., Jian, Z.: A comparative assessment of malware classification using binary texture analysis and dynamic analysis. In: ACM Workshop on Security and Artificial Intelligence (2011)
9. Nataraj, L., Karthikeyan, S., Jacob, G., Manjunath, B.S.: Malware images: visualization and automatic classification. In: Proceedings of the 8th International Symposium on Visualization for Cyber Security (2011)
10. Kirat, D., Nataraj, L., Vigna, G., Manjunath, B.S.: Sigmal: a static signal processing based malware triage. In: Computer Security Applications Conference (2013)
11. Raff, E., Barker, J., Sylvester, J., Brandon, R., Nicholas, C.: Malware detection by eating a whole EXE (2017)
12. Yue, S.: Imbalanced malware images classification: a CNN based approach (2017)

Privacy Protection Sensing Data Aggregation for Crowd Sensing

Yunpeng Wu, Shukui Zhang$^{(\boxtimes)}$, Yuren Yang, Yang Zhang,
Li Zhang, and Hao Long

School of Computer Science and Technology, Soochow University,
Suzhou 215006, China
ypwu@stu.suda.edu.cn, zhangsk@suda.edu.cn

Abstract. The emergence of the crowd sensing solves the problem that the traditional perception mode is hard to deploy on a large scale and at a high cost. However, users are exposed to the risk of privacy leakage when participating in crowd sensing. In order to solve this issue, this paper protects the user's privacy through the dynamic group collaborative data submission mechanism and the method of adding noise perturbation, solves the privacy protection problem in the case of collusion attack. While implementing privacy protection and taking into consideration performance, this solution further reduces the cost of the system through batch verification. Safety analysis and simulation show the effectiveness and efficiency of the proposed method.

Keywords: Crowd sensing · Privacy protection · Batch verification ·
Aggregation statistics

1 Introduction

Due to the popularity of mobile smart devices and the improvement of performance, the emerging human-centered sensing method of mobile crowd sensing has emerged [1, 2]. It solves the problem of high cost of the large-scale deployment of traditional sensing modes, so it has broad application prospects in many fields, such as intelligent transportation [3], environmental monitoring [4], medical health [5]. However, the data collected by the user will contain specific private information. If the data is obtained by malicious third-party, it will extract the sensitive information, which will seriously threaten the user's personal and property security. Therefore, it is especially important to protect the privacy of users, this is an important prerequisite for people to accept and participate in the perception of the mobile crowd sensing [6].

In order to ensure the user's safe participation in the sensing task, the contributions of this paper mainly include: introducing random noise with certain attributes as a key for lightweight encryption, and using a data submission mechanism that the user can dynamically join and exit the group management mechanism for group cooperation, the user's private data is further protected. The user can ensure the privacy of the data at a lower computing cost, and can also protect the user's private information in the face of collusion attacks and the like. A certificateless signature scheme based on [7] is used

© Springer Nature Switzerland AG 2019
E. S. Biagioni et al. (Eds.): WASA 2019, LNCS 11604, pp. 622–630, 2019.
https://doi.org/10.1007/978-3-030-23597-0_52

for signature to ensure data integrity and non-repudiation. Therefore, the third-party cloud does not need to verify the identity certificate and can perform batch signature verification, which reduces the burden on the cloud.

2 Related Work

The issue of privacy protection in mobile crowd sensing has received wide attention. At present, the main technologies can be divided into three categories: anonymization, data perturbation, and cryptography for the privacy protection problem in crowd sensing [2]. Gisdakis et al. [8] implemented identity privacy protection based on k-anonymity in crowd sensing, so that users are hidden in the crowd, data and users are not linked. Papers [9] and [10] by introduced third-party cloud and used homomorphic encryption, which prevented the cloud and the requestor from directly contacting sensing data, thus protect the privacy of users. Wang et al. [1] hide the user's true identity in the Ad-Hoc network and use the tree routing between users to hide the true source of the message. Chen et al. [6] implemented 2ε-differential privacy protection by introducing specific random noise perturbation data.

3 Preliminaries and Background

3.1 System Model

The proposed scheme mainly consists of five entities, which are trusted institutions (TA), mobile users, group managers (GM), clouds and requester.

Trusted Authority (TA): The TA is responsible for system initialization, generating various initialization parameters and registering other entities. Generate anonymous identity and certificateless signing keys for mobile users, generate encryption and decryption keys for mobile users and requesters, and more.

Mobile User: The mobile user is the owner of a smart device, a participant in a sensing task. They collect various sensing data through smart devices and report the data to the cloud for processing.

Group Manager (GM): The GM groups the users participating in the task, so that the user can conveniently submit data for group collaboration privacy protection.

Cloud: The cloud is responsible for accepting, storing, and processing the data uploaded by the mobile user, and transmitting the result to the requester.

Requester: The requester is the owner of the sensing task, the consumer of the sensing data. Which delegates the processing of the data to the cloud due to the requester's storage and computational capabilities.

3.2 Security Objective

Assuming TA and GM do not collude with any entity. All entities are honest but curious, they will strictly enforce the prescribed actions, but may try to mine the user's private information. Our security objectives as follows:

Identity privacy protection: User anonymous participation in sensing tasks, other users, clouds, requesters and external attackers cannot obtain the user's true identity.

Data privacy security: No attacker can mine the user's private information within the scope of their own information. At the same time, data privacy can be well protected when the collusion attack occurs.

Message integrity and authentication: User-contributed messages are valid and have not been illegally modified or corrupted. It should be detectable when there is modification and destruction. The anonymous identity of the user should be real and effective, and the illegal user cannot forge identity to participate in the perceived task.

Replay resistance: The malicious third party may attempt to replay a message to interfere when the original message is invalid by collecting the user's message.

4 Privacy Protection Sensing Data Aggregation

4.1 Initialization

First, the system generates some necessary initial parameters. TA selects a large prime number p to determine the limited domain $GF(p)$ and selects $a, b \in GF(p)$ to construct an elliptic curve $y^2 = x^3 + ax + b \bmod p$. At this time, an additive group whose order is q is constructed by all the solution points and the infinite point O. Select one of the generators and record it as G. Then, TA selects a random number $\alpha \in Z_q^*$, and calculates $P = \alpha G$, α is the private key, P is the public key of the TA. Next, TA selects a random number $\beta_i \in Z_q^*$ and calculates $UID_i = \beta_i G$ to obtain the anonymous identity UID_i of user. The private key $psk_i = \beta_i + h(UID_i, \tau, T) \cdot \alpha \,(mod\,q)$ for signing is calculated for the user U_i after obtaining the anonymous identity UID_i, where T is the anonymous identity validity period, $h()$ is the secure hash function of $\{0, 1\}^* \rightarrow Z_q^*$. Then, TA randomly generates $n + 1$ large numbers $x_1, x_2, \cdots, x_n, rsk \in Z_p^*$ such that $(x_1 + x_2 + \cdots + x_n + rsk)\,mod\,p = 0$, x_i is used as the key sk_i of user U_i, rsk is used as the requester's private key to obtain the final aggregated result. Finally, TA sends (sk_i, UID_i, psk_i, T) to the user U_i through the secure channel.

4.2 Data Collection and Group Collaboration Data Submission

When a user participates in the task, it first selects an anonymous identity obtained from the TA to hide the real identity, then notifies the GM of the anonymous identity. The GM randomly divides the user into groups, each group forming a ring, and the users in the group will collaborate with the previous and next users to complete the submission of the data. Assume that the user U_i is in the group GID_j, the previous user in the user group is U_{i-1}, and the next user is U_{i+1}.

After U_i collects the data m_i, the data is desensitized by adding the noise data by the noise key sk_i obtained from the TA, and the following ciphertext is obtained:

$$c_i = m_i + sk_i \bmod p. \tag{1}$$

After obtaining the ciphertext c_i, the ciphertext is divided into two parts to become $c_{i,i}$ and $c_{i,i+1}$, where $c_i = c_{i,i} + c_{i,i+1}$. Suppose there are five users in the group, and the operation is as shown in Fig. 1. When U_i receives $c_{i-1,i}$ sent by U_{i-1}, it aggregates with $c_{i,i}$ reserved by itself, and obtains the ciphertext c_i' after cooperation, that is,

$$c_i' = c_{i,i} + c_{i-1,i}. \tag{2}$$

In order to ensure the integrity and verifiability of the message sent by the user to the cloud, the user will sign the message $\{c_i', GID_j, UID_i, \tau, T, t\}$, where t is the time stamp. First, the user U_i selects a random number $r_i \in Z_q^*$, calculates $R_i = r_iG$ and $s_i = h(c_i', GID_j, UID_i, \tau, T, t) \cdot r_i + psk_i(\bmod q)$. Finally, the certificateless signature $\sigma_i = (R_i, s_i)$ of the message is obtained.

Then the message that the U_i send to the cloud is $\{c_i', GID_j, UID_i, \tau, T, t, \sigma_i\}$.

The group collaboration scheme in this paper solves the problem of user dynamic joins and exits. When a user quits or a new user joins, only two neighbors are updated, which has lower communication overhead. Suppose U_i quit the task, it needs to report to the GM, GM only needs to update the two nodes U_{i-1} and U_{i+1} to re-form the ring, as shown in Fig. 3. When the new user U_i joins, the GM only needs to update the two nodes U_{i-1} and U_{i+1} to re-form the ring, that is, the reverse process of Fig. 2.

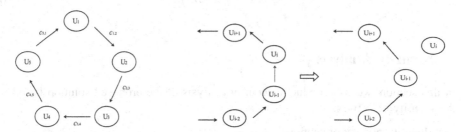

Fig. 1. Group collaboration   **Fig. 2.** Dynamic departure of users in the group

4.3 Batch Verification and Aggregation Statistics

After receiving the message $\{c_i', GID_j, UID_i, \tau, T, t, \sigma_i\}$ delivered by the user U_i, the cloud first calculates whether the difference between the signature time t and the current time is less than Δt, and whether the signature time is within the validity period of the pseudonym identity, that is, whether t is within T. If it is satisfied, it can be judged whether the message is accepted by verifying Eq. (3).

$$s_i \cdot G = h(c_i', GID_j, UID_i, \tau, T, t) \cdot R_i + UID_i + h(UID_i, \tau, T) \cdot P \tag{3}$$

Since the signature scheme in this article supports aggregate signature verification, the TA can be batch verification. Assuming a total of n participating users, TA first calculates $h_{i,1} = h(UID_i, \tau, T)$ and $h_i = h(c_i', GID_j, UID_i, \tau, T, t)$, where $i = 1, 2, \ldots, n$. Then perform batch signature verification according to Eq. (4).

$$\left(\sum_{i=1}^{n} s_i \right) \cdot G = \sum_{i=1}^{n} (h_i \cdot R_i) + \sum_{i=1}^{n} UID_i + \left(\sum_{i=1}^{n} h_{i,1} \right) \cdot P \tag{4}$$

After the cloud successfully verifies all the signatures, the aggregation result is calculated as C on the ciphertext, and the calculation is as follows:

$$C = \sum_{i=0}^{n} c_i' \bmod p. \tag{5}$$

After the cloud completes, signed the result by ECDSA, and then the aggregated result C and the signature are transmitted to the requester through the secure channel.

4.4   Result Acquisition

After the requester receives the result C and the signature, the signature is first verified, and the result is accepted only when the verification is passed. The decryption private key rsk is then obtained from the TA over the secure channel. Finally, using its own key rsk, it can decrypt and obtain the statistical summation result.

$$S = C + rsk \bmod p. \tag{6}$$

5   Security Analysis

In this section, we will conduct a security analysis of the proposed solution based on the security objectives.

(1) Identity privacy protection

In the proposed scheme, the user participates in the task using an anonymous identity UID, which is generated by the TA through random numbers β and G. Since the use of anonymous identity to participate in the sensing task makes its real identity only known to the TA, other users and entities cannot obtain the true identity of the user, and the attacker cannot obtain any information according to the anonymous identity, the user is hidden in many participating users, realized the identity privacy protection.

(2) Data privacy security

In this article, when the requester illegally eavesdrops, although it has the decryption private key rsk, since the data contributed by the user to the cloud passes the encryption of the noise key and the disturbance of the group cooperation, the requester cannot obtain the collaborative user of the user from among the many users, cannot possible to split the pieces of data of the user from the collaborative user and the user. Even in the case where each piece of data is obtained, since a large integer noise key is used, it is much larger than the real data, so that the requester cannot obtain the real data. Similarly, the cloud, other users and external attackers will not be able to capture the user's real data and dig out private information.

For the collusion attack between the cloud and the requester, the cloud and some users, and the requester and some users, due to the limited information of each other, similar to non-collusion, the user's real data will not be obtained. The most threatening when users collaborate with each other is the collusion attack between two users U_{i-1} and U_{i+1} adjacent to U_i, but they are difficult to know each other's. When U_{i-1} and U_{i+1} know each other, since U_i shares information with them, they will get the containing noise data of user U_i, but due to the existence of large integer noise keys, they are also difficult to obtain the user's true sensing data.

Therefore, the scheme in this paper implements privacy protection well, preventing attackers from mining private information from sensing data.

(3) Message integrity and authentication

The message delivered by the user is signed by the certificateless signature scheme. When signing, the random number r_i is used to calculate $R_i = r_i \cdot G$, and the signature private key psk_i and r_i are used to calculate s_i, where $psk_i = \beta_i + h(UID_i, \tau, T) \cdot \alpha \, (mod\, q)$ and $UID_i = \beta_i G$. Because of the difficulty in solving the ECDLP problem, attacker cannot obtain the signature private key of the user, and the forgery modification of the signature cannot be implemented. Therefore, when the attacker makes any modification to the message, the verification will fail and the certifier will find the modification, so guarantees the integrity of the message.

Since the user's anonymous identity is used for signing and verification, the validity of the user's anonymous identity is verified when the signature verification is successful. At the same time, due to the anonymous identity $UID_i = \beta_i G$, the signature key $psk_i = \beta_i + h(UID_i, \tau, T) \cdot \alpha \, (mod\, q)$ is composed of β_i and the private key α of the TA. According to the difficulty of solving the ECDLP problem, even if the attacker can forge UID, the corresponding signature key psk cannot be forged. Therefore, the attacker cannot forge the anonymous identity of the user, realized the verifiability and unforgeability of the user identity.

(4) Replay resistance

For replay attacks, since the message $\{c_i', GID_j, UID_i, \tau, T, t, \sigma_i\}$ has a timestamp t, when the attacker replays the message, the cloud can check the validity of the message according to the timestamp. Assume that the attacker replays the attack with a timestamp of t', which may exceed the validity period of the user's anonymous identity. In this case, the message will be invalid. Even if t' is within the validity period of the user's anonymous identity, because the timestamp changes, the user cannot forge an anonymous identity, the signature verification is not valid, and the message will be invalid. Therefore, this scheme can resist replay attacks.

6 Performance Analysis and Simulation

This section will perform performance analysis and simulation on the proposed method. The proposed method was compared with the other three methods [1, 8] and [10], these three methods were recorded as PPS, SPIP, and PPAS. The above algorithm is implemented based on the OpenSSL library, and the selected elliptic curve is secp256k1. Simulated on a PC equipped with an Intel i7-8750H 2.2 GHz CPU and 8 G RAM. All simulation results are averages of multiple executions.

First, a comparative analysis of the cost of the user, as shown in Fig. 3(a). For the cost of encryption, our solution uses group collaboration and noise perturbation, which has lower overhead than Paillier homomorphic encryption used by PPS and PPAS. Our solution only needs 0.003 ms; while PPS takes 6.447 ms; PPAS needs 31.907 ms (When the number of intervals divided is 5). PPAS and SPIP adopt the ECDSA signature scheme, which is the same cost as the scheme in this paper. The total cost of the solution in this paper is much smaller than that of PPS and PPAS. Since SPIP uses plaintext transmission, only the message is signed, so the total cost of the user is similar to the scheme of this paper, but the security of this scheme is much higher than PPAS.

Next, the cost of the requester is analyzed. Since both our solution and PPAS use the third-party cloud for aggregation statistics, PPS uses the primary node for aggregation statistics, so the aggregation statistics cost is zero. SPIP needs to aggregate statistics by itself. It can be observed in Fig. 3(b) that the decryption cost of this paper is much lower than that of PPS and PPAS. In this paper, the requester only needs to perform a modular addition operation of a large integer to obtain aggregated statistical results, but PPS and PPAS need to decrypt to obtain the result. The requester's verification cost is shown in Fig. 3(c). PPAS, SPIP, and this article, the signatures used by the requester are ECDSA. Since we and PPAS only need to verify the result for the third-party cloud. The requester of the SPIP needs to verify all the messages transmitted by the user, so when there are n users, it is necessary to perform n time of verification (In Fig. 3(c), n is 200). Therefore, the cost of the requester in this scheme is better than PPS, PPAS and SPIP.

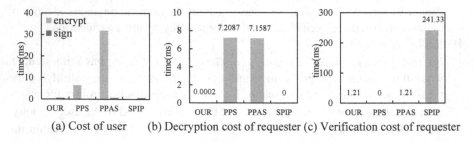

(a) Cost of user   (b) Decryption cost of requester (c) Verification cost of requester

Fig. 3. Cost of user and requester

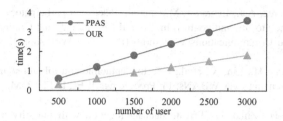

Fig. 4. Third-party cloud verification cost under different users

Finally, the advantages of using batch verification in this article are demonstrated. The cost of single signature verification in PPAS is $T_h + 2T_{p\_mul} + T_{p\_add}$ (T_h is hash operation time, T_{p_add} is two-point addition operation time in ECC, T_{p_mul} is point multiplication operation time in ECC), this paper is $2T_h + 3T_{p\_mul} + 2T_{p\_add}$, so the efficiency of single verification is lower than ECDSA. However, since the batch verification scheme is adopted in this paper, for n users, the cost is $2n \cdot T_h + (n+2) \cdot T_{p\_mul} + (2n+2) \cdot T_{p\_add}$. In the PPAS, the cost is $n \cdot T_h + 2n \cdot T_{p\_mul} + n \cdot T_{p\_add}$. Since T_{p_mul} is much larger than T_{p_add}, the verification cost in the cloud is gradually lower than PPAS with the increase of participating users, as shown in Fig. 4.

7 Conclusion

This paper we proposed a privacy protection sensing data aggregation scheme for crowd sensing. Through the method of dynamically collaborative data submission and noise perturbation, the problem of privacy leakage when users participate in sensing tasks is solved, especially in the case of collusion attacks. While solving the privacy protection problem, it is also taken into account the performance, and system cost is reduced through batch verification.

Acknowledgements. This work is partially supported by Prospective Application Foundation Research of Suzhou of China (No. SYG201730), Blue Project of Jiangsu of China, Science and technology project of Xuzhou of China (No. KC17074).

References

1. Wang, Z., Huang, D.: Privacy-preserving mobile crowd sensing in ad hoc networks. Ad Hoc Netw. **73**, 14–26 (2018)
2. Ganti, R.K., Ye, F., Lei, H.: Mobile crowdsensing: current state and future challenges. IEEE Commun. Mag. **49**(11), 32–39 (2011)
3. Gisdakis, S., Manolopoulos, V., Tao, S., et al.: Secure and privacy-preserving smartphone-based traffic information systems. IEEE Trans. Intell. Transp. Syst. **16**(3), 1428–1438 (2015)

4. Mendez, D., Perez, A.J., Labrador, M.A., et al.: P-sense: a participatory sensing system for air pollution monitoring and control. In: 2011 IEEE International Conference on Pervasive Computing and Communications Workshops (PERCOM Workshops), pp. 344–347, IEEE (2011)
5. Zhang, Z., Wang, H., Lin, X., et al.: Effective epidemic control and source tracing through mobile social sensing over WBANs. In: Proceedings IEEE INFOCOM, pp. 300–304, IEEE (2013)
6. Chen, J., Ma, H., Zhao, D.: Private data aggregation with integrity assurance and fault tolerance for mobile crowd-sensing. Wirel. Netw. 23(1), 131–144 (2017). https://doi.org/10.1007/s11276-015-1120-z
7. Cui, J., Zhang, J., Zhong, H., et al.: An efficient certificateless aggregate signature without pairings for vehicular ad hoc networks. Inf. Sci. 451, 1–15 (2018)
8. Gisdakis, S., Giannetsos, T., Papadimitratos, P.: Security, privacy, and incentive provision for mobile crowd sensing systems. IEEE Internet Things J. 3(5), 839–853 (2016)
9. Zhuo, G., Jia, Q., Guo, L., et al.: Privacy-preserving verifiable data aggregation and analysis for cloud-assisted mobile crowdsourcing. In: INFOCOM 2016 - The 35th Annual IEEE International Conference on Computer Communications, pp. 1–9. IEEE (2016)
10. Chen, J., Ma, H., Wei, D.S.L., et al.: Participant-density-aware privacy-preserving aggregate statistics for mobile crowd-sensing. In: 2015 IEEE 21st International Conference on Parallel and Distributed Systems (ICPADS), pp. 140–147. IEEE (2015)

A New Outsourced Data Deletion Scheme with Public Verifiability

Changsong Yang[1,2], Xiaoling Tao[2(✉)], Feng Zhao[2], and Yong Wang[2]

[1] School of Cyber Engineering, Xidian University, Xi'an 710071, China
csyang02@163.com
[2] School of Computer Science and Information Security,
Guilin University of Electronic Technology, Guilin 541004, China
{txl,fengzhao,wang}@guet.edu.cn

Abstract. In the cloud storage, the data owner will lose the direct control over his outsourced data, and all the operations over the outsourced data may be executed by corresponding remote cloud server, such as cloud data deletion operation. However, the selfish cloud server might maliciously reserve the data copy for financial interests, and deliberately send a false deletion result to cheat the data owner. In this paper, we design an IBF-based publicly verifiable cloud data deletion scheme. The proposed scheme enables the cloud server to delete the data and return a proof. Then the data owner can check the deletion result by verifying the returned deletion proof. Besides, the proposed scheme can realize public verifiability by applying the primitive of invertible bloom filter. Finally, we can prove that our proposed protocol not only can reach the expected security properties but also can achieve the practicality and high-efficiency.

Keywords: Cloud storage · Data deletion · Invertible bloom filter · Public verifiability · Data confidentiality

1 Introduction

Cloud computing can connect large-scale resources together via the Internet [20], and offer many high-quality services, for instance, data sharing service [11], verifiable database service [7], cloud storage service [12], and so on. Thanks to many advantages, these cloud services have been widely applied, specifically data storage service. In the cloud storage, the tenant outsources his personal data to the cloud server, which can greatly reduce the local storage overhead [19].

Despite many advantages, cloud storage unavoidably suffers from some new security issues, such as data privacy disclosure, data pollution and malicious data reservation. In particular, the malicious data reservation has become a severe challenge [14]. To be specific, the data owner loses the direct control over his outsourced data, which prevents him from executing the operations over the data directly. All the operations over the outsourced data (e.g., data deletion)

© Springer Nature Switzerland AG 2019
E. S. Biagioni et al. (Eds.): WASA 2019, LNCS 11604, pp. 631–638, 2019.
https://doi.org/10.1007/978-3-030-23597-0_53

will be executed by the cloud server. But the selfish cloud server might not delete the data honestly for economic benefits [16].

A great many of solutions have been proposed to solve this problem [10,15, 17,18], but there still exist some security challenges in processing the cloud data deletion. Firstly, lots of the existing deletion methods are very inefficient because they might cost plenty of computational overhead and transmission bandwidths to reach data deletion. Especially the schemes that achieve deletion by over-writing [3,4,6,13]. Secondly, some investigations show that most of the existing deletion schemes work as the "one-bit-return" protocol [1,5]. They delete the data according to the data owner's command and return a deletion result. Then the data owner has to trust the result since he cannot verify it. However, the selfish cloud server might return a wrong result to mislead the data owner maliciously. Recently, although a few schemes can reach verifiability of deletion result, most of them need some data owner's personal information in the verification process [8,9]. That is, only the data owner can verify the deletion result. But in real-application, the property of public verifiability should be introduced in data deletion scheme. To the best of our knowledge, it seems that there is no research work on invertible Bloom filter-based publicly verifiable cloud deletion scheme.

Our Work. In this paper, we put forward a new invertible Bloom filter-based data deletion scheme for cloud storage, which can deal with the problems mentioned above. To be more specific, our paper has three contributions. First of all, our proposed scheme is able to offer the data owner the ability to check the results of the storage and deletion operations. Therefore, if the cloud server does not perform honestly, the data owner can detect the cloud server's malicious behaviors by verifying the corresponding evidences. Secondly, our new proposed scheme can realize public verifiability by taking the advantages of the invertible Bloom filter. Finally, our novel scheme not only can reach the desired security requirements, but also can satisfy the high-efficiency and practicality.

The rest of this paper is organized as follows: In Sect. 2, we briefly describe the preliminaries of invertible Bloom filter, and followed by the detailed design of our novel outsourced data deletion scheme in Sect. 3. After that we present the security analysis in Sect. 4 and the efficiency evaluation of our scheme in Sect. 5. Finally, we conclude our paper in Sect. 6.

2   Preliminaries

Invertible Bloom filter (IBF) was an extend version of counting Bloom filter (CBF) [2], which can list all the given elements in the set that it represents. The main idea is that there are some pure cells whose values may be merely influenced by a data item. Once a pure cell is found, we divide its $idSum$ by its count to recover the data item. Besides, the CBF only needs k hash functions $h_1, \cdots, h_k$, where $h_i : [1, n] \rightarrow [1, m]$ and $i \in [1, k]$. However, except these k hash functions, the IBF still needs other three hash functions: $f_1, f_2 : [1, n] \rightarrow [1, m]$ and $g : [1, n] \rightarrow [1, n^2]$. Finally, there are three fields in every cell of the IBF: a *count* field, an *idSum* field and a *hashSum* field. In the following, we describe the construction of IBF in detail.

Algorithm 1. Insert(x)

Input: an element x
Output: an invertible Bloom filter IBF
for $i \in [1, k]$ **do**
> 1. Increment $B[h_i(x)]$.count by one;
> 2. Add the value x to $B[h_i(x)]$.idSum;
> 3. Add the hash value $g(x)$ to $B[h_i(x)]$.hashSum.

for $i = 1, 2$ **do**
> 1. Increment $C[f_i(x)]$.count by one;
> 2. Add the value x to $C[f_i(x)]$.idSum;
> 3. Add the hash value $g(x)$ to $C[f_i(x)]$.hashSum.

return IBF.

- A *count* field, which maintains the sum of the insert and deletion operations. In other word, it records the amount of the data items which are contained in the cell.
- An *idSum* field, which maintains the total of all data items y, where the data items ys map to the cell $B[i]$. Specifically, if $B[i]$ merely maintains n backups of a data item y, then $B[i].idSum = ny$.
- A *hashSum* field, which maintains the total of all the hash values $g(y)$. Specifically, if $B[i]$ merely maintains m backups of data item y, then the value of $B[i].hashSum$ will be $mg(x)$.

Algorithm 2. Delete(x)

Input: an element x
Output: a new invertible Bloom filter IBF
for $i \in [1, k]$ **do**
> 1. Decrement $B[h_i(x)]$.count by one;
> 2. Subtract the value x to $B[h_i(x)]$.idSum;
> 3. Subtract the hash value $g(x)$ to $B[h_i(x)]$.hashSum.

for $i = 1, 2$ **do**
> 1. Decrement $C[f_i(x)]$.count by one;
> 2. Subtract the value x to $C[f_i(x)]$.idSum;
> 3. Subtract the hash value $g(x)$ to $C[f_i(x)]$.hashSum.

return IBF.

In the IBF, we build an additional Bloom filter (BF) C, whose construction is similar to B. But C only uses f_1 and f_2 to map the data items to its cells. To insert an element x into the IBF, we should get k cells that x maps to firstly. Then we increase their *count* field by one, add x and $g(x)$ to their *idSum* field and *hashSum* field, respectively. Similarly, to delete an element y, we need to subtract one, y and $g(y)$ from their *count* field, *idSum* field and *hashSum* field, respectively. Figure 1 describes the detailed insert and deletion operations.

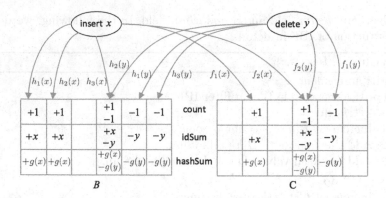

Fig. 1. An example of IBF with insert and deletion

3 Our Scheme

3.1 Overview

System and Threat Model. There are three entities in our system: a data owner O, a cloud server S and a third party auditor TPA, as shown in Fig. 2. O uploads his personal data to S. Then S maintains the data for O and deletes the data when O will not need them anymore. Finally, O checks the deletion result by verifying the deletion proof. Since S may cheat O and there must be one to solve the dispute, the existing of the TPA is reasonable.

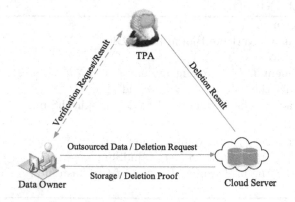

Fig. 2. The system model

Design Goals. There are three design goals for our scheme. The first one is *data confidentiality*. It means that the privacy information contained in the outsourced file should be protected. Any adversary cannot obtain the plaintext information without the encryption/decryption keys. The second one is *public verifiability*.

That is, any verifier (not only the data owner) can check the data deletion result by verifying the returned data deletion proof. Finally, the data deletion and result verification operations should be efficient for the data owner.

3.2   The Concrete Construction

For simplicity, we assume that O has become a legal tenant of S. Besides, O and S has a ECDSA key pair (pk_o, sk_o) and (pk_s, sk_s), respectively. $H(\cdot)$ is a secure hash function. Furthermore, we choose hash functions $h = (h_1, \cdots, h_k)$, f_1 and f_2 that satisfy $[1, N] \rightarrow [1, m]$. Finally, we still need a function $g : [1, N] \rightarrow [1, N^2]$. Without loss of generality, we can assume that O would like to outsource file F to S, whose name is n_f.

- *Data outsourcing.* To protect the privacy, O should encrypt the outsourced file, and upload the corresponding ciphertext to S.
  1. Firstly, O divides F into n blocks $(m_1, \cdots, m_n)$. Then O randomly chooses a distinct integer tag_i from Z_N as index of m_i. After that, O encrypts the blocks as $C_i = Enc_{k_i}(m_i)$, where $i \in [1, n]$, Enc is an IND-CPA secure encryption algorithm and $k_i = H(sk_o \| tag_i \| n_f)$. Finally, O sends the data set $C = ((C_1, tag_1), \cdots, (C_n, tag_n))$ to S.
  2. Upon receiving C, S maintains C and inserts all tag_i into IBF according to Algorithm 1, where $i \in [1, n]$. Then S computes $sig_s = Sign_{sk_s}(storage \| IBF)$, where $Sign$ is an ECDSA signature generation algorithm. Finally, S sends storage proof $\lambda = (sig_s, IBF)$ to O.
- *Storage check.* On receiving λ, O can check the storage result by verifying λ. Firstly, O checks the validity of the signature sig_s. If sig_s is invalid, O aborts and returns $Failure$; otherwise, O uses $(tag_1, \cdots, tag_n)$ to reconstruct a new CBF_o, and checks the equation $CBF_o = CBF$ (the IBF's first level can be seen as a CBF). If $CBF_o \neq CBF$, O aborts and returns $Failure$; otherwise, O deletes the local backup.
- *Data Deletion.* When O will not need the data anymore, he will require S to delete the data permanently.
  1. Firstly, O computes $sig_e = Sign_{sk_o}(erase \| tag_i \| T_e)$, where T_e is a timestamp. Then O generates a deletion request $R_e = (erase, tag_i, T_e, sig_e)$, and sends R_e to S to delete the data block (C_i, tag_i), where $i \in [1, n]$.
  2. On receipt of R_e, S checks the validity of R_e. If R_e is invalid, S aborts and returns $Failure$; otherwise, S deletes (C_i, tag_i) from disk by overwriting, and deletes tag_i from IBF to obtain a new IBF' according to Algorithm 2. Then S computes $sig_d = Sign_{sk_s}(delete \| R_e \| IBF')$ and sends deletion proof $\tau = (IBF', R_e, sig_d)$ to O.
- *Deletion Check.* On receiving τ, O checks the validity of the deletion proof.
  1. Firstly, O checks the validity of signature sig_d. If sig_d is invalid, O aborts and returns $Failure$; otherwise, O verifies $CBF'(tag_i) \overset{?}{=} 0$, determines whether tag_i belongs to CBF'. If $CBF'(tag_i) = 0$ (that is, at least one equation $h_i(tag_i) = 0$ holds for $1 \leq i \leq k$), O aborts and returns $Success$; otherwise, goes to 2.

2. O sends tag_i and τ to the TPA. Then according to Algorithm 3, TPA lists all the elements that included in IBF'. If tag_i is included in IBF', TPA returns $Failure$ to O; otherwise, TPA returns $Success$ to O. After that, if C_i appears again, O can be entitled to compensation.

Algorithm 3. Element Listing

Input: IBF
Output: stack O
while $g(B[i].idSum/B[i].count) = B[i].hashSum/B[i].count$ **do**
   if $B[i].count > 0$ **then**
      1. Push $y = B[i].idSum/B[i].count$ into an output stack;
      2. Call Delete(y) algorithm to delete all $B[i].count$ backups of y.
   else
      1. Exit all $-B[i].count$ falsely-deleted;
      2. Call Insert(y) algorithm to insert y into IBF.

if $count = 0$ **then**
   Output the data items in the output stack and then insert every data items back into B and C.
else
   1. Use the C to replace B to repeat the above while loop;
   2. Output the data items in the output stack and then insert every data item back into B and C.

---

4   Security Analysis

Data Confidentiality. In our scheme, O uses the IND-CPA secure AES algorithm to encrypt the file, and keeps the keys so secret that any attacker cannot obtain them maliciously. Further, any attacker cannot get any plaintext information. Hence, our scheme can reach data confidentiality.

Public Verifiability. Our scheme can reach public verifiability. Specifically, the verifier V checks the validity of sig_d firstly. If sig_d is valid, V verifies $CBF'(tag_i) \overset{?}{=} 0$. If $CBF'(tag_i) = 0$, V trusts tag_i does not belong to CBF'; otherwise, V sends tag_i and τ to TPA. Then the TPA tries to list all the elements of IBF' to check that whether tag_i belongs to CBF'. The verification doesn't need any privacy information so that any V can check the deletion result.

Note that the deletion verification may be failed for two reasons: (1) the BF's false positive, which means CBF' doesn't contain tag_i, but $CBF'(tag_i) \neq 0$ still holds with a very small probability ε. (2) TPA fails to list all the elements. The probability for TPA fails to list the elements isn't larger than $\varepsilon/4$ according to [2]. So, the final failure probability is at most $\varepsilon^2/4$, which is negligible.

5   Simulation and Performance Evaluation

In this section, all the simulations are executed with PBC and OpenSSL library on a Linux machine with Intel(R) Core(TM) i5-6200U processors running at

2.4 GHz and 8 GB main memory. For simplicity, we assume that the ratio of the data block number and the length of IBF is fixed 1 : 29, k is fixed 20.

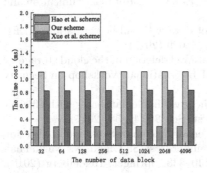

Fig. 3. Time cost of data deletion   **Fig. 4.** Time cost of deletion check

Figures 3 and 4 show the time cost of data deletion and result verification processes. Compared with Hao et al. scheme [5] and Xue et al. scheme [16], our scheme might cost a little more time cost. However, the data deletion and result verification operations are one-time, and they can be executed off-line. Additionally, the time cost of our scheme is acceptable since it is very small. Hence, our scheme is still very efficient.

6   Conclusion

In the cloud storage, the data owner may not believe that the selfish cloud server would delete the data honestly. To solve this problem, we propose an IBF-based cloud data deletion scheme with public verifiability. In the proposed scheme, we use the IBF to deal with the problem of public verifiability in cloud data deletion. By applying the IBF, the proposed scheme can offer the data owner the capacity to verify the data deletion result. Besides, we prove that our novel scheme can realize all the excepted security requirements.

Acknowledgements. This work was supported by the Natural Science Foundation of Guangxi (No. 2016GXNSFAA380098) and the Science and Technology Program of Guangxi (No. AB17195045).

References

1. Boneh, D., Lipton, R.: A revocable backup system. In: Proceedings of the 6th Conference on USENIX Security Symposium, vol. 6, pp. 91–96 (1996)
2. Eppstein, D., Goodrich, M.T.: Straggler identification in round-trip data streams via Newton's identities and invertible Bloom filters. IEEE Trans. Knowl. Data Eng. **23**(2), 297–306 (2011)

3. Gutmann, P.: Secure deletion of data from magnetic and solid-state memory. In: Proceedings of the Sixth USENIX Security Symposium, vol. 14, pp. 77–89 (1996)
4. Hall, B., Govindarasu, M.: An assured deletion technique for cloud-based IoT. In: Proceeding of the 27th International Conference on Computer Communication and Networks (ICCCN 2018), pp. 1–9 (2018)
5. Hao, F., Clarke, D., Zorzo, A.: Deleting secret data with public verifiability. IEEE Trans. Dependable Secure Comput. **13**(6), 617–629 (2016)
6. Luo, Y., Xu, M., Fu, S., Wang, D.: Enabling assured deletion in the cloud storage by overwriting. In: Proceedings of the 4th ACM International Workshop on Security in Cloud Computing, pp. 17–23 (2016)
7. Miao, M., Wang, J., Ma, J., Susilo, W.: Publicly verifiable databases with efficient insertion/deletion operations. J. Comput. Syst. Sci. **86**, 49–58 (2017)
8. Paul, M., Saxena, A.: Proof of erasability for ensuring comprehensive data deletion in cloud computing. In: Meghanathan, N., Boumerdassi, S., Chaki, N., Nagamalai, D. (eds.) CNSA 2010. CCIS, vol. 89, pp. 340–348. Springer, Heidelberg (2010). https://doi.org/10.1007/978-3-642-14478-3_35
9. Perito, D., Tsudik, G.: Secure code update for embedded devices via proofs of secure erasure. In: Gritzalis, D., Preneel, B., Theoharidou, M. (eds.) ESORICS 2010. LNCS, vol. 6345, pp. 643–662. Springer, Heidelberg (2010). https://doi.org/10.1007/978-3-642-15497-3_39
10. Rahumed, A., Chen, H.C., Tang, Y., Lee, P.P., Lui, J.C.: A secure cloud backup system with assured deletion and version control. In: Proceedings of the 40th International Conference on Parallel Processing Workshops, pp. 160–167 (2011)
11. Shen, J., Zhou, T., Chen, X., Li, J., Susilo, W.: Anonymous and traceable group data sharing in cloud computing. IEEE Trans. Inf. Forensics Secur. **13**(4), 912–925 (2018)
12. Tian, H., et al.: Dynamic-hash-table based public auditing for secure cloud storage. IEEE Trans. Serv. Comput. **10**(5), 701–714 (2017)
13. Wei, M.Y.C., Grupp, L.M., Spada, F.E., Swanson, S.: Reliably erasing data from flash-based solid state drives. In: Proceedings of the 9th USENIX Conference on File and Storage Technologies (FAST 2011), pp. 105–117 (2011)
14. Wang, Y., Tao, X., Ni, J., Yu, Y.: Data integrity checking with reliable data transfer for secure cloud storage. Int. J. Web Grid Serv. **14**(1), 106–121 (2018)
15. Xiong, J., et al.: A secure data self-destructing scheme in cloud computing. IEEE Trans. Cloud Comput. **2**(4), 448–458 (2014)
16. Xue, L., Ni, J., Li, Y., Shen, J.: Provable data transfer from provable data possession and deletion in cloud storage. Comput. Stand. Interfaces **54**, 46–54 (2017)
17. Yang, C., Chen, X., Xiang, Y.: Blockchain-based publicly verifiable data deletion scheme for cloud storage. J. Netw. Comput. Appl. **103**, 185–193 (2018)
18. Yang, C., Tao, X.: New publicly verifiable cloud data deletion scheme with efficient tracking. In: Yang, C.N., Peng, S.L., Jain, L.C. (eds.) SICBS 2018. AISC, vol. 895, pp. 359–372. Springer, Cham (2020). https://doi.org/10.1007/978-3-030-16946-6_28
19. Yang, C., Wang, J., Tao, X., Chen, X.: Publicly verifiable data transfer and deletion scheme for cloud storage. In: Naccache, D., et al. (eds.) ICICS 2018. LNCS, vol. 11149, pp. 445–458. Springer, Cham (2018). https://doi.org/10.1007/978-3-030-01950-1_26
20. Yang, C., Ye, J.: Secure and efficient fine-grained data access control scheme in cloud computing. J. High Speed Netw. **21**(4), 259–271 (2015)

DPSR: A Differentially Private Social Recommender System for Mobile Users

Xueling Zhou[1,2], Lingbo Wei[1,2(✉)], Yukun Niu[1], Chi Zhang[1(✉)],
and Yuguang Fang[3]

[1] School of Information Science and Technology,
University of Science and Technology of China,
Hefei 230027, Anhui, People's Republic of China
{wxzxl,xiaoniu}@mail.ustc.edu.cn, {lingbowei,chizhang}@ustc.edu.cn
[2] State Key Laboratory of Information Security,
Institute of Information Engineering, Chinese Academy of Sciences,
Beijing 100093, People's Republic of China
[3] Department of Electrical and Computer Engineering, University of Florida,
Gainesville, FL 32611, USA
fang@ece.ufl.edu

Abstract. Recommender systems, which provide users with suggestions for selecting items that is of potential interest to them, are widely used to assist mobile users in reducing information overload and making better choice quickly in their daily life. Social recommender systems, which have the potential to mitigate the new user cold-start problem, utilize social relationships as an extra source of information. As recommendation results depend on users' individual data, privacy breaches may occur. Although several differentially private social recommender systems have been proposed, their application scopes or protection strengths are limited. In this paper, we propose a differentially private social recommender system for mobile users named *DPSR* to block curious users from inferring the existence of someone else's numeric rating or social relationship. Empirical evaluations on two real-world datasets are conducted, and the results show that *DPSR* can balance the utility of recommendations with the privacy of users' data in both normal and cold-start test view.

Keywords: Differential privacy · Social recommendation · Deep learning

1 Introduction

Recommender systems provide users with suggestions for selecting items that they may like from an enormous amount of alternatives, and they play a vital role in reducing information overload. Nowadays, many users depend on mobile devices to access online service. Therefore, considering the task of making recommendations for mobile users is of great significance. Traditional recommender

© Springer Nature Switzerland AG 2019
E. S. Biagioni et al. (Eds.): WASA 2019, LNCS 11604, pp. 639–646, 2019.
https://doi.org/10.1007/978-3-030-23597-0_54

systems gather users' ratings and recommend in view of users' past rating patterns. However, these systems suffer from the cold-start problem which is hard to make relevant predictions for a new user or a new item due to the lack of sufficient ratings. Social recommender systems [10] utilize social relationships as extra information and assume users' preference is similar to or impacted by connected users. Under this assumption, recommendations for a user depend on not only his rating history but also ratings of those the user trusts. As one of their advantages, social recommendations mitigate the new user cold-start problem.

Recommender systems depend on users' data to provide suggestions and may cause privacy breaches. Even if a system gathers, stores, and manipulates users' data securely, the visible results make it possible for a curious user to infer others' information [2]. Furthermore, social recommender systems are more vulnerable to privacy-inference attacks because recommendations for a user are based on the connected users who are more targeted and known by the given user.

Differential privacy [4] provides a rigorous notion to quantify the privacy loss, and a few differentially private social recommender systems [7,9,12,13] have been proposed. However, these systems are confined in application scopes or protection strengths. Some systems [7,9,12] are only applied to binary ratings which just reflect whether a user likes an item or not. Although the system proposed by Meng et al. [13] can handle numeric ratings, it protects only the privacy of rating scores not including the existence of ratings, which means the existence of a rating can be inferred. Unfortunately, the existence of a rating may be sensitive. For example, a rating of a medicine may reflect the user's health condition. Besides, the system divides ratings into sensitive and non-sensitive ratings, protects sensitive ratings, and sets non-sensitive ratings public. However, non-private ratings also need privacy protection since their statistics may leak users' preference.

In this work, we first propose a differentially private social recommender system predicting numeric ratings for mobile users named *DPSR* that can block curious users from inferring the existence of others' rating or social relationship. Second, *DPSR* can provide different records with privacy guarantees of different strengths. Finally, we experiment on two real-world datasets, and we are the first to evaluate differentially private social recommendations in cold-start settings.

The rest of this paper is organized as follows. We describe the problem statement in Sect. 2. The algorithm of our system is proposed in Sect. 3. Privacy analysis and experimental results are shown in Sects. 4 and 5 respectively. Conclusion is given in Sect. 6.

2 Problem Statement

As shown in Fig. 1, there are two types of entities: *mobile users* and the *recommender*. A mobile user can rate items and follow or make friends with others. The recommender predicts users' preferences based on records gathered.

The security assumptions of our system are as follows. The recommender is assumed to be trusted, and mobile users are assumed to trust the recommender and transmit records honestly. Adversarial users are honest-but-curious,

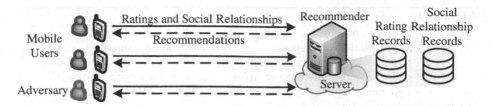

Fig. 1. Architecture of *DPSR*.

i.e. they try to infer other users' privacy. We consider an adversary knowing all other records except one, and his goal is to infer whether the one exists or not. To achieve this, he can create multiple user accounts and receive all recommendations returned. This setting also considers the collision between adversarial users. Besides, the adversary knows the system's algorithm.

We take two contradicting objectives into consideration: the privacy of users' data and the utility of recommendation results.

Privacy. We introduce differential privacy to measure the strength of privacy protection. Differential privacy limits the influence caused by one record.

Definition 1. *(differential privacy) [4]. An algorithm M is (ϵ, δ)-differentially private if for all $S \subseteq Range(M)$ and for all neighboring datasets of D and D':*

$$Pr[M(D) \in S] \le e^{\epsilon} Pr[M(D') \in S] + \delta.$$

Parameter ϵ implies the similarity of the outputs computed on two neighboring datasets, and a smaller value of ϵ means a stronger privacy guarantee.

Utility. We adopt root mean square error (RMSE) to measure the utility of recommendations. A smaller RMSE value implies predictions are more accurate.

3   Algorithm of *DPSR*

3.1   Overview

A mobile user transmits rating records including his ID, items' IDs, and rating scores to the recommender. The recommender gathers all uses' ratings and generates the rating network R which contains users' IDs and items' IDs as its nodes and ratings as directed numerical edges from user nodes to item nodes. A user also transmits social relationships including his ID and other users' IDs, and all users' social relationships form social relationship network S which contains users' IDs as its nodes and social relationship as binary edges. The recommender stores R and S, predicts rating scores, and sends mobile users recommendations from which adversaries cannot infer others' private records.

We present the algorithm on the recommend's side in Algorithm 1. In the following, we describe the two main components of this algorithm in detail.

Algorithm 1. $\mathcal{DPSR}$ algorithm

Input: R_{sen} - subset of sensitive ratings, R_{ord} - subset of ordinary ratings,
          S - social relationship network, γ - regularization parameter,
          α - probability ratio between sampling an ordinary and a sensitive rating,
          β - probability ratio between sampling a trust and a sensitive rating,
          C - clipping bound, σ - noise scale, I - iteration times
Output: Predicted rating scores
1: Transform S to trust network T
2: Give T trust weights equaling to $\gamma \cdot r_{max}$ and combine the rating records and trust
   relationship records, where r_{max} represents the highest rating score
3: Calculate the sampling probabilities of a record in R_{sen}, R_{ord} and T, denoted by
   p_{sen}, p_{ord} and p_T, according to α and β
4: **for** i from 1 to I **do**
5:    Sample a batch B according to records' computed sampling probabilities
6:    For every record x_k in B, compute its gradient $g(x_k)$ based on last iteration's
      weight values and get a clipped gradient $\bar{g}(x_k) = g(x_k)/\max(1, \|g(x_k)\|_2/C)$
7:    Compute the perturbed average gradient of this batch $\tilde{g} = \frac{1}{|B|}(\sum \bar{g}(x_k) +$
      $\mathcal{N}(0, \sigma^2 C^2 \mathbf{I}))$ and use $\tilde{g}$ to update weight values, where $\mathcal{N}$ is the Gaussian dis-
      tribution with mean 0 and variance $\sigma^2 C^2$ in every dimension
8: **end for**
9: Predict rating scores based on the trained neural network

3.2   Data Processing

We first transform S to directed binary graph T which represents the trust
network. If S is unidirectional, one social relationship corresponds to one trusts
in T. Otherwise, one social relationship corresponds to two symmetric trusts.
Then, using rating and trust data together as the training data, Dang and Ignat
[3] give scores equaling the highest rating score r_{max} to trust records. To improve
their method, we add a regularization parameter γ to adjust the social influence,
and a larger γ means considering more effect from the social relationship.

To reasonably utilize privacy budget, we provide a stronger protection for
sensitive ratings, which motivates us to give an ordinary rating record or a trust
record a higher sampling probability and use α or β to set the probability ratio.
We compute p_{sen}, p_{ord}, and p_T, which correspond to sampling probabilities of a
record in R_{sen}, R_{ord}, and T, according to

$$\begin{cases} p_{sen} = 1/(|R_{sen}| + \alpha|R_{ord}| + \beta|T|) \\ p_{ord} = \alpha/(|R_{sen}| + \alpha|R_{ord}| + \beta|T|). \\ p_T = \beta/(|R_{sen}| + \alpha|R_{ord}| + \beta|T|) \end{cases}$$

3.3   Neural Network Training

After processing records from users, we use the link weight and nodes' IDs in R
and T to train a deep learning network in which weight values are differential
private. Figure 2 shows the network structure.

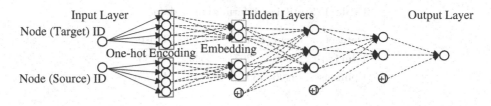

Fig. 2. The recommender's deep learning network. The dotted lines mean the weight values satisfy differential privacy. Nodes with +1 are bias terms.

Two technologies are used in this component. The first one is node embedding, which corresponds with the left two layers in the network structure in Fig. 2. Nodes' IDs are treated as categorical variables, and then a one-hot vector is created for each. However, one-hot vectors' dimensions are very high due to the large amount of users and items, so we use embedding vectors based on the neural network, which is also used in [8]. Then these vectors will be input to a fully connected neural network and the link weight acts as the regression label.

The second one is computing differentially private weights. Abadi et al. [1] propose a privacy-preserving deep learning approach by using differentially private stochastic gradient descent. Besides, moments accountant is used to achieve a tighter privacy budget bound, instead of advanced composition theorem [5]. However, Abadi et al. [1] treat records equally, which ignores the fact that records' sensitivities may be diverse. Considering this issue, we give different sampling probabilities to different records, therefore sensitive records have a smaller effect on final weight values which will bring about stronger privacy protection.

4   Privacy Analysis of $\mathcal{DPSR}$

Theorem 1. *Algorithm 1 satisfies (ϵ, δ)-differential privacy, and the values of ϵ can be different for different types of records.*

Proof. The recommender depends on computed weight values and IDs to predict ratings. So, if weight values satisfy (ϵ, δ)-differential privacy, according to the post-processing property in [5], final results also satisfy (ϵ, δ)-differential privacy.

We denote the operation in every iteration by f and denote the operation including all iterations by F. For any neighboring datasets D and D', as mentioned in [1], the distribution of $f(D)$ and $f(D')$ can be formulated as

$$f(D) \sim q_1 = \mathcal{N}(0, \sigma^2),\ f(D') \sim q_2 = (1 - |B|p)\mathcal{N}(0, \sigma^2) + |B|p\mathcal{N}(1, \sigma^2),$$

where $|B|$ is the batch size, and p is the record's sampling probability, i.e. p_{sen} for a sensitive record, p_{ord} for an ordinary record, and p_T for a trust record.

Given parameter I and δ, the value of ϵ can be calculated as below:

$$\epsilon = \min_{\lambda} \max \left\{ \frac{I(\int q_1^{\lambda+1}q_2^{-\lambda}dx - 1) - \ln\delta}{\lambda}, \frac{I(\int q_2^{\lambda+1}q_1^{-\lambda}dx - 1) - \ln\delta}{\lambda} \right\}.$$

Table 1. Statistical information of datasets.

Dataset	Users	Items	Ratings	Trusts
FilmTrust	1508	2071	35497	1853
Epinions	49290	139738	664824	487181

Different records match different ϵ due to sampling probabilities. Thus, strengths of privacy protection vary. According to [1], using the ϵ above, F satisfies (ϵ, δ)-differential privacy. Therefore, Algorithm 1 satisfies (ϵ, δ)-differential privacy.

5   Experiments

We use FilmTrust (www.librec.net/datasets.html) and Epinions (www.trustlet. org/epinions.html) as experimental datasets, both containing numerical ratings and asymmetric binary trusts. Statistical information is shown in Table 1.

In our neural network, we use 16-dimensional embedding vectors and 2 hidden layers both containing 16 units. In experiments on FilmTrust, we set C to 0.01 and B to 8. In experiments on Epinions, we set C to 0.1 and B to 256. Besides, all experiments' learning rate is 0.01, the iteration time is 4000, and δ is 10^{-5}.

We split ratings randomly into training set consisting of 80% ratings and test set consisting of the remaining, and trust records are all included in training set.

When we do not distinguish sensitive and ordinary ratings, records are treated equally. When we divide ratings into sensitive and ordinary ratings, we randomly select 10% rating records as sensitive ratings with the setting $\alpha = \beta = 10$.

Besides the normal test view, similar to [6], we use a cold-start test view on which only users rating less than five items could be involved in the testset.

To evaluate *DPSR*'s performance, we check performances of several non-private state-of-the-art approaches: PMF [14], SoReg [11], and TrustSVD [6].

We use Gaussian noise with different variances to control ϵ. As shown in Fig. 3, when we add less noise, predictions are closer to actual scores, but it also means a higher risk to leak privacy. This reflects a trade-off between privacy and utility. Figure 3 shows on Epinions dataset, *DPSR* performances comparably with SoReg on normal test view and better than PMF and SoReg on cold-start test view. Comparing experiments on two datasets, we find that γ has a larger impact in experiments on Epinions than in experiments on FilmTrust. We also observe the performance of *DPSR* in the setting where we distinguish sensitive and ordinary ratings is similar to that in the setting where we treat records equally, but in the latter we reduce the privacy leakage of sensitive ratings. For example, in Fig. 3(c), with standard deviation 0.01, ϵ for an ordinary rating is 0.77, while its value for a sensitive rating is 0.58.

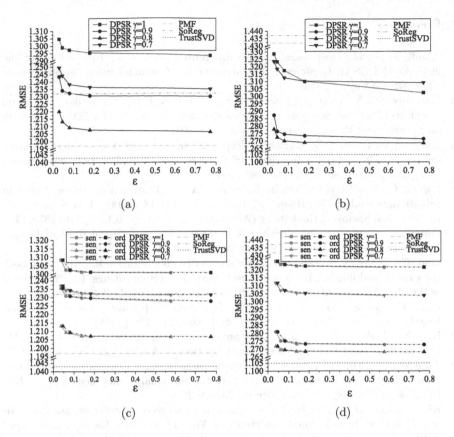

Fig. 3. The performance on Epinions dataset. Records are treated equally in (a) and (b), while ratings are divided into sensitive and ordinary ratings in (c) and (d). Performances on normal test view are shown in (a) and (c), while performances on cold-start test view are shown in (b) and (d).

6   Conclusion

In this paper, as existing systems' application scopes or protection strengths are limited, we propose a differentially private social recommender system for mobile users named *DPSR* that can predict numeric rating scores while protecting the existence of users' records and providing different types of records with privacy guarantees of different strengths. We empirically evaluate it on two real-world publicly available datasets and show that *DPSR* achieves a good balance between utility and privacy on both normal test view and cold-start test view.

Acknowledgement. This work was supported by the National Key Research and Development Program of China under Grant 2017YFB0802202, and by the Natural Science Foundation of China (NSFC) under Grants 61702474 and 61871362.

References

1. Abadi, M., et al.: Deep learning with differential privacy. In: Proceedings of the 2016 ACM SIGSAC Conference on Computer and Communications Security, New York, USA, October 2016
2. Calandrino, J.A., Kilzer, A., Narayanan, A., Felten, E.W., Shmatikov, V.: "You might also like:" privacy risks of collaborative filtering. In: 2011 IEEE Symposium on Security and Privacy, Berkeley, USA, July 2011
3. Dang, Q.V., Ignat, C.L.: dTrust: a deep learning approach for social recommendation. In: The 3rd IEEE International Conference on Collaboration and Internet Computing, San Jose, USA, October 2017
4. Dwork, C., McSherry, F., Nissim, K., Smith, A.: Calibrating noise to sensitivity in private data analysis. In: Halevi, S., Rabin, T. (eds.) TCC 2006. LNCS, vol. 3876, pp. 265–284. Springer, Heidelberg (2006). https://doi.org/10.1007/11681878_14
5. Dwork, C., Roth, A.: The algorithmic foundations of differential privacy. Found. Trends Theoret. Comput. Sci. 9(3–4), 211–407 (2014)
6. Guo, G., Zhang, J., Yorke-Smith, N.: TrustSVD: collaborative filtering with both the explicit and implicit influence of user trust and of item ratings. In: Proceedings of the 29th AAAI Conference on Artificial Intelligence, Austin, USA, January 2015
7. Guo, T., Luo, J., Dong, K., Yang, M.: Differentially private graph-link analysis based social recommendation. Inf. Sci. **463–464**, 214–226 (2018)
8. Hou, Y., Holder, L.B.: Deep learning approach to link weight prediction. In: 2017 International Joint Conference on Neural Networks, Anchorage, USA, May 2017
9. Jorgensen, Z., Yu, T.: A privacy-preserving framework for personalized, social recommendations. In: Proceedings of the 17th International Conference on Extending Database Technology, Athens, Greece, March 2014
10. King, I., Lyu, M.R., Ma, H.: Introduction to social recommendation. In: Proceedings of the 19th International Conference on World Wide Web, Raleigh, USA, April 2010
11. Ma, H., Zhou, D., Liu, C., Lyu, M.R., King, I.: Recommender systems with social regularization. In: Proceedings of the fourth ACM International Conference on Web Search and Data Mining, Hong Kong, China, February 2011
12. Machanavajjhala, A., Korolova, A., Sarma, A.D.: Personalized social recommendations: accurate or private. Proc. VLDB Endow. 4(7), 440–450 (2011)
13. Meng, X., et al.: Personalized privacy-preserving social recommendation. In: Proceedings of the 32nd AAAI Conference on Artificial Intelligence, New Orleans, USA, February 2018
14. Mnih, A., Salakhutdinov, R.R.: Probabilistic matrix factorization. In: Advances in Neural Information Processing Systems, Vancouver, Canada, December 2008

Author Index

Printed in the United States
By Bookmasters